N   ndows

V   tration

IONY T. **VELTE**
LENDENNING
TOBY J. **VELTE**

McGraw Hill

New York   Chicago   San Francisco
Lisbon   London   Madrid   Mexico City   Milan
New Delhi   San Juan   Seoul   Singapore   Sydney   Toronto

The **McGraw·Hill** Companies

Cataloging-in-Publication Data is on file with the Library of Congress

McGraw-Hill books are available at special quantity discounts to use as premiums and sales promotions, or for use in corporate training programs. For more information, please write to the Director of Special Sales, Professional Publishing, McGraw-Hill, Two Penn Plaza, New York, NY 10121-2298. Or contact your local bookstore.

Microsoft® Windows Vista™ Administration

1234567890 DOH DOH 01987

ISBN-13:   978-0-07-149303-1
ISBN-10:   0-07-149303-4

Sponsoring Editor
Jane Brownlow

Editorial Supervisor
Patty Mon

Project Manager
Madhu Bhardwaj
(International Typesetting and Composition)

Acquisitions Coordinator
Jennifer Housh

Technical Editors
Rich Harmer
Steve Makousky

Copy Editor
Lisa McCoy

Proofreader
Surendra Nath Shivam

Indexer
Kevin Broccoli

Production Supervisor
George Anderson

Composition
International Typesetting and Composition

Illustration
International Typesetting and Composition

Art Director, Cover
Jeff Weeks

Toby and I would like to dedicate this book to Mr. Robert Elsenpeter and his wife Janet and their growing family—Henry, Lizzie, and Charlie. While performing his substantial contributions to this book, Bobb saw the birth of his third child, Charlie. A growing family and a book project represent a lot of work, but Bobb didn't miss a beat. His craftsmanship can be seen throughout the book and, as always, is superb. So we want to acknowledge and thank him for being so deeply involved in yet another Velte Publishing project.

We also dedicate this book to Anne Marie and Sandra and the "little crew"—Luke, Jack, Joey, Olivia, and Connor.

Dennis offers his dedication with great affection to his wife Melissa. For your support, thank you to Darren Gutwein, John Harris, Chris Balk, Anthony Velte, and Toby Velte.

ABOUT THE AUTHORS

Anthony T. Velte, CISSP, CISA, has over 16 years in the information systems industry. He is co-founder of Velte Publishing, Inc. and the co-author of more than a dozen books published by McGraw-Hill and Cisco Press.

Mr. Velte is a senior security engineer for an industry-leading security software company. He frequently speaks at seminars and helps companies large and small protect their information systems infrastructure. He holds a variety of business and technical certifications. He can be reached at atv@velte.com.

Dennis R. Glendenning, MA, MBA, PMP, MCSE, is a principal consultant in the technology infrastructure practice of Avanade, the joint venture firm of Accenture and Microsoft that provides systems integration for large-scale technology implementations across the globe.

Mr. Glendenning has successfully lead technology teams for more than 10 years while specializing in infrastructure optimization and automation.

Toby J. Velte, Ph.D., is an international, best-selling author of business technology articles and books. He is co-founder of Velte Publishing, Inc. and the co-author of more than a dozen books published by McGraw-Hill and Cisco Press. Dr. Velte is currently part of Avanade's North Central practice focused on helping thriving companies with their Microsoft-based initiatives. He can be reached at tjv@velte.com.

About the Technical Editors

Rich Harmer has a long history of working with computers and operating systems, starting with the venerable Apple II+ back in 1981. He attended Iowa State University, majoring in computer science. Over the years, he's specialized in PC and server hardware, Linux, UNIX, Novell, and Microsoft support and systems design. Rich currently works in the healthcare industry as a lead operating systems analyst and manages and maintains a 30,000-user Active Directory domain, along with being a partner in PHCommunications Consulting.

Rich enjoys traveling, taking photos, snowmobiling, and ATVing. He is married and has three wonderful "children"—one dog and two cats.

Stephen C. Makousky, CISSP, MCP, CNE, has been involved in computing in one way or another since the early '80s. Since then, he has watched Microsoft Windows evolve from Windows 1.0 to its current form. Stephen regularly participates in beta programs for Microsoft products, including Windows Vista and Windows Server "Longhorn." In his current position as a lead information system security analyst, he is responsible for VPN, firewall, intrusion prevention, vulnerability scanning, and switch security.

He is also actively involved in the Minnesota ISSA chapter and currently serves as their communications director.

When Stephen is not geeking out, he enjoys spending time with his family (wife Jennifer, daughter Josephine, and son Nicholas), riding his Harley Davidson Softail, and cooking for friends and family.

CONTENTS

Part I

Windows Vista Basics

v

Part II

Networking

Part III

Security

FOREWORD

The Velte brothers and I have been in the same market for many years. We are helping system administrators to keep all those Windows systems up and running. When we first met, Anthony and his brother Toby were running a startup company that developed a policy-based Quality of Service (QoS) system management package. But since that time, they have been actively writing books on networking, operating systems, smart homes, and more techie stuff. This is their thirteenth book project, and this one is a particularly good and timely one.

I was given the early galleys so that I could read chapters before they went to print. It's an excellent piece of work, and you could call this the "Vista Manual That Microsoft Never Wrote." This book is special because it includes third-party tips and tools and also covers the process of deployment and management, going way beyond just the technology. Even so, they go into great detail about Vista, how to keep it running, and, more importantly, how to keep it secure.

If you are a systems analyst, network architect, desktop and server admin, or professionally interested in this latest flavor of Windows, this book is for you. If you are tasked with having to roll out Vista, you definitely need to read this book. The authors clearly demonstrate what has changed under the hood and how to get the most out of these new features.

Many chapters explain how you can use those features to improve your own network. They go into configuration details, how to deploy Vista images, and how to hook it up and troubleshoot. But apart from the normal nuts and bolts, this book goes into depth about Vista's advanced features that were included to increase network performance and stability.

For instance, Vista has useful new diagnostics code built in, and it tells you about hardware problems before trouble hits the fan. Things like this are important for system admins, and make the case for migrating to Vista. This book will help you make sense of it all and help you deploy and manage Vista quickly and easily.

Another highlight of the book is that you can just jump into a chapter without having to read all the preceding pages. This aspect of the book makes it actually useful in a work setting, where you are putting out fires on a regular basis.

Having written an industry newsletter about Windows system management for 11 years now, I have reviewed many books. I highly recommend this book, since it has everything about Vista that you need and nothing you don't.

—Stu Sjouwerman, Editor, WServerNews, www.wservernews.com

Founder, Sunbelt Software

ACKNOWLEDGMENTS

The first edition of any book is the most challenging—even more so when the subject is brand new and evolving as the book is being written. That said, the people we acknowledge here made it look easy once again. First off is Mr. Robert Elsenpeter, who has worked with us on many projects and to whom this book is dedicated. Once again, he wrote and edited and reworked text with efficiency and his usual finesse. We also acknowledge Dennis Glendenning for his marvelous contributions—as a savvy writer, yet first-time author, he did a great job of stepping up to the plate and delivering prose week after week.

We also want to offer our appreciation to Steve Makousky and Rich Harmer, our technical editors. They were involved in the project from start to finish and made some excellent recommendations that extended beyond their thorough and timely technical edits.

Of course, all of us want to offer a special acknowledgement to our families for supporting us as we worked on this book. Writing a book is a challenging and time-intensive activity that knows no particular time of day or particular day of the week. It may not have seemed like it at the time, but we all know who was there, holding up the fort, while we were working all of those evenings and weekends.

And, as always, it was a pleasure working with the team at McGraw-Hill. To this edition's executive editor, Jane Brownlow, and acquisitions editor, Megg Morin, we say thank you for involving us in another great McGraw-Hill project. Also, congratulations to Jane, who during this project, had a brand-new baby boy named Holden.

To acquisitions coordinator, Jennifer Housh, thanks again for being there every time and for keeping the beat as we worked through this project. Finally, to everyone else on the McGraw-Hill production team, we say thank you very much.

INTRODUCTION

I t was almost midnight, and the crowd's excitement was palpable. The line had wrapped around the electronics store, getting longer with each passing hour. As the clock ticked closer to midnight, the pack grew more and more electric. In just a few minutes, it would be in their hands. Was the crowd waiting to buy a new CD? Was a new *Star Wars* movie opening? Was there some new game console about to go on sale? Believe it or not, people were lined up to get a copy of the new Microsoft Windows operating system—and, yes, some people did line up for Vista; it happened. However, the rabid fan base didn't really need to wait in line for Vista—thousands upon thousands got it early, via the beta program or a TechNet subscription, or they got their hands on it when it was released to corporations some two months before the consumer release.

Still, Windows Vista came with all the hype and fanfare you'd come to expect from a new Windows release. Millions were spent on the launch, and it was clear that Microsoft had a lot at stake in Vista. The good news was that Vista made some great strides with new and improved features, especially in security. As an IT professional, you'll appreciate its ease of configuration and deployment to your users. With all its new security features, you'll probably be able to sleep a little better at night. Users will appreciate the slick new graphical user interface—even if they will have to learn some new places to point and click.

One might think that the development of new operating systems at Microsoft is a fairly linear process: Release Windows XP one day; celebrate the release with a nice dinner and a few cocktails that evening, play *Halo* for a few days and try not to be noticed by the boss, and then roll up your sleeves and get cracking on Windows Vista.

That wasn't the case for Vista. In fact, you almost need a dry-erase board and hand puppets to understand how it finally came to fruition. Vista took the longest amount of time to develop in Microsoft's history.

Microsoft started working on Vista in May 2001 (at that time, it was known as "Longhorn"). The intention was for it to be released in 2003 as an intermediate step between Windows XP and Windows Vienna—the operating system Microsoft intended to be the big new release.

Over time, Vista absorbed the advanced features that were meant for Vienna. In addition, security was being beefed up in the wake of issues found in Windows XP. By August 2004, Microsoft decided to scrap their original game plan and decided to turn "Longhorn" into its next server product. By fall 2005, Vista was out for beta testing, and by early 2006, it seemed the overall product was ready, but it needed a few more tweaks to get it just right.

Microsoft's original intention was to release Vista in time for Christmas 2006. Much to the chagrin of computer makers, who were hoping for Vista to help drive the sales of new PCs during the holiday season, the release was pushed back until January 2007.

So when it finally did come out, why weren't there more people lined up to get Vista? Well, in some ways, earlier versions of Windows made many more radical changes than Vista does. While the face of Windows changes a bit with Vista, there just wasn't the sex appeal with Vista that Windows 95 and XP enjoyed. In addition, Vista was much more readily available in beta and release-candidate form than earlier versions. As such, it was much more talked about, and we knew a lot more about Vista a lot sooner than we did the other operating systems. We also heard about what worked and what didn't. Perhaps because the process was drawn out, it just wasn't as exciting as the others.

Whether or not Vista got all the attention that its predecessors did is irrelevant. The fact of the matter is that it's the new version of Windows, and it's going to be on most business desktops, if not sooner, then definitely later. This book explains how you, the IT professional, can make Vista a part of your network. We'll talk about what's new, what's improved, and how this humble little operating system can help your organization do big things.

WHO SHOULD READ THIS BOOK

Microsoft Windows Vista Administration was written for the systems analyst, network architect, desktop and server administrator, or anyone with a professional interest in Microsoft Windows and networking.

If you are in the position to decide how Windows Vista should be deployed in your organization, then this book is definitely for you. Even if all you want is a better understanding of Windows Vista, this book is for you. There's a lot going on under Vista's hood—this book can help you get a better feel for what's new, what has changed from previous versions of Windows, and how to get the most out of this substantial evolution of the Windows platform.

WHAT THIS BOOK COVERS

This book explains how you can use Vista's new features to make your organization's network more productive and effective. It talks about all aspects of Vista that are useful for your organization—from configuration and deployment of a Vista image all the way through networking and troubleshooting Vista.

While the book covers the conventional, meat-and-potatoes issues of the operating system, like using the Web browser, it also covers Vista's advanced features that will make your network more reliable and stable. For example, Vista introduces a technology called built-in diagnostics. In essence, it checks your hardware and memory for problems. If a problem arises, it can tell you or the user about the problem so that you can handle it before a catastrophe occurs. This book covers this and many other Vista tools and technologies.

Part I: Windows Vista Basics

The first section of this book examines Windows Vista, what's new, and how you can best deploy it to your organization with as little headache as possible:

▼ **Chapter 1, Introduction to Windows Vista** The first chapter takes a look at the new and improved features of Microsoft's newest version of Windows. Before you start buying Vista, we'll talk about system requirements and what needs to be done to ensure that systems can properly run Vista. The chapter compares the different versions of Vista, allowing you to see which edition is best for your computers. We'll also look at some of the new, sexy features in Vista, like gadgets, Flip, and Flip 3-D.

■ **Chapter 2, Planning a Windows Vista Deployment** There are a couple of ways you can get Vista into your organization's computers: You can buy Vista pre-installed on new computer; you can take an install DVD around to your computers; or you can create an image and send it, via the network, to all your computers. This chapter examines these options and explains the ins, outs, ups, and downs of these scenarios. Beyond that, it also explains what you need to do to prepare for a deployment. Rather than just start a deployment, there are a great many considerations to keep in mind to ensure as little pain as possible.

▲ **Chapter 3, Deploying Windows Vista** Once you've planned for your Vista deployment, it's time to get your hands dirty. This chapter examines the best ways to actually get Vista onto your organization's desktops. We'll look at scenarios for both migration and deployment. We'll talk about tools Microsoft has that you can use to deploy Vista across your organization.

Part II: Networking

You probably don't have just one computer in your organization. As such, you need to know about the new networking features in Windows Vista. This section is about connecting your Vista systems to the organization's network and how you can utilize these new networking features:

▼　**Chapter 4, TCP/IP and Name Resolution**　While the subject of TCP/IP and name resolution aren't really new to the seasoned IT professional, Vista introduces some new capabilities. This chapter explains how TCP/IP and name resolution operate in Vista.

■　**Chapter 5, Creating Network Connections**　Vista introduces some new networking features, and this chapter examines and explains them. The bulk of the discussion, however, centers on how you can make sundry network connections. This includes connecting to the Internet or connecting to a corporate network using a wired or a wireless connection.

■　**Chapter 6, Network Navigation**　Microsoft introduced a new way to view and navigate a network with Windows Vista. This chapter examines such new tools as Network Map and Network Details. If you have several networks that your users need to connect to using a single computer, you'll find this chapter will explain how you can manage those connections more simply and efficiently than in earlier versions of Windows.

■　**Chapter 7, Collaboration and Communication**　A computer network isn't very useful if the people and computers on it cannot collaborate. While being able to share common files among users is sort of a basic level of functionality for any computer network, Vista broadens the network's features and makes it possible to do a host of new and exciting things, like conducting online meetings and sharing calendars. Microsoft has also revamped its basic e-mail application, integrating more features and making it easier and more powerful to use.

▲　**Chapter 8, Remote Control**　Users might want to share their computers for any of a number of reasons. First, if the user is having trouble with the computer, it's nice to be able to ask someone for help—it's even better if help comes quickly, something that is more likely if the user's desktop can be accessed remotely. A user might also need to log on to his or her computer from a remote location and use it as if sitting in front of it. This chapter examines Vista's remote functionality tools, explaining what's new in Vista, as well as how you can best use them.

Part III: Security

Security in Windows Vista is a huge issue and certainly a subject matter on which an entire book could be written. While this book doesn't dedicate all its real estate to the issue of security, it does examine the more relevant and germane issues of network security that you will likely run into on a regular basis:

▼ **Chapter 9, User Accounts**   One of the main ways to keep your network and computers safe is to keep out people whom you don't want to have access. This chapter examines how you can set up user and group accounts (useful when managing lots of people with similar rights and privileges) in Windows Vista. In Vista, accounts aren't just useful for keeping people out or letting people in—they're also useful when deciding which applications and processes can be run on a Vista system.

■ **Chapter 10, System Security**   Windows Vista adds a lot of new features to its security arsenal. This chapter looks at such features as the improved Windows Firewall, along with new tools like BitLocker, Trusted Platform Modules, and Windows Defender. In addition, Microsoft has made it easier to find and use its security applications with the Windows Security Center.

▲ **Chapter 11, Network Security**   While Vista itself isn't necessarily thought of as being a security hub for a network, it is still a component. Vista includes a number of security features that are designed to ensure a safe and secure network. In this chapter, we'll talk about such features as Network Access Protection, which limits or prevents an "unhealthy" or otherwise untrusted computer from trying to connect to your network. We'll also talk about how the venerable Group Policy can be used with Vista to ensure a safe network.

Part IV: Working with Windows Vista

Once you've got Vista set up and running, you'll need to do some regular tweaks, tuning, and other sorts of work on your systems. This last section examines the tools and techniques you can use to manage Windows Vista:

▼ **Chapter 12, Internet Applications**   More and more, the Internet needs to be a part of a typical workplace. Vista includes several applications that help you leverage the usefulness and utility of the Internet. We start the chapter with a discussion on Internet Explorer 7, the latest version of Microsoft's Web browser that was redesigned with Vista in mind. If you have your own Web site or have another need for Web services, Microsoft has also included Internet Information Server 7 with Vista. We'll talk about both of these tools and how you can use them most effectively.

■ **Chapter 13, Mobile Devices**   It is quite likely that many of your users aren't tethered to your desktops via "normal" PCs. If you use laptops or Table PCs, this chapter explains what's new in the world of power management, along with the tools that make your Tablet PC even cooler to use. When a computer is reconnected to a network, a user may need to synchronize with those computers on the network. We'll talk about that, too.

■ **Chapter 14, Supporting Vista**   In this, the penultimate chapter, we talk about the applications on Vista that you can use to manage the day-to-day operations of your Vista system. The chapter examines how you can configure a computer running Vista with tools via the Microsoft Management Console (MMC). We'll also talk about how you can monitor a system and respond to events that require it. The chapter also examines some of the tools you can use to minimize loss of data. And, if the worst does happen, we'll talk about backing up and restoring your computer.

▲ **Chapter 15, Troubleshooting**   While it's nice to think that nothing bad will ever happen, the truth of the matter is that not only will bad things happen, but sometimes they will be hard to correct. In the last chapter of this book, we'll talk about what you can do to identify and quickly fix problems when they arise. A review of this chapter can also help you learn how to avoid many typical problems. Microsoft has made nice progress in this regard with its built-in diagnostics tools that will help you avoid catastrophe. We'll talk about these tools, as well as how to stop frozen applications, analyze printer problems, and deal with system crashes.

HOW TO READ THIS BOOK

Books like this can be a little challenging, organizationally speaking. Once we cover "the basics," you might have different needs and specific interests that won't necessarily follow the chapters in any sort of linear fashion. As such, the book has been written so that you can pick it up, flip to any chapter, and find the information you need. For example, if you want to know how Windows Vista can be used to manage Network Access Protection, flip ahead to Chapter 11. If you want to know about using IPv6 in harmony with IPv4, take a look at Chapter 4. If you prefer, you can sit down and read the whole thing cover to cover. By the way, thank you very much for taking the time to read this and for purchasing this book—we have worked very hard to create a valuable source of information for you, and we appreciate your patronage. Enjoy!

PART I

Windows Vista Basics

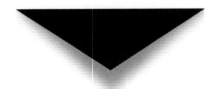

CHAPTER 1

Introduction to Windows Vista

We know: You're a Pepsi guy. You've always played your video games on a PlayStation. You'd drive a Chevy to the grave before you'd set foot in a Ford. And you prefer boxers instead of briefs. You also prefer Linux or Mac or some other non-Windows operating system. But whether you love it or hate it, Windows is the big dog in business. Whether it was your choice, your boss's, or the edict of a committee, you're implementing a migration to the latest flavor of Windows, Windows Vista. You may not be enamored with Windows, but with each successive Windows release, Microsoft's flagship product has an indelible impact on the workplace. On the other hand, you may love Windows, and the prospect of deploying the newest version across your organization is great news for you. In either case, you need to know how to make the best of Microsoft's newest operating system (OS) offering.

This first chapter serves two purposes: First, we explain how Windows Vista can be an important, useful, and productive tool for your organization. Second, we examine some of the new features in Windows Vista and tell you how you can use them to your advantage.

HOW WILL VISTA HELP YOUR ORGANIZATION?

Vista offers enhancements for everyone in your organization. Administrators can deploy and manage an OS that is, by default, more secure than any previous release. In many cases, IT and business managers will find an attractive total cost of ownership (TCO) and value proposition, while almost every Vista user will be excited about a new desktop that is sure to please both the eye and the mind of today's well-organized worker. Before we walk through the list of new Vista features, here is a quick run-down of how Vista can benefit an organization.

Usability Enhancements

User productivity remains the central factor in IT decisions surrounding desktop deployments, and Vista has a rich set of new productivity features that makes it easier to decide to upgrade. Over time, users will notice that their workstation runs more reliably, requires fewer restarts, and provides a more stable work platform. However, the most visceral impact of Vista comes from the new glossy graphic interface.

One of the most striking user enhancements is the new user interface, called Windows Aero. Based on WinFX, the open application programming interface (API) for Vista, the Aero interface presents a rich environment that is both responsive and helpful. In addition to rendering a translucent, multilayered display of the Vista universe, Aero makes the desktop appear professional and attractive as it scales icons and windows, without distorting icons and text, to fit a range of screen resolutions.

Look around and you'll find that the enhancements extend to many of the basic user operations. Vista's new navigation tools enable users to manipulate information with relative ease. It integrates a new Desktop Search tool into the improved Windows Explorer, helping users find and launch almost any item from any location. The Windows Explorer navigation pane allows users to easily search their desktop with keywords or phrases.

Also in Windows Explorer, Vista provides custom command bars that display only the tasks that are appropriate for the files seen in the Windows Explorer window. To make navigation even simpler, file icons can display the first page of documents, a thumbnail image, or the album art for a music file. All these capabilities are intended to improve a user's ability to interact with the work environment. This should ultimately reduce the amount of time needed to accomplish a given task which, in turn, should reduce user frustration (and help desk calls).

Vista streamlines data management through SyncManager. Through SyncManager, users manage data synchronization across a wide range of devices, portable audio players, personal digital assistants (PDAs), mobile phones, and files between networked computers.

These features are just a short list of the productivity and usability enhancements that provide Vista users with the freedom to focus more on their job-related tasks and less on learning new software. We'll talk more about Aero and some of Vista's features later in this chapter.

Security Enhancements

One of the most complex challenges in maintaining a computing environment is desktop security. Many of the issues that plague an IT support staff can be traced back to undetected attacks or to intrusive workers with excessive user privileges. User mistakes or attacks by malicious parties can bring down a single station or an entire network, costing companies dearly in lost productivity or worse. When developing Vista, Microsoft took advantage of the opportunity to rearchitect their flagship OS. One of their main priorities was to incorporate security deeply into the product. To accomplish this, Vista was built using Microsoft's Security Development Lifecycle (SDL), a methodology that makes security a priority from the very start of the development process. In addition, Vista has been independently tested in third-party labs using criteria set by the International Standards Organization (ISO) for security. In a general sense, Vista improves security by adding several layers to a "defense-in-depth" strategy, defending several attack points, ranging from domain membership to Internet protection.

One of the most interesting topics when talking about security improvements is Internet Explorer version 7. Vista introduces Internet Explorer 7 as a major step forward in browser security and privacy protection, helping keep user information, the workstation, and the network safe and running. The program includes many usability enhancements that bring it up to speed with competitive browsers, such as the tabbed browsing feature that bundles many sites into one window. One example among many of the security improvements includes detection of *phishing* sites while browsing the Internet—sites that look legitimate but capture personal information. We take a closer look at this important facet of Vista in Part IV: Managing Vista in the Enterprise.

User Account Control (UAC) protects corporate resources by enabling standard user privileges. Running applications at the lowest required level of privilege reduces the attack surface of the operating system, limiting the ability of malicious software to cause harm. In the past, administrators gave users elevated rights on their workstations because most applications demanded it. In Vista, file and registry virtualization isolate the core file system and registry from applications, allowing users to install and operate many applications without administrator privileges. When an application does require administrative credentials, the user is prompted for them, as is shown in Figure 1-1.

Vista helps keep data confidential by supporting data encryption at the disk, directory, or file level. Administrators can control the level of protection that makes sense for the way the computer will be used.

Vista has a number of platform innovations that make security much easier to manage. The improved Windows Firewall includes bi-directional, application-aware filtering to help prevent distributed denial of service (DoS) attacks. Unlike the firewall found in Windows XP, the outbound filtering in Windows Firewall enables you to selectively block both outbound and inbound traffic. To centralize administration, Vista's firewall can be configured using Group Policy settings. The firewall works closely with another new feature, Windows Service Hardening, to restrict what services can do on the system. Together, Windows Firewall and service hardening provide defense-in-depth by restricting access to files, registry, and network resources to block malicious software from hijacking Windows services.

The last feature in this abridged list of security enhancements that we introduce is Vista's implementation of Network Access Protection (NAP)—Microsoft's workstation quarantine solution. NAP ensures that only qualified workstations are permitted

Figure 1-1. User Account Control manages access to restricted resources.

to interact within a subnet. Working with Microsoft's new Windows Server 2007, long known under the code name "Longhorn," Vista allows administrators to specify the minimum requirements for local area network (LAN) access and block unsecured workstations from connecting to otherwise-healthy workstations. It can also work with third-party products to perform IEEE 802.1X enforcement, locking down access at a network switch port, or even assigning a connection to a specific virtual local area network (VLAN). There's much more here that we'll talk about in greater depth when we cover Vista's security traits and how you can use them in Part III: Security.

Networking Enhancements

Vista improves network services to include self-managed quality of service (QoS) and also includes some terrific management applications. The result is a functional set of troubleshooting tools for administrators. This also benefits users, in that they get a clearer sense of what they are doing when using a network.

Vista provides users with self-help for network issues that should reduce the number of administrator calls. The Network Diagnostics Framework (NDF) provides problem resolution for network-related issues. For example, when unable to connect to a network resource, Vista has special heuristics that can fix many of the common problems. If that fails, users are given simple repair options and clear directions. Armed with NDF, Vista users receive a natural boost in productivity and your administrative team enjoys reduced support costs.

Vista's authentication options are updated to reflect today's security technology, such as integrated support for fingerprint scanners and smart cards. Integrated deployment and management tools make smart cards easier to manage and deploy. Certificate and credential roaming and certificate lifecycle management are handled by the powerful new Digital Identity Management Service (DIMS). Combined with the latest in wireless authentication protocols, such as WiFi Protected Access 2 (WPA2), DIMS provides a new level of secure and flexible authentication options for wireless networks. To add to its authentication capability and extend its viable life span, Vista supports authentication using either Internet Protocol version 6 (IPv6) or Web services.

Network performance is given a boost in Vista, too. Vista's rearchitected TCP/IP stack was tuned to optimize throughput, reducing the need for specialized engineering and manual updates. It can make dynamic adjustments that enable faster transfers, improved bandwidth use, and fewer retransmissions of lost data. The result is faster, more reliable communication across the network.

The Vista networking stack also fully leverages IPv6 when available. Once you have fully converted your network to IPv6, you can immediately retire your Dynamic Host Configuration Protocol (DHCP) servers and leverage Vista as a rich IPv6 client. Even so, with IPv6, you still have the option to use DHCPv6.

This brings along additional benefits; IPv6 supports a larger network address space, while eliminating the need for DHCP and for network address translation (NAT); it also supports integrated Internet Protocol Security (IPSec) capabilities. Vista was designed to allow IPv4 and IPv6 to coexist in a symbiotic way. This makes it possible to deploy IPv6 without upgrading your network with interface appliances to support the new traffic on an IPv4 infrastructure.

Infrastructure Optimization

Third-party studies indicate that because Vista is easier to deploy, manage, and support, it reduces TCO. One of the frameworks that Microsoft has developed for decreasing TCO for the Windows platform is called the Infrastructure Optimization Model (IOM). IOM identifies phases of IT management maturity based on the number of best practices in use by the management team. Using third-party studies, Microsoft argues convincingly that moving into the progressively more *dynamic* phases of management maturity can save substantially on the per-PC resource requirements. It says that companies can save 66 percent in labor costs, for example, when moving from the first stage of the IOM optimization model to the third stage. Table 1-1 shows what those cost savings might look like.

Vista networks incorporate more of the best practices that define the higher stages of the IOM. They also reduce complexity, another key factor in TCO figures. Key best practices that are well supported in a Vista enterprise include:

▼ **Standardize on a single operating system**   The most compelling justification for multiple operating systems is compatibility between the OS and applications. Vista offers a virtualized registry and directory, greatly increasing the compatibility.

■ **Manage PC software and configuration centrally**   With previous OS versions, users often operated using elevated rights because software operations require administrator rights. With elevated rights, users install and configure their workstations without restriction, often in violation of IT policy. Vista's UAC and virtualization allow applications to install and run with nominal user rights.

▲ **Manage network traffic policies centrally**   Vista's improved firewall and extended Group Policy options enable administrators to centrally manage network ports, applying IPSec rules and packet filters.

In addition, Vista supports a level of automation and provides simple deployment paths that can help raise a company's ranking in the IOM. Vista reduces the need to

	Windows 2000 Professional	Windows XP Professional	Windows XP Professional (SP2)	Windows Vista
Basic optimization	$178	$177	$162	$127
Mature optimization	$380	$380	$380	$380
Total	$558	$557	$542	$507

Table 1-1.   Optimized IT Cost Savings

create, test, and maintain separate OS images with the new disk-imaging tool called ImageX that uses a new file-based format for imaging called Windows Imaging Format (WIM). This means that those deploying Vista now have a native and enhanced, and highly flexible, alternative to the familiar Norton Ghost. Using ImageX, administrators can now create and deploy a single image to different types of workstations, with modules aligned with the different hardware, regions, and languages in a global enterprise. In effect, an entire level of engineering is nearly removed from what is typically a complex phase of upgrading desktops. ImageX and WIM should be of great benefit to all Vista administrators.

Finally, enhancements to self-help capabilities give Vista users the ability to diagnose and resolve their own support issues. The list of new features includes Network Diagnostics; an improved Event Viewer; and automation for resolving hardware failures, networking problems, client performance issues, resource exhaustion, power transition issues, unbootable systems, and service crashes. With improved management tools, security, and automation, Vista offers enterprises a powerful means by which to get the benefits of the advanced phases of the IOM. As you climb toward the more dynamic phases of the IOM, you substantially reduce your TCO standing.

Now that we've looked at a business case for Windows Vista, let's take a peek under the hood and examine what, specifically, this new OS will bring to your organization.

VERSIONS OF VISTA

Back in 1985, there was one version of Windows—Windows 1.0. This was the only flavor of Microsoft Windows available; it offered a bare-bones set of applications, and it didn't know a thing about networks, but it did allow for basic multitasking. In 1987, Windows 2.0 came along, with new processor support and a better graphical user interface (GUI). As simple as these versions look to us now, even then it was clear that Microsoft was on to something.

Then, over the years, as more versions of Windows were introduced to the public—and to business—Microsoft diversified its product portfolio. In 1993, they added Windows NT 3.1 and the "networkable" Windows 3.11, commonly known as Windows for Workgroups. Then the pace picked up. In 1995, we saw Windows 95; in 1996, Windows NT 4.0; and from 1998 to 2000, three upgrades to the original Windows 95 platform came along: Windows 98, 98SE, and Windows ME. One release and one product every year or so. It was all very simple and very serial.

Something else happened in 2000—you guessed it: the release of Windows 2000 Professional. It's here that things started to get a bit more complicated. You see, Windows 2000 wasn't a one-trick pony like its predecessors. The Windows 2000 family included Windows 2000 Server and Windows 2000 Advanced Server. Since Windows XP rolled out, there have been all sorts of variants, including Windows XP Professional, Windows XP Media Center, Windows XP 64-bit Edition, and even Windows XP Starter Edition, which is marketed to countries like Thailand and Ecuador.

It took several years for Windows XP to add all its siblings. Fast-forward to today, and we see that Windows Vista launched with five versions right out of the chute. It was a concerted effort by Microsoft to deliver its new core OS in flavors best suited to what it now knows about its user base. These versions—which we'll examine in more depth in a moment—are targeted at varying business and home environments. Let's take a closer look at the current crop of Windows Vista editions.

Windows Vista Business

Windows Vista Business Edition is targeted at all sizes of businesses. Microsoft has designed it to offer smoother and more secure operation over previous Windows versions. For small businesses, this reduces the reliance on dedicated IT staff to manage and support the OS. Larger organizations will benefit from new infrastructure features that allow IT staff to spend less time maintaining workstations. In addition, business functions are enhanced through new ways to organize, locate, and share information.

Although not without controversy, Microsoft has included built-in protection against malware. While a debate continues about how it's been implemented, we see it as an important step in keeping business PCs safe and secure. Other key features include Vista's ability to warn users of impending hardware failure before important data is lost or compromised. If the unthinkable does happen, new backup technologies promise to make data retrieval easier and more reliable.

Larger organizations will benefit from Windows Vista Business Edition's deployment and management features. A new, streamlined, image-based deployment system reduces the number of images required for deployment in an organization. That means it'll be a faster, less headache-inducing rollout.

For organizations that do not have a dedicated IT staff, Windows Vista Business Edition includes Small Business Resources. This is a built-in guide that walks the user through everyday tasks and troubleshooting jobs in nontechnical language.

For users on the move, Windows Vista Business Edition allows them to connect through a WiFi connection, or even using a cellular telephone to connect to the Internet.

Windows Vista Enterprise

The next step up in the business world of Windows Vista is Windows Vista Enterprise Edition. This version is targeted at large organizations and those with complex IT infrastructures. In addition to all the features included in Windows Vista Business, this version includes technology for higher levels of data protection, tools to improve application compatibility, and ease of deployment by again using a single deployment image.

NOTE   Windows Vista Enterprise is only sold to Microsoft Volume License Customers who have PCs covered by Microsoft Software Assurance or a Microsoft Enterprise Agreement.

Windows Vista Enterprise protects data with its Windows BitLocker Drive Encryption technology. This helps secure data if the computer is lost or stolen. BitLocker uses hardware-based data encryption to encrypt the entire hard drive.

NOTE   We'll talk about BitLocker in greater detail in Chapter 10.

Windows Vista Enterprise also improves application compatibility with earlier versions of Windows, as well as with UNIX applications. One of the tools—Virtual PC Express—allows you to run an application in a legacy Windows environment from the Windows Vista Enterprise desktop.

Windows Vista Home Premium

Microsoft created a Vista version aimed at home users as well. Windows Vista Home Premium Edition is the top-shelf version of Vista for the home.

The organization capabilities of Windows Vista make it ideal for home entertainment needs, such as categorizing photos, music, and video. In addition, laptop and tablet users will benefit from Vista's ability to easily access WiFi hotspots.

While Windows Vista Home Premium Edition contains all the features that mark an improved version of Windows (security, data organization, and so forth), what really sets this edition apart from other versions is its emphasis on digital entertainment, including photo sharing, video, TV, movies, music, and games. Users can even record HDTV on their Windows Vista Home Premium systems. Windows Vista Home Premium systems can also be connected to an Xbox 360 to extend its media capabilities to other rooms of the house.

Windows Vista Home Basic

Windows Vista Home Basic Edition is for homes that need basic computing functions. It boasts easy setup, improved security, and enhanced reliability.

One of the features that all versions of Windows Vista include is a Parental Controls feature that allows you to monitor your family's use of games, the Internet, and instant messaging.

In essence, Windows Vista Home Basic provides exactly what the name describes: basic features. That's not to say, however, that what Microsoft calls "basic" is less of an improvement over earlier versions of Windows.

Windows Vista Ultimate

Last, but not least, is the Windows Vista Ultimate Edition. This version combines all the features that we've mentioned in this section. It mixes business-based needs with mobility features and throws in the digital entertainment features of the home edition.

This OS is targeted at the person who wants to do it all: they want to bring their computer to work, use it on the road, and then use it for entertainment. It could also be used by someone who wants the home entertainment features of the home edition, but also wants to connect to their corporate network from home.

HARDWARE REQUIREMENTS

Chances are you'll be buying Windows Vista and installing it on existing computers within your organization. If you're in the lucky position of buying brand-new computers with Vista preinstalled, you don't need to worry about system requirements.

However, if you're installing Vista on existing computers, you need to make sure your computers are capable of running the OS.

Microsoft has two levels of computer operability with Windows Vista. Vista will run in a basic, no-frills sort of way on a computer that is classified as "Vista Capable." To get your money's worth out of Vista, however, you'll need a computer that's "Vista Premium Ready."

Computers that are Vista Capable will deliver the core duties of Windows Vista, including new organization tools, security, and reliability. However, some features, like Windows Aero, require the Vista Premium level of configuration.

A computer that is Vista Capable needs at least an 800-MHz processor and 512 MB RAM, as well as a DirectX 9 graphics card. Computers that are Vista Premium Ready must have at least 1-GHz processors, 1 GB RAM, and a DirectX 9 graphics processing unit with Hardware Pixel Shader 2.0.

Table 1-2 compares the complete list of system requirements for both Vista Capable and Vista Premium Ready computers.

	Vista Capable	Vista Premium Ready
Processor	800 MHz (32-bit or 64-bit)	1.0 GHz (32-bit or 64-bit)
Memory	512 MB RAM	1 GB RAM
Graphics Card	DirectX 9-capable	DirectX 9-capable GPU with Hardware Pixel Shader v2.0 and WDDM driver support
Graphics Memory	32 MB RAM (SVGA-capable)	128 MB RAM, up to 2,304,000 total pixels (e.g. 1920 × 1200) or 256+ MB for greater resolutions
Hard drive capacity	20 GB	40 GB
Hard drive free space	15 GB	15 GB
Hard drive type	Normal	Normal, but hybrid flash memory/hard disk recommended
Other drives	CD-ROM	DVD-ROM
Other requirements	n/a	Audio output Internet connectivity

Table 1-2.   Hardware Requirements for Windows Vista

We've certainly come a long way from the system requirements for Windows 1.0. But as Microsoft continues to evolve its flagship product, it always necessitates beefier hardware.

There is quite a bit required of a computer running Windows Vista. If yours is an environment where not every computer is identically configured, or if you just aren't sure what your computers have under the hood, you will probably find yourself using the Windows Vista Upgrade Advisor. When run on a computer, you'll get a report like the one shown in Figure 1-2.

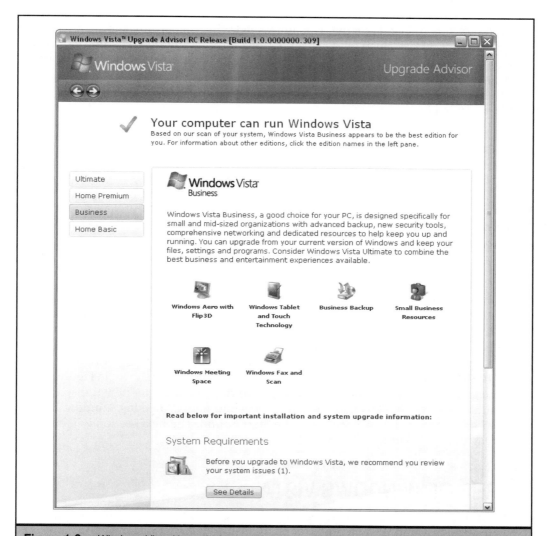

Figure 1-2.   Windows Vista Upgrade Advisor can tell you if your computer can run the new OS.

We'll talk about this tool in more depth in Chapter 2. But if you want to check it out right now, it can be downloaded for free from Microsoft at www.microsoft.com/windowsvista/getready/upgradeadvisor/default.mspx.

HOW YOU'LL INTERFACE WITH VISTA

Even though Windows Vista features a slew of new features and improvements, the first thing you'll experience is the graphical user interface (GUI). Again, this connection between the user and the OS has undergone many changes over the years, starting with the "classic" look of Windows that was unleashed with version 1.0, and then changing with each major release. Such releases as Windows 95 and Windows XP came with a new look and feel—they also gave users the opportunity to relearn their OS and get frustrated when applications and tools weren't where they used to be.

Basic User Interface

Computers that are Vista Capable will run with the so-called Basic User Interface. The Basic User Interface shouldn't be considered the red-headed stepchild of the Vista user interfaces, however. It's not as polished and shiny as its big brother, Aero, but it's still a step above what you have been working with in Windows XP.

The Basic User Interface provides new ways of organizing and finding information, security, and improved reliability. However, systems configured with less than 1 GB of RAM will not be able to provide the premium experience including the new Aero User Interface. Vista's Basic User Interface is shown in Figure 1-3.

Aero

For computers that are Vista Premium Ready, the new look and feel has been named Aero. Aero is the top-shelf GUI for Windows Vista and incorporates a number of aesthetically pleasing elements.

Microsoft's marketing department spent some time and effort coming up with the name and getting some positive, proactive words to fit with each letter. As such, Aero is an acronym for Authentic, Energetic, Reflective, and Open. The Aero interface is shown in Figure 1-4.

Aero gives a glass-like appearance to one's desktop and includes new transparencies and animations. But the changes in Aero go beyond simply making window corners rounded or changing the appearance of the Start button. The next section will examine the new features of Windows Vista.

FEATURES OF WINDOWS VISTA

With Windows Vista, Microsoft has changed all sorts of ways that you interact with its GUI. Buttons, options, dialog boxes, wizards, Control Panel, icons, fonts, and user notifications have all changed. Even the tone of the text has changed to be less insulting and technocratic.

Figure 1-3.   Vista's Basic User Interface is what you'll encounter when using a Vista Capable computer.

Microsoft has introduced some new things, improved other things, and moved around existing items. Let's examine some of the things that are new and improved.

Wizards

Wizards have followed the same look and feel since 1997, but they are substantially different in Windows Vista. The most overt change is, of course, the wizards' look. However, there are also changes to the way in which a user interacts with the wizard itself. Changes include:

▼ The purpose of a wizard is more clearly defined at the top of the page.

■ The concept of *commit pages* is implemented. These pages make it clear that the next step will be the actual process that the wizard will execute. Commit pages typically have a button in the lower-right corner that is labeled with the action to be taken, like "Configure device."

- ■ The Back button has been moved to the upper-left corner of the page. This gives more focus to the commit choices, and the Next button is only shown on pages where necessary.

- ■ The Welcome and Completion pages are no longer used. This was done to increase the wizards' efficiency.

- ▲ Wizards can be resized.

Vista does another thing to be user-friendly: When a wizard has been completed, a follow-up page can be used to tell the user about related tasks he or she might want to pursue. For example, if the user has burned a DVD-ROM, the wizard might ask if he or she wants to copy the disc.

An example of the new wizard look is shown in Figure 1-5.

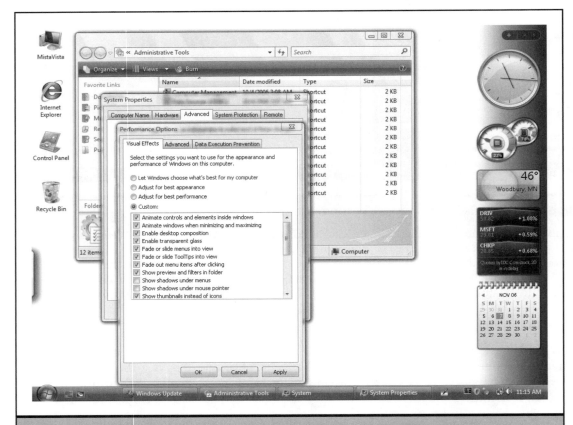

Figure 1-4.   Windows Vista's Aero desktop gives a new look and feel to the OS.

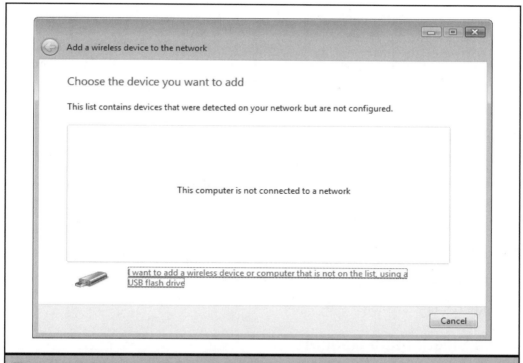

Figure 1-5. Microsoft has revamped the venerable wizard in Windows Aero.

Notifications

Introduced in Windows 2000, notification balloons pop up in the system tray, telling you about a system event or a problem. For instance, if your printer runs out of paper, a balloon will appear to let you know. If you connect to the network, it will let you know.

Some people don't like these balloons, because they tend to pop up out of nowhere and are a minor nuisance. Plus, if you are using a full-screen application, like a game, they could disrupt that application. Notifications, like the one in Figure 1-6, are present in Vista, but Microsoft aims to make them less intrusive.

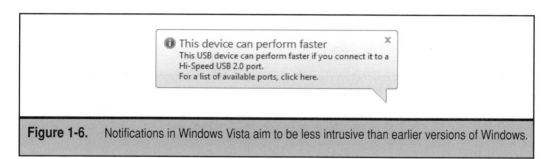

Figure 1-6. Notifications in Windows Vista aim to be less intrusive than earlier versions of Windows.

NOTE Naturally, you can disable notifications, but if you still like seeing the information they present, the Vista version is a little less "in your face."

In Aero, these windows gradually fade in and out, and won't display if you're in a full-screen application or screensaver. The notification balloons also feature larger icons, varying font sizes, and colors.

Tone

There's an even more subtle change to the GUI that the casual computer user might not be aware of—Microsoft has changed the way Windows talks to you. This means that the phrasing of text used for Vista to communicate with the user has changed.

Microsoft performed research and determined that users were finding Windows difficult to understand. In fact, some users felt insulted by the tone Windows took with them. Specifically, computer terminology and jargon were overused or used inconsistently, causing newer users to be confused.

With Vista, Microsoft has sought to provide technically accurate information in an objective and positive manner. For instance, Vista is embracing the use of first person and the active voice. Is it a big change? Not really, but you might not find your computer as condescending anymore.

Windows Sidebar and Gadgets

After the new look of Windows Vista, the next thing you'll likely notice is the new Windows Sidebar. This tool is located on the right side of your monitor and provides a launching point for performing common tasks and to organize information coming into your computer.

Windows Sidebar provides a number of useful tools and allows you to see quick information through applications called *gadgets*. The Windows Sidebar and some gadgets are shown in Figure 1-7.

By default, Windows Sidebar and gadgets are not displayed. However, this setting can be changed by following these steps:

1. From the Start menu, point to All Programs.
2. Select Accessories.
3. Select Sidebar.

Once the Sidebar has been activated, you can start using the gadgets Windows Vista has to offer.

Gadgets

The gadgets, which are housed in the Windows Sidebar, can be used to perform all sorts of useful tasks. You can check the time, convert currency, play a game, or even bid on eBay items. Several gadgets are included with Windows Vista, but you can also download hundreds more through the Internet. Some of the gadgets that are included are:

▼ **CPU Meter**   Shows the current percentage utilization of the computer's CPU and memory.

■ **Feed Viewer**   Displays information from a Really Simple Syndication (RSS) feed that has been configured in Internet Explorer.

■ **Slide Show**   Shows pictures from a folder as a continuous slide show.

▲ **Weather**   Displays a window pane with a background image representative of the local weather. This information is culled from MSN.com, based on the location information you entered during configuration.

Other gadgets include the Recycle Bin, a clock, and a calculator.

Figure 1-7.   The Windows Sidebar contains applications called gadgets.

Adding Gadgets to the Sidebar

To add a gadget to the Windows Sidebar, follow these steps:

1. Click the plus (+) button at the top of the sidebar.

2. In the Add Gadgets dialog box, double-click the gadgets you want to add to the Sidebar.

3. You can find additional gadgets by clicking Get More Gadgets Online. This launches Microsoft's gadgets site (www.microsoftgadgets.com), where you can download custom gadgets. These are gadgets made by Microsoft or other gadget enthusiasts.

4. Click the Close button when you're done adding gadgets.

NOTE   You can add the same type of gadget more than once. For instance, you can add the clock gadget several times, each one set to a different time zone. If you want more than one slide show running, you can do that, too.

Gadgets can be worked with in a couple of ways:

▼   They can be detached from Windows Sidebar and moved around the desktop by right-clicking the gadget and selecting Detach From Sidebar. If you decide to move it back to Windows Sidebar, just right-click the gadget and select Attach To Sidebar.

▲   When gadgets are detached, you can elect to have them on top of other windows by right-clicking the gadget and selecting Always On Top.

Make Your Own Gadgets

There's another way to get gadgets—you can make your own. While this is a cool, geeky thing to do, don't overlook how useful this can be in a business environment. For instance, you can design and create your own gadgets based on a particular organizational need. In an accounting firm, for example, you could create a gadget that adds or calls up information from your database. Rather than starting the entire database session, the specific information you want to call up can be done right from a gadget.

To create a gadget, you need two items:

▼   A *manifest* file named gadget.xml. This contains the settings for the gadget, including the gadget's name, author, and information about the HTML page that comprises the gadget. This is the information that will appear when you are selecting gadgets from the Gadget Picker dialog box.

▲   An HTML file. Gadgets are, in essence, HTML files. You just create an HTML file and then add the requisite tags and code.

Let's talk about these files in a little more depth.

Manifest file   While an HTML file is reasonably straightforward and well known, what's a manifest file? This is just a basic text file that you can create with Notepad or another text editor. The file should look something like the following code:

```
<?xml version="1.0" encoding="utf-8" ?>
<gadget>
 <name>SuperGlobalMegaCorp Systems Gadget</name>
 <author>Mike Bolton</author>
 <copyright>2006 SuperGlobalMegaCorp</copyright>
 <description>A gadget simulating a red Swingline stapler.</description>
 <icons>
 <icon>icon.png</icon>
 </icons>
 <version value="1.0.0.0" MinPlatformVersion="0.1"></version>
 <sidebar>
 <type>html</type>
 <permissions>full</permissions>
 <code>swingline.htm</code>
 <website>www.SuperGlobalMegaCorp.com </website>
 </sidebar>
</gadget>
```

That's it. That's all you need. Best of all, you can just copy this code, change the name and description data as needed, and use it for your own gadgets. But remember: the file must be named gadget.xml.

Table 1-3 explains what's going on with each tag.

Tag	Description
<name>	The gadget's name as it will appear in the Gadget Picker dialog box
<author>	Author name
<copyright>	Copyright information
<description>	A brief description of the gadget and what it does
<icon>	The name of the icon file
<code>	The name of the HTML file for your gadget
<website>	A Web site associated with your gadget

Table 1-3.   Manifest File Tags

HTML Script   The second file is your HTML file that contains the actual functionality of the gadget. Creating a gadget is a fairly straightforward affair, but it does require some knowledge of HTML scripting. If you're new to scripting, we're sorry to say that it's a little out of the scope of this book, but encourage you to experiment and learn more using the Web and other resources.

> **NOTE**   To learn more about scripting, take a look at *HTML & XHTML: The Complete Reference* by Thomas Powell or www.htmlgoodies.com.

Since gadgets are just HTML files, you can do as little or as much coding as you want, depending on what you want the gadget to do and how involved you want it to be.

When you're all done, simply put the manifest and HTML files into the gadgets folder, located at: %userprofile%\appdata\local\microsoft\windows sidebar\gadgets\gadget-name.gadget. For example, if your gadget is called helloworld, you would create a folder under the gadget folder listed and call it helloworld.gadget. This is where your manifest and HTML files should be placed.

Taskbar

When you have a program running in Windows, a button at the bottom of the screen shows you what's running, and it also allows you to click back and forth between applications. The taskbar has been enhanced in Windows Vista so that when you point your mouse at a taskbar button, Windows Vista displays a live thumbnail view of the window, showing the contents.

> **NOTE**   If you have multiple types of windows open (for example, if you're visiting several Web pages in multiple Internet Explorer windows), they are all grouped together. When you point the mouse at that button, a thumbnail of the most recently accessed window is displayed.

Flip and Flip 3D

Another Windows feature—one that not too many people use—that has been expanded upon in Windows Vista is the ALT+TAB key combination. In earlier versions of Windows, the ALT+TAB key combination would let you move through your open applications. In Windows Vista, however, the ALT+TAB combination displays a *flip* view containing the live thumbnails of all the open windows.

Holding down the ALT key keeps Windows Flip active, while pressing Tab while holding down Alt allows you to cycle through your open windows.

A similar feature is Windows Flip 3D. Basically, this provides the exact same feature as Windows Flip; however, the thumbnails are displayed in a 3D view. This is accomplished by holding down the Windows logo key. Pressing the Tab key while holding down the Windows logo key allows you to cycle through the windows. When you release the Windows logo key, the currently viewed window is selected. This is shown in Figure 1-8.

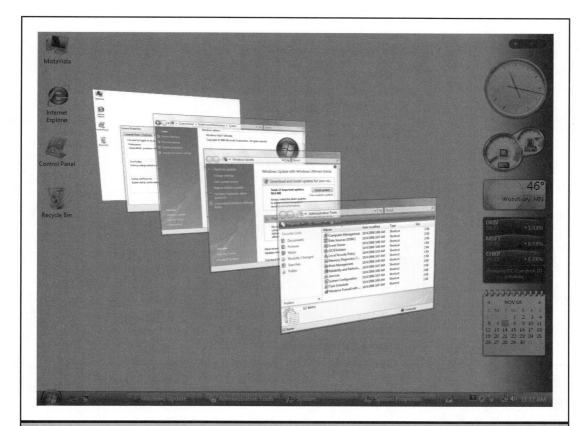

Figure 1-8.   Windows Flip 3D provides the same functionality as Windows Flip, but with a cool 3D interface.

Start Menu

Let's take a quick look at one of the most active areas on your Windows desktop: the Start menu.

When you click the Start button on the taskbar, the Start menu appears. This is shown in Figure 1-9.

The Start menu is comprised of three areas:

▼ **Programs list**   A display of recently used programs and programs that you've pinned to the menu. Up to eight recent programs are displayed, as well as Internet Explorer and Windows Mail.

■ **Search box**   Allows you to search your computer for specific files, folders, or applications.

▲ **Right pane**   Used to access commonly used folders and features. The right pane also includes the Lock and Options buttons.

Figure 1-9.   The Start menu is the launching point in Windows Vista.

Instant Search

A new feature added to the Start menu is a feature called Instant Search. This tool can help you find and launch files and applications on your computer. You just type a keyword, name, or phrase into the tool, and it will search your computer for it.

Instant Search prioritizes the results of your search. That is, results of your search will be optimized based on your current activity. For example, if you've been searching through your gadgets folder for a specific gadget, those results will be listed first.

Instant Search can be accessed from several places in Windows Vista:

▼   **The Start menu**   Instant Search is located at the bottom of the Windows Vista Start menu. Just open the Start menu, and type the keyword into the Instant Search field. As you type, Windows Vista starts looking for and displaying matching items, including bookmarked Web pages, documents, media, contacts, calendar events, or e-mails.

■   **Explorers**   The Instant Search tool is located in the upper-right corner of every Windows Explorer window.

■   **Control Panel**   As with the Windows Explorers, the Instant Search tool is located in the upper-right corner of Control Panel. Type the keyword for what you want to do, and the tool will search for the most relevant options.

▲   **Advanced Search pane**   If you want more precise or powerful search options, the advanced Search pane can perform a search based on multiple criteria. For example, if you are looking for a document in a specific folder that was created on a specific date, enter those parameters and the search tool will go looking for it.

Windows Vista also utilizes *Search Folders*. These are searches you've already conducted and are likely to run again. Just click the desired Search Folder, and Instant Search will go looking for results.

Turning Off and Shutting Down

One of the key performance features of Windows Vista is how it turns off and shuts down. In earlier versions of Windows, both actions accomplished the same thing: Windows ceased what it was doing, saved what needed to be saved, parked the hard drive heads, and turned itself off. Turning off and shutting down a computer running Windows Vista, however, are not synonymous actions. Let's take a closer look at what Vista does when you are done working.

Turning Off   When you turn off a computer running Windows Vista, the computer enters a sleep state. Entering a sleep state causes Windows Vista to do the following:

▼   Saves all work.

■   Turns off the display.

▲   Enters the computer into sleep mode.

When in sleep mode, the computer doesn't power off entirely; rather, it stops the PC's fan, the hard drive stops spinning, and the computer enters a low-power mode. This is useful, because when you "start" the computer again, it fires right up and is ready for action.

To enter sleep mode, click the Start button, and then click the GUI's Power button. To wake the computer up, press the computer's Power button or a button on the keyboard.

Keep in mind that not every computer is capable of entering sleep mode. It depends on your hardware configuration, whether updates requiring a reboot have been installed, or whether sleep mode has been administratively disabled.

NOTE   Because the computer is still drawing power in sleep mode, don't try to add or remove any internal hardware during this time. Make sure the computer is completely shut down and unplugged from the power source; otherwise, the last thing you'll see is a bright blue flash.

Shutting Down   As opposed to turning off a computer, shutting down the computer completely shuts it off.

To shut down a computer running Windows Vista:

1.   Click Start, and then click the Options button to the right of the Power and Lock buttons.

2.   Click Shut Down.

Not much more to say about that, but you may want to consider educating your users on these nuances so that they don't assume that they have truly shut down the computer when they selected the "Turned Off" option.

SuperFetch

When Windows is running, there's a lot going on behind the scenes that you don't even know about. It's cleaning up system files, running virus scans, and so forth. Windows tries to keep this impact as minimal as possible by using *fetch* technology.

In Windows XP, it used *Prefetch*. This loaded the majority of files and data needed by an application into memory so that they could be quickly accessed when needed. In Windows Vista, Microsoft has introduced *SuperFetch*.

SuperFetch not only preloads information, it also builds a profile of the applications, incorporating information about how you use them. As such, that data is also preloaded. It also analyzes when you use different applications and preloads them based on when you use them. For example, if you open up the expense report every Friday at 2 p.m., SuperFetch will remember that and get it ready for you.

ReadyBoost

Windows uses virtual memory to, in essence, give your computer more memory. That is, it utilizes so-called page files on the hard drive to temporarily store data from system memory. The problem with this scenario is that accessing the page file on a hard drive is much slower than accessing the same information stored in physical memory. This can be especially challenging for a tool like SuperFetch, which is really affected by a slow page file.

Microsoft has figured out a way to increase the speed of the paging file by implementing its ReadyBoost technology. ReadyBoost uses the popular USB 2.0 sticks and flash drives to store the active paging file. These drives are pretty inexpensive. You can pick up a 2-GB stick for about $50. And they are getting larger and cheaper by the day. USB drives are still not as efficient as physical memory, but they're much faster than hard drives. Here's how you can set up ReadyBoost on your users' computers:

1. Insert a USB 2.0 memory stick into the computer. An AutoPlay dialog box will appear.

2. You'll be asked to indicate how much storage space you want to designate to SuperFetch.

3. The stick can be removed at any time without losing data, and you can still use it for other files.

NOTE   On the memory stick, your SuperFetch data is encrypted, so it is not accessible when the stick is used on another computer.

Restart Manager

One of Windows more aggravating traits is having to reboot the computer when new software or an update is installed. Microsoft seems to be working on this issue, because one of Windows Vista's most highly touted features is Restart Manager.

The system needs to be rebooted after an installation or update because some of those files being updated are being used by the running application or service. The Restart Manager shuts down all but the most critical system services. Once the new files are installed, the processes can be restarted.

Internet Explorer 7

Internet Explorer 7 was expected to be part of a Microsoft one-two punch, but when it was released in October 2006, it turned out to be a leading left. Initially, Microsoft had intended to release Internet Explorer 7 and Vista at the same time. As a number of Internet Explorer features are only available on Vista, its capabilities would have been in the spotlight. However, since Internet Explorer 7 was kept on track to be made public and Vista was delayed a few months, the two did not get the symbiotic release that Microsoft initially intended. Regardless, Vista includes Internet Explorer 7, and you can take advantage of those capabilities. Chances are you've been using Internet Explorer 7 for several months already, as Microsoft's adjusted strategy was to push upgrade to Internet Explorer 7 as part of its automatic update service for Windows XP and Windows Server 2003.

The program is available as a separate download and can be installed on a compatible Windows XP computer. Certain features, however, will only be available when Internet Explorer 7 operates on Vista. Regardless of the operating system used, the program presents terrific improvements in both usability and security. Microsoft is confident that these enhancements will address criticism leveled against previous versions of Internet Explorer, including complaints that those versions provide clunky, sluggish experience of content and considerable security vulnerabilities. Figure 1-10 shows what Internet Explorer 7 looks like.

Internet Explorer 7 is substantially more secure than Internet Explorer 6. By default, Internet Explorer 7 leverages Vista's UAC feature to provide users with a secure environment from which to browse the Internet. This "Protected Mode" gives the user enough access to browse Web sites, but not enough to damage the operating system or data. While in Protected Mode on a computer running Vista, Internet Explorer 7 cuts off access to the system registry, blocks installation of software, blocks hijacking of Internet Explorer 7 settings, and filters malicious sites that "phish" for user and system information.

In addition to the security enhancements, Internet Explorer 7 offers a rethought and refined interface. New features bring it up to speed with most competitive browsers. Tabbed browsing is finally brought to the Microsoft platform with Internet Explorer 7, affording a set of controls to browse multiple sites through an easy-to-navigate set of tabs that can be grouped and stored for quick retrieval.

Internet Explorer 7 also includes a native RSS client, making RSS feeds available from anywhere in the operating system. Users can select Delete Browsing from the Tools menu and wipe out the entire browsing history, including the URL history, cookies, temporary files, Web site form data, and Web site passwords. Enhanced printing options allow for partial page prints and rescaling of full Web pages to fit into the margins of a page.

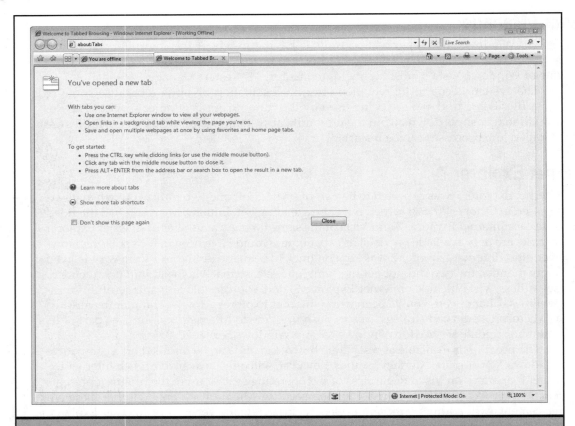

Figure 1-10. Internet Explorer 7 has been revamped and has features available only in Windows Vista.

Internet Explorer 7 has several enhancements for manageability, too. It includes an application compatibility tool that will confirm compatibility with legacy sites visited by Internet Explorer 7. An updated Internet Explorer Administrators' Kit (IEAK) includes documentation and tools to package the program for deployments in almost any environment. Another feature that can greatly affect administrators is that every aspect of Internet Explorer 7 can be set and managed centrally in Group Policy.

NOTE Internet Explorer 7 is examined in more depth in Chapter 12.

While this isn't the complete list of all the new stuff Windows Vista has to offer, it's enough to get us started. As we proceed through the coming chapters, we'll expand on some of the aforementioned features and introduce you to some others that will help your organization, your IT infrastructure, and your users.

CHAPTER 2

Planning a Windows Vista Deployment

Now that you know what's new and significantly changed in Windows Vista, you need to figure out how to get it into your organization with the least negative impact possible. This chapter goes hand-in-hand with Chapter 3 to help you deploy Windows Vista across your organization. The focus of this chapter—as you have probably deduced from the cleverly crafted title—is planning for a deployment.

True, you could just take a DVD of Vista around to all your computers and start installing, assuming every desktop had a DVD reader. Let's say each did—in a large organization, that could take more time than expected, and you might not get what you planned for. At best, it would take a long time, but when you were done, everything would be running fine. This might be acceptable if the organization is willing to accept the risk. However, the worst case might be that you lose important data and your applications may not work. You could suffer the long, unforeseen delays and unexpected costs that are the hallmarks of a poorly planned project. Initially, your best course of action is to take a step back, look at your organization, and consider the wisest way to deploy Windows Vista.

Some of the many things to consider are whether you should migrate or upgrade to the new operating system (OS). Equally important will be doing the groundwork to ensure that you know exactly which of your applications will be compatible with Vista and which won't. Once you know this, you'll be well equipped to decide how to remedy any incompatibilities. You'll also need an easy and trustworthy way to check your computers to ensure that they are Vista-compatible.

DECIDING WHETHER TO MIGRATE OR UPGRADE

There are two routes you can follow when implementing Windows Vista across your organization: migration or upgrade. The words might seem synonymous, but they aren't. What's the difference? The difference adds up to dollars and time. In some organizations, migration is going to save both time and money. In another organization, just the opposite will be true. This section examines both scenarios and helps you decide which path makes the most sense for your organization.

Understanding Migration

A migration is a scenario where you get brand-new computers with Windows Vista either preinstalled or you perform an installation yourself. Where the real action takes place is moving all the users' applications, settings, bookmarks, documents, and anything else unique to them from the old computer to the shiny new one. In days past, this was a horrendous chore. Now, thanks to Microsoft's Systems Management Server (SMS) and other migration tools, you can easily transfer these settings automatically.

Migration Methods

Windows Vista offers three methods to perform a migration. You can transfer your files and settings via:

▼ A network connection

■ Removable media, like a Universal Serial Bus (USB) flash drive or an external hard disk

▲ Recordable CD or DVD

The easiest method is to simply transfer settings across the network. This requires the minimum amount of effort, since everything will be plugged in and ready to go. On the other hand, you might not have the new computer networked yet, so transferring files and settings might be best on a flash drive or a recordable CD or DVD, depending on how much data you need to move. Which method you choose to use is dependent on your organization, your computers' configuration, and—to a large extent—personal preference.

Migration Tools

Microsoft has made a couple of tools available that you can use to transfer your files and settings, including:

▼ **Windows Easy Transfer**   This tool is available on the Windows Vista DVD. Figure 2-1 shows this tool. This is a good tool for a small handful of computers. It can move user accounts, files and folders, program settings, Internet settings and favorites, and e-mail settings.

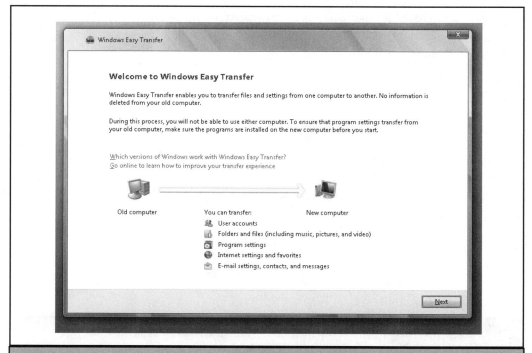

Figure 2-1.   Windows Easy Transfer allows files and settings to be transferred from an older version of Windows to Windows Vista.

▲   **User State Migration Tool (USMT)**   This is used to migrate files and settings for a number of users and multiple computers. You configure this tool for your unique environment using the migration rule (.xml) files to control which user accounts and files and settings are migrated. Your migration can be automated using the two USMT command-line tools. These control collecting and restoring user files and settings.

NOTE   There is a nice tool called Desktop DNA that also works well. Some of you might remember it as a Miramar Systems product. They were acquired by Computer Associates back in mid-2004, so it is now a CA Unicenter product. More information on it can be found at www3.ca.com/solutions/Product.aspx?ID=4920.

We'll explain how to use these tools in more depth in Chapter 3. But for now, as you plan your migration, upgrade, or combination deployment, think about which tools will be ideal for your individual solution.

Understanding an Upgrade

An upgrade uses your existing computers (assuming they're Vista-capable) and replaces Windows 2000 or XP with Windows Vista. All your users' settings should still be the same, the applications should still be there, and (hopefully) everything will work the way you want it to. This basic process is illustrated in Figure 2-2.

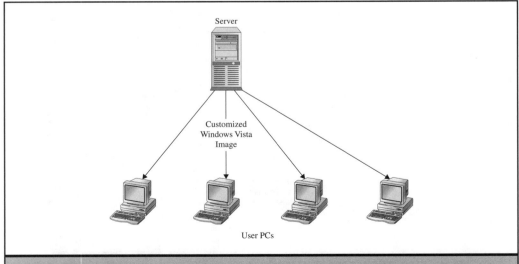

Figure 2-2.   Upgrading is simplified with Windows Vista's built-in imaging tools.

NOTE   An upgrade is only possible to Windows 2000 or XP computers. Earlier versions of Windows cannot be upgraded to Windows Vista.

Before starting an upgrade, you need to ensure that your computers are Vista-capable. We can't stress this enough, because if your computers don't meet the basic minimum requirements and you still want Windows Vista, you're going to have to beef up the lagging components on the computer; otherwise, you'll wind up shelling out money for new computers. If you buy new computers on which to install Windows Vista, go ahead and flip back to the migration section.

NOTE   We'll probably say this a few times, and it will certainly be apparent to you when running Vista with a few active applications: 512 megabytes (MB) of random access memory (RAM) is not enough. This is especially true if you are planning to run new applications, like Microsoft Office 2007. When you are planning, plan for as much RAM as you can reasonably get. One gigabyte (GB) is good; two is better.

As a reminder, Table 2-1 lists the basic minimums for a Windows Vista system.

	Vista Capable	Vista Premium Ready
Processor	800 MHz (32-bit or 64-bit)	1.0 GHz (32-bit or 64-bit)
Memory	512 MB RAM	1 GB RAM
Graphics card	DirectX 9-capable	DirectX 9-capable GPU with Hardware Pixel Shader v 2.0 and WDDM driver support
Graphics memory	32 MB RAM (SVGA-capable)	128 MB RAM up to 2,304,000 total pixels (e.g. 1920 × 1200) or 256+ MB for greater resolutions
Hard drive capacity	20 GB	40 GB
Hard drive free space	15 GB	15 GB
Hard drive type	Normal	Normal, but hybrid flash memory/hard disk recommended
Other drives	CD-ROM	DVD-ROM
Other requirements	n/a	Audio output Internet connectivity

Table 2-1.   Hardware Requirements for Windows Vista

Batch Rollouts vs. a Big Bang

Anyone who has had a rollout blow up on them will tell you that few things are worse. It's not even fun to imagine what it would be like to be in the limelight while deploying your new, untested OS organization-wide, only to find out that systems aren't compatible, you've misconfigured the image, your application doesn't work, drivers don't work, and a host of other gut-wrenching problems crop up. After all, if something goes wrong and user computers are down, business probably won't be getting done and fingers are going to point at you. Some would even call it an "automatic resume-generating event."

Rollout Phases

As such, we recommend rolling out your Vista deployment in phases. Consider the organization shown in Figure 2-3. Here, once Windows Vista has been tested and prepped, it is rolled out only to a handful of clients—clients that are as nonessential to the day-to-day running of the business as possible. You are planning to "learn something" during this phase, so don't include your CEO or his/her administrative assistant as part of the first rollout.

Once the first computers have been upgraded, spend some time checking out the devices, and make sure they work properly. Better yet, delegate some of the duty to the actual users, and get their real-life impressions on the usability of their new environment. They should use their computers as they normally would, poke around their lesser-used applications, make sure that everything works, and then tell you what doesn't work. If there are any problems during this phase, you can go back and double-check your work, and try again.

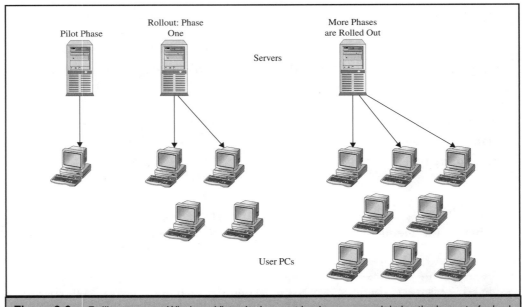

Figure 2-3. Rolling out your Windows Vista deployment in phases can minimize the impact of a bad image design.

Doing It All at Once

Alternately, you can take life by the horns and get it all done in one fell swoop. This is often called taking the 'Big Bang' approach. The payoff here is that if everything is configured properly and there are no problems, you can roll out the OS to everyone all at once and be done with it. It's sort of like ripping off a Band-Aid. Do it once, quickly, and be done with it.

The problem, as we already noted, is that if there are any problems, most likely, everyone will have problems, including the CEO, CIO, etc., so not only will you run the risk of costing your organization stacks of money in lost productivity, you also won't be doing much to help your professional image.

Rollout Methods

Microsoft has taken great efforts to make an image-based deployment an easy process. And that's what we're going to spend the bulk of our time and space discussing in this chapter and the next. It's a great way to deploy if you have lots of computers to upgrade. This is sort of a middle-of-the-road solution and, depending on the size of your organization, there may be other ways in which you deploy Vista.

Really Big Environments

If you're planning on deploying Vista in a particularly large organization, you can use Windows Deployment Services (WDS), which is the Vista version of Remote Installation Services (RIS) in Windows Server 2003. You might also want to use Microsoft's Solution Accelerator for Business Desktop Deployment (BDD). This includes templates to help with your planning, building, testing, and rolling out of your deployment. Your organization may have already done this before, so don't forget to leverage any existing deployment resources that were used for Windows XP where you can.

Smaller Environments

On the other hand, your organization might be relatively small. Imaging is still a good option in this case, but you can do a more traditional unattended setup, using Windows System Image Manager (WSIM) to create the unattend.xml files and distribution shares. Preboot Execution Environment (PXE) is used to boot the clients into Windows PE. The clients are connected to the distribution shares across the network, and then Vista is installed.

Really Small Environments

If yours is a particularly small environment (only a handful of computers), then don't even bother with an image—you can do it right from the Vista installation DVD. Why overcomplicate the whole process when you don't need to?

INTRODUCTION TO DEPLOYMENTS

In French, ROI means *king*. In business, ROI might as well mean the same thing. ROI is an acronym for *return on investment*. If you're going to invest in something new (like, oh, I don't know, a new, organization-wide operating system), you want to make sure you

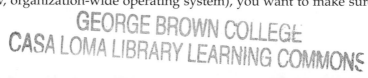

get something back for the investment. Happily, you'll get a much better ROI on a Vista deployment than you may have on earlier Windows releases.

In the past, deploying a new OS could be a complicated and time-consuming process. The IT department had to design the new client platform to meet organizational security needs, ensure compatibility with existing applications, and then, finally, deploy the OS. Thankfully, Microsoft seems to have smoothed out a lot of the rough edges on a Vista deployment, ultimately reducing the cost of a deployment.

Engineering the Client

Vista makes client-image engineering much easier than with Windows XP. This is because Vista uses new imaging technologies and tools to develop and customize the image. This smoothes out the process, because you and your IT department don't have to spend as much time engineering the client image to meet your system requirements.

The process of developing the distributable image is facilitated with some special applications that are available on Microsoft's Web site in conjunction with content and applications that are already on the Windows Vista DVD.

Application Compatibility

Microsoft has tried to ensure that Windows Vista supports the majority of applications that already run on Windows XP and earlier versions of Windows. This, again, saves your IT department time in assessing which applications will run on Vista and which won't.

NOTE In testing Vista, you'll probably find that some software does not work, especially older versions of antivirus software. Don't forget to check with all your software vendors for Vista-compatible versions and updates.

If you happen to use a specialized piece of software or hardware that is unique to your company, you want to ensure that it still works—otherwise, why bother upgrading? For example, companies that perform closed-captioning work use specific software for that very purpose. Car dealerships and hospitals have their own applications as well. If those applications won't work with Vista, upgrading isn't much of an upgrade.

You don't need to take Microsoft's word on it. There are a number of tools that you can use to ensure that your applications will work on Windows Vista. We'll talk about these tools in more depth later in this chapter.

Deployment

In earlier versions of Windows, you either had to run around with the install CD-ROM or a mapped network share and touch all of your computers, or use a third-party imaging product to deploy the OS image *en masse*. Because imaging is now built into Windows Vista, you can easily deploy it across your organization. Again, the cost savings here is not only the manpower of your IT department, but also the cost of that third-party imaging system.

The bad news is that companies making applications for deployment are going to take a financial hit. The good news is that those organizations deploying Vista to their users will save money, as deployment is better integrated into Windows.

DEPLOYMENT PROCESS OVERVIEW

Deploying any new OS is stressful and prone to cause headaches and pain. That said, the discomfort can at least be minimized if you follow some basic steps in your deployment.

As with any migration to a new OS, the process is anything but a simple matter of inserting the installation media into the drive bay and letting the computer do all the work. The process requires careful planning, meticulous testing, and a well-designed rollout.

The easiest way to migrate to Windows Vista is to buy workstations with it preinstalled. This avoids any configuration problems. However, since you're likely to be operating on some sort of budget and probably have specific requirements beyond the standard install, this might not be the most feasible plan.

If you decide to migrate from an existing Windows platform, there are four basic steps you should follow. Those steps are broken down in Table 2-2 and illustrated in Figure 2-4. These steps are explained in greater detail in the following sections.

NOTE   Obviously, for just one or two PCs, this is overkill. These steps are meant for large organizations with PCs that have a standard configuration.

Logical Design

The logical design stage involves picking the preferred features and configuration options of your "ideal" Windows Vista system configuration for both desktop and mobile users. This is the stage at which you should consider network parameters and protocols, as well as your file system structure and applications that will be used on the system.

Design Stage	Purpose
Logical design	To determine the fundamental features and framework of the preferred Windows Vista configuration
Lab test	To build, configure, and test your design in a controlled environment
Implementation design	To evaluate and select Windows Vista automated installation methods
Pilot design	To approve the pilot Windows Vista configuration and implementation process

Table 2-2.   Design Stages for Migration to Windows Vista

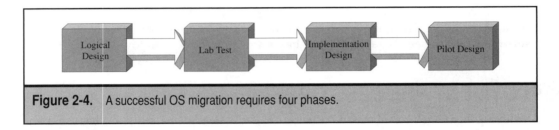

Figure 2-4. A successful OS migration requires four phases.

For instance, if you will be using a certain word processor, will it be compatible with Windows Vista? It's best to check with the Microsoft Web site to make sure everything will run properly.

NOTE   We'll talk about application compatibility tools later in this chapter.

Test System

The next stage is to build a test system. At this stage, you will take your "ideal" system and install it on a few computers in an isolated lab in preparation for constructing the final image. Make sure that you have computers that represent the hardware standard(s) for your organization and that you do this process for each of them. Don't connect this test lab to your production network. You want to test your system and applications to ensure that it operates properly and that you have all the necessary device drivers.

NOTE   Windows Vista is compatible with a slew of device drivers right out of the box. However, in the event that a peripheral or two is not supported by Windows Vista, it is a good idea to go to your peripheral manufacturer's Web site and check for updated device drivers.

Implementation Design

Once you've tweaked your Windows Vista systems in an isolated lab, you should decide how you will deliver the new OS. Again, this method should be tested in your lab to ferret out any problems that might arise.

You could run around from computer to computer with an installation disk and a list of product keys, but with Windows Vista, you can install the OS automatically from your administration PC. As we've noted, one of Vista's best features is its ability to be distributed across a network from a single image or set of images.

Pilot Design

In the last phase, you should roll out Windows Vista to one computer and then to progressively more users, performing any last-minute checks before making the final rollout. Once those PCs are running properly, you can implement your final rollout strategy. Again, you don't need to upgrade all your computers at once. There's something to be said for being a bit cautious and deploying Vista in phases.

PLANNING

The aforementioned section highlighted the broad strokes of a Windows Vista deployment. Let's drill down a little deeper and take a look at some of the specifics that are involved in a Vista deployment.

While earlier versions of Windows could be a headache when it came to deploying them, Microsoft aims to make deployment much less of a problem with Vista. Some of the improvements in Vista that should make the deployment process smoother include:

▼　Modularization of device features. This means that you only deploy what you want to, which keeps the images as streamlined as possible.

■　A single answer file (unattend.xml), which uses the standard eXtensible Markup Language (XML) format.

■　A standard imaging format called Windows Imaging Format (WIM). This employs compression and single-instance storage to keep the image as small as possible. WIM is file-based, rather than sector-based, like most disk image formats. This makes it possible to mount WIM images to folders so you can easily add and remove components without having to rebuild the entire image.

▲　A disk-imaging tool called ImageX that can be run from the command line or within the Windows PE environment.

We'll cover the basic steps here to help you plan and prepare for a complete deployment. We'll tell you exactly what to click and what to press in Chapter 3.

Build a Lab

Once you've figured out your organization's needs and what you've already got in place, it's time to start getting your hands dirty. It's time to build a lab environment in which you can create your Vista image.

Your lab needs two pieces of equipment, with specific software and hardware configurations, as shown in Figure 2-5:

▼　**Technician computer**   This is the computer on which you will need to download and install Windows Automated Installation Kit (AIK), which is available from Microsoft. The computer can be running Windows XP, Windows Server 2003, or Windows Vista. It needs a DVD-ROM drive and a CD-RW drive (or a combination drive that does both). The technician computer is where you will design and configure your Vista image.

▲　**Master computer**   This computer is also known as a reference computer, and is a fully assembled computer on which you will install a customized version of Windows Vista using the Windows Vista DVD and a customized answer file. When it is installed, you will then capture and store an image of that installation on a network share. The computer must have a DVD-ROM drive, network card, floppy drive, or USB support. You don't need any specific software installed.

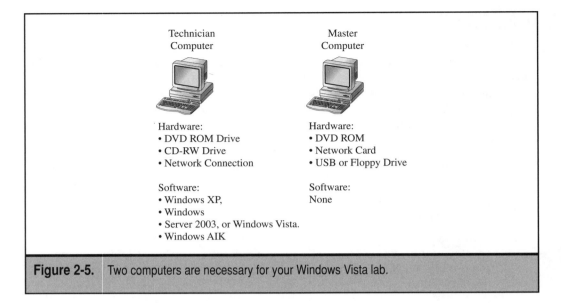

Figure 2-5. Two computers are necessary for your Windows Vista lab.

Answer File

When you have your lab in place, you'll need an important document called an *answer file*. This contains the information necessary to complete a mass Vista deployment. The process requires five basic steps:

▼ Creating a new answer file.

■ Adding components to the file.

■ Changing values or settings in the file.

■ Validating the file.

▲ Saving the file to distributable media.

In Chapter 3, we'll show you exactly how to make an answer file.

Building a Master Installation and Creating an Image

The master computer is where the customized installation of Vista is created that you will duplicate on your target computers. The master installation can be accomplished by using the Windows Vista DVD and the answer file you just created.

Once a master installation is completed, you can deploy that image to your organization's computers. To accomplish this, you'll need ImageX and Windows PE:

▼ **ImageX**   This is a command-line tool that allows you to capture, modify, and apply disk changes.

▲ **Windows PE**   This is an environment from which you can capture and deploy an image.

In this step, you are actually capturing the image that will be deployed across your organization's PCs.

Proof of Concept

Once you've plotted out your deployment and developed your image, you want to test it to make sure it's what you want. At this stage, you'll enter the piloting phase of the deployment, as we noted earlier. Once the OS has been piloted, you can check out the deployment and tweak it as necessary.

Piloting the Solution

When you pilot your Windows Vista image, you should first send it to a single computer to ensure that everything is working properly. Be as thorough as you can in checking out how the computer works. Are there any driver conflicts? Are there any question marks in Device Manager? Are essential applications running properly? Are nonessential applications running properly?

Refining Plans and Assets

If, in the course of your pilot test, you find that there are any problems with your deployment, now is the time to go back and tweak the image before you start rolling it out to the entire organization.

DEPLOYING

Getting ready for deployment tasks includes selecting a deployment tool and technique. Deployment technologies are either script-based or traditional imaging and deployment tools from third-party vendors. Script-based solutions are flexible across a wide range of hardware platforms and tend to be slow, with only a few standard methodologies. Imaging technologies are a quick way to deploy operating systems, though, to date, they can be rigid, have a steep learning curve, and place a burden on administrators to maintain an image library.

Deployment Tools

You will need a deployment tool to get your image out and installed to your workstations. Microsoft does provide its own Vista-specific deployment tool; however, there are also third-party options you can consider.

The deployment tool is a software package that facilitates packaging, distribution, installation, and reporting. Selecting the right software can be tough. A blend of variables goes into the decision, including the scale of your enterprise, the makeup of the desktop fleet, and the skill sets of your IT group, to name a few. At the same time you select your deployment tool set, you decide which technique to use. Before we review some of the well-known deployment tools, let's look at the techniques.

Deployment Techniques

Several deployment techniques and tools are available for deploying Vista. The four techniques covered here are:

▼ **Basic or manual**   Pack up your CD case, and off you go. Insert your latest image on DVD or CD into the workstation, and settle into comfortable few hours where you click your mouse and check off the boxes on your list. No matter which technique or tool you choose, you have to do a manual install at least once to establish your base installation. Using installation media, you install the operating system, device drivers, service packs, hotfixes, and applications and configure the user's profile (file and print services, etc.) using a checklist, your engineering skill, and a mouse. This takes a lot of time and has a heightened risk of failures deriving from missteps and bad luck.

■ **Standardized**   Image-based installs present plenty of opportunities to preconfigure major portions of the desktop, such as common profiles for virtual private network (VPN) client software or Microsoft Office, for example. To take the process to the next level, each manual step in the build process can be further automated using scripts and support tools. Using a base image plus automation scripts, the standardized installation can be a reliable, repeatable process.

■ **Lite touch install (LTI)**   As with the standardized method, LTI starts with a base image—further application installations and user profile configurations are accomplished either almost or totally through automation and with minimal input by the user. You distribute your solution through a custom-made installation disk, network share, disk cloning, or other method. The distinguishing point is that the imaging and installation process are activated manually. The LTI process includes three steps: gather pre-engineered configuration settings, prompt the user for missing data or ask the user to validate settings, and, last, execute the installation process. LTI is the best choice when you have a fully automated install process but you don't have the necessary heuristics to determine all the settings automatically. LTI is a pretty good solution, but it's not optimal.

▲ **Zero touch install (ZTI)**   As the name implies, you have no physical interaction with the target systems, and neither does the user (during installation). Unlike the other options, you never have to be in the same room as the client computer. ZTI is a deployment solution where your users activate the process by which your solution is delivered with minimal human interaction. The goal is to develop a reliable, scalable, secure, and manageable enterprise self-service deployment framework.

The time it takes to upgrade a system to Vista manually can range from 2 to 10 hours. The time it takes to upgrade a system using ZTI is reduced substantially, to a range of one to three hours, with as little as five minutes of actual screen time. A "real-world" rule of thumb, using imaging over a 100-Mb (megabit) switched local network, is that it will take approximately 10 minutes per GB. The time savings is dropped, sometimes considerably, given the infrastructure and engineering investments required to reach an optimized deployment solution. Everyone has to understand where the marginal investments meet the marginal rewards and when spending money on infrastructure fails to yield a return that covers the costs, as Figure 2-6 illustrates.

Finding that threshold is an important step in deciding which deployment technique and which tool to use. Table 2-3 illustrates the different situations in which deployment techniques shine and where they may not work as well.

Table 2-3 illustrates the optimal use of the available deployment technologies, although most of the options can be used for other purposes. The OSD, for example, can deploy server images. Use this table as a guideline only. Another important factor in selecting your tool includes the not-so-distant roadmap for the Microsoft options.

In their next forms, Systems Management Server (SMS) and Automatic Deployment Services (ADS) will be consolidated into the Unified Enterprise OS Deployment solution in the form of the System Center Configuration Manager (SCCM) 2007 and the Windows Deployment Service. SCCM is really SMS 2007 (informally referred to as SMS v4) wrapped into the new System Center platform. ADS 1.1 will roll into SCCM as well, although it was also supposed to be integrated into WDS, which will be around for some time to come.

Hard Disk Drive Cloning

With this option, you copy your "sysprepped" image onto one or more hard disk drives using a duplicator. A disk duplicator of this type can be a handheld unit that duplicates one disk at a time or a floor-standing model that duplicates 10 drives simultaneously.

Cloning technology has kept pace with storage technology, supporting the full range of drive bus technology, including ATA, Serial ATA (SATA), Small Computer System Interface (SCSI) and USB drives, with standard transfer rates of 1 to 4 GB per minute. A couple of options for this kind of distribution include Logicube's Omniclone line (www.logicube.com) and Kanguru's KCLONE models (www.kanguru.com).

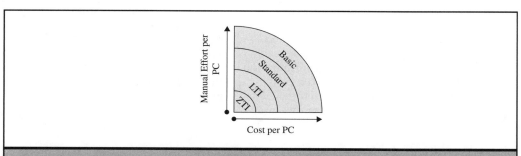

Figure 2-6.   The effort and cost for deployment techniques vary.

Image Deployment Options	Category	Sweet Spot	Pros	Cons
CD or DVD media	Basic	Occasional, one-time use, no network connectivity	Low-cost engineering No reliance on system management infrastructure	Highest cost per PC Most disruptive to users Inflexible
Disk cloning	Standard	Desktops or servers, batch deployments with basic or standard infrastructures	Low-cost engineering No reliance on system management infrastructure	High cost per PC Disruptive to users Inflexible
Microsoft Windows DS	LTI/ZTI	Desktops and simple servers, user-managed, small-scale deploys	Lower cost per PC Leverages AD infrastructure Supports future unified deployment and past operating systems (Windows 2000 – Longhorn/Vista)	Limited kinds of install packages Does not multicast
Microsoft SMS 2003 OSD	LTI/ZTI	Desktops and simple servers, self-service or administrator-managed in a rationalized or dynamic infrastructure	Lowest cost per PC Least disruptive to users Push/pull options	Requires high levels of engineering Relies on a rich, complex infrastructure
Microsoft Automated Deployment Services (ADS)	ZTI	Servers only, with a scripted, sequenced configuration in a rationalized or dynamic infrastructure	Highly customizable Multicast up to 128 computers simultaneously Relies on a simple infrastructure	Requires highest levels of engineering

Table 2-3.   Deployment Technologies

Windows Deployment Services

Windows Deployment Services (WDS) is a more comprehensive and viable solution than its predecessor Remote Installation Services (RIS), which failed to get a foothold at the enterprise level. You can add and remove servers in WDS and configure a variety of options, including computer naming rules, DHCP settings, and PXE response settings. You can add and remove installation and boot images, and organize images into image groups. WDS also leverages Windows PE, including the Vista-only version, 2.0. WDS can be scripted using a command-line interface. Figure 2-7 shows the WDS management console.

The WDS management console gives you full control over the image groups and images you add to them. You can configure permissions for each image group and for individual images, too. Unlike RIS, you can also associate an answer file (unattend.xml) with each image. You can associate different boot programs and boot images with x86-, x64-, and Intel Itanium-based systems.

For most, using WDS means first upgrading to WDS from RIS; for others, it means installing it from scratch. That is a simple matter of downloading WDS and installing it on a computer running Windows Server 2003 or higher. A great thing about WDS is that it is integrated into Microsoft's Solution Accelerator for Business Desktop Deployment (BDD). The BDD has guides that will walk you through the detailed steps of using WDS for user-activated installs. You can get WDS with BDD from the Microsoft Download Center at www.microsoft.com/downloads.

In addition to the server, there are a few more services that need to be hosted for WDS to work. These include a PXE server and a Trivial File Transfer Protocol (TFTP) server for network-booting a client to load and install an operating system. Both these servers can be hosted on the same computer as the WDS server or on separate systems.

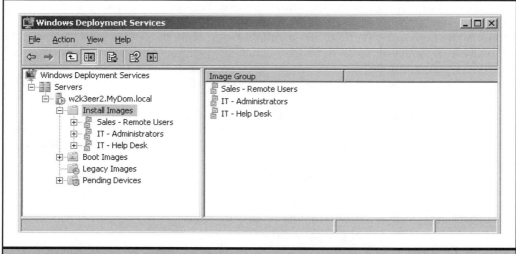

Figure 2-7.   Windows Deployment Services is managed via this console.

You will also need a shared folder and image repository to store boot images, installation images, and other files for network booting.

Some of the additional requirements which you should be aware of before you elect this option include:

▼   **Windows Server 2003**   The WDS server must run on Windows Server 2003, with Service Pack 1 or higher. In addition, IIS and RIS must be installed on the host server.

■   **Active Directory**   A WDS server must be either a member or a domain controller within an Active Directory domain. Any system within a domain can serve as a WDS server.

■   **DNS and DHCP**   Your network must have a Domain Name System (DNS) server for the local domain, which is required for Active Directory. Your network must also have an IPv4 or IPv6 dynamic addressing service to support Windows Preboot Execution Environment (Windows PXE).

■   **NTFS**   Windows Deployment Services requires a New Technology File System (NTFS) partition for the image repository. You cannot create the image repository on the partition containing the operating system files.

▲   **Rights**   Installing and administering WDS requires local administrator's rights on the WDS server.

Systems Management and Desktop Deployment Suites

Today's administrator has a lot of options from which to pick when it comes to enterprise desktop deployment tools. Commercial offerings include a range of software, including some specifically targeted toward deployments, and continue through to robust solutions that address the spectrum of desktop management. Venders are updating their offerings quickly for compatibility with Vista. Once you develop interest in a deployment technique, you should have no problem finding a suitable tool. Though Vista is new platform, the established deployment tools have long-standing pedigrees in this space, so you can purchase with confidence.

While SMS appears at the top of many ratings lists of deployment tools, other vendors have some terrific options that are widely adopted. A few products worth considering in this space include, in no particular order, Desktop Authority by ScriptLogic (www.scriptlogic.com), HP's OpenView (www.hp.com), and IBM's Tivoli Software (www.ibm.com). For the purposes of illustration, we focus on SMS 2003, which integrates smoothly with the Microsoft Vista platform and is the first to do so. No matter if you elect to use an alternate tool, whatever incidental tips you may pick up about SMS 2003 will be useful, we promise. Figure 2-8 shows an example of an SMS site diagram.

SMS Capabilities   SMS is a useful tool for a variety of network management needs. Some of the main capabilities of SMS 2003 include:

▼   **Image Capture**   SMS walks administrators through the process of capturing an image of a reference computer in the WIM format.

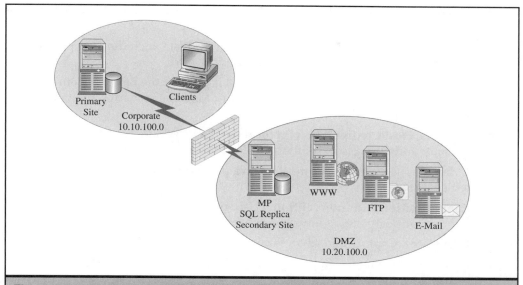

Figure 2-8. An example of an SMS 2003 site diagram shows relevant information about the network.

- **OS package management**   SMS customizes and manages the settings for individual deployments, including notifications, distribution settings, and network settings. You can manage replication across distribution points in a distributed enterprise.

- **User state migration**   SMS also integrates with USMT 2.6.1 and 3.0 to preserve user profiles when installing new operating systems.

- **Image deployment**   SMS deploys OS images using a highly customizable task-based infrastructure.

- **Inventory-based targeting**   Select target stations based on characteristics from the SMS enterprise inventory.

- ▲ **Reporting**   Centralize status and tracking reports on specific deployments to help troubleshoot and demonstrate deployment success.

SMS 2003 with the OSD feature pack is a turnkey solution. This combination makes it possible to manage the capture of an image, map report data for planning, distribute image files, kick off and track installations, and opens up the desktop for additional tasks with supplemental scripts.

SMS System Requirements   Before you consider using SMS 2003, here are some of the requirements you will need:

- ▼ **SMS 2003 Service Pack 2 (SP2) or above**   Ensure that every SMS server within the Vista infrastructure has SMS 2003 SP2.

- **Operating System Deployment (OSD) feature pack**   At least one server must have the OSD feature pack.

- **OSD feature pack update**   Brings support for Vista, including support for the .wim file format and 64-bit image capture.

- **Windows PE**   Windows PE environment is used by the target system to contact the SMS store. Version 1.6 will work for some scenarios, but version 2.0 is what is supported.

- **Dynamic Host Configuration Protocol (DHCP)**   Windows PE requires dynamic addressing, so a solution for IP addressing is required.

- **C drive**   The system drive must be on a partition named "C" and formatted with NTFS.

- **User initiation and intervention**   User notification balloons allow users to approve or postpone deployment processes.

- **User state**   Capture and restore user states with USMT.

- **SMS advertisements**   Support additional applications for self-service installs by users.

- ▲ **Task sequencing**   Bundle a package as part of a larger set of tasks.

For more information on obtaining, installing, and managing Service Pack 2 and the OSD feature pack and the feature pack update, see the SMS center at www.microsoft.com/smserver.

Microsoft Automated Deployment Services (ADS)

ADS is a rich, complex application for deploying Windows server operating systems on to bare-metal servers across large networks. With support for mass server administration using scripts, ADS also enables you to administer hundreds of servers simultaneously. It enables and requires a high level of engineering and automation for complex server builds. It is restricted to the server operating system, and is mentioned here for the sake of completion. There are components of ADS, however, that are reusable in a desktop scenario, such as the Automated Deployment Toolkit (ADT), which includes the same task sequencer that will be the core of future versions of WDS and SMS. At the time of this writing, version 1.1 is the current release.

Microsoft Solution Accelerator for Business Desktop Deployment (BDD)

This incredible asset is Microsoft's ongoing effort to help you deploy their operating systems. The asset started in 2001 and has been redesigned for every operating system release since Windows 2000. The accelerator for BDD is a centralized collection of end-to-end guides, templates, and tools. It covers the whole range of deployment scenarios and is completely updated for the new Vista platform and for the 2007 Office system. The BDD includes major assets for conducting network-wide inventories for planning, building out labs and image creation, and, of course, deployments. It has step-by-step guides for planning and executing lite touch and zero touch installs. The 2007 version includes support for:

▼   Windows Preinstallation Environment (Windows PE) 2.0

■   Windows PE CDs as boot disks

■   USMT for capturing and restoring user data

■   Microsoft Application Compatibility Toolkit 5.0 for gathering application inventory and for testing and remediation of application-compatibility issues

■   Office Professional Edition 2007 as cornerstone enterprise applications

■   Office Professional Edition 2007 Resource Kit for creating the custom-deployment packages

■   Windows Vista as the deployed computer operating system:

    ■   Windows Automated Install Kit (WAIK)

    ■   Guidance for User Account Control (UAC) and BitLocker technologies

    ■   Support for .wim images

    ■   Support for the SMS 2003 OSD feature pack update for Vista

▲   XML configuration files make it easy to update and customize

For the next-generation enterprises, BDD has been rethought. First, Microsoft recognizes that its deployment support is scattered across an unwieldy array of portal pages. Microsoft has put a stake in the ground and dubbed BDD as *the* deployment asset going forward. For centralized deployment advice and assets in the future, you will turn to BDD. When you do so, you will find that the 2007 version is simplified compared to previous versions. LT and ZT installs are merging, sharing many of the same tools and workflows. The current incarnation of LTI is less idiosyncratic than in the past—it looks more like a ZTI, so there is less to learn. Figure 2-9 shows what BDD looks like.

Microsoft's Solution Accelerator for BDD is an essential part of the planning process for just about any Vista deployment project. At a minimum, the guides will help you understand the scope of your deployment and manage it accordingly. For most, BDD will provide guidance and reusable tools that will accelerate the process and help you move forward competently.

Planning for Lite Touch and Zero Touch Installation Deployments

Using LTI or ZTI-based deployments means that you will be using some form of enterprise-class system management to distribute a highly engineered image. Using those two main components and leveraging a rich IT infrastructure, you can deploy Vista across the organization without ever being in the room. Planning for an LTI or ZTI includes the following key tasks:

▼   **Identify and assign roles and responsibilities**   Partition the work into work streams, and assign responsibility for them. Make sure you cover testing, security, and user experience in addition to designing and deploying. Design a communication plan and escalation path so the responsible parties can work as a team.

■   **Select your distribution method**   Two obvious choices include WDS and SMS.

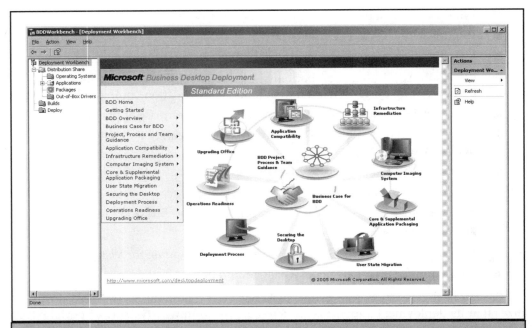

Figure 2-9. Microsoft's Business Desktop Deployment management console is the starting point for a system-wide deployment.

- **Ensure that your distribution method complies with Vista** WDS and SMS Operating System Deployment feature pack update are compatible with Vista's new platform technologies.

- **Validate your infrastructure readiness** Make sure you have a stable network environment, with enough bandwidth and storage capacity to pull off the deployment:

    - **Deployment service** For ZTI, install the SMS 2003 OSD feature pack, the OSD feature pack update, and any additional support files. Make sure you have a fully functioning WDS or SMS infrastructure, which includes healthy DNS, DHCP, and Active Directory services and reliable network connectivity among your target sites.

    - **Determine storage needs for user and user state data** When refreshing or upgrading a system, you will need to decide where to store the user data during the installation so that it can be restored upon completion. When affecting a sizable amount of workstations, the required space for user data can skyrocket to 10, 50, 100 GB, or more.

    - **Determine storage needs for deployment logs** Deployment logs will not need a lot of space, though they will need to be placed in a safe, secure location.

- ■ **Determine the bandwidth requirements**   Look at sites with slow links and work around the requirement for high bandwidth by offloading storage to a local server when possible.

- ■ **Categorize your workstations**   Identify the differences between the workstations in your organization. Important differences include hardware platforms, site locations, user roles (such as finance users), and any other category that may affect which image is deployed.

- ▲ **Train**   Get the knowledge you need to move forward with competence. If no one in your team has solid experience in deployments of this kind, make arrangements to have an escalation path to someone who does.

This is as far as we go into the process for now. We pick this up in the next chapter and offer details on how to leverage your deployment assets while executing your Vista deployment.

EXAMINING YOUR ORGANIZATION

Discovery is a key part of the planning process for any deployment project. What if, during an installation of Vista, you discovered that a user has installed a business-critical application that is incompatible with Vista? By proceeding, you would effectively block your entire company from conducting business. Progressing through installations without understanding the details, the context of how each workstation operates within the greater network and business, can be disastrous. You need to ensure that the new state will work for your users. You need to identify where it will fail and design a workaround before you deploy. You also need to ensure that the transformation process does not destroy key functionality for a user, such as access to important files and services. Before you begin transforming your network into a new state, you need to define—in detail—the current state. Discovery is the process by which the network, servers, and clients are enumerated. Pushing past elements that are indirectly related, such as Active Directory, you can define your environment in terms of applications, hardware, and network nodes.

Network Discovery

If you have more than 100 workstations, you should consider conducting a network discovery, even if you have topology records in your library. If you have more than a few sites, you should strongly consider refreshing your data before you deploy Vista. A fact of life is that inventory records quickly become stale. Networks are rarely static. People add or change nodes more than once a year, sometimes once a month, and do not always update records.

What to Gather

Network discovery has a couple of challenges in particular. First, you may need enterprise administrator rights in your network to navigate through network services. Second, some discovery tools will only report on hosts in the local subnet. Crossing over into other subnets may require special consideration. Valuable data to capture includes:

▼ Site name and/or site ID

■ Site location (city)

■ Site link speed

■ Gateway addresses

■ Active Directory site link metrics

■ Core infrastructure services, including versions and their IP addresses (DNS, DHCP, WINS, Active Directory)

■ Network print server addresses and models

▲ Number of nodes per operating system

Collection Tools

The following list includes options for network discovery. If your need is to simply update your diagrams for your deployment project, and you do not see yourself reusing the tool in the next year, and you have the skills and patience to work with an open-source tool, consider Nmap. If you can invest between $100 and $1,500, you can choose a richer option and get the support, integration, and documentation that will accompany the purchase:

▼ **Nmap ("Network Mapper")**   Nmap is an open-source utility for network exploration or security auditing. It uses raw IP packets to discover hosts on a network, the services (application name and version) those hosts offer, the operating systems and versions, the type of packet filters/firewalls in use, and many other characteristics. Nmap runs on most types of computers, though a Linux platform offers the best performance. Nmap is available under the terms of the GNU General Public License (insecure.org/).

■ **Security Tool Distributor (STD)**   STD is a Linux-based security tool. It's a Live Linux Distro, which means it runs from a bootable CD in memory without changing the native operating system of the host computer. Its purpose is to provide a Linux-based platform from which to execute security applications. You can find STD at s-t-d.org/.

■ **IPsonar**   For state-of-the-art visual analyses that bring the unknown aspects of IT infrastructure into focus, IPsonar is a hallmark solution for those that are serious about network node management. The Lumeta MapViewer network intelligence application provides an accurate baseline understanding of network connections, routes, and hosts through predefined views and interactive visual analyses—unique maps with supporting information that provide a holistic network view. Check out IPsonar at www.lumeta.com/solutions/ipsonar.asp.

▲ **SolarWinds toolset**   The toolset includes a suite of tools for network discovery. You can downsize or upsize your toolset, though the following list will suffice for deployment discovery. You can learn more about SolarWinds at www.solarwinds.com. The more relevant offerings include:

- **IP Network Browser** Allows you to perform a detailed discovery on one device or to scan a range of subnets.

- **Network Sonar** Uses a Simple Network Management Protocol (SNMP) discovery engine to create a detailed discovery database of a high-speed data network.

- **Subnet List** Discovers all subnets and masks on a network.

- **SNMP Sweep** Queries a defined IP address range and then locates both used and unused IP addresses.

- **DNS Audit** Inventories an IP address and validates the correct forward and reverse resolution of domain names.

Regardless of the toolset you choose, run impact tests on virtual or screened networks before executing the discovery tools on your production environment. Ensure that your discovery tool does not cause slow service or denial of service for your users.

NOTE You should inform your intrusion detection and security teams, as well as the relevant application personnel and server teams responsible for the computers that will be discovered. If you don't inform them of your scan(s), you will likely cause at least some panic as various alarms show up on their monitoring screens and alerts are sent to their pagers.

Hardware Inventory

A hardware inventory can be as simple as counting the number of workstations and recording the model numbers. From there, you can research compatibility with Vista using the manufacturer's Web site. Doing this, however, can be time-consuming if you have more than 10 models, and will lack the comprehensive benefits of a full analysis provided by a complete inventory. You may also lose out on some opportunities to optimize your workstation fleet. For example, if some of the models have the *minimum* but not the *recommended* memory, you may overlook that. If the workstation user is a power user, you would be doing the user a great disservice by underfitting their workstation memory. If you have a typical, complex, heterogeneous fleet of workstations, you will want to know more than just the model numbers.

Key factors that can help you decide whether you need to remediate any hardware deficiencies include:

- ▼ IP address and NetBIOS name (to identify the station)
- Location and users (also to identify the station)
- Workstation manufacturer and model
- Main board (manufacturer, model)
- Main board BIOS (vendor, name, and version)
- Processor (manufacturer, type, speed, and stepping)
- Memory (type and size)
- Network interface (manufacture, model, type, and network settings)

- Hard disk drive (type, size, free space, and file system)
- Operating system name and version
- ▲ Peripherals, such as personal printers and scanners

Hardware Tracking

Ideally, you have a systems management solution already in place that reports on your hardware, in which case, inventory is a snap. If that is not the case, then you have some research to do. If your workstations are running Windows 2000 or higher—and you have the time, skill, and patience—you can use home-grown scripts to capture this data. Keep in mind, however, that the time it takes to launch the script on each workstation in the environment, collect, and parse the results can be substantial, and you won't get any support from a manufacturer if your script fails.

The following tools can help track your system's hardware:

▼ **Microsoft Systems Management Server (SMS) 2003**   This has grown into one of the more widely adopted and respected options for systems management. The range of functions that it provides is beyond the scope of this book, but suffice it to say that any investment in SMS will yield benefits that span the range of desktop management. The current version is the first option to support Vista, and future versions will be part of Microsoft's new System Center and the unified deployment platforms. You can learn more about SMS by going to www.microsoft.com/smserver.

■ **Quest Reporter**   This tool comes either as part of one of Quest's award-winning suites or as a standalone product. The feature set may not be as full as other tools, and it may be more complex to configure. The Quest Reporter is a great tool if you already have a suite from Quest or if you find the feature set uniquely suited for your environment. Learn more about it at www.quest.com.

▲ **Ecora Auditor Professional**   Ecora offers reporting solutions, with an intuitive interface, a simple installation, and configurable reports. Ecora Auditor collects critical configuration data from Windows, Unix, Linux, NetWare, Cisco, MS-SQL Server, Exchange, Internet Information Server (IIS), Active Directory, Citrix, Oracle, and Lotus Domino platforms into a Microsoft Development Environment (MSDE) database, creating a cross-platform configuration repository. The Ecora Auditor Lite version is free and reports on a subset of data. You can learn more at www.ecora.com.

Some of the other options in use today are provided by Altiris (www.altiris.com) and NetIQ (www.netiq.com), both of which are great vendors for enterprise systems, including inventory solutions. Also, current patching solutions like BigFix and Patchlink have fantastic software and hardware inventory tools, and are certainly worth looking into.

Windows Vista Upgrade Advisor

Microsoft has made a tool that, when run, will tell you exactly where your computers are lacking—if at all—and which version of Vista would be most appropriate. This can be a real headache-reduction tool. It's recommended that you run the Windows Vista Upgrade Advisor on your standard systems to help you identify potential issues. This step can't hurt and may help ensure that your computers are Vista-compatible.

The Tool   Windows Vista Upgrade Advisor scans your computer to create a report of all system, device, and program compatibility issues, and then recommends how to correct them. It is a small, 6-MB application that can also advise you as to which version of Vista is most appropriate for your computer. At this time of this writing, it is available as a free download at go.microsoft.com/fwlink/?linkid=65926&clcid=0x409, but if the page has moved, a quick keyword search for the application name should help you find it.

> **NOTE**   Before running the Windows Vista Upgrade Advisor, plug in any peripheral devices—like printers, scanners, external hard drives, and so forth—so that these can be checked for compatibility as well.

The Windows Vista Upgrade Advisor is a nice tool, but it isn't perfect. It only works with 32-bit versions of Windows XP Service Pack 2. It will not work with Windows 98, Windows 2000, and 64-bit versions of Windows XP or Windows XP *without* Service Pack 2.

Usage   Once you download the application, you go through the standard installation wizard. Once installed, click Start Scan, and your computer will be examined for Windows Vista compatibility. A screen like the one in Figure 2-10 is shown while the Windows Vista Upgrade Advisor scans your computer.

When the scan is complete, you will see a window like the one in Figure 2-11.

The Windows Vista Upgrade Advisor will tell you if your computer's processor is zippy enough, if there is enough hard drive space, if the video card is robust enough and, ultimately, what version of Windows Vista would be best for the computer.

Application Inventory

The number-one issue that can hold a deployment project back is application compatibility. Compatibility remediation is covered elsewhere, though we would be remiss if we did not mention the key descriptions that you can collect on your applications to help identify the sticking points in advance. For details on common compatibility issues, see www.microsoft.com/technet/windowsvista/appcompat/entguid.mspx.

Microsoft says it has done a number of things to keep Vista compatible with existing applications:

▼   Vista was designed with application compatibility in mind. It was tested against 800 applications on daily builds.

■   Vista can automatically make basic compatibility changes via the Program Compatibility Assistant.

■   The Application Compatibility Toolkit helps customers understand the application environment, identifying those that need correction and helping to make those corrections.

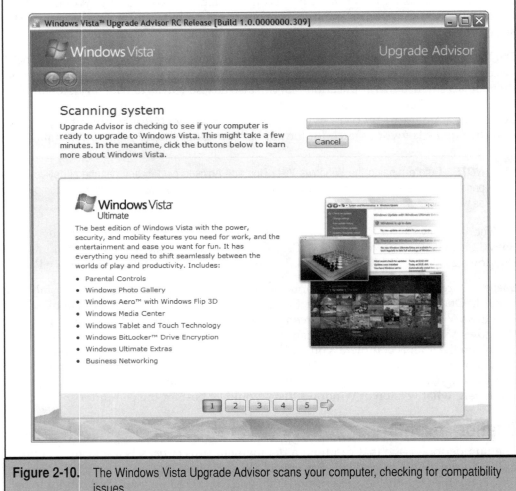

Figure 2-10.   The Windows Vista Upgrade Advisor scans your computer, checking for compatibility issues.

- ■ Vendors and customers can share compatibility test results online, giving an opportunity to learn from compatibility information.

- ▲ "Bridging" technologies can assist during the migration process. Microsoft Virtual PC, Virtual Server, and Terminal Server environments will help users use existing applications in a virtual OS environment.

Still, collecting data about applications can be a detailed process.

Collection

Collecting an inventory of every application and workstation in your organization can take time, but the benefits outweigh the costs. Vista is drastically different in the way it works on a network and the way it allows applications to interact with

Figure 2-11.   The Windows Vista Upgrade Advisor presents you with a list of compatibility issues if any are found.

local hardware. There will be a lot of compatibility issues—that is virtually guaranteed. You can also be sure that your deployment of Vista will suffer from disaster after disaster if you don't identify and remediate the issues in advance.

If you elect to perform lot sampling to build an inventory, select the workstations to inventory based on the following:

▼ Operating system version

■ Service pack level

■ Geographic location

■ Computer manufacturer model and type

■ Installed applications

■ Business unit in which the computer is used

▲ Organizational role that the user performs

Although you can use lot sampling to create a useful inventory, you do increase your risk of failure by overlooking applications that are installed on a workstation that did not make it into your sample group. Automated inventory tools can get you the data you need to more completely reduce the risks at a lower cost.

An automated analysis is also in your best interest, given the complexity involved. Key data points to collect and analyze about your applications include:

▼ Installation and setup

■ Registry keys

■ User configuration

■ Security requirements

■ Firewall traffic

■ Distributed Component Object Model (DCOM) details

■ Heap management

■ Use of forbidden kernel mode drivers

▲ The presence of Microsoft Internet Explorer

Collection Tools

Most of the tools mentioned in the section "Hardware Inventory" will also collect information on applications. Additional tools include the following.

Microsoft Application Compatibility Toolkit (ACT) 5.0. The toolkit does a good job of identifying Win32 applications and their characteristics. It includes a collection tool to scan workstations and a central repository based on Microsoft SQL to store results. ACT will analyze the data in the repository and identify any incompatible applications for you. When applications are found to be unsuited for Vista, ACT lets you know which part of the application will fail and why; whether it is a registry key created in a secure hive or access to kernel drivers that is not allowed in Vista. What sets the tools within ACT apart is that many are specially configured to identify compatibility issues specific to Vista. This tool is shown in Figure 2-12. It includes:

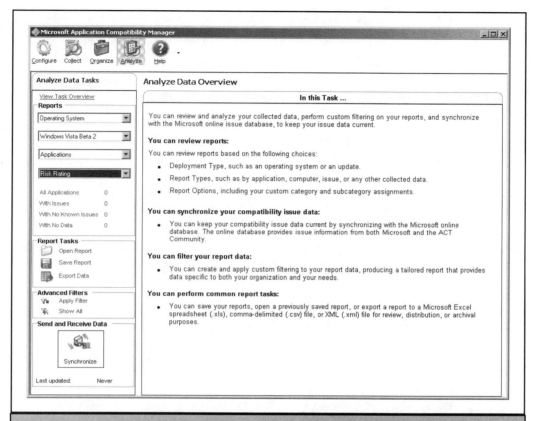

Figure 2-12. The Application Compatibility Toolkit 5.0 analysis engine examines your applications and their compatibility with Windows Vista.

▼   **Inventory Collector**   Used to generate an inventory of your installed software.

■   **Internet Explorer Compatibility Evaluator (IECE)**   Lists potential incompatibility details for internal and external Web sites.

■   **Update Impact Analyzer (UIA)**   Identifies potential application incompatibility details due to updates provided by Windows Update.

▲   **User Account Control Compatibility Evaluator (UACCE)**   Discovers potential application incompatibility details due to users running an application with low rights and permissions.

ACT breaks down its process into three phases:

▼   **Evaluate**   This is the most in-depth portion of the process and the one where your system's applications are studied. This step is broken into three sub-steps:

■   **Inventory**   A list of all applications on the PC are collected.

- **Prioritize**   Applications are ranked according to business priorities.
- **Test**   The applications are tested for compatibility with Windows Vista.

  When the evaluation phase is completed, you will have a list of "must-fix" application issues. From there, you move on to the next phase.

- **Mitigate**   This phase begins by reviewing the "must-fix" issues found in the Evaluate phase and determining how to resolve them. This phase takes place in your test environment. You will use Windows documentation, the ACT, and good old-fashioned trial-and-error to create compatibility solutions for each of the issues on the "must-fix" list. Ultimately, you'll have a tested solution package that can be deployed.

- **Deploy**   The final phase is to deploy the project into your production environment, along with any fix packages that you developed during the Mitigate phase.

Windows Vista Program Compatibility Assistant   The Program Compatibility Assistant (PCA) that was introduced with Windows XP is still present on Windows Vista. So if there is an application that doesn't run on Windows Vista, an easy way to try and work around the problem is to right-click the Application, select Properties from the context menu, and then click the Compatibility tab, as shown in Figure 2-13.

This feature isn't exactly the same as it was in Windows XP. For starters, when you try to run an application in Vista, the PCA attempts to automatically figure out the compatibility mode settings the program needs. It will either automatically configure said settings or it will prompt you for some information.

Another new feature in Vista is the use of file system and registry virtualization. Legacy applications often fail to run correctly because they try to write to protected areas of the file system or to restricted parts of the registry. In order to write to these areas, the user needs administrator credentials. So, in order to use those applications, administrators had to make domain users members of the local Administrators group on their desktop computers for third-part applications to install and run. Vista negotiates around this issue by allowing applications to write to corresponding per-user virtual areas of the file system and registry. That is, file system and registry virtualization allow non-administrators to install and run applications on their computers.

Microsoft Standard User Analyzer   Since a lot of compatibility problems stem from a simple issue—they need to be installed and run by someone with administrator privileges—Microsoft has developed a tool, called the Standard User Analyzer, to help identify applications that need to be installed or run with such privileges.

This application for Windows XP, Vista, and Windows Server 2003 is the next step up on the application compatibility food chain. This tool is really targeted more at developers, but can also be used by any IT professional to help diagnose issues that would prevent a program from running properly without administrator privileges.

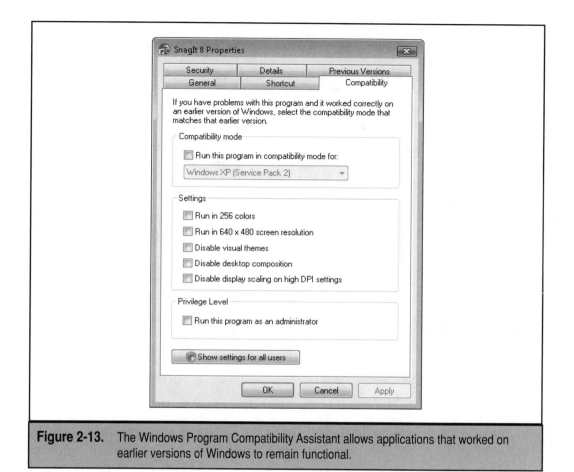

Figure 2-13.   The Windows Program Compatibility Assistant allows applications that worked on earlier versions of Windows to remain functional.

The Standard User Analyzer can help test your application to identify administrator dependencies for the following areas:

▼   File access

■   Registry access

■   INI files

■   Token issues

■   Security privileges

■   Namespace issues

▲   Other issues

Standard User Analyzer, shown in Figure 2-14, can be used in tandem with ACT. ACT includes a User Account Control (UAC) agent that you can deploy to desktops and use to locate applications that require administrator privileges.

The Standard User Analyzer is supposed to be run on the developer or tester's workstation to analyze specific applications. When Standard User Analyzer identifies any issues, the information can be included in the ACT database so you can track the application across your network.

Altiris Wise Package Studio   If your organization has a license for the Wise Package Studio, you may have a cost-effective solution for capturing application data. The studio keeps a software repository, a central database of details on applications. Analysis for compatibility, however, would have to be either scripted or done manually.

NOTE   Free expert tools for checking file and registry issues are available from Microsoft at www.microsoft.com/technet/sysinternals/default.mspx.

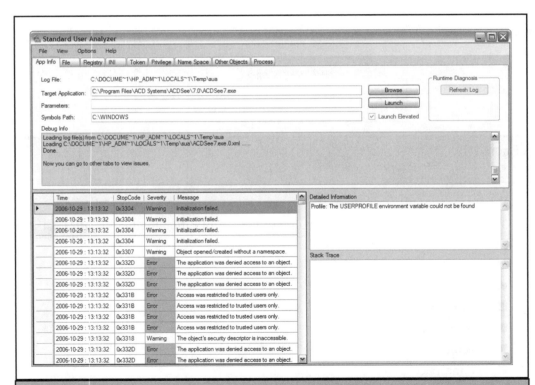

Figure 2-14.   The Standard User Analyzer checks applications to see whether administrator privileges are needed to install and run them.

User and Group Data

Another factor to consider in deployment planning is *data*. Users often store data on their local workstation and on network shares. Your users may also make use of group data—data that users read, update, and share among other users during the course of their working day. The more you understand how users store and use their data, the less likely you will be to cut off their access during your Vista deployment. A few options for collecting configuration information on data include:

▼ **Somarsoft's Dumpsec**   Use Dumpsec to export file and folder names, along with the access control entries (ACE) that compose the access control lists (ACLs) for each file and folder. Dumpsec is shown in Figure 2-15.

▲ **Microsoft's USMT Scanstate.exe**   The Scanstate.exe tool, which is part of USMT, captures user data and application descriptions on workstations and describes what it finds in an .xml file. The tool is customizable and scriptable, allowing you to target a particular user and specific applications or to capture them all. The tool will analyze and package the data, getting it ready for migration. For planning purposes, however, you can target the tool for reporting only.

Deploying Windows Vista won't be an instant, overnight undertaking. It will, and should, take some time to plan and deploy. The Gartner Group, for instance, thinks that a rollout will take 18 months to accomplish, from beginning to end. They're factoring such issues as ensuring that your organization's key applications will be functional on Vista and that the vendors will support Vista usage.

We don't know if you're going to take 18 months to completely move to a Vista environment, but no matter how long it's taking you to progress through these steps, let's go ahead and assume you've got a solid deployment plan in place and you're ready to start upgrading some computers. In the next chapter, we'll do just that.

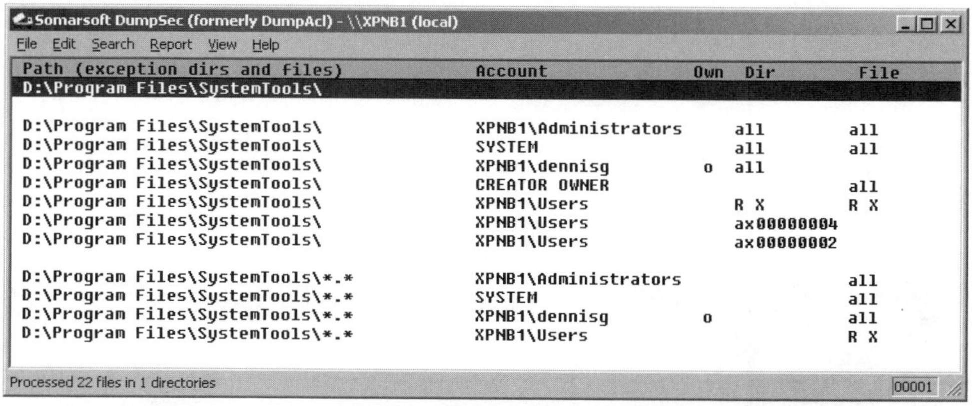

Figure 2-15.   Somarsoft's Dumpsec is used to gather information on data configuration.

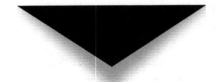

CHAPTER 3

Deploying Windows Vista

I n Chapter 2, we talked about all the things you need to do to get ready for a Windows Vista deployment. Now that you've done some homework on your network, computers, and users, it's time to make the move. In this chapter we'll talk about the options that you have, the tools that you can use, and the steps that you can follow to upgrade or migrate to Windows Vista.

First, we'll talk about migrating user settings to a new computer running Windows Vista. Next, we'll look at the process of creating a Windows Vista image and deploying it to PCs across your network. Finally, we'll talk about the powerful Business Desktop Deployment (BDD) tool and how you can use it to conduct your organization's deployment.

IMAGE TOOLS

To perform either a migration or a deployment, there are a handful of tools you'll need. A couple of them come with Windows Vista (like Windows PE, for instance); others you'll need to download from Microsoft (like Windows Automated Installation Kit). You can download all of these applications in a large package called the Business Desktop Deployment (BDD) kit from www.microsoft.com/technet/desktopdeployment/default.mspx. Before you read on, you might want to stop here and start that download—at 700+ megabytes (MB), it can take awhile to transfer. We'll be discussing it later in the chapter.

Since we don't want to get bogged down in so much alphabet soup (Windows AIK, BDD, PE, etc.), let's spend some time explaining what these tools are and what they're used for.

Migration

The first sets of tools are relevant if your organization has computers to which you will be migrating existing user data onto a new Windows Vista installation. There are two applications you can use: one if you have a lot of users to migrate, another if you have only a handful.

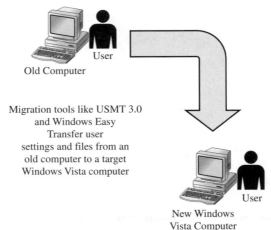

Old Computer

Migration tools like USMT 3.0 and Windows Easy Transfer user settings and files from an old computer to a target Windows Vista computer

New Windows Vista Computer

User State Migration Tool

The User State Migration Tool (USMT) 3.0 allows you to migrate user accounts during large Windows Vista deployments. USMT captures user accounts and related user state data from an old computer, including:

▼   Documents

■   Desktop settings

▲   Application settings

USMT 3.0 includes better procedures for identifying user data that should be migrated and improves migration through scripting.

Windows Easy Transfer

Included on your Windows Vista DVD, Windows Easy Transfer is used to migrate user data and settings. It is similar to USMT in that it transfers settings from an old computer to a new Windows Vista install. Unlike USMT, however, Easy Transfer is used for small-scale migrations. If you are migrating five or fewer computers, Easy Transfer is the best choice.

Deployment

If you've elected to deploy Windows Vista to existing computers, you won't need to migrate user settings—rather, you'll have to create a Windows Vista image and then dole that out to your computers. This is a simple-sounding process—and, indeed, Microsoft has made it easier than earlier processes—but there are a lot of tools you need to get the job done.

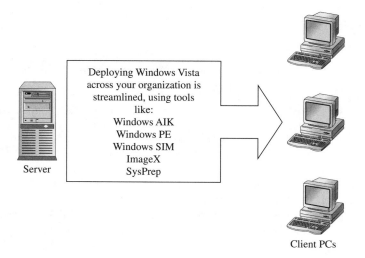

Server

Deploying Windows Vista across your organization is streamlined, using tools like:
Windows AIK
Windows PE
Windows SIM
ImageX
SysPrep

Client PCs

Windows Automated Installation Kit

The Windows Automated Installation Kit (AIK) is the platform on which you will create your Windows Vista image. This application can be downloaded from Microsoft, but, again, it's a really good idea just to download BDD. It allows you to create the images and add and remove Windows components as you see fit.

ImageX

When you've finished creating the Windows Vista image in Windows AIK, the next step is to use ImageX. This is a command-line tool that captures, modifies, and applies installation images for deployment.

Windows System Image Manager

Windows System Image Manager (SIM) allows you to create answer files (unattend.xml) and network shares or to modify the files contained in a configuration set. You use Windows SIM on the technician computer, and then transfer your unattend.xml file to the master computer before creating your installation image.

Sysprep

Sysprep helps with image creation and prepares an image for deployment to groups of computers that have an identical hardware configuration. It can clone a computer, capturing all of its specific settings, allowing it to be deployed to other computers. It also removes the System Identifier (SID) found on the reference computer so that each newly imaged computer will have its own unique SID.

Windows PE

Windows Preinstallation Environment (PE) is a lightweight version of Windows that was initially intended as a deployment platform. Since its inception in 2001, Windows PE has evolved into a platform for:

▼ Workstation deployment

■ Preinstallation of workstations and servers by system builders

■ An operating system (OS) recovery platform

▲ An MS-DOS replacement used by technicians for system diagnostics and repair

In Windows Vista, if the OS fails to start because of a corrupted system file, Windows PE allows you to access and run the Startup Recovery tool. Windows PE can also be manually started to use its troubleshooting tools.

Windows PE runs from the command line, as shown in Figure 3-1.

Windows PE is a replacement for MS-DOS as the preinstallation environment. It is built from Vista components and can run many Windows Vista applications, but it can also detect and enable most hardware devices and communicate across Internet Protocol (IP) networks. Windows PE can be run from system random access memory

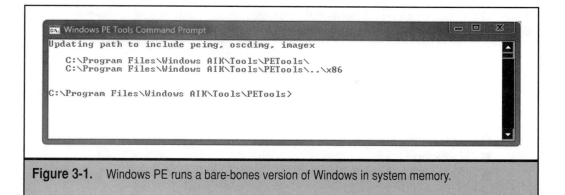

Figure 3-1. Windows PE runs a bare-bones version of Windows in system memory.

(RAM), allowing you to run it on computers that do not have a formatted hard drive or installed OS.

Windows PE includes important management tools, including:

▼ **DiskPart** Used for managing disks, partitions, and volumes.

■ **Drvload** Used for adding device drivers and dynamically loading a driver after Windows PE has started.

■ **Net** Used for managing local users, starting and stopping services, and connecting to shared folders.

▲ **Netcfg** Used for network configuration.

Customized Windows PE images can be created with configuration scripts that customize the deployment process. When a new computer is connected to the network, the Preboot Execution Environment (PXE) client connects to a Windows Deployment Service server and then downloads the customized Windows PE image. The new computer loads Windows PE into memory and then launches the configuration script.

MIGRATION

If you've decided to migrate user settings to a newly installed Windows Vista environment, the process is a little simpler than an upgrade, but there's still a fair amount of work to be done. The following sections describe the steps that should be followed.

Plan the Migration

Yes, we did spend the last chapter talking about planning, but there are two final, hands-on planning steps you need to consider.

First, you need to decide what you'll migrate. The USMT tool migrates the following items by default:

▼ Individual user folders, including:
- My Documents
- My Video
- My Music
- My Pictures
- Desktop files
- Start menu
- Quick launch settings
- Favorites

■ Folders from the "All users" profile, including:
- Shared Documents
- Shared Video
- Shared Music
- Shared Desktop files
- Shared Pictures
- Shared Start menu
- Shared Favorites

▲ File types with the following extensions: .qdf, .qsd, .qel, .qph, .doc, .dot, .rtf, .mcw, .wps, .scd, .wri, .wpd, .xl?, .csv, .iqy, .dqy, .oqy, .rqy, .wk?, .wq1, .slk, .dif, .ppt, .pps, .pot, .sh3, .ch3, .pre, .ppa, .txt, .pst

NOTE In the file type list, "?" represents all letters. For instance, .wk? represents .wka, .wkb, .wkc, and so forth.

Access control lists (ACLs) for files and folders are also migrated. For instance, if a file is marked as "read-only" for User A and as "full control" for User B, those settings will be carried over to the new computer.

The following Windows settings are migrated with USMT:

▼ Microsoft Internet Explorer settings
■ Microsoft Outlook Express mail files
■ Remote access service (RAS) connection phone book files
■ Dial-up connections
■ Phone and modem options

- Accessibility settings
- Classic desktop
- Command prompt settings
- Favorites
- Fonts
- Folder options
- Taskbar settings
- Microsoft Open Database Connectivity (ODC) settings
- Mouse and keyboard settings
- Screen saver selection
- Multimedia settings
- Remote access
- Regional settings
- ▲ Wallpaper settings

When you decide which settings to migrate, you should think about which settings you want users to be able to configure and which settings you want to standardize for all your users. Many organizations use migration as a time to update their policies, which allows them to create, implement, and operate in alignment with new technologies, requirements, and standards. For example, if you have allowed users to set their own desktop wallpapers and Internet Explorer settings in the past, you might want to use the migration as a time to standardize a wallpaper and Internet Explorer security settings as per a new human resources directive.

You might also want to reduce the complexity of your migration by determining a standard operating environment. That is, all your users will have the same environment, rather than trying to migrate each and every setting for each and every user. This distributes the same hardware drivers, OS features, business applications, and utilities.

Creating a standard operating environment can make the migration process simpler and smoother.

Storage Options

When you've decided what you're going to migrate, you then need to determine where you're going to store the data. You're going to be storing operating system settings, e-mail, personal documents, and applications for each user. The best way to estimate how much storage you'll need is to survey a few PCs.

One of the determiners of storage space size is how your organization stores data. For example, one of the big things that's going to take up space is the amount of e-mails a user is storing. However, if your organization stores e-mails centrally, the sizes of migration files will be smaller. If the data is stored locally, migration files will be larger.

NOTE   As a rule of thumb, you can expect mobile users to have larger migration files than workstation users.

When estimating storage space, keep these issues in mind:

▼ **E-mail**   Take into consideration where e-mail is stored. As noted earlier, if e-mails are stored on the users' computers instead of on a mail server, e-mail can take up as much space as all the users' other files combined. It can help to ask users to clean up their e-mail by archiving and purging deleted or unwanted e-mails prior to the migration. Don't forget to mention the Sent Items folder—there can be plenty of e-mail and attachments there that users didn't even know were there and can live without. As you probably know, e-mail problems really irritate end users, so before migrating user data, you should make sure that users who store e-mail on their computers synchronize their inboxes with their mail server.

■ **User documents**   You can estimate that most users' documents will fit into 50 MB worth of space. This estimate assumes "normal" office work. However, if your organization uses larger files—for instance, a business that deals with multimedia—you'll need more storage space. If your files are stored on a server, you won't need to migrate those documents; you just need to ensure that users will be able to access those folders after the migration.

▲ **System settings**   As a rule of thumb, 5 MB is generally enough space to save registry settings. The size will change based on the number of installed applications, but it's rare for the registry to be larger than this.

Taking all the aforementioned into consideration, Table 3-1 gives a rough estimate as to how much space your various users will need for a migration. Again, this is an estimate. Your organization's needs and individual usage will vary.

The next question to answer is where you should store migration files until they are put onto the new computer. The answer lies in your network design, computers' capacity, and personal preference.

User	Storage Space (Plus Any Additional Files)
Workstation storing e-mail on server	50 MB to 75 MB
Workstation with local e-mail storage	120 MB to 200 MB
Laptop	150 MB to 300 MB

Table 3-1.   Space Requirements for Migration Scenarios

Store Files Locally

If there is enough disk space, and if you are migrating the user back to the same computer, then the best idea is to keep user files on the PC. This can reduce server storage costs and network performance problems. The migration data can be stored on a different hard drive partition or on a Universal Serial Bus (USB) drive.

NOTE If you are saving data to the local computer, have users store their data within their %UserProfile%\My Documents and %UserProfile%\Application Data folders. This improves the chance that USMT will find the data to be migrated.

Store Files Remotely

You may not have enough disk space to store user data locally, or you could be migrating to a brand-new computer. If that is the case, then you'll have to store the data remotely. Options for remote storage include:

▼ A network drive

▲ Removable media, like a USB drive, CD-ROM, or DVD-ROM

ScanState and LoadState

There are two processes within USMT that you'll use to perform a migration: ScanState and LoadState.

The applications can be run on computers using these operating systems:

▼ Microsoft Windows 2000 Professional with Service Pack 4

■ Microsoft Windows XP Home

■ Microsoft Windows XP Professional

■ Microsoft Windows XP Professional x64 Edition

▲ Microsoft Windows Vista

ScanState

ScanState is used on the computer from which you want to migrate. This application—run from the command line and shown in Figure 3-2—collects information about all the migration components that need to be migrated and saves it to a data store called USMT3.mig.

NOTE A migration component is a group of files, registry keys, and values. For instance, a set of files, registry keys, and values that store the settings for Microsoft Word are grouped into a single migration component.

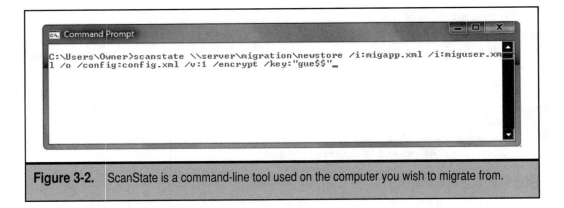

Figure 3-2. ScanState is a command-line tool used on the computer you wish to migrate from.

ScanState runs in three phases:

▼ **Scanning phase**   ScanState checks each component. If the current user profile is the system profile and the component type is "System" or "UserAndSystem," the component is selected for this user. The component is ignored, otherwise.

■ **Collecting phase**   ScanState creates a master list of the migration units by combining the lists that were generated for each selected user profile.

▲ **Saving phase**   ScanState writes the collected migration to the store location.

Table 3-2 lists the options available for the ScanState command.

LoadState

The LoadState process is similar to ScanState. But whereas ScanState collects migration units from the source computer and then saves them to a store, LoadState collects the migration units from the store and applies them to the destination computer. Figure 3-3 shows the LoadState command-line process.

Like ScanState, LoadState operates in distinct phases. It gathers information for the application settings components and user data components from the migration .xml files that are specified in the LoadState command line. On a computer running Windows Vista, migration settings can be managed by modifying a Config.xml file. We'll talk about this file in the next section.

Next, LoadState determines which user profiles should be migrated. The default setting is to migrate all user files on a source computer. However, users can be included or excluded using options in the command line.

In the scanning phase, each component in the user profile is checked. If the current user profile is the system profile and the component type is "System" or "UserAndSystem," the component is selected for the user. Otherwise, the component is ignored.

In the apply phase, LoadState writes the migration units that were collected onto the destination computer.

Option	Description
/config	Specifies the Config.xml file to be used in creating the data store.
/efs:copyraw	Generates EFS certificates (only valid when migrating to Windows Vista).
/encrypt	Encrypts the data store with the specified key.
/genconfig[: *StorePath*]	Generates a Config.xml file, but does not create a store. You can specify an optional store path to use when later generating the data store by using /config.
/nocompress	Disables compression of data (meant only for testing).
/targetxp	Optimizes ScanState for destination computers running Windows XP. When Windows XP is the destination, USMT 3.0 does not migrate user cookies, network drive settings, or printers.
/ue	Excludes specific users, domains, or both from the migration. Specified user accounts and domains are not migrated.
/uel	Excludes user accounts based on user logon. User accounts that have not been logged on to within the specified time period are not migrated.
/ui	Includes specific users, domains, or both from the migration. Specified user accounts and domains are migrated.

Table 3-2. ScanState Options

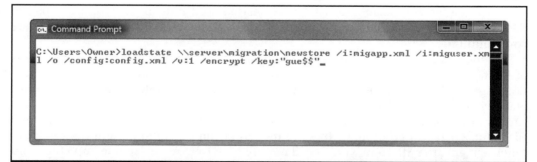

Figure 3-3. LoadState is executed from the command line to migrate user data.

Option	Description
/config	Specifies the Config.xml file that LoadState should use.
/decrypt	Decrypts the data store with the specified key.
/md	Modifies old domain names to new domain names during the migration.
/mu	Modifies old user names to new user names during the migration.
/nocompress	Specifies that the store is not compressed.
/ue	Excludes the specified users, domains, or both from the migration.
/uel	Excludes user accounts that have not been logged on to within the specified time period.
/ui	Migrates the specified users, domains, or both.

Table 3-3.   LoadState Usage Options

NOTE   Some settings—like wallpaper, screensavers, and so forth—will not take effect until the next time the user logs on. Once LoadState has been run, you should log off.

Table 3-3 explains the options for the LoadState command.

Usage

To run ScanState and LoadState and use any of the migration .xml files, you must specify them on both command lines using the /i option.

Once you've run ScanState with your desired .xml files, if you want to migrate the entire store with no alterations, specify the same set of files on the LoadState command line.

On the other hand, once you've run ScanState, you might decide not to migrate some of the files or settings to the destination computer. This can be done by modifying the necessary .xml files and specifying them when you run LoadState. By doing this, Load-State will only migrate the files and settings you choose.

For example, during the ScanState process, you might have elected to store all .mp3 files. But when you go to move them to the target computer, you might decide not to migrate them after all. Here, you would modify MigUser.xml to exclude .mp3 files, and then specify this updated MigUser.xml file on the LoadState command line.

To modify the migration to suit your needs, you will need to do one of the following:

▼ **Create and modify a Config.xml file**   Do this if you want to exclude a component from migration. For instance, you might want to exclude My Documents/My Music from migration. Excluding components using this file is simpler than modifying the migration .xml files because you don't have to know the correct migration rules.

■ **Modify the migration .xml files**   Do this if you want to exclude a portion of a component (for instance, you want to migrate everything except .mp3 files). Also use it if you want to move data to a new location on the target computer. The difficulty with these sorts of files is that you must be familiar with the migration rules and syntax. If you use these files, they must be specified on both the ScanState and LoadState command lines.

▲ **Create custom .xml files**   Do this to migrate settings for another application. For ScanState and LoadState to use this file, you need to specify it on both command lines.

If you choose to modify the migration .xml files and create custom .xml files, you can modify MigUser.xml and MigApp.xml. To modify operating system settings that are to be migrated, you must create and modify a Config.xml file.

We've only just scratched the surface with regards to developing custom migration .xml files. Unfortunately, we simply don't have the space to go into the complete nuts and bolts of .xml file creation and modification. However, you can find XML editing tips, tools like XML Notepad, and a lot more XML-related information on Microsoft's Developer Network Web site at msdn.microsoft.com/xml/.

Gathering Files and Settings

If you've modified any migration .xml files, or if you've decided to perform a straightforward migration, the next step is to actually get your hands dirty. To perform your migration:

1. Back up the source computer.

2. Close all running applications. If applications are left running when ScanState or LoadState runs, they may not be properly migrated.

3. Run ScanState on the source computer to collect files and settings using the ScanState command-line options. Be sure to specify all the .xml files you want ScanState to use. For example:

```
scanstate \\fileserver\migration\mystore /config:config.xml
/i:miguser.xml /i:migapp.xml /v:1 /l:scan.log
```

In the previous example, the destination, `\\fileserver\migration\mystore`, could be on a network share, or you could very easily take the share and burn it to a CD or DVD.

Restoring Files and Settings

Now that you have the user files and settings from the source computer, it's time to put them on the new computer.

1. Install the operating system on the target computer.

2. Install all applications that were on the source computer. It's a good idea to do this first, because it will ensure that migrated settings are preserved.

3. Close all running applications. As with ScanState, if applications are running while LoadState is run, applications may not migrate properly.

4. Modify .xml files, if you choose (see the previous section for more information on this). If you want to migrate the entire store with no changes to the data, specify the same set of files on the LoadState command line.

5. Run LoadState on the target computer using the LoadState command-line options. Be sure to specify any .xml files you want LoadState to use. For example:

```
loadstate \\fileserver\migration\mystore /config:config.xml
/i:miguser.xml /i:migapp.xml /v:1 /l:load.log
```

When you're done with the migration, be sure to log off the computer and log back on again. Several settings—especially desktop environment settings—won't be valid until the user logs back on.

Windows Easy Transfer

Windows Easy Transfer can be started from the System Tools menu. Click Start, point to All Programs, point to Accessories, point to System Tools, and then click Windows Easy Transfer.

Alternately, the application can be started when you put the Windows Vista DVD into the DVD drive. At the bottom, the splash screen prompts you to run Easy Transfer.

Easy Transfer can transfer files and settings from the following Windows environments:

▼ Microsoft Windows 2000 Professional with Service Pack 4

■ Microsoft Windows XP Home

■ Microsoft Windows XP Professional

■ Microsoft Windows XP Professional x64 Edition

▲ Microsoft Windows Vista

Windows Easy Transfer migrates the same set of data as USMT 3.0. As such, flip back to the section on USMT 3.0, and you can see what sorts of data this includes. Also, as with USMT 3.0, you want to reinstall your applications before migrating user files and settings.

Getting Ready

To get started with Windows Easy Transfer:

1. Log on to the computer running Windows Vista to which you plan to transfer files and settings.

2. Click Start, point to All Programs, point to Accessories, point to System Tools, and then click Windows Easy Transfer.

3. The screen shown in Figure 3-4 appears. Click Next.

4. You should have all programs closed; if you don't, you will be prompted to close any running programs. Click Close All to shut them down.

5. On the Do You Want To Start A New Transfer Or Continue One In Progress page, click Start A New Transfer.

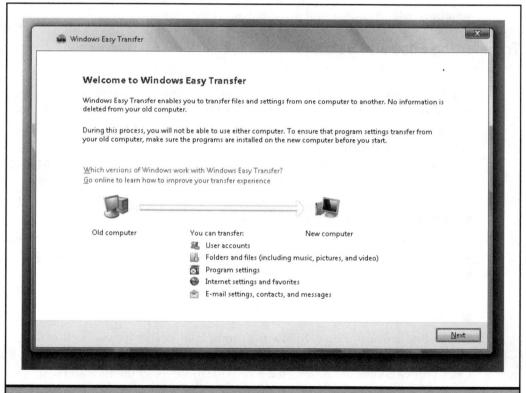

Figure 3-4. Windows Easy Transfer can help migrate user information for a small number of PCs.

6. On the Which Computer Are You Using Now page, click This Is My New Computer.

7. On the Do You Have A Windows Easy Transfer USB Cable page, do one of the following:

   ■ Click Yes if you have an Easy Transfer cable. Connect the cable between your old and new computers when prompted, and then follow on-screen instructions. You can then skip the rest of these steps.

   ■ Click No if you don't have an Easy Transfer cable. Follow the rest of these steps.

8. Since Windows Easy Transfer is a new application, computers running Windows 2000 or Windows XP will not have Windows Easy Transfer installed. On the Did You Install Windows Easy Transfer page, click I Need To Install Windows Easy Transfer.

9. You'll be prompted to select the media, drive, or folder to which you'll save Windows Easy Transfer, and then click Next.

Transferring Files and Settings

The next step is to commence the transfer of files and settings.

1. Log on to the old computer. If you are transferring just one account, log on as that user. If you are transferring all accounts, log on with administrator privileges.

2. Insert the media, attach the drive, or connect to the shared folder that you elected in the preceding procedure.

3. Windows Easy Transfer should start automatically. If it does not, open the MigWiz folder in the media, drive, or shared folder, and then double-click MigWiz.exe.

4. You shouldn't have any programs running, but if you do, you'll be prompted to close them. Click the Close All button.

5. On the How Do You Want To Transfer Files And Program Settings To Your New Computer page, select one of the options presented. You can chose between:

   ■ Using a network

   ■ Using a removable device

   ■ Saving to a folder

6. Depending on your choice, follow the prompts to establish a connection or select a save location.

7. Once you've connected or selected a save location, select the files and settings to transfer, as shown in Figure 3-5. On the What Do You Want To Transfer To Your New Computer page, to transfer files and settings for all users, select Everything—All User Accounts, Files, And Program Settings. To transfer files and settings for the currently logged on user only, select Only My User Accounts, Files, And Program Settings.

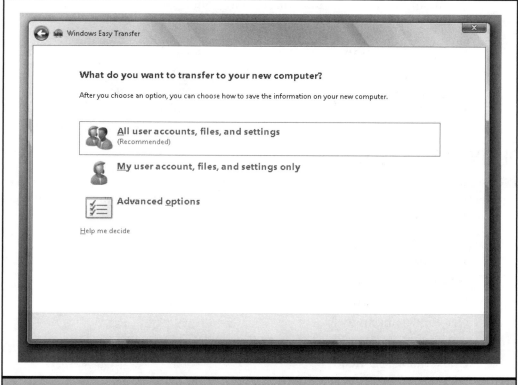

Figure 3-5.   You can select which files and settings to transfer using Windows Easy Transfer.

8. Click Start Transfer to begin the transfer.

9. You may be prompted to insert a blank, writable CD or DVD, or to plug in a USB flash device. When you do this, click Next and then click Close.

The migration is finalized in the next section.

Completing the Migration

To finish the migration process:

1. Log on to the computer running Windows Vista to which you plan to transfer files and settings.

2. Click Start, point to All Programs, point to Accessories, point to System Tools, and then click Windows Easy Transfer.

3. Click Next on the Introduction screen.

4. You shouldn't have any programs running, but if you do, you'll be prompted to close them. Click the Close All button, and then click Next.

5. On the Do You Want To Start A New Transfer Or Continue One In Progress page, click Continue A Transfer In Progress.

6. On the Are You Using A Home Network page, specify whether the old computer and new computer are on the same network. Click Yes or No, as appropriate, and then follow the prompts to complete the migration.

DEPLOYMENT PROCESS

Deploying Windows across your organization is much simpler with Windows Vista than with earlier incarnations of Windows, but there's still a lot to be done. Before we get started, let's run down a list of things you'll need:

▼ A Windows Vista product DVD

■ The Windows Automated Installation Kit (AIK)

■ Your technician computer

■ Your master computer

■ Network connectivity

■ A floppy disk or Universal Flash Device (UFD), such as a USB memory key

▲ One writable CD-ROM

When you've got all those components ready, let's move on.

Answer File

A key component in a Vista deployment is an answer file. This contains information necessary to complete a mass Vista deployment. The deployment process requires five basic steps:

1. Create a new answer file.

2. Add components to the file.

3. Change values or settings in the file.

4. Validate the file.

5. Save the file to distributable media.

Create the Answer File

First, you must build a catalog (a binary file containing the states of all settings and packages in the Windows image) and then a blank answer file.

1. On your technician computer, insert the Windows Vista DVD.

2. From the desktop, navigate to the DVD's \sources directory.

3. Copy install.wim from the product DVD to a location on your technician computer. This will probably take a few minutes because install.wim is a couple of gigabytes in size.

4. Open Windows SIM, as shown in Figure 3-6.

5. From your desktop, click Start, point to Programs, point to Microsoft Windows AIK, and then click Image Manager.

6. On the File menu, click Select Windows Image.

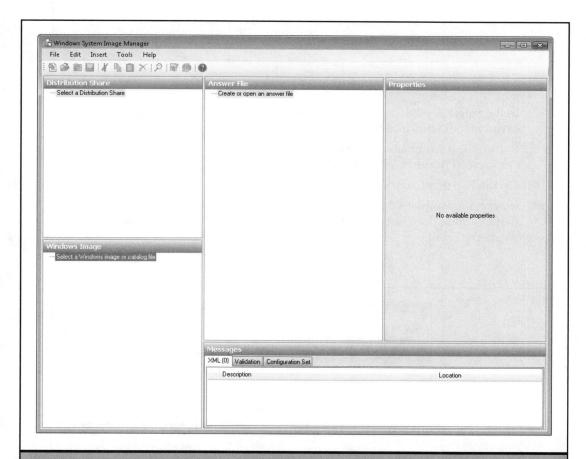

Figure 3-6. Use Windows SIM to create the answer file, which is a key component of a deployment.

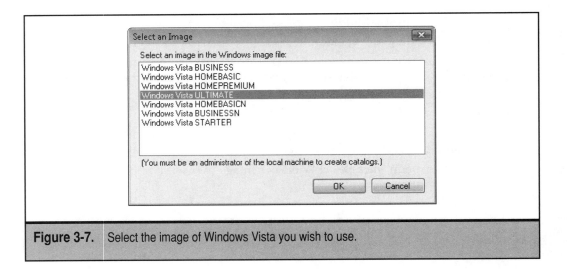

Figure 3-7.   Select the image of Windows Vista you wish to use.

7. In the Select A Windows Image dialog box, navigate to the location where you saved install.wim, and then click Open.

8. In the Select An Image dialog box, shown in Figure 3-7, select the appropriate version of Windows Vista, and then click OK.

9. On the File menu, click New Answer File.

10. When you complete the final step, a warning message will appear, telling you that a catalog does not exist. It soon will, as Figure 3-8 shows. Click OK to create the catalog.

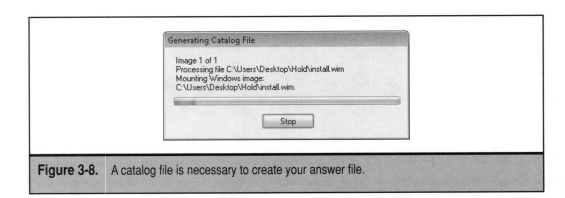

Figure 3-8.   A catalog file is necessary to create your answer file.

Add Modules

With the basic file created, you can now add the components you want to make it unique and appropriate for your organization. To add the modules you want:

1. In Windows SIM, in the Windows Image pane, expand the Component node to display available settings.

2. The list of components will be shown in the middle pane of SIM. That pane is shown in Figure 3-9. You can add components to or remove them from your answer file by right-clicking the component and selecting the desired configuration pass. This is shown in Figure 3-10. A configuration pass is a phase of Windows installation, and different parts of Vista are installed in different phases.

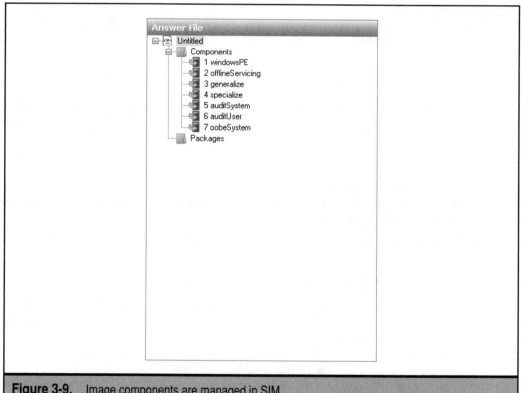

Figure 3-9.   Image components are managed in SIM.

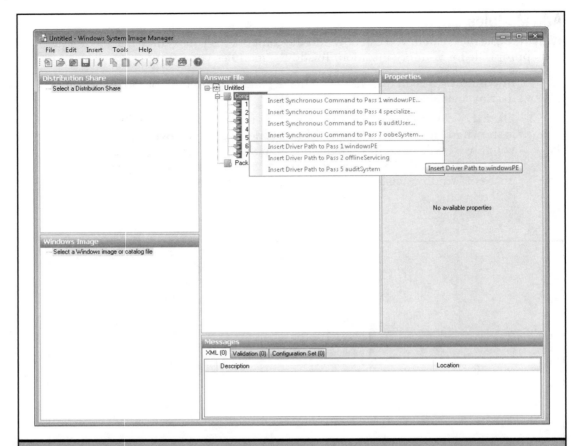

Figure 3-10. Manage component attributes in SIM.

Table 3-4 shows the components and their configuration passes.

1. Expand the component list until you see the lowest setting listed in Table 3-4, and then add that setting to the answer file. This adds the setting and all parent settings to the answer file in one step.

2. When you've added your desired settings, they will appear in the Answer File pane. Configure each setting as shown in Table 3-5.

NOTE In Table 3-5, you probably noticed the acronym OOBE pop up a few times. OOBE stands for "Out-Of-Box Experience."

Component	Configuration Pass
Microsoft-Windows-Setup\DiskConfiguration\Disk\CreatePartitions\CreatePartition	1 windowsPE
Microsoft-Windows-Setup\DiskConfiguration\Disk\ModifyPartitions\ModifyPartition	1 windowsPE
Microsoft-Windows-Setup\ImageInstall\OSImage\InstallTo	1 windowsPE
Microsoft-Windows-Setup\UserData	1 windowsPE
Microsoft-Windows-Shell-Setup\OOBE	7 oobeSystem
Microsoft-Windows-Shell-Setup\AutoLogon	7 oobeSystem
Microsoft-Windows-International-Core-WinPE	1 windowsPE

Table 3-4.   Components That Can Be Added to Your Answer File

Component	Value
Microsoft-Windows-Setup\DiskConfiguration	WillShowUI = OnError
Microsoft-Windows-Setup\DiskConfiguration\Disk	DiskID = 0 WillWipeDisk = true
Microsoft-Windows-Setup\DiskConfiguration\Disk\CreatePartitions\CreatePartition	Extend = false Order = 1 Size = 20000 (this creates a 20-GB partition) Type = Primary
Microsoft-Windows-Setup\DiskConfiguration\Disk\ModifyPartitions\ModifyPartition	Active = true Extend = false Format = NTFS Label = Vista Letter = C Order = 1 PartitionID = 1

Table 3-5.   Settings That Can Be Managed In Your Answer File

Component	Value
Microsoft-Windows-Setup\ImageInstall\OSImage\	WillShowUI = OnError
Microsoft-Windows-Setup\ImageInstall\OSImage\InstallTo	DiskID = 0 PartitionID = 1
Microsoft-Windows-Setup\UserData	AcceptEula = true
Microsoft-Windows-Setup\UserData\ProductKey	Key = <product key> WillShowUI = OnError
Microsoft-Windows-Shell-Setup\OOBE	HideEULAPage = true ProtectYourPC = 3 SkipMachineOOBE = true SkipUserOOBE = true
Microsoft-Windows-International-Core-WinPE	InputLocale = <Input Locale> SystemLocale = <System Locale> UILanguage = <UI Language> UserLocale = <User Locale>
Microsoft-Windows-International-Core-WinPE\SetupUILanguage	UILanguage = <UI Language>
Microsoft-Windows-Shell-Setup\AutoLogon	Enabled = true LogonCount = 5 Username = Administrator
Microsoft-Windows-Shell-Setup\AutoLogon\Password	<strongpassword>

Table 3-5.   Settings That Can Be Managed In Your Answer File *(Continued)*

Once the answer file is complete, no user input will be needed during the deployment.

Validate the File

Before you're done, you have to validate the file to ensure that you haven't made a mistake somewhere along the line.

1. In Windows SIM, click Tools and then click Validate Answer File. This compares the setting values in the answer file with the available settings in the Windows image.

2. If the answer file validates successfully, you'll get a message telling you so in the Message pane. If there are any problems, an error message appears.

3. If there are errors, double-click the error in the Message pane, change the setting to correct the error, and then revalidate.

4. When the file checks out, on the File menu, click Save Answer File. Save the answer file as unattend.xml.

5. Copy unattend.xml to the root of a floppy disk or UFD.

Building a Master Installation

The master computer is where the customized installation of Windows is created that you will duplicate onto your target computers. The master installation can be accomplished by using the Windows Vista DVD and the answer file you just created.

Install Windows Vista

To install Windows Vista:

1. Turn on the new computer.

2. Insert removable media containing the answer file (unattend.xml) and the Windows Vista DVD into the master computer.

3. Press CTRL+ALT+DEL to restart the computer. In this example, we're assuming that the hard drive is blank and that Windows Vista Setup will automatically begin. Windows Vista Setup will search all removable media for the answer file.

4. When Setup finishes, check to ensure that all customizations were applied.

5. Shut down the computer.

6. From a command prompt, type: `c:\windows\system32\sysprep\sysprep .exe /oobe /generalize /shutdown`.

The Sysprep application will finalize the image for capture by cleaning up user and computer settings and log files. The master image is now complete and ready to be imaged.

Create an Image

Once a master installation is completed, you can deploy that image to your organizations' computers. To accomplish this, you'll need ImageX and Windows PE. As a reminder:

▼ **ImageX**   This is a command-line tool that allows you to capture, modify, and apply disk changes.

▲ **Windows PE**   This is an environment from which you can capture and deploy an image.

In order to create and save the image, you'll create a bootable Windows PE CD or a network share.

Creating Bootable Windows PE Media At this point, you will create a bootable Windows PE CD. This CD will be used to capture an image of your master computer and then later deploy that image to your destination computers.

1. From your technician computer, run the copype.cmd script to create a local Windows PE build directory. For example, from a command prompt, type:

```
cd Program Files\Windows AIK\Tools\PETools\
copype.cmd <arch> <destination>
```

Where <arch> can be x86, amd64, or ia64 and <destination> is a path to local directory. For example:

```
copype.cmd x86 c:\winpe_x86
```

2. Copy additional tools, like ImageX, to your Windows PE build directory. For example:

```
copy "c:\program files\Windows AIK\Tools\x86\imagex.exe" c:\winpe_x86\iso\
```

You can also create a configuration file called wimscript.ini. The configuration file, using a simple text editor, will instruct ImageX to exclude certain files during the capture operation. The following example excludes certain system files as well as .mp3, .zip, and .cab files:

```
[ExclusionList]
ntfs.log
hiberfil.sys
pagefile.sys
"System Volume Information"
RECYCLER
Windows\CSC
[CompressionExclusionList]
*.mp3
*.zip
*.cab
\WINDOWS\inf\*.pnf
```

3. Save the configuration file to the same location as ImageX was saved in the previous step. For example:

```
c:\winpe_x86\iso\
```

ImageX will automatically detect wimscript.ini, if it is in the same location.

4. Create an image (.iso) file using the Oscdimg tool. For example:

```
cd program files\Windows AIK\Tools\PETools\
oscdimg -n -bc:\winpe_x86\etfsboot.com c:\winpe_x86\ISO
c:\winpe_x86\winpe_x86.iso
```

5. Burn the image (winpe_x86.iso) to a CD-ROM.

Storing the Image to a Network Share   To save your image to a network share:

1. On your master computer, insert your Windows PE media, and restart the computer. Windows PE will start, launching a command-prompt window.

2. Capture an image of the master installation by using ImageX located on your Windows PE media. For example:

```
d:\tools\imagex.exe /compress fast /capture c: c:\newimage.wim
"my Vista Install" /verify
```

3. Copy the image to a network location. For example:

```
net use h: \\network_share\images
copy c:\newimage.wim h:
```

Deploying the Image

Here's what it all comes down to: getting that Vista image to your target computers. Follow these steps, and your computers will be running your customized version of Windows Vista in no time.

1. Insert the Windows PE media on your target computer, and restart. Windows PE will start and launch a command-line window.

2. Use the diskpart command to format the hard drive to replicate the necessary disk configuration. For instance, from the command prompt, enter:

```
diskpart
select disk 0
clean
create partition primary size=20000
select partition 1
active
format
exit
```

3. Copy the image from your network share to the local hard drive.

NOTE   Remember, Windows PE allows network access, so you won't be disconnected from the network and your network share.

For example:

```
net use H: \\network_share\Images
copy H:\Newimage.wim c:
```

4. Using ImageX located on your Windows PE CD ROM, apply the image. For example:

```
D:\Tools\Imagex.exe /apply C:\Myimage.wim c:
```

At this point, your computers have been successfully installed with Windows Vista. However, Microsoft offers another means to deploy Vista across your network. The next section examines how BDD can be used to deploy Vista.

DEPLOYMENT SERVICES

When deploying Vista, you should consider leveraging a deployment service, a tool for automated distribution and installation. Even if your current scope includes deploying only a few workstations, you are sure to deploy Vista workstations more and more as time goes on. Having a reliable, efficient deployment solution saves you valuable time, freeing you to focus more on engineering a better image and improving your operations. In this section, we cover two deployment service options and the terrific assets wrapped up into the Microsoft Business Desktop Deployment (BDD) accelerator.

The BDD is the Vista workstation deployment asset. You can use it to:

▼   Leverage the Deployment Wizard to sequence the deployment

■   Use the USMT to save user profile and data to a server

■   Back up the entire workstation to a server

■   Wipe the hard disk system partition

■   Deploy a new image

■   Customize images for hardware-specific needs

■   Install supplemental applications

▲   Use USMT to restore user profile and data

NOTE   This section does not develop any solutions around hard disk drive cloning. Essentially, the process for deployments using cloning as a distribution mechanism is the same as any other—up to a point. You can still make use of the BDD accelerator for preparing the images for cloning and then add subsequent tasks to your plan for getting the newly imaged drives out into production using cloning hardware as opposed to Windows Deployment Services (WDS) or Microsoft Systems Management Server (SMS).

Vista Deployment Process Overview

Before getting into the details of the deployment services, it is a good idea to quickly review the deployment process. The following list covers a generic deployment at a high level:

▼   **Validate your infrastructure**   Ensure that your IP addressing, name resolution, and Active Directory substructures are stable and have the capacity for the increased load. Ensure high-speed connections between the distribution points and target hosts. Finally, ensure that any firewalls that may be crossed have the correct TCP/UDP ports opened.

- **Install Microsoft's BDD accelerator**   Install the BDD on at least two computers, a technician's workstation and on the deployment servers:

  - The BDD will aid technicians in analyzing applications and packaging drivers and will provide process guidance.

  - You will also need major components on your deployment servers. Install the Windows AIK, which accompanies the BDD download, for the Windows PE tools.

  - For lite touch and zero touch installations (LTI and ZTI), consider installing Windows Deployment Services (WDS), which accompanies the BDD download. WDS requires Internet Information Server (IIS) and Remote Installation Service (RIS) for Windows Server 2003 platforms.

- **Establish a deployment infrastructure**   BDD includes the deployment scripts, deployment configuration files, computer imaging wizards, and other files necessary for using LTI to successfully deploy operating systems. As a part of this step, install USMT 3.0. Also, configure Deployment Workbench, creating the deployment point, operating system images, applications, updates, and other deployment options.

- **Prepare the images**   You can use the native tool, ImageX, and the Windows SIM to capture an image. If you have SMS, the OSD Feature Pack is responsible for the creation and delivery of images. The SMS OSD Feature Pack has phases based on your scenario, which includes validation, state capture, preinstall, postinstall, and state-restore phases.

- **Identify your targets**   Using a variety of descriptors, set conditions that will filter your target hosts. Descriptors include Active Directory group membership, processor type, and more.

- **Deploy images**   Using the BDD Deployment Wizard, WDS or SMS 2003, execute the command to deploy the images onto the target hosts.

- ▲ **Transition into operations**   Begin using your new Vista deployment.

Microsoft Solution Accelerator for Business Desktop Deployment (BDD)

Building on the current version 2.5, the new BDD for the Vista era includes configuration management, application management, and security scenarios that constitute the best starting point from which to launch a Vista deployment project. The BDD 2007 is a step toward consolidating Microsoft's best bets for deployment into one portal and one asset. The following sections are not meant to replace the documentation that accompanies the BDD. They are offered with the goal of demonstrating the breadth and intricacies, the width and potential, of this great tool. The BDD consolidates and covers technologies for Vista, including:

▼ **Guides and templates:**

- ■ **Feature Team Guides**   Documents for all phases and technologies within the deployment spectrum covered by the BDD.

- ■ **Job Aids**   Templates that help establish and manage scope, quality, and schedule for your project.

■ **The BBD Workbench**   Centralized management console where you can configure and launch almost any deployment task.

■ **Automation scripts**   These include:

- ■ The task sequencer (TS.WSF) file, which executes each task involved in a build according to the build stage. TS.WSF is a core asset, derived from Microsoft's Automated Deployment Toolkit (ADT), and is reborn to play a major role in both WDS and System Center Configuration Manager 2007.

- ■ Other Windows script files (.wsf) that automate the build process and are called by the task sequencer.

■ **The Windows Automated Installation Kit (AIK)**   The AIK is reviewed in the previous sections on creating an image, and it's important to note the major components, which are:

- ■ **Windows System Image Manager (SIM)**   The tool used to mount and modify images in the .WIM format.

- ■ **Windows PE (WinPE) 2.0**   The preinstallation environment with management and support documentation.

- ■ **Windows Deployment Services (WDS)**   The Active Directory–integrated service for deploying operating systems, service packs, and applications. WDS is discussed in detail in an upcoming section.

■ **User State Migration Tool (USMT) 3.0**   Capture and restore user profile settings and data, covering well-known locations where users store data and common application settings. The USMT is reviewed in more detail in an upcoming section.

▲ **Application Compatibility Toolkit (ACT) 5.0**   A rich suite of tools used to capture application data from deployed workstations and to centralize findings into a common SQL store. It analyzes the application data and recommends a migration path, if one is available.

Along with tools and technology, the BDD provides end-to-end guidance for efficient planning, building, testing, and deploying methodologies. This covers the configuration and automation of the build process, the installation of applications and drivers, and patching and service pack options. Wrapping all those technologies into one download, the BDD also includes new tools for managing applications, drivers, and patch deployments.

Installing the BDD

If you have not done so already, you can download the BDD 2007 installer package from the Microsoft desktop deployment center at www.microsoft.com/technet/desktopdeployment/default.mspx. Before installing, you need to ensure that the target system has:

▼   Microsoft Windows Installer 3.1

■   Microsoft Core Extensible Markup Language (MSXML) Services 6.0, from the Windows AIK (part of the BDD)

▲   Microsoft .NET Framework 2.0, from the Windows AIK (part of the BDD) or (x86)

NOTE   These applications can be found on www.microsoft.com.

Upon fulfilling the requirements and obtaining the BDD download package, complete the following steps to install the BDD:

1. Double click the installer package (.MSI) to launch the installer wizard.
2. Click Next on the Welcome page.
3. On the License Agreement page, review the license agreement. If you agree to its terms, select I Accept The Terms In The License Agreement, and then click Next.
4. On the Custom Setup page, choose the features you want to install, and then click Next. The available features are:

   ■   **Documents**   This installs the project guides and job aids. By default, this feature is installed in C:\Program Files\BDD 2007\Documentation.

   ■   **Tools and templates**   This installs the wizards and template deployment files, such as Unattend.xml.

   ■   **Distribution share**   This creates a distribution share. By default, the installer creates the distribution folder in D:\Distribution, where D is the volume with the greatest amount of free disk space.

5. Click Install to install the solution.
6. Click Finish to complete the installation.
7. On systems where you wish to manipulate .WIM images without the SMS OSD Feature Pack, install the Windows AIK by right-clicking C:\Program Files\BDD 2007\WAIK\waikplatform.msi (where "platform" is either x86 or amd64), and then click Install. Install the Windows AIK in its default installation folder, which is C:\Program Files\Windows AIK.
8. On systems where you wish to manage application migrations, install ACT 5.0 by launching the file C:\Program Files\BDD 2007\Application Compatibility Toolkit.msi.

Upon installing the BDD components, locate the BDD Document Explorer and the BDD Workbench in the Programs folder in the Start menu. When you run it, the Explorer looks like the one shown in Figure 3-11.

Because the BDD covers the breadth of the distribution services, it's worth it to step through the major technologies and provide some of the details involved in using then. Unlike some of the documentation you will find in the BDD, this section offers a smooth, high-level overview, which can help you understand the whole of a Vista deployment. For more details on each section, consult the BDD documentation.

Job Aids

The BDD provides a great set of starter templates to use during a Vista deployment project. These templates can give your project the benefit of a sophisticated approach, allowing you to control the scope, quality, and schedule, while minimizing risk. Known as

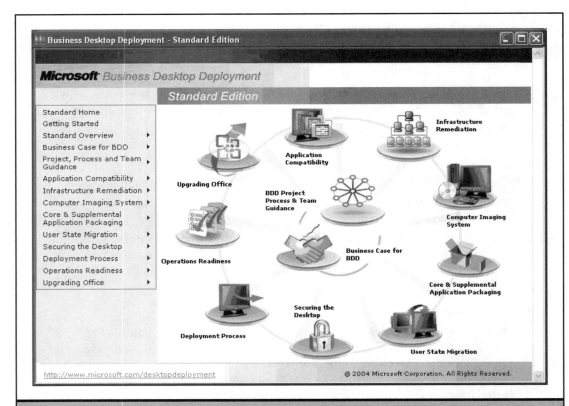

Figure 3-11.   The BDD Document Explorer provides quick navigation.

"job aids," they are stitched into the phases and appear at the appropriate points in the deployment flow. You can review these documents before you start:

▼ Vision Scope.doc

■ Migration Plan.doc

■ Communications Plan.doc

▲ Pilot Plan.doc

You can wrap your preliminary and ongoing plans into a Microsoft Project template, Site Deployment Project Plan.mpp. Included in the template bundle are a set of inventory starter files:

▼ Assessment Template.xls

■ Inventory Template.xls

▲ Application Knowledge Sheet.doc

After completing these templates, you can move on to some of the more useful planning documents. The BDD includes two files: Client Build Requirements.doc and Functional Specification.doc. Together, these two files allow you to specify, in detail, the particulars of your Vista builds. These build specifications should accompany each of the images you manage.

The BDD Topology

A Vista deployment using the BDD includes a routing infrastructure, servers for networking infrastructure, and the target hosts:

▼ **Network router and switches** Hosts in the network should be connected to a suitable network switch or hub and routed to other networks with a high-speed link. For labs, all network traffic should be isolated from any production environment.

■ **Network infrastructure servers** You need a network infrastructure based on the Windows Server 2003 platform or higher. For lab environments, you can centralize core services onto one box, including Dynamic Host Configuration Protocol (DHCP), Domain Name Server (DNS), Windows Internet Naming Service (WINS), and Active Directory. For production environments, these services are normally distributed among many servers.

■ **The BDD server** This is a server running Windows Server 2003 Standard or Enterprise Edition or higher with a recommended minimum of 30 GB of available hard disk space. Considerably more space would be necessary if you wish to include images for operating systems other than Vista.

■ **Deployment server** Either a WDS or SMS 2003 OSD server where the command to deploy images is executed.

▲ **Target host** Any computer that is compatible with Vista and is PXE-capable.

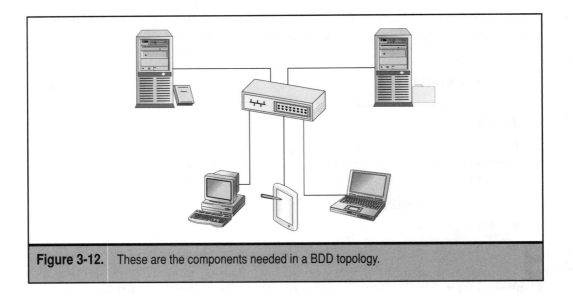

Figure 3-12. These are the components needed in a BDD topology.

Figure 3-12 shows an example of the components in a BDD topology, including file servers, switches, and different types of PCs.

Doing the Heavy Lifting with the BDD Workbench

The BDD Workbench creates and deploys builds from a centralized management console, giving you all the tools needed to:

▼ Consolidate operating systems, applications, and device drivers into the BDD distribution points.

■ Connect operating-system source bits with an answer file (unattend.xml or unattend.txt) and with a task sequence. The task sequence screen gives you the chance to establish the order of operations, such as the sequence of application installations.

■ Create replicas of deployment points. You can help balance bandwidth and input/output (I/O) load on a deployment server by creating replicas.

■ Build Windows PE image files, with imbedded instructions to automatically connect to the BDD deployment point upon launch.

■ Capture images from a reference workstation as a custom image for use in your deployment service solution (for example, SMS or WDS).

▲ Install a build from the distribution share onto a target host.

As you can see from the list, the BDD Workbench is the place where you conduct most of your business when it comes to Vista deployments. Figure 3-13 shows the BDD Workbench.

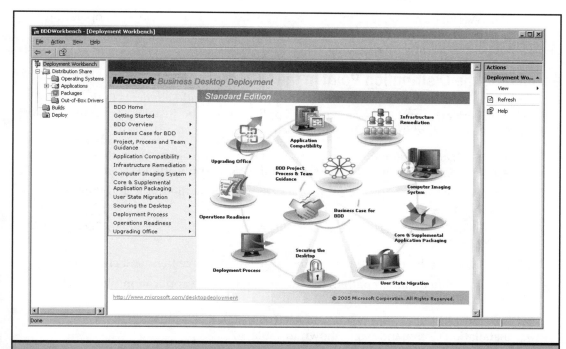

Figure 3-13.   The BDD Workbench shows the components used in the BDD.

Using the BDD Workbench to Establish a Distribution Point

The BDD manages images, application packages, and drivers required to deploy your customized Vista workstations. Deployment bits are stored and managed from a file share on the BDD deployment server. After BDD 2007 is installed, create the deployment point by using the Deployment Point Wizard in the Deployment Workbench. The Deployment Point Wizard allows you to manage the following four types of deployment points:

▼   **Default deployment point**   This default type creates a deployment point shared as Distribution$.

■   **New deployment point on a network share**   Use this option to create a network share as a deployment point. The share can be local or remote.

■   **A shared folder to use for removable media deployment**   Use this option to create a shared folder for use in creating images for deployment on removable media, including deploying from DVDs, external hard disks, or USB storage devices.

▲   **A shared folder to use for SMS 2003 OSD Feature Pack**   Use this option to create a shared folder for use in creating SMS 2003 OSD Feature Pack–managed images. This option should only be used for ZTI-based deployments.

The BDD Workbench manages this share, and is used to import the Vista operating systems stored in the .WIM format, manage applications or patches and their installation options, and automatically import and catalog driver files.

Populating the Distribution Point in the BDD Workbench

Before you deploy a Vista image, you have the opportunity to add elements to the build, including drivers and applications. Add the applications to be installed by using the New Application Wizard in the BDD Workbench.

1. In the BDD management console, expand Distribution Share, right-click Applications, and then click New to start the New Application Wizard.

2. Specify whether to copy the source files from a remote file share, and then click Next.

3. Complete the Specify The Details For This Application page, shown in Table 3-6, and then click Next.

4. Provide the fully qualified path to the application source files, and click Next.

5. Type the fully qualified path to the folder to which the application files will be copied, and click Next.

6. Provide additional parameters you need to install the application in the Installation Command page, shown in Table 3-7.

Upon completing the wizard, the new application name appears in the details pane.

In addition to applications, you can add other installation packages that need to be added after the operating system is set up. Add the packages to be installed by using the

In This Field	Provide
Publisher	Type the name of the software publisher or vendor.
Application Name	Type the user-friendly name of the application.
Version	Type the version of the application.
Languages(s)	Type the languages that the application supports.
Platforms(s)	Select the processor type that the application supports. Options are: ■ All platforms ■ Only X86 platform ■ Only X64 (or amd64) platform ■ Only ia64 platform

Table 3-6. Application Details

In This Field	Provide
Command Line	The command, with parameters, to launch the installation of the application.
Working Directory	The folder to use as the default directory when starting the installation by running the command.

Table 3-7.   Additional Parameters Needed to Install the Application

New Package Wizard in the Deployment Workbench. The following are some examples of packages:

▼   Security updates

■   Service packs

▲   Language packs

To add packages:

1. In the console tree, expand Distribution Share and right-click Packages to start the New Package Wizard.

2. On the Select The Location Of The Package Files page, in the Package Source Directory box, type the fully qualified path to the package source files, and click Add.

3. When the New Package Wizard finishes, the new package name appears in the details pane of the Pages node in the BDD Workbench.

You can add device drivers to the distribution point that must be installed with the operating system on the host workstation. Add the drivers to be installed by using the New Driver Wizard in the BDD Workbench. To add drivers:

1. In the BDD Workbench management console, expand the Distribution Share node, right-click the Out-Of-Box Drivers node, and click New to start the New Driver Wizard.

2   On the Select The Location Of The Driver Files page, in the Driver Source Directory box, type the fully qualified path to the driver source files, and then click Finish.

When the New Driver Wizard finishes, the new driver name appears in the details pane.

Configuring Builds in the BDD Workbench

Builds specify the operating system source and version of Vista that should be used, settings specific to the build (including the unattend.xml answer file), and any tasks that

In This Field	Provide
Build ID	The build number, used as a short, unique identifier for the build.
Build Name	The user-friendly name of the build.
Build Comments	A description of the build that helps identify the purpose, limits, and special details for the build.

Table 3-8.   Build Description Information

should be run as part of the installation. You specify any number of build configurations based on the information available from the distribution share.

The deployment configurations are used to create customized Windows PE boot images and to set the rules by which the BDD implements user state migration using the USMT. You create the builds to be deployed by using the New Build Wizard in the BDD Workbench.

1. In the BDD Workbench management console, right-click Builds and click New to start the New Build Wizard.

2. Provide some description of your new build using the general information fields listed in Table 3-8.

3. Select the image to be deployed with this build, and click Next.

4. Select one of the options listed in Table 3-9 for your license model.

5. Specify settings regarding the build, completing the fields listed in Table 3-10, and then click Create. The New Build Wizard is shown in Figure 3-14.

When the New Build Wizard finishes, the new build name appears in the details pane.

Option	Select This Option To
Use The Specified Product Key	Enter a product key to be used when deploying the build. In the Product Key field, type the product key to be used during deployment.
Do Not Use A Product Key When Installing	Select this option when using a volume license key or to manually specify the product key during the deployment process.

Table 3-9.   License Options

In This Field	Provide
Organization	The name of your organization to be configured during the deployment process.
Full Name	The full name of the user to be configured during the deployment process.
Internet Explorer Home Page	The URL for the Web site to be configured as the home page for Microsoft Internet Explorer during the deployment process.

Table 3-10.   Organizational and Internet Explorer Information

More Requirements for Deploying on a Target Host

The target systems on which you wish to deploy Vista must support these technologies:

▼   Microsoft Windows 2000 Professional SP4, Windows XP SP2, or a later Windows operating system (if not a bare-metal deploy using Windows PE)

▲   MSXML 3.0 (versions 4.0 and 6.0 are not compatible with the BDD scripts)

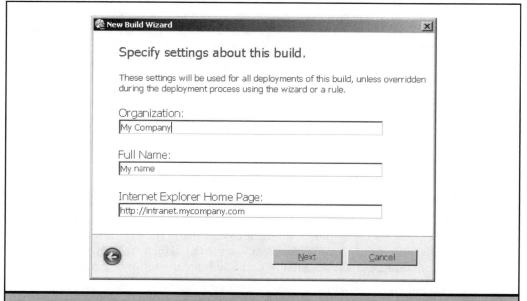

Figure 3-14.   Starting the New Build Wizard requires basic information to get started.

Because of the size of the images being distributed to the target computers (500 MB to 4 GB), computers must have a high-speed, persistent connection to the servers used in the deployment process. These servers include:

▼ WDS and/or SMS 2003 OSD Feature Pack servers

▲ File servers hosting shared folders (distribution points) used to store deployment images, shared folders used to store user state migration data, and shared folders used to store deployment logs

These servers should be on adjacent subnets to the target computers to ensure high-speed connectivity. If the organization cannot provide sufficient network capacity to deploy the BDD solution to computers, perform one of the following actions:

▼ Store user state migration data locally on the target host.

■ Place a distribution server closer to the target host for the duration of the migration.

■ Move the target host to a staging area where the computers can be deployed, and then move the host to the production location.

▲ Use a combination of a Vista or Windows PE image CD configured by the BDD or by the SMS OSD Feature Pack.

Windows Deployment Services

Windows Deployment Services (WDS) comes with the latest Microsoft server, and is available as an add-on for Windows Server 2003. Improving upon its predecessor, Remote Installation Services (RIS), WDS is the next generation of platform-integrated deployment services. Use it to install Vista, service packs, patches, and any packaged application to any member workstation in the Active Directory domain. WDS integrates with Active Directory for storing configuration and for defining distribution groups.

With WDS, you can add and remove servers, and configure a variety of options, including computer naming rules, DHCP settings, and PXE response settings. You can add and remove installations and boot images, and organize images into image groups. WDS also leverages Windows PE. An interesting capability of WDS is that it can be scripted using a command-line interface.

Use the BDD Workbench to create Vista or Windows PE images that can be stored on the BDD distribution point or on the WDS server. You can use WDS to deploy Vista for bare-metal installations, upgrades and replacement scenarios.

Preparing the WDS Server

In the absence of SMS 2003, WDS is responsible for initiating the deployment process for PXE boot-enabled target computers. You install WDS using the windows_deployment_services_update.exe provided with the Windows AIK, which accompanies the BDD download. Before you install WDS, ensure that you have the following requirements:

▼ **Active Directory** The WDS server must be a member of an Active Directory domain or be a domain controller.

- **DHCP** WDS uses PXE, which requires DHCP.
- **DNS** A working DNS server on the network is required to run WDS.
- **Windows Server 2003 SP1 with RIS** RIS does not have to be configured, but it must be installed.
▲ **Administrative Credentials** You have to install WDS as local administrator for member servers and as a domain administrator for domain controllers. To boot a host target into the WDS client, you must be a member of the Domain Users group.

You have two options for configuring WDS. Upon installation, there are a couple of management console snap-ins: the Windows Deployment Service and the Windows Deployment Service Legacy snap-ins. Use the latter snap-in for managing WDS with legacy RIS tools. Use the former for managing WDS in mixed or native modes. Your second option is the command-line interface, WdsUtil.exe. Use the /allhelp command argument for Wdsutil to get a full list of available commands.

TIP You can bring up the WDS snap-in by clicking the Start menu and typing "WdsMgmt.msc" into the run command. Your second option is the command-line interface, WdsUtil.exe.

To use WDS for LTI, run it in mixed mode or native mode. You decide which operational role a WDS server plays when installing it. Table 3-11 lists the operational modes of WDS.

TIP You can manage network loads across more than one distribution point by creating BDD distribution "sites," which are a collection of points grouped together in the LocationServer.xml file. By grouping points into a site, you give WDS the ability to balance the network and I/O load among all the servers.

Adding Images to the WDS Server

WDS supports the following types of images:

▼ **Install images** Install images are operating system images that are installed to client computers, which will boot to a WDS server. Types of install images include:

- **Windows Image Format (WIM)** WIM is a new file format that contains one or more compressed Windows images.
- **RIPREP images** RIPREP images are legacy RIS images. WDS in legacy or mixed mode is capable of deploying RIPREP images. Remember that unlike .wim images, RIPREP images are both hardware abstraction layer (HAL)-dependent and language-dependent.
- **RISETUP images** Copies of the CD directory structure (i386 directory) on a file share on the RIS server. RISETUP images are not HAL-dependent.

▲ **Boot images**   Boot images are Windows PE images containing the WDS client, and are used to present an initial boot menu when a client contacts a WDS server. The types of boot images include:

■ **Setup images**   The default image that contains the new host. When a client boots to a setup image, Windows Setup is launched and the host builds.

■ **Capture images**   An alternative to ImageX.exe when capturing an image prepared with the utility Sysprep.exe. When a booting to a capture image, the WDS Capture Utility walks the user through the process of capturing a new image.

■ **Discover images**   Boot images that are copied to a CD for use when PXE boot services are not available. When booting to a discover image, you get a WDS client-side menu in place of the PXE setup and Windows Setup launches to build the host.

Pre-staging Hosts for WDS

WDS can be configured to image computers that are pre-staged, which means that the host is authorized to receive an image from WDS. Depending on the WDS configuration,

Mode	Description
Legacy	Emulates RIS. This mode supports: ■ OSChooser as the boot operating system. ■ Images created by RISSETUP and RISREP. ■ Administration by using the normal RIS tools.
Mixed	Compatibility mode, with RIS and WDS functionality. This mode supports: ■ OSChooser or Windows PE as the boot operating system. ■ Images created by RISSETUP, RISREP, or ImageX/SIM (WIM format). ■ Administration via RIS or WDS management tools. ■ SMS 2003 OSD Feature Pack and ZTI.
Native	Supports WDS only. This mode only supports: ■ Windows PE as the boot operating system. ■ Images created by ImageX/SIM (WIM format). ■ Administration using the WDS management tools.

Table 3-11.   WDS Operational Modes

the team may need to pre-stage the target computers. Doing so authorizes WDS to deploy operating system images to the target computer.

To pre-stage a workstation:

1. Create the computer account in the Active Directory Users And Computers management console.

2. Select This Is A Managed Computer in the Managed dialog box in the Creation Wizard.

3. Provide the workstation's globally unique identifier (GUID). To find the GUID, visit Microsoft's TechNet Web site at technet.microsoft.com.

4. In the Host Server dialog box, select Any Available Remote Installation Services (RIS) or The Following RIS Server, and provide a resolvable name for the WDS server.

Running the WDS Deployment Wizard

After attending to all the planning and tasks reviewed so far, you are ready to deploy an image. The process prompts you for any configuration settings that are not already specified. To initiate the deployment of a Vista build to target hosts, you can use the Windows Deployment Wizard from WDS or launch the build manually.

Before you launch a deployment manually, ensure that any previous pass is removed. If a remnant of that process remains, it will interfere with your deployment. Be sure these two directories are empty:

▼ **%SystemDrive%\MININT**   Holds deployment state data, including user state migration and migration logs.

▲ **%SystemDrive%_SMSTaskSequence**   Contains task sequencer (TS.WSF) state information.

You can initiate deployments from a network share, local drives, or from a Vista DVD. Initiate the Lite Touch Installation Wizard by using one of the following methods:

▼ Manually connect to the appropriate deployment point (for example, *servername*\Distribution$\Scripts), and type **cscript litetouch.vbs**.

▲ Initiate the process through WDS and automatically run cscript litetouch.vbs.

The Windows Deployment Services Wizard launches. For bare-metal builds, complete the User Credentials page, providing the user name, password, and domain of an account with administrator rights on the target host, and then click OK. For all types of builds, the first task is to identify the distribution point. If the DeployRoot property does not specify a distribution point, you can specify the name of a server hosting the point or a BDD site name, if one has been created, to balance the network and I/O load across distribution points.

If the SkipDeploymentType property is set to Yes, you will not be asked to select the type of install. You will not be asked for a type if the DeploymentType property is set to NewComputer for bare-metal installations. Otherwise, the next page appears, prompting you to select one of the options listed in Table 3-12.

Option	Select This Option To
Refresh This Computer	Save the existing user state data (optional).
	Deploy the desktop image, including operating system and applications.
	Restore user state data (optional).
Upgrade This Computer	Upgrade the host by using the upgrade features as supported by the target host operating system.
Replace This Computer	Save the existing user state data.
	Deploy the desktop image, including operating system and applications, on a new computer.
	Restore user state data.

Table 3-12. Deployment Options

Next, answer a series of questions about the host and environment. Provide data on the host name, whether it should remain in a workgroup or join a domain upon completion, the domain name, and the credentials needed to join the target domain.

From there, you get a chance to specify where data will be saved. First up are the user state data and application data. You can leverage the BDD rules to automatically decide where on the target host the data can be safely stored, specify a location (local or remote), or choose not to store data at all—which applies if there is no existing user. When deploying to a new computer, the next page allows you to confirm that there is no data to restore. If replacing a host, you can elect not to restore data or provide a fully qualified path to the location where the backup files are stored.

Next, you have the option to back up the system drive before the new image is applied. As with user data, you can leverage the BDD rules to automatically determine the best location, specify a location yourself, or elect not to back up the host.

Following the data management, you identify the image to install if the BuildGUID property is left blank. The next step is to enter license key options, which are listed in Table 3-13.

You will get a chance to add a language module to suit the locale of the workstation. On the Packages page, in the Packages box, select the language pack to be installed, and then click Next.

NOTE This page of the wizard appears when the SkipPackageDisplay property is empty, the DeploymentType property is something other than REPLACE, and the first character in the ImageBuild property is 6, which indicates a Vista build. For Vista Ultimate and Enterprise Editions, select more than one language. For all other versions, select only one language. You can add extra language packs when upgrading hosts. If the languages are not already installed, problems in displaying the fonts may arise.

Option	Select This Option To
No Product Key Is Required	Assign product keys to target computers by using a Key Management Service (KMS).
Activate The Target Computer By Using A Multiple Activation Key (MAK)	Assign a MAK to the target computer and activate the computer over the Internet. In the Multiple Activation Key box, type the MAK to be assigned to the target computer.
Use A Specific Product Key	Assign a specific license key for installation or retail activation. In the Product_key box, type the product key to be assigned to the target computer.

Table 3-13.   License Key Options

When upgrading a host, the WDS Deployment Workbench prevents selecting a regional locale. During an upgrade, Vista will reuse the same language that is currently installed.

Next, you have the option to install applications. The applications must have been imported into the distribution point using the BDD Workbench. On the Select One Or More Applications To Install page, in the Applications list box, select the appropriate applications to deploy, and then click Next.

Finally, you are asked whether you wish to install the build as you have configured it, and then capture the result as a reference image. For normal deployments, you will be better off using the BDD tools or SMS 2003 to build your reference image. Nonetheless, WDS offers that functionality. Review the information on the Ready To Begin page, and then click Begin. As the WDS Deployment Wizard finishes, the deployment begins.

Systems Management Server 2003

As an alternative to using WDS alone, you can leverage SMS 2003 with the Operating System Deployment (OSD) Feature Pack, which has been updated since its original release to serve Vista installs. SMS is a great way to elevate your Vista deployment into the highly automated ZTI program. SMS and the OSD Feature Pack is a rich topic beyond the scope of this book. However, we want to give you an initial sense of what is involved so that you can at least be somewhat aware of the benefits and weaknesses of using an industry-leading solution. The overall process of preparing and deploying Vista using SMS includes the following steps:

1. Configure the master computer as a reference host:
   - Install Vista, any service packs, and hot fixes.
   - Install common applications (Office, VPN client, etc.).
   - Install the SMS Advanced Client.

2. Insert the SMS 2003 Capture CD into the reference host:

■ Provide settings answers, such as where to store the image.

■ Add drivers for any known hardware that is not on the hardware list.

■ Execute Sysprep and restart the computer.

■ Image Capture Wizard completes the capture and posts the file to the target share in about 30 to 45 minutes.

3. Distribute images among the SMS distribution points:

■ Import the .wim file into SMS.

■ Create an image program, licensing, domain settings, and target organizational unit (OU) for the computer object.

■ Specify distribution points.

■ Create a collection of target systems.

4. Deploy the images and install the build:

■ Notify the user. He or she can continue or postpone the install (optional).

■ Validation. Confirm that the system is compatible with the image.

■ Capture state. This include computer, SMS, and user settings.

■ Preinstall. Prepare the system for update by standing services down and unlocking files.

■ Install. Stand up the new image.

■ Postinstall. Apply computer, domain, and SMS settings.

■ State restore. Restore the system to the state, plus install additional packages.

Figure 3-15 shows the phases for a ZTI deployment.

For more information about SMS, consult the Help files that accompany the installation or the online SMS portal (www.microsoft.com/smserver/default.mspx).

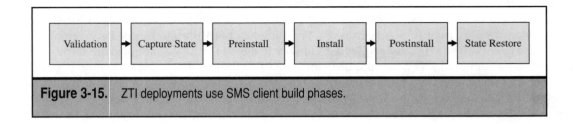

Figure 3-15.   ZTI deployments use SMS client build phases.

PART II

Networking

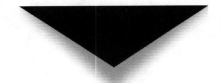

CHAPTER 4

TCP/IP and Name Resolution

A s you know, you can't simply put two computers running Windows Vista next to each other, plug in their network interfaces, and expect them to communicate. Those computers need some sort of common language, and that's where the Transmission Control Protocol/Internet Protocol (TCP/IP) comes into play. Furthermore, those computers need some way to find each other, whether on a network, intranet, or the Internet. That's where name resolution comes into play.

This chapter examines two necessary tools for networking: TCP/IP and name resolution. While the overall topic is not necessarily specific to Windows Vista, it is important to developing your Windows Vista network. Plus, we'll take a look at how these technologies are put into use in a Windows Vista environment.

NOTE   The first part of this chapter is really for readers who may not understand TCP/IP and the OSI model. If this is nothing new to you, please skip ahead to the last portion of this chapter, where we really get into the nuts and bolts of how this all relates to Windows Vista.

TCP/IP

Like Velcro and freeze-dried ice cream, TCP/IP was created as part of a larger U.S. government interest. It was developed by the Defense Advanced Research Projects Agency (DARPA) in the 1970s. The idea was to allow dissimilar computers to freely exchange data, regardless of location. At the time, there wasn't a computer on every desktop, so consumer or big-scale business application of the protocol wasn't even a glimmer in the developers' minds. The TCP/IP suite was first developed on UNIX computers. As the protocol was packaged inside each computer, its popularity grew.

To understand how TCP/IP works—and to establish a vocabulary that we'll revisit throughout this book—we need to take a step back and first understand the Open Systems Interconnect (OSI) reference model.

OSI Model

The OSI reference model was developed in the 1970s to provide the standard by which computers could communicate with each other. It has seven functional layers, each one defining a function performed when data is transferred between applications across a network. Each protocol communicates with the same protocol on a remote system. This is illustrated in Figure 4-1.

For example, Hypertext Transfer Protocol (HTTP) is an application-layer protocol that communicates with peer Web browser applications on remote systems. The applications do not care whether the physical layer is a dial-in modem or an Ethernet connection. It is only concerned with functions within HTTP.

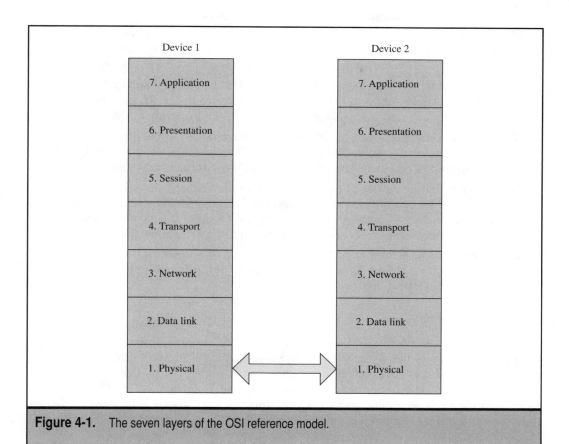

Figure 4-1.   The seven layers of the OSI reference model.

The seven OSI layers include the following:

▼ **Layer 1**   The *physical layer* deals with the actual transport media that are being used. It defines the electrical and mechanical characteristics of the medium carrying the data signal. Some examples include coaxial cable, fiber optics, twisted-pair cabling, and serial lines.

■ **Layer 2**   The *data link layer* governs access on to the network and the reliable transfer of packets across the network. It controls the synchronization of packets transmitted, as well as the error checking and flow control of transmissions. Token-passing techniques work at this layer.

- **Layer 3**   The *network layer* is concerned with moving data between different networks or subnetworks. It's responsible for finding the destination device for which the data is destined. IP and IP routing is a function of this layer.

- **Layer 4**   The *transport layer* takes care of data transfer, ensuring that the data reaches its destination intact and in the proper order. The Transmission Control Protocol (TCP) and User Datagram Protocol (UDP) operate at this layer.

- **Layer 5**   The *session layer* establishes and terminates connections and arranges sessions to logical parts. The Lightweight Directory Access Protocol (LDAP) and Remote Procedure Call (RPC) provide some functions at this layer.

- **Layer 6**   The *presentation layer* is involved in formatting data for the purpose of display or printing. Data encryption and character set translation, such as ASCII to EBCDIC, are also performed by protocols at this layer. Examples of presentation layer protocols are Basic Input Output System (BIOS) and Telnet.

- **Layer 7**   The *application layer* defines the protocols to be used between the application programs. Examples of protocols at this layer are protocols for e-mail, HTTP, and File Transfer Protocol (FTP).

How TCP/IP Works

So why the preceding foray into the world of the OSI reference model? As you might have picked up from our description of the layers, TCP/IP maps to the OSI reference model at layers 3 and 4, as illustrated in Figure 4-2.

The idea behind mapping the two stacks in this way is to leave networking technologies up to the local area network (LAN) vendors. TCP/IP's goal is to move messages through any LAN product and establish a connection using any network application.

TCP/IP Layers

TCP/IP functions because it links to the OSI reference model at its two lowest levels: the data link and physical layers. This allows TCP/IP to speak with just about any networking technology and, as a result, any computer platform. It contains four abstract layers:

- **Network interface**   Allows TCP/IP to interact with all modern network technologies by complying with the OSI model.

- **Internet**   Defines how IP directs messages through routers and over internetworks, such as the Internet.

- **Transport**   Defines the mechanics of how messages are exchanged between computers.

- **Application**   Defines network applications to perform tasks such as file transfer, e-mail, and other useful functions.

TCP/IP has become the Internet's standard protocol—not by design, but because of popularity and prevalence. A computer implementing an OSI-compliant layer network

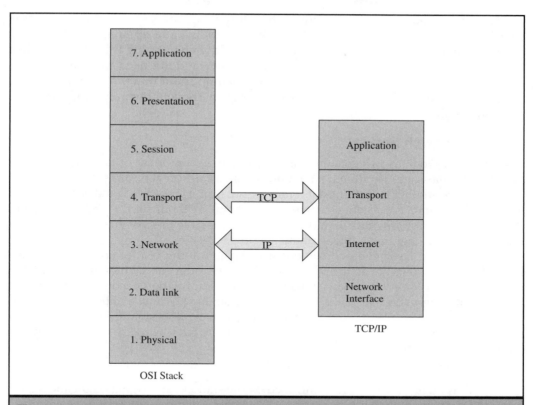

Figure 4-2.   The TCP/IP stack is compliant with the OSI seven-layer reference model.

technology (such as Ethernet) will be able to connect with other devices. This is useful not only in your organization's network, but also when you want to connect to the Internet and to other networks.

Datagrams

All this conceptual talk about the OSI reference model and TCP/IP's layers is nice and all, but how does it come together in practical terms? When data works its way through a network, it must be in a format that both sender and receiver can understand. TCP/IP accommodates this communication with its Internet layer. This layer maps directly to the OSI model's network layer and is based on a fixed-message format called the *IP datagram*.

Think of a datagram as a basket that holds all the parts of your message. For instance, when you download a Web page to your browser, what you finally see was delivered piece by piece inside datagrams.

Datagrams and packets are easily confused: A datagram is a unit of data, whereas a packet is the physical message entity (created at levels 3 and up) that actually passes through a network. Although the terms are used interchangeably (like "engine" and "motor"), they really are two different things—but we don't need to bore you with anything other than a high-level explanation. The important thing to note here is that messages are broken into pieces, sent across the network, and then reassembled at the receiving station.

The IP Datagram Format

Taking a closer look at a IP version 4 datagram, we see a number of fields for both the payload and message-handling data. Figure 4-3 illustrates a datagram's layout.

If you take another look at the datagram format from Figure 4-3, you'll notice that the leftmost fields are a consistent size in each datagram. Without some standardization in these fields, the resulting bits would be an undecipherable mess of zeroes and ones. To the right of the datagram are the variable-length packets.

There are two basic components on each datagram: the header and the data portion. Think of a datagram as the Space Shuttle. The header can be thought of as all the computers in the shuttle's cockpit. It handles all the information needed by the various routers and computers that will send the packet on its way, and will be used to maintain order when it's time to bring this packet together with its siblings to form the message. The payload is like the Shuttle's cargo bay—it's what's being carried, either by the Shuttle or the datagram.

This is what the various datagram fields do:

▼ **VER**   The version of IP being used by the station that originated the message. The current version is IP version 4. This field lets different versions coexist in an internetwork.

■ **HLEN**   For *header length*, this tells the receiver how long the header will be so that the central processing unit (CPU) knows where the data field begins.

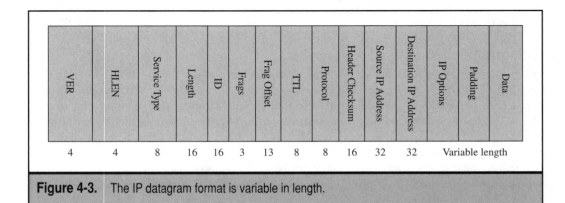

Figure 4-3.   The IP datagram format is variable in length.

- **Service type**   A code to tell the router how the packet should be handled in terms of level of service (reliability, precedence, delay, and so on).

- **Length**   The total number of bytes in the entire packet, including all header fields and the data field.

- **ID, frags, and frags offset**   These fields identify for the router how to handle packet fragmentation and reassembly, and how to offset for different frame sizes that might be encountered as the packet travels through different LAN segments using different networking technologies, such as Ethernet, Fiber Distributed Data Interface (FDDI), and so on.

- **TTL**   Short for Time to Live, a number that is decremented by one each time the packet is forwarded. When the counter reaches zero, the packet is dropped. TTL prevents router loops and lost packets from endlessly wandering internetworks.

- **Protocol**   The transport protocol that should be used to handle the packet. This field almost always identifies TCP as the transport protocol to use, but certain other transports can be used to handle IP packets.

- **Header checksum**   A *checksum* is a numerical value used to help ensure message integrity. If the checksums in all the message's packets don't add up to the right value, the station knows that the message was garbled.

- **Source IP address**   The 32-bit address of the host that originated the message (usually a PC or a server).

- **Destination IP address**   The 32-bit address of the host to which the message is being sent (usually a PC or a server).

- **IP options**   Used for network testing and other specialized purposes.

- **Padding**   Fills in any unused bit positions so that the CPU can correctly identify the first bit position of the data field.

- ▲ **Data**   The payload being sent. For example, a packet's data field might contain some of the text making up an e-mail.

So why bother with breaking the message into pieces and then transmitting them? It's sort of the same reason why the president and vice president don't fly together. If a bird gets sucked into Air Force One's engine and it goes down, we still have the vice president to lead the country. If a message is corrupted during transmission, only that portion of the message needs to be resent, not the entire thing. Another benefit is that no lone host needs to wait an inordinate amount of time before being able to send its own message.

Datalink Protocols

Layer 2 of the OSI reference model is where computers formulate how they're going to talk on the physical layer. That is, maybe they're communicating via a dial-in modem or Category 5 cabling, so the computers need a way to converse over that medium. When we talk about connecting the computers in your organization's Windows Vista environment, there are a few common datalink protocols that your network is likely using. Let's look at them a little more closely.

NOTE There's a datalink protocol that you might expect to see in our list: Asynchronous Transfer Mode (ATM). However, you are probably never going to run into ATM at the desktop or server, and since ATM is very nearly dead, we're not going to waste precious ink on it.

Ethernet

The most common network technology is *Ethernet,* which carries data at a rate of 10 or 100 megabits per second (Mbps). (We'll get to Gigabit Ethernet in a second.)

NOTE You'll often hear 100-Mbps Ethernet referred to as *Fast Ethernet.*

Ethernet operates by contention. Devices sharing an Ethernet LAN segment listen for traffic being carried over the wire and defer transmitting a message until the medium is clear. If two stations send at about the same time and their packets collide, both transmissions are aborted, and the stations back off and wait a random period of time before retransmitting.

Ethernet is inherently less expensive, thanks to the random nature of its architecture. In other words, the electronics needed to run Ethernet are easier to manufacture because it doesn't try to control everything on the LAN.

The obvious disadvantage of Ethernet is that a lot of raw bandwidth is sacrificed to aborted transmissions. Theoretical maximum effective bandwidth from Ethernet is estimated at only 37 percent of raw wire speed. However, the equipment is so inexpensive that Ethernet has always been, on balance, the cheapest form of effective bandwidth.

Gigabit and 10 Gigabit Ethernet

Gigabit Ethernet and *10 Gigabit Ethernet* are 1- and 10-gigabytes per second (GBps) extensions of the Ethernet standard. The big draw for these faster Ethernet specifications has been largely motivated by their inherent compatibility with earlier Ethernet specifications.

Its greatest advantage is familiarity, given that Ethernet is the pervasive technology. Many network managers are naturally biased in favor of Gigabit Ethernet because they and the people they work with know and trust the technology. While Gigabit Ethernet over copper is becoming a common method of connecting servers in the datacenter, 1 and 10 Gigabit Ethernet are also supported and used over a variety of fiber-optic cable types.

Token Ring

Token Ring used to be Ethernet's biggest competition, but not anymore. Still, there are a handful of Token Ring networks out there. Architecturally speaking, Token Ring is quite different from Ethernet. It takes its name from the fact that it defines attached hosts into a logical ring. Token Ring is described as *logical* because the LAN segment behaves like a ring by passing signals in a round-robin fashion as if the devices were actually attached to a looped cable. This is illustrated in Figure 4-4.

Token Ring can use up to 75 percent of raw bandwidth, compared to Ethernet's theoretical maximum of about 37 percent. That sounds great and efficient, but in order for them to pay off and reach maximum efficiency, they must be deployed across large networks.

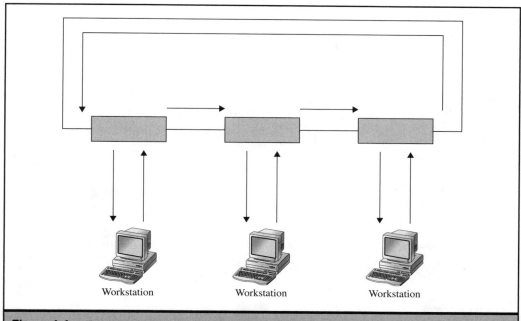

Figure 4-4. Token Ring LANs use logical rings, not literal physical loops.

This is a problem, because most LANs tend to be small, since most enterprises are small. Moreover, even big companies have their networks segmented into smaller LANs, which are too petite to receive much of the bandwidth benefit of a Token Ring.

FDDI

Fiber Distributed Data Interface (FDDI) is a 100-Mbps protocol that runs over fiber-optic cable media. Like Token Ring, FDDI uses a token-passing architecture to control media access, yielding high effective bandwidth from its 100-Mbps wire speed. You may still see it from time to time, mostly in the datacenter.

FDDI's architecture made it attractive for use as backbone LANs, especially for office campuses and other large-area applications. FDDI uses dual rings to provide additional reliability because of their redundant paths. The secondary ring goes into action when the primary ring fails. As Figure 4-5 shows, FDDI isolates the damaged station by wrapping around to the secondary ring and looping back in the other direction—thus keeping the ring intact.

NOTE You might also use Copper Distributed Data Interface (CDDI). This technology works the same way as FDDI, but as you might gather from the name, it does so over copper cabling, not fiber optic.

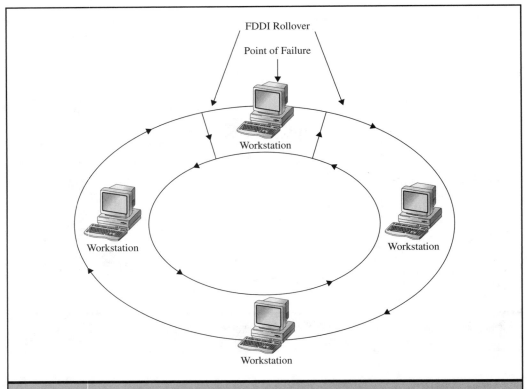

FDDI Rollover

Point of Failure

Workstation

Workstation

Workstation

Workstation

Figure 4-5.   FDDI uses fiber-optic cabling to carry its messages.

Host-to-Host Transport Layer Protocols

When an IP message travels across a network, it does so using one of two *transport* protocols: TCP or UDP. As mentioned, TCP stands for Transmission Control Protocol and is the first half of the TCP/IP acronym. UDP stands for User Datagram Protocol and is used in place of TCP for less-critical messages. Either protocol serves to transport messages as needed through TCP/IP networks. There is a major difference between the functionality of TCP and UDP messages, however:

▼   TCP is called a *reliable* protocol because it checks with the receiver to ensure that the packet was received.

▲   UDP is called an *unreliable* protocol because no effort is made to check with the receiver and verify delivery.

The important thing to remember is that only one transport protocol can be used to manage a message. For instance, if you download a web page, the packets are managed by TCP. On the other hand, a Trivial File Transfer Protocol (TFTP) upload or download is accomplished via the UDP protocol.

The transport protocol used is dependent on the application type—it isn't just a random determination. UDP is used whenever possible because it cuts down on overhead traffic. On the other hand, TCP makes more efforts to ensure delivery and transmits more packets than UDP. Figure 4-6 shows a brief list of network applications, illustrating which ones use TCP and which use UDP.

For example, FTP and TFTP do basically the same thing. However, TFTP is generally used to download firmware or images to a device on the network or to perhaps back up network device software. It's a simple job, not very complicated, so UDP works fine. Another example is a voice/video session, which can utilize ports for both TCP and UDP sessions. For instance, a TCP session will be initiated to share information while setting up the call, whereas the actual call will be sent via UDP. This is because of the speed involved with streaming voice and video. In the event a packet is dropped, it makes no sense to resend it, as it will no longer fit in with the datastream.

IPv4

Much like your home address, devices on a computer network use addresses to locate one another. But computers don't use a format like 1312 Mockingbird Lane, Anytown U.S.A. to identify themselves. They use IP addresses.

The most prevalent kind of IP addresses are 32-bit addresses known as IP version 4 (IPv4) addresses. An up-and-coming IP addressing scheme is IPv6. This section looks at IPv4. In the next section, we'll look at IPv6 and what it means for Windows Vista.

Elements of an IP Address

IPv4 addresses use a 32-bit notation scheme. That is, they contain four sections of 8 bits each. An example of an IPv4 address is:

192.11.203.122

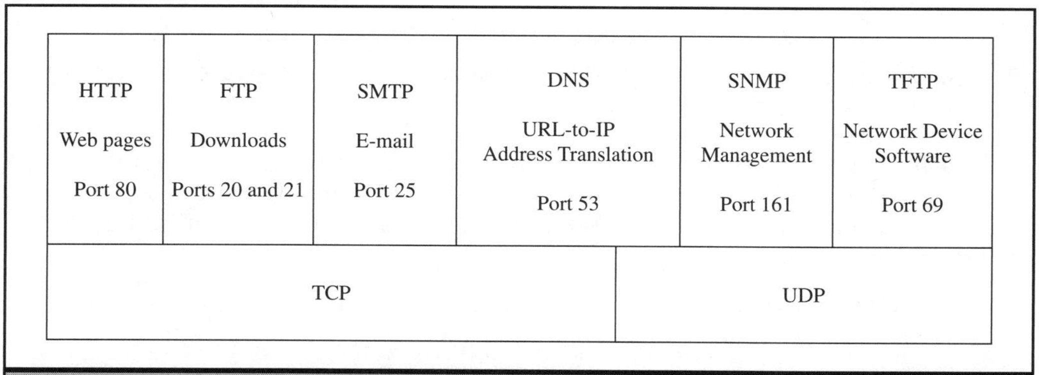

HTTP	FTP	SMTP	DNS	SNMP	TFTP
Web pages	Downloads	E-mail	URL-to-IP Address Translation	Network Management	Network Device Software
Port 80	Ports 20 and 21	Port 25	Port 53	Port 161	Port 69
TCP				UDP	

Figure 4-6.   Applications use TCP or UDP, depending on their need.

As a result, there are about 4 billion addresses available. Believe it or not, we're running out of unique IPv4 addresses, so the next notation scheme, IPv6, was developed. Windows Vista includes both IPv4 and IPv6 in its architecture.

NOTE These examples assume a 24-bit mask. We'll explain masks later in this chapter.

There are two parts of each IPv4 address:

▼ **Network ID** The network ID identifies each network. All the hosts in a single network will have the same network ID. For example, in the IP address 192.11.203.122, the network ID is 192.11.203. A router analyses only the network ID portion of an IP address for datagram forwarding.

▲ **Host ID** The host ID identifies a host on a network. Two hosts on two different networks can have the same ID (but, as the name suggests, the network IDs will be different). For instance, an IP address of 192.11.203.122 has 122 as its host ID.

Let's take a closer look at how those addresses are managed.

IPv4 Address Classes

As a network professional, you probably know all about IP addresses. You might be able to recite which computers on your networks have which IP addresses. ("Oh, yeah, Eric in marketing is 192.169.2.100.") On the other hand, if the nuts and bolts of IP addressing are still fuzzy to you, let's take some time to understand it.

The Internet Engineering Task Force (IETF), the organization that oversees the Internet, divides IP addresses into three generalized classes. Each class differs in the way the octets are designated for addressing networks as opposed to hosts. Figure 4-7 shows the first octet number ranges. The shaded octets show how much of the IP address space is reserved for addressing networks. As the shaded portion proceeds to the right, more networks are possible, but there are fewer possible hosts.

NOTE The IETF also divides IP addresses into two specialized addresses, one for multicasting and one for research, which we don't discuss here.

This division of ranges is known as the *first octet rule*. Any router in the world can read the first octet of an IP address and interpret the bits as network addresses versus host addresses. Most networks are numbered using either Class B or Class C IP addresses. The octet ranges are as follows:

▼ **0 to 127** Class A, range of network numbers is 0.0.0.0 to 127.0.0.0 for 128 networks. However, the network must not consist of only 0s, and 127.0.0.0 is reserved for loopback. What remains are 126 networks—1 to 126. There are 16,777,214 possible host addresses (16,777,216 minus 2).

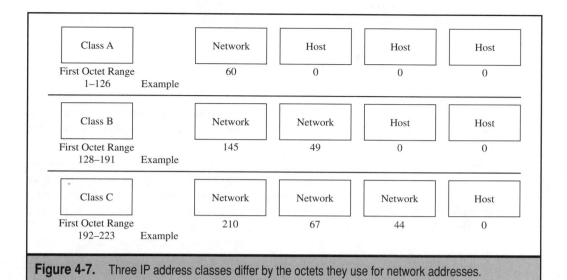

Figure 4-7.   Three IP address classes differ by the octets they use for network addresses.

- **128 to 191**   Class B, range of network numbers is 128.0.0.0 to 191.255.0.0, for 16,384 networks. There are 65,534 possible host addresses (65,536 minus 2).

- **192 to 223**   Class C, range of network numbers is 192.0.0.0 to 223.255.255.0, for 2,097,152 networks. There are 254 possible host addresses (256 minus 2).

NOTE   In order to perform host calculations, two reserved addresses must be deducted: 0 for "this network" and 255 for broadcast. Addresses 1 through 254 can be assigned to hosts.

Looking at the preceding list—you might surmise that only a few very large organizations can have Class A addresses—only 126 of them, to be exact. Most users, whether they know it or not, use a unique, publicly addressable Class B or Class C IP address when they connect to the Internet.

Subnet Masks

Subnetting an IP network allows a single network to be broken into several smaller networks. A *subnet mask* is a mask that is used to tell how many bits in an octet identify the subnetwork and how many bits provide room for host addresses.

Normally, a subnet mask is used to determine whether to send a packet to the Media Access Control (MAC) address of the default gateway or to a specific host.

Format

To make the issue of subnetting more confusing, binary subnet masks are represented in the same format as IP addresses: the IPv4 dotted-decimal format.

Here's an example of a binary subnet mask:

11111111.11111111.11111111.11000000

This mask can be written in octet form as:

255.255.255.192

Subnet masks are easy to spot, however, because you'll see the same eight numbers: 0, 128, 192, 224, 240, 248, 252, 154, and 255. These numbers represent a series of all ones followed by all zeroes.

NOTE A subnet mask will always end with one of those eight numbers, because they are all a series of ones to the left and a series of zeroes on the right, which is necessary for a mask. A subnet would never end in .10, for instance, because its binary number is 00001010—as you can see, the ones and zeroes are mixed together. Likewise, a subnet mask would never end with a number like .15. In this case, the binary equivalent of 15 is 00001111. While the ones and zeroes are all together, they are on the wrong sides.

CIDR

Rather than write out the dotted-decimal version of a subnet mask, there's a quick and easy way to show your IP address's subnet mask. A form of notation called Classless Inter-Domain Routing (CIDR) gives the network number, followed by a "/" and the number of "one" bits in the network number.

Using our example of 255.255.255.192, CIDR notation for an IP address with that subnet mask would be something like:

192.0.2.100/26

Putting It Together

An IP address, remember, is comprised of two parts: the network portion and the host portion. Subnetting takes bits from the host portion and adds them to the network portion.

For instance, giving the class A network of 10.0.0.0 a subnet mask of 255.255.0.0 would break it into 256 subnetworks. In this case, the first network would be 10.0.0.0 to 10.0.255.255, and the last network would be 10.255.0.0 to 10.255.255.255.

NOTE Subnet masks are not limited to whole octets. For instance, applying a subnet mask of 255.254.0.0 (or /15) to a Class A address would create 128 subnetworks.

You can figure out the number of available hosts and subnets on a given network rather simply if you know the subnet mask. For example, let's say you have a network address of 155.7.32.0 and a subnet mask of 255.255.255.0. This can be written as 155.7.32.0 /24.

Decimally, the mask 255.255.255.0 looks like:

11111111.11111111.11111111.00000000

Remember, the mask portion is the ones. So in this case, the subnet mask has 24 bits for the network portion of the address and 8 bits for the host portion.

In this case, if 24 bits have been allocated for the network portion and 8 bits have been allocated for the host portion, then this subnet mask allows 256 hosts.

Private Addresses

If you connect a Windows Vista device to your LAN, it will have to be assigned an IP address. However, if the Internet uses IP addresses to connect, what prevents some weirdo from typing in your IP address and getting at your personal files? Among other reasons, the use of private addressing allows different LANs to employ the same IP addresses. This is because these addresses are only used within the confines of your LAN.

The Internet Assigned Numbers Authority (IANA) reserves three blocks of IP addresses for private usage. This keeps the world from running out of IP addresses (because more than one organization can reuse the same IP network and its addresses for devices it doesn't want on the Internet anyway).

NOTE   When privately addressed devices need to connect to the internet, they usually do it by way of a "proxy" that performs network address translation (NAT). This is a mechanism whereby the private IP address is "converted" into a common public IP address for the sole purpose of communicating outside the private network. It's best looked at as a "one to many" relationship, where perhaps thousands of private IP addresses are able to use one public IP address. The proxy keeps track of all of the private IP addresses using the connection to make sure that the return traffic is sent back to the correct private IP address. These days, this is a process typically managed by a firewall.

The three blocks of reserved private addresses are as follows:

▼ **10.0.0.0 through 10.255.255.255**   The *10 block* is a single Class A network number.

■ **172.16.0.0 through 172.31.255.255**   The *172 block* is 16 contiguous Class B network numbers.

▲ **192.168.0.0 through 192.168.255.255**   The *192 block* is 256 contiguous Class C network numbers.

There are no official rules for when to use a particular private-network IP address block. The IP address police won't come and arrest you for using the 172 block when you should be using the 192 block. Generally speaking, the one with the most suitable size is used. For obvious reasons, there is no need to use 10.x.x.x if it is unthinkable that your LAN will ever grow to more than 254 hosts. However, when using private addresses, the network administrator can be liberal on the usage of the addresses when assigning them to the different parts of a network, as the strict rules that govern public IP address assignment do not apply.

Once the network uses a device that is a boundary to the Internet (a so-called *edge device*), then a public IP address must be assigned. The use of private IP addresses is meant only to link hosts that do the bulk of their connections from within the private network.

Private IP addresses can be assigned in two ways:

▼ **Automatic private IP addressing**   If a user wants to connect multiple computers running Windows Vista, he or she can use the Automatic Private IP Addressing (APIPA) feature. This allows each computer to automatically assign itself a private IP address. The user need not configure an IP address for each computer, and a Dynamic Host Configuration Protocol (DHCP) server is not necessary. Computers with authorized private IP addressing can connect to the Internet by using another computer with proxy or NAT capabilities.

▲ **Unauthorized private IP addressing**   If he or she is so inclined, a user can manually configure a private IP address. This is only recommended if there is a relative certainty that the devices will never go on the Internet. In the event these computers do connect to the Internet, you might have to run around and change the IP addresses of each host.

Default Gateways

Earlier, we talked about the slick way network engineers are able to get around the limitations on the number of IP addresses available by implementing subnets. However, as nice as this is, subnetting raises another problem—the inability to get from one subnet to another (for instance, a computer in accounting might not be able to access a server in administration). To ameliorate this problem, routers, or *gateways*, are placed between LAN segments. If a device wishes to contact another device on the same segment, it transmits to that station directly using a simple discovery technique. If the destination station does not exist on the same segment as the source station, then the source can't figure out how to get to the destination.

One of the configuration parameters needed by each network device is its *default gateway*. The default gateway is what is most often used to get a workstation's or server's network traffic from one subnet to another. The default gateway is simply a router's IP address, configured by the network administrator. This router is usually running a special route protocol that helps it know how to get to other networks near and far. So if the destination station does not exist on the same subnet, or if it doesn't know exactly which gateway is the next hop on a route to the destination, the workstation can send its traffic to the default gateway.

NOTE   A generally easy way to tell if your default gateway is incorrectly configured is if you are able to communicate with other devices on the same subnet (normally in the same building or same floor) but cannot access devices outside your subnet. However, a 10.x.x.x network is easier to type and generally easier to remember.

When making your TCP/IP connections, DHCP can be configured to provide the default gateway address. However, if you are configuring your network manually, you'll need to ensure that you have a correctly assigned IP address and subnet mask, and know which default gateway to use.

IPv6

An introduction to Vista's Next Generation TCP/IP Stack, which we'll explain in the next section, requires an in-depth look at IPv6. IPv6 is a set of network standards defined within the network-interface layer of OSI reference model. It follows IPv4 and offers evolutionary improvements over IPv4 that will ensure its adoption in networks across the globe, although IPv4 will continue to be supported for the foreseeable future.

IPv6 was authored by Steve Deering and Craig Mudge at Xerox PARC and was adopted by the IETF in 1994. Originally named "IP Next Generation," or IPng, IPv6 was given its official name by the IETF after the IPv5 name was assigned to an experimental suite of protocols that support video and audio transmissions.

IPv6 has seen only minor adoption in the private and public domains. However, the pool of available public IPv4 addresses is expected to run out as early as 2009, which will necessitate adoption of the great address space provided by IPv6.

IPv6 is similar to IPv4 in many respects, and reflects the next step in improvements over its pervasive predecessor. This new version of IP services holds promise, though not enough for networks to rush to update to it. Reaching past 10 years as an accepted standard, IPv6 is mature enough to warrant feasibility studies, and you may soon be preparing possible upgrade paths. In the meantime, you should realize that IPv6 has a foothold that will grow quickly with each implementation of Vista.

NOTE   Because most security hardware appliances and host-based intrusion detection programs have not been programmed to inspect IPv6 packets in depth, data can bypass most network security. Though you may not have plans for deploying IPv6, your security systems should be updated as soon as possible to accommodate the growing threat.

IPv6 Characteristics

IPv6 is a rich extension of IPv4, and many of the details are beyond the scope of this book. We encourage you to do additional reading on the subject—one of the best places to start is at www.microsoft.com/technet/itsolutions/network/ipv6/default.mspx. Before we dig into some interesting engineering traits of IPv6, we will talk about the characteristics relevant to Vista networking, including Internet Protocol Security (IPSec) and the new IP addressing solution.

Streamlined IP Packets

Even though the IPv6 header is larger, it is purposefully streamlined to keep overhead to a minimum. IPv6 addresses are four times as large, but the IPv6 header is only twice as large as the IPv4 header. This streamlined header is designed to be efficiently processed by IPv6-capable router infrastructures. It's important to keep in mind that IPv4 headers and IPv6 packet headers are not interoperable, and IPv6 is not a superset of functionality that is backward-compatible with IPv4. A host or router must use an implementation of both IPv4 and IPv6 in order to recognize and process both header formats.

IP Addresses for Everyone and Everything

The pool of IPv4 addresses is expected to run dry sometime around 2009. IPv4 provides for 4.3 billion addresses using a 32-bit addressing scheme. Using a 128-bit scheme, IPv6 provides for 340,282,366,920,938,463,463,374,607,431,768,211,456 or 2^{128} or 3.40282366920938E+38 or 50,000,000,000,000,000,000,000,000,000,000 unique addresses per person on Earth—that should be enough (for now).

The downside is that 128-bit addresses require more overhead. That should be supplanted as computer platforms move toward 64-bit architecture, which handles the larger addresses exceedingly well. The large pool of addresses ensures that, for the foreseeable future, end-to-end communications will continue without the need of helper technology, such as NAT. The relatively large size of the IPv6 address is designed to be subdivided into hierarchical routing domains that reflect the topology of the modern-day Internet. The use of 128 bits allows for multiple levels of hierarchy and flexibility in designing hierarchical addressing and routing, which is currently lacking in the IPv4-based Internet.

The drawback of the large address size is that IPv6 is less efficient in bandwidth usage, which may hurt regions where bandwidth is limited. The benefits of the larger address space include less fragmentation and easier administration of the pool, since organizations can be allocated large blocks, which, in turn, leads to smaller routing tables. Unfortunately, IPv6 makes it harder to conceal an organization's addressing scheme, where all hosts multicasts and Directory Service tables list which IPv6 addresses in a range are assigned, and it will be much harder to track down those rogue computers if they occupy an address that has not been legally assigned.

Stateless and Stateful Autoconfiguration

Dynamic configuration does not require a DHCP service for a host with IPv6. IPv6 routers can manage the settings for all hosts within the local internetwork served by the router using a native feature called stateless autoconfiguration. Workstations or other devices send a broadcast request for configuration parameters, which is met with a router advertisement packet sent by an IPv6 router that contains IP network-interface layer configuration parameters. If you need to manage IP configurations in ways that are not accommodated by the IPv6 router, install the DHCPv6 service on the network to provide stateful autoconfiguration and the necessary management options.

Built-In IPSec

IPv6 easily enables secure channels for routers that use the Border Gateway Protocol (BGP) by encrypting the route protocol when it's transmitted from one router to another. And while IPSec support for IPv6 traffic in Windows XP and Windows Server 2003 is limited, Vista's support is much more robust. Previous operating systems do not support Internet Key Exchange (IKE) or data encryption. IPsec security policies, security associations, and keys are configured through text files and activated through a command-line tool, IPsec6.exe. In Vista, IPSec support for IPv6 traffic is the same as that for IPv4, including support for IKE and data encryption with AES 128/192/256. The IP Security Policies snap-in now supports the configuration of IPsec policies for

IPv6 traffic in the same way as IPv4 traffic, using either the IP Security Policies snap-in or the new Windows Firewall With Advanced Security snap-in.

IPv6 Addressing Overview

Rendering more IP addresses was a key factor in moving toward the IPv6 design. The address schema of an IPv6 address is quite different and requires more study to assign than with IPv4. Before we explore how IPv6 communication works, we should cover some fundamental questions you may have about address types.

Nodes, Hosts, and Interfaces

As we know from IPv4, host addresses are assigned to network interfaces or network adapters. A single network host or node can either have multiple interfaces or a single interface with multiple addresses. All interfaces have to have at least one unicast address, which is explained in an upcoming section.

Address Types

Under IPv4, address types include unicast for point-to-point communication, broadcast for network-wide blasts, and multicast addresses for parallel communications. In IPv6, we have unicast and multicast addresses, as before, plus "anycast" addresses. Broadcast addresses are replaced in IPv6 with multicast addressing. That said, one needs to be aware that in many network implementations, multicast may not be enabled unless there is, or was, as specific application requiring it.

IPv6 Unicast Addresses   Unicast addresses in IPv6 are similar to the ones in IPv4—a single address identifying a single interface. There are four types of IPv6 unicast addresses: global unicast, link-local, unique local, and special addresses:

▼   **Global unicast addresses**   Figure 4-8 shows the structure of global unicast addresses currently being allocated by IANA, as defined in RFC 3587.

The makeup of the global unicast address is:

■   **001**   The three high-order bits are set to 001.

■   **Global Routing Prefix**   The prefix for a specific organization's site.

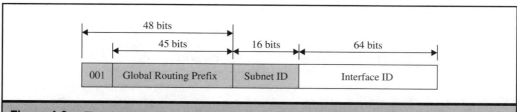

Figure 4-8.   The global unicast address.

- **Subnet ID** Identifies the subnet within the IPv6-defined site with a 16-bit suffix. Each organization, or site, can have up to 65,536 subnets.

- **Interface ID** The 64-bit field that identifies a unique interface on a host in a specific subnet within a site.

- **Link-local addresses** The link-local address is a non-routable address reserved for private networks. These are not meant to be routed and confined to a single network segment.

- **Unique local addresses** Unique local addresses also support non-routable private addressing, with the addition of being unique within an organization.

▲ **Special addresses** Special addresses are those that are not normally configurable and provide a consistent basis for integrating nodes into a routed network. Special addresses include the loopback addresses, IPv4 address-mapped spaces, and a technique called "6to4" that is used for communicating between two nodes running both IPv4 and IPv6 (more on that later). See the following section for specifics on special unicast addresses.

Multicast Addresses Multicast addresses in IPv6 operate the same as in IPv4. Packets sent to a multicast address are accepted by all interfaces in the multicast group. IPv6 multicast is routable, and routers will not forward multicast packets unless there are members of the multicast groups to forward the packets to. Figure 4-9 shows the IPv6 multicast address.

Beyond the first 8 bits, multicast addresses include additional components identifying their flags, scope, and multicast group. The components of a multicast address are:

▼ **1111 1111** The first 8 bits of a multicast address are set to 1111 1111, or "FF," which makes it easy to identify.

- **Flags** This 4-bit field will have future use. For now, only the "T" flag is used. It identifies whether the multicast address is permanently assigned by IANA or if the address is privately assigned. A "T" flag set to 0 indicates a permanent address (well-known) allocated by IANA. When set to 1, the T flag shows that the multicast address is transient, which simply means it's not a permanently assigned address.

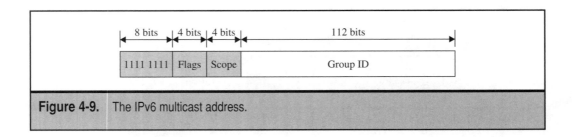

Figure 4-9. The IPv6 multicast address.

- **Scope**   Another 4-bit field, the scope field indicates the scope of the destination IPv6 internetwork. Routers use the multicast scope to determine whether multicast traffic can be forwarded. The common values are the interface-local scope, the link-local scope, and the site-local scope. For example, traffic with the multicast address of FF02::2 has a link-local scope. An IPv6 router never forwards this traffic beyond the local link.

▲ **Group ID**   Identifies the multicast group and is unique within the scope. The size of this field is 112 bits. Permanently assigned group IDs are independent of the scope. Transient group IDs are only relevant to a specific scope. Multicast addresses from FF01:: through FF0F:: are reserved, well-known addresses. With 112 bits for the group ID, it is possible to have 2,112 group IDs in each multicast scope. However, by using only the low-order 32 bits, each group ID maps to a unique Ethernet multicast MAC address.

Anycast Addresses   An anycast address is assigned to multiple interfaces. Packets addressed to an anycast address are forwarded by the routing infrastructure to the nearest interface within the anycast group. To facilitate delivery, the routing infrastructure must be aware of the interfaces assigned to anycast addresses and their "distance" in terms of routing metrics. Anycast addresses are assigned out of the unicast address space, and their scope is the scope of the type of unicast address from which the anycast address is assigned.

The subnet-router anycast address is predefined and required for an IPv6 routed network. It is created from the subnet prefix for a given interface. To construct the subnet-router anycast address, the bits in the subnet prefix are fixed at their appropriate values, and the remaining bits are set to 0. All router interfaces attached to a subnet are assigned the relevant subnet-router anycast address. The address is used for communication with one of multiple routers attached to a remote subnet IPv6 anycast addresses containing fields that identify them as anycast. All you need to do is configure your network interfaces appropriately. The IPv6 protocol itself takes care of getting the packets to their final destinations. It's a lot simpler to administer than shared unicast addressing.

IPv6 Addressing Principles

When you look at an IPv6 address, your first feeling might be one of sheer terror. Don't sweat it. If you can understand some basic principles, IPv6 addressing isn't so frightening. These principles include the following.

Colon-Hexadecimal Format   An IPv6 address consists of 128 bits, broken into four 16-bit hexadecimal digits, separated by colons. They are divided along 16 boundaries, which are written as eight groups of four hexadecimal digits. The coined phrase for describing the format is *colon-hexadecimal*. For example:

2001:0000:4136:e378:3000:3dd3:3f56:ffa4

Replace the Zeroes   Contiguous blocks of 0000 can be replaced by double colons (0000 = ::).
For example, if a four-digit group (0000) is present, then the zeros can be omitted. For
example, the address:

```
2001:4136:0000:e378:3000:3dd3:3f56:ffa4
```

can be expressed as:

```
2001:4136::e378:3000:3dd3:3f56:ffa4
```

Extending this rule, contiguous groups of consecutive 0000 groups may be reduced
to two colons, as long as there is only one double colon used in an address. More than
one double-colon abbreviation in an address is not valid. The following addresses are
synonymous:

```
2001:4136:0000:0000:0000:3dd3:3f56:ffa4
2001:4136::0000:0000:3dd3:3f56:ffa4
2001:4136::0000:3dd3:3f56:ffa4
2001:4136::3dd3:3f56:ffa4
```

Omit Leading Zeros in a Group   If a digit group is lead by a 0, the 0 can be truncated. For
example, the IPv6 address:

```
2001:0300:4136:e378:3000:3dd3:3f56:ffa4
```

can be expressed as:

```
2001:300:4136:e378:3000:3dd3:3f56:ffa4
```

Addresses Include a Network ID and an Interface ID   Like IPv4 addresses, IPv6 addresses are
typically composed of two logical parts: a 64-bit network prefix and a 64-bit interface ID.
The interface ID is automatically generated from the network adapter MAC address, or
it can be assigned from an address block manually or through DHCPv6.

Addresses Include a Network Prefix   An IPv6 network (or subnet) is a contiguous group of
IPv6 addresses, the size of which must be a power of two; the initial bits of addresses that
are identical for all hosts in the network are called the network's prefix.

NOTE   A special concern arises when IP addresses are derived from consistent factors, such as
the site prefix and MAC address. User traffic and their use of the Internet can be traced, eliminating
the anonymity that users have under IPv4 and creating privacy issues. To address this concern and
provide a level of anonymity, an alternative IPv6 interface identifier that is randomly generated and
changes over time is described in RFC 3041. The resulting IPv6 address is known as a temporary
address. Temporary addresses are generated for public-address prefixes that use stateless address
autoconfiguration. They are valid for a duration specified by the IPv6 router. Default values are either
one week or one day, depending on whether the host requests a preferred lifetime. More information
is found in RFC 3041.

Denote Networks Using CIDR   An IPv6 network is identified using the first host address in the network and the network prefix size in bits. The two identifiers are separated by a slash. For example, the IPv6 network:

```
2001:300:4136:e378::/64
```

incorporates the network that begins at address:

```
2001:300:4136:e378::
```

and terminates at address:

```
2001:300:4136:e378:FFFF:FFFF:FFFF:FFFF
```

Denote Hosts with a 128-Bit Length   To distinguish a single host, add a slash and 128. For example:

```
2001:300:4136:e378::/128
```

Enclose IPv6 Addresses in URLs in Brackets   In a URL, the IPv6 address is enclosed in brackets. For example:

```
http://[ 2001:300:4136:e378:3000:3dd3:3f56:ffa4]/
```

This notation allows parsing a URL without confusing the IPv6 address and port number:

```
http://[ 2001:300:4136:e378:3000:3dd3:3f56:ffa4]:443/
```

For more information, see RFC 2732 "Format for Literal IPv6 Addresses in URLs" and RFC 3986 "Uniform Resource Identifier (URI): Generic Syntax."

Write IPv6 Networks Using CIDR Notation   IPv6 addresses use CIDR subnetting, alleviating the rigid class system that can interfere with the practical partitioning of address spaces and artificially inflate an address block. Using CIDR allows for routing prefix aggregation, also known as *summarization* or *supernetting*, where multiple continuous address blocks are advertised as one.

Compatible Addresses   IPv6 hosts will continue to communicate with devices that offer only IPv4. Compatible addresses enable communication crossover between the two implementations if fed into a translation mechanism:

▼   **IPv4-compatible address**   The IPv4-compatible address—0:0:0:0:0:0: w.x.y.z or ::w.x.y.z (where w.x.y.z is the dotted-decimal representation of an IPv4 address)—is used by IPv6/IPv4 nodes that are communicating using IPv6. IPv6/IPv4 nodes have both IPv4 and IPv6 protocols. When the IPv4-compatible address is used as an IPv6 destination, the IPv6 traffic is automatically encapsulated with an IPv4 header and sent to the destination using the IPv4 infrastructure. ::/96—the zero prefix—is used for IPv4-compatible addresses (see "Tunneling and Transition Mechanisms").

- **IPv4-mapped address**   The IPv4-mapped address—0:0:0:0:0:FFFF:w.x.y.z or ::FFFF:w.x.y.z—is used to represent an IPv4-only node to an IPv6 node. It is used only for internal representation. The IPv4-mapped address is never used as a source or destination address of an IPv6 packet. The ::ffff:0:0/96 prefix is used for IPv4-mapped addresses (see "Tunneling and Transition Mechanisms").

- **6to4 address**   The 6to4 address is used for communication between two nodes running both IPv4 and IPv6 over an IPv4 routing infrastructure. The 6to4 address is formed by combining the prefix 2002::/16 with the 32 bits of a public IPv4 address, forming a 48-bit prefix. This tunneling technique is described further in RFC 3056.

Other Special Addresses   There are a number of addresses with special meaning in IPv6:

- **::/128**   The address with all zeroes is an unspecified address, and is only to be used in software.

- **::1/128 or 0000:0000:0000:0000:0000:0000:0000:0001**   The loopback address of the local host. If an application in a host sends packets to this address, the IPv6 stack will loop these packets back to the same host (corresponding to 127.0.0.1 in IPv4). Remember, the /128 prefix length indicates a host address.

- **2001:db8::/32**   This prefix is used in documentation (per RFC 3849). Anywhere that an example IPv6 address is given, addresses from this prefix should be used.

- **fc00::/7**   Unique local IPv6 unicast addresses are only routable within a set of cooperating sites. They were defined in RFC 4193 as a replacement for site-local addresses (see the following section). The addresses include a 40-bit pseudo-random number that minimizes the risk of conflicts if sites merge or packets somehow leak out.

- **fe80::/10**   The link-local prefix specifies that the address only is valid in the local physical link. This is analogous to the APIPA address 169.254.x.x in IPv4.

- **ff00::/8**   The multicast prefix is used for multicast addresses.

- **3FFE::/16**   These addresses were for the 6Bone test network, which shut down in June 2006. Addresses in this network are not valid.

There are no address ranges reserved for broadcast in IPv6—applications are supposed to use multicast to the all-hosts group instead.

NOTE   If you want more information on the IPv6 addressing architecture, or if you just need a good read, check out "RFC 4291 – IP Version 6 Addressing Architecture."

Tunneling and Transition Mechanisms

For an IPv6 host or network to operate on the Internet or other non-IPv6 domain, the IPv6 traffic uses the existing IPv4 infrastructure to transport packets using a technique known as *tunneling*. Tunneling encapsulates IPv6 packets within IPv4 and, as such, the

IPv6 application considers IPv4 as a data link layer within the network stack. Tunneling examples that you may be familiar with include Layer 2 Tunneling Protocol (L2TP) for virtual private network (VPN) tunnels and IPSec. The tunneling technologies used to bridge IPv6 to IPv4 are transition mechanisms. They are how a network with IPv6 hosts communicates with backwards compatibility while other networks upgrade to IPv6. They are not meant to be permanent, but you can figure on them being around for a long time nonetheless.

Automatic Tunneling   Tunnel endpoints are determined by IPv6 routers. Three automatic tunneling options include 6to4, Teredo and ISATAP:

▼   **6to4 tunneling**   The recommended technique for automatic tunneling is *6to4 tunneling*. Tunnel endpoints are determined by using a well-known IPv4 anycast addresses on the remote side and embedding IPv4 address information within IPv6 addresses on the local side. This type of tunneling is widely available in modern routing infrastructures.

■   **Teredo**   This type of tunneling uses UDP encapsulation, which most NAT devices can forward. IPv6 hosts behind NAT services can be used as Teredo tunnel endpoints even when they don't have a dedicated public IPv4 address. Using Teredo, IPv6 hosts on separate IPv4 networks can communicate without any alteration to the routing infrastructure. Though not yet widely available, Teredo is enabled by default in Vista, but is inactive.

NOTE   Teredo was first released with the Advanced Networking Pack for Windows XP with Service Pack 1, and is also included with Windows XP Service Pack 2 and Windows Server 2003 Service Pack 1.

Teredo IPv6 addresses are global in scope and unique within the Internet. To activate it, simply use an application that requires it, or configure a rule in Windows Firewall to allow edge traversal.

Vista's implementation of Teredo includes the following characteristics:

■   It is enabled for domain member computers, where Teredo for Windows XP and Windows Server 2003 automatically disabled itself if the computer was a member of a domain.

■   It can now work if there is one Teredo client behind one or more symmetric NATs. A symmetric NAT maps the same private address to different public addresses, depending on the external destination address. Teredo for Windows XP and Windows Server 2003 disables itself if it detects that it is behind a symmetric NAT. This new behavior allows Teredo to work between a larger set of Internet-connected hosts.

▲   **Intrasite Automatic Tunnel Addressing Protocol (ISATAP)**   ISATAP is defined in RFC 4214. Cisco and Microsoft are developing an implementation of it at the time of this writing. With ISATAP, IPv4 network hosts emulate a logical IPv6 subnet scheme. This enables ISATAP nodes located on the IPv4 network to tunnel to each other with logical IPv6 connectivity through an ISATAP router. IPv4 infrastructures can provide unicast IPv6 connectivity with the addition of an ISATAP router.

Configured Tunneling Configured tunneling is a technique whereby the tunnel endpoints are configured explicitly, either by a human operator or by an automatic service known as a *tunnel broker*. A tunnel broker provides IPv6 tunnels to end users/end sites using manual, scripted, or automatic configuration. Tunnel brokers offer "protocol 41," or "proto-41," tunnels, which encapsulate IPv6 inside IPv4 packets and update the IPv4 header. The header's protocol field is set to 41, which is IPv6.

NOTE Configured tunneling is usually more deterministic and easier to debug than automatic tunneling, and is, therefore, recommended for large, well-administered networks.

Configured tunneling typically uses a protocol 41 tunnel (recommended) or raw UDP encapsulation.

IPv6 and the Domain Name System

IPv6 addresses are four times larger than IPv4 addresses, so they are represented in DNS forward-lookup zones by "AAAA" records, or "quad-A" records. Here is an example of an IPv6 host record:

```
host1.mydomain.com   IN   AAAA   2001:0:4136:e378:3000:3dd3:3f56:ffa4
```

The IPv6.ARPA domain has been created for IPv6 reverse queries. Also called pointer queries, reverse queries determine a host name based on the IP address. To create the namespace for reverse queries, each hexadecimal digit in the fully expressed 32-digit IPv6 address becomes a separate level, in inverse order and in the reverse domain hierarchy.

For example, the reverse lookup domain name for the address:

```
2001:0:4136:e378:3000:3dd3:3f56:ffa4
```

is:

```
4.a.f.f.6.5.f.3.3.d.d.3.0.0.0.3.8.7.e.6.3.1.4.0.0.0.0.1.0.0.2.IP6.ARPA
```

Computers that use both IPv4 and IPv6 might not be able to resolve names and connect to Internet resources if DNS servers are configured incorrectly. When a mis-configured DNS server receives a request to resolve a name to an IPv6 addresses and the DNS server does not support IPv6, the name query will fail. A subsequent request for an IPv4 version of the record is requested, but the misconfigured DNS server will drop the subsequent DNS query for IPv4 addresses and the entire name resolution attempt will fail, resulting in impaired network connectivity for the requesting node. If you are experiencing this problem, ask your DNS administrator to reconfigure his or her DNS server to accept the subsequent DNS query for A records after failing the DNS query for AAAA records.

IPv6 in Vista

More great news for IPv6 fans is that it is already highly integrated into the Microsoft platform. The capture and parsing of IPv6 traffic is supported by Microsoft Network Monitor, found in Systems Management Server (SMS) version 2.0 and Windows Server 2003. Within the Microsoft platform, you can use IPv6 without affecting IPv4 communications.

IPv6 hosts are all *logically* multihomed, with at least two addresses with which they can receive packets—a link-local address for local link traffic and either a routable site-local or a global address, depending on the routing infrastructure. By default, every host is addressable and receives traffic on these multicast addresses:

▼ The interface-local scope all-nodes multicast address (FF01::1)

■ The link-local scope all-nodes multicast address (FF02::1)

■ The solicited-node address for each unicast address on each interface

▲ The multicast addresses of joined groups on each interface

An IPv4 host typically has a single IPv4 address assigned to each network interface. In contrast, IPv6 hosts have several IPv6 addresses for each interface. IPv6 hosts are assigned these unicast addresses:

▼ A link-local address for each interface

■ Unicast addresses for each interface (which could be a site-local address and one or multiple global unicast addresses)

▲ The loopback address (::1) for the loopback interface

Figure 4-10 illustrates the multiple addresses assigned in a workgroup environment.

Configuration   In Windows XP and Windows Server 2003, you manually configure IPv6 using **netsh interface IPv6** commands. Vista allows you to also configure IPv6 settings through the properties of the IPv6 component in the Connections And Adapters folder.

MLDv2   Vista supports Multicast Listener Discovery version 2 (MLDv2), specified in RFC 3810, which allows IPv6 hosts to register interest in source-specific multicast traffic with their local multicast routers.

LLMNR   Vista also supports Link-Local Multicast Name Resolution (LLMNR), which allows for name resolution without a DNS server for IPv6-enabled interfaces. This capability is useful for single-subnet networks and ad hoc wireless networks. Workstations with LLMNR send their DNS queries to a multicast address on which

```
Command Prompt                                                    _ □ X

Windows IP Configuration

Ethernet adapter Local Area Connection:

    Connection-specific DNS Suffix  . :
    Link-local IPv6 Address . . . . . : fe80::c8e5:588b:855b:1ec6%8
    IPv4 Address. . . . . . . . . . . : 192.169.0.91
    Subnet Mask . . . . . . . . . . . : 255.255.255.0
    Default Gateway . . . . . . . . . : 192.169.0.254

Tunnel adapter Local Area Connection* 6:

    Connection-specific DNS Suffix  . :
    Link-local IPv6 Address . . . . . : fe80::200:5efe:192.169.0.91%9
    Default Gateway . . . . . . . . . :

Tunnel adapter Local Area Connection* 7:

    Media State . . . . . . . . . . . : Media disconnected
    Connection-specific DNS Suffix  . :

Tunnel adapter Local Area Connection* 9:

    Connection-specific DNS Suffix  . :
    Temporary IPv6 Address. . . . . . : 2002:c0a9:5b::c0a9:5b
    Default Gateway . . . . . . . . . :
```

Figure 4-10. IPv6 and IPv4 addresses for a sample host.

all the LLMNR-capable nodes of the subnet are listening. The destination owner sends a unicast response to the source host. IPv4 nodes can also use LLMNR instead of NetBIOS lookups.

IPv6 over PPP Vista's remote-access client supports IPv6 over the Point-to-Point Protocol (PPP). Referred to as PPPv6, it is defined in RFC 2472. PPPv6 support allows you to connect with an IPv6-based Internet service provider (ISP) through either dial-up or PPP over Ethernet (PPPoE). PPPv6 also supports L2TP, which is used for VPN connections.

DHCPv6 The DHCP client service in Vista supports Dynamic Host Configuration Protocol for IPv6 (DHCPv6). This new version of DHCP is defined in RFCs 3315 and 3736. Vista IPv6 workstations can negotiate both stateful and stateless DHCPv6 configuration on IPv6 networks.

Random Interface IDs To prevent address scans of IPv6 addresses based on well-known interface ID roots, Vista will, by default, generate random interface IDs for permanent, autoconfigured IPv6 addresses, including public and link-local addresses. A public IPv6 address is a global address that is registered in DNS and is typically used by server applications for incoming connections, such as a Web server.

Note that this new behavior is different than that for temporary IPv6 addresses, as described in RFC 3041. Temporary addresses also use randomly derived interface IDs. However, they are not registered in DNS and are typically used by client applications when initiating communication, such as with a Web browser. You can disable this behavior using the following command:

```
netsh interface ipv6 set global randomizeidentifiers=disabled
```

You can enable this behavior using this command:

```
netsh interface ipv6 set global randomizeidentifiers=enabled command
```

Disabling IPv6   Unlike Windows XP, IPv6 in Vista cannot be uninstalled, although it can be disabled. To disable IPv6 on a specific connection, clear the check box next to the Internet Protocol version 6 (TCP/IPv6) component on the properties pane of the network connection. This disables IPv6 on your LAN interfaces and connections, but does not disable IPv6 on tunnel interfaces or the IPv6 loopback interface. To selectively disable IPv6 components and configure behaviors for IPv6 in Vista, create and configure the following registry value (DWORD type):

```
HKEY_LOCAL_MACHINE\SYSTEM\CurrentControlSet\Services\tcpip6\Parameters\
DisabledComponents
```

DisabledComponents is set to 0 by default. Restart the computer for the changes to the DisabledComponents registry value to take effect. This registry value is a bit mask that controls the following series of flags, starting with the low-order bit (Bit 0):

▼   **Bit 0**   Set to 1 to disable all IPv6 tunnel interfaces, including ISATAP, 6to4, and Teredo tunnels. Default value is 0.

■   **Bit 1**   Set to 1 to disable all 6to4-based interfaces. Default value is 0.

■   **Bit 2**   Set to 1 to disable all ISATAP-based interfaces. Default value is 0.

■   **Bit 3**   Set to 1 to disable all Teredo-based interfaces. Default value is 0.

■   **Bit 4**   Set to 1 to disable IPv6 over all non-tunnel interfaces, including LAN interfaces and PPP-based interfaces. Default value is 0.

▲   **Bit 5**   Set to 1 to modify the default prefix policy table to prefer IPv4 over IPv6 when attempting connections. Default value is 0.

To determine the value of DisabledComponents for a specific set of bits, convert the registry bits to hexadecimal. For example, if you want to disable 6to4 interfaces, disable Teredo interfaces, and prefer IPv4 over IPv6, you would construct the following binary number: 101010. When converted to hexadecimal, the value of DisabledComponents is 0x2A.

THE NEXT GENERATION TCP/IP STACK IN VISTA

Microsoft refers to the core TCP/IP processing services as *The Next Generation TCP/IP Stack*. This is an homage to the code name for IPv6, which was once referred to as "IP Next Generation," or IPng. Not only is IPv6 included as a bona fide service in the new stack, but both the IPv4 and IPv6 network services have been completely rewritten. While IPv4 was last revised for Windows 2000, IPv6 was introduced with Windows XP, with an introductory feature set. Vista's refined network stack includes enterprise-class services and is optimized for today's environment, where high bandwidth is required and low latency and low packet loss are desired on today's wired and wireless networks. Figure 4-11 shows how the Next Generation TCP/IP is structured.

Packets are sent and received by the new stack using Network Driver Interface Specification (NDIS) v6.0. The mechanisms and application programming interfaces (APIs) used to access the Next Generation TCP/IP Stack include:

▼ **Windows Socket Kernel (WSK)** WSK is a new kernel-mode network programming interface (NPI).

■ **Windows Sockets** The Windows Sockets API operates through the ancillary function driver (AFD) to perform socket functions with TCP/IP.

▲ **Transport Driver Interface (TDI)** For NetBIOS over TCP/IP (NetBT) and other legacy TDI clients.

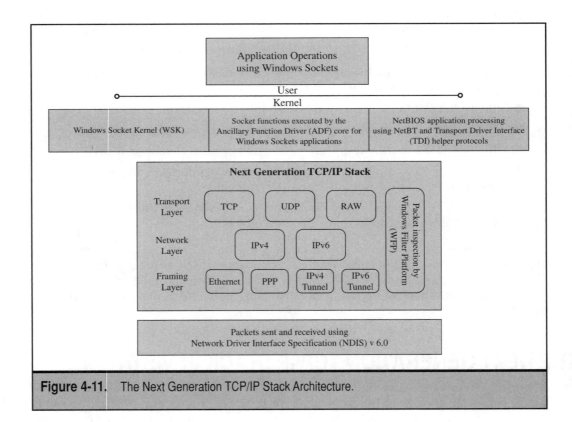

Figure 4-11. The Next Generation TCP/IP Stack Architecture.

Windows Filter Platform (WFP) provides API access to packets throughout the architecture, allowing inspection or data modification of packet contents at the network and transport layers.

The layer model for the Next Generation TCP/IP Stack includes the following layers:

▼ **Transport layer**   Implements TCP and UDP, and raw (headerless) IP packets.

■ **Network layer**   Implements IPv4 and IPv6 in a dual IP layer architecture.

▲ **Framing layer**   Components that frame IP packets. Packets are framed for IPv4 and IPv6 and are packaged for transport through various physical and logical technologies. Physical transport technologies include Ethernet IEEE 802.3, Wireless IEEE 802.11, and FireWire IEEE 1394. Logical interfaces include the loopback interface, IPv4-based, and IPv6-based tunnels.

The following sections introduce some of the main enhancements of Vista's new network stack.

Native IPv6 Support Added to IPv4

For Windows XP and Windows Server 2003, using IPv6 meant installing separate IP, TCP, and UDP protocols through the Network Connections folder and then updating both the Tcip.sys driver for IPv4 and the Tcpip6.sys driver for IPv6. The protocols remain separate in what is referred to as dual IP layer architecture.

Vista's Next Generation TCP/IP Stack leverages the dual IP layer architecture such that the IPv4 and IPv6 implementations share common IP, TCP, and UDP layers. It has both IPv4 and IPv6 enabled by default. There is no need to install a separate component to activate IPv6, and the layer of translation overhead between the protocols is no longer required. For Windows XP and Windows Server 2003, the operating system was a "native" IPv4 "speaker" and was just learning how to "speak" IPv6, with the pauses and mistakes that come with being a novice. Vista "speaks" IPv4 and IPv6 as a native of both protocol suites, switching between the two without noticeable effect.

NOTE   Learn the IPv6 addressing nomenclature as soon as you can. It appears today in the `IPConfig` results in Vista by default.

By default, the Next Generation TCP/IP Stack prefers the use of IPv6. While locating peers with which to communicate, the stack will work with DNS servers, attempting to communicate using IPv6 addresses first over IPv4 addresses, subject to the address selection rules that are defined in RFC 3484. IPv4 communication is not affected, however, as IPv6 traffic is not commenced unless an application that is IPv6-aware initiates it.

A Reliable Hook into the TCP/IP Stack

Windows Filtering Platform (WFP) for Vista is a new API and architecture that allows access to the TCP/IP stream. Packets are examined and updated by WFP in several TCP/IP layers and throughout the operating system, affording unprecedented access. Using the structured access into the TCP/IP stream provided by WFP, common applications for workstation management will increase in quality and, perhaps, fall in price. Applications such as firewalls, antivirus software, diagnostic software, and other types of applications and services will benefit from the WFP API, which offers a well-documented, built-in filtering mechanism. Major benefits for Vista users of applications based on WFP include the following:

▼   Prices for management software may be affected, because WFP already provides an IPv4 and IPv6 filtering engine. Application developers can focus on value-added components and save the cost of filter development for either IP versions.

■   Vista is easier to update because with WFP, there is much less risk of service pack incompatibilities and failures.

▲   Vista will be more stable, since many applications will move out of kernel mode and into user mode, where a component crash does not affect the entire system.

Updated Kernel Mode Programming

Vista introduces Windows Socket Kernel (WSK) to Microsoft networking. This is a new kernel-mode NPI for legacy networking clients using TDI for NetBT applications. With WSK, kernel-mode software modules can perform network communication using programming similar to the user-mode Windows Sockets semantics, although without the insecurities and overhead of the legacy TDI helper protocol.

NOTE   While TDI is supported in Windows Vista for backward compatibility, TDI clients (Windows NT, Windows 2000, Windows XP, and Windows Server 2003) should be updated to use WSK to achieve the best performance.

Multihome Security Enhancement

Vista validates traffic better using a strong-host model for authenticating network packets. A strong-host model implies that packets destined for an IP address that does not match the address assigned to a network interface are refused, regardless if the address is assigned to a different network interface in the same computer. In a weak-host model, like that used for previous Microsoft operating systems, IP implementations accept any locally destined packet. This happened regardless of the interface on which the packet was received and, thus, led to susceptibility to network attacks based on multihome logic.

Vista uses audit packets with the strong-host model by default for both IPv4 and IPv6 layers. Changing to a weak-host model will enhance Vista's connectivity, although it will also make the workstation more vulnerable to multihome network attacks.

Multiprocessors Process Several Network Receipts

The architecture of NDIS 5.1 and earlier versions limits network receive processing to a single CPU. Vista introduces Receive Side Scaling (RSS) as part of NDIS 6.0. Put simply, RSS allows faster network performance by spreading the packet reception-processing load across multiple processors. It supports dynamic load balancing across processors, includes validation using a secure hashing mechanism, and traffic management with parallel processor interrupts.

Portability

For Vista's performance and reliability enhancements to work, the operating systems of both the sending and receiving workstations need to support many of the functions found in the Next Generation TCP/IP Stack. Microsoft has distribution packages for improved portability of the stack to other Microsoft operating systems and devices, such as Windows CE, Xbox, and Windows Embedded.

Offloading TCP/IP Processing

Vista also supports the offloading of TCP/IP processing away from the system CPU on to miniport drivers and network interface adapters. This is based on *TCP Chimney*, a processing architecture released by Microsoft in 2004 as part of the Scalable Networking Initiative, which formalizes the process partitions and API semantics. For high-bandwidth environments, like peer-to-peer applications and large file transfers, processing TCP/IP can be a system bottleneck that drags down performance. By offloading it to a network interface adapter outfitted with a TCP/IP processor, Vista relieves the CPU from network traffic processing, which enables it to scale better under load.

Automatic Tuning

Vista's Next Generation TCP/IP Stack dynamically self-adjusts configuration settings based on environmental factors. This new feature set comes with benefits and complexities, which you will want to know about before you deploy Vista in your organization. Vista includes auto-tuning capabilities that better manage important network parameters, like TCP/IP Receive Window Size and the Send Window Size. These automatic changes can be made based on advanced congestion detection and other factors, as the following sections explain.

Congestion Management

With previous Microsoft network stacks, the stack would see network congestion as caused by the transmission of too many packets. When a workstation with those earlier stacks lost packets, it assumed that to alleviate congestion, transmitting fewer packets was a good idea. The problem is that packets are lost for reasons other than the workstation itself generating too many. Oftentimes, a workstation will stall for no good reason, assuming network congestion when none exists. To better understand the network conditions, Vista uses Explicit Congestion Notification (ECN), an Internet standard, which calls for packet updates during router congestion. When routers suffer from overwhelming traffic, where delays and lost packets become probable, an ECN router stamps each packet with an ECN warning mark as it forwards the packet. Being ECN-aware, when Vista checks packets for an ECN stamp and finds it, transmission of TCP packets across the router is scaled back.

With ECN, Vista does not stall as often based on false congestion alarms, it proactively participates in congestion avoidance when warned, and it helps throughput for the entire network to rise. ECN requires an ECN-aware router. Use the netsh command to enable ECN in Vista, which is disabled by default.

Auto-Tuning

Another performance management feature is Receive Window Auto-Tuning, which continually determines the optimal receive window size—that is, the number of packets received in buffer—before processing up to the next layer and sending an acknowledgment to the sender. To manage flow rates, a receiver posts the required receive window size in the TCP connection and forces the sender to set a transmission burst rate and then wait for an acknowledgement after sending the required number of packets. Adjusting the size positively impacts throughput, and is an effective way in which to manage high latencies and to take advantage of low latencies. Although previous operating systems supported adjustments to the receive window size, the adjustment is fixed (unless specified by an application) and works well for some traffic and penalizes others.

NOTE   Use the netsh command to enable ECN in Vista—for example:
netsh interface tcp set global ecncapability=enabled.

Vista enables dynamic scaling of the window size for each TCP connection separately, basing the size on available bandwidth and round-trip calculations (i.e., the bandwidth-delay product) and the rate that the applications process the packets. The upper bound of the window size is 16 megabytes (MB). The result of dynamically tuning the receive window sizes is a connection that is optimized for both the current capacity of the network and the performance of the network applications. Of benefit to everyone on the network is a greater overall yield from your network topology.

NOTE   Scaling windows requires a routing infrastructure that supports it, which some legacy appliances (routers and firewalls, for example) do not. Some legacy appliances drop packets that are not part of the segment size negotiated during the initial TCP handshake. Upon discovering a network routing failure in which other routes operate as expected, use the Network Diagnostics tool to examine the route in question. Compatibility with scaling windows should also be checked.

Segment Management

Vista also supports enhanced management and control over of the size of TCP segments from the sender's point of view. Previous operating systems use algorithms, based on a concept called slow start and congestion avoidance, to set the TCP send window size when initiating TCP connections. With Vista's predecessors, the send window size is continually adjusted based on the size of packet segments sent successfully. That is, the send window size grows until packets are lost, at which time the size is reset and the optimization process begins anew. The reality of this architecture is that scaling the send window size lags behind the real capacity of the network in high-latency networks when the window size is constantly reset to the slow start level.

Vista introduces Compound TCP (CTCP) to solve the problem in high-bandwidth, high-delay networks. CTCP manages the send window size aggressively, monitoring the variations in delays and losses to keep the window size from lagging behind the real capacity of the network. The result is that large file-transfer times can be reduced to almost half the time. Together, CTCP and Receive Window Auto-Tuning can deliver significant enhancements in network performance.

Neighbor Unreachability Detection

Vista supports a new approach to managing dead gateways. Neighbor Unreachability Detection (NUD) is a native feature of IPv6, and is brought into Vista's updated implementation of IPv4. It uses connection results, Address Resolution Protocol (ARP), and upper-layer TCP to track availability of nodes on the local network. When a gateway fails to respond and packets are resent, Vista sends an ARP connection request first. If the request is not acknowledged, then Vista fails over to the next on the list of configured gateways. Unlike previous operating systems, Vista is empowered to distinguish between failures on local routers and failures on remote routers, which keeps it from attempting a dead gateway recovery when a remote router fails and traffic is not destined for the remote network. Also, Vista can now recover from secondary gateway failures by failing back to the primary gateway.

Configuring the IP Address

We've given you a lot to chew on with regards to IP addressing—both old and new. But how do you actually configure this setting on Windows Vista? As we mentioned earlier, there are two ways in which IP addresses can be configured: automatically and manually. To configure IP addresses, either IPv4 or IPv6:

1. Select Control Panel | Network and Internet Connections | Network and Sharing Center.

2. In the left pane, select Manage Network Connections.

3. Right-click the icon of the network you wish to manage, and then select Properties from the context menu.

4. Depending on which IP version you are using, select Internet Protocol Version 4 (TCP/IP) or Internet Protocol Version 6 (TCP/IP).

5. Click the Properties button. The resulting window for IPv4 is shown in Figure 4-12.

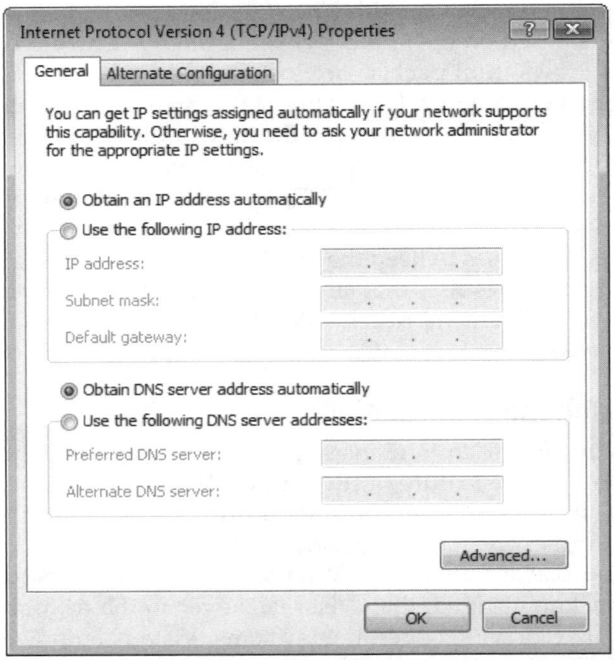

Figure 4-12.   Configure your device's IP address through the connection's Properties window.

From here, there are different routes you can take, depending on your network's configuration and whether you're using IPv4 or IPv6:

▼ If you're using a DHCP server to automatically dole out IP addresses, select the Obtain An IP Address Automatically option.

■ If you need to manually enter the device's IP address, for IPv4, enter the IP address, subnet mask, and default gateway information in the relevant boxes.

▲ Manually entering the IP address in IPv6 requires the IP address, subnet prefix, and default gateway information.

NAME RESOLUTION

In addition to setting the TCP/IP address, you must set up name resolution services. As we noted earlier, computers and devices use IP addresses to identify one another, but humans rely on computer names for identification. It's easier to remember that the computer ID for Dave in accounting is "SuperDave" rather than 192.168.1.212. Windows Vista provides four methods to resolve names to IP addresses:

▼ **Domain Name System (DNS)**   This is used for applications and services requiring host name-to-IP address resolution. This is broadly used, of course, and is the underlying name resolution protocol found in Active Directory.

■ **Windows Internet Name Service (WINS)**   This is Microsoft's proprietary name resolution service and isn't used, by default, in Windows 2000 or beyond. However, for the sake of backward compatibility, it is included in Windows Vista. It offers compatibility with services and applications that require NetBIOS-to-IP address resolution. Be aware, however, if you're using IPv6 that you won't be able to use WINS.

■ **Hosts and Lmhosts files**   These provide host name-to-IP address resolution and NetBIOS name-to-IP address resolution using locally maintained files.

▲ **Subnet broadcasts**   These can be used for NetBIOS name resolution within the local subnet.

NOTE   NetBIOS (short for Network Basic Input/Output System) is a program allowing applications on different computers to communicate within a LAN. It was created by IBM for its early PC network, was then adopted by Microsoft, and has since become a de facto industry standard.

Choosing a Name Resolution Method

Depending on your network components, you will need to determine whether your Windows Vista clients need to be configured to use DNS, WINS, or a combination of both. You should use DNS if the following conditions are present:

▼ The Windows Vista client is a member of an Active Directory domain.

■ The client is connected to a network that uses a DNS server.

▲ The client connects to the Internet.

Failing the use of a DNS server, other means of name resolution should be used, as follows:

▼ WINS is only used for the sake of backward compatibility. If your network has a WINS server to meet a specific requirement, then you'll probably need to configure your name resolution service for WINS.

▲ If a WINS server is unavailable, configure your Windows Vista clients to use Lmhosts for NetBIOS name resolution. If this option is not available, name resolution must be performed by broadcasts. Unfortunately, this does not work outside the local subnet.

The good news is that if you use a DHCP server, you can configure the name resolution method appropriate to your environment, and all DHCP clients will be automatically configured. However, if you do not use a DHCP server, then all this information must be manually configured.

Setting and Changing the DNS Host Name

If you've upgraded from an earlier version of Windows, Vista saves you some trouble and automatically rolls over the old DNS name into the new operating system. With new installations, the Setup tool will ask you to enter the DNS name for this client. With DNS, the host name can be up to 63 characters long, and is used in conjunction with the primary domain name to supply the *fully qualified domain name* (FQDN).

NOTE There are compatibility issues between long-named computers and older computers that still utilize NetBIOS. For example, if WINS is still used in your environment, you may see issues with licensing and communications between computers.

For instance, if a client computer is named "gilligan" and is part of the domain castaways.com, then the FQDN is gilligan.castaways.com.

The NetBIOS name is only 15 characters long, and when Windows Vista needs to assign a NetBIOS name, it takes the DNS name and shortens it to 15 characters.

For example, as *Star Wars* fans will probably note, the computer shown in Figure 4-13 would most accurately be referred to as "The Forest Moon of Endor," rather than simply

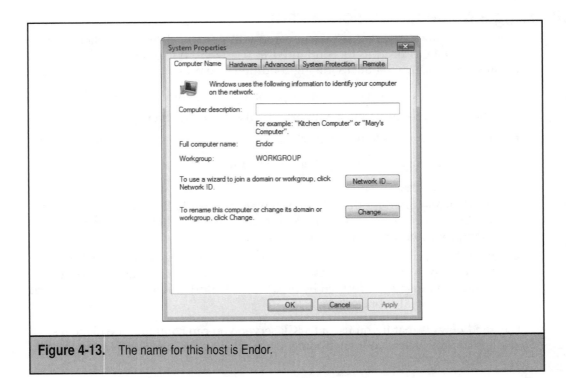

Figure 4-13. The name for this host is Endor.

"Endor." However, because NetBIOS only allows 15 characters, this was originally concatenated to "The_Forest_Moon." This cramped our style a bit, so we went with the more aesthetically pleasing "Endor."

After installation, you can change your DNS host name (which, in turn, will change your NetBIOS name):

1. From the Start menu, select Control Panel | System and Maintenance | System.

2. Click Change Settings.

3. Select the Computer Name tab. The resulting window is shown in Figure 4-14).

4. Click the Change button.

5. Enter the new host name, and click OK.

6. You will have to restart the computer for the name change to be finalized. Click Yes to restart.

NOTE   You can only use the characters a–z, A–Z, 0–9 and -. If any other characters are present in your name, Windows Vista will issue a kindly warning message.

Changing the Primary DNS Suffix

The primary DNS suffix is the name of the DNS domain to which the client is attached. If you are using Active Directory domains, the Windows Vista client's domain name is

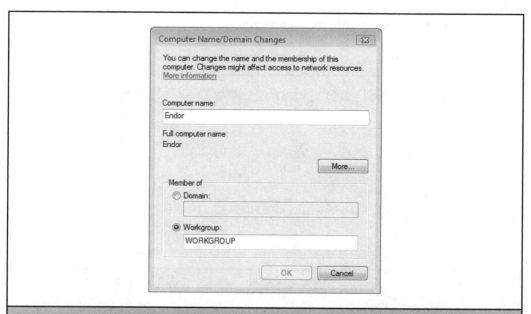

Figure 4-14.   The Computer Name tab can allow you to change your host's identity.

automatically set to the Active Directory DNS name. However, if the client is a member of a Windows NT domain, a DNS suffix is not automatically selected. The primary DNS suffix can be changed as follows:

1. Select Control Panel | System and Maintenance | System.
2. Click Change Settings.
3. Select the Computer Name tab.
4. Click Change | More. The result is shown in Figure 4-15.
5. In the text box, enter the primary DNS suffix.
6. Click OK.

In the event you are connecting your Windows Vista clients to a Windows NT domain but plan on migrating to Windows 2003 server in the future, then the client can automatically change its DNS suffix when you migrate. Simply ensure that the Change DNS Domain Name When Domain Membership Changes check box is selected. (This is the default setting.)

Connection-Specific Domain Names

Windows Vista allows you to name your computer differently, depending on the network to which you're connecting. This is known as a *connection-specific domain name*. For example, if your organization's suffix is castaways.com and your computer is named "gilligan," your FQDN is gilligan.castaways.com. However, when you connect to your ISP (dobiegillis.net), you can set your DNS name to "maynardgkrebs," which would give you the FQDN of maynardgkrebs.dobiegillis.net.

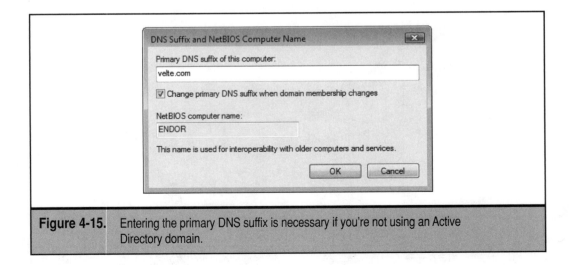

Figure 4-15. Entering the primary DNS suffix is necessary if you're not using an Active Directory domain.

Connection-specific domain names for each network interface card (NIC) can be assigned either automatically or manually. To configure them manually:

1. Select Control Panel | Network and Internet Connections | Network and Sharing Center.

2. In the left pane, select Manage Network Connections.

3. Right-click the icon of the network you wish to manage, and then select Properties from the context menu.

4. Depending on which IP version you are using, select Internet Protocol Version 4 (TCP/IP) or Internet Protocol Version 6 (TCP/IP).

5. Click the Properties button.

6. Click the Advanced button, and then select the DNS tab. This is shown in Figure 4-16.

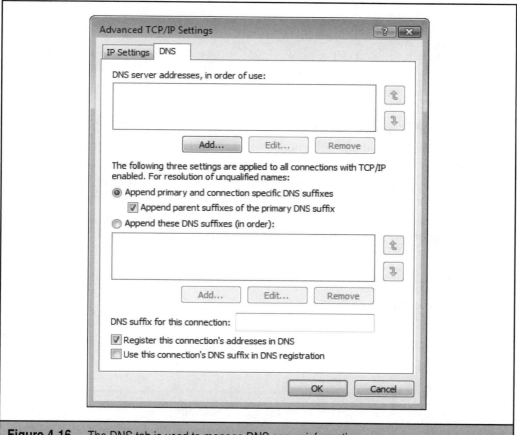

Figure 4-16. The DNS tab is used to manage DNS server information.

NOTE Depending which version of IP you are using, this window will look a bit different. This figure is shown representing an IPv6 configuration. The steps are the same for an IPv4 configuration, however.

7. In the DNS Suffix For This Connection box, enter the domain name for the connection.

Preferred and Alternate DNS Servers

Depending on your network, you may have one DNS server, a dozen, or even more. Windows Vista allows you to pick which DNS server you will primarily access for name resolution. In addition, you can set an unlimited number of alternates, in case you are unable to query the preferred DNS server.

To specify a preferred and alternate DNS server:

1. Select Control Panel | Network and Internet Connections | Network and Sharing Center.
2. In the left pane, select Manage Network Connections.
3. Right-click the icon of the network you wish to manage, and then select Properties from the context menu.
4. Depending on which IP version you are using, select Internet Protocol Version 4 (TCP/IP) or Internet Protocol Version 6 (TCP/IP).
5. Click the Properties button.
6. Select the General tab, and choose the method you will use to access the DNS server:

   ■ Select Obtain DNS Server Address Automatically if a DHCP server is available for automatic IP addressing.

   ■ Select Use The Following DNS Server Addresses if you wish to manually configure the DNS server, and then enter the appropriate IP address of your DNS server.

To specify additional alternate servers:

1. Click the Advanced button.
2. Select the DNS tab. This is the same window shown earlier in Figure 4-16.
3. Under DNS Server Addresses, in order of use, click Add.
4. Enter the IP address of your alternate DNS server.
5. Click Add.

You can remove a DNS server from the list by selecting it and then clicking Remove.

WINS

WINS is a name resolution service for NetBIOS name-to-IP address mappings. It can be used either on its own or in conjunction with DNS. It is useful in reducing the number of local name resolution broadcasts and allows users to locate computers on remote networks. In addition, DHCP can be used for autoconfiguration if a DHCP server is available on the network.

Configuration

If you are using IPv4 and need to configure WINS, the following steps are used to configure a Windows Vista client to employ WINS for name resolution:

NOTE WINS will only work for IPv4. It is not compatible with IPv6.

1. Select Control Panel | Network and Internet Connections | Network and Sharing Center.
2. In the left pane, select Manage Network Connections.
3. Right-click the icon of the network you wish to manage, and then select Properties from the context menu.
4. Select Internet Protocol Version 4 (TCP/IP).
5. Click the Properties button.
6. If a DHCP server is operational, select Obtain An IP Address Automatically.
7. If a DHCP server is neither available nor operational, follow this path:
   a. Select the Alternate Configuration tab.
   b. Select the User Configured option.
   c. Enter your preferred and alternate WINS servers in the relevant boxes.

Search Order

Like DNS servers, you can have more than one WINS server on your network.

1. Select Control Panel | Network and Internet Connections | Network and Sharing Center.
2. In the left pane, select Manage Network Connections.
3. Right-click the icon of the network you wish to manage, and then select Properties from the context menu.
4. Select Internet Protocol Version 4 (TCP/IP).
5. Click the Properties button.
6. Select the Advanced button.

7. Select the WINS tab.

8. Under WINS Addresses, in the Order Of Use box, select the IP address of the WINS server you wish to move around.

9. Use the up and down buttons to change the order of the WINS servers.

Understanding IP addressing (both IPv4 and IPv6) can be somewhat daunting. However, when you do get a grasp on the topic, it is helpful as you deploy Windows Vista. At the close of this chapter, we showed you how to configure IP addressing, DNS servers, and so forth on your Windows Vista devices. In the next chapter, we'll take a closer look at configuring your clients.

CHAPTER 5

Creating Network Connections

Networking computers is a task that comes in different shapes, sizes, and configurations. For example, if you're handling the network of a Fortune 500 company, you're going to be dealing with clients that are logging on to different networks, depending on where in the company they work. On the other hand, if yours is a small organization, you may be connecting only a few computers to a single network. These scenarios are vastly different, but they aren't the only ones. There are countless scenarios in between—yours is likely somewhere in that vast gray area.

Even the smallest network connection scenarios don't encompass joining a hard-wired corporate network. A network client might also need to connect to the Internet or to a wireless LAN (WLAN). Whatever your particular client connection need, this chapter addresses the issues germane to the sundry ways a computer running Windows Vista can connect to "the network."

Before we get into the nuts and bolts of making those network connections, let's take a look at what is new in Windows Vista with regards to networking. It's not enough to make the network connection—Vista has a number of new ways to make the most of those connections.

NEW NETWORKING FEATURES IN VISTA

Vista brings a new set of features to network management. The improvements in the network capabilities are some of the more valuable and complex changes from previous versions of the operating system. The improvements covered in this section are focused on network connections, and range from enhanced security, updates for managing network connectivity, and rich improvements in architecture. The addition of IPv6 and the Next Generation TCP/IP Stack are also profound changes (see Chapter 4).

Architecture

When it comes to networking architecture, Microsoft made good use of the five years between the release of Windows XP and Vista. We could write a book just on the improvements to the network architecture in Vista, illustrating the application programming interface (API) hooks and development options, but that would be of little use to networking professionals, who need to know more about how to use a networking service than how to write one. Instead, we highlight a few key improvements to the network services architecture to help you better integrate them into your environment.

Policy-Based Quality of Service (QoS)

Essentially, Quality of Service (QoS) is about partitioning available bandwidth among your users in such a way as to optimize the user experience. Bandwidth, or access to it, can be an issue for almost everyone at some point in time. This is true for just about every organization. In the past, QoS was made available to applications through an API embedded in the Windows platform. By and large, your users' network bandwidth was managed only if their applications were written to participate in the process. This and other past limitations have always been a bit disappointing, because QoS has the potential to enhance the user experience by protecting bandwidth when it's needed and giving it up when it's not.

NOTE   You can have QoS at the desktop and QoS on the wide area network (WAN), but just one piece of networking equipment not supporting QoS can "break the chain" and cause issues for anyone trying to implement it across an enterprise network.

With the next-generation platform, which includes Vista, QoS is now something that you can control as an administrator using Active Directory Group Policies. You can put all the network-bound traffic under the tutelage of QoS. QoS Group Policies for Vista allow you to prioritize the sending rate for outgoing network traffic. You can set policies to apply to specific applications, specific addresses (IPv4 or IPv6), and Transmission Control Protocol (TCP) or User Datagram Protocol (UDP) ports. Because QoS operates at the network layer, applications do not need to directly support QoS capabilities—nearly all traffic can be managed by a Group Policy.

Here is more detail on how you deploy QoS in Vista: First, you can throttle traffic. Throttling traffic causes it to be transmitted at a reduced rate, which remains capped and is consistent in the absence of any failures. For example, you can restrict the transmission rates coming from a file server so that file copies do not bog down your network. Second, you can provide a priority metric that will rank traffic within the QoS traffic queues. Qualifying traffic is prioritized by Vista and marked by routers with a Differentiated Services Code Point (DSCP) value, which is a metric that measures priority. The traffic is then directed to routing queues for differentiated delivery based on the priority value. Using a DSCP, for example, you can place a higher priority on e-mail traffic than on file transfers. In this case, you could ensure that file transfers do not interfere with e-mail while avoiding a cap on file transfer traffic. Figure 5-1 shows where QoS policies are managed in Active Directory.

NOTE   Users and administrators often have different priorities. Be sure that your users agree with any priorities that you set, or you risk creating a network that is not responsive in the way that allows your users to do their jobs well. Like any policy, QoS policies should reflect a compromise between business and technology goals.

Just like any Group Policy object, QoS policy settings are part of the User Configuration or Computer Configuration Group Policy, are configured with the Group Policy Object Editor, and are linked to Active Directory containers with the Group Policy management console. This is shown in Figure 5-2.

Vista also introduces qWave—Quality Windows A/V Experience. qWave brings QoS to streaming audio and video feeds, allowing Vista to de-prioritize traffic that is not as time-sensitive as a contiguous file stream. qWave is not managed through Group Policy; rather, it is integrated as a set of QoS technologies in the Next Generation TCP/IP Stack.

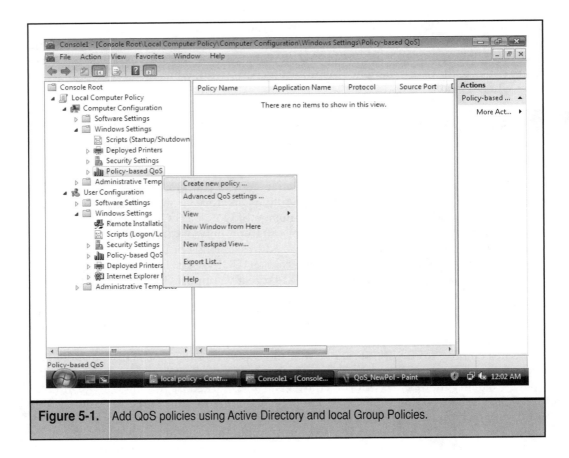

Figure 5-1. Add QoS policies using Active Directory and local Group Policies.

There is no doubt that QoS on the desktop is "coming of age" in Vista. What has not changed, however, is the requirement that all the network devices in the path support QoS, especially those that sit at network bottlenecks, like those found in remote broadband and DSL connections.

Server Message Block 2.0

Since 1991, Server Message Block (SMB) 1.0 has been the standard for file transfers. All Microsoft operating systems, including Vista, leverage SMB in the network clients, which are called Client for Microsoft Networks and File and Printer Sharing. Unlike previous operating systems, however, Vista's implementation of SMB leverages version 2.0, although it is compatible with version 1.0. With this update, Vista leapfrogs 15 years into the present.

SMB 2.0 is a redesigned transfer protocol for modern file sharing. It supports sending multiple commands within a packet, which dramatically reduces the traffic sent between an SMB client and server. Key improvements over SMB 1.0 include the following:

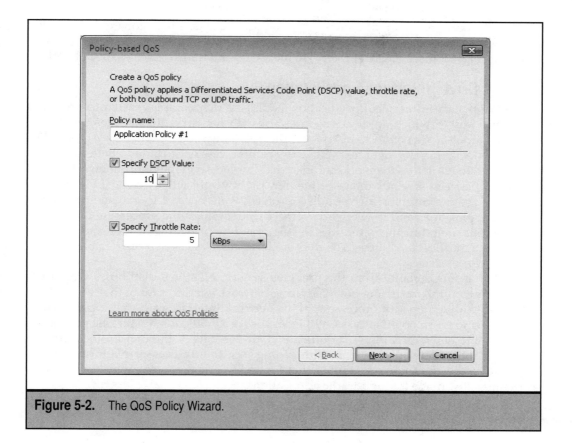

Figure 5-2.   The QoS Policy Wizard.

▼   SMS 2.0 supports larger buffer sizes than SMB 1.0.

■   It extends the number of concurrent open file handles on a server without service degradation, increasing the number of file shares that a server can support.

■   It supports durable connections that can withstand short interruptions in network availability.

▲   SMS 2.0 supports symbolic links. In Vista, New Technology File System (NTFS) files and folders can be accessed by referring to a new kind of file system object, called a symbolic link. A symbolic link is a pointer to another file system object. It sounds like another word for a shortcut, but they are not synonymous. The difference between a shortcut and a symbolic link is that a shortcut only works from within the Windows shell. To other programs and applications, shortcuts are just another file, whereas with symbolic links, the concept of a shortcut is implemented as a feature of the NTFS file system.

Vista workstations support both SMB 1.0 and 2.0. Vista tries to negotiate up to version 2.0 if the peer computer supports it. Where both sides of the connection support it, SMB 2.0 will bring a faster, more reliable protocol to file access and transfers across the network.

Network Driver Interface Specification 6.0

The Network Driver Interface Specification (NDIS) is a rich, complex set of protocols that affects the way in which applications interface with networks. It manages processing between kernel-mode network drivers and the operating system. Whereas Windows XP relies on NDIS 5.1, Vista includes NDIS 6.0. The new version includes a better distribution of workloads across the workstation and a simpler development framework.

Developers can take advantage of the new Lightweight Filter Driver (LFD) as well. Previously, both a miniport driver and a protocol were needed to manage processing between applications and the network. NDIS 6.0 streamlines the processing framework into one context and further simplifies development by providing deeper stack integration and diagnostics capabilities. The LFD model also offers faster, more reliable processing of network tasks.

Updating functionality from the previous service, NDIS 6.0 distributes workloads between the central processing unit (CPU) and network interfaces for both IPv4 and IPv6 traffic. Offloading network processing to the network interface card frees up the workstation CPU to work on other tasks. While Windows XP offloads IPv4 traffic processing to compatible network cards, Vista offloads both versions of Internet Protocol (IP). In addition, NDIS 6.0 enables true multithreading in a multiprocessor platform. For the first time, processing network traffic is not limited to one processor, which will offer a substantial advantage for high-traffic applications.

Management

Identifying opportunities to optimize network connections and resolve issues automatically is a universal ideal. Everyone appreciates a faster connection with fewer interruptions. In the absence of a perfect world, your challenge is to give your users the best experience and keep them functioning. Vista's networking improvements include several additions to help you gain more control over the quality of network connections.

Policy-Based Network Management

Vista extends support for Active Directory Group Policies to include settings for network connections and the Windows Firewall. The new policies enable administrators to configure settings for both wired and wireless connections. Using the Group Policy snap-in for the Microsoft Management Console (MMC), you can define how workstations connect to and operate within your network. For example, you can define a policy that requires all wireless connections to use a certain security configuration, that all connections must be limited to a certain wireless network, or that the connection can only be made to secured networks. Any updates made by users to settings managed by Group Policy are reset to the settings found in the policy upon the next Group Policy update,

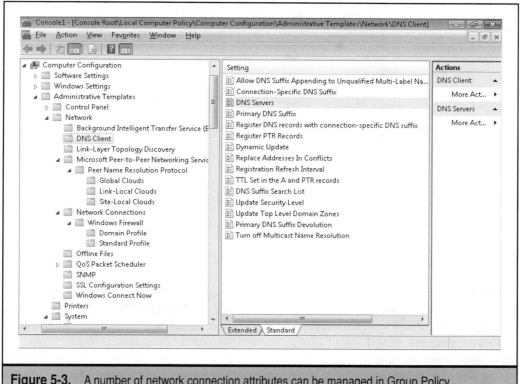

Figure 5-3.   A number of network connection attributes can be managed in Group Policy.

enforcing your centralized configuration across your network. An example of Group Policy management is shown in Figure 5-3.

What used to be a locally managed or scripted activity is completely centralized in Vista. The available settings include Domain Name System (DNS) server assignments, primary DNS prefix, Dynamic Host Configuration Protocol (DHCP), and program exceptions for traffic managed by Windows Firewall. The settings take precedence over what may be provided locally or by DHCP. DNS server properties are shown in Figure 5-4, while Windows Firewall management is shown in Figure 5-5.

Network Awareness

Vista tracks the status of the workstation's network connections using a rich vocabulary of descriptors. The status is made available to applications through a network awareness API. Any application that wishes to be informed of the network connection status can register with Vista to be on the distribution list. As the status changes, applications can adjust accordingly, helping to optimize performance and making for a smooth user experience.

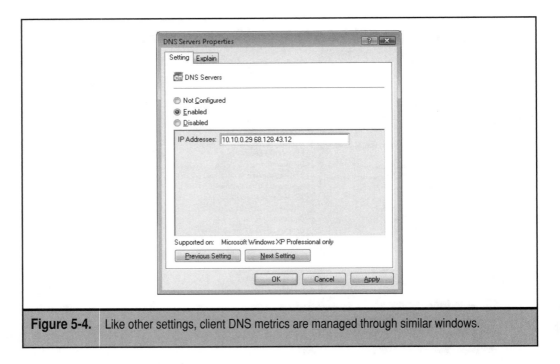

Figure 5-4. Like other settings, client DNS metrics are managed through similar windows.

Firewall settings and Group Policies are updated based on your Network Awareness API. Vista will keep the applications up to date on connectivity, including the connection status and access level (Internet, intranet, WLAN, etc.).

Network Diagnostics Framework

Workstations in and out of the workplace will occasionally disconnect from a network or otherwise suffer from degraded performance. Network Diagnostics Framework (NDF) is a set of technologies that will help users learn what ails the connection and give advice on how to further troubleshoot and resolve the issue—without calling in to the help desk. Figures 5-6 and 5-7 show how Windows Vista identifies a problem and then diagnoses the problem, respectively.

NDF will give users better details then Internet Explorer's famous message, "The page you are looking for is currently unavailable. The Web site might be experiencing technical difficulties, or you may need to adjust your browser settings." Users get something that helps them navigate through the network layers and components without being network engineers. When tasks fail that require network connectivity, NDF will ask the user if he or she wishes to diagnose the issue. Diagnostics and advice are conducted within the context of the task, which makes the process less generic and far more helpful than in the past. Vista will attempt to fix the problem, and then let you know when the problem has been worked out, as shown in Figure 5-8.

Diagnostics are executed using Vista "helper classes," which hold a library of resolution techniques to employ based on the application (URL, e-mail, etc.) and the task type.

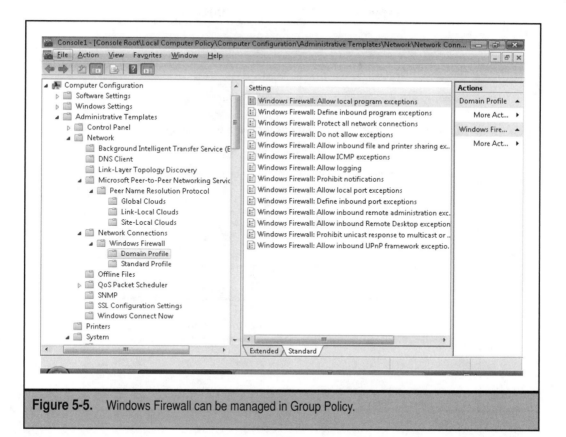

Figure 5-5.   Windows Firewall can be managed in Group Policy.

NDF is a client-side diagnostic, so any server issues or end-to-end traffic may be beyond its reach. If it fails to fix a problem, NDF offers the user options on how to report the issue or, if appropriate, reconfigure settings.

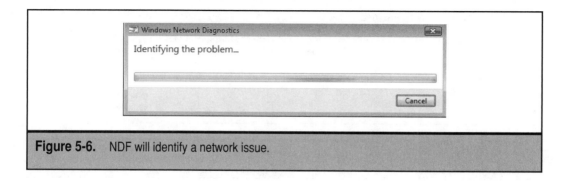

Figure 5-6.   NDF will identify a network issue.

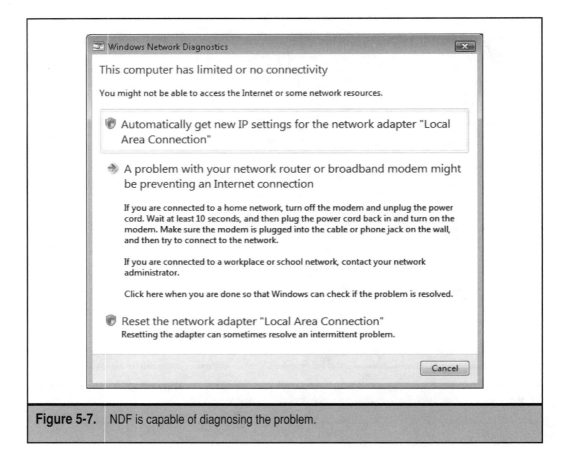

Figure 5-7.   NDF is capable of diagnosing the problem.

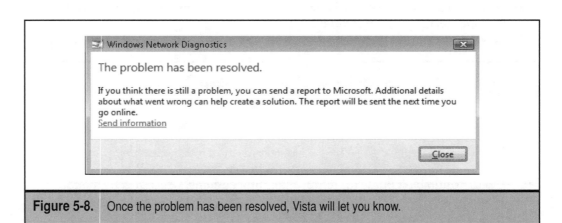

Figure 5-8.   Once the problem has been resolved, Vista will let you know.

The helper classes are part of another Vista layer that is available to NDF and other Vista services, called Windows Diagnostics Infrastructure (WDI). A helper class can determine the state of a specific network layer or component functionality. It plugs into the NDF, along with other helper classes from other network components. This allows the helper class to work within a common framework and determine the root cause of a networking problem.

For example, there is a helper class for wireless connectivity. The wireless helper class plugs into NDF, which, in turn, plugs into WDI. The role of the wireless helper class is to be the expert for wireless connectivity issues by collecting and analyzing information about wireless connectivity and providing the results of the analysis, with repair options to, WDI through NDF. NDF is an application that looks up your issue in the WDI library and can act on your behalf based on what it finds.

Windows Peer-to-Peer Networking

Today's users can leverage peer-to-peer (P2P) networks for file distribution and collaboration. Unlike a classic client/server architecture, where a centralized server acts as the hub of activity, P2P networks distribute the burden across the participating workstations. For example, once a user receives a file from a peer workstation, the user makes that file available to other users who are also designated to receive it. As each workstation receives a copy of the file, it becomes a distribution point. Creating P2P connections to all the participating clients, a workstation can receive the file faster than if it were served by a single file server. P2P networking support was first introduced in the Microsoft family with the advanced networking pack for Windows XP. With P2P, you can efficiently distribute presentations and applications while reducing the burden of maintaining designated file servers. Improvements in Microsoft's P2P implementation include the following:

▼ **Group Policy configuration**   You can configure P2P settings with Group Policy from the Computer Configuration\Administrative Templates\Network\Microsoft Peer-To-Peer Networking Services node.

■ **Command-line configuration**   You can configure P2P settings from commands in the **netsh p2p** context. This can be scripted, too, allowing you configure P2P in logon scripts.

▲ **PNRPv2**   The new version of the Peer Name Resolution Protocol (PNRP) is more scalable and uses less network bandwidth. In Vista, P2P applications can access PNRP name publication and resolution functions through a simplified API, which makes it easier for application developers to hook into PNRP. The new name resolution protocol also includes IPv6 addressing, which opens up P2P to the fantastic set of IPv6 scalability and performance. The pnrp.net domain is a reserved domain in Vista for PNRP name resolution. The PNRPv2 protocol is incompatible with the protocol used by computers running Windows XP. At the time of this writing, Microsoft has not released a distributable update for legacy operating systems, which means that the advantages of PNRPv2 are exclusive to Vista-to-Vista connections.

P2P is the basis for a few applications that are part of the Vista platform, including Windows Meeting Space and People Near Me.

End-to-End Security

Privacy and security are the issues that define today's network computing environment. Vista was written using the Security Development Lifecycle (SDL), a methodology that makes security a top priority from the very start of the development process. Vista manages network traffic using coded applications that were rewritten for a more secure platform.

Windows Firewall

In Part III: Security, we review in detail the care and feeding of the updated version of Windows Firewall. A key highlight of the new firewall service is that outgoing traffic is subject to firewall policies, not just incoming traffic. That alone makes the firewall far more effective than previous versions.

IPSec Improvements

IP Security (IPSec) is one of the most popular and prevalent methods for creating a secure communications tunnel between two participating hosts:

▼ **Integrated firewall and IPSec configuration** Formerly, Windows Firewall and IPSec were configured using separate graphical user interfaces (GUIs). Furthermore, each GUI offered different options and different limitations. For example, while you can specify exceptions to policies in Windows Firewall based on the application name, you cannot do the same when configuring IPSec policies. This might not be a problem, except that the firewall policies and the virtual private network (VPN) policies need to work together to create a secure connection. So the result of these dueling policies often included conflicting settings, and more than a little confusion, that stalled security policy deployments. To solve the problem, Vista integrates Windows Firewall and IPSec configuration into a single interface and provides a common set of settings. The new Windows Firewall with Advanced Security snap-in controls both firewall and IPSec configurations. This is shown in Figure 5-9.

With both tools combined into a single interface, you can configure when to block traffic and how to protect it. In addition, you can set configuration options using a command-line interface. Commands within the netsh advfirewall context can be used for configuration of both firewall and IPSec policies. The integration of Windows Firewall with IPSec provides Vista workstations with what can be thought of as an authenticating firewall.

▲ **Additional configuration options** In the new Windows Firewall and Advanced Security MMC snap-in, the options available for new IPSec rules are now on par with the options available for Windows Firewall. IPSec configuration options are shown in Figure 5-10.

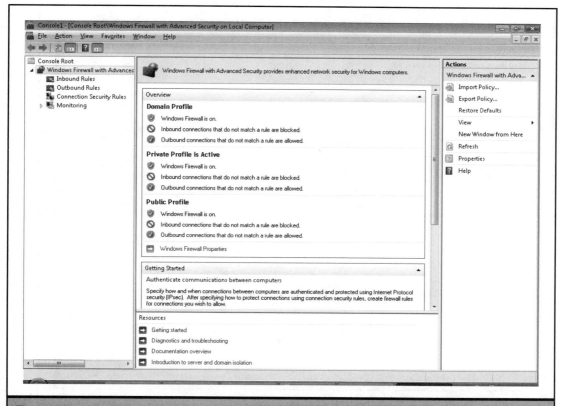

Figure 5-9.   The consolidated Windows Firewall and Advanced Security console.

You can filter the application of IPSec policies by:

▼ **Application name**   You no longer have to configure ports for an application, which greatly simplifies configuration.

■ **Ports**   You can specify all TCP or UDP ports or multiple TCP or UDP ports in a comma-delimited list.

■ **Address range**   You can specify a range of IP addresses, such as 10.1.17.23 to 10.1.17.219.

■ **Addresses on the local subnet**   You can specify individual addresses.

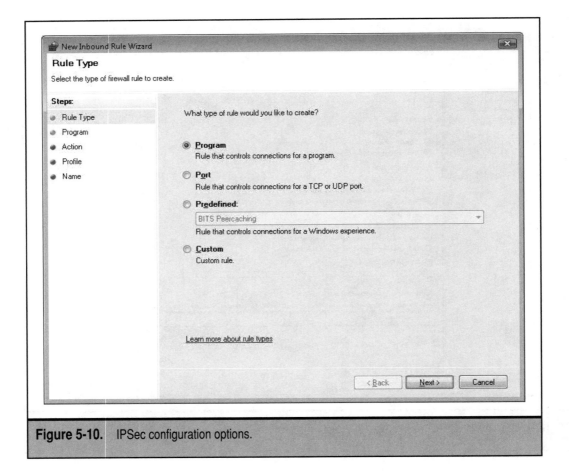

Figure 5-10. IPSec configuration options.

- **Connection type** You can base IPSec policies on the interface type, which includes wireless, LAN, and remote access.

- **Active Directory group, user, or computer** You can specify the list of computers, users, or groups that are authorized to initiate protected communication. You can specify that only members of a group can access a secured server and specifically deny users that cannot, which gives you granular control of the application of policies.

- **Services** Specify rules or exceptions for a process or service.

- **Parallel IPSec/clear negotiation** When a Vista workstation initiates communication with another host, two lines of traffic are started. In previous implementations of IPSec, only one line is started. The first line provides for the initiation of an IPSec tunnel, while Vista's second channel is a clear line without encryption. If the target host does not respond to the IPSec handshake, then the second line becomes the venue by which the two computers communicate. This sidesteps the delay commonly suffered when an IPSec host attempts to communicate with a target and the target fails to respond. The initiating host waits three seconds for the target to respond using IPSec before starting a new, clear line without encryption. Because Vista begins two lines simultaneously, there is no three-second delay when the target fails to respond—Vista immediately fails over to the clear line.

- **Client-to-DC IPSec**   In previous implementations of IPSec, only domain controller-to-domain controller (DC-to-DC) traffic can be encapsulated with IPSec. Tunneled traffic between domain controllers and member hosts is not supported. One problem with this is that hosts that have yet to join a domain can never get past the IPSec policy to reach the domain controller (IPSec requires domain-based authentication). Vista supports a robust filter that enables a flexible implementation of IPSec policies that can apply to domain controllers without blocking normal traffic and requiring complex configuration. You can safely apply IPSec to your domain controllers without running the risk of denying normal traffic.

- **Extended IPSec authentication**   You can integrate a second authentication into IPSec, which adds to the flexibility and security of the solution. This ensures that only specific users and specific computers can initiate communication with a server containing sensitive information. With both computer and user authentication, the risk of attack by trusted computers is greatly reduced. Layered authentication is not new, although in Vista you have more options. For example, you can layer the nominal authentication options of Kerberos, certificates, and preshared keys with a second layer of authentication against the certificate of health provided by the new Network Access Protection (NAP).

- **Integrated IPv4 and IPv6 support**   In Chapter 4, we covered TCP/IP and how IPv6 is integrated into the Next Generation TCP/IP Stack in Vista and is active by default. In Vista, IPSec supports Internet Key Exchange (IKE) and end-to-end encryption for both IPv4 and IPv6.

- **New cryptography**   Vista supports additional key derivation and encryption algorithms to improve high-end security solutions for government and sensitive applications. Vista supports the following additional algorithms to negotiate the master key material derived during main-mode negotiation:

  - Diffie-Hellman (DH) Group 19, which is an algorithm using a 256-bit random curve group

  - DH Group 20, an algorithm using a 384-bit random curve group

Adding to the popular Data Encryption Standard (DES) and Triple-DES (3DES) encryption technologies, Vista supports these additional algorithms for encrypting data:

- Advanced Encryption Standard (AES) with cipher block chaining (CBC) and a 128-bit key size (AES 128)
- AES with CBC and a 192-bit key size (AES 192)
- AES with CBC and a 256-bit key size (AES 256)

TIP The limit of these new algorithms is that previous Microsoft operating systems cannot participate in IPSec tunnels with Vista using these technologies. Until your entire network is outfitted with Vista and the latest server, you should be extremely careful about rolling out these new options into your production network.

▲ **Network Diagnostics Framework (NDF)** If IPSec negotiation fails, NDF prompts a user with an option to identify and correct the problem. The NDF engine for IPSec then attempts to discover the source of the failed connection and either automatically corrects the problem or advises the user to update the configuration.

CONNECTING CLIENTS TO THE WORKGROUP

Connecting a Windows Vista client to your network can be done in one of three ways. The first way, if you've updated your operating system, has already been done for you. When you deploy the OS, the settings should remain the same and will be carried over to your new environment.

The two other ways are by allowing Vista to do it for you or via manual configuration. Which way you decide to connect is largely up to you, your style, and your needs. Letting Vista do it for you is the quickest, easiest way. However, you may have specific settings you want to configure, or maybe automatic setup just isn't working the way you want it to. In those cases, you can configure your network adapter manually.

Before you can start either configuration, you need to install your network interface card (NIC) and its driver, and then plug the NIC into an open switch port. Let's take a look at how to configure Vista to operate on the network.

Automatic Configuration

In previous versions of Windows, adding a client to a network was a matter of learning IP addresses, right-clicking here, clicking there, and entering a host of information. In Windows XP, the process became much easier, with a wizard that took care of a lot of the heavy lifting. In Windows Vista, the process is downright foolproof.

To connect a client to your workgroup:

1. Plug the computer into a hub, switch, or router, and then turn it on.

    That's it. You're done.

    To confirm that the connection has been made:

2. Click the Start button.

3. Click Network.

You should see icons for the computer you added and for other computers and devices on your network, as shown in Figure 5-11.

If, for some reason, you are not connected, you can start a wizard that will connect you to your workgroup.

1. Right-click Computer and then select Properties.

2. Click Change Settings.

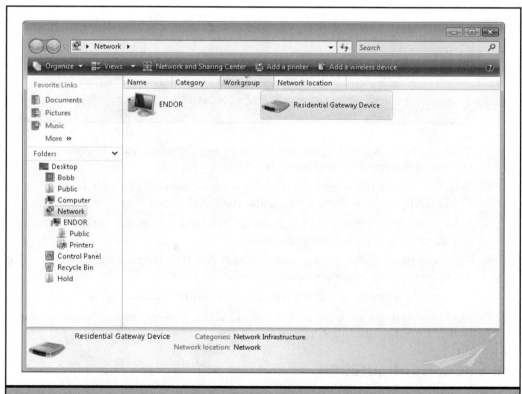

Figure 5-11.   Adding a computer to your network is reflected on the client.

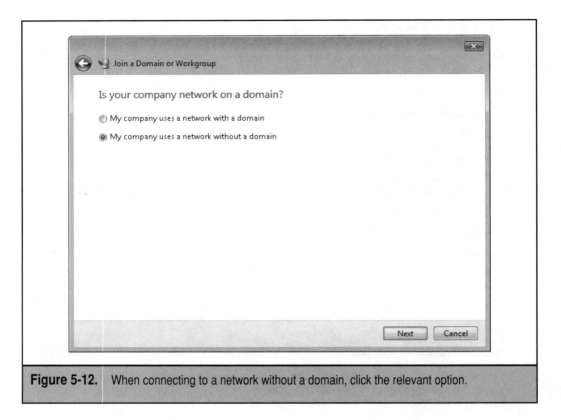

Figure 5-12.   When connecting to a network without a domain, click the relevant option.

3. Click the Network ID button in the Computer, Domain, And Workgroups section of the window, and then click Next.

4. Select the This Computer Is Part Of A Business Network; I Use It To Connect To Other Computers At Work option, and then click Next.

5. Select the My Company Uses A Network Without A Domain option, as shown in Figure 5-12, and click the Next button.

6. Enter the name of the workgroup to which you'll be connecting. In Figure 5-13, we're connecting to the workgroup "REXKWONDO."

7. Click the Next button, and the wizard performs its installation.

8. On the next page, click the Finish button. You will be prompted to restart the computer for the changes to take effect.

Manual Client Configuration

In an automatic configuration, Vista takes care of the dirty work in configuring a Vista client. However, there might be times when you'll need to manage some details to form

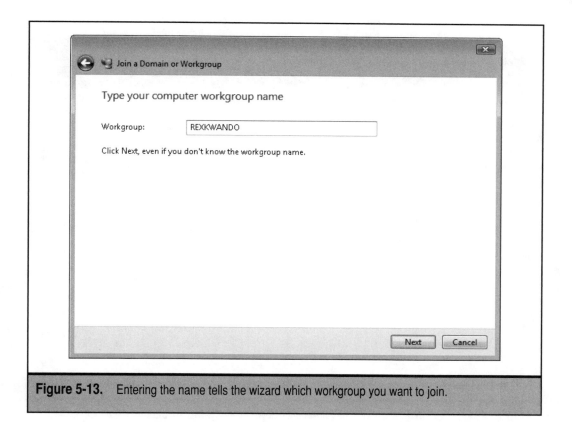

Figure 5-13.   Entering the name tells the wizard which workgroup you want to join.

a connection. For example, some connections might require the installation or removal of network components, like clients, protocols, or services.

Within each network connection listed in the Network Connection window are certain properties that can be examined and configured.

1. Click Start | Control Panel.

2. Click Network And Internet.

3. Click Network And Sharing Center.

4. Click Manage Network Connections. A list of available network connections is shown, like the one in Figure 5-14.

5. Right-click your desired network connections, and select Properties from the context menu. This brings up the Local Area Connection Properties dialog box, shown in Figure 5-15.

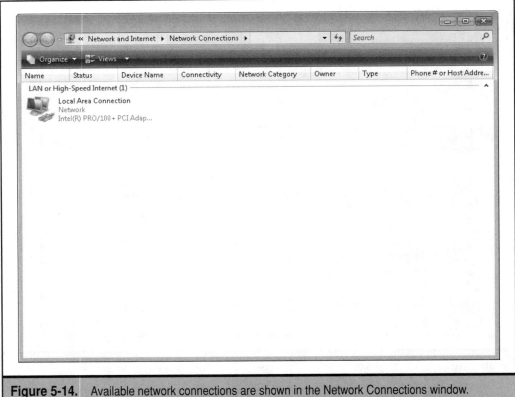

Figure 5-14. Available network connections are shown in the Network Connections window.

As Figure 5-15 shows, the connection's NIC is displayed, along with its clients, protocols, and services. In a conventional TCP/IP-based, Windows Vista LAN, seven components are automatically installed:

▼ **Client for Microsoft Networks** The client that enables the computer to be part of a native Microsoft network.

■ **File and Printer Sharing for Microsoft Networks** The service that allows Microsoft computers to share files and printers.

■ **QoS Packet Scheduler** The service that establishes when packets are to be sent, based on QoS standards.

■ **Internet Protocol version 4 (TCP/IPv4)** The TCP/IP version 4 protocol suite

■ **Internet Protocol version 6 (TCP/IPv6)** The TCP/IP version 6 protocol suite

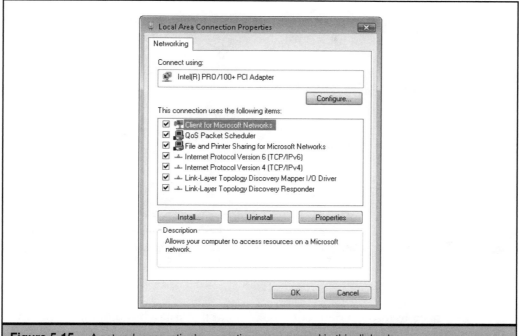

Figure 5-15.   A network connection's properties are managed in this dialog box.

■ **Link-Layer Topology Discovery Mapper I/O Driver**   Used to discover and locate other PCs, devices, and network infrastructure components on the network. Also used to determine network bandwidth.

▲ **Link-Layer Topology Discovery Responder**   The component that allows the PC to be seen on the network.

In Windows XP, this dialog box included clients, protocols, services, and the QoS packet scheduler. In Windows Vista, it also includes the Link-Layer Topology tools. We'll talk about the Link-Layer Topology tools a little later in this chapter. For now, however, let's turn our attention to clients, protocols, and services.

Clients

The client component of your network connection identifies on which type of network you'll be connecting. By default—and since this is a Microsoft product—Vista installs the Client for Microsoft Networks. However, if you are going to be connecting to a NetWare environment, for instance, you can change this setting. To see which clients are installed on your computer, examine the This Connection Uses The Following Items dialog box (see Figure 5-15).

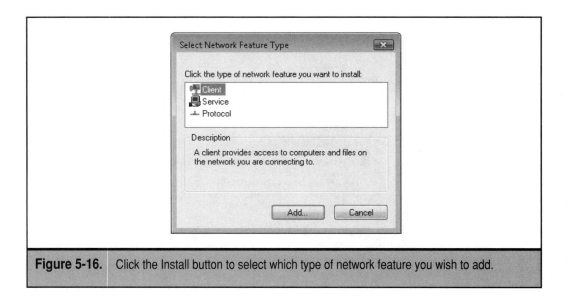

Figure 5-16.   Click the Install button to select which type of network feature you wish to add.

You may need to install a different type of client that is not listed in the connection's properties box.

1. Click Start | Control Panel.

2. Click Network And Internet.

3. Click Network And Sharing Center.

4. Click Manage Network Connections. A list of available network connections is shown.

5. Right-click your desired network connections, and select Properties from the context menu. This brings up the Local Area Connection Properties dialog box.

6. Click the Install button, and a dialog box appears, asking if you want to install a client, protocol, or service. This is shown in Figure 5-16. Select Client and then click Add.

7. Select the client you wish to install. If you are installing a third-party client, insert the disk containing the protocol, and click the Have Disk button. Click OK.

Protocols

The TCP/IP protocol suite is, by default, installed on your Windows Vista client. This is a fairly obvious setting, simply because the protocol is so prevalent. That's not to say, however, that it's the only protocol in town. There might be other protocols you wish to install, for example, Internetwork Packet Exchange/Sequenced Packet Exchange (IPX/SPX).

Installation   To install a protocol:

1. Click Start | Control Panel.

2. Click Network And Internet.

3. Click Network And Sharing Center.

4. Click Manage Network Connections. A list of available network connections is shown.

5. Right-click your desired network connections, and select Properties from the context menu. This brings up the Local Area Connection Properties dialog box.

6. Click the Install button, and a dialog box appears, asking if you want to install a client, protocol, or service. Select Protocol and then click Add. The resulting dialog box is shown in Figure 5-17.

7. Select the protocol you wish to install. If you are installing a third-party client, insert the disk containing the protocol, and click the Have Disk button. Click OK.

Link-Layer Topology   New to Windows Vista is Microsoft's Link-Layer Topology protocol. This is used by Microsoft and third-party vendors to help identify network components. For example, in Figure 5-17, we showed the Link-Layer Topology Discovery Mapper I/O Driver and the Link-Layer Topology Discovery Responder.

The Responder, as we noted earlier, is used to announce the computer on the network. As such, other computers that are capable can "see" the computer and add it to their

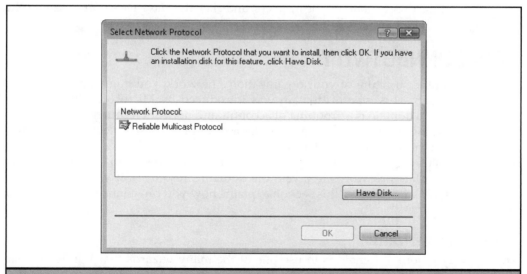

Figure 5-17.   You can add network protocols that are either already part of Vista or from a third party.

inventory of devices. The Mapper is used to cull information taken from devices announcing their presence with their own Responders. Thus, a computer with a Mapper (like Vista) can make a map of a network—something we'll see more of in the next chapter.

Services

The last type of network component you can add and manage is services. These are the mechanisms that allow you to share a computer's resources on the network. Unlike protocols and clients, services are optional. You don't need a service to make a basic network connection. However, if you want to do things like use a printer or share files, then you'll need to install requisite services.

To install a service:

1. Click Start | Control Panel.

2. Click Network And Internet.

3. Click Network And Sharing Center.

4. Click Manage Network Connections. A list of available network connections is shown.

5. Right-click your desired network connections, and select Properties from the context menu. This brings up the Local Area Connection Properties dialog box.

6. Click the Install button, and a dialog box appears, asking if you want to install a client, protocol, or service. Select Service and then click Add.

7. Select the service you wish to install. If you are installing a third-party client, insert the disk containing the protocol, and click the Have Disk button. Click OK.

DOMAIN CONNECTIVITY

Depending on the structure of your organization's network, you might have an Active Directory domain. This type of domain was introduced by Microsoft with Windows 2000. In essence, a domain is a grouping of accounts and network resources that are organized under a single domain name (army.mil, for example). These devices and accounts also fall within the security boundary that the domain affords. That is, if the Secretary of the Army is trying to log on to the army.mil domain, he'll be required—just once—to give the appropriate passwords to access the domain's resources. If your organization utilizes a domain architecture, this section explains how you can connect clients to your domain.

Joining via a Wizard

An easy way to join a domain is to use one of the many wizards that Windows Vista supplies. In this case, you would use the Join A Network Or Domain Wizard just as you would to join a workgroup. This wizard provides a means to connect Windows Vista clients to Windows 2000- or 2003-based domains.

NOTE   Often, companies will deny regular users the right to do this and will have already defined the appropriate domain.

To start the Network Identification Wizard:

1. Click Start.
2. Right-click Computer, and then select Properties.
3. Click Change Settings.
4. Click the Network ID button in the Computer, Domain, And Workgroups section of the window, and then click Next.
5. Select the This Computer Is Part Of A Business Network; I Use It To Connect To Other Computers At Work option, shown in Figure 5-18, and then click Next.
6. Select the My Company Uses A Network With A Domain option, and click the Next button.

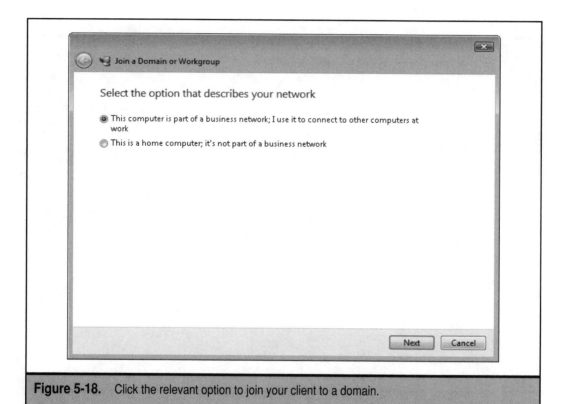

Figure 5-18.   Click the relevant option to join your client to a domain.

7. The wizard will give you instructions to gather certain information that will be needed to complete it. The information includes:

■ User name

■ Password

■ User account domain

■ Computer name

■ Computer domain

Figure 5-19 shows the Network Identification Wizard seeking the user's name, password, and domain.

Joining Manually

As with connecting to a workgroup, you needn't run a wizard to configure your client. To join a Windows domain manually:

1. Right-click Computer and then select Properties.
2. Click Change Settings.

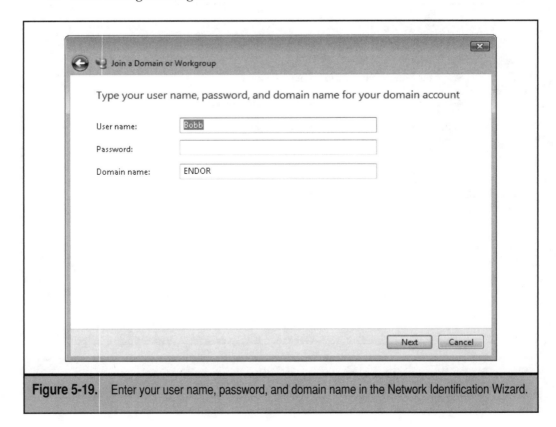

Figure 5-19. Enter your user name, password, and domain name in the Network Identification Wizard.

3. Click the Change button in the middle of the box, and then click Next. The Computer Name/Domain Changes dialog box appears (this is shown in Figure 5-20).

4. If the computer account has been created and is on the domain controller, enter your user name, password, and domain name. Click Next.

   –Or–

   If the computer account has not been created at the domain controller:

   a. Type the user name, password, and domain name, and then click Next.

   b. When prompted, enter the user name and password of an administrator account, and then click OK.

5. Click OK three times.

6. You will be prompted to restart the computer. Click Yes.

When you've finished these steps, you should verify your membership in the domain. You do this by restarting the computer and pressing CTRL + ALT + DEL. This opens the Log On To Windows dialog box. To the right of the box is an arrow. Click that arrow to get a list of available domains. The list should contain the domain you just added.

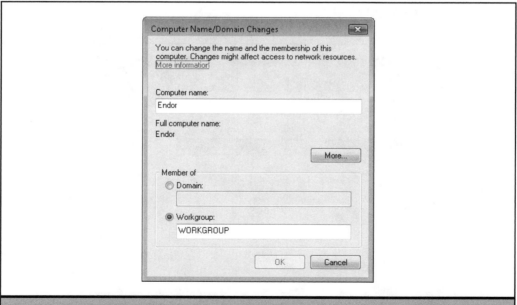

Figure 5-20. You can manually elect to join a workgroup or a domain.

CONNECTING TO THE INTERNET

If yours is a large organization, your clients are probably already connecting to the Internet through the network. However, if your organization is such that your clients need to connect to the Internet through modems or a broadband connection (like mobile users or home users, for instance), Windows Vista make the connection using the Set Up A Connection Or Network Wizard.

With this wizard, you tell Vista what type of connection you're using and how it should be configured. This is used for analog, DSL, Integrated Services Digital Network (ISDN), or cable modem connections. This section explains how to use the wizard to configure your client for Internet connectivity.

Using the Set Up A Connection Or Network Wizard

The Set Up A Connection Or Network Wizard makes the process of establishing a new connection easier than it had been in previous incarnations of Windows. To activate the wizard:

1. Click Start | Control Panel.

2. Click Network And Internet.

3. Click Network And Sharing Center.

4. In the tasks pane, click Set Up A Connection Or Network. The resulting wizard is shown in Figure 5-21.

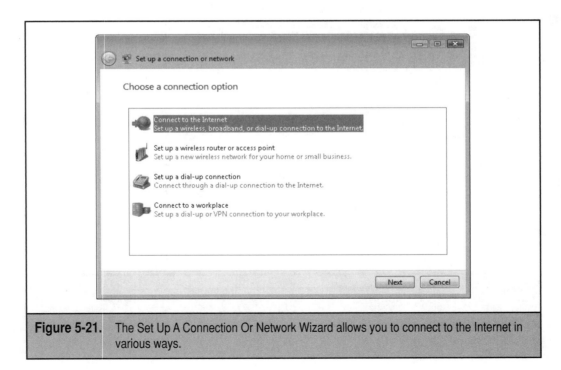

Figure 5-21. The Set Up A Connection Or Network Wizard allows you to connect to the Internet in various ways.

When you start the wizard, it allows you to build one of four types of network connections:

▼ Internet connection

■ Wireless router or access point

■ Dial-up connection

▲ Connection to your workplace using VPN

These connections are explored in more depth in the following sections.

Internet Connection

This selection helps you build your connection for Internet access. This connection automatically assumes you'll be connecting via a broadband (DSL or cable) connection. Vista examines your computer and asks what type of device you'll be using for a connection. For example, in Figure 5-22, we're using a DSL modem to connect.

You can tell Windows Vista what type of technology you'll be using for your broadband connection, but if you do not, it will automatically search your system and configure the connection, assuming that the device is already in place on your computer.

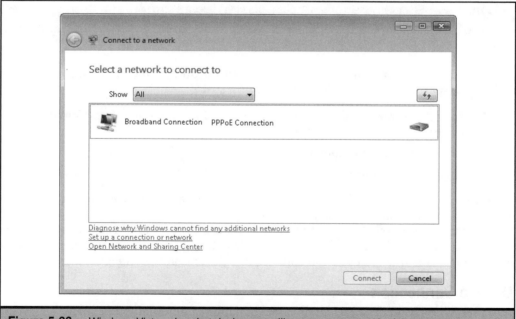

Figure 5-22. Windows Vista asks what device you will use to connect to the Internet.

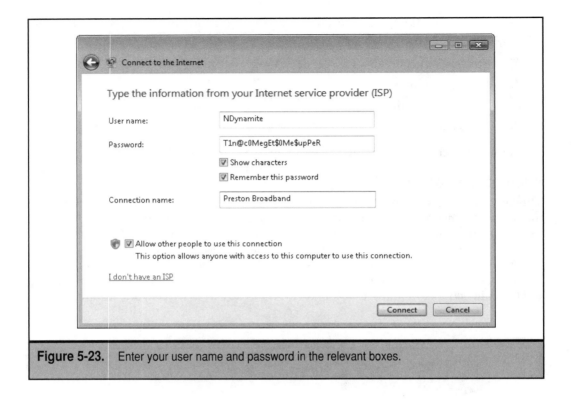

Figure 5-23. Enter your user name and password in the relevant boxes.

Even so, it is recommended that you call your ISP and get the following information before you set up your broadband connection:

▼ Your IP address (or at least know if the IP address is assigned dynamically or statically)

■ DNS addresses and domain names

▲ Other relevant information

When prompted, you should enter your user name and password, along with a description of the connection, as shown in Figure 5-23.

The next step is to click the Connect button, and the connection will be configured. To connect to the Internet, all you need to do is click Start | Connect To, and then you'll see a list of networks to which you can connect, like the one shown in Figure 5-24.

Dial-Up Connection

A dial-up connection uses a telephone line for a limited amount of time, namely conventional analog modems or ISDN. By selecting this access route, you should have details of your connection (ISP telephone numbers and so forth) on hand.

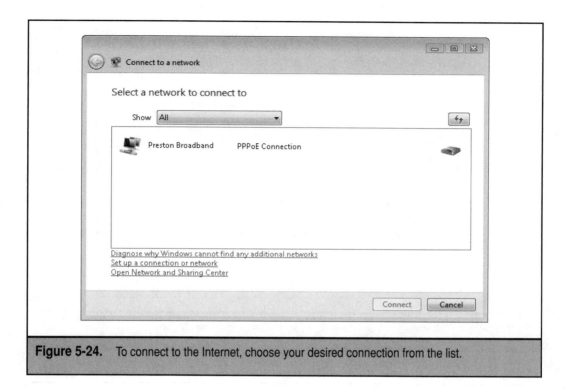

Figure 5-24.   To connect to the Internet, choose your desired connection from the list.

When you start this wizard, you're asked for some basic information, including your user name, password, and the ISP's dial-in number. This is shown in Figure 5-25.

Connect to the Network at My Workplace

This selection allows you to connect to a LAN from home, the field, or any other location. When you select this option, two more subcategories are presented. If you already have preconfigured ISP connections, either broadband or dial-up, you'll be asked if you want to use one of those connections or if you want to configure a new connection. If you don't have an existing connection—or if you decide to configure a new one for this purpose—you're asked if you want to connect using an Internet connection or via a dial-in connection, as Figure 5-26 shows.

Use My Internet Connection (VPN)   The first way to connect to your organization's network is via VPN, across the Internet. You will have to connect to the Internet first, and then your connection will be tunneled to your organization's network.

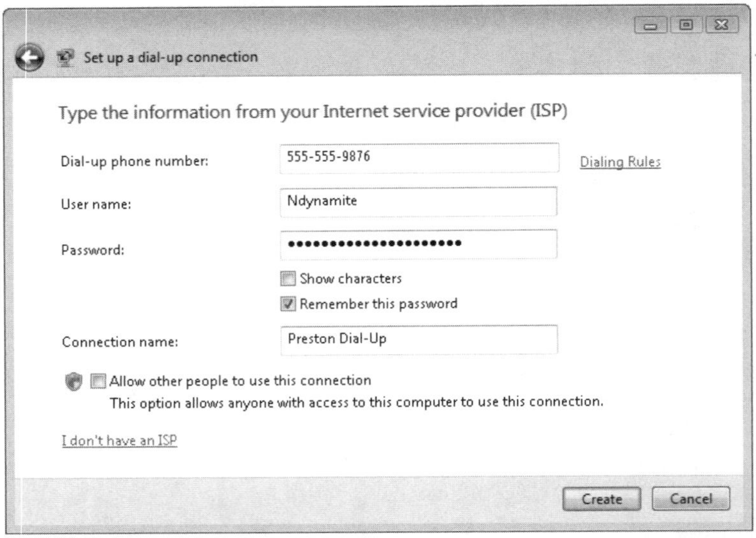

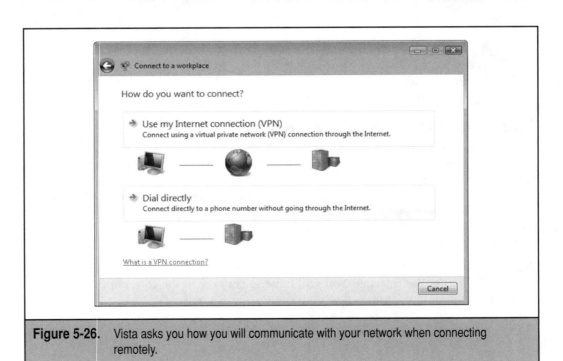

Figure 5-25. The wizard to dial in to an ISP requires basic information.

Figure 5-26. Vista asks you how you will communicate with your network when connecting remotely.

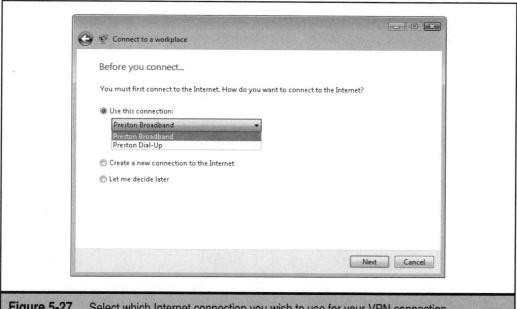

Figure 5-27.   Select which Internet connection you wish to use for your VPN connection.

In configuring the VPN, you're asked which connection you wish to use. If you don't have a connection, the window shown in Figure 5-27 gives you the option to create one.

Once connected to the Internet, Vista needs to know what IP address your organization uses for the connection. Enter it as shown in Figure 5-28.

Finally, you're asked for your user name and password. Enter these, and the connection will be complete.

Dial Directly   Dialing directly is another way to configure a dial-in connection. But rather than connecting to an ISP, you'll be dialing the phone number that allows you to connect to your organization's network, assuming there is a computer set up to accept incoming calls. The configuration steps are just like those we covered for configuring a dial-in connection.

By the time you've completed the various types of connections Vista allows, you can make those connections easily enough by clicking Start | Connect To. You'll be shown a list of your connections, with various icons indicating the type. The ones we've configured as examples throughout this chapter are shown in Figure 5-29.

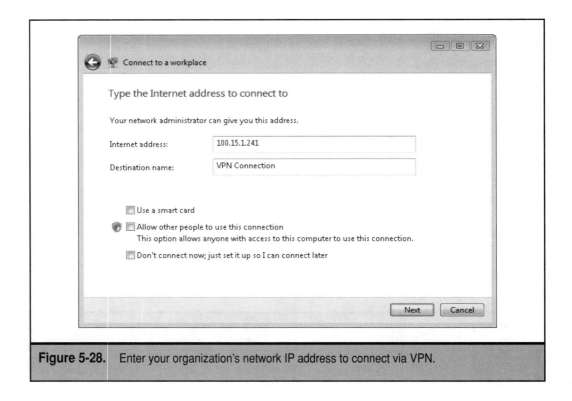

Figure 5-28.   Enter your organization's network IP address to connect via VPN.

WIRELESS CONNECTIONS

In the past, wireless connectivity has been slow (compared to Ethernet), expensive, and notoriously hard to configure. Recently, however, wireless components have become less expensive (they're even included in most laptops), faster, and easier to configure. In Windows Vista, wireless connectivity has been overhauled from its earlier incorporation in Windows XP. This section takes a look at what's new and improved, and how you can configure your wireless clients.

Wireless Networking Updates in Vista

Wireless networking is a wonderful technology that's making networking a lot easier for admins and computer users alike. Unfortunately, wireless can be inherently tricky to use. Microsoft added a number of great wireless tools and applications in Windows XP. They continue to make wireless easier to use with Windows Vista. Let's take a look at what's new in Windows Vista.

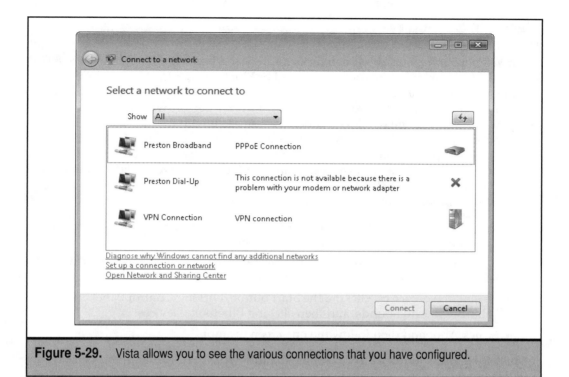

Figure 5-29. Vista allows you to see the various connections that you have configured.

Native Wireless Fidelity Architecture

In earlier incarnations, wireless connections in Windows were designed to emulate Ethernet connections and were extended using Extensible Authentication Protocol (EAP) types for IEEE 802.1X authentication. In Windows Vista, a new architecture is employed, called the Native Wireless Fidelity (WiFi) architecture.

This architecture allows Vista to represent wireless connections as a media type separate from Ethernet. This enhances Vista's flexibility by allowing hardware vendors to support features specific to 802.11 networks, like a larger frame size than Ethernet.

Hardware vendors will be able to extend the built-in wireless client for new wireless capabilities. This allows them to provide customized configurations, dialog boxes, and wizards.

Wireless Network Setup Wizard

The Wireless Network Setup Wizard is used in Windows Vista to configure a wireless client. The wizard will examine the wireless network adapter and recommend the strongest security setting that is supported by it. For instance, if the adapter is capable of both Wi-Fi Protected Access (WPA) authentication and Wired Equivalent Privacy (WEP) encryption, the wizard will automatically select WPA, because it provides a stronger, more secure environment.

Bluetooth Support

There are a few different ways in which wireless connectivity happens. When we talk about WiFi, we're talking about network adapters and access points that use the 802.11 standard. However, you can also use infrared or Bluetooth devices.

Bluetooth—as anyone knows who's stood next to someone seemingly talking to themselves at the grocery store, only to find out that person was wearing a wireless headset—is a short-range wireless technology. You see it with the aforementioned cellular telephone/headset solution, and there are also toys that can be run from a Bluetooth-enabled cellular phone. But it isn't just the phones that use Bluetooth. There's plenty of computer gadgetry that you can use thanks to Bluetooth, like keyboards, mice, and personal digital assistants (PDAs).

To set up a Bluetooth-enabled device:

1. Install a Bluetooth adapter. Normally, this is a simple process of plugging a Universal Serial Bus (USB) Bluetooth dongle into an open USB port.

2. Turn on the device, and make it discoverable. How you do this will vary from device to device, so check your manufacturer's instructions.

3. Install the device by clicking the Start button, clicking Control Panel, clicking Hardware And Sounds, and then clicking Bluetooth Devices.

4. Click Add, and then follow the on-screen prompts.

Installing a Bluetooth printer is somewhat different. The first steps are the same: install the dongle, and then turn on the printer and make it discoverable. When that's done, open the Add Printer Wizard. This is done by clicking the Start button, clicking Control Panel, clicking Hardware And Sound, clicking Printers, and then clicking Add A Printer.

Making a Connection

There are three different types of wireless networks you'll encounter. Actually, you'll only encounter two of them, unless you know to look for the third type. They are:

▼ **Unsecured** These networks do not require authentication or encryption. They may, however, require a password to connect, but they aren't using encryption or protection.

NOTE Since unsecured networks present a good chance of your data being compromised, Windows Vista will give you a friendly reminder before allowing you to connect to an unsecured network. When you attempt to connect, Vista will ask you to verify that you do, in fact, want to connect to the network.

■ **Secured** These networks require passwords and utilize encryption to keep data secure and safe. Generally speaking, the stronger the encryption, the more protection is afforded.

▲   **Hidden**   These networks do not advertise their network names, so the only way you'd know they are out there—and be able to connect to them—is if you know the exact name.

Non-Broadcasting Wireless Networks

If a hacker doesn't know about a network, he can't try and break into it. That's the logic behind not broadcasting a Service Set Identifier (SSID). By not broadcasting an SSID, a casual hacker doesn't know that there's anything there to mess with.

> **NOTE**   A skilled hacker can "see" the network anyway, because packet-laden frames are flying somewhere, SSID or not. Still, this basic security concept is used in Windows Vista to help maintain a WLAN's safety from most people, certainly from the casual but curious WLAN user looking for a free ride on your wireless network.

Previous versions of Windows did not allow you to indicate a preferred wireless network as hidden; however, that has been changed in Windows Vista. Now, you can indicate that a preferred network is hidden by configuring it as a non-broadcast network.

Wireless Network Configuration Methods

Connecting to a WLAN is easy in Windows Vista. Vista (via your network interface) will scan the airwaves to find available networks. From there, it's a simple matter of clicking the desired network (assuming it's not hidden, of course).

But you don't have to run through a list of available networks every time you attempt a connection with Windows Vista. You can select the preferred wireless networks with which the client will attempt to connect.

In previous versions of Windows, if preferred wireless networks were not found, or if connections to preferred networks were not successful, the wireless client would prompt you to connect to any detected wireless network. In Windows Vista, Group Policy settings allow administrators to set lists of allowed and denied wireless networks:

▼   **Allow**   This list specifies the wireless networks to which clients are allowed to connect.

▲   **Deny**   This list specifies the wireless networks to which clients are not allowed to connect. This prevents connection to unsecured networks, along with any other wireless network that the administrator does not wish to allow access to.

The Connect To A Network Dialog Box

To see a list of available wireless networks and connect to the network of your choice:

1.   Click Start, and then click Connect To. A list of the wireless networks currently available is displayed.

2.   Select a network and then click Connect.

Naturally, you'll only see networks that aren't being blocked by a Group Policy setting. However, if you are expecting to see a network and you don't:

1. Click the I Don't See The Networks I Am Looking For link.

2. On the Select A Connection Option page, select the Show All Connection Options check box.

3. Select the type of connection that you are trying to use, and then follow the instructions to configure the connection.

Connecting to Public Networks

You just can't have a cup of coffee without lugging that laptop along and checking your e-mail. If you're out and about and trying to connect to a public network, you'll follow the same steps that you would follow to connect to a private network; however, you might be asked to set up an account and save some files to your computer. Before just accepting that at face value, double-check a few things:

▼ Make sure you know which files are being saved to your computer.

■ Know what type of information the network provider is gathering from your computer.

■ Read the service provider's privacy statement.

▲ Although you may be creating an account, the connection may not be secure.

Once you're satisfied that the files and account creation are correct, connect to the network.

1. Click Start, and then click Connect To. A list of the wireless networks currently available is displayed.

2. Select a network and then click Connect.

When connecting to a WLAN that supports Wireless Provisioning Service (WPS) technology, you will be asked to download some files that are meant to allow your computer on the network. Typically, these files are safe, but there are a few things you should understand before clicking OK:

▼ Ensure that the Web site from which the files are being downloaded is one you expected them to come from, based on your location or the organization. These files don't contain personal information about yourself or your computer; rather, they are configuration details about the network. If you don't accept the files, you won't be able to connect to that network.

■ Once the provisioning files have been downloaded, the Wireless Network Registration Wizard asks you for more information. This might be credit card information or simply accepting the provider's usage terms.

▲   If you're going back to the same public network, you can elect to have the provisioning files on your computer updated automatically. Typically, these updates are conducted on a regular schedule, and your computer will attempt to connect to the wireless network provider to download the updates. This normally occurs while the computer is already connected to the Internet and won't interfere with your Internet usage.

Disconnecting

When you're done with your wireless connection, it's a good idea to disconnect. To do so, right-click the network icon in the notification area, if it is displayed, or follow these steps:

1. Click Start and then click Control Panel.

2. In Control Panel, under the Network And Internet area, click View Network Status And Tasks.

3. If you have a connection to the network, click Personalize under Network Details. The Status dialog box appears.

4. The Connections In Use list shows the connections you are using. Click the wireless connection, and then click Disconnect.

Managing a Connection

Group Policy settings can also be used to configure fast-roaming and automatic connections.

Fast-Roaming Connections

A fast-roaming connection allows wireless clients to quickly roam from one access point to another by using preauthentication and Pairwise Master Key (PMK) caching.

Automatic Connections

Wireless auto-configuration dynamically selects the wireless network to which the computer will connect. This is done based on preferences or default settings. This can also include disconnecting from one network and connecting to a preferred one once it becomes available.

Connecting a client to your network, the Internet, or a wireless network is an important task. Happily, Windows Vista makes it easier than ever to form such connections. Better yet, Microsoft has made some nice strides toward improving the quality and manageability of network connections.

Once you've connected your clients to the network, it's time to check out your network and see what's going on. In Chapter 6, we'll talk about the new ways you can manage your network with Windows Vista.

CHAPTER 6

Network Navigation

As a systems professional, there's one thing that is almost always on your mind: the network. It matters to you when it's down. It matters to you when it's up (it could be running better, of course...). And it matters to you when a new way to do an old trick comes around.

There's some good news. With Windows Vista, Microsoft has made big improvements on what have become old yet familiar technologies. In the process, they've made connecting to and navigating networks much easier. Have they invented the perfect operating system? No, of course not, but what they do offer is a lot better than what was there before.

This chapter is all about what's new in the Vista world of networking and also explains how to teach the new dog some old tricks. We'll talk about how you can navigate your network, and examine and manage its various and sundry settings. We'll also take a closer look at wireless networks, which takes a huge leap in accessibility and configuration in Windows Vista. Before we get into the nuts and bolts, let's take a quick look at some of the new technologies that promise to make your network a better place to work.

WHAT'S NEW IN VISTA NETWORKING

While the obvious differences between Windows XP and Vista are cosmetic, there's a lot going on under Vista's hood. Vista—along with its server partner, currently code-named "Longhorn," but slated to be called Windows Server 2007—features a number of improvements in the way networking takes place. We have already talked about its Next Generation TCP/IP Stack, which uses both IPv4 and IPv6.

New and Improved

The first stop is to examine what is new to Windows Vista. Depending on your organization and its networking needs, some of these things may not be as important as others. On the other hand, some may be exactly the sorts of things you've needed to get the most out of your network.

QoS

Audio and video traversing a network is becoming more commonplace, both on home and corporate networks. Because audio and video packets generally need priority over other packets to avoid playback problems, Microsoft has enhanced Quality of Service (QoS) in Vista. Of course, it isn't just multimedia that benefits from Vista's policy-based QoS mechanisms. Networks of any complexity and with any need can prioritize which packets get preferential treatment.

For example, if yours is a network routinely used for transferring large files to workstations, you might use the new QoS tools to tell the network to give those packets priority over such packets as e-mail or Web traffic.

SMB

The Windows file-sharing protocol Server Message Block (SMB) 1.0 was introduced more than 15 years ago. As time has marched by and networks evolved, SMB's shortcomings needed to be addressed. With Vista, SMB is reintroduced with version 2.0, and it allows such enhancements as:

▼ Multiple commands can be handled within one packet. This reduces the amount of traffic that traverses the network between the server and client.

■ Larger buffer sizes are allowed over SMB 1.0

■ Support for symbolic links is provided

▲ It can handle short interruptions in network availability.

Http.sys

Http.sys, the kernel-mode driver that services Hypertext Transfer Protocol (HTTP), has also been improved over earlier versions. Ultimately, HTTP is enhanced for users, providing a smoother, more robust experience. Improvements include:

▼ Server-side authentication

■ Logging

■ Netsh commands, which will be examined later in this chapter

▲ Performance counters

Peer-to-Peer Networking

Initially introduced with the Advanced Networking Pack for Windows XP, Windows Peer-to-Peer Networking is an operating system platform and application programming interface (API) that allows the development of peer-to-peer (P2P) applications. In Vista, Windows Peer-to-Peer Networking includes:

▼ An easy-to-use API

■ A new version of the Peer Name Resolution Protocol (PNRP)

■ The dynamic discovery of other users on the local subnet

■ Netsh configuration support

▲ Group Policy configuration support, that allows P2P settings to be managed from Group Policy

Retired Technologies

While Vista adds some new and interesting technologies, it removes several others. The following networking technologies were available up until Windows XP, but you won't find them in Vista:

▼ Bandwidth Allocation Protocol (BAP)

■ X.25

- Serial Line Interface Protocol (SLIP)
- Asynchronous Transfer Mode (ATM)
- IP over IEEE 1394
- NWLink IPX/SPX/NetBios Compatible Transport Protocol
- Services for Macintosh (SFM)
- Open Shortest Path First (OSPF) routing protocol in Routing And Remote Access
- Basic Firewall in Routing And Remote Access
- ▲ Static IP filter APIs in Routing And Remote Access

This section gave just the quickest overview of what's brand new in Vista that was worth mentioning and what was removed. Let's take a closer look at the applications that you'll regularly come into contact with while using Vista on your network.

THE NETWORK AND SHARING CENTER

Unless you have intimate knowledge of a network's design, unless you've committed its topology to memory, and unless there have been no changes made to said design, just sitting down at a PC and trying to discern everything about that network can be difficult. Microsoft has tried to make network navigation easier in Windows Vista, thanks to a component called the Network And Sharing Center. The Center makes it a lot easier to gather information about how a workstation is connected to its network and how you can configure that workstation to work with the network.

Like so many other things in Vista, the Network And Sharing Center has its roots in earlier versions of Windows. If you hop in your time machine and set the dial for 1995, you might remember seeing Network Neighborhood in Windows 95. That tool gradually evolved into My Network Places in Windows XP. In Windows Vista, the tool is called simply Network. To start this option, simply click the Start button, and then click Network. The resulting screen looks like the one in Figure 6-1.

In many ways, Network behaves a lot like Network Neighborhood—clicking it displays all the computers in the current domain. By double-clicking any of the computers, you can access its shared resources.

By clicking the Network And Sharing Center option, a screen like the one in Figure 6-2 appears.

As you can see in the figure, the Network And Sharing Center is made up of a few components, which we will discuss in the next section.

Meet the Network And Sharing Center

There are several ways to access the Network And Sharing Center. In addition to the aforementioned method, you can start the Network And Sharing Center as follows:

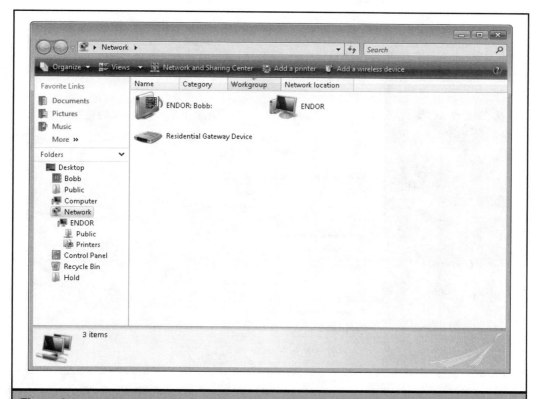

Figure 6-1.   Windows Vista's Network is reminiscent of Network Neighborhood from Windows 95.

1. Click Start and then click Control Panel.
2. In Control Panel, under Network And Internet, click View Network Status And Tasks.

When you've started the Network And Sharing Center, you can use it to manage your network settings and status.

There are four areas within the Network And Sharing Center:

▼   **Network map**   This presents a visual representation of the network's infrastructure. This map shows if you are connected to a network and whether you can access the Internet through that connection. If you click View Full Map, an extended network map is displayed.

■   **Network details**   This presents details about the network to which the computer is connected. By following the links, you can manage the connections and the networks to which they are linked.

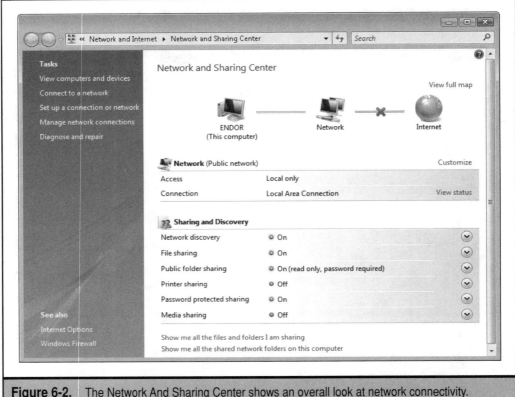

Figure 6-2.   The Network And Sharing Center shows an overall look at network connectivity.

- ■ **Sharing and discovery**   This presents a summary of the computer's firewall, detection, and sharing settings. These options will vary, depending on the computer's configuration, and include Block, Allow, and View Sharing Settings.

- ▲ **Tasks**   These are additional tasks, listed in the left pane, that can be started from elsewhere in Windows Vista, but are convenient to have handy in this context.

Let's examine these sections in more depth.

Network Map

Consider again the Network And Sharing Center. It shows the workstation you're using passing through a local network, with a subsequent connection to the Internet. Above the Internet icon, there is an option to view a full map of the network. If you click the View Full Map link, you'll see all the devices on your network. This is shown in Figure 6-3.

Vista does this by using Microsoft's link-layer protocol. As you may remember from Chapter 5, the protocol is used to both announce a device's presence on the network and map out devices on the network.

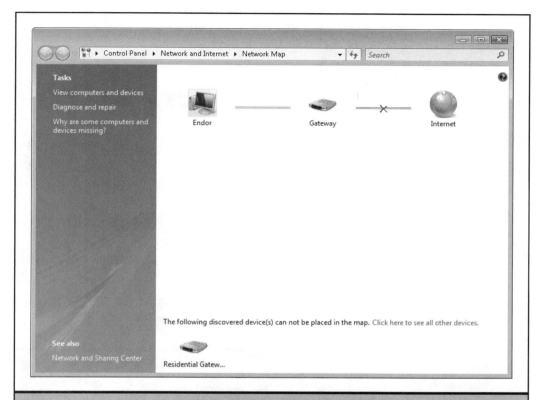

Figure 6-3.   Clicking the View Full Map link gives a comprehensive overview of devices on your network.

NOTE   If you have an Xbox plugged into your network, it will be shown on this map, as it also uses the link-layer protocol to announce its presence.

Network Details

By clicking the View Status link, you'll see a dialog box like the one shown in Figure 6-4.

The box should look familiar to Windows XP users—it's basically the Properties dialog box that so many of us have seen. However, here, it has been retooled for a Vista environment, including IPv6 details.

Sharing and Discovery

There are a couple of differences in how resource sharing works in Vista when compared to Windows 2000/XP. Vista uses the Public folder, unlike the user's Shared Documents folder in Windows XP, to simplify file sharing. In fact, simple file sharing is enabled by default in

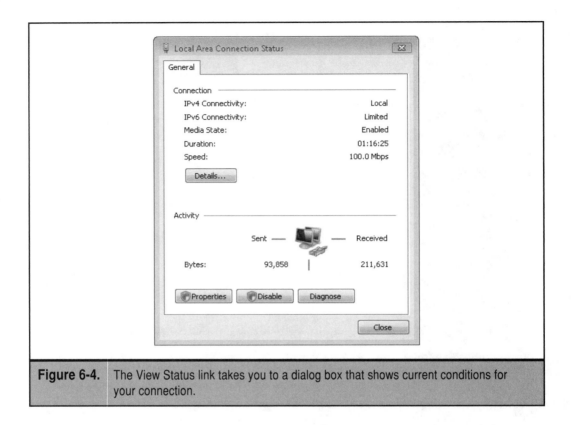

Figure 6-4. The View Status link takes you to a dialog box that shows current conditions for your connection.

Windows XP Home Edition and XP Professional when not joined to an Active Directory domain. By default, Vista does not allow simple file sharing. Access to shared folders requires a user name and password. The Sharing And Discovery area is shown in Figure 6-5.

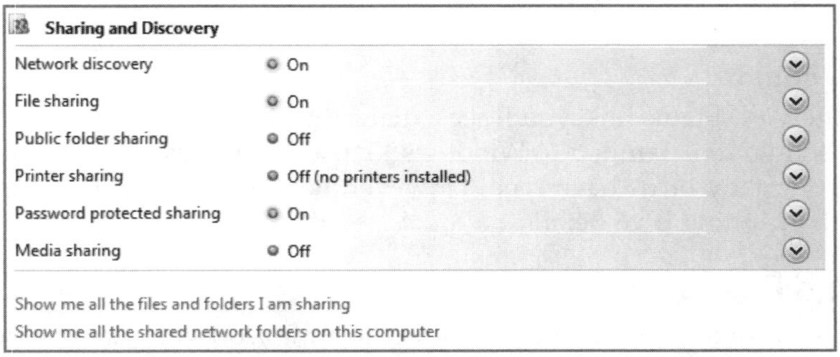

Figure 6-5. The Sharing And Discovery area centralizes resource-sharing configuration.

Your options for configuring resource sharing in the Sharing And Discovery area are explained in the following sections. Each area includes two or more options that are displayed by clicking the down arrow to the right of the option line.

Network Discovery   By setting Network Discovery to "on," you activate the network map and make the workstation visible on the network maps of other workstations. The workstation can see other members of the workgroup or domain, and it can be seen by those other stations. Network Discovery is a requirement for sharing files and printers, as well as for accessing shared resources on other workstations. When connecting to a network, you choose the network location (domain, private, or public), and Vista sets Network Discovery to "on" or "off" based on your choice. For domain-controlled networks, Network Discovery is turned off by default and is managed by Group Policy. For private locations, Network Discovery is on by default.

When you select the network location, Windows Firewall will open the necessary ports to allow resource-sharing traffic. If you manage Windows Firewall using Group Policy, you will want to ensure that the ports in Table 6-1 are set according to your needs. If you use a firewall other than Windows Firewall, you must configure it to allow network discovery and file and printer-sharing traffic. The network ports used to support resource sharing include those listed in Table 6-1.

File Sharing   Turn on file sharing to make files and printers that you have shared accessible to other workstations and devices on your network. You can access shared folders and devices on other workstations and servers, although the local sharing may be disabled. Turning file sharing on for the local workstation is not required if you wish to access network resources. The File Sharing option in the Network And Sharing Center affects whether the local workstation will advertise and allow access to local resources.

Purpose	Ports
For network discovery of other computers running Vista	UDP 3702 TCP 5357 TCP 5358
For network discovery of computers running Windows XP, as well as file and printer sharing for both Vista and Windows XP	UDP 137 UDP 138 TCP 139 TCP 445
For network discovery of network devices	UDP 1900 TCP 2869

Table 6-1.   Resource Sharing Ports Managed by the Windows Firewall

The File Sharing feature is turned off by default. For domain network locations (domain member workstations), File Sharing is managed by Group Policy. To turn File Sharing on:

1. In the Sharing And Discovery section of the Network And Sharing Center window, click the down arrow next to File Sharing.

2. Within the File Sharing settings area, select Turn On File Sharing, and then click Apply.

After enabling file sharing, you then must configure each folder that you wish to share. Chapter 7 has more details on how to share files and devices.

Public Folder Sharing   Vista provides a quick and easy way for all users that log on to a workstation to share files. Although it can be administratively disabled, by default, each installation of Vista includes a folder named "Public" that resides in the Users container. The Public folder is configured to enable all interactive, or locally logged on, users to read and write to a shared repository. By sharing it, the public folders and all of the folders within it are automatically shared.

Sharing files through the Public folder does not replace traditional file sharing. You can always share files directly from any folder on the workstation without copying or moving them to the Public folder (provided that file sharing is enabled). This method gives you more control over who you share files with on your network. It allows you to select people on an individual basis and set the level of sharing permissions for each person.

The Public folder (which is shown in Figure 6-6) contains no files by default. Any user who logs on locally can add files. The Public folder contains several subfolders to organize files, including:

▼   Public Documents

■   Public Downloads

■   Public Music

■   Public Pictures

▲   Public Videos

As a shared storage area, no one should store files in the Public folder that they do not wish others to see. The Public folder is a good place for any file you want to share with the people who have given access to it. Settings for sharing the Public folder are shown in Figure 6-7.

You can control who will have access to the Public folder. You can also set the level of access by choosing between the three options:

▼   Turn On Sharing So Anyone With Network Access Can Open Files

■   Turn On Sharing So Anyone With Network Access Can Open, Change, And Create Files

▲   Turn Off Sharing (People Logged On To This Computer Can Still Access This Folder)

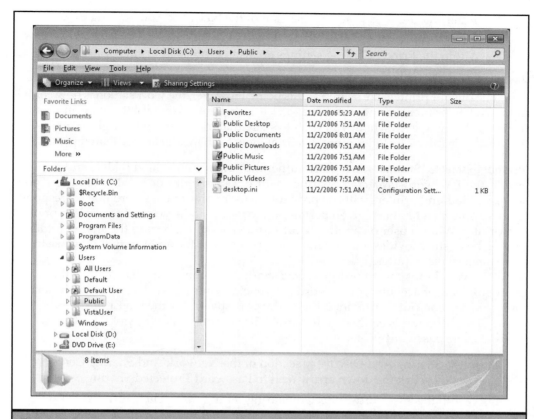

Figure 6-6. Public folder sharing gives you the option to share files quickly and simply.

Printer Sharing Until the Printer Sharing feature is enabled, no local printers can be shared. By enabling it, any personal or workgroup printers that are attached directly to the Vista workstation can be accessed by any user on your network. To enable printer sharing:

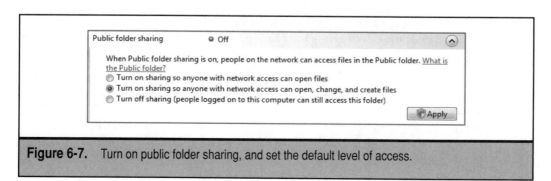

Figure 6-7. Turn on public folder sharing, and set the default level of access.

1. In the Sharing And Discovery section of the Network And Sharing Center window, click the down arrow next to Printer Sharing.

2. Within the Printer Sharing settings area, click Turn On Printer Sharing, and then click Apply.

None of your printers are shared at this point. However, the workstation is now configured to allow printer sharing. You have to visit each printer you wish to share and configure it, establishing with whom you wish to share the printer and what rights you wish to give them. Chapter 7 includes more details on how to share and access shared printers.

Password-Protected Sharing   To require authentication to your shared folders and printers, enable the Password-Protected Sharing feature. Users will not be able to access your shared folders and printers without providing a user name or password that corresponds to an account that has been given permission to view, modify, or add to a folder or print to a printer. When a user on another workstation tries to connect to the shared folder or printer, he or she provides a user name and password of the account that they use to log on to their own computer.

When you disable password-protected sharing, the computer sharing the folder does not require a user account or password. Anyone on your network can access the shared folders of the computer (provided the folder was shared for the Guest or Everyone account). This behavior is equivalent to simple file sharing in Windows XP.

To disable password-protected sharing:

1. In the Sharing And Discovery section of the Network And Sharing Center window, click the down arrow next to Password-Protected Sharing.

2. Within the Password-Protected Sharing settings area, click Turn Off Password-Protected Sharing, and then click Apply.

Media Sharing   Sharing music, video, and pictures may be appropriate for a workstation. You can stream these items from your workstation to devices that are connected to the wired or wireless home network. You may have a library of presentations for any number of business functions, such as product demonstrations, sales presentations, or other training. Windows Media Player 11 is specially enhanced to navigate media sharing on the Vista platform. By default, the Media Sharing feature is disabled in all network locations. To enable it:

1. In the Sharing And Discovery section of the Network And Sharing Center window, click the down arrow next to Media Sharing. This is shown in Figure 6-8.

2. Within the Media Sharing settings area, click Change.

3. In the new Media Sharing window that opens, select the Share My Media With check box, and click OK. Another new window opens, with any media player devices available on your network that can potentially access your files. Media player devices can be any workstation, personal digital assistant (PDA), or other handheld device with Windows Media Player 11 installed and configured accordingly.

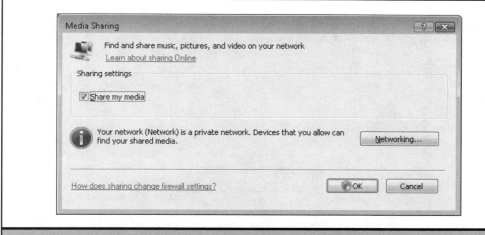

Figure 6-8.   Windows Vista allows you to select whether you will share media content.

4. Among the items that appear in the box, select those that you wish to share media with, and click the Allow button. This is shown in Figure 6-9.

5. You can be more specific about what you would like to share by clicking the Customize button. You can choose to share only pictures, video, or music files. By selecting the Allow New Devices And Computers Automatically check box, you will open your media to all users on any network you may join. The types of media you can share are shown in Figure 6-10.

In addition to computers on your network, media devices attached to computers or the network will be able to access your content. Vista warns you about this, as Figure 6-11 shows.

You can share nearly any digital media file in your Media Player library, including protected Windows Media files that you have downloaded from online stores. To share a file in your library, the original file must be stored in one of your monitored folders (by default, the folders where digital media files are stored, including the My Music, My Pictures, and My Videos folders). For information about monitored folders, see Windows Media Player Help. In addition, the file must be of one of the following types:

▼ Music files, such as Windows Media Audio (.wma), MP3 (.mp3), and WAV (.wav) files. Note that audio CDs that are inserted into your workstation cannot be shared.

■ Video files, such as Windows Media Video (.wmv), AVI (.avi), MPEG-1 (.mpeg, .mpg), and MPEG-2 (.mpeg, .mpg) files. Note that DVD-video discs that are inserted into your workstation cannot be shared.

Figure 6-9.   You can select with whom you will share media content.

- ■ Picture files, such as JPEG (.jpeg, .jpg), portable network graphics (.png), and Windows Media Photo (.wpd) files.
- ▲ Playlists, such as Windows Media playlist (.wpl) and MP3 playlist (.m3u) files.

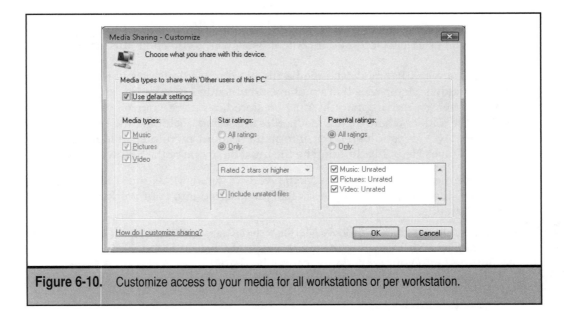

Figure 6-10.   Customize access to your media for all workstations or per workstation.

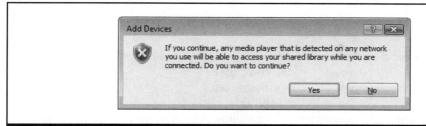

Figure 6-11. Allow computers to automatically access your media only after careful consideration of the security implications.

Depending on how your computer is configured, Media Player might be able to share other music, video, and picture file types in addition to those listed here.

Windows Vista makes the process of configuring common network access and sharing tasks simple through its Sharing And Discovery settings area. The relevant settings are described in Table 6-2, along with their options.

At the bottom of the Network And Discovery section of the dialog box are two links that allow you to see which folders you are sharing on the network and all shared network folders that are on the computer (see Figure 6-12).

Tasks

In the leftmost pane of the Network And Sharing dialog box is a list of tasks that can be performed. We've already discussed a few of these tasks in Chapter 5—connect to a network, set up a connection or network, and manage network connections—but we'll touch on them a bit more in this section. However, there are a couple of other tasks that we haven't talked about yet.

By clicking Windows Firewall at the bottom of the pane, you can manage your computer's firewall settings. Clicking that link brings up a screen like the one shown in Figure 6-13.

To change the firewall's configuration, click the Change Settings link, and the resulting dialog box appears like the one shown in Figure 6-14.

By clicking Block, Windows Firewall blocks all access to the network, and you cannot access other computers on the network or the Internet. Likewise, no other computers will be able to access your computer.

You can unblock the computer by clicking Allow. This sets the computer's firewall to a normal configuration. In this mode, you can access other computers on the network or the Internet. Likewise, other computers can access your computer.

NOTE Windows Firewall can be configured from the Network And Sharing Center by clicking View Sharing Settings. This opens the Windows Firewall dialog box, which you can use to manage its configuration.

Setting	Description	Options
Network Discovery	When this setting is turned on, the computer can see other devices on the network, and this computer will be visible to other devices.	On or off.
File Sharing	When this setting is turned on, files and printers that you have designated as sharable will be available on the network.	On or off.
Public Folder Sharing	When turned on, people on the network can access files in the Public folder.	Turn on sharing so that anyone with network access can open files, change, or create files. Turn off sharing (anyone logged on to the computer can still access files).
Printer Sharing	When turned on, people connected to the network can access printers connected to this computer.	On or off.
Password-Protected Sharing	When turned on, only people with a user account on this computer can access shared files, printers attached to the computer, and the Public folder.	On or off.
Media Sharing	When turned on, others connected to the network can access shared music, pictures, and video, and this computer can find those types of files on the network.	On or off. If this setting has not already been configured, Vista will ask you whether you want to share your media and with whom you want to share it, as explained earlier.

Table 6-2. Network And Sharing Center Settings

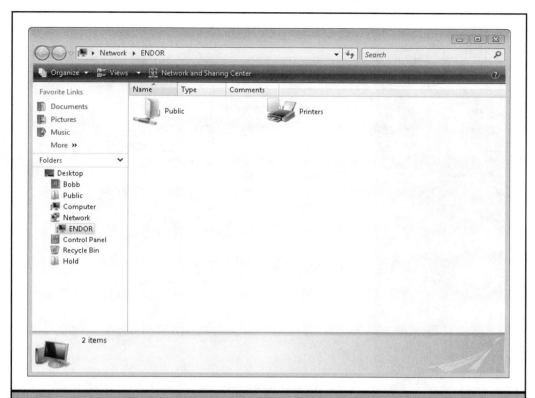

Figure 6-12. In the Network And Discovery area of the Network and Sharing dialog box, you can see which folders and printers are shared by your computer.

Troubleshooting

When your computer is disconnected from a network, the Network And Sharing Center shows an X through the connection. This is an obvious way of letting you know that you aren't connected to the Internet or a network.

To fix this problem, you start troubleshooting as you would with any other type of network—check network cables and wireless adapters. If they are appropriately plugged in, click Diagnose And Repair in the left pane to start the new Windows Network Diagnostics Tool, as shown in Figure 6-15.

This tool provides step-by-step instructions to fix your networking problem. For example, Figure 6-16 shows a window telling the user to connect a network cable to the network adapter. Once you plug in the cable and click the Diagnostics button, the tool will complete the repair. If the tool still detects a problem, it will continue troubleshooting the connection. Ideally, however, you'll see a message that the problem has been fixed.

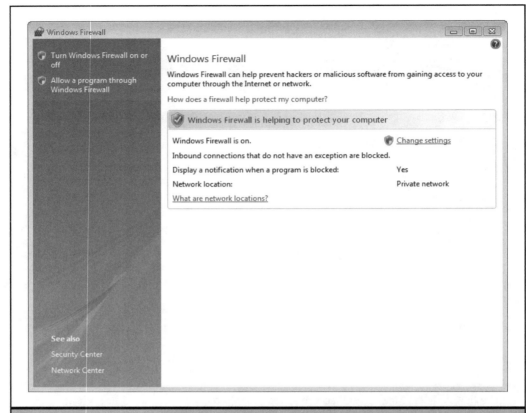

Figure 6-13. Windows Firewall settings can be managed from the Tasks pane on the Network and Sharing dialog box.

Managing Networks

Computers and devices in your network can be examined in the Network Center by clicking Browse The Network in the left pane. Depending on the type of network you have (domain or workgroup), your interaction will vary:

▼ If yours is an Active Directory domain, options in the Network View toolbar allow you to search Active Directory, connect to a domain, or return to Network Center.

▲ If yours is a workgroup, options in the Network View toolbar allow you to connect to a network or return to the Network Center.

Double-clicking a computer while browsing a network will allow you to see devices associated with the computer, like printers, external hard drives, and so forth.

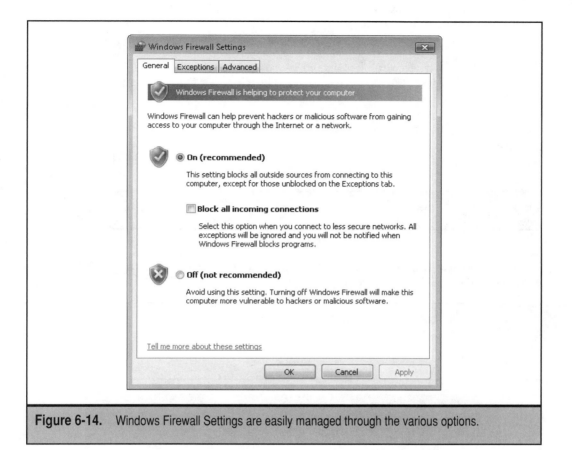

Figure 6-14. Windows Firewall Settings are easily managed through the various options.

Network connections can be created in the Network Center by clicking Connect To in the left pane and then clicking Create A New Connection in the Connect To A Network dialog box. This opens the Connect To A Network Wizard, which is shown in Figure 6-17.

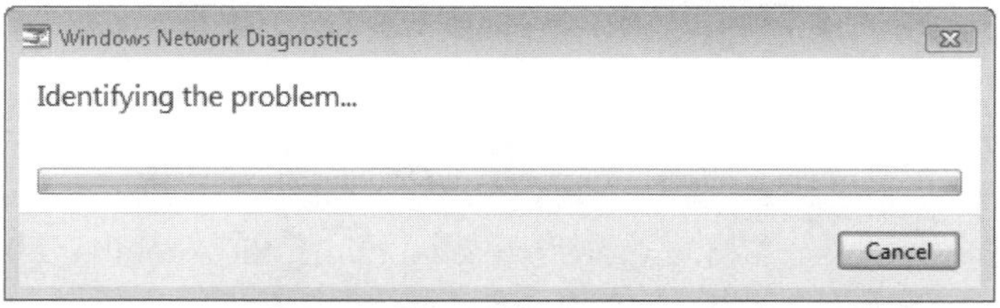

Figure 6-15. The Windows Network Diagnostics tool scans your computer to determine what's wrong with your network connection.

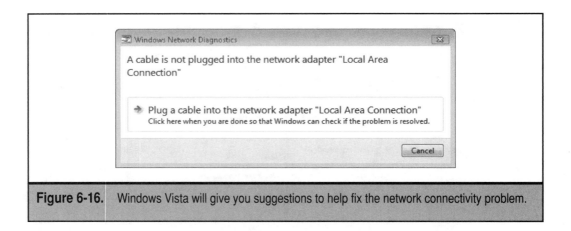

Figure 6-16.   Windows Vista will give you suggestions to help fix the network connectivity problem.

This wizard is used to add a network, create virtual private network (VPN) connections, or make a dial-up connection.

NOTE   For more detail on forming these connections, see Chapter 5.

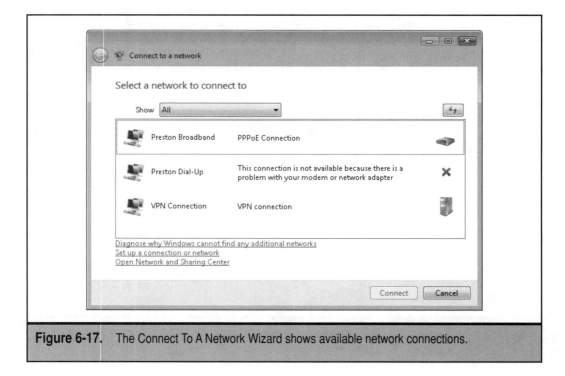

Figure 6-17.   The Connect To A Network Wizard shows available network connections.

Network Connections

Connecting to a network in a new location creates a new network profile. Vista will automatically save this new network connection and settings, and will use them the next time you connect to this network.

Depending on how your computer is configured, there might be different ways in which you want to connect to the network. For instance, you might want to connect wirelessly, or you might have multiple network interface cards (NICs) installed but want to use a specific NIC for connection. You can configure which devices and connections are to be associated with the network.

1. Click Start and then click Control Panel.

2. In Control Panel, under the Network And Internet area, click View Network Status And Tasks.

3. If you have a working connection to the network, click the Customize link above the Network Details section of the dialog box.

4. The Set Network Location dialog box gives details about the network to which you're currently connected. This is shown in Figure 6-18.

5. The Network text box shows the name of the profile associated with the network. You can change it by typing a new name.

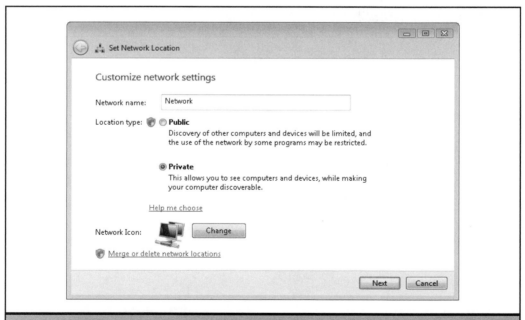

Figure 6-18.   The Set Network Location dialog box offers many details that can be customized for a network connection.

6. The Location Type options indicate the category of the network. This is either public or private.

7. The Network Icon shows the current icon selected for the connection. You can change the icon by clicking the Change button next to this setting.

8. Click OK to close the Set Network Location dialog box.

Customization

The Set Network Location dialog box allows you to customize a network connection to meet your specific needs. It doesn't really sound like an earth-shattering achievement, but the idea behind it was to help people who are connecting to various wireless networks. This allows you to assign a specific name to each wireless network that you might connect to, rather than having to use whatever name is part of the network's Service Set Identification (SSID). For example, consider the laptop user in Figure 6-19.

NOTE If you're connecting to a "hidden" wireless network that is not broadcasting an SSID, this is a way to indicate—at least to yourself—which network it is.

As you can see from the example, there are five different networks to which our user, Kip, can connect. A couple of these don't really concern him; the rest have names that make sense to the network administrator or to the administrator's overall naming plan, but they aren't meaningful to Kip. As such, Kip can personalize the connection names in Network Details to make them relevant.

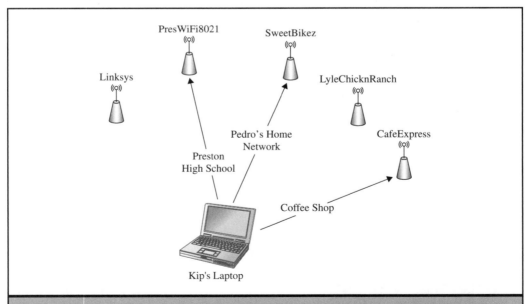

Figure 6-19. Users can give available wireless networks their own names to make the connections more meaningful.

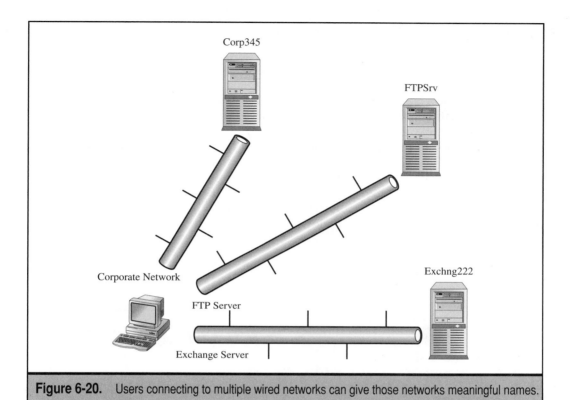

Figure 6-20.   Users connecting to multiple wired networks can give those networks meaningful names.

Now, instead of names like PresWiFi8021, SweetBikez, and CafeExpress, Kip can re-name them to be more readily understandable, like Preston High School, Pedro's Home Network, and Coffee Shop.

But the Personalize feature isn't just for wireless networks—it's also for wired connections. This isn't too crucial of a feature for computers with just one network connection, but laptop users or those who have more than one network to which they can connect will find this feature useful.

For example, consider the user in Figure 6-20. His workplace uses three networks to which he connects at various times during the day. The convenience of Vista, however, keeps him from having to remember which network is which. By giving the networks his own names, it's easier to keep track of what he's doing.

WIRELESS NETWORK CONFIGURATION

We touched on connecting to a wireless network in Chapter 5, but let's take a closer, more in-depth look at configuring a Windows Vista wireless network. This section looks at two ways you can configure your wireless connection: through the Connect To A Network dialog box and using the **netsh** command on the command line.

The Connect To A Network Dialog Box

The way most wireless local area networks (LANs) are configured is through the Connect To A Network dialog box. This is the standard, point-and-click way to configure such a connection. The dialog box can be called up in a number of ways, but for the sake of this exercise, click Start and select Connect To. This displays the Connect To A Network dialog box, which is used to select a wireless network to which you'll connect. An example is shown in Figure 6-21.

The dialog box is a somewhat retooled version of the wireless network dialog box from Windows XP Service Pack 2 (SP2). This dialog box not only handles wireless connections, but also VPN and dial-up connections.

To connect to a listed network, simply double-click its relevant icon.

If the network you wish to connect to is not listed, click Set Up A Connection Or Network, and Vista will display a dialog box. There are several options from which you can choose, including:

▼   Connect to the Internet

■   Set up a wireless router or access point

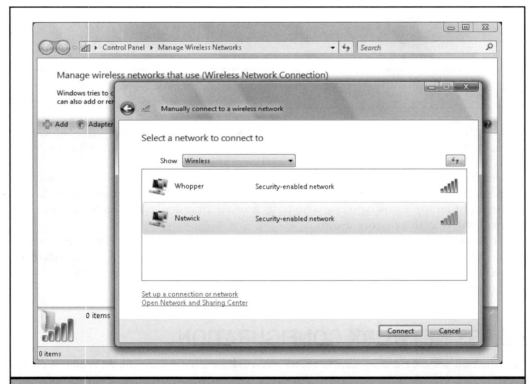

Figure 6-21.   The Connect To A Network dialog box allows you to select the wireless network to which you'll connect.

- Manually connect to a wireless network
- Set up a wireless ad hoc (computer-to-computer) network
- Set up a dial-up connection
- ▲ Connect to a workplace

So, not only can you configure wireless connections, but other types as well. For more information on these other types of connections, see Chapter 5.

Manual Configuration

To manually configure a wireless connection, click Manually Connect To A Wireless Network, and then click Next. The resulting dialog box looks like the one shown in Figure 6-22.

Vista asks you various questions about the wireless network's configuration settings. The settings and requested information is listed in Table 6-3.

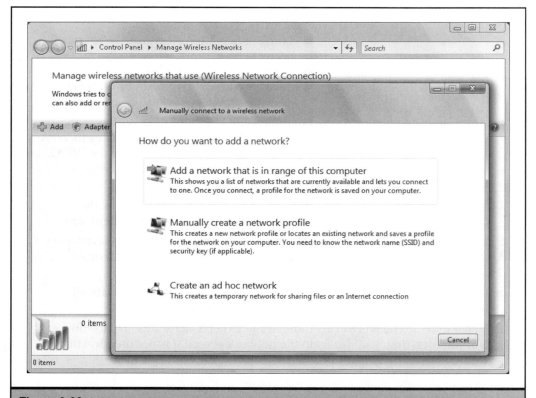

Figure 6-22.   Connecting manually to a wireless network requires you to enter information about it.

Setting	Description
Network Name	Enter the name of the wireless network.
Security Type	Select the type of authentication you want to use to connect to the network. This is shown in Figure 6-23. Choices are: ■ No Authentication (Open) ■ WEP ■ WPA-Personal ■ WPA-Enterprise ■ WPA2-Personal ■ WPA2-Enterprise ■ 802.1x
Encryption Type	Select which method should be used to encrypt data sent over the network. The choices will depend on your security type. You can choose from: ■ None (when No Authentication is your security type) ■ WEP (when WEP is the security type) ■ TKIP or AES (when a form of WPA is the security type)
Security Key/Passphrase	Enter the WEP key (assuming WEP was chosen as the security type), the preshared key (if WPA-Personal was the security type), or the WPA2 preshared key (if you picked WPA2-Personal as the security type).
Display Characters	Indicates whether you want to view the security key characters as they are entered.
Save This Network For All Users Of This Computer/Save This Network For Me Only	Indicates whether this profile will be available for all users on the computer or just the current user.
Start This Connection Automatically	Indicates whether Vista will automatically connect to this network.
Connect Even If The Network Is Not Broadcasting	Indicates whether Vista should try to connect to the network even if it is not broadcasting its name.

Table 6-3.   Configurable Settings for a Wireless Network

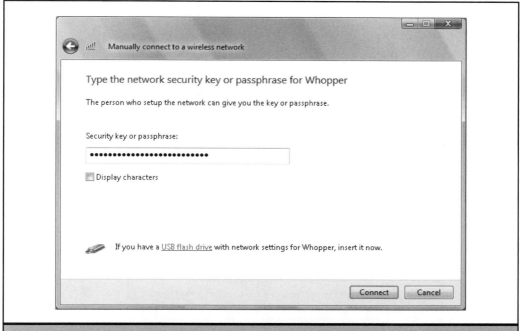

Figure 6-23.   Depending on the type of security your network is using, you'll need the appropriate key or passphrase.

Connecting to the Network

You can connect to the network that you just configured by clicking Connect To and then double-clicking the network's icon in the Connect To A Network dialog box. Once the connection has been created, you can manage it right-clicking the connection icon and selecting Properties. You'll see a properties box like the one shown in Figure 6-24.

In this box, you can select:

▼   The Connection tab   This allows you to view the wireless network's name, SSID, network type (access point for infrastructure networks or computer-to-computer for ad hoc networks), and availability. You can also opt to automatically connect when the network is in range, connect to a more preferred network, or connect if the network is not broadcasting. This tab is shown in Figure 6-25.

▲   The Security tab   This allows you to manage the security settings that were detailed in Table 6-3. This tab is shown in Figure 6-26.

You can manage your wireless networks from the Manage Wireless Networks dialog box, as shown in Figure 6-27.

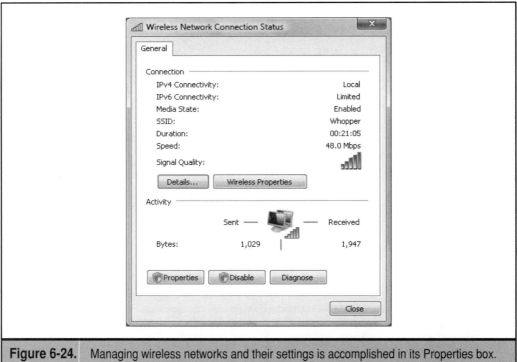

Figure 6-24. Managing wireless networks and their settings is accomplished in its Properties box.

To display this dialog box:

1. Click Start.
2. Click Control Panel.
3. Click Manage Wireless Networks.

This dialog box allows you to add and remove wireless networks and manage the properties of a connection.

COMMAND LINE

In addition to the very visual, easy-to-follow interface provided by the Vista graphical user interface (GUI), you can configure clients using the command line. Netsh—short for network shell—is a utility that was provided with Windows 2000 and XP. It allows for local or remote configuration of network settings. Netsh is commonly used to reset the TCP/IP stack to default settings that are known to be good.

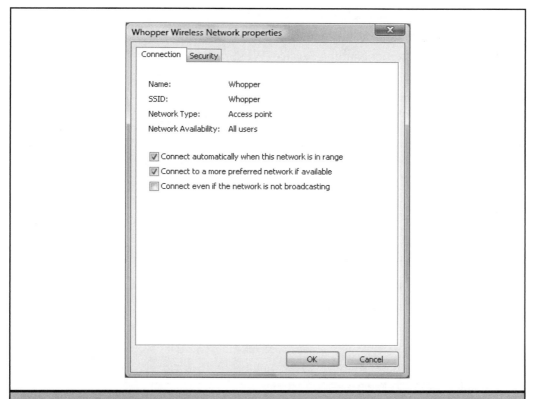

Figure 6-25.   The Connection tab shows various connection details and allows you to manage them.

Netsh

Netsh is a powerful networking tool, but Window's flashier GUI brother seems to get more of the action than this frumpy command-line tool.

NOTE   You can also use Netsh to connect remotely to other systems by using the –r parameter.

Contexts

Netsh is used in different *contexts*. Contexts are specific areas within the network that can be managed by Netsh. Commands are context-sensitive, and the same command can exist in different contexts. As such, it's important to know which context you're working in. Contexts include:

▼   Dynamic Host Configuration Protocol (DHCP) server administration

■   LANs

■ Wireless local area networks (WLANs)

■ Routing and administrations

▲ Windows Internet Naming Service (WINS)

Netsh is a big topic, and not one we can cover in its entirety here. For the sake of our discussion, we're going to talk about two specific contexts: LAN (for wired networks) and WLAN (for wireless networks).

It's important to know that each context can have a subcontext. For example, the interface context includes these subcontexts:

▼ ip

■ ipv6

▲ portproxy

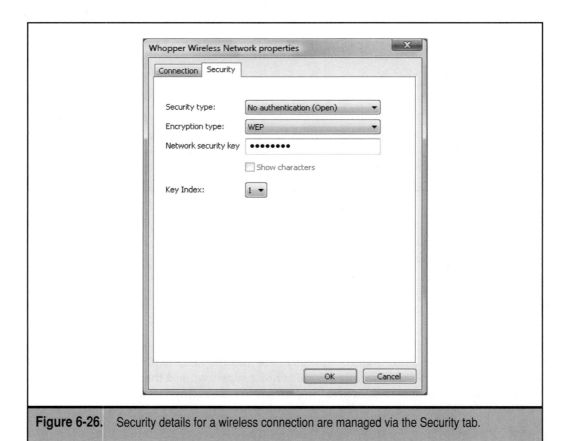

Figure 6-26. Security details for a wireless connection are managed via the Security tab.

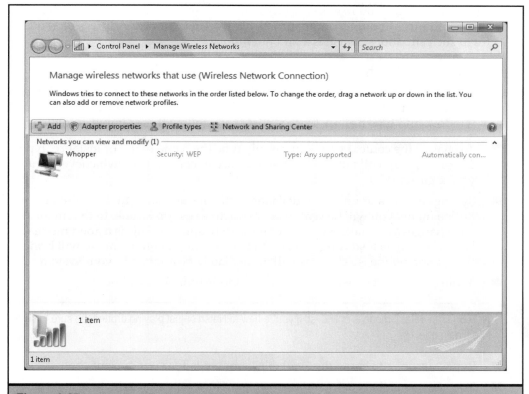

Figure 6-27.   The Manage Wireless Networks dialog box helps you manage your wireless networks and gives at-a-glance information.

The point is that it is important to know which context you're working in so that you aren't issuing commands that are harming your system's configuration.

TCP/IP

Netsh can be used to make dynamic IP address changes from a static IP address to DHCP by importing a file. Netsh can also bring about the complete configuration, including:

- ▼   TCP/IP address
- ■   DNS settings
- ■   WINS settings
- ▲   IP aliases

This is helpful when you're working on different networks, some with DHCP servers, and others without. Although Automatic Private Internet Protocol Addressing (APIPA) is useful in such situations, Netsh is a far better tool.

Getting Around Netsh

Getting around Netsh can seem daunting, but there are some easy, basic rules that will help you once you understand them. Starting Netsh is easy—just open the command prompt window, and type `netsh`. Once you're there, follow these simple guidelines:

▼ To change the context you're in, simply type the name of it. For instance, typing `interface ip` will take you to the interface ip context from whichever context you're currently in.

■ Typing `offline` or `online` will change what mode you're in. If you're in offline mode, you will be sent to an interactive session offline. In that mode, any changes you make won't be immediately applied. This is a good mode to be in if you're just starting to learn Netsh. Working in online mode will bring the session online, so changes will immediately be applied to your system.

■ Typing `show mode` displays the current mode (online or offline).

NOTE   The default mode is online, so if you're new to Netsh or just playing around, be sure to switch to offline mode.

■ Type `?` or `help` to show the available commands for your current context.

■ You can use global commands anywhere. These commands include `online`, `offline`, and `quit`.

▲ Within a context, typing **set** and **show** displays context-sensitive command options.

Wired

To use Netsh to manage your wired network connections, enter the **netsh** LAN context.

1. Click Start.
2. Click Run.
3. Type `cmd` and then click OK to open a command prompt window.
4. Type `netsh` and then press ENTER.
5. Type `lan` and then press ENTER.

Once you're in this context, you can use the commands listed in Table 6-4 to manage your wired connection.

Command	Description	Syntax	Usage Examples
?	Displays a list of commands or parameters	*CommandName*/?	? add /?
Add	Adds a profile to the specified interface on the computer	add profile filename= *PathAndProfileName*interface=*InterfaceName*	add profile filename=C:\ configfiles\ "lanprofile.xml" interface="LAN Connection"
Delete	Removes a LAN profile from the computer interface	delete profile interface=*InterfaceName*	delete profile interface="LAN Connection"
Dump	Creates and saves a script containing the current configuration	dump >*PathAndFileName*	dump >C:\configfiles\ lanconfig.txt
Export	Saves LAN profiles as XML files	export profile folder=*PathAndFileName* [[interface=]*InterfaceName*]	export profile folder=C:\configfiles\ interface="Local Area Connection" export profile folder=C:\configfiles\
Help	Shows a list of commands	*CommandName*help	Add profile help
Reconnect	Reconnects to the network	reconnect[[interface=] *InterfaceName*]	reconnect interface="LAN Connection"
Set	Sets wired configuration	set autoconfig enabled= {yes | no}interface=*InterfaceName*	set autoconfig enabled=yes interface="LAN Connection"

Table 6-4.   Netsh Commands for a Wired Network

Command	Description	Syntax	Usage Examples
Show	Displays information for various settings	show interfaces show profiles[[interface =]*InterfaceName*] show settings show tracing	show interfaces show profiles interface="LAN Connection" show settings show tracing

Table 6-4. Netsh Commands for a Wired Network *(Continued)*

Wireless

To use Netsh to manage your wireless network connections, enter the netsh WLAN context.

1. Click Start.
2. Click Run.
3. Type cmd and then click OK to open a command prompt window.
4. Type netsh and then press ENTER.
5. Type wlan and then press ENTER.

Once you're in this context, you can use the commands listed in Table 6-5 to manage your wireless connection.

Networking your organization's computers is a crucial way to share information. With Windows Vista, users can access information on the network and on others' computers much more easily than they could with earlier versions of Windows. In addition, Vista introduces some exciting new ways to share information, such as integrated media sharing.

But while simply sharing information is the cornerstone of networking, the next level is actually being able to communicate and collaborate with coworkers. In Chapter 7, we'll show you how your users can collaborate using some tried and true Windows technologies, along with some new items introduced with Vista.

Command	Description	Syntax	Usage Examples
?	Displays a list of commands or parameters	*CommandName* / ?	? add / ?
Add filter	Adds a wireless network to an allowed or blocked list	add filter permission={allo w | block | denyall} ssid=*WirelessNetworkName* networktype={infrastructure | adhoc}	add filter permission=allow ssid="PrestonWiFi" networktype=infrastructure
Add profile	Adds a profile to the specified interface on the computer	add profile filename=*PathAndFileName* [[interface=]*InterfaceName*] [[user=]{all | current}]	add profile filename=C:\configfiles\"wlanprofile1.xml" Interface="Wireless Network Adapter"
Connect	Connects to a wireless network	connect[[ssid=]*SSIDName*] name=*ProfileName*interface= *InterfaceName*	connect ssid=PrestonWiFi name=Kip
Delete filter	Removes a wireless network from an allowed or blocked list	delete filter permission= {allow | block | denyall} ssid= *WirelessNetworkName*networkt ype={infrastructure | adhoc}]	delete filter permission=allow ssid=PrestonWiFi networktype=infrastructure

Table 6-5. Netsh Commands for Wireless Networks

Command	Description	Syntax	Usage Examples
Delete profile	Removes a LAN profile from the computer interface	delete profile name=*ProfileName* [[interface =]*InterfaceName*]	delete profile name="Kip" interface="WLAN Connection"
Disconnect	Disconnects from a wireless network	disconnect interface=*InterfaceName*	disconnect interface="WLAN Connection"
Dump	Creates and saves a script containing the current configuration	dump >*PathAndFileName*	dump >C:\configfiles\wlanconfig.txt
Export	Saves LAN profiles as XML files	export profile folder=*PathAndFileName* [[name=]*ProfileName*] [[interf ace=]*InterfaceName*]	export profile folder=C:\profiles name="Kip" interface="WLAN Connection"
Help	Shows a list of commands	*CommandName*help	Add profile help

Table 6-5.   Netsh Commands for Wireless Networks *(Continued)*

Command	Description	Syntax	Usage Examples
Set	Sets configuration on interfaces	set autoconfig enabled={yes|no} interface=*InterfaceName*	set autoconfig enabled=yes interface="WLAN Connection"
		set blockednetworks display={show|hide}	set blockednetworks display=show
		set profileorder name=*Profile Name*interface=*InterfaceName* priority=*integer*	set profileorder name="Kip" interface="WLAN Connection" priority=1
		set tracing [[mode=]{yes|no |persistent]]	set tracing mode=persistent
Show	Displays information for various settings	show all	show all
		show autoconfig	show autoconfig
		show blockednetworks	show blockednetworks
		show drivers[[interface=]*Inte rfaceName*]	show drivers interface="WLAN Connection"
		show filters[[permission=]{al low|block}]	show filters permission=allow
		show interfaces	show interfaces
		show networks[[inte rface=]*InterfaceName*] [[mode=]{ssid|bssid}]	show networks interface="WLAN Connection"
		show profiles[[name=]*Profil eName*] [[interface=]*Interface Name*]	show profiles name= "Kip" interface="WLAN Connection"
		show settings	show settings
		show tracing	show tracing

Table 6-5.   Netsh Commands for Wireless Networks *(Continued)*

CHAPTER 7

Collaboration and Communication

At its core, networking is a convenient way to share files among people in your organization. It could be as simple as pulling a Word document from a shared folder. It could be the ability to send an e-mail to someone else in your company. That basic functionality is nice, but Microsoft aims to make the network even more useful with a number of communication and collaboration tools.

In this chapter we take a look at the communication and collaboration tools that are new and improved in Windows Vista. For example, where basic networking provides the ability for different people to look at the same file, Windows Vista supplies the tools that allow you to view a file—along with a half dozen other members of your team—each one making changes to the document while the others watch.

In addition to the tools that Vista provides, we'll take a look at some of the new server products that Microsoft is introducing, which promise to keep your network communicating, collaborating, and productive.

SHARING NETWORK RESOURCES

Like previous Microsoft operating systems, Vista enables you to share files, folders, and printers. In Vista, you will find a new Network And Sharing Center (accessed from the Control Panel). Like the Network Setup Wizard found in Windows XP, Vista's Network And Sharing Center provides you with a master switch for turning sharing of all sorts on and off. You need to have sharing enabled and the right ports open on the Windows Firewall, and you can make both of those actions happen from the Network And Sharing Center.

Authorization Using NTFS and Share Permissions

When you share resources, whether files, folders, or printers, you need to pay attention to two sets of security configurations. First, you should review the New Technology File System (NTFS) permissions that are assigned to the resource you are sharing. NTFS access control lists (ACLs) are the best way to manage authorization, setting the level of access per security group and per account. To view and adjust NTFS permissions, right-click the file or folder of interest, and choose Properties from the pop-up menu; then select the Security tab at the top of the properties window. You have a great many options for configuring access in the default security window, and you can click the Advanced button (as shown in Figure 7-1) for even more granular options.

The other way that security is applied to a shared resource is through the share itself. In addition to the NTFS permissions, you can configure share permissions that will authenticate a user. Regardless of what a user is authorized to access in NTFS permissions, a user will not have access to anything, unless the share itself is configured to authenticate the user. You can modify share permissions remotely if you have been granted full control (which administrators have by default). For other users, you must modify permissions using an account that is logged on locally and has full control over the resource. To modify a share, right-click the resource and select Share from the pop-up menu. Click Change Sharing Permissions and then choose an account or group to add or remove, and click Add. You can set the account's access using the toggle in the Permissions column.

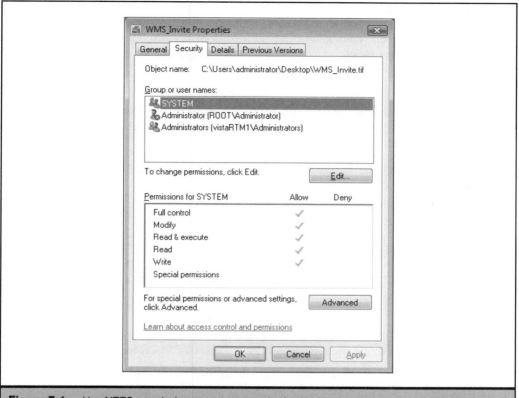

Figure 7-1.   Use NTFS permissions to manage authorization levels.

You have a few options when setting permissions:

▼ **Reader**   Allows the user or group to view resources

■ **Contributor**   Allows the user or group to view and add resources

■ **Co-Owner**   Allows the user or group to view, add, and edit resources

▲ **Remove**   Removes the user or group from the permissions set, disabling explicit access to shared resources

After adding a user or group and configuring permissions in the Permissions column, click the Share button at the bottom of the share window when finished.

NOTE   Leave the default share permissions in place in most cases. NTFS should be the primary way in which you manage authorization for any resource.

You can share your files with all the users across your network or with selected users on the same computer. When sharing files from your local computer, you have two options. You can share from Vista's default public folders or from another folder anywhere on your hard disk drive.

Public Folders

To share files on a network, one Vista-only option is to copy or move the files that you want to share into your Public folder (similar to the Shared Documents folder in Windows XP). To access the Public folder on your computer:

1. From the Start menu, open the Documents folder. If only the Favorite Links are displayed, click the Folders button.

2. On the left "folder" pane, scroll down to almost the bottom of the list of components and folders, and then click the Public folder icon in the navigation pane to display all subfolders within the Public folder on your computer. This is shown in Figure 7-2.

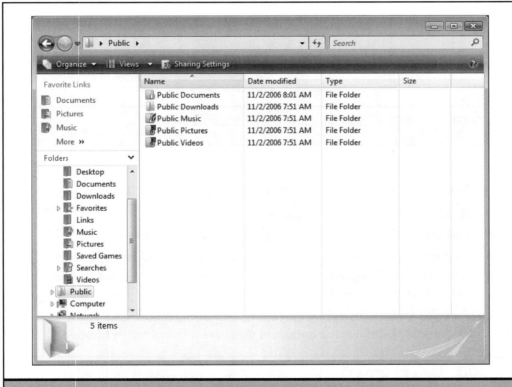

Figure 7-2. Use Vista's Public folder to quickly share files.

Vista creates six default subfolders within your Public folder: Public Documents, Public Downloads, Public Music, Public Pictures, and Public Videos. You can enable sharing of these public folders using the Network And Sharing Center applet in Control Panel. Once you open the applet, find the Sharing And Discovery section in the center of the window. Note the status for sharing files, printers, media, and public folder sharing. Turn on any sharing features you need.

Once you turn sharing on, Vista automatically configures the Windows Firewall for you. The ports needed to pass sharing traffic are enabled automatically. When activating public folder sharing, Vista also sets sharing permissions on your public folders. By default, the Everyone group is given read permissions and the local Administrators group is given full-control permissions. This is a good best-practice–based approach to permissioning shares, but if you want to change them, navigate through Computer\ %SystemDrive%\Users and right-click the Public folder. Select Sharing from the pop-up menu, and configure them according to your needs.

NOTE We will cover Windows Firewall in more detail in Chapter 10. However, you should be aware that enabling file and printer sharing will automatically configure Windows Firewall to open several services and their associated ports. These include ICMP (ping), NetBIOS (UDP 137 and 138, TCP 139), SMB (TCP 445), and RPC (dynamic endpoint mapper).

Step-by-Step Sharing

The next sections walk you through the exact steps you can take to share resources in Vista.

Share a File or Folder Using Public Folders

1. From the Start menu, open the Documents folder.

2. Copy or move your file or folder into one of the sub-folders.

3. Your file or folder will inherit share permissions from the Public folder. To adjust share permissions, right-click the file or folder, and select Sharing. A new window opens, giving you the choice to adjust sharing or stop sharing. Click Change Sharing Permissions, and update the share permissions as necessary. This is shown in Figure 7-3.

NOTE You must be a member of the Administrators or Power Users group to adjust share permissions for public folders.

Share a File, Folder, or Drive Using Windows Explorer

1. Open Windows Explorer by clicking Start and selecting Explorer from the top of the Start menu.

2. Once the new Windows Explorer window opens, navigate to the shared file, folder, or drive to which you want to add a new share.

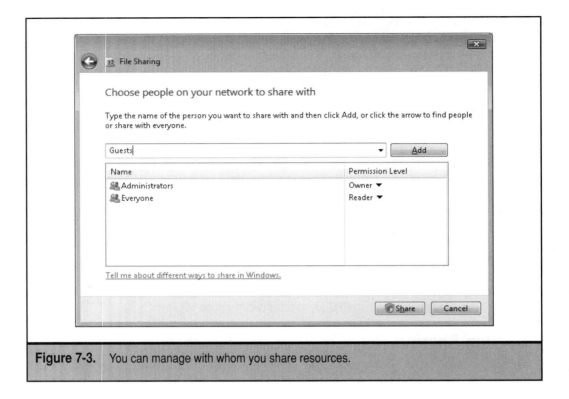

Figure 7-3. You can manage with whom you share resources.

If you are logged on to a domain, do the following:

1. Right-click the shared folder or drive, and then click Share.

2. Click Share This Folder.

3. Set any other options that you need, and then click OK.

If you are not logged on to a domain, do the following:

1. Right-click the shared folder or drive, and then click Properties.

2. On the Sharing tab, click Share This Folder On The Network.

3. Set any other options that you want, and then click OK.

Share a File, Folder, or Drive Using a Command Line

1. Open a command prompt, click Start and type **cmd** into the search box at the bottom of the Start menu. Then press the RETURN or ENTER key.

2. In the command window, type the **net share** command into the prompt. The syntax is:

```
net share [Share Drive Letter]: [Share Path]
```

For example:

```
net share Z: \\192.168.0.50\Public
```

> **NOTE**   To view the complete syntax for this command, at a command prompt window, type:
>
> ```
> help share
> ```

You can use public folders to manage shared resources on both local and re-mote computers. Windows Explorer and the command line allow you to manage shared resources on your local computer only.

You can hide a shared resource from users by typing $ as the last character of the shared resource name. Users can map a drive to this shared resource, but they cannot see the shared resource when they browse to it in Windows Explorer or in My Computer, or when they use the net view command on the remote computer.

Share Encrypted Files

You can share encrypted files with other users and between computers. To do so, you need to add the other user's encryption certificate to your local store of cer-tificates.

1. First, have the other user export his or her Encrypting File System (EFS) certificate using the Certificate Manager:

   a. Open the Certificate Manager by typing **certmgr.msc** into the Search field in the Start menu.

   b. Click the arrow next to the personal folder to expand it, and then select the EFS certificate you wish to export.

   c. Select the user's certificate, click the Action menu, point to All Tasks, and then click Export. (You can also right-click the certificate and choose All Tasks from the context menu, as shown in Figure 7-4.)

   d. In the Export Wizard, click Next and then click Next again to confirm the default option: No, Do Not Export The Private Key.

   e. On the Export File Format page, click Next to accept the default format (DER encoded binary X.509).

   f. Provide a file name and path for your new certificate file, and click Finish.

2. Second, after acquiring the file (through e-mail or a USB flash drive), import the certificate into your local store:

   a. Open Certificate Manager by typing **certmgr.msc** into the Search field in the Start menu.

   b. Select the Personal folder, and click the Action menu.

   c. Point to All Tasks, and click Import.

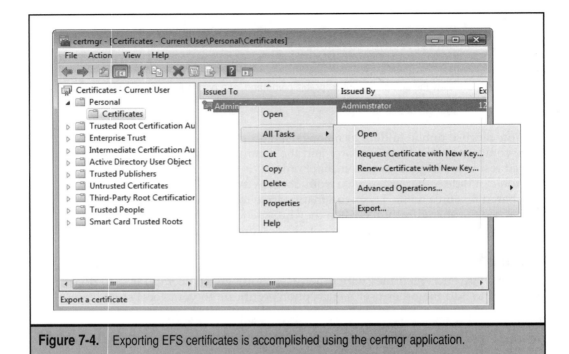

Figure 7-4. Exporting EFS certificates is accomplished using the certmgr application.

    d. In the Certificate Import Wizard, click Next.

    e. Type the location of the file to import, and click Next.

    f. Type the certificate owner's password, and click Next.

    g. Click Place All Certificates In The Following Store, browse to Trusted People, and then click Next.

3. Add the other user's certificate that you have stored locally to the encrypted file:

    a. Right-click the encrypted file that you want to share, and choose Properties from the context menu.

    b. In the General tab of the Properties window, click Advanced.

    c. In the Advanced Attributes dialog box, click the Details button.

    d. In the Details dialog box, click the Add button.

Share Encrypted Files Between Two Computers

If you want to use your encrypted files on two computers, you need to first export the EFS certificate and related key on the computer that contains your encrypted files, and then import them to the computer to which you want to add the files.

1. From the other user's computer, export the user's private key:

    a. Open Certificate Manager by typing `certmgr.msc` into the Search field in the Start menu.

    b. Select the Personal folder.

    c. Click the Action menu, point to All Tasks, and then click Export.

    d. In the Certificate Export Wizard, click Next.

    e. Click Yes, export the private key, and then click Next.

    f. Click Personal Information Exchange, and then click Next.

    g. Type the password you want to use, confirm it, and then click Next.

    h. The export process creates a file to store the certificate in. Type a name for the file and the location.

    i. Click Finish.

2. Import the other user's private key:

    a. Click the arrow next to the Personal folder to expand it.

    b. Click the Action menu, point to All Tasks, and click Import.

    c. In the Certificate Import Wizard, click Next.

    d. Type the location of the file that contains the certificate; or click Browse, navigate to the file's location, and then click Next.

    e. If you navigate to the right location but don't see the certificate you are importing, in the list next to the File Name box, click Personal Information Exchange.

    f. Type the password, select the Mark This Key As Exportable check box, and then click Next.

    g. Click Place All Certificates In The Following Store, choose Personal, and then click Next.

Sharing Printers

To share your locally attached printers (printers attached directly to your workstation by a cable), you can turn printer sharing on in the Network And Sharing Center applet in Control Panel.

NOTE   If you have no printers attached, or if the printer is unplugged, the sharing dialog box will be grayed out.

1. Click the Start button, and select the Network option from the Start menu.

2. Click the Network And Sharing Center icon.

3. Under Printer Sharing, click the down arrow button to expand the section, click Turn On Printer Sharing, and then click the Apply button. Your printers are now shared.

Enabling printer sharing through the Network And Sharing Center is a quick way to open access to your locally attached printer. To get more control over how the printer is shared by setting permissions and management access, you need to use one of the printer management tools, including the Print Management Console.

Print Management Console

The Print Management Console is a centralized printer management center. It is a snap-in available for the Microsoft Management Console (MMC). It enables you to install, view, and manage all of the printers in your organization from any computer running the latest server (Windows Server 2003 R2 and above) and the Vista operating system. You can use the Print Management Console on a Windows XP workstation, although some of the functionality is disabled.

To open the console, click the Start menu and select Control Panel. Choose System And Maintenance, then Administrative Tools, and then click Print Management. The Print Management Console is shown in Figure 7-5.

Configuration

The Print Management Console provides up-to-the-minute details about the status of printers and print servers on the network. You can use it to install printer connections to a group of client computers simultaneously. The console can help you find printers that have an error condition by using filters. It can also send e-mail notifications or run scripts when a printer or print server needs attention. On printer models that provide a Web page, the Print Management Console has access to more data, such as toner and paper levels, which you can manage from remote locations, if needed.

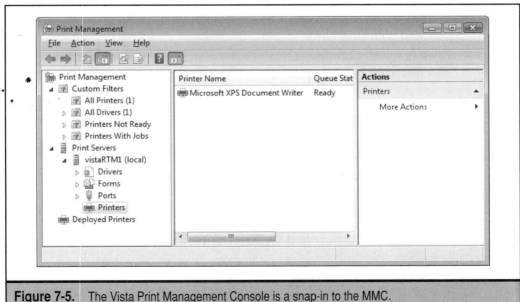

Figure 7-5. The Vista Print Management Console is a snap-in to the MMC.

To configure sharing for a printer using the Print Management Console:

1. Open the Print Management Console by clicking Start menu, selecting Control Panel, selecting System And Maintenance, selecting Administrator Tools, and then clicking Print Management.

2. In the tree in the left pane, locate and expand the Print Server node by clicking the arrow next to it.

3. From the print servers that appear in the Print Server node, locate your workstation, and click on the arrow next to it to expand the print modules for your workstation.

4. Locate and click the Printers node among the print modules for your workstation. Note the installed printers that appear in the center pane.

5. Select the printer for which you wish to manage share permissions, and right-click it.

6. From the pop-up menu, select Manage Sharing, and configure the permissions much like you would for file and folder permissions.

PEOPLE NEAR ME

While sitting in a conference room, disconnected from your network, with People Near Me (PNM), you can connect to other workstations in the room to share applications without entering Internet Protocol (IP) addresses or computer names. PNM is a new capability of Vista's peer-to-peer (P2P) functionality that allows users to dynamically discover other users, their published PNM-capable applications, and easily invite users into a collaboration activity without core IP infrastructure services, such as Domain Name System (DNS) and Dynamic Host Configuration Protocol (DHCP). For all that it does, it is remarkably easy to set up. To open PNM:

NOTE   People Near Me shows up directly in the Control Panel in the classic view.

1. Click the Start button, select Control Panel, click Network And Internet, and then click People Near Me.

2. Edit the name that is automatically entered in the Type The Name You Want Other People To See text box.

3. If you don't want Vista to sign you into PNM each time you start the computer, make sure that the Sign Me In Automatically When Windows Starts check box is cleared.

4. Select the Include My Picture When Sending Invitations check box, if desired.

5. Click Trusted Contacts on the Allow Invitations From drop-down list if you wish to restrict participants to trusted contacts.

6. Select the Sign Me In Automatically When Windows Starts check box, if it is not already checked.

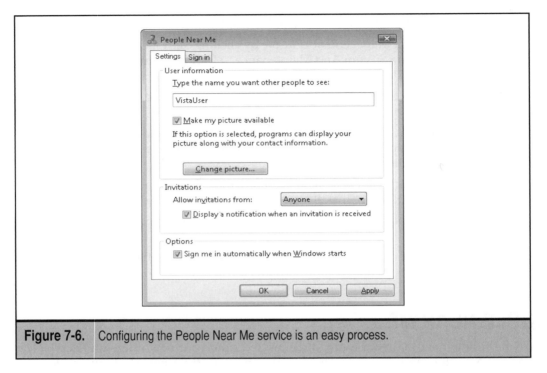

Figure 7-6. Configuring the People Near Me service is an easy process.

7. After reviewing your choices to set up PNM, click the Sign In tab, click Sign In To People Near Me, and then click OK. If you are prompted for an administrator password or confirmation, type the password or provide confirmation. The confirmation dialog box is shown in Figure 7-6.

8. If this is the first time that you are signing in to People Near Me, you'll see an additional dialog box. In that dialog box, shown in Figure 7-7, click OK.

After setup, PNM remains in a passive state. When receiving a Windows Meeting Space invitation while disconnected from your local area network (LAN), PNM launches an application on the invited user's computer, and the two workstations can begin participating in a collaboration activity, such as chatting, file sharing, or even gaming.

WINDOWS MAIL

Windows Mail is an e-mail and newsgroup client that replaces Outlook Express. Why are we including a discussion of it in a chapter on collaboration tools, rather than in a chapter about Internet tools? One of the big architectural changes to the component is that it is no longer considered part of Internet Explorer.

NOTE Since Windows Mail is not a component of Internet Explorer, it will not work on earlier versions of Windows, and is not going to be included with Windows Server "Longhorn."

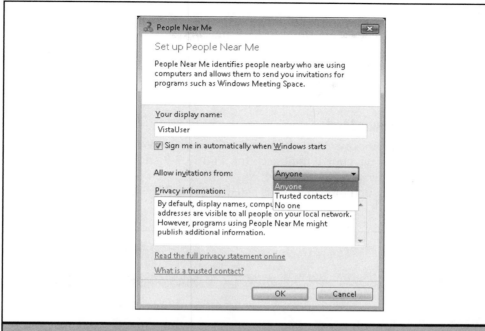

Figure 7-7. Setting up the People Near Me service indicates how you will be seen to others.

Windows Mail shares a lot of common functionality with Outlook Express. However, you'll see differences in the iconography, which has been changed to fit in with Vista's overall theme. Also, Windows Mail features the reading pane on the right that you'll recognize from Outlook 2003. But, again, the most important changes aren't the ones that step up and slap you in the face. Functional changes include:

▼ Mail messages are now stored as individual files. In Outlook Express, they were stored as a single, large, database file. A transactional index database allows for real-time searching. If the database becomes corrupted, the indexes can be rebuilt from the mail files.

■ Account information is no longer stored in the registry. It is stored next to the mail, which makes it possible to copy a Windows Mail configuration and mail store in a single step.

■ Junk mail and phishing filers. Windows Mail uses Microsoft's SmartScreen technology to filter junk e-mail and keep it out of your Inbox.

■ Top-level domain and encoding blocking.

▲ Microsoft Help Groups have been added. These are preconfigured links to Microsoft's newsgroups.

Using Windows Mail

To start Windows Mail, click Start, point to All Programs, and then click Windows Mail. Figure 7-8 shows the basic Windows Mail interface.

When you start Windows Mail for the first time, you need to configure it for your personal settings. Once this is done, you can use it to send and receive e-mail, as well as to browse Microsoft's Help newsgroups.

Configuring Windows Mail

When you start using Windows Mail, the Internet Connection Wizard takes you through the process of configuring your e-mail account. Figure 7-9 shows where you need to enter that information.

You'll need to enter such information as listed in Table 7-1.

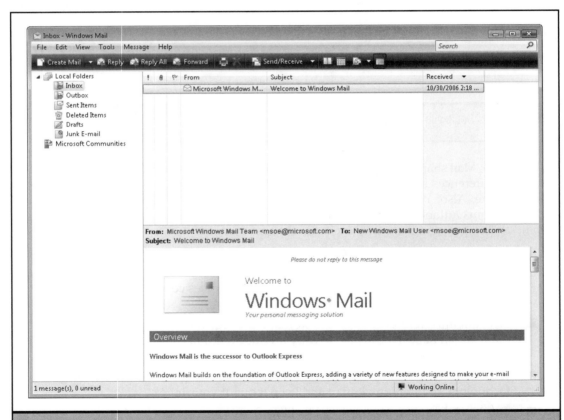

Figure 7-8. Windows Mail has a similar look to Outlook Express.

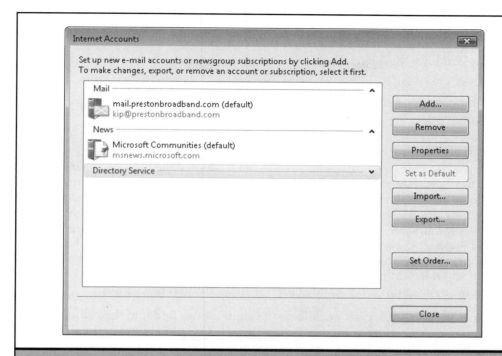

Figure 7-9. The Internet Connection Wizard guides you through the process of e-mail configuration.

Required Information	Example
Display Name	Kip Dynamite
E-mail Address	kip@prestonbroadband.com
Incoming Mail Server Name	mail.prestonbroadband.com
Outgoing Mail Server Name	smtp.prestonbroadband.com
E-mail User Name And Password	Kdynamite L@wf0nd@h

Table 7-1. Information Required by the Internet Connection Wizard

There may come a time when you need to change e-mail account settings. This is a simple enough process.

1. In Windows Mail, click Tools and then click Accounts.

2. Under the Mail heading, click your account and then click Properties.

3. You can now change e-mail account settings, such as user information, server information, and type of connection.

Help Newsgroups

Microsoft has had help newsgroups for a while, but it was a challenge for some users. First, they had to know they were there. Second, they had to know how to configure Outlook Express to take them there. Microsoft has given users a little nudge with Windows Mail, preconfiguring the newsgroups so that users have somewhere to go and get help.

The newsgroups are useful if you are having trouble with your computer and the Help And Support Center doesn't have the information you need. You can browse the newsgroups, and, chances are, someone else has already had the same problem, posted a message about it, and got help. Before you can access those newsgroups, you need to configure the newsgroup service and subscribe to the desired newsgroups.

1. In Windows Mail, click the Microsoft Communities folder in the Folders view.

2. If this is the first time you've accessed the Microsoft Communities, you'll see a Windows Mail dialog box, stating that you've not subscribed to any newsgroups (see Figure 7-10). Click Yes to see a list of available newsgroups.

3. Windows Mail will connect to the Internet to download a list of available newsgroups. The available newsgroups are then displayed in the Newsgroup Subscriptions dialog box.

4. To subscribe to a newsgroup, click the newsgroup on the All tab, and then click the Subscribe button.

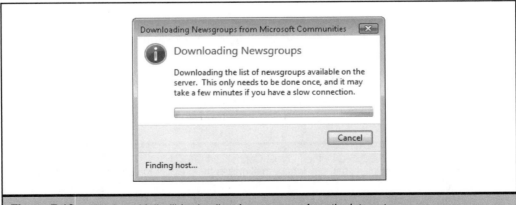

Figure 7-10. Windows Mail will fetch a list of newsgroups from the Internet.

When you've decided newsgroups you want to subscribe to, they are listed in the Folders view under the Microsoft Help Groups folder. Just double-click the newsgroup, and you can access it. You can also access newsgroups through the Subscribed tab in the Newsgroup Subscriptions dialog box. Once subscribed, you can search for answers to your questions or ask questions of your own.

> **NOTE**   Just who is answering the questions posted on the Microsoft Help newsgroups? Usually, it's a Most Valuable Professional (MVP). The MVP program was developed by Microsoft to identify people who actively participate in online communities to share their knowledge with others. You can find out more about the MVP program at mvp.support.microsoft.com.

Searching Your E-mail

It's no secret that the ability to search is a huge component of Windows Vista. It's part of the Start menu and on every Explorer window. It's everywhere, including Windows Mail.

You can use the Search box to scour your messages for specific correspondence containing the text you've entered. The Search feature will match complete or partial words in both the message header and body. As such, the complete text of your messages is searched, including the From, To, Subject, and Sent fields.

To start a search:

1. Click in the Search box.
2. Type your search text.

In Figure 7-11, we searched e-mails for the word "election." It returned two results: an e-mail with an address containing "election" and an e-mail with "election" in the subject line.

Matches are returned as you type. If you want to search newsgroups, select the Newsgroups folder, and then start your search.

Contacts

While Windows Mail allows you to create e-mail messages for contact and create new contacts, the Contacts window allows you to create and manage individual contacts or groups of contacts.

To open the Contacts window, click Start, point to All Programs, and click Contacts. The Contacts window is shown in Figure 7-12.

Contacts and contact groups are stored in the *%UserProfile%\Contacts* folder. Like e-mail messages, which are their own unique files, contacts are also stored in individual contact files. Groups are stored in .group files.

> **NOTE**   Storing contacts separately from e-mail makes them easier to use with other programs. For instance, if you use Outlook and Windows Mail, both programs can use the same set of contacts without having to import them into one or the other program.

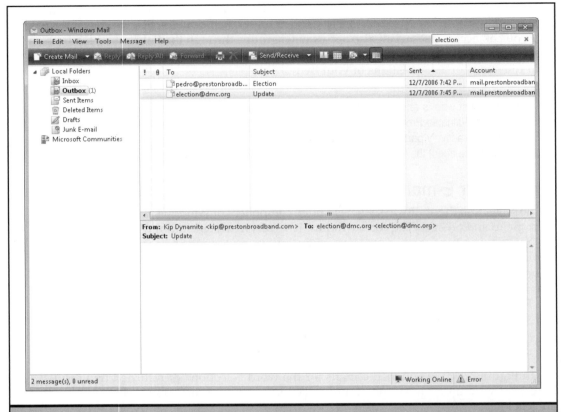

Figure 7-11. Windows Mail allows you to easily search your mail folders for messages.

You can create a new contact or contact group by clicking New Contact or New Contact Group. These dialog boxes are shown in Figures 7-13 and 7-14, respectively.

To edit contacts and groups:

1. Open the Contacts window.
2. Double-click the contact entry to display a Properties dialog box.
3. Make the necessary changes in the Properties dialog box.
4. Click OK.

WINDOWS CALENDAR

New to Windows Vista is Windows Calendar. As its name suggests, it is a calendar application used for managing appointments and tasks. There are enough third-party calendars to go around, and certainly the same sort of functionality can be found in Outlook.

Figure 7-12.   Individual and group contacts are managed in the Contacts window.

However, its inclusion in Windows Vista allows you similar functionality but without having to buy a server product or configuring it on a large scale. It's also a nice feature for organizations where a user wants a scheduling tool but the organization doesn't want to spend extra money on such a tool.

Using Windows Calendar

Windows Calendar can be used to manage appointments and tasks using personal and shared calendars. The application also allows you to create multiple calendars for different people or different tasks. These calendars can then be published and shared with others.

To start Windows Calendar:

1. Click Start and then point to All Programs.
2. Click Windows Calendar.

Figure 7-15 shows the Windows Calendar interface.

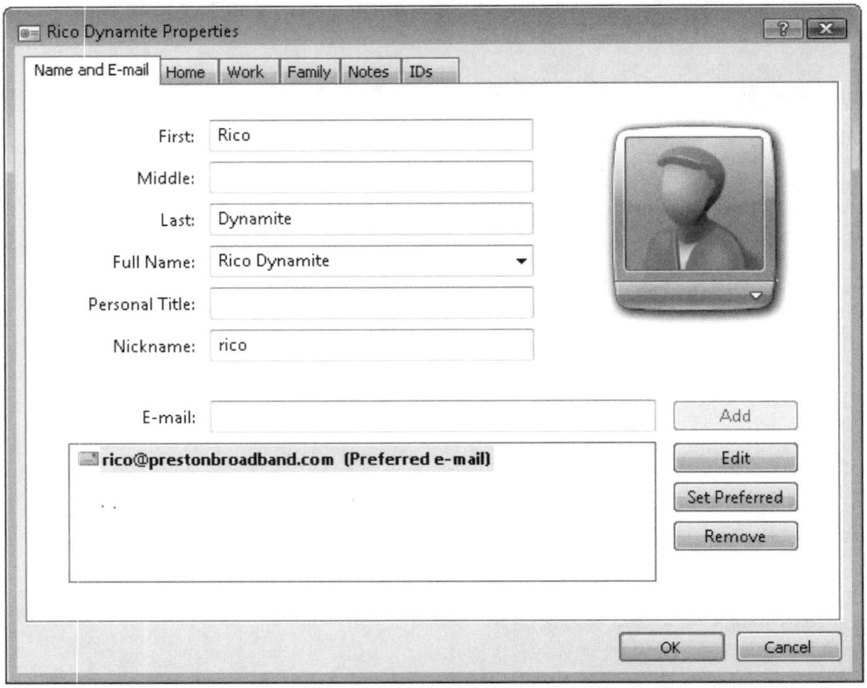

Figure 7-13. A dialog box asks for various pieces of information for a new contact.

Calendars, appointments, and tasks are color-coded so that you can quickly distinguish one person's appointments and tasks from another. It is also possible to quickly access someone else's calendar and for others to access your calendar. To see another's calendar, ask him or her to publish it so that you can subscribe to it. Conversely, if you want to share your calendar with others, you need only publish it. We'll explain how to publish calendars—along with performing other features—later in this section.

Searching the Calendar

Remember the Search feature in Windows Explorer, Windows Mail, and the Start menu? Well, Windows Calendar has a Search feature, too. You can use the Search box to look for appointments and tasks containing the text you've entered. The Search feature matches partial or complete words in the details for the appointment or task in all of the calendars which you've created and to which you've subscribed.

To perform a search:

1. Click in the Search box.

2. Type your search text.

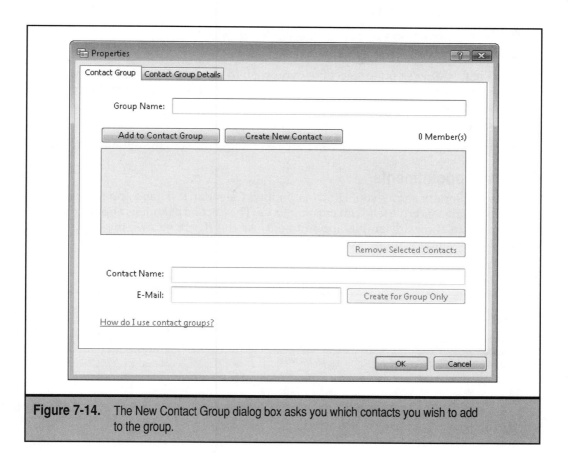

Figure 7-14.   The New Contact Group dialog box asks you which contacts you wish to add to the group.

Matches are returned as you type; they become more specific the more characters and words you enter.

Once an item you are interested in appears in the search results, double-click that item. Windows Calendar displays the calendar view and item details.

Working with Calendar

The toolbar in the main Calendar window is used to navigate the calendar, change views, and perform various tasks. The toolbar is shown in the illustration. The buttons are:

- ▼   **New Appointment**   Creates a new appointment in a calendar
- ■   **New Task**   Creates a new task in a calendar

■ **Today**   Accesses the current date in the calendar

■ **Delete**   Deletes the currently selected entry

■ **View**   Allows you to select how you wish to view the calendar: by day, work week, week, or month. This button also includes options for hiding or displaying the navigation and the details panes.

■ **Subscribe**   Manages the calendar subscriptions

▲ **Print**   Prints appointments on the calendar according to the options you select

Creating Appointments

There are two sorts of entries you'll find in Windows Calendar: tasks and appointments. The next section will concern itself with creating tasks. This section examines appointments.

Figure 7-16 shows a sample appointment. As the figure shows, the appointment includes a title and location.

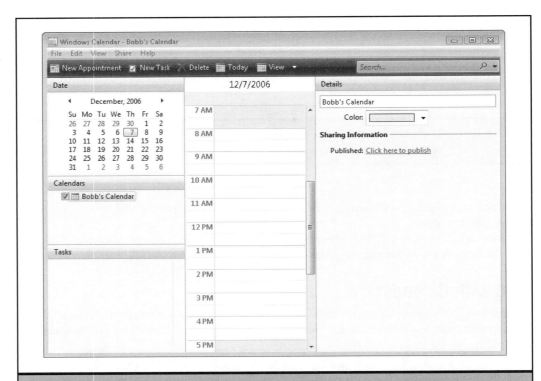

Figure 7-15.   Windows Calendar provides the ability to organize and share your schedule.

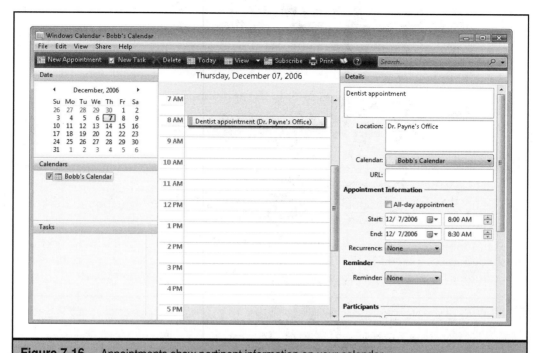

Figure 7-16. Appointments show pertinent information on your calendar.

When you create an appointment, you can indicate start and end times. Alternately, you can indicate that it runs all day. As with other calendar applications, you can also:

▼ Indicate whether an appointment repeats daily, weekly, monthly, or yearly

■ Set alarms so that you are notified prior to an appointment

■ List and invite other attendees

▲ Add notes to an appointment

To create an appointment:

1. Start Windows Calendar.

2. Under the Calendars section, select the calendar you want to work with.

3. In the Day or Week view, right-click the date and time of the appointment, and then select New Appointment from the context menu.

4. If you'd rather work in the Month view, right-click the date on which the appointment occurs, and then select New Appointment from the context menu.

5. Click the Details button in the Day, Week, or Month view on the right.

6. In the text box at the top of the details pane, type a title for the appointment.

7. In the Location text box, type the location for the appointment.

8. Use the Appointment Information options to set the start and end times for the appointment.

9. If your new appointment should repeat, set the relevant repeat options.

10. If you want to be reminded prior to the appointment, use the Reminder options.

11. If you want to specify participants, click the Attendees button. You can select the contacts or contact groups you want.

12. If you want to send invitations to attendees, click Invite. You will then be able to send an e-mail message to the attendees.

13. If you want to add notes to the appointment, type this information in the boxes provided under the Notes heading.

The appointments you've created on your calendar or calendars to which you've subscribed are displayed in the Day, Week, and Month views. If the details pane is hidden, double-clicking an appointment displays the details of the appointment.

NOTE If you are working with multiple calendars, it's a good idea to use color-coding to help you distinguish between calendars. Clicking a calendar under the Calendars heading allows you to indicate what color to associate with the calendar.

Tasks

The second type of information tracked in Windows Calendar is tasks. Tasks are listed under the Tasks heading, as shown in Figure 7-17.

Tasks have two states:

▼ **Open** An open task has not yet been completed.

▲ **Completed** A completed task has been finished.

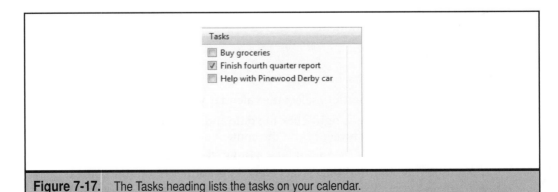

Figure 7-17. The Tasks heading lists the tasks on your calendar.

When you create a task, you indicate a priority level to quantify how important it is. Windows Calendar also allows you to:

▼ Specify a start date.

■ Specify a due date for the task's completion.

■ Add reminders to let you know that a given task is coming up or that it needs to be completed soon.

▲ Add notes to the task.

To create a task:

1. Start Windows Calendar.

2. Under the Calendars section, select the calendar you want to work with.

3. Click the New Task button on the toolbar.

4. Click the Details button in the Day, Week, or Month view on the right.

5. If you want to add notes to the task, type them in the boxes under the Notes heading.

6. In the text box at the top of the details pane, type a title for the task.

7. Use the Priority list to indicate the task's priority level.

8. Use the Start options to set the task's start date.

9. Use the Due Date options to indicate the task's completion date.

If you want to be reminded prior to the task's start date, use the Reminder options. A dialog box like the one shown in Figure 7-18 will appear, reminding you of the event.

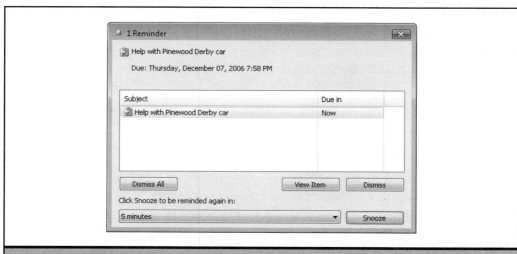

Figure 7-18.   Windows Calendar will remind you when a task is due.

Tasks on your calendar or calendars to which you've subscribed are shown under the Tasks heading. If the details pane is hidden, double-clicking the task shows them.

When a task is completed, you can mark it as such by using the check box under the Tasks heading. In the details pane, select the Completed check box under Task Information.

Managing Multiple Calendars

There may come a time when you decide you need more than one calendar. For example, you might need to break down tasks and appointments based on a project. You might also need a calendar to track personal items. Windows Calendar allows this, and it is easy to set up.

NOTE Windows Calendar allows you to have up to 100 calendars at a time.

To create a new calendar, click File | New | Calendar. Alternately, you can right-click an open area under the Calendars heading and click New | Calendar.

A new calendar entry is added under the Calendars heading. When created, the entry is highlighted so that you can enter a new name for the calendar by typing it in and pressing ENTER.

There are two main properties you can manage in your overall calendar view: title and color. You can edit calendar details by selecting the calendar under the Calendars heading and then displaying the details pane.

Publishing Calendars

The key to collaboration with Windows Calendar is the ability to publish your own calendar. The task sounds more headache-ridden than it really is. In fact, publishing and subscribing to calendars is quite simple.

NOTE Windows Calendar uses Web Distributed Authoring and Versioning (WebDAV) to upload, download, view, and edit. Users need appropriate permissions to access the Web server to perform these tasks. Both Internet Information Services (IIS) 6 and 7 support WebDav.

Any calendars you've created can be published to a folder on a Web server so that they can be easily accessed. To share a folder:

1. Open Windows Calendar.
2. Click the calendar you want to work with under the Calendars heading.
3. If the details pane is hidden, press CTRL+D to display it.
4. Under the Sharing Information heading, select Click Here To Publish.
5. Use the Publish Calendar dialog box to publish the calendar and associated information to a designated folder on a Web server, as shown in Figure 7-19.
6. Click Publish.

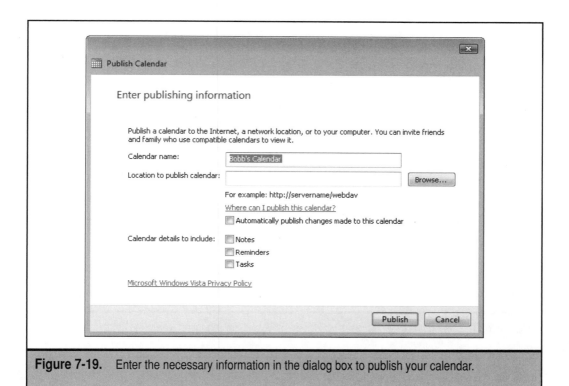

Figure 7-19.   Enter the necessary information in the dialog box to publish your calendar.

Subscribing to a Calendar

Once a calendar has been published, users must subscribe to it in order to view it. To subscribe to a calendar:

1. Open Windows Calendar.
2. Click the Share button on the toolbar, and then click Subscribe. The Subscribe To A Calendar dialog box, shown in Figure 7-20, appears.
3. In the Calendar To Subscribe To text box, enter the Uniform Resource Locator (URL) path to the folder in which the calendar is published—for instance, www.prestonbroadband.com/pedroscalendars.
4. Click Next and then follow the prompts.

WINDOWS MEETING SPACE

Windows 2000 and Windows XP have a desktop sharing and collaboration tool called NetMeeting. In Vista, the distributed desktop sharing tool is known as Windows Meeting Space (WMS). Available in all versions of Vista except for the Starter Edition, WMS is

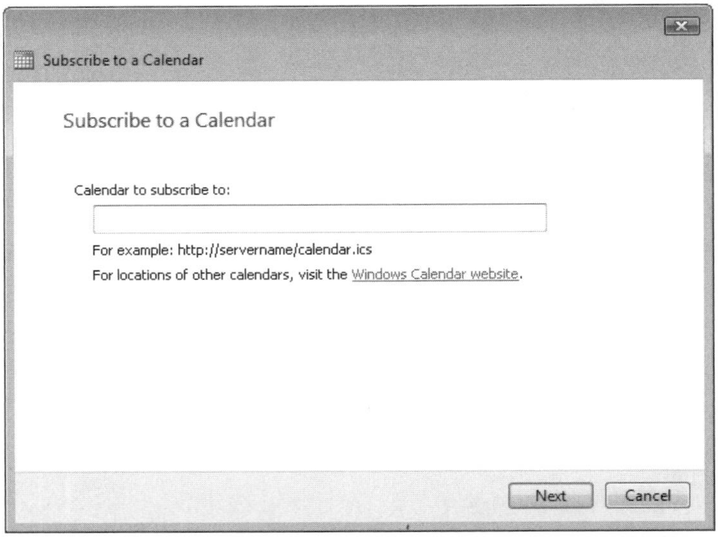

Figure 7-20.   Windows Calendar asks you for the URL path for the folder where the calendar is published.

a new peer-to-peer–based application that allows users to conduct online meetings and collaborate across digital networks. You can share your desktop, including applications, take notes on a shared chalkboard, and co-author documents in real time.

With WMS, you can move to a conference room or a wireless hotspot and collaborate as if you were connected to full network. WMS uses Windows Peer-to-Peer Networking functionality. If you are away from a network, you can connect your workstations directly to each other, either using a wired or a wireless ad hoc network that WMS will activate and manage for you. WMS supports connections for network locations ranging from computer to computer (ad hoc), home, managed/corporate, and Internet. If you do not have network connectivity, you can still create a session if your wireless network card supports computer-to-computer wireless network connections.

Managing connections, invite lists, and other tools make WMS a nifty application. More key features of WMS include:

▼ Organize, invite, and view participants

■ Include local and remote attendees

■ Distribute agendas, attendee lists, notes, and documents

■ View shared presentations

▲ Support unsecured environments (such as customer sites and hotspots) that have no infrastructure by using the Microsoft P2P infrastructure

WMS requires a network connection and a few services, which have to be enabled by an administrator. The required services are:

▼   Distributed File System Replication (DFS Replication) service, which replicates files among multiple PCs, keeping them in sync. This is used by roaming clients to provide high availability and local access across a wide area network (WAN).

■   People Near Me/Peer to Peer Collaboration Foundation

■   Network Projection services

■   Network Connections service

▲   Manages objects in the Network And Dial-up Connections folder, in which you can view both local area network and remote connections

You also need to set up Windows Firewall to allow WMS traffic, if Windows Firewall is enabled. The ports and applications to enable as exceptions include those listed in Table 7-2.

Before launching a WMS session, you will be asked to configure the People Near Me (PNM) service, which is a new Vista option for network infrastructures, including name resolution and IP addressing, without servers. If you intend to use WMS offline from an enterprise network, you may want to configure PNM.

NOTE   For more information on PNM, see the section "People Near Me."

Starting a WMS Session

Starting a WMS session is easy once you have the services up and have either a wired or wireless network connection. To start a session, click the Start menu, click All Programs, and then click Windows Meeting Space. Once WMS opens, select Start A New Meeting. This is shown in Figure 7-21.

Stack	Port
TCP	801, 3587
UDP	1900, 3540, 3702
Application Name	**Application Path**
Network Projection	%SystemRoot%\System32\netproj.exe
P2P Host	%SystemRoot%\System32\p2phost.exe

Table 7-2.   Windows Firewall Configuration Information for Windows Meeting Space

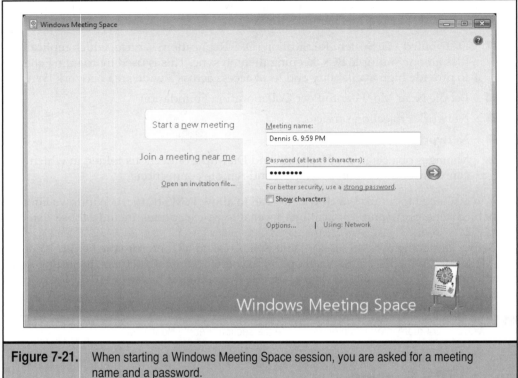

Figure 7-21. When starting a Windows Meeting Space session, you are asked for a meeting name and a password.

Enter a name for the session and a password. The default name is comprised of the user's name and a date stamp. Once a proper password is provided, the gray arrow turns green. Under the Password box, find the line that reads "Options… | Using [network]." Click the Options link to make available the visibility and network options for the WMS session. This is shown in Figure 7-22.

If your WMS session will rely on an ad hoc wireless network, be sure to choose that option. When you create a session, you specify a name and password for it. For wireless sessions, WMS creates a computer-to-computer ad hoc network connection by taking the Service Set Identifier (SSID) from the session name and the Wired Equivalent Privacy (WEP) key from the password you entered. You can also force the application to create a computer-to-computer wireless network connection using the Network Options dialog box on the start page of WMS. The main screen for Windows Meeting Space is shown in Figure 7-23.

Inviting Attendees to a Windows Meeting Space Session

WMS is an invitation-only meeting application. Before anyone joins a WMS session, a connected member has to invite participants. There are a few methods that you can use to invite people to join your session, including file, e-mail, and People Near Me.

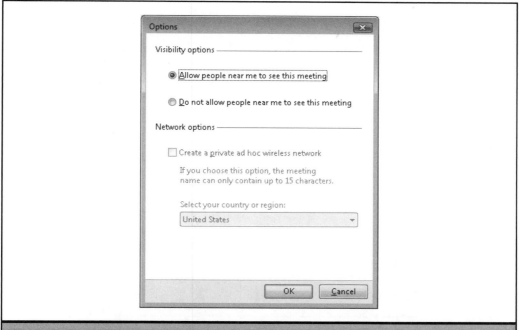

Figure 7-22.   WMS allows you to manage how visible your meeting will be to others on the network.

The WMS feature makes use of People Near Me. This allows signed-on users to publish their presence and view other peoples' presences. Users that are published in the peer-to-peer directory managed by the People Near Me service can be invited to join WMS sessions.

Any user in the session can invite a nearby user by simply launching the Windows Meeting Space invitation dialog box and selecting a user. The dialog box is shown in Figure 7-24. After clicking Send Invitations, the remote user will receive an invitation dialog box. The invitation box allows the user to accept, decline, or dismiss the invitation. To invite someone near you to a Windows Meeting Space session using the People Near Me Directory:

   a.   Click Invite in People Near Me or from the button bar

   b.   Select a person to invite

   c.   Click Send Invitations

If you need to send invitations through e-mail or file sharing, you can click Invite Others and select whether you wish to send the invitation file through e-mail or save it to your hard disk drive. The invitation file has a .wcinv extension. Recipients open the invitation file to join the WMS session.

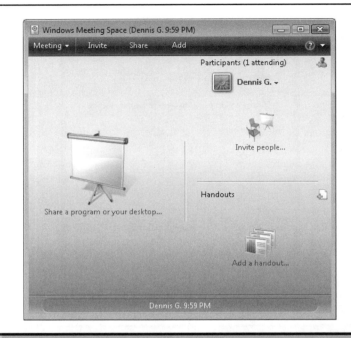

Figure 7-23. When Windows Meeting Space opens, you can manage the content and level of interaction in your meeting.

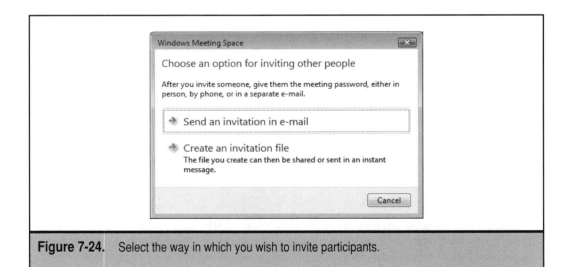

Figure 7-24. Select the way in which you wish to invite participants.

Sharing Resources

Once you have a session and your participants have joined, you can share documents, applications, or your desktop using one of the two following options:

▼ **Share**   To enable participants to view your applications, click the Share button found on the top WMS menu. Alternately, click the projector screen with the label Share A Program Or Your Desktop, and then click what you wish to share. Only currently executing programs and your desktop are available. Click the Share button at the bottom after you make your selection.

■ **Add**   To send documents as handouts to the session participants, click the Add button found on the WMS top menu. Members can make changes to the document one at a time during the session.

▲ **Meeting**   When it is time to stop the session, click on the Meeting button found on the top WMS menu. On the context menu, click Leave Meeting to terminate your session.

Handouts

Before you share a document as a handout, you have to add items to the handouts cache. Click the plus sign on the right side of the handouts pane to open a browser from which you select files you want to add to the handouts cache. To collaborate with your participants, right-click the icon for the file in the Handouts section of your WMS window, click Share To Meeting from the pop-up menu, click the name of the program in the dialog box, and then click OK. As you manipulate your shared file, all members will see your actions.

To hand control of the handout to another participant, click the Give Control icon, located next to the Windows close button in the upper-right corner. You can take control of a shared document by clicking the same icon, which will read Take Control when another member has control.

When finished, click the Options menu in the upper-right area of your screen, choose Show Windows Meeting Space Window in the upper-right corner of the application in which the file is open, and then click the Stop Sharing link in the middle of your WMS window. You can then close the document.

Speech Recognition

Speech recognition is a technology that has yet to reach the mainstream. The Speech Recognition feature in Vista enables you to set up your computer to receive voice commands as well as to dictate text in application programs such as Microsoft Word and Excel. In addition, you can configure the Text To Speech feature, which reads aloud text in dialog boxes when you turn on the narrator function. To start the narrator function, click Start | Control Panel | Ease Of Use, and then click Start Narrator. The resulting dialog box is shown in Figure 7-25.

Before you can use the speech recognition feature to dictate actions to your workstation, you have to get a microphone connected and installed. A unit with headphones

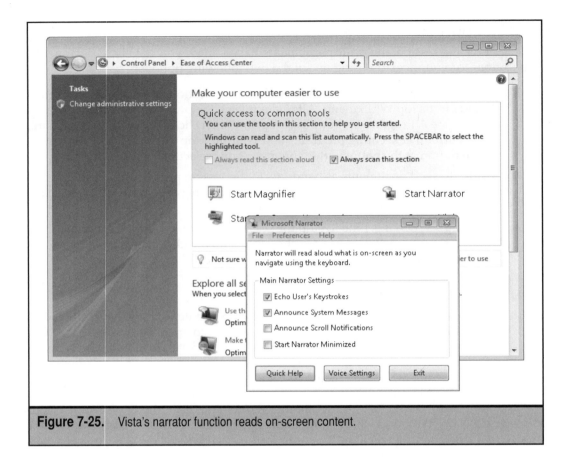

Figure 7-25.   Vista's narrator function reads on-screen content.

may help increase the quality of your experience. Once you have a microphone installed, you can set up the Speech Recognition feature.

1. Open the Speech Recognition window by clicking Start | Control Panel | Ease Of Access | Start Speech Recognition.

2. Click Next and then in the Select The Type Of Microphone You Would Like To Use dialog box, choose the Headset Microphone, Desktop Microphone, or Other option.

3. Click Next and then position your microphone for use. Click Next in the Set Up Your Microphone dialog box.

4. Read the passage into your microphone as requested in a normal voice. Click Next when finished.

If your presentation of the passage qualifies, "The microphone is ready to use with this computer" appears in the Your Microphone Is Now Set Up dialog box. If you see a message indicating that the computer did not hear you very well, click the Back button and read the passage again. Make sure your microphone is connected properly if you have any difficulty. Once the microphone is properly set up, follow these steps:

1. Click Next in the Your Microphone Is Now Set Up dialog box.

2. In the Improve Speech Recognition Accuracy dialog box, click the Enable Document Review option, and then click Next.

3. To learn more about how to use speech recognition, click the topics such as Basics, Top 10 Commands, and Commanding Windows. Vista will display tables of commands for each. Print the command tables using the Print button for reference. Click the Close button in the Windows Help And Support window to close it.

4. Launch the tutorial by clicking the Start Tutorial button. Run the Speech Recognition Tutorial, which is necessary to train the computer to understand your voice and vocabulary.

Vista returns you to the main Speech Recognition window after you finish the Speech Recognition Tutorial. The Speech Recognition toolbar now appears docked in the center at the top of the Windows desktop, with a status of "Sleeping." The toolbar is shown in the illustration.

To move the Speech Recognition toolbar, drag it by clicking and holding down your mouse in any area outside the microphone icon, the level meter, or the Close and Minimize buttons. To reduce the toolbar to an icon in the Windows taskbar, click the Minimize button on the toolbar. Say "Start Listening" into your microphone when you want the Speech Recognition feature to wake up and start listening.

COMMUNICATION TOOLS

While Windows Vista contains some really useful tools for communications and collaboration, Microsoft has even more robust tools that it released right around the same time as Vista. These tools—Outlook, SharePoint, and Exchange—are nothing new to business. However, this section looks at the latest versions of these tools and explains what's new and how they could benefit your Windows Vista environment.

Outlook 2007

While Microsoft Mail and Calendar provide a lot of built-in productivity tools, there are times when your organization needs a broader scope of capabilities. You might consider adding Outlook 2007 to your organization's core application portfolio. If you've used older versions of this software, upgrading to Outlook 2007 can be helpful, especially if you're deploying Windows Vista.

NOTE If you have or will be upgrading to Office 2007, then you'll have Outlook 2007—it's included as one of the tools in the suite of applications.

If you're already using Outlook 2003 or an earlier version, you already know what it has to offer. Microsoft has introduced a number of new features in Outlook 2007, including:

▼ **Instant search**   Users can quickly search through e-mail, e-mail attachments, calendars, contacts, and tasks.

■ **To-do bar**   Your daily priorities are presented in a consolidated view, integrating tasks, flagged e-mails, appointments, and calendar information.

■ **Flagging mail**   Mail can be flagged as tasks in one easy step.

■ **Calendar task integration**   Tasks and flagged mail can be dragged onto the calendar to schedule time to complete them.

■ **Improved interface**   E-mail is easier to respond to, because composing and formatting is more intuitive. Also, a color-coding scheme can help organize tasks.

■ **Attachment preview**   You can preview attachments in the reading pane so that you can see what the attachment is without having to open it.

■ **Scheduling**   Scheduling meetings for large groups is improved by suggesting the best times and locations.

■ **Integration with SharePoint**   You can connect to documents, calendars, contacts, or tasks stored on SharePoint Services sites.

■ **Calendar improvements**   You can easily post or share calendar information through Microsoft Office Online Calendar. These provide a way to share calendar information with those outside of your organization. The calendar overlay mode allows you to manage multiple calendars simultaneously.

■ **RSS integration**   Really Simple Syndication (RSS) feeds are delivered directly to your inbox.

■ **Mobile services**   Outlook can send and receive text and picture messages with mobile phones.

■ **Exchange Server 2007**   Outlook can understand messages of all types, so voice mail and faxes can be delivered to your Inbox.

▲ **Anti-phishing and junk mail**   Phishing and junk mail filtering has been improved.

Exchange Server 2007

The next communication and collaboration tool that will be released around the time of Windows Vista is the latest version of Microsoft Exchange Server. Exchange 2007's main features include e-mail, shared calendars and tasks, and support for mobile and Web-based information access.

Exchange 2007 includes voice mail integration and improved search services for the Web. But probably the biggest change in Exchange 2007 is that is will run only on 64-bit versions of Windows. Microsoft made this decision, citing the performance benefits inherent with a 64-bit system.

NOTE   While a 64-bit system is required to host Exchange Server 2007, clients accessing the server need not be 64-bit clients.

Key improvements to Exchange 2007 include:

▼ **Multifront protection**   Antispam, antivirus, clustering with data replication, improved security, and encryption. This allows information coming in and going out of your organization to be vetted and approved by Exchange 2007 to ensure safety.

■ **Access**   Exchange 2007 includes improved calendaring, unified messaging, improved mobility, and enhanced Web access.

■ **Deployment and performance**   IT professionals will appreciate the server's 64-bit performance and scalability, command-line shell, and improved graphical user interface (GUI). Deployment has also been enhanced with this release.

■ **Exchange Management Shell**   The server features a new command-line shell and scripting language based on the Windows PowerShell language. Shell users can perform all the GUI tasks and can create custom scripts.

■ **Unified messaging**   This feature allows users to receive voice mail, e-mail, and faxes in their Inboxes. Furthermore, users can access their Inboxes from cellular telephones and other wireless gadgets. In addition, voice commands can be used to manage and listen to e-mails over the phone and send basic messages.

■ **Database size**   Database sizes are now only limited by hardware capability.

▲ **Storage group increase**   The maximum number of storage groups and mail databases per server have been increased to five for the Standard Edition (up from one in Exchange 2003) and to 50 for the Enterprise Edition (from four groups and 20 databases in Exchange 2003 Enterprise).

SharePoint 2007

The last of the communication and collaboration tools we'll look at is SharePoint 2007. This is a collaborative portal that allows online publishing of files and allows your organization to store information in one easy-to-navigate, central location.

It uses SQL Server for back-end data storage, while the front end is accessed via Web pages that are served using IIS 6.

NOTE   We'll talk about IIS 6 in more depth in Chapter 12.

Like the other tools we've talked about in this section, SharePoint is being enhanced and improved for its 2007 version. Let's examine what's new and improved for its latest release:

▼   **Consistent user interface**   SharePoint Server 2007 has been integrated with other Microsoft applications—like e-mail and Web browsers—to ensure a consistent user interface. This simplifies how users interact with the tool.

■   **Document control**   Customized document management policies can be created to control access rights in accordance with your organization's access policies. You can store and organize documents and content in a centralized location, with users having a consistent way to navigate and find information.

■   **Improved partner relationships**   Business information can be culled from partners and customers through intelligent, standards-based forms. The information can be sorted, managed, and stored in a way that's easy for you to interact with. Since it uses the Lightweight Directory Access Protocol (LDAP) standard, it can work with non-Active Directory directory service sources. This aids in extranet setups.

■   **Searches**   The Enterprise Search feature in SharePoint Server 2007 incorporates content like contact information for users and business data, along with information about the documents and Web pages. This makes overall search results more complete and relevant.

■   **Sharing**   Users can create and use personal networks, both inside and outside the organization. This allows them to share information efficiently.

■   **Interoperability**   SharePoint Server 2007 incorporates a number of standards, including eXtensible Markup Language (XML) and Simple Object Access Protocol (SOAP). This allows for interoperability with a number of files. In addition, it features application programming interfaces (APIs) and event handlers for lists and documents. This allows for integration with existing systems, and improves compatibility with non-Microsoft products.

▲   **Improved system monitoring**   Monitoring tools are improved to help find and fix performance problems as quickly as possible.

Communication and collaboration tools are greatly enhanced over earlier versions of Windows. Ideally, these tools and their implementation in your organization will help your users become more efficient and have an easier time collaborating and working.

CHAPTER 8

Remote Control

Twenty years ago, there were more typewriters than computers in the average office, and what computers there were tended to bewilder the workers. As time has marched on, computers have not only become more prevalent in the workplace, but they are also critical to daily duties. Twenty years ago, most users were petrified of the computer. By now, you'd think that users would have become more tech savvy and rarely intimidated by those once-mystical beige and black boxes.

To be fair, workers are generally more comfortable around their computers. It's pretty safe to say that they work well with applications that are critical to their jobs—at least, the ones in which they have extensive training and plenty of time at the mouse and keyboard. However, there are times when their computers are not responding like they need or expect, and having to venture into the configuration world of their operating system is likely to be overwhelming. As an IT professional, you've gotten the call to go look at someone's computer and fix it a time or two. You know that fixing their problem can be reasonably straightforward (depending on the problem, of course), but you also know that it's still a hassle to traipse over to their computer and work on the problem. And if they happen to be in another building across town or in a facility across the country, your little visit may be impractical, if not nearly impossible. Not surprisingly, Microsoft introduced a solution in Windows XP that makes it possible for you to take control of another's computer without having to leave your desk. In this chapter, we'll look at Windows Vista's implementation of Remote Assistance.

We'll also talk about Remote Desktop. Remote Desktop is a great tool that allows you to operate your computer from another computer. In fact, once the Remote Desktop connection is made, what you see on the computer screen is exactly what you would see on the remote computer, but we are still trying to figure out where they came up with the name. Let's get started with a look at Remote Desktop.

REMOTE DESKTOP

Remote Desktop is a feature that was initially rolled out with Windows XP. It allows the user to access his or her computer remotely, as the name suggests. For instance, if the user needs to access his or her computer from home or from another computer on the company network, Remote Desktop allows the user to access everything on the remote computer, including files, applications, and network connections. Remote Desktop not only allows the user to access the remote computer's files, but in addition, the desktop appears exactly as it does on the remote computer.

Remote Desktop is based on Terminal Services technology. This means that it allows you to run applications on a remote computer using Windows Vista from any other client using a Windows operating system. Remote Desktop connections are typically established across a local area network (LAN) or wide area network (WAN), and may or may not be encrypted over a virtual private network (VPN). In addition, Remote Desktop connections can be configured to encrypt the client-to-server communication channel independent of any external encryption, such as an Internet Protocol Security (IPSec) connection between two remote networks (more on that later). And, as you might expect, the speed of your connection will have a significant impact on your Remote Desktop experience.

There are two components to a Remote Desktop connection:

▼ **Server** The remote computer to which you will be connecting. It could be your office desktop computer or a special computer setup for road warriors to access when they're out and about.

▲ **Client** The computer you will use to form your connection with the server. It could be a PC at home, a road warrior's laptop, or even a coworker's PC in a neighboring cubicle.

Remote Desktop Features

There are a number of features that make Remote Desktop not only useful, but also practical. Its main features include console security, color support, and resource redirection.

Console Security

When you use Remote Desktop, you need not worry that someone will be able to sit down at the remote computer and watch your every mouse click. Remote Desktop utilizes *console security*. When a Remote Desktop session has been initiated, the active user is logged off of the client computer and, by default, Windows Vista disables the screen. That is, when a Remote Desktop session is active, the only thing visible on the client's screen is the user's icon and an indication of how many applications are running. A user on the other end can take control of the PC; however, it will start with his or her desktop and settings, not those of the user who was using the PC remotely.

Color Support

Remote Desktop supports up to 32-bit color depth. In essence, whatever is displayed on the Remote Desktop server is what is displayed on the Remote Desktop client. Primarily for performance reasons, the depth of color displayed can be adjusted by the remote user.

Resource Redirection

Using a Remote Desktop session is useful, because you actually get to use the components and tools of the remote computer, including plugged-in Universal Serial Bus (USB) devices, printers, and so forth. This is possible because Remote Desktop employs *resource redirection*, allowing the user to function as if he or she were sitting in front of the remote computer. Resource redirection applies to many components of a remote computer, including utilizing the computer's file system as if it were a shared resource.

As we'll see in this chapter, it isn't just the file-system nuts and bolts of the remote computer that are accessed. Resource redirection can also be applied to such features as audio redirection, which allows the client computer to play the sounds that the server computer generates. For example, if two applications are playing sound, the two audio streams are combined and both are delivered.

Remote Desktop Protocol 6.0

The heart and soul of Remote Desktop is the Remote Desktop Protocol (RDP). Windows XP initially utilized version 5.2 of the protocol, while Vista has bumped up to version 6.0. RDP is a presentation protocol that allows communication between client and server devices. New features of RDP 6.0 include:

▼ A front-end Internet Information Services (IIS) server can accept connections for back-end Terminal Service servers via a Hypertext Transfer Protocol Secure socket (HTTPS) connection. This is similar to how Remote Procedure Call (RPC) over HTTPS allows an Outlook client to connect to a back-end Exchange server.

■ Support for the Aero glass theme.

■ Support for remotely controlling Windows Presentation Foundation applications. Clients using .NET Framework 3.0 are able to display Windows Presentation Foundation effects on a local computer.

■ Device redirection improvement so that more devices can be accessed.

■ Support for displays that can be spread across multiple and widescreen monitors.

■ Implementation of network-level authentication prior to the RDP session being established.

▲ To top it off, it also requires fewer remote computer resources.

Security Settings

It's disturbing enough when someone is able to access a network in an unauthorized manner. However, it's downright scary if someone is able to access your desktop. It's sort of like having your house broken into and then also finding that they have dug through your underwear drawer.

That is why security is so important with Remote Desktop. But it isn't just a worry that a hacker will access a user's computer; there are also concerns about what a legitimate remote user should be able to access remotely.

Security in Remote Desktop can be managed through several techniques. The subsequent sections explain how you can keep your system secure at varying levels using Remote Desktop. These settings are managed using the Terminal Services section of the Group Policy Microsoft Management Console (MMC) snap-in.

Terminal Services is located by activating the MMC, adding the Group Policy snap-in, and then double-clicking Computer Configuration. Next, click Administrative Templates, click Windows Components, and then click Terminal Services. This tool is shown in Figure 8-1.

By double-clicking the Security folder, there are a number of settings you can manage. The following are some of the settings that can be managed based on your organization's needs and wants.

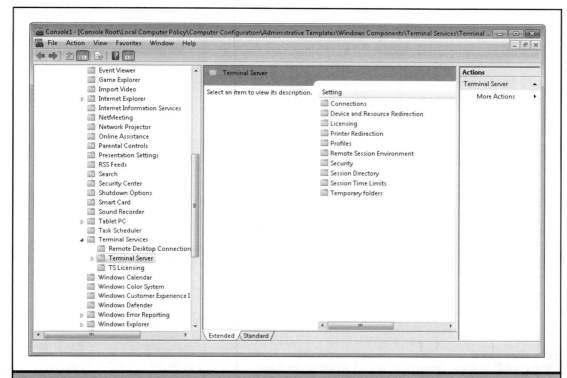

Figure 8-1.   The Terminal Services portion of the Group Policy snap-in is where security settings can be managed.

Encryption

You can enable and manage encryption levels between your Remote Desktop client and server by using the Terminal Services Group Policy setting. There are two encryption levels that you can choose between (as shown in Figure 8-2):

▼ **High Level**   The highest level of encryption encodes data between the client and server using strong 128-bit encryption. This level should only be chosen if you are certain that both computers can use 128-bit encryption (for instance, if both computers are using Windows Vista). If your client does not support this level, it will not be able to connect.

▲ **Client Compatible**   At this level, data is encrypted at the highest level supported by the client computer.

If your encryption settings are incompatible—for instance, if your server is using strong 128-bit encryption and the client can only handle 56-bit encryption—the connection will not be established.

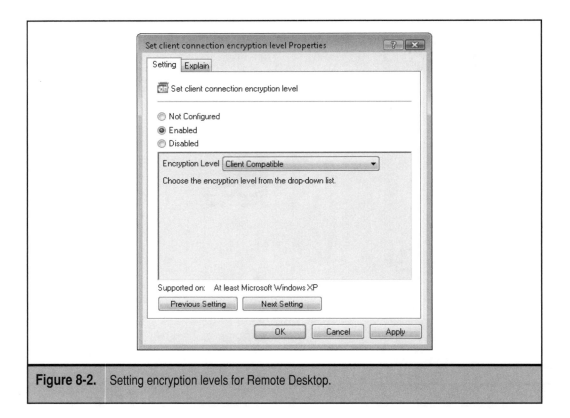

Figure 8-2. Setting encryption levels for Remote Desktop.

NOTE Examining encryption settings is a good place to start the troubleshooting process if your Remote Desktop session does not work.

Password Authentication

You can elect to have the user's password automatically sent during a client logon, or you can prompt the user for the password. A best-practices choice for security is to prompt the user for his or her password upon logon. In the Terminal Services Group Policy setting, this is managed under Always Prompt Client For Password.

Disabling the Clipboard

Clients can cut or copy content to their Clipboards. However, if you decide to prevent users from sharing a Clipboard between the Remote Desktop client and server, this can be disabled in the Terminal Services Group Policy setting under Do Not Allow Clipboard Redirection.

Disabling the Printer

Whether or not to allow users remote printer access is another setting that can be made. Printer redirection is managed in the Terminal Services Group Policy setting by enabling the option Do Not Allow Printer Redirection.

Disabling Files

Just because a user has access to a computer remotely doesn't necessarily mean he or she gets *carte blanche* to the whole file system. If you want to prevent remote users from rifling through the file system connected to the Remote Desktop server, in the Terminal Services Group Policy setting, select the Do Not Allow Drive Redirection Policy option.

USING REMOTE DESKTOP

Before you can use Remote Desktop, it's necessary to prepare your server and client computers. It's also a really good idea to test your connection to make sure that everything is working the way you want it to. After all, once you're away from the server, the computer cannot be accessed to perform any tweaks or to fine-tune it.

Remote Desktop Server

When configuring a Remote Desktop server, you will be indicating which user accounts will be authorized access. These user accounts must have passwords. If the computer to which the client will be accessing does not normally utilize a password, you will have to create one for Remote Desktop.

When you configure your server for Remote Desktop, you will enter the user account name in the Object Name field, located in the Select Users dialog box. To configure a Remote Desktop server:

1. Select Start | Control Panel | System And Maintenance.

2. Click the Allow Remote Access icon from the System portion of the dialog box.

3. In the Remote Desktop portion of the dialog box, you can make two selections, based on your connection and security needs (see Figure 8-3):

   ■ Allow Connections From Computers Running Any Version Of Remote Desktop (Less Secure)

   ■ Allow Connections Only From Computers Running Remote Desktop With Network Level Authentication (More Secure)

   Network Level Authentication (NLA) is a new form of authentication that completes user authentication before a remote connection is made. This is a more secure method of authentication and can protect the remote computer from attacks and malware.

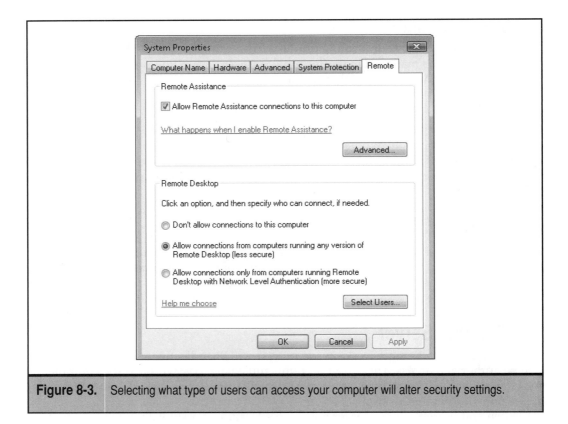

Figure 8-3. Selecting what type of users can access your computer will alter security settings.

The best choice is to select the second option, allowing connections only with NLA-enabled computers. However, if your connecting computers don't have NLA, or if you just don't know if they do, you should select the first option.

NOTE How do you know if your computer is using NLA? Open the Remote Desktop connection, click the small icon in the upper-left corner of the dialog box, and then click About. If you are running Windows XP or Server 2003 and want NLA support, you can download Terminal Services Client 6.0 from Microsoft's Web site.

4. Click the Select Users button. This calls up the Remote Desktop Users dialog box in which you add users who will be allowed to remotely access this computer. Administrative accounts are automatically given access.

5. Click Add. This calls up the Select Users dialog box, as shown in Figure 8-4. User accounts have three identifying components: Object Type, Location, and Name.

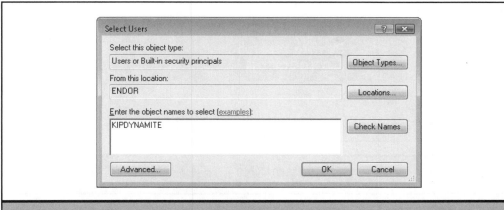

Figure 8-4. Adding a user to the Remote Desktop server determines who can access the computer.

6. If you want to locate a user account from the Remote Desktop server, make sure the Select This Object Type option is set to Users, and type an account name in the Enter The Object Names To Select box. If you wish to enter a user from another computer on an Active Directory–based LAN, click the Locations button, select the domain, and then enter the user account name.

7. Click Check Names. This gives Windows Vista a chance to enter the name in the *computername\username* format.

8. Click OK. The user you just indicated will be added to the list of users permitted to remotely access your Remote Desktop server. To add more users, repeat steps 6–9.

9. Click OK twice to exit all the dialog boxes.

Remote Desktop Client

The Remote Desktop tool is installed by default, and is located by selecting Start | All Programs | Accessories | Remote Desktop Connection. When you start the tool, it looks like the one shown in Figure 8-5.

We're talking specifically about Windows Vista and Remote Desktop here, but Remote Desktop works with versions of Windows other than Vista and even Mac OS X. The tool was introduced in Windows XP, but if you have older versions of Windows that need to connect remotely, Microsoft provides a tool that can be used on Windows 95, Windows 98 and 98 Second Edition, Windows Me, Windows NT 4.0, and Windows 2000. The Remote Desktop client is a 3.4-MB file that you can download from www.microsoft .com/windowsxp/pro/downloads/rdclientdl.asp. When installed, this client allows older versions of Windows to connect to a Windows Vista Remote Desktop server.

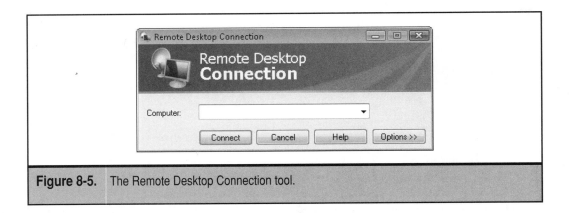

Figure 8-5. The Remote Desktop Connection tool.

Establishing a Connection

Once your Remote Desktop server and client have been configured, you should test the connection to make sure it works the way you want. The first step is to ensure that the Remote Desktop server is turned on and you're connected to the network.

If someone is logged on locally, the client trying to access the server will see a message telling them that the local user must first disconnect. Simultaneously, at the remote computer, the user will see a message allowing him or her to prevent the Remote Desktop session from taking place. If the user fails to respond to the request after a certain amount of time, Windows assumes that the user is away, and he or she is automatically logged out.

Next, start the Remote Desktop client.

1. Select Start | All Programs | Accessories | Remote Desktop Connection. Another way is to select Start | Run (search box), type **mstsc**, and press ENTER.

2. From the Computer drop-down list, pick the name of the server computer or enter its IP address. If the drop-down list does not contain any computer names, click Browse For More to see the available computers in your domain or workgroup. This list will only show computers that have been enabled for Remote Desktop.

NOTE If you don't know a computer's IP address, you can find it by selecting Start | My Network Places, and then clicking View Network Connections. Right-click your LAN or Internet connection, choose Status, and then click the Support tab.

3. Click Connect.

4. When Remote Desktop is done forming its connection with the remote computer, you'll see a Windows Vista–style splash screen. The screen contains

icons for the users who have been authorized to remotely access the computer. Click your icon, and then enter your password.

5. Click OK. The connection has now been formed, and you'll see the remote desktop, as shown in Figure 8-6.

Once connected, the client will see what the server's desktop looks like, and he or she can use it as if they were sitting at that computer. The main difference, however, is at the top of the screen. There is a special toolbar that can be used to minimize, maximize, or close the Remote Desktop view. For example, if you wish to work on your client computer, you click the Minimize button. To return to the Remote Desktop connection, click the Maximize button. The pushpin icon locks the menu in place.

But your desktop doesn't have to look exactly like that on the server. For example, you can choose to access the Remote Desktop server in full-screen view, as shown in Figure 8-6. However, you can control the size and location of the window as you would for any other Windows application.

Using Remote Desktop

Once you've established a Remote Desktop connection, you can use the server computer locally, just as you would if you were sitting in front of it. If you are using a Remote

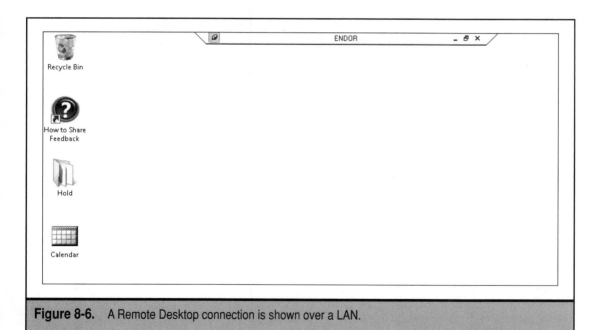

Figure 8-6. A Remote Desktop connection is shown over a LAN.

Desktop session, you might find it necessary to transfer information from one system to another. For instance, you might need to merge database content from the Remote Desktop server with a document stored on your Remote Desktop client.

Remote Desktop provides a number of ways in which you can use your Remote Desktop client in conjunction with your Remote Desktop server:

▼ **Cut and paste**   Information displayed on your Remote Desktop window can be cut and pasted into an application on the client computer or vice versa.

■ **Use local files**   Users can, by default, use local files. Local drives will appear in My Computer under Other. They will also be in any application's Open and Save dialog boxes.

▲ **Use a local printer**   The logistics of printing are somewhat complicated. Here's how it works: A print job will be sent to the default local printer, as long as the server computer contains the driver for your client computer's printer.

NOTE   Whether or not you want your users to be able to cut and paste, access local files, or use a printer are all security settings that you can manage, as we noted earlier in this section.

Other Remote Desktop Settings

Remote Desktop seems like a fairly clean, easy-to-use little tool—and it is. Even so, you have a good deal of flexibility and control over its various features. In addition to user name and password, a number of other preferences can be set by clicking the Options button. The resulting window is shown in Figure 8-7.

Table 8-1 explains the tabs, important settings, and a description of each.

Once these settings have been established, you can save them under a specific name. This is helpful if you use multiple Remote Desktop servers and have preferred settings for each. Your preferences are saved by clicking the Save As button on the General tab of the Remote Desktop.

REMOTE ASSISTANCE

In the first section, we talked about how you or another user can access a computer and use its resources via Remote Desktop. Well, Microsoft has provided another useful tool for users who are having trouble getting their computers to work properly: Remote Assistance. Remote Desktop and Remote Assistance sound alike, but they are used in different ways.

The names tip you off as to their functions: Remote Assistance is used when a user needs help with his or her computer. Remote Desktop, on the other hand, is called upon when a user needs to access resources on a remote device. Distinctions between the two include the following:

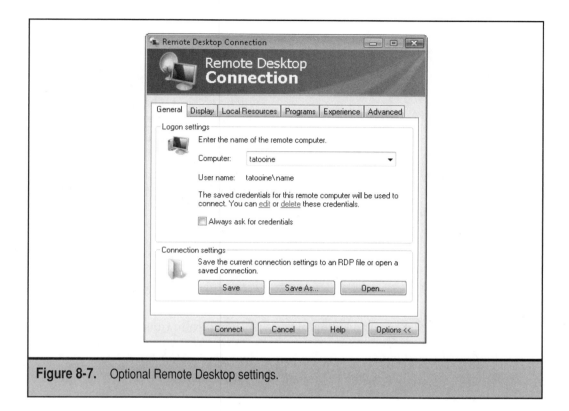

Figure 8-7.   Optional Remote Desktop settings.

▼ Remote Desktop establishes new connections, but Remote Assistance calls
someone in to be part of an existing connection.

▲ Remote Desktop locks out the remote computer from being used locally during
a remote session. Remote Assistance, on the other hand, requires a local user to
be present.

In this section, Remote Assistance and its functionality are explained in more depth. In
addition, we'll explain how to use Remote Assistance and how connections are formed.

Remote Assistance Features

There are a number of features in Remote Assistance that simplify access to a user's
computer, whether that be a help desk caller, a friend, a family member, or anyone else.
As you can imagine, having the ability to directly access a remote computer can be invaluable in isolating a user's technical difficulties. Not only can an expert access the
computer and provide help, but that person can also use a number of troubleshooting
tools in his or her endeavors to assist you.

Tab	Setting	Description
General	Always Ask For Credentials	Indicates if the user's name will be maintained on the computer or if it will be entered whenever a Remote Desktop connection is formed.
Display	Remote Desktop Size And Colors	Indicates the screen size and colors used for the Remote Desktop.
Local Resources	Remote Computer Sound	Indicates if the Remote Desktop client will play the sounds that the Remote Desktop server would play.
Local Resources	Keyboard	Indicates if ALT+key combinations apply to the Remote Desktop server or the Remote Desktop client.
Local Resources	Local Devices	Indicates which devices you can connect to on the Remote Desktop server.
Programs	Start The Following Program On Connection	Automatically runs a specified program when you connect to the Remote Desktop server.
Experience	Allow The Following (Desktop Background, Show Contents Of Window While Dragging, Menu And Window Animation, Themes, And Bitmap Caching)	Indicates which items will appear in your Remote Desktop server view. Items can be selected or cleared based on your preferences.
Advanced	Server Authentication	Helps ensure that you are connecting to the correct computer.
Advanced	Connect From Anywhere	If you need to connect remotely and are behind a firewall, you'll need to configure a Terminal Services gateway. This is where you indicate those gateway settings. This dialog box is shown in Figure 8-8.

Table 8-1. Optional Remote Desktop Settings

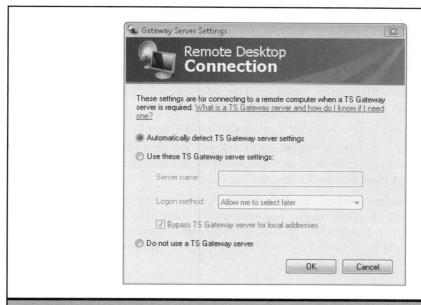

Figure 8-8. The Advanced tab allows you to manage security settings and Terminal Services gateways.

Desktop Control

You can call upon a friend or expert to help track down and fix a problem on your computer running Windows Vista. Similarly, if a user is having problems with his or her computer, you could be called upon to provide help. Remote Assistance is useful in a number of scenarios:

▼ **Problems that are hard to reproduce** It seems that the best way to cure yourself of a physical malady is to go to the doctor's office. The throbbing pain in your shoulder always seems to disappear as soon as you walk into the doctor's office. It's the same for computer users. They can call you and tell you there's a problem, but given the endless ways a computer can be configured, sometimes, the best way to really understand the problem is to see the problem in its native environment. With Remote Assistance, you can see what's going on, but without having to leave your office.

▲ **Resolutions that are complicated** Unless your instructions for fixing a problem are simple, chances are that as you start explaining the resolution, the user's eyes are going to gloss over and all they'll hear is, "Blah, blah, blah, right-click… blah, blah, blah, click." Remote Assistance provides you with the mechanism to fix the problem yourself and the user with the chance to see what you did. Best-case scenario: They'll be able to fix the problem should it arise again. Worst-case scenario: They've just learned enough to really screw up their computers.

Troubleshooting Tools

While Remote Assistance is a helpful basic tool for the user and expert alike to figure out what's wrong with a computer, it also provides some features that can expedite the communication and resolution process, including:

▼ **File transfers**   Files can be transferred between the user's and helper's respective computers.

■ **Chat**   The user and expert can type text messages to each other.

■ **Voice over IP**   Assuming the user and helper have microphones and speakers connected to their computers, and assuming there's enough bandwidth, the two can speak to each other across the connection.

▲ **Bandwidth management**   Remote Assistance will gauge how much bandwidth is available and manage settings for color depth and sound quality. If there's enough bandwidth, color depth and audio quality will be improved. If bandwidth is tight, sound and color quality will be diminished.

Security

While giving control of your computer to a friend or expert is meant to solve your technical difficulties, there is still the chance for security problems. You should bear these issues in mind before allowing a Remote Assistance connection.

In most cases, there will be a different level of permissions and access between administrators and standard users. That is, what the expert is able to do with his or her permissions is probably a lot more than what a user is able to do with his or her permissions. This can be an issue in problem-solving, because the expert assisting the user accesses at the user's security level. As such, any actions the helper makes will be limited to what the user is allowed to do.

If the user is seeking help from someone across an Internet connection, it's a good idea to use a VPN connection. This is a safe practice, because it effectively scrambles the communication between the two computers on the off chance that someone with access anywhere along the network is monitoring the connection for interesting information.

Using Remote Assistance

To use Remote Assistance, you invite someone (a friend or an expert in your organization) to take control of your computer. This invitation is extended via either Windows Messenger or an e-mail. If the other person accepts the invitation, he or she can control the mouse and type as if sitting in front of your computer. You can also share information back and forth, either by text or using microphones.

Configuring Remote Assistance

The first step in using Remote Assistance is to make sure it has been enabled on your computer. This can be verified by clicking Control Panel | System And Maintenance, and then clicking the Allow Remote Access icon. The icon is shown at the far right of the dialog box (see Figure 8-9).

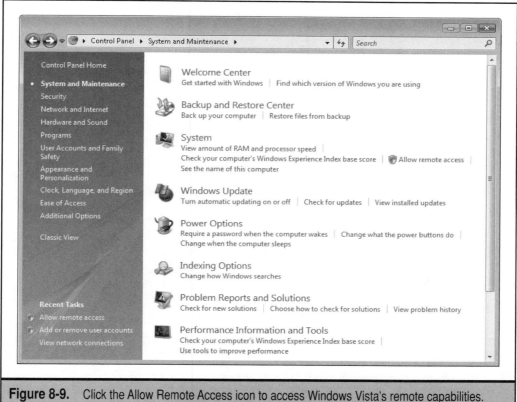

Figure 8-9.   Click the Allow Remote Access icon to access Windows Vista's remote capabilities.

This calls up the System dialog box with the Remote tab (shown in Figure 8-10) selected. In the Remote Assistance area, select the Allow Remote Assistance Invitations To Be Sent From This Computer check box, and then click OK.

Extending an Invitation

To ask someone to help you via Remote Assistance, you'll need to send an invitation. The most common way to initiate Remote Assistance is via an invitation. However, the process can also work in reverse. That is, a person can offer to help, rather than waiting for an invitation.

Sending the Invitation   To send an invitation:

1. Select Start | All Programs | Maintenance | Windows Remote Assistance. A dialog box like the one in Figure 8-11 appears.
2. Click Invite Someone You Trust To Help You in the next window.

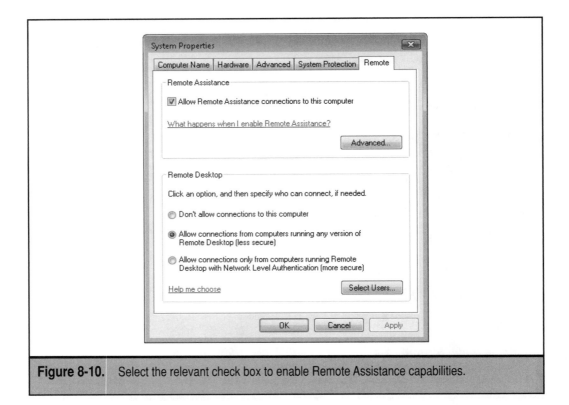

Figure 8-10. Select the relevant check box to enable Remote Assistance capabilities.

3. Next, as Figure 8-12 shows, choose whether you want to send your invitation via e-mail or save the invitation as a file. Selecting the e-mail option calls up your system's e-mail system. However, if you use a Web-based e-mail system, save the invitation as a file, and attach it to your Web-based e-mail. For this example, we're using Send Your Invitation Via E-mail.

4. Next, you'll enter a password that must be at least six characters in length. Your helper will enter this password to access your computer.

5. Then Windows Vista will generate an e-mail message, like the one in Figure 8-13. You enter your helper's e-mail address and make any changes you want to the e-mail message. You'll notice that there is also an attachment with your e-mail. This is the file your helper will open to initiate the help session.

6. Click the Send button.

7. Call your helper and tell him or her that an invitation is on the way. This is a good time to share the password with your helper.

8. When your helper gets the invitation and enters the password to access the invitation ticket, you'll see a dialog box asking "Would you like to allow (*the user*) to connect to you computer?" Click Yes to proceed.

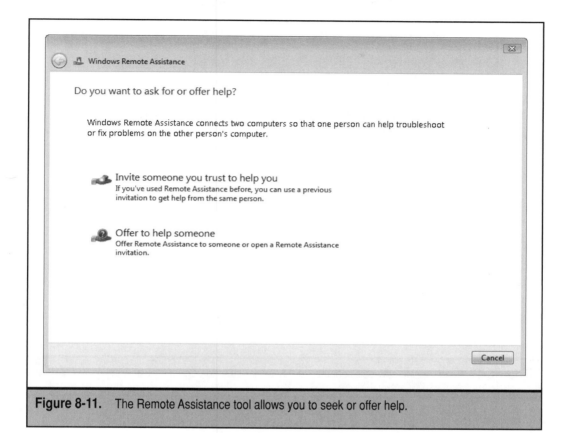

Figure 8-11.   The Remote Assistance tool allows you to seek or offer help.

9. As Figure 8-14 shows, the Remote Assistance window opens. You can chat with your helper on the left side of the window, and the actual desktop appears on the right.

10. If you didn't already explain the problem you're experiencing, you can share the specific details in the Message Entry area in the lower-left corner of the Remote Assistance window.

When your helper establishes a Remote Assistance session, there are three things that you can do:

▼ **Share control of your computer**   This is the final step before your helper takes control of your computer. When you are using Remote Assistance, it's a good idea not to type or move the mouse. Since someone else is trying to use these controls, it can be troublesome for both parties when you are trying to use them at the same time. To end the Remote Assistance session, press ESC or click Stop Control.

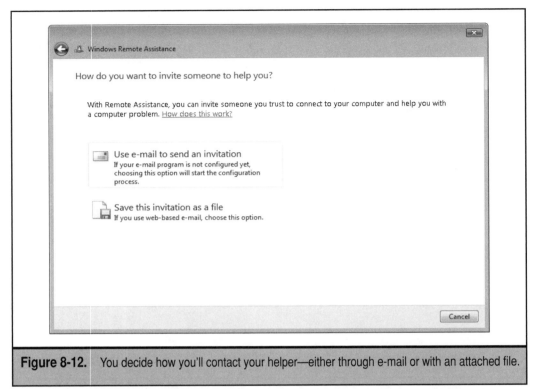

Figure 8-12. You decide how you'll contact your helper—either through e-mail or with an attached file.

- ■ **Send a file** By clicking this button, you can send a file to the person with whom you are sharing your computer. After clicking this button, you'll be prompted to enter the name of the file you want to send.

- ▲ **Voice chat** If you and your helper have microphones, speakers, and speedy-enough connections, you can talk about your problem. Audio quality can be managed by clicking Settings. If your helper clicks Start Talking before you do, a message is sent to the other computer, asking if a voice chat is desired.

When the session is over, either you or your helper can click Disconnect to wrap things up.

Invitation Restrictions Since invitations can be the ticket into a system, some security mechanisms are built in to keep the invitation from being used for evil purposes. For the ticket to be valid, two conditions must be present:

- ▼ The ticket must not be expired. Each ticket is given a time limit, established by the user. If the user anticipates that help is needed just once, the ticket can be set to expire in a day. If the user wants to keep the invitation open longer, that period can be adjusted accordingly.

- ▲ The IP address of the expert's computer must not have changed since the ticket was issued.

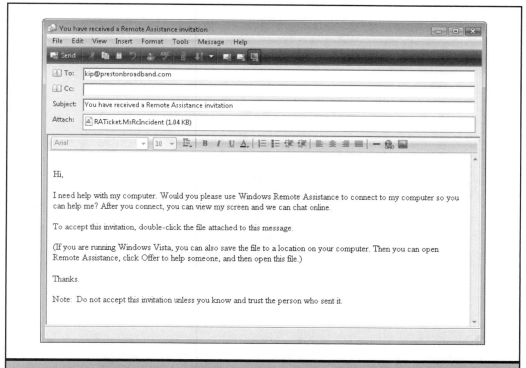

Figure 8-13.   Remote Assistance will create an e-mail invitation for you to send.

Offering Assistance

Remote Assistance doesn't just work one way. That is, it isn't just the user who can ask for help. Experts or friends can extend the offer of help to the user. The Offer Remote Assistance feature allows anyone with administrator privileges to initiate a Remote Assistance session without first having to be invited.

Enabling Offer Remote Assistance   On Windows Vista, Offer Remote Assistance is disabled by default, but it can be activated as follows:

NOTE   Offer Remote Assistance can only be used within an organization, not across the Internet.

1. Open the Group Policy snap-in to the MMC.
2. Expand Local Computer Policy.
3. Expand Computer Configuration.
4. Expand Administrative Templates.
5. Expand System.

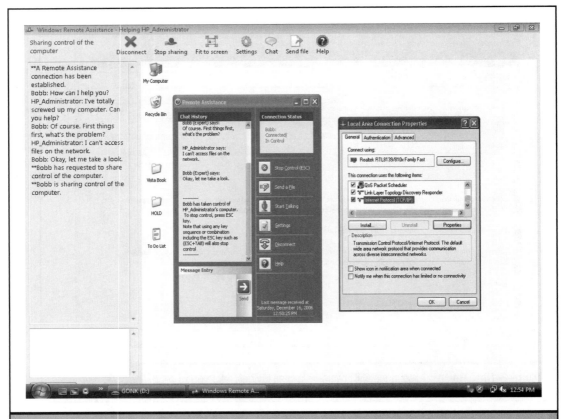

Figure 8-14.   Remote Assistance allows you to help fix a user's problem and chat with them at the same time.

6. Expand Remote Assistance

7. Double-click Offer Remote Assistance

8. Click Enabled

9. Click OK

The preceding steps grant Offer Remote Assistance privileges to administrators; however, others in the organization can be granted this privilege. To grant the privilege to others:

1. Open the Group Policy Object Editor snap-in to the MMC

2. Expand Local Computer Policy

3. Expand Computer Configuration

4. Expand Administrative Templates.

5. Expand System.

6. Expand Remote Assistance.

7. Double-click Offer Remote Assistance.

8. Click Enabled.

9. Click Show and then click Add.

10. In the Add Item dialog box, enter the name of the user or group to whom you want to grant this privilege. The entry should be made in either of the following formats: *domain\username* or *domain\groupname*.

11. Click OK.

Offering Help   Once you've enabled Offer Remote Assistance, you first tell the user that you are offering help. Then follow these steps:

1. Click Start | All Programs | Maintenance | Windows Remote Assistance.

2. In the dialog box, click Offer To Help Someone.

3. The resulting dialog box, shown in Figure 8-15, shows different ways in which you can offer help. At the top of the box is a tool that allows you to access the connection file that has already been sent to you. Or, on the right side of the box, previous connection sessions are shown. Since you're attempting to solicit help, enter the name or IP address of the computer you wish to connect to.

4. A message will appear on the user's screen, informing him or her of the connection attempt, stating who is trying to connect, and asking if he or she wishes to permit it. If the user clicks Yes, the session is initiated.

NOTE   The user must be present at his or her computer to accept the connection attempt. Remember, Remote Assistance is a joint effort.

Accepting an Invitation

In the preceding sections we covered the steps involved in initiating a Remote Assistance session. We'll wrap up this chapter with a discussion about what happens when you are asked for help in a Remote Assistance session.

When you are asked for help, you are on the receiving end of an invitation, identical to the one we prepared and sent earlier. The message will also include an attached file (usually called RATicket.McRcIncident) containing the *invitation ticket*. If you'd like to accept the invitation and have the password the user has entered, follow these steps:

1. Make sure that you are connected either to the Internet or the LAN (assuming the person you are helping is on the LAN with you).

2. Open the attached file. The Remote Assistance dialog box appears.

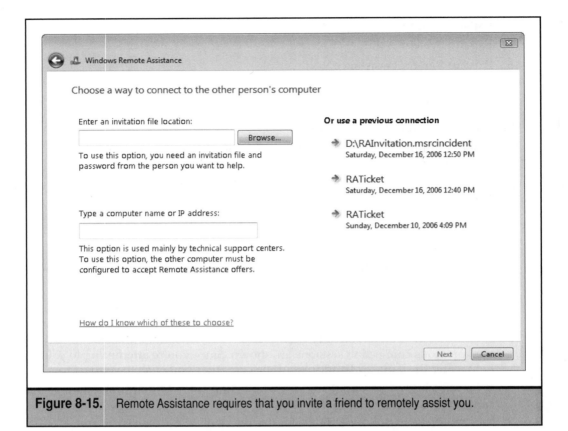

Figure 8-15. Remote Assistance requires that you invite a friend to remotely assist you.

3. Enter the password and click Yes to connect. Remote Assistance handles the niggling details of forming the connection across your LAN.

4. In the Message Entry area in the lower-left corner of the screen, you can enter text messages that will be shared with the other computer. Once you've entered your message, click Send to speed the message on its way.

Whether your users need to connect remotely, or if they need your help, Remote Desktop and Remote Assistance are useful tools. However—and this can't be stressed strongly enough—they must be preconfigured before they are used. You also need to make sure that you have tested them out and are comfortable that they work the way you want them to before you have to depend on them. Lastly, care should be exercised in how everything is configured, how access is controlled, and who is allowed to deploy and use the tools so that security is assured.

PART III

Security

CHAPTER 9

User Accounts

Computer security is a lot like the multiple layers of an onion. When you peel away one layer, there is another beneath it, and another beneath that. There are security issues that pertain to Web access. There are security issues that pertain to authentication. There are security issues that pertain to the data saved on your hard drives. In this chapter we'll look at security issues as they pertain to user accounts.

Naturally, different users will have different needs on the network. There are some areas where you don't want some users poking around and changing settings, while other users might need to access those very same areas. As such, managing user accounts is important.

Managing user accounts in Windows Vista is extremely similar to earlier flavors of Windows—but it's not exactly the same. In this chapter we'll examine how to create user accounts and how to manage them. We'll also look at what Vista brings to the user account party—namely, its new User Account Control (UAC) feature, which is meant to patch some holes in Windows security.

USERS AND GROUPS

User accounts exist in two places on a network: on the network itself and on individual computers. When a user sits down in front of the computer and tries to log on to that computer, Windows Vista checks to see if, in fact, the user has permission to even be at that computer. If he or she does, the user can access the computer's resources—inasmuch as the network administrator has allowed access to that computer.

The next place accounts exist is on the network itself. If a user tries to access a shared drive, printer, or other network resources, Windows will check to ensure that he or she is authorized to do so. This first section sets the stage, so to speak, about user accounts. It describes where they exist and how they can be managed.

The Local Users And Groups Tool

A local user or group is a type of account that can be given permissions and rights on the local computer. Local Users And Groups is a tool that is used to manage rights and permissions on the local computer. It is a useful security feature that allows you to limit the ability of users and groups to perform certain actions on a computer by assigning rights and permissions.

Rights and permissions are distinct functions and can be differentiated in the following ways:

▼ **Rights** A right authorizes a user to perform actions on a computer, like shutting it down or playing a CD.

▲ **Permissions** These are rules associated with an object, like a file, folder, or printer. Permissions control which users are allowed to access the object and to what degree they are allowed access.

NOTE Local users and groups cannot be added to global groups.

Other types of groups are managed at the network level. Domain and global users are managed by the network. Local users, global users, or global groups can be added to local groups.

NOTE Local Users And Groups is not available on domain controllers. Active Directory Users And Computers (ADUC) is used to manage global users and groups.

The Active Directory Users And Computers Tool

While the Local Users And Groups tool is used to manage rights and permissions on the local computer, Active Directory Users And Computers is used to manage rights and permissions on the network.

Windows servers use a user or computer account to authenticate the user or computer's identity (ID) to allow or deny access to domain resources. User and computer accounts can be added, disabled, reset, or deleted using the Active Directory Users And Computers tool.

User, computer, and group accounts are also known as security principals. Security principals are directory objects that are assigned a security ID (SID). A SID is used to access domain resources. Accounts are used for:

- ▼ **Authenticating identity**   Users and computers can be authenticated to the domain when they appropriately log on to an account.

- ■ **Authorizing access to domain resources**   Once authenticated, a user's level of permissions indicates to which network resources he or she will be allowed access and at what level.

- ■ **Administering other security principals**   A foreign security principal is created in the local domain to represent security principals from trusted external domains.

- ▲ **Auditing user and computer accounts**   Auditing is useful in monitoring account security.

In addition, user accounts can be used as service accounts for some applications. In other words, a service can be configured to log on as a user account, and is then given access to specific network resources through that account.

Profile Types

Three different types of profiles are used in the creation of a user account. These profile types prevent unwanted interference with the local system:

- ▼ **Local profile**   A local profile is maintained on the local computer and is automatically created the first time a user logs on to a computer and then logs off. The profile is stored in the *\%SystemRoot%\Profiles* folder and maintains all the settings made to it while the user was logged on. This profile is maintained only on a single computer and does not follow the user from computer to computer.

- ■ **Roaming profile**   Unlike a local profile, a roaming profile does, in fact, follow users from computer to computer. Roaming profiles are ideal for users who move to different workstations in the organization. In addition to their rights and permissions, personal settings can move with them. Since this profile must be available at different computers, profiles must be downloaded across the network when logon occurs. Upon logoff, changes are saved back to the server. Because of these additional steps, logon and logoff can take extra time.

▲ **Mandatory profile**   To cut down on the logon and logoff times demanded by roaming profiles, mandatory profiles are set as read-only. It is possible to log on from any computer in the organization, but users cannot change the profile.

CREATING USER ACCOUNTS

Windows Vista presents two ways in which you can create new local user accounts. As a network administrator you likely will use the second option—through the Microsoft Management Console (MMC)—more often than you would by actually sitting down in front of a local computer and performing the actions there. However, let's examine both processes so that you can get an idea of how accounts are set up, managed, and—if need be—deleted.

In addition, we'll talk about how you can create new user accounts for a domain environment using the Active Directory Users And Computers tool. Finally, we'll talk about the different types of accounts that can be created in Windows Vista and the differences between them.

Create a User Account from Control Panel

Creating a new user account in Vista is almost identical to the process in Windows XP. The biggest challenge—if that word can even be used in this context—is figuring out where to go once you're in Control Panel.

To create a new user account:

1. Click Start and click Control Panel.
2. Click User Accounts And Family Safety.
3. Under User Accounts, click Add Or Remove User Accounts.
4. Click Create A New Account. The resulting dialog box is shown in Figure 9-1.
5. Type the account name.
6. Select the account type: Standard or Administrator.
7. Click Create Account.
8. The User Accounts dialog box will reappear, now with your newly created user added to the list of users. Select the account you just created, and then click Create A Password.
9. Type a password for the user account and an optional password hint.
10. Click Create Password.

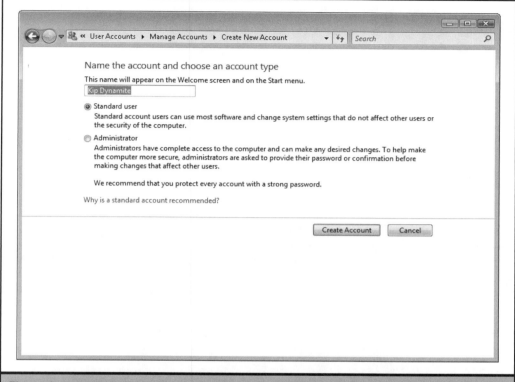

Figure 9-1.   When creating a new account, you are asked for the account name and whether it will be a Standard or Administrator account.

The user can now log on to the computer using the newly defined user name and password.

Create a New User Account from Local Users And Groups

To create a new user account using the Local Users And Groups snap-in to the MMC:

1. Open the command prompt by clicking Start and then typing `lusrmgr.msc` in the Run/Search prompt, otherwise known as the UAC prompt. Press ENTER to then launch the Local Users And Groups snap-in, shown in Figure 9-2.

2. In the console tree, click Users.

3. On the Action menu, click New User.

4. Type the appropriate information in the dialog box, shown in Figure 9-3.

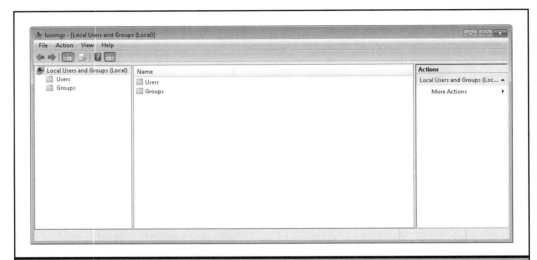

Figure 9-2. The Local Users And Groups snap-in allows you to add and manage users and groups on the local computer.

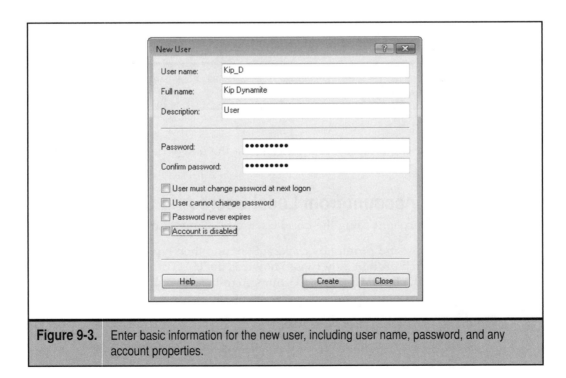

Figure 9-3. Enter basic information for the new user, including user name, password, and any account properties.

5. Select or clear the following check boxes:
   - ■ User Must Change Password At Next Logon
   - ■ User Cannot Change Password
   - ■ Password Never Expires
   - ■ Account Is Disabled
6. Click Create and then click Close.

As you can see from the options in step 5, there are some account management processes you can engage in, including disabling an account, without fully deleting it. However, if you care to completely delete the account, that's simple enough—just right-click the user's account, and select Delete from the context menu.

Add a User Account from Active Directory Users And Computers

As nice a tool as lusrmgr.msc is, if you are trying to add users to an Active Directory domain, you'll get an error telling you that you cannot use it. In order to add users in this scenario, you must use the Active Directory Users And Computers tool.

You also need to use this tool if you are trying to add a computer to your Active Directory domain. The following steps illustrate the process of adding users and computers to your domain.

Adding a User

Assuming your computer running Vista is part of a domain, adding a user is accomplished by following these steps:

1. Select Start | All Programs | Administrative Tools | Active Directory Users And Computers.
2. Expand your domain name in the left pane.
3. Click Users. You will see all of the automatically created users.
4. Right-click the Users folder, and select New from the context menu.
5. Click User from the next context menu.
6. A new dialog box will appear, asking for:
   - ■ First name
   - ■ Last name
   - ■ Initials
   - ■ Full name
   - ■ User logon name and the domain to which they will belong

   Once you've entered this information, click Next.

7. The next screen shows password settings. Enter the password twice (to confirm the entry), and then you'll be presented with such settings as:

- User Must Change Password At Next Logon
- User Cannot Change Password
- Password Never Expires
- Account Is Disabled

8. Click Finish to complete the process.

Adding a Computer

To add a computer to your Active Directory domain:

1. Select Start | Administrative Tools | Active Directory Users And Computers.

2. Expand your domain name, and right-click Computers.

3. Select New and then click Computer.

4. In the resulting dialog box, enter the name of the computer you wish to add.

5. Click Next, and you'll see a final report of what you just added. Click Finish, and you're done.

ACCOUNT SECURITY

Once an account has been created, you can manage users' rights and permissions via the Security Configuration Management Console. It is here where you can establish whether or not you want users to be able to do such things as rename their accounts, shut down the computer, and a zillion other behind-the-scenes settings.

First, let's look at an area of security that runs largely behind the scenes, but is important to know about because of the benefit it has on overall system security. Windows Service Hardening is meant to secure services that have access to your system. Once we talk about improvements that have been made to it, we'll take a closer look at security policies and what you can do with them in Windows Vista.

Account Policies

The main way in which user rights and permissions are managed is through Group Policy—as has been the case in Windows for quite some time. Microsoft bolsters many areas of local security in Vista with improvements to the security settings for local policies, which are managed through Active Directory Group Policies (if you are working in an Active Directory environment) or the Group Policy Object Editor (if your network is not part of an Active Directory environment).

To manage Group Policy on a local computer, you can access security settings by using the Security Configuration Management Console. The following sections explain the usage and setting of changes to Audit Policy, User Rights Assignment, and Security Options.

To manage each of these settings, you must first start the Local Security Settings Console. The quickest way to get there is as follows:

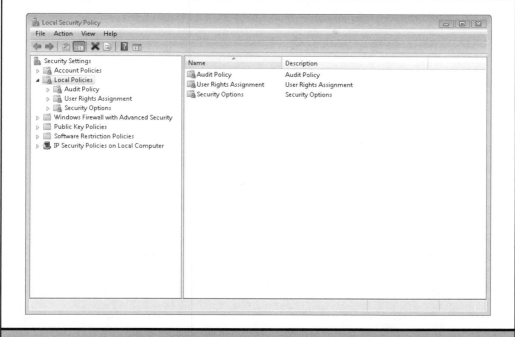

Figure 9-4.   The Local Security Settings Console is used to manage local security settings for individual users.

1. Click Start and then type **secpol.msc** in the Run/Search box.

2. Press ENTER. The Local Security Settings Console (which is part of MMC) is shown in Figure 9-4.

Audit Policy Changes

The Audit Policy feature is used to collect information about resource and privilege use. If you enable auditing policies, you can track security events, such as when a user logs on or when an object has been accessed.

Once you've opened the Local Security Settings Console, you can access the Audit Policy portion by expanding the Local Policies node in the left pane and then clicking the Audit Policy node. This is shown in Figure 9-5.

To view or change a policy, right-click it and then select Properties from the context menu. An example of the Audit Object Access policy is shown in Figure 9-6.

Audit Policy contains several events that can be tracked. Table 9-1 lists those policies and their default settings.

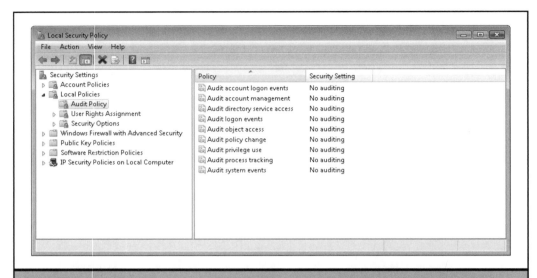

Figure 9-5.   The Audit Policy feature can help you manage which events will be logged.

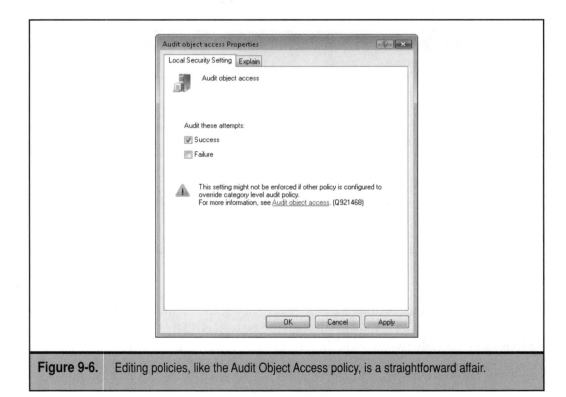

Figure 9-6.   Editing policies, like the Audit Object Access policy, is a straightforward affair.

Policy	Default Setting
Audit Account Logon Events	No auditing
Audit Account Management	No auditing
Audit Directory Service Access	No auditing
Audit Logon Events	No auditing
Audit Object Access	No auditing
Audit Policy Change	No auditing
Audit Privilege Use	No auditing
Audit Process Tracking	No auditing
Audit System Events	No auditing

Table 9-1.   Audit Policy Default Settings

User Rights Assignment Changes

User Rights Assignment policies establish what a user or group can do on a local computer. These settings can be managed by accessing the User Rights Assignment feature in the Local Security Settings Console.

First, open the Local Security Settings Console. Next, expand the Local Policies node in the left pane, and then click the User Rights Assignment node. This is shown in Figure 9-7.

Windows Vista adds several new settings for User Rights Assignment that were not provided in Windows XP. A major reason for these changes is due to User Account Control, which provides a thicker layer of protection for computers. It ensures that there is a separation of user and administrator accounts.

NOTE   We'll talk about User Account Control later in this chapter.

An example policy—Adjust Memory Quotas For A Process—is shown in Figure 9-8. Table 9-2 lists the settings for User Rights Assignment, along with their default settings.

One change in Windows Vista is that the Power Users group has been eliminated, and is only maintained for backward compatibility with legacy applications. As such, the Power Users group is not granted user rights in Vista.

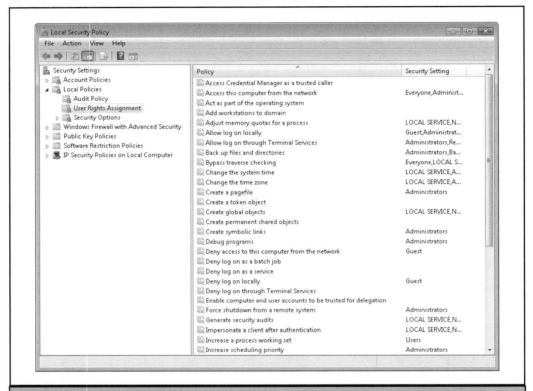

Figure 9-7. The User Rights Assignment portion of the Local Security Settings Console allows you to manage what users and groups can do on a computer.

Vista has added a number of new rights, including:

▼ **Access Credential Manager As A Trusted Caller**   A user or group can establish a connection to Credential Manager. Credential Manager is used—as the name implies—to manage credentials, which are associations of all of the information needed for logon and authentication.

■ **Allow Log On Locally**   A user or group is allowed to log on at the keyboard. This existed before in Windows XP as Log On Locally, but has been renamed in Vista, as there are Allow Log On Locally and Deny Log On Locally user rights.

▲ **Change The Time Zone**   A user or group is allowed to change the time zone.

Changes in Security Options

Security Options are used to enable or disable a computer's security settings. To access Security Options, first open the Local Security Settings Console. Next, expand the Local Policies node in the left pane, and then click the Security Options node. This is shown in Figure 9-9.

An example policy—Devices: Allowed To Format And Eject Removable Media—is shown in Figure 9-10.

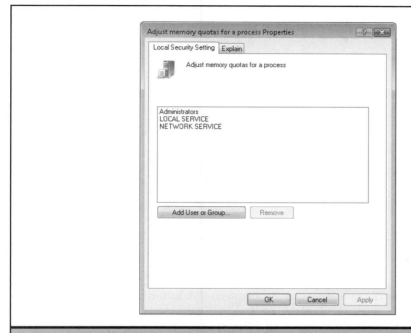

Figure 9-8.   The Adjust Memory Quotas For A Process policy allows you to define who can adjust the amount of memory used for a process.

Table 9-3 lists the security settings you can manage in Security Options, along with their default settings. As was the case with User Rights Assignment, the changes in Windows Vista are largely because of User Account Control.

Changes to Security Options include the following:

▼ **Remote registry access**   In earlier versions of Windows, multiple registry paths were remotely accessible by default. Now, the default setting has been changed, shoring up registry security.

■ **Anonymous access to named pipes and shares**   This option was added to restrict anonymous access to named pipes and shares.

▲ **Sharing and security model for local accounts**   Earlier versions of Windows authenticated local users as guests. In Vista, local users are authenticated as themselves, ensuring that appropriate rights and permissions are applied to users.

USER ACCOUNT CONTROL

User Account Control (UAC) is a new feature in Vista and is a big change in how Windows provisions user and application security. UAC prevents unauthorized changes to workstations. Whenever an application or task requires access to protected systems,

Policy	Default Setting
Access Credential Manager As A Trusted Caller	No default setting
Access This Computer From The Network	Everyone, Administrators, Users, Backup Operators
Act As Part Of The Operating System	No default setting
Add Workstations To Domain	No default setting
Adjust Memory Quotas For A Process	LOCAL SERVICE, NETWORK SERVICE, Administrators
Allow Log On Locally	Guest, Administrators, Users, Backup Operators
Allow Logon Through Terminal Services	Administrators, Remote Desktop Users
Back Up Files And Directories	Administrators, Backup Operators
Bypass Traverse Checking	Everyone, Administrators, Users, Backup Operators
Change The System Time	LOCAL SERVICE, Administrators
Change The Time Zone	LOCAL SERVICE, Administrators, Users
Create A Pagefile	Administrators
Create A Token Object	No default setting
Create Global Objects	Administrators, SERVICE
Create Permanent Shared Objects	No default setting
Create Symbolic Links	Administrators
Debug Programs	Administrators
Deny Access To This Computer From The Network	Guest
Deny Logon As A Batch Job	No default setting
Deny Logon As A Service	No default setting
Deny Logon Locally	Guest
Deny Logon Through Terminal Services	No default setting

Table 9-2.   User Rights Assignment Default Settings

Policy	Default Setting
Enable Computer And User Accounts To Be Trusted For Delegation	No default setting
Force Shutdown From A Remote System	Administrators
Generate Security Audits	LOCAL SERVICE, NETWORK SERVICE
Impersonate A Client After Authentication	Administrators, SERVICE
Increase A Process Working Set	Users
Increase Scheduling Priority	Administrators
Load And Unload Device Drivers	Administrators
Lock Pages In Memory	No default setting
Log On As A Batch Job	Administrators, Backup Operators
Log On As A Service	No default setting
Manage Auditing And Security Log	Administrators
Modify An Object Label	No default setting
Modify Firmware Environment Values	Administrators
Perform Volume Maintenance Tasks	Administrators
Profile Single Process	Administrators
Profile System Performance	Administrators
Remove Computer From Docking Station	Administrators, Users
Replace A Process Level Token	LOCAL SERVICE, NETWORK SERVICE
Restore Files And Directories	Administrators, Backup Operators
Shut Down The System	Administrators, Users, Backup Operators
Synchronize Directory Service Data	No default setting
Take Ownership Of Files Or Other Objects	Administrators

Table 9-2.   User Rights Assignment Default Settings *(Continued)*

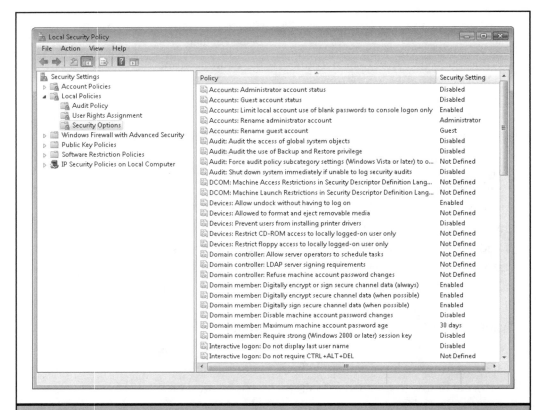

Figure 9-9. The Security Options feature in the Local Security Settings Console allows you to enable or disable various security settings.

UAC displays a pop-up message and asks the logged-on user for confirmation or an administrator's password. Users and applications are monitored by Vista, and when someone attempts an action that exposes important system data or system services, Vista steps in. Vista affects which privileges users and applications have, how applications are installed and run, and more. In earlier versions of Windows, malicious software and users could exploit the fact that most user accounts are configured as local computer administrators. This allows malicious software to install and use elevated privileges to wreak havoc on the computer. Programs installed by administrators can write to secure sections of the registry and file system.

To protect against the threat of malicious software, administrators require users to log on to workstations using standard user accounts. Users are more secure, but have limited capabilities. Companies with higher security standards even require their administrators to log on using standard user accounts. To do their jobs, administrators have to switch to an administrator account or use the Run As command. Users logged on as a standard user under Windows XP cannot perform some of the most basic tasks, such as changing the system clock, calendar, time zone, or power management settings.

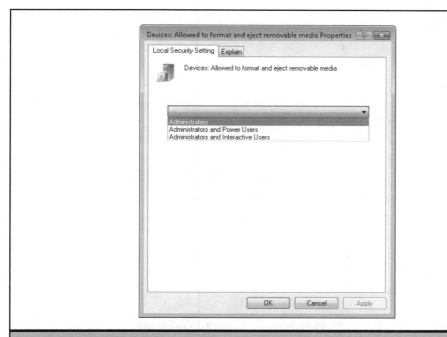

Figure 9-10.   Devices: Allowed To Format And Eject Removable Media lets you allow or deny users the ability to format or eject removable media.

Many applications operating on Windows XP will not function properly without adminis-trator rights to write to system locations during installation and normal operations.

Blocking users from all secure areas of their workstation and forcing administrators to bounce back and forth between accounts is heavy-handed and overkill; it cuts into productivity and sometimes produces a frustrated user. With Vista, UAC limits the scope of administrator-level access and requires applications to run in a specific user mode. This stops users from making changes to system settings and locks down the computer to prevent unauthorized applications from installing or performing malicious actions while enabling a much better user experience.

The component responsible for UAC is the Application Information service. This service facilitates the running of interactive applications with an "administrator" access token. To understand the workings of UAC, you have to first come to terms with the new account mode paradigm.

User Modes: Standard and Administrator

User Mode is a new term to express an old idea. In Vista parlance, User Mode simply refers to the level of access granted based on whether the user is an administrator or an end user. As in the past, Vista has a range of accounts, with varying levels of access privileges. Guests, Users, Power Users, and Administrators are present in Vista, as in Windows XP and other Windows operating systems.

Policy	Default Setting
Accounts: Administrator Account Status	Enabled
Accounts: Guest Account Status	Disabled
Accounts: Limit Local Account Use Of Blank Passwords To Console Logon Only	Enabled
Accounts: Rename Administrator Account	Administrator
Accounts: Rename Guest Account	Guest
Audit: Audit The Access Of Global System Objects	Disabled
Audit: Audit The Use Of Backup And Restore Privilege	Disabled
Audit: Shut Down System Immediately If Unable To Log Security Audits	Disabled
DCOM: Machine Access Restrictions In Security Descriptor Definition Language (SDDL) Syntax	Not defined
DCOM: Machine Launch Restrictions In Security Descriptor Definition Language (SDDL) Syntax	Not defined
Devices: Allow Undock Without Having To Log On	Enabled
Devices: Allowed To Format And Eject Removable Media	Not defined
Devices: Prevent Users From Installing Printer Drivers	Disabled
Devices: Restrict CD-ROM Access To Locally Logged-On User Only	Not defined
Devices: Restrict Floppy Access To Locally Logged-On User Only	Not defined
Devices: Unsigned Driver Installation Behavior	Silently Succeed
Domain controller: Allow Server Operators To Schedule Tasks	Not defined
Domain controller: LDAP Server Signing Requirements	Not defined
Domain controller: Refuse Machine Account Password Changes	Not defined
Domain member: Digitally Encrypt Or Sign Secure Channel Data (Always)	Enabled
Domain member: Digitally Encrypt Secure Channel Data (When Possible)	Enabled

Table 9-3.   Security Options Default Settings

Policy	Default Setting
Domain member: Digitally Sign Secure Channel Data (When Possible)	Enabled
Domain member: Disable Machine Account Password Changes	Disabled
Domain member: Maximum Machine Account Password Age	30 Days
Domain member: Require Strong (Windows 2000 or Later) Session Key	Disabled
Interactive Logon: Do Not Display Last User Name	Disabled
Interactive Logon: Do Not Require CTRL+ALT+DEL	Not defined
Interactive Logon: Message Text For Users Attempting To Log On	Not defined
Interactive Logon: Message Title For Users Attempting To Log On	Not defined
Interactive Logon: Number Of Previous Logons To Cache (In Case Domain Controller Is Not Available)	10 Logons
Interactive Logon: Prompt User To Change Password Before Expiration	14 Days
Interactive Logon: Require Domain Controller Authentication To Unlock Workstation	Disabled
Interactive Logon: Require Smart Card	Disabled
Interactive Logon: Smart Card Removal Behavior	No action
Microsoft Network Client: Digitally Sign Communications (Always)	Disabled
Microsoft Network Client: Digitally Sign Communications (If Server Agrees)	Enabled
Microsoft Network Client: Send Unencrypted Password To Third-Party SMB Servers	Disabled
Microsoft Network Server: Amount Of Idle Time Required Before Suspending Session	15 Minutes
Microsoft Network Server: Digitally Sign Communications (Always)	Disabled

Table 9-3.   Security Options Default Settings *(Continued)*

Policy	Default Setting
Microsoft Network Server: Digitally Sign Communications (If Client Agrees)	Disabled
Microsoft Network Server: Disconnect Clients When Logon Hours Expire	Enabled
Network Access: Allow Anonymous Sid/Name Translation	Disabled
Network Access: Do Not Allow Anonymous Enumeration Of SAM Accounts	Enabled
Network Access: Do Not Allow Anonymous Enumeration Of SAM Accounts And Shares	Disabled
Network Access: Do Not Allow Storage Of Credentials Or .NET Passports For Network Authentication	Disabled
Network Access: Let Everyone Permissions Apply To Anonymous Users	Disabled
Network Access: Named Pipes That Can Be Accessed Anonymously	SQL\QUERY, SPOOLSS, Netlogon, Lsarpc, Samr, Browser
Network Access: Remotely Accessible Registry Paths	Not defined
Network Access: Remotely Accessible Registry Paths And Sub-Paths	Not defined
Network Access: Restrict Anonymous Access To Named Pipes And Shares	Enabled
Network Access: Shares That Can Be Accessed Anonymously	Not defined
Network Access: Sharing And Security Model For Local Accounts	Classic – Local Users Authenticate As Themselves
Network Security: Do Not Store LAN Manager Hash Value On Next Password Change	Enabled
Network Security: Force Logoff When Logon Hours Expire	Disabled
Network Security: LAN Manager Authentication Level	Send NTLMv2 Response Only
Network Security: LDAP Client Signing Requirements	Negotiate Signing

Table 9-3.   Security Options Default Settings *(Continued)*

Policy	Default Setting
Network Security: Minimum Session Security For NTLM SSP–based (Including Secure RPC) Clients	No Minimum
Network Security: Minimum Session Security For NTLM SSP–Based (Including Secure RPC) Servers	No Minimum
Recovery Console: Allow Automatic Administrative Logon	Disabled
Recovery Console: Allow Floppy Copy And Access To All Drives And All Folders	Disabled
Shutdown: Allow System To Be Shut Down Without Having To Log On	Enabled
Shutdown: Clear Virtual Memory Pagefile	Disabled
System Cryptography: Force Strong Key Protection For User Keys Stored On The Computer	Not defined
System Cryptography: Use FIPS-Compliant Algorithms For Encryption, Hashing, And Signing	Disabled
System Objects: Default Owner For Objects Created By Members Of The Administrators Group	Object Creator
System objects: Require Case Insensitivity For Non-Windows Subsystems	Enabled
System Objects: Strengthen Default Permissions Of Internal System Objects (For Example, Symbolic Links)	Enabled
System Settings: Optional Subsystems	Posix
System Settings: Use Certificate Rules On Windows Executables For Software Restriction Policies	Disabled
User Account Control: Behavior Of The Elevation Prompt For Administrators In Admin Approval Mode	Prompt For Consent
User Account Control: Behavior Of The Elevation Prompt For Standard Users	Prompt For Credentials
User Account Control: Detect Application Installations And Prompt For Elevation	Enabled
User Account Control: Only Elevate Executables That Are Signed And Validated	Disabled
User Account Control: Run All Administrators In Admin Approval Mode	Enabled

Table 9-3.   Security Options Default Settings *(Continued)*

Policy	Default Setting
User Account Control: Switch To The Secure Desktop When Prompting For Elevation	Enabled
User Account Control: Virtualize File And Registry Write Failures To Per-User Locations	Enabled

Table 9-3.   Security Options Default Settings *(Continued)*

Note that the Power Users group in Vista is around only to support operations in legacy domains. The Power Users group in past platforms enabled users to perform system tasks without being administrators. However, using the Power Users group in this way still elevated applications with unnecessary privileges. For that reason, UAC does not use the Power Users group, and the permissions granted to the Power Users group on Windows XP have been removed from Vista altogether (you can restore them with a security template). In the Vista era, UAC enables standard users to perform all common configuration tasks and restricts all system tasks to administrators.

User Mode

UAC treats all accounts the same during logon and while performing normal tasks. All users—regardless of group membership—are given a User Mode token, that is a key that unlocks all the doors that end users typically need to operate their workstations normally and securely. Users can launch nonadministrative applications, print, search the desktop, and browse the Internet. Users cannot do things such as audit the security log, remove devices, install or uninstall applications that install into %systemroot%, change system settings, and launch many of the administrator tools. The following list shows how Vista revamps what standard users can do:

▼ **Desktop**   Install fonts, view the system clock and calendar, change the time zone, and change the display settings

■ **System**   Change power management settings, add printers, activate devices (when the required drivers are installed), download and install updates

▲ **Communications**   Create and configure virtual private network (VPN) connections and install Wired Equivalent Privacy (WEP) to connect to secure wireless networks

When a user tries to access a secure part of the workstation, he or she is informed that access is denied and asked if he or she wants to provide administrator credentials. Vista, unlike in the past, informs the user about access issues with a pop-up message. The same holds true for any applications that are either launched by the user or by itself. When the application tries to access restricted areas, the user is notified with a pop-up message and given the chance to provide elevated credentials.

Administrator Mode

When administrators log on, they are given the User Mode token, just as any other user. In addition, they are given a second token that identifies them as administrators. To make the workstation safe to operate for administrators, Vista also blocks administrators from accessing restricted areas in exactly the same way as if the administrator were a simple user. By default, all users present their User Mode tokens first. This solves the problem of running a workstation as a full-time administrator. The difference is that the pop-up message does not prompt an administrator for administrator credentials; rather, the administrator is asked to approve the action. If the logged-on administrator confirms that the access is legitimate, Vista checks the administrator's second token. The following list illustrates some of the tasks that only administrators can typically authorize:

▼ **Desktop**   Browse to another user's directory

■ **System**   Add or remove a user account, install and uninstall applications, open the Windows Firewall control panel, and install a driver for a device

▲ **Communications**   Configure Remote Desktop and configure parental controls

In Vista, even the administrators act as standard users during normal operations. Administrators are blocked from secure areas of the workstation because they only make use of their administrator tokens when needed and when approved. A pop-up message will appear, requiring confirmation that you are the one who seeks access, not some rogue application. You can see the difference between the administrator user and standard user access tokens by opening two command prompt windows, one run with elevation (right-click and select Run As Administrator) and one run as a standard user. In each window, type **whoami /all** and compare the results. User Mode privileges and Administrator Mode privileges are shown in Figures 9-11 and 9-12, respectively.

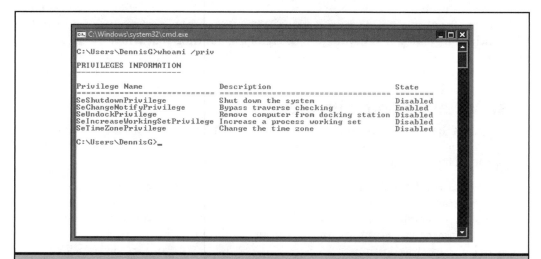

Figure 9-11.   User Mode privileges are shown by using the whoami /all command at the command prompt.

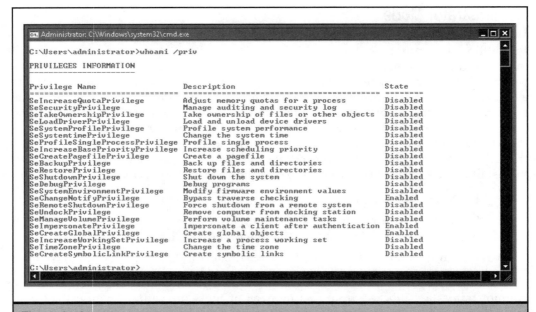

Figure 9-12. Administrators have, naturally, far more privileges than users.

Both access tokens will have the same SIDs, but the elevated administrator user access token will have more privileges than the standard user access token.

Even with UAC, it is still the best practice to log on with a standard user account to perform your normal activities. You can surf the Internet, send e-mail, and use a word processor, all without an administrator account. When you want to perform an administrative task, such as installing a new program or changing a setting that will affect other users, you don't have to switch to an administrator account. Windows Vista will prompt you for permission or an administrator password before any administrator tasks are launched.

User Account Control Prompts

The prompts that you see from UAC are based on where you are in Vista, what application you launched, and what part of the workstation you are accessing. Some of the common prompts you will encounter include:

▼ **Windows needs your permission to continue**   A Windows function or program that can affect other users of this computer needs your permission to start. Check the name of the action to ensure that it's a function or program you want to run. An example of this prompt is shown in Figure 9-13.

■ **A program needs your permission to continue**   A program that's not part of Windows needs your permission to start. It has a valid digital signature indicating its name and its publisher, which helps to ensure that the program is

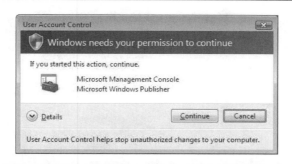

Figure 9-13.   If a Windows program or function is activated that affects other users on the computer, Vista will prompt you to continue.

what it claims to be. Make sure that this is a program that you intended to run. An example of this prompt is shown in Figure 9-14.

■ **An unidentified program wants access to your computer**   An unidentified program is one that doesn't have a valid digital signature from its publisher to ensure that the program is what it claims to be. This doesn't necessarily indicate danger, as many older, legitimate programs lack signatures. However, you should use extra caution and only allow this program to run if you obtained it from a trusted source, such as the original CD or a publisher's Web site. An example of this prompt is shown in Figure 9-15.

▲ **This program has been blocked**   This is a program that your administrator has specifically blocked from running on your computer. To run this program, you must contact your administrator and ask to have the program unblocked. An example of this is shown in Figure 9-16.

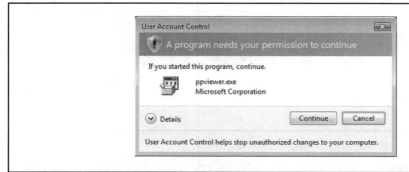

Figure 9-14.   Programs that are not part of Windows but that have valid digital signatures require your permission to start.

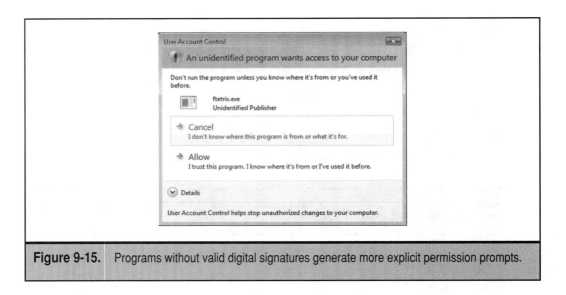

Figure 9-15. Programs without valid digital signatures generate more explicit permission prompts.

Managing UAC User Mode with Admin Approval Mode and Group Policy

Admin Approval Mode is the key component of UAC. It manages how administrators are prompted when running administrator applications (programs that access protected areas of the files system, registry, and system settings). By default, Admin Approval Mode works as follows:

▼   All administrator accounts—local and domain—operate in Admin Approval Mode.

▲   All administrators see the elevation prompt whenever they run administrator applications before the Administrator Mode token will be applied to grant access.

Figure 9-16. Administrators can block certain programs from running on Windows Vista.

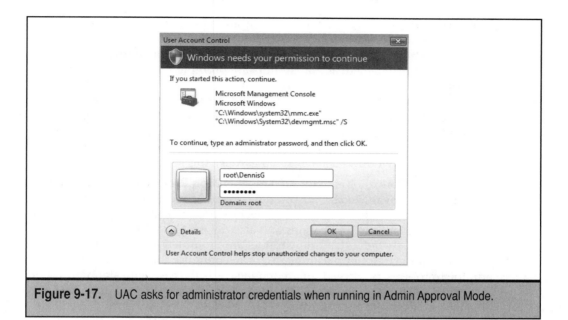

Figure 9-17.   UAC asks for administrator credentials when running in Admin Approval Mode.

Running certain applications will require the administrator password. This is shown in Figure 9-17.

Security Settings

Five security settings determine how Admin Approval Mode and elevation prompting are applied to administrators. These settings are found in either Group Policy or local security policies. These security settings are:

▼   **User Account Control: Behavior Of The Elevation Prompt For Standard Users**   Controls whether standard users see an elevation prompt when running administrator applications and can then provide administrator credentials to continue. By default, users logged on with a standard user account are prompted for administrator credentials when running administrator applications. You can configure this option so that users are not prompted and are prevented from using UAC to elevate their access. Note: This won't prevent users from using Run As.

■   **User Account Control: Switch To The Secure Desktop When Prompting For Elevation**   The secure desktop restricts application access to the desktop environment, isolating the new application thread. This keeps the any rogue application from gaining access to the process being elevated. By default, this security option is enabled. You can disable this setting if you wish to allow access to the launching thread for other monitoring or logging tools. Without the secure desktop setting in place, the workstation is exposed to attack and should be restored as soon as possible.

■ **User Account Control: Run All Administrators In Admin Approval Mode**   Sets administrators to run in Admin Approval Mode, which ensures that administrators are challenged when executing administrative tasks. With this feature enabled, administrators are prompted to confirm any access to protected systems that requires use of the Administrator Mode token. If you disable this setting, users logged on with an administrator account are not subject to administrator approval, are not prompted for elevation, and the Administrator Mode token is used. If disabled, administrators are given unfettered access to administrator applications. When Vista is a member of a legacy domain (Windows 2003 SP1 and earlier), this setting is disabled.

■ **User Account Control: Behavior Of The Elevation Prompt For Administrators In Admin Approval Mode**   If Admin Approval Mode is enabled, this determines whether administrators subject to it see an elevation prompt when running administrator applications and also determines how the elevation prompt works. By default, administrators are prompted for consent when running administrator applications. You can configure this option so that administrators are prompted for credentials, as is the case with standard users. You can also configure this option so that administrators are not prompted at all, in which case, the administrator will not be able to elevate privileges. This doesn't prevent administrators from right-clicking an application shortcut and selecting Run As Administrator.

▲ **User Account Control: Admin Approval Mode For The Built-In Administrator Account**   Determines whether actions taken while running as the built-in local administrator account are run in Admin Approval Mode. Enabled by default, the setting ensures that the built-in local administrator account is subject to the elevation prompt when administrator applications or tasks are executed. If you disable this setting, users and processes running as the built-in local administrator will not run in Admin Approval Mode and will not be subject to the elevation prompt.

Location

You can find these settings as part of the Computer policy in the Computer Configuration node, under Windows Settings\Security Settings\Local Policies\Security Options. For workstations managed as part of an Active Directory domain, you can use the Active Directory Users And Computers (ADUC) Console (dsa.msc) or the Group Policy Management Console (GPMC) to deploy the settings in your environment. You can also configure these settings on a per-computer basis using the local security policy. To disable or enable either of these settings:

1. Launch the Local Security Policy (secpol.msc) Console. From the Start menu, type **secpol.msc** in the Search text box, right-click the Local Security Policy program once it appears in the search results, and choose Open.

2. In the Local Security Policy Console tree, expand the Security Settings node, expand Local Policies, and select Security Options.

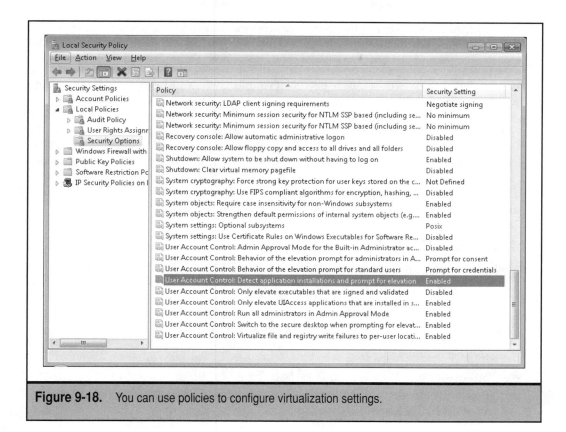

Figure 9-18.   You can use policies to configure virtualization settings.

3. Open the setting of interest, make any changes, and then click OK. An example is shown in Figure 9-18.

Application Run Levels: Standard and Administrator

Just as user accounts have two distinct User Modes, Vista distinguishes between two different run levels for applications: standard and administrator. If an application has been written for Vista (for example, it has the Vista-compliant logo), then it will leverage UAC to decrease the attack surface for the operating system by cutting back on the privileges required to run it. If the application was written for legacy operating systems, then, in all likelihood, it will not work smoothly with UAC and the end user will be asked repeatedly to approve the request operations of the application. The two run levels are broken up in the following ways:

▼   **Standard user applications**   Do not need or receive elevated privileges to run. The application writes data only to nonsystem locations of the registry and file system. Standard applications must request elevated privileges to perform administration tasks. If the currently logged-on user is an administrator, he or she can approve the request.

▲ **Administrator user applications** Require elevated privileges to run and perform core tasks. Administrator applications can perform tasks that require administrator privileges and can write to system locations of both the registry and file system.

Vista determines whether a user needs elevated privileges to run a program by supplying a security token for each application and any associated processes. All applications that run on Vista derive their security context from the logged-on user's access token. UAC treats all users as standard users, even if the user is an administrator, until the user or the application seeks access to protected systems. If an application has a standard token, Vista assumes that elevated (administrator) privileges are not required to run the application and launches it as a standard application. If an application has an administrator token, Vista understands that elevated privileges are required to run the application and prompts the user for permission or confirmation prior to running the program.

Monitoring Installations

Installation technologies can often access protected areas of the workstation, including the system directories and registry. The mission of UAC regarding software installations is to protect the user and workstation from unauthorized or harmful entities. To this end, UAC monitors common installation points and will raise a notice and post a log entry when it detects an installation. UAC monitors the following:

▼ 32-bit executables

■ Applications without an exposed requested Execution Level property

▲ Interactive processes running as a standard user with Least-Privileged User Account (LUA) enabled

If a 32-bit executable is launched, the thread is checked for the characteristics that qualify it as an installation process:

▼ The file name includes keywords like "install," "setup," "update," etc.

■ Keywords are in the following Versioning Resource fields: Vendor, Company Name, Product Name, File Description, Original File Name, Internal Name, and Export Name.

■ Keywords in the side-by-side manifest are embedded in the executable.

■ Keywords in specific StringTable entries are linked in the executable.

■ Key attributes in the Emacs Configuration Record (RC) data are linked in the executable.

▲ There are targeted sequences of bytes within the executable.

If these conditions are met, UAC will halt the execution of the installer process and prompt the currently logged-on user for administrator credentials or for confirmation that the installation is authorized.

File System and Registry Virtualization

Applications written expressly for Vista will integrate smoothly into the daily task of your workstation users. These Vista-compatible applications promise to run smoothly and securely. To be a viable desktop platform, Vista has to accommodate the library of legacy applications in an equally secure way.

Software that is not written for Vista is launched at a standard run level by default and in a special compatibility mode. This compatibility mode creates an isolated version of the workstation file system and registry—the application is free to read and modify this copy while the actual reference file system and registry remain untouched. When an application writes to a system location, Vista gives the application a private copy of the file or registry value. Any changes are then written to the private copy, and this is stored in the user's profile. If the application attempts to read or write to this system location again, it is given the private copy from the user's profile to work with. If there is any kind of issue as a result of the system manipulation, the notification and logging will point to the virtualized location rather than to the actual location.

A consequence of this compatibility mode is that changes to protected systems are, for the most part, going to be user specific. Since the changes made are stored in the user's profile, no other user on the workstation will be affected by the update. If you are using a legacy application to install a printer, for example, only the logged-on user will be able to access the printer. You may have to find a way to facilitate these kinds of changes through a logon script or other automation options if more than one user profile is regularly used on the workstation.

Before we move on to the next section, there are a couple of notes to share. First, Vista-compatible applications will always be accompanied with a manifest file (.xml) that holds the User Mode and application run levels necessary to install and operate the application. Using the manifest, UAC will know how to support the application to find a balance between reducing the security exposure and ensuring a good user experience. The second note is that virtualization of the file system and registry is not included in the 64-bit version of Vista. Any application that is installed on such a platform is expected to be Vista compatible and to include a manifest.

Managing UAC Application Run Levels with Application Properties

You can mark an application run level by updating the application's properties. You can establish the run level by marking an application or process to always run using elevated credentials without prompting the user for consent. You simply have to access the Properties menu and set the security context.

1. Log on to the workstation as an administrator.

2. Find the program of interest by using the Vista desktop Search feature in the Start menu.

3. When the program appears in the search results, right-click the application's shortcut, and click Properties.

4. In the Properties window, click the Compatibility tab.

5. Under Privilege Level, select the Run This Program As An Administrator check box, and click OK.

Managing UAC Application Run Levels with Policies

There are two Group Policy settings of UAC that can be deployed:

▼ **User Account Control: Detect Application Installations And Prompt For Elevation**   Activates Vista's management of software installations. When applied, Vista automatically detects application installations and prompts for elevation or consent. This setting is enabled by default. Vista automatically detects installations and prompts users for elevation or consent to continue. If you disable this setting, users will not be able to elevate the run level by supplying administrator credentials.

▲ **User Account Control: Virtualize File And Registry Write Failures To Per-User Locations**   Activates file and registry virtualization. This setting is also enabled by default. When enabled, error notifications and error logging related to virtualized files and registry values are written to the user's isolated location rather than to the actual location. When this setting is disabled and an application attempts to access protected systems, then the task will fail without notification.

You can find these settings as part of the Computer policy in the Computer Configuration node, under Windows Settings\Security Settings\Local Policies\Security Options. For workstations managed as part of an Active Directory domain, you can use the Active Directory Users And Computers (ADUC) Console (dsa.msc) or the Group Policy Management Console (GPMC) to deploy the settings in your environment. You can also configure these settings on a per-computer basis using the local security policy. To disable or enable either of these settings:

1. Launch the Local Security Policy (secpol.msc) Console. From the Start menu, type **secpol.msc** in the Search text box, right-click the Local Security Policy program once it appears in the search results, and choose Open.

2. In the Local Security Policy Console tree, expand the Security Settings node, expand Local Policies, and select Security Options.

3. Open the setting of interest, make any changes, and then click OK.

User accounts are just the outer layer of our computer security onion—as we peel one away, there are deeper ones within. In the next chapter, we'll discuss the next layer of our onion's security: system security.

CHAPTER 10

System Security

Microsoft has taken a lot of lumps over security holes in Windows. Whether it's susceptibility to viruses and spyware or flaws in the operating system, there is a lot to worry about. But despite widespread criticism, Microsoft really is taking a big step with new security enhancements. One of the biggest—if not the biggest—set of improvements in Windows Vista has to do with its security features. Some of the improvements are smaller and embedded in seemingly unrelated parts of the operating system, while still others are whole new applications.

This chapter examines some of the more prominent security features that are designed to keep your system safe. We'll talk about securing data on your hard drive using new technologies like BitLocker and Trusted Platform Modules (TPMs). We'll also talk about the new and improved Windows Firewall with Advanced Security. Vista keeps all its security features accessible from one place, which we'll also examine. Finally, we'll talk about preventing spyware from invading your system by using Windows Defender.

> **NOTE**   There are other third-party drive-encryption solutions out there that one could consider. One of the market leaders, particularly in the business space, is Pointsec. A popular open-source solution for disk encryption is TrueCrypt. Although we don't go into detail on them here, more information can be found at www.pointsec.com and www.truecrypt.org, respectively.

TRUSTED PLATFORM MODULES

A new layer of security introduced in Windows XP—and continuing with Windows Vista—is the Encrypting File System (EFS). Using EFS, data is encrypted on your hard drive so that only you could access it. It stores encryption certificates as part of the user profile. If users on the computer have access to their profiles, then those files can be accessed.

But while EFS is a nice security measure, it isn't foolproof. If an attacker still has physical access to the computer, then the data can still be compromised. For example, if a laptop is stolen, or if the attacker is logging on at the keyboard, EFS isn't totally secure, because the attacker could access the computer before Windows starts up, change to a different operating system, and access the data.

Windows Vista shores up your computer from this type of physical attack by introducing the Trusted Platform Module Services architecture. It uses a hardware component called a TPM, which is a microchip built into the motherboard used to enhance data protection. It also ensures validation of the boot file's integrity and checks to see if a disk has been altered while the operating system was offline.

TPM employs three technologies:

▼   **Sealing**   This encrypts data such that it can only be decrypted by the same computer that encrypted it and while using the same software.

▲   **Binding**   This encrypts data using the TPM endorsement key, a unique key installed on the chip during its production.

NOTE   A third technology is called remote attestation. This isn't especially relevant for our discussion of TPM as it relates to Vista, but it is nice to know what it is. Remote attestation creates an unforgeable summary of the software on a computer. This allows a third party, like a digital music store, to make sure that the software has not been compromised. This feature has created some furor amongst privacy advocates.

When used together, BitLocker and TPM seal the boot manager and boot files of a computer. Those files can only be unsealed if they remain unchanged since they were last sealed.

NOTE   TPM is not something the inexperienced user or administrator should fiddle with. If you don't know what you're doing or aren't sure, make sure that you invest some time in educating yourself on how it works and is configured. If you make a mistake in configuring it, you run a good chance of losing data.

Using TPM

Remember, if you want to use TPM, you need a computer that already has the TPM chip installed. If your computer(s) running Vista isn't TPM version 1.2–compatible, and it doesn't have a Trusted Computing Group (TCG)–compliant Basic Input Output System (BIOS), this feature won't work and you'll see a message as shown in Figure 10-1.

To see if a computer is capable of using TPM:

1. Click Start, point to All Programs, point to Accessories, and then click Command Prompt.
2. Type **tpm.msc** in the Open text box, and then click ENTER. The resulting console is shown in Figure 10-1 when a TPM chip is either not present or is not enabled in BIOS.

When the chip is present and enabled in BIOS, TPM is configured and managed by using the commands listed under the Actions menu.

Initializing the TPM

Before using the TPM for the first time, you must initialize it and then turn it on. Initializing a TPM configures it for use on a computer. This process involves activating the TPM and then establishing ownership of it.

To initialize the TPM:

1. Using administrator credentials, log on locally to the computer.
2. Start the Trusted Platform Module Management console, as described in the previous section.
3. Under Actions, click Initialize TPM to start the TPM Initialization Wizard. On the Welcome page, click Next.

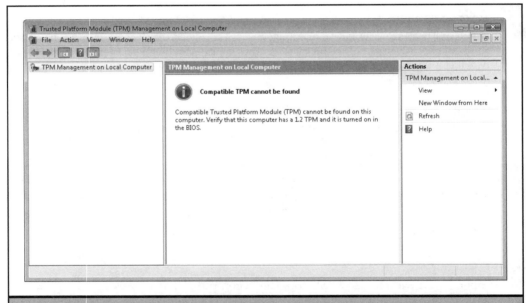

Figure 10-1. The TPM console is used to manage Vista's TPM functions.

4. The next step depends on the state of the TPM:

- If the TPM Initialization Wizard detects a BIOS that doesn't meet Vista's TPM requirements, the wizard will not continue.

- If the TPM is turned off, the wizard will show the Turn On The TPM Security Hardware page. At this point, you'll have to follow the instructions for turning on the TPM. This will involve shutting down the computer and following BIOS screen prompts. When the computer restarts, Vista will prompt you to turn on the TPM.

- If the TPM is turned on, you'll see a Create The TPM Owner Password page.

The next phase of TPM initialization is setting ownership. Setting ownership involves assigning a password so that only the authorized TPM owner can manage the TPM.

NOTE The TPM password is also required if you choose to deactivate the TPM.

To establish the ownership of TPM:

1. Using administrator credentials, log on locally to the computer.

2. Start the Trusted Platform Module Management console, as described in the previous section.

3. Under Actions, click Initialize TPM to start the TPM Initialization Wizard. On the Welcome page, click Next.

4. On the Create The TPM Owner Password page, select Automatically Create The Password (Recommended), and then click Next.

5. On the Save Your TPM Owner Password page, click Save and then select a location to save the password. The best practice is to save the TPM ownership password to removable media, like a Universal Serial Bus (USB) flash drive.

6. Click Save. The password file is saved as *computer_name*.tpm.

7. Click Print if you want to print a hard copy of your password.

NOTE   Obviously, you don't want this printout taped to the wall next to your computer.

8. Click Initialize.

9. When initialization is finished, click Close.

Turning Off TPM

Since TPM is a reasonably new hardware feature, new computers might have TPM turned on by default. If you elect not to use TPM, it's a good idea to turn it off. Also, if you want to reconfigure or recycle a computer, you should turn off TPM.

To turn off the TPM:

1. Using administrator credentials, log on locally to the computer.

2. Start the Trusted Platform Module Management console, as described in the previous section.

3. Under Actions, click Turn TPM Off.

4. In the Turn Off The TPM Security Hardware dialog box, select one of the following methods for entering your password and turning off the TPM:

   ■ If you have your TPM owner password on removable media, insert the media and click I Have A Backup File With The TPM Owner Password. In the Select Backup File With The TPM Owner Password dialog box, click Browse and then use the Open dialog box to locate the .tpm file saved on your removable media. Click Open and then click Turn TPM Off.

   ■ If you don't have the removable media with your owner password, click I Want To Type The TPM Owner Password. In the Type Your TPM Owner Password dialog box, enter your password and then click Turn TPM Off.

   ■ If you don't know your TPM owner password, click I Don't Have The TPM Owner Password, and then follow the on-screen instructions. Since you are logged on locally, you'll be able to turn off TPM.

Clearing the TPM

Turning off isn't the final thing you can do to deactivate TPM. That just stops it from running. Clearing the TPM cancels the TPM ownership and completes TPM shutdown.

To clear the TPM:

1. Using administrator credentials, log on locally to the computer.

2. Start the Trusted Platform Module Management console.

3. Under Actions, click Clear TPM.

4. The Clear The TPM Security Hardware dialog box appears, and you are asked for a method for entering your password and clearing the TPM:

   - If you have your TPM owner password on removable media, insert the media and click I Have A Backup File With The TPM Owner Password. In the Select Backup File With The TPM Owner Password dialog box, click Browse and then use the Open dialog box to locate the .tpm file saved on your removable media. Click Open and then click Turn TPM Off.

   - If you don't have the removable media with your owner password, click I Want To Type The TPM Owner Password. In the Type Your TPM Owner Password dialog box, enter your password and then click Turn TPM Off.

   - If you don't know your TPM owner password, click I Don't Have The TPM Owner Password, and then follow the on-screen instructions. Since you are logged on locally, you'll be able to turn off TPM.

BITLOCKER DRIVE ENCRYPTION

Losing a notebook with confidential data can be a disaster for any business. The consequences can affect every facet of a company, and can wreak havoc long after the event. Such a catastrophe can be damaging to the reputation and viability of a firm, resulting in loss of goodwill, lost revenue, a weakened competitive position, and loss of consumer confidence. With such a devastating impact, it is no wonder that data theft is one of the major concerns among security experts and corporate executives alike.

Another aspect for today's administrators to contend with is government regulations that focus on corporate data protection and privacy. Recent legislation in this area has had a strong impact on organizational storage policies, especially for devices that are easily lost, stolen, or compromised.

BitLocker Drive Encryption is a data-protection feature available in the Enterprise and Ultimate versions of Vista. It protects user and system data on the operating system volume when the computer is turned off or hibernated, that is while the computer is offline. BitLocker addresses the very real threats of data theft or exposure from lost, stolen, or inappropriately decommissioned devices with a security solution that is tightly integrated with Vista. It provides both mobile and office workers with enhanced data protection if their systems are lost or stolen and secure data deletion when computers are decommissioned. BitLocker provides data protection by bringing together two major functions:

▼ Full drive encryption, including:

  ■ All user files

  ■ All system files, including the swap and hibernation files

▲ Checking the integrity of early boot components, including:

  ■ System BIOS

  ■ Master Boot Record (MBR)

  ■ Boot sector

  ■ Boot manager

For a BitLocker-protected system to boot, the protected volume will be decrypted only after the early boot components are tested. Checking the integrity of early boot components helps ensure that the system boots, only if those components are pristine, were not tampered with, and that the protected drive is homed in the original host. Note, however, that the boot files on the system volume are important elements of the integrity checking; they are not encrypted.

The benefits of BitLocker are the reasons why it was developed and the value offered for IT administrators. BitLocker prevents a malicious user from:

▼ Booting BitLocker-protected drives in another operating system

■ Running a software-hacking tool to break Vista file and system protections

▲ Performing offline viewing of the files that are stored on the protected drive

At the end of the workstation lifecycle, BitLocker offers benefits that simplify the recycling process:

▼ Data on the encrypted volume can be rendered useless by deleting the TPM key store.

▲ Data can be made permanently unusable, which takes seconds instead of hours.

NOTE   Encrypting a drive volume is not the same as using Microsoft's EFS technology. EFS allows you to encrypt sections of a volume—or an entire volume—using cryptography as a feature of the operating system. Encrypting a drive as BitLocker does so using TPM is a pre-boot technology.

Technical Overview

BitLocker encrypts your storage area with a full-volume encryption key (FVEK), that, in turn, is encrypted with a volume master key (VMK). The addition of the VMK allows BitLocker to easily rekey when encryption keys upstream in the trust chain are lost or compromised. VMK is bound, or sealed, to the TPM 1.2 security hardware. BitLocker leverages the 1.2-specification TPM chip and the TCG specification for the Static Root of Trust Measurement (SRTM) to provide a high level of tamper detection to early boot code. This, combined with integrated disk encryption, provides the most resilient data-at-rest operating system solution ever offered for a Windows environment.

Access to data on the protected operating system volume is possible if the TPM successfully validates the integrity of early boot components on the protected drive. The default TPM platform validation profile secures the VMK against changes to the MBR code (workstationR 4), the New Technology File System (NTFS) boot sector (workstationR 8), the NTFS boot block (workstationR 9), the NTFS boot manager (workstationR 10), and the volume key and critical components (workstationR 11). This process is shown in Figure 10-2.

The Vista loader searches for usable keys for each enrolled option in turn until it finds a key that can decrypt the volume. When a BitLocker-enabled operating system volume boots, BitLocker attempts to unlock a volume in this sequence:

1. Clear key: Protection has been disabled and the VMK is freely accessible. No authentication is necessary.

2. Authentication without user input:
   - TPM: The TPM successfully validates early boot components to unseal the VMK.
   - TPM plus startup key: The TPM successfully validates early boot components, and a USB flash drive that contains the startup key is inserted.

3. Authentication that requires user input:
   - TPM plus personal identification number (PIN): The user must enter the correct PIN before the TPM can be successfully validated.
   - Recovery key and/or startup key: The user must insert the USB flash drive that holds the recovery key or startup key.
   - Recovery password: The user must enter the correct recovery password.

Steps for Deploying BitLocker

In selecting which devices might require encryption, look to your corporate security policy. Generally speaking, a good candidate device for BitLocker is one that has valuable data where the loss or revelation of that data would have a significant, negative impact on the company, its customers, shareholders, or staff.

Requirements for BitLocker

The following list includes some of the requirements for BitLocker:

▼ The system volume hard disk drive must be formatted with NTFS rather than File Allocation Table (FAT) or FAT32 file systems.

■ A separate volume must be partitioned and given a drive letter. The partition must:
   - Be formatted using NTFS

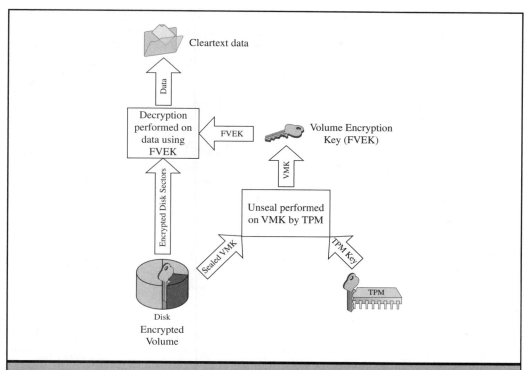

Figure 10-2.   Windows Vista uses BitLocker and TPM-enabled protection to secure data on your hard drive.

- Not be encrypted and be used to support the authentication process to start the computer.

- Be, at a minimum, 450 megabytes (MB), although Microsoft recommends a minimum of 1.5 gigabytes (GB). Use your judgment on this, but remember that the more space you have, the better equipped you'll be to accommodate future requirements.

▲ Your system must support and be equipped with either a separate TPM version 1.2 module or a USB flash drive on which BitLocker stores a recovery key.

To find out if your computer has TPM security hardware:

1. Open BitLocker Drive Encryption by clicking the Start button, clicking Control Panel, clicking Security, and then clicking BitLocker Drive Encryption. If you are prompted for an administrator password or confirmation, type the password or provide the confirmation.

2. If the TPM administration link appears in the left pane, your computer has the TPM security hardware. If this link is not present, you will need to either update the computer BIOS to support TPM or use a removable USB memory device to turn on BitLocker and store the BitLocker startup key that you'll need whenever you restart your computer.

Some details that are good to know about BitLocker:

▼ An administrator needs to turn BitLocker on.

■ You will have to use the function keys (F1 through F10) to enter the 48-character recovery key. Only F1 through F10 keys are universally available pre-boot, across all original equipment manufacturers (OEMs) and languages. However, where available, the numeric keys 0 through 9 are also usable now.

■ BitLocker optionally leverages an existing Active Directory infrastructure to remotely escrow recovery keys.

▲ BitLocker uses Advanced Encryption Standard (AES) as its encryption algorithm, with configurable key lengths of 128 or 256 bits. These options can be configured by using Group Policy.

Multifactor Authentication

If you choose, you can integrate multifactor authentication solutions with BitLocker to make your computer security more resilient. BitLocker supports a few options for multifactor authentication through choices for key storage. A protected volume must be configured for, or enrolled in, at least one storage method. An authentication provider protects a key storage file from any read or write activity, except by a trusted, authenticated source. An authentication provider secures the startup key file for either:

▼ TPM-plus-startup-key authentication scenarios

▲ Startup-key-only authentication scenarios

The Vista pre-boot loader searches for keys in all the enabled options until it finds a key that can decrypt the volume. Figure 10-3 shows a dialog box generated by a system looking for a key. The key storage options for Vista include:

▼ Recovery password (for recovery only)

■ TPM

■ TPM plus PIN

■ TPM plus startup key (such as a USB or other storage devices)

▲ Startup key (such as a USB or other storage devices)

The more authentication factors you include, the more secure the computer. Of course, each factor has a maintenance element that should be considered. Management and recovery of authentication factors is no simple endeavor. With that in mind, a relatively manageable but secure way to configure BitLocker is to use TPM 1.2 with a TCG-compliant

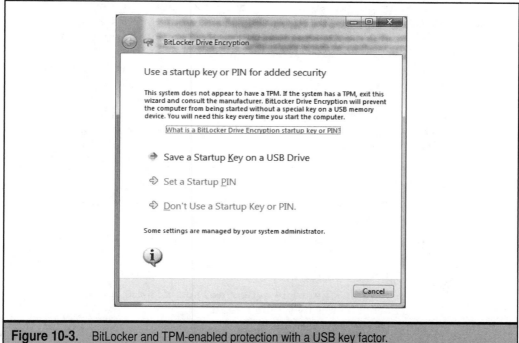

Figure 10-3. BitLocker and TPM-enabled protection with a USB key factor.

BIOS implementation, plus a startup key. A startup key provides an additional factor of authentication by requiring either an additional physical key (a USB flash drive with a machine-readable key written to it) or a PIN entry that was set by the user.

You configure volumes for BitLocker protection and enroll key files into a storage method using the BitLocker Drive Encryption Microsoft Management Console (MMC), found in the Security applet of Control Panel, or by using the Windows Management Instrumentation (WMI) administrative interface. Each enrolled key storage method has a key file, and the Vista boot loader has to be able to find the file. The Vista loader looks for key container files in the root directory of each storage device listed in the BIOS that is formatted with NTFS.

For information on how to enhance BitLocker with custom authentication provider, visit www.microsoft.com/whdc/system/platform/hwsecurity/BitLockerExt.mspx and download the white paper.

Building the BitLocker Partition on a Computer with No Operating System

BitLocker requires a separate partition for exclusive use that must have at least 450 MB and be set as the active partition. When installing Vista on pristine hard disk drives without an operating system, you need to configure two partitions. Essentially, the process involves starting your computer using the Vista media and interrupting the normal installation to access diskpart.exe to partition and format your volumes. If the target drive has an operating system installed, do not perform this procedure. Instead, you will need to repartition the drive, as discussed in the following section.

To partition a drive with no operating system for BitLocker Drive Encryption:

1. While installing Vista, enter Setup:

   a. Turn on the computer with the Vista installation media in the CD-ROM or DVD-ROM drive. When prompted, press any key to boot from the Vista installation media.

   b. After Vista mounts the Setup environment, the Installation Windows dialog box appears. In the dialog box, choose System Recovery Options.

   c. Clear any operating systems listed in the System Recovery Options list, and then click Next.

   d. Click Command Line Window. In the command-line window, type **diskpart.exe**.

2. Create the BitLocker Partition:

   a. Select the hard disk for use by typing **select disk 0**, and then erase the existing partition table by typing **clean**.

   b. Create a primary partition by typing **create partition primary**. Set the drive letter by typing **assign letter=C**.

   c. Format the partition by typing **Format FS=NTFS QUICK**. Then set the minimum partition size to 450 MB by typing **Shrink minimum=450**.

NOTE If Vista is already installed, you can use Compmgmt.msc to access the Disk Management Console and accomplish the same tasks.

3. Create the system partition:

   a. After the Shrink command completes for the C volume, create a primary partition in the space remaining by typing **Create partition primary**.

   b. Set the new partition as active by typing **Active**.

   c. Set the drive letter by typing **assign letter=D**. You can use drive letters other than D if you need to.

   d. Format the new partition by typing **Format FS=NTFS QUICK**.

4. Quit the Diskpart application by typing **exit**. Close the Command Prompt window by typing **exit**.

5. Restart the computer and then press any key to boot from the installation media when prompted. Select Install Now, accept the license agreement, and proceed with the installation. Install Vista on drive C.

6. If the computer BIOS is TPM 1.2–compliant and TPM module is active, you will need to initialize it as described in the "Initializing the TPM" section later in this chapter.

Creating the BitLocker Partition on a Computer with an Operating System

If you have a computer running Vista already and would like to integrate BitLocker Drive Encryption, you have to follow a different course. You will need to have another partition available, either by using unallocated space on an existing drive or by adding an additional hard disk drive to the system. Once you have the additional storage area:

1. Boot the computer running Vista into the Vista Setup environment using the installation media in the CD-ROM or DVD-ROM drive:

    a. Choose to boot from the drive hosting the Vista installation media, proceed through the loader screens, and enter System Recovery Options.

    b. Clear any operating systems listed in the System Recovery Options list, and then click Next.

    c. Click Command Line Window. In the command-line window, type **diskpart.exe**.

2. Create the BitLocker partition on the new hard disk drive by launching Diskpart from the search bar in the Start menu:

    a. Once in the interactive Diskpart window, select the hard disk for use by typing **Select disk 1**—assuming that one (1) is the new disk number. You can detect the disk number by logging on to Vista, launching compmgmt.msc, and viewing the disk configuration.

    b. Create a primary partition by typing **create partition primary**. Set the drive letter by typing **assign letter=D**, or assign it another drive letter if D is not available.

    c. Format the partition by typing **Format FS=NTFS QUICK**. Then set the minimum partition size to 450 MB by typing **Shrink minimum=450**.

    d. Quit the Diskpart application by typing **exit**. Close the Command Prompt window by typing **exit**.

NOTE   You can use Compmgmt.msc to access the Disk Management Console and accomplish these tasks. You will need to reboot Vista into the installation media to accomplish the following tasks.

3. Transfer the early boot components to the new partition:

a. Make new boot sectors at the beginning of the new partition. Use the Bootsect.exe tool, found in the Boot folder on the Vista installation media. Type `x:\boot\bootsect /nt60 ALL`. The /nt60 switch applies the master boot code that is compatible with Vista to all partitions.

b. Prepare the boot manager files by removing the read-only, system, and hidden attributes. Type `Attrib -r -s -h c:\bootmgr`. Copy the boot manager files to the system drive by typing `Xcopy C:\bootmgr d:\`.

c. Restore the read-only, system, and hidden attributes to the boot manager files on both drives by typing the following commands into the command window:

- `Attrib +r +h +s c:\bootmgr`
- `Attrib +r +h +s d:\bootmgr`
- `Attrib +r +h +s d:\boot`

d. Make a copy of the boot files on drive C by typing `Xcopy d:\boot c:\boot\ cherky`. Copy the boot manager files to the C drive by typing `Xcopy x:\bootmgr c:\`.

e. Close the Command Prompt window by typing `exit`. Return to the main installation screen by clicking Close.

f. Remove the installation media, and then restart the computer.

g. If you are integrating a TPM, you will need to initialize it, as described in the "Initializing the TPM" section later in this chapter.

For a full list of technical requirements, visit technet.microsoft.com/en-us/windows-vista/aa906017.aspx.

Turning BitLocker On

1. Open Bitlocker Drive Encryption by clicking the Start button, clicking Control Panel, clicking Security, and then selecting BitLocker Drive Encryption.

2. Click Turn On BitLocker.

3. Follow the instructions in the BitLocker Setup Wizard.

Recovering Data Protected by BitLocker

If the TPM fails validation due to a necessary upgrade, if the system board that contains the TPM is replaced, or if the hard disk drive that contains the operating system is moved to another computer, you can use a recovery key that is stored on a USB key to reset access to the encrypted drive.

The recovery password can be saved to a folder or to one or more USB keys. A domain administrator can also configure Group Policy to automatically generate recovery passwords and transparently escrow them to Active Directory. Administrators can handle recovery keys in whatever manner is most appropriate to their infrastructure. In enterprise environments, the most efficient way to handle key material is to use BitLocker's ability to escrow the keys in Active Directory. This can be enabled via Group Policy or WMI. Domain administrators can access recovery keys whenever they are needed by using scripts or simple Lightweight Directory Access Protocol (LDAP) commands. Another option is to store recovery keys on USB media. The USB devices can be kept separate from the computer, and the enterprise administrator can implement an extra layer of physical access control to help protect those keys.

To unlock the computer by typing your recovery key:

1. Turn on the computer, and let the system conduct the Power On Self Test (POST).

2. The computer starts the BitLocker Drive Encryption Recovery console, as shown in Figure 10-4.

3. Type the recovery password, and then press ENTER. The computer will unlock and restart automatically.

To unlock the computer by using a startup or recovery key stored on a USB memory drive:

1. Turn on the computer, and let the system conduct the POST. The computer starts the BitLocker Drive Encryption Recovery console.

2. When prompted for the USB drive, insert the drive that stores the startup or recovery key, wait a moment for the drive to mount, and then press the ENTER key.

3. The computer will unlock and restart automatically. You will not need to enter the recovery key manually.

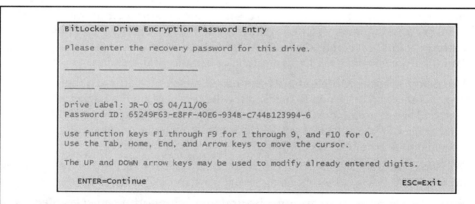

Figure 10-4.   You must use the function keys to enter the 48-character recovery key for BitLocker.

If the computer locks, as it will if you enter an incorrect key, press ESC twice to exit the recovery prompt and turn off your computer. If the computer locks because the early boot components were modified, or if there is a TPM error, then the locked computer will not accept standard keyboard numbers. In this case, use the function keys to enter the recovery key password. Function keys F1 through F9 represent digits 1 through 9, and the F10 function key represents 0.

Limitations

The following limitations are consequences of deploying BitLocker. Read on and ensure that you accommodate these points when planning your deployment so that you are not caught off guard:

▼ **Dependence on a recovery key**　The most obvious limitation of a BitLocker solution is that if you lose your recovery key and the protected system is modified, the drive becomes unrecoverable. Of course, this is by design. If at all possible, escrow the recovery password to either Active Directory or another safe location. However, this is a valuable feature when a workstation asset is decommissioned. BitLocker will place the computer into a recovery state so that only the recovery key holder can access the disk's contents. This can be of value to you when a workstation is sold or redeployed.

NOTE　Brute-force attacks against the volume encryption keys are currently computationally unfeasible, just as with any other AES 128-bit or 256-bit protected data.

■ **Additional authentication factors add complexity and risk**　BitLocker also has an optional PIN or USB multifactor authentication feature that can be used in conjunction with a TPM for added layers of security. The consequence of adding authentication factors is that if any one of these is lost, the system will be locked, a support request will be created, and an administrator must use a recovery key. Until resolved, the computer will be completely unusable. Also, adding factors can create a less secure system, as is the case when using a PIN, and the user records the PIN in a public or easy-to-find location.

■ **BitLocker is susceptible to hardware-based attacks**　Naturally, there are systems that can be aimed to break BitLocker encryption if a hacker has physical access to the protected computer. Configurations that do not take advantage of the additional authentication factors (external key authentication options) may be more susceptible to hardware-based attacks.

■ **Weak passwords**　When using BitLocker with Vista, the security of the operating system still relies on users choosing strong passwords for logon and recovery.

▲ **Enterprise support systems must be updated**　Supporting an encrypted computer will be little different from administering an unencrypted drive. The differences include diagnostic knowledge and new processes for storing and accessing recovery keys.

WINDOWS SECURITY CENTER

While many of the Vista security components work independently of each other, Microsoft has provided a unified interface for the management of these tools. The Windows Security Center, shown in Figure 10-5, is activated by clicking Start and then clicking Control Panel. In Control Panel, click Security and then click Check This Computer's Security Status.

Windows Security Center will work differently, depending on how your computer is configured: as part of a domain or a standalone computer in a workgroup.

In a domain environment, administrators handle the various computer security tasks, but users can still use this application to get information on their computer's security settings, although they can't take any action. In a workgroup, however, individual users manage security settings. Windows Security Center will also report the current status of the security applications.

In the Windows Security Center, you can track various features, each in a different panel of the center. The details that are tracked include the following.

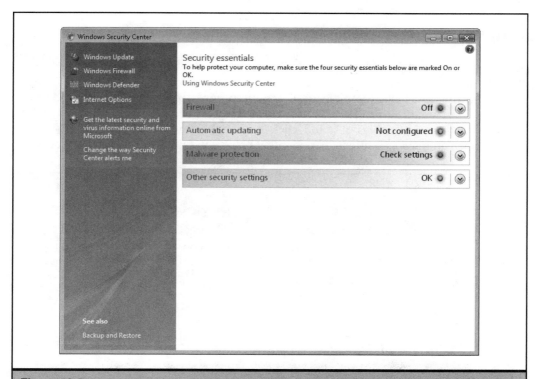

Figure 10-5. Windows Security Center allows you to manage the security tools in Windows Vista.

Firewall Protection

This section of the Center shows the status of Windows Firewall. If the firewall is off or in an unknown state, a red button is shown and you'll see a link titled Show Me My Available Options when the Firewall panel is expanded. If you click the link, a dialog box appears, as shown in Figure 10-6.

You can elect to turn on the firewall by clicking Turn On Windows Firewall. However, if you'd rather not use Windows Firewall, or if you have another firewall that you'd rather use, select I Have A Firewall Solution That I'll Monitor Myself.

Automatic Updating

This portion of the Windows Security Center shows the status of automatic updating. Automatic updating is particularly important, because as security threats are made known to Vista, Microsoft will develop a solution and include it as part of regular updates.

If automatic updating is not configured, you'll see a button that reads Change Settings. Clicking this button will display a dialog box, like the one in Figure 10-7, which allows you to tell Vista to automatically check for updates.

Malware Protection

This portion of the application shows the status of your computer's malicious software protection. Malware is subdivided into two camps:

▼ **Antivirus**   Vista doesn't include its own antivirus application. You should install and maintain a third-party solution for protecting your system against viruses. If antivirus software is not found, click the Find A Program button, and Vista will open an Internet Explorer window that helps you find an antivirus product.

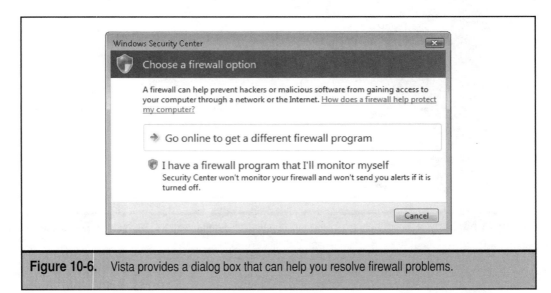

Figure 10-6.   Vista provides a dialog box that can help you resolve firewall problems.

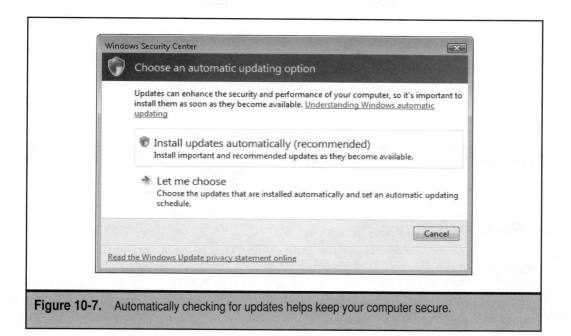

Figure 10-7. Automatically checking for updates helps keep your computer secure.

▲ **Spyware**   Later in this chapter, we'll talk at some length about Windows
Defender. It is an application included with Vista that helps protect your
computer against spyware threats. If Defender is not turned on, you will be
reminded of that fact. If it is out of date, as the one in Figure 10-8 is, you will be
notified and given the opportunity to update it.

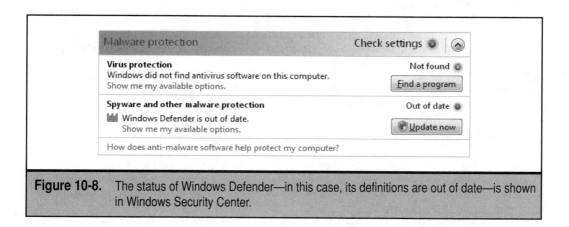

Figure 10-8. The status of Windows Defender—in this case, its definitions are out of date—is shown
in Windows Security Center.

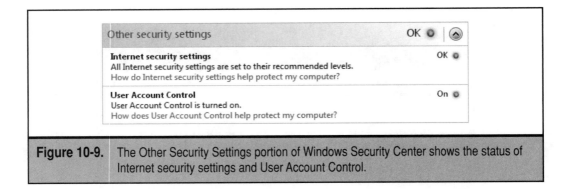

Figure 10-9. The Other Security Settings portion of Windows Security Center shows the status of Internet security settings and User Account Control.

Other Security Settings

This portion of the Center shows the status of Internet security settings and User Account Control (UAC). This is shown in Figure 10-9. If Internet security settings are set below recommended levels, or if user accounts are configured too liberally, you'll get a warning message.

WINDOWS FIREWALL

One of the chief ways to prevent attackers from assaulting your computer is to place a firewall between your computer and an Internet connection. While you can use a hardware solution, like a Cisco 3825 router, to protect your organizations, you can also use a software solution to protect individual computers.

In Windows XP, Microsoft introduced its own firewall product: Windows Firewall. Like so many other parts of Windows, this application is improved in Vista.

Vista includes two different versions of the firewall: Windows Firewall and Windows Firewall with Advanced Security. In a nutshell, Windows Firewall provides the same sort of support and features that the Windows XP firewall provided. Windows Firewall with Advanced Security allows you to be a lot more granular with your firewall functionality. Let's take a closer look at these two products and how you can use them in your organization.

NOTE You don't have to use Windows Firewall, but it's a nice feature in Vista. If you prefer to use a third-party product, you can simply deactivate Windows Firewall and use the other product.

Firewall Features

As you probably remember from Windows XP or Windows 2003 Server, Windows Firewall is installed and enabled by default. It protects the computer by blocking incoming network connections (wired or wireless), allowing only designated exceptions for specific programs, services, and ports.

Windows Firewall can be accessed by selecting Start | Control Panel | Security | Windows Firewall. When the product starts, you see a screen like the one in Figure 10-10.

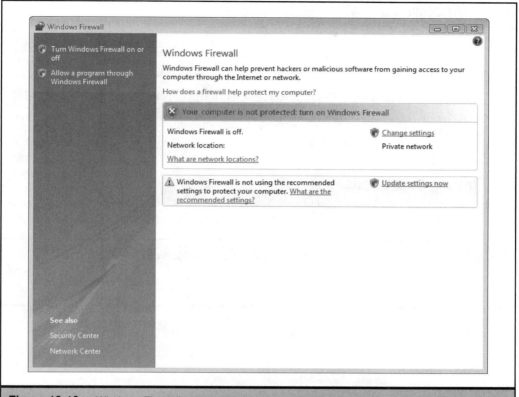

Figure 10-10.   Windows Firewall starts by showing a status overview.

When Windows Firewall starts, click Change Settings. Windows Firewall configuration and management is accomplished using three tabs:

▼   **General**   Used to configure general firewall settings, including whether the firewall is turned on.

■   **Exceptions**   Used to designate programs and services that are allowed to access the network.

▲   **Advanced**   Used to configure protected connections, control messages, and logging services.

Let's take a close look at the configuration and management of your Windows Firewall. Remember, in order to make changes to the firewall settings, you must be logged on as a local computer administrator. If your computer is part of a domain, specific Group Policy rules might also apply and limit what you can do to Windows Firewall.

Using Windows Firewall

To turn on Windows Firewall:

1. Click Start and then click Control Panel.
2. In Control Panel, click Security and then click Windows Firewall.
3. On the General tab, select On (Recommended). This is shown in Figure 10-11.
4. To block incoming connections to all programs, select the Block All Programs check box.
5. Click OK.

Configuring Exceptions

Windows Firewall works by blocking incoming network connections. Exceptions are made for programs, services, and ports that the administrator decides to allow.

NOTE Only one program is granted permission to make an incoming connection by default: Remote Assistance.

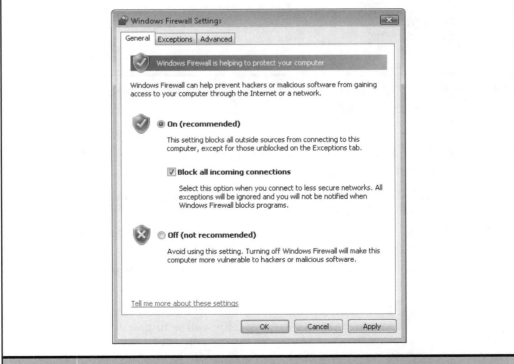

Figure 10-11. Turning on Windows Firewall can help secure your computer against attack.

To allow specific programs and services to establish connections to your Vista computer:

1. Open Windows Firewall (which we explained in the previous section).

2. On the Exceptions tab, shown in Figure 10-12, programs and services that you can allow or deny are shown. Selecting or clearing the check box next to the program or service allows you to manage the connection's permissions.

3. If the program you want to allow isn't listed, click Add Program and then use the Add A Program dialog box to pick the program you want to allow.

4. If a specific Transmission Control Protocol (TCP) or User Datagram Protocol (UDP) port isn't listed, click Add Port and then use the Add A Port dialog box to pick the port you want to allow.

5. Windows Firewall will tell you when it blocks a program. This notification can be deactivated by clearing the Tell Me When Windows Firewall Blocks A Program check box.

6. If you want to block every incoming connection, including those for Remote Assistance, select the Block All Programs check box in the General tab.

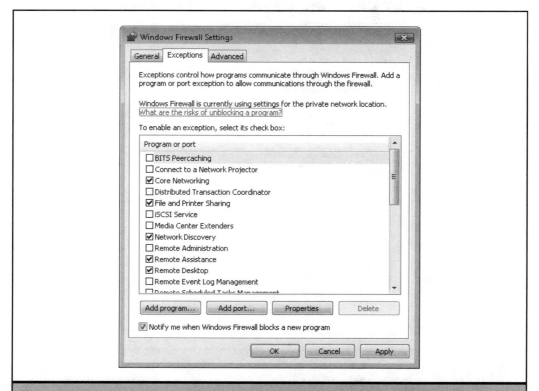

Figure 10-12. Manage exceptions using the Exceptions tab in Windows Firewall.

Configuring Connections

Windows Firewall protects all connections to your computer by default. However, you can stop Windows Firewall from doing this.

1. Open Windows Firewall.
2. On the Advanced tab, shown in Figure 10-13, under Network Connection Settings, clear the check boxes for the connections you don't want Windows Firewall to protect.
3. Click OK.

Windows Firewall with Advanced Security

While the original flavor of Windows Firewall provided adequate protection for your system, Microsoft has improved upon it. Windows Firewall with Advanced Security offers new features, including:

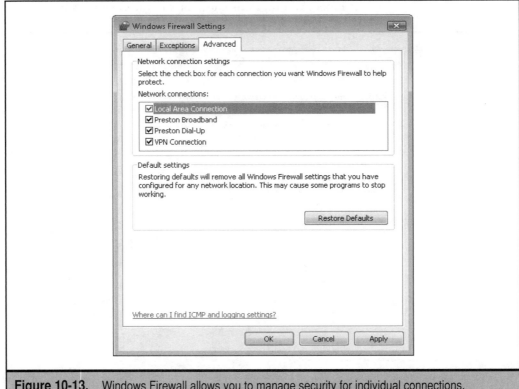

Figure 10-13.   Windows Firewall allows you to manage security for individual connections.

▼ Support for incoming and outgoing traffic filtering

■ An MMC snap-in

■ Built-in firewall filtering and Internet Protocol Security (IPSec) protection settings

▲ Exceptions can be configured for Active Directory accounts and groups, source and destination IP addresses, IP protocol numbers, source and destination TCP and UDP port, interfaces, and Internet Control Message Protocol (ICMP) and ICMP for IPv6 traffic

NOTE   There's a lot going on with Windows Firewall with Advanced Security—far more than we have space to examine here. We'll hit on some of the high points that you'll most likely use.

Features

Windows Firewall with Advanced Security offers a number of features that will help give you the sort of firewall protection you want. Whereas Windows Firewall, for the most part, is a blunt instrument, Windows Firewall with Advanced Security gives you precise control over your firewall settings.

Incoming and Outgoing Traffic   Windows Firewall with Advanced Security supports isolating incoming traffic, and will drop incoming unsolicited traffic, along with solicited traffic that does not correspond to a request of the computer.

The firewall also supports firewalling outgoing traffic. That is, the firewall can be configured with a set of rules to block all traffic sent to specific ports, such as the ports known to be used by virus software, or to addresses that contain sensitive or questionable content.

By default, Windows Firewall with Advanced Security blocks all incoming traffic, unless it is solicited, and allows all outgoing traffic.

MMC Interface   The basic Windows Firewall uses a graphical user interface (GUI) accessed from Control Panel. Windows Firewall with Advanced Security is managed through a snap-in to the MMC. With this snap-in, you can configure settings for remote computers, which is not possible using the basic Windows Firewall product.

Command-line configuration of advanced settings is possible using the netsh advfirewall command. This is a new feature and not available for computers running Windows XP or Windows Server 2003.

Group Policy–based configuration of Windows Firewall is accessed by going to Computer Configuration\Windows Settings\Security Settings\Windows Firewall with Advanced Security in the Group Policy Editor snap-in.

The new Windows Firewall with Advanced Security will apply Group Policy settings configured for the current Windows Firewall at Computer Configuration\Administrative Templates\Network\Network Connections\Windows Firewall.

NOTE   If you have computers running both Vista and XP on your network, the computers running XP will ignore the firewall settings you establish for your computers running Vista.

Firewall and IPSec Integration   IPSec is a set of Internet standards for the cryptographic protection of IP traffic. Normally, IPSec and your firewall are configured separately. As such, sometimes they overlap one another with contradictory rules. Windows Firewall with Advanced Security resolves this problem because IPSec has been integrated into the firewall.

Configuring Rules

Rules can be configured in Windows Firewall with Advanced Security in granular ways. The following lists some of the ways in which you can specify rules:

▼   **Active Directory users and groups**   Rules that specify traffic must be protected with IPSec can indicate the specific accounts or groups that are authorized to communicate in a protected mode.

■   **IP addresses**   With the previous Windows Firewall product, you could specify a scope of excepted incoming traffic based on IP address. Windows Firewall with Advanced Security allows you to configure source and destination addresses for incoming and outgoing traffic. This allows you to be precise with what type of traffic comes and goes from a specific IP address.

■   **IP protocol number**   Windows Firewall with Advanced Security allows you to select protocols by name or to manually enter the value of the IPv4 protocol or IPv6 Next Header fields. In previous versions of Windows Firewall, you could only create rules for TCP- or UDP-based traffic.

■   **TCP or UDP ports**   The new version of Windows Firewall allows you to configure both source and destination TCP or UDP ports for both incoming and outgoing traffic.

■   **Interfaces**   Rules are applied to specific interfaces or types of interface, including local area network (LAN), remote access, or wireless interfaces.

▲   **Services**   Windows Firewall with Advanced Security allows you to create rules for specific threats.

Using Windows Firewall with Advanced Security

To start Windows Firewall with Advanced Security:

1. Click Start.
2. Select Control Panel.
3. Click System And Maintenance.
4. Click Administrative Tools.
5. Double-click Windows Firewall with Advanced Security.

The MMC plug-in is shown in Figure 10-14.

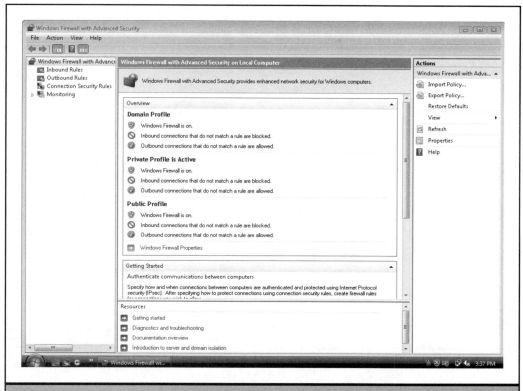

Figure 10-14.   Windows Firewall with Advanced Security is a snap-in to the MMC.

Management

You can manage whether the Windows Firewall is on or off (its *state*), IPSec settings, and the firewall's overall behavior and logging setting by right-clicking Windows Firewall with Advanced Security in the console tree and then clicking Properties. The resulting dialog box is shown in Figure 10-15.

You'll notice that in Figure 10-15 there are Domain Profile, Private Profile, and Public Profile tabs (in addition to an IPSec Settings tab). The distinction between them and how you would use them includes the following:

▼ **Domain**   This profile is used when a computer is a member of a domain.

■ **Private**   This profile is used when a computer is not connected to its domain, but is connected to a different private network—for instance, when you use your laptop on another organization's network.

▲ **Public**   This profile is used when a computer is not connected to its domain or another private network. For instance, when you use your laptop to connect to a public network, like a Wi-Fi hotspot.

Figure 10-15.   Managing overall settings on Windows Firewall with Advanced Security.

Navigation

Windows Firewall with Advanced Security looks like most MMC plug-ins and is navigated the same way. The Windows Firewall with Advanced Security tree has four nodes:

▼   **Inbound Rules**   Maintains a set of rules for incoming traffic

■   **Outbound Rules**   Maintains a set of rules for outgoing traffic

■   **Connection Security Rules**   Maintains a set of rules for protected traffic

▲   **Monitoring**   Displays information about firewall rules, connection rules, and security associations

By selecting Windows Firewall with Advanced Security in the tree, three panes are shown:

▼   **Overview**   Displays the current state of the firewall for the domain and standard profiles. It also shows which profile is active

■   **Getting Started**   Displays links to topics to help you start configuring rules

▲   **Resources**   Includes links to documentation for Windows Firewall

Configuring Windows Firewall with Advanced Security involves the following processes.

Configuring Inbound Rules

To create an inbound rule:

1. Right-click Inbound Rules in the tree.
2. Click New Rule. This starts the New Inbound Rule Wizard, as shown in Figure 10-16.

NOTE   You could also click Inbound Rules in the tree and then click New Rule in the action pane.

The Rule Type page on the New Inbound Rule Wizard allows you to establish rules for different programs, ports, predefined services, or a customization. Table 10-1 explains when to set these different rules.

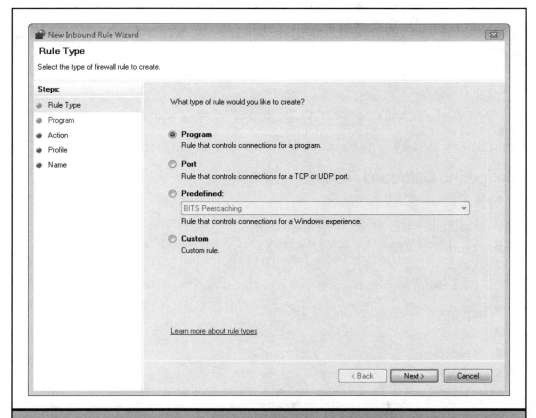

Figure 10-16.   The New Inbound Rule Wizard is used to create a new rule for inbound traffic.

Rule	Explanation
Program	Used to specify a rule for incoming traffic based on a program name. You must also provide an action (allow, block, or protect), the profile to which the rule applies (domain, public, or private), and a name for the rule.
Port	Used to specify a rule for incoming traffic based on TCP and UDP ports. You must also provide an action (allow, block, or protect), the profile to which the rule applies (domain, public, or private), and a name for the rule.
Predefined	Used to specify a rule based on a predefined service. A name must also be specified for the rule.
Custom	Used to create a customized rule. Use this option when you want to manually configure rule behavior. A name must be specified for this rule.

Table 10-1. The rules on the Inbound Rules Page

When the New Inbound Rule Wizard has finished, a new inbound rule with the name you created is added to the details pane. You can configure advanced properties for the rule by right-clicking the name of the rule and clicking Properties.

Configuring Outbound Rules

To create an outbound rule:

1. Right-click Outbound Rules in the tree.
2. Click New Rule. This starts the New Outbound Rule Wizard, which looks a lot like the Inbound Rule Wizard shown in Figure 10-16.

The wizard allows you to create four types of rules:

▼ Program

■ Port

■ Predefined

▲ Custom

Table 10-2 explains when to use these outbound rules.

When the New Outbound Rule Wizard has finished, a new outbound rule with the name you created is added to the details pane. You can configure advanced properties for the rule by right-clicking the name of the rule and clicking Properties.

Rule	Explanation
Program	Used to specify a rule for outgoing traffic based on a program name. You must also provide an action (allow, block, or protect), the profile to which the rule applies (domain, public, or private), and a name for the rule.
Port	Used to specify a rule for outgoing traffic based on TCP and UDP ports. You must also provide an action (allow, block, or protect), the profile to which the rule applies (domain, public, or private), and a name for the rule.
Predefined	Used to specify a rule based on a predefined service. A name must also be specified for the rule.
Custom	Used to create a customized rule. Use this option when you want to manually configure rule behavior. A name must be specified for this rule.

Table 10-2.   Rules on the Outbound Rule Page

Settings for Inbound and Outbound Rules

Once your rule—whether inbound or outbound—has been created, you can fine-tune its functionality. Right-click the rule to display its properties box. An example is shown in Figure 10-17.

From the properties dialog box for the rule, you can configure settings for the tabs listed in Table 10-3.

Connection Security Rules

To create a new connection security rule:

1. Right-click Connection Security Rules in the tree.
2. Click New Rule.

The New Connection Security Rule Wizard starts, as shown in Figure 10-18. Table 10-4 lists the types of rules you can choose from and what they do.

When the New Connection Security Rule Wizard has finished, a new rule with the name you created is added to the details pane of the Connection Security Rules node. You can configure advanced properties for the rule by right-clicking it and clicking Properties.

In the properties dialog box for the rule, you can configure the settings listed in Table 10-5.

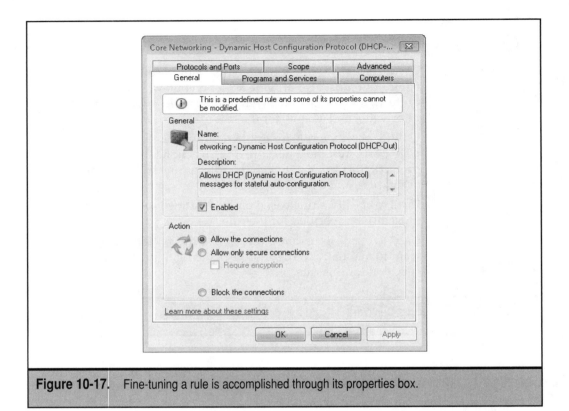

Figure 10-17. Fine-tuning a rule is accomplished through its properties box.

WINDOWS DEFENDER

One of the biggest knocks Windows has against it is its susceptibility to viruses and spyware. In response to the spyware portion of that threat, Microsoft introduced Windows Defender, which is a free product. Defender is downloadable for Windows XP, but it comes included with Windows Vista.

Defender is based on GIANT AntiSpyware, initially developed by GIANT Company Software, Inc., and acquired by Microsoft in December 2004. In addition to the features that other free spyware products include, Defender includes several real-time security agents that monitor various areas of Windows for changes that might be brought on by spyware. It also makes it possible to remove ActiveX applications that may be causing problems. Furthermore, it includes support for Microsoft's SpyNet network. SpyNet allows users to report spyware to Microsoft, which is added to their database and distributed to other users.

In Vista, Defender works a little differently than in other flavors of Windows. Vista automatically blocks all startup items that require administrator privileges to run. Blocking is related to the UAC (which we covered in Chapter 9), and requires the user to manually run each startup item each time he or she logs on.

Tab	Explanation
General	The rule's name and its actions (allow the connections, allow only secure connections, or block)
Programs And Services	The programs and services to which the rule applies.
User And Computers (Inbound) or Computers (Outbound)	If the rule is to allow only secure connections, this shows the user or computer accounts that are authorized to make connections.
Protocols And Ports	The rule's IP protocol, source and destination TCP or UDP ports, and ICMP settings.
Scope	The rule's source and destination addresses.
Advanced	The profiles or interface types to which the rule applies. For inbound rules, this also indicates whether traffic allowed for this exception is to be passed through the router performing network address translation using Taredo.

Table 10-3.   Additional Settings for Inbound and Outbound Rules

Windows Defender Operation

The startup screen for Windows Defender is shown in Figure 10-19. It has two operating modes:

▼   **Real-time protection**   Defender runs in the background, attempting to stop spyware from trying to install itself. This type of security check secures the computer from known spyware.

▲   **Scanning**   Defender checks your system, attempting to locate spyware that may have slipped past the real-time mode or that was installed if Defender was ever deactivated.

Defender is, by default, configured to use real-time protection and then perform daily scans.

Defender uses definition files to maintain current information about spyware. That is, it downloads so-called *signatures* from Microsoft. Signatures are what Defender uses to check and see if spyware is trying to install itself or if it has already been installed. Current signatures are acquired from Microsoft as part of Defender's regular updating process.

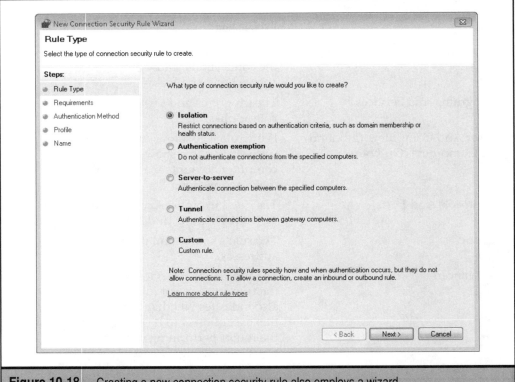

Figure 10-18. Creating a new connection security rule also employs a wizard.

NOTE Defender will automatically download signatures at a predetermined time, but you can also elect to manually download signatures whenever you choose.

Using Windows Defender

Windows Defender is started by clicking Start and then clicking Control Panel. From Control Panel, click Security and then click Windows Defender. Defender may be turned off or be out of date, as shown in Figure 10-19. If this is the case, you'll see a warning message, telling you that the computer is at risk. Click Turn On And Open Windows Defender to enable Windows Defender.

The Windows Defender home page, shown in Figure 10-19, shows an overview of your system's current status, based on a three-color code:

▼ **Green** Ideally, you want to see this color. This indicates that all of Defender's definitions are up to date and that no known spyware has been installed.

■ **Orange** If the Defender definitions are not up to date but there is no known spyware installed, an orange status indicates that your definitions need to be updated. Click the Check For Updates Now button that is provided as part of the warning.

▲ **Red** This tends to be the universal color for trouble, and it's no different here. This color indicates that your computer is possibly compromised or that there is unwanted software installed on your computer. You'll be given the option to scan or quarantine the spyware.

Rule	Explanation
Isolation	Used to isolate computers by limiting connections based on domain membership or health status. You must also indicate: ■ When authentication should occur (for incoming or outgoing traffic, for example) ■ Whether you want to require or request secure connections ■ The authentication method for protected traffic ■ A name for the rule
Authentication Exemption	Used to indicate computers that need not authenticate or protect traffic. This is based on IP address.
Server-To-Server	Used to specify traffic protection between servers. You must indicate: ■ The endpoints that will exchange protected traffic by IP address ■ When authentication is to occur ■ Authentication method to be used ■ A name for the rule
Tunnel	Used to specify traffic protection that is tunneled. Normally, this is used when sending packets via the Internet between two gateway computers. You must indicate: ■ The tunnel endpoints by IP address ■ The authentication method ■ A name for the rule
Custom	Used to create a rule that does not specify an authentication behavior. Select this option when you want to manually configure a rule.

Table 10-4. Specifics of New Connection Rules

Setting	Explanation
General	The rule's name, a description, and the rule's status (enabled or disabled).
Computers	The IP addresses for computers for which traffic is protected.
Authentication	The authentication method used for protected traffic.
Advanced	The profiles and interface types to which the rules apply. This also maintains IPSec tunneling behavior.

Table 10-5. Advanced Properties for Connection Rules

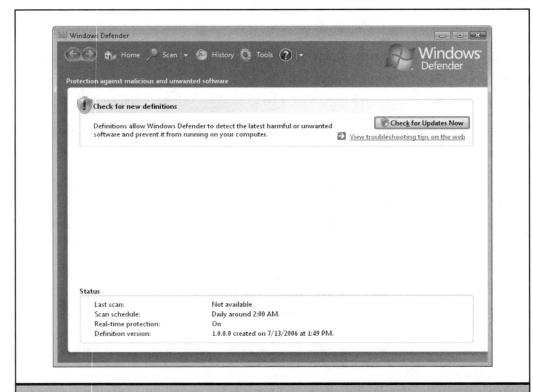

Figure 10-19. Windows Defender is a component of Windows Vista that fights spyware.

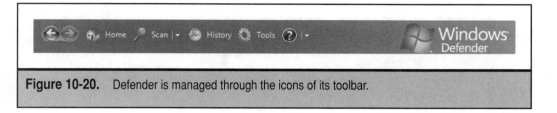

Figure 10-20. Defender is managed through the icons of its toolbar.

Defender's features are accessed through the toolbar on the top of the window. The toolbar's icons are shown in Figure 10-20.

The buttons perform the following functions and, from left to right, are:

▼ **Forward/Back**   Like the forward and back buttons on a Web browser, this allows you to navigate to locations you've already visited

■ **Home**   Takes you to the Defender home page

■ **Scan**   Initiates a quick scan of your computer and shows its progress

■ **History**   Shows the History page. This page includes a summary of all Defender activity based on programs detected and the action that's been taken

■ **Tools**   Displays the All Settings And Tools page. The page allows you to manage settings, show quarantined programs, view allowed items, and so forth

■ **Windows Defender Help**   Shows Help topics for Defender

▲ **Windows Defender Help Options**   Shows an options list allowing you to display additional Help topics

The Status section of the home page, located at the bottom, displays general status information about Defender. Information includes:

▼ **Last Scan**   The date, time, and type of the last scan

■ **Scan Schedule**   The schedule for automatic scans, such as Daily at 2:00 AM

■ **Real-Time Protection**   The status of real-time protection

▲ **Definition Version**   The version, time, and date of the most current definitions file

When you work with Defender, you'll perform common tasks. The following sections explain these tasks and how you can initiate them in Windows Vista.

Setting Configuration

You can manage Defender's operation by configuring its settings. This is accomplished by following these steps:

1. Open Defender (this was explained earlier in this section).

2. Click Tools and then click Options. The resulting page is shown in Figure 10-21. Within the page are several sections that contain different settings.

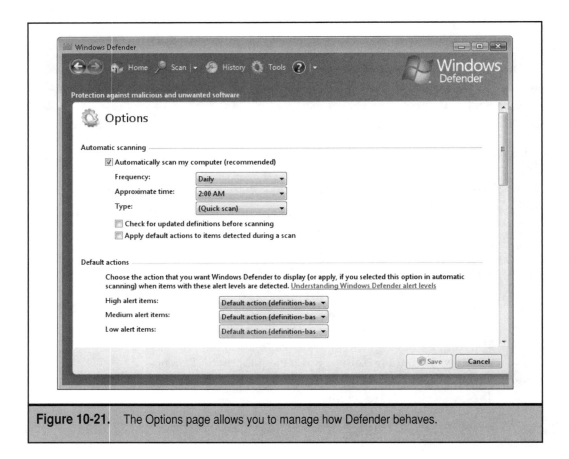

Figure 10-21. The Options page allows you to manage how Defender behaves.

Automatic Scanning

This section contains settings that are used to manage automatic scanning and updating processes. If you want Defender to automatically scan, select the Automatically Scan My Computer (Recommended) check box. Next, establish scan frequency, time of day, and type of scan. You can also elect to have Defender check for updates before starting its scan. If you want to do this, select the Check For Updated Definitions Before Scanning check box.

Default Actions

This section contains the settings used to establish what action should be taken based on the alert level of detected spyware. There are three spyware alert levels:

▼ **High** This is considered to be the most serious and has a high probability of causing damage to the computer.

■ **Medium** This is a modest level of danger, but could still cause damage to your computer.

▲ **Low** At this level, spyware is more of an annoyance than anything else.

By selecting the Apply Default Actions To Items Detected During A Scan check box under Automatic Scanning, Defender will perform the prescribed action when an automatic scan is completed. Actions include:

▼ **Ignore**   Items are—as the name implies—ignored.

■ **Remove**   Items are quarantined.

▲ **Signature Default**   Items are handled based on the setting in the signature.

Real-Time Protection Options

This setting is used to turn real-time protection on or off. Defender monitors a number of system settings and components, and each of those areas can be individually managed by selecting or clearing the relevant check boxes.

Advanced Options

This section contains the settings needed for advanced detection of spyware. Settings allow you to scan inside archives to detect spyware.

Administrator Options

Use this setting to indicate whether Defender is turned on or off. This is also used to indicate whether normal users are allowed to perform scans and remove spyware. The default setting is to allow this behavior.

Scanning for Spyware

If you suspect spyware has infiltrated your computer, you can use Defender to perform one of three types of scans:

▼ **Full scan**   Defender checks all areas of the memory, the registry, and the file system for spyware. A full scan can be initiated by clicking the Scan button on the toolbar and selecting Full Scan.

■ **Custom scan**   Defender checks selected areas of the file system for spyware. To initiate a custom scan:

 a. Click the Scan button on the toolbar.

 b. Select Custom Scan.

 c. On the Select Scan Options page, click Select and indicate which drives and folders you wish to scan.

 d. Click OK.

 e. Click Scan Now to initiate the scan.

▲ **Quick scan**   Defender checks memory, the registry, and the file system for any spyware or harmful processes. A quick scan can be initiated by clicking the Scan button on the toolbar.

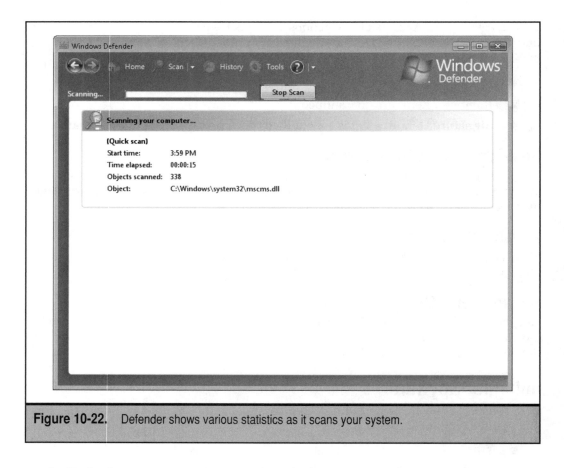

Figure 10-22. Defender shows various statistics as it scans your system.

As Defender scans your computer, it shows various information, as shown in Figure 10-22. Information includes the start time of the scan, the elapsed scan time, the location or item currently being examined, and the total number of files scanned.

Once the scan is complete, Defender shows final results, as shown in Figure 10-23.

Updating Defender

Spyware creators are a devious bunch. As soon as you've figured out how to beat back their unwanted ads or stop them from monitoring your browsing habits, they figure out a different way to do it. To keep up on their tactics, you should regularly update your spyware definitions, as you would with antivirus definitions.

Defender's default setting is to check for updated definitions before performing an automatic scan. However, you can manually update spyware definitions by clicking Check For New Definitions in the Defender home page.

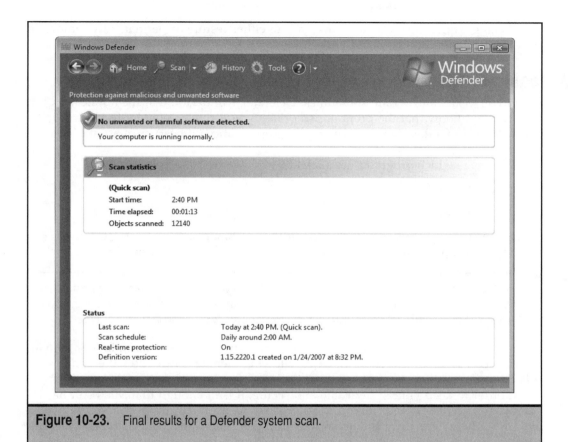

Figure 10-23.   Final results for a Defender system scan.

NOTE   In order for Vista to download spyware definitions, the computer must be connected to the Internet or to an update server.

For large organizations with several thousand computers, it is not as efficient to use Defender for each computer and update its definitions individually. It's a better practice for the definitions to be automatically pushed to the client computers.

Quarantined Items

If Defender finds something suspect, it will quarantine the item. This means that it has been disabled and moved to a secure area on the computer. If you believe the quarantined item is okay and you want to check it out, follow these steps:

1. Click Tools.
2. Click Quarantined Items.

Clicking a quarantined item allows you to either restore or permanently remove it. To remove all quarantined items, click Remove All.

Managing Programs

When you install a program, sometimes, Defender will decide that the application is a threat. If you know that the program isn't risky, you can tell Defender to allow it to be run without Defender "helping" by popping up a notice (at best) or quarantining it (at worst).

To manage which programs are allowed:

1. Click Tools.
2. Click Allowed Items.

On the Allowed Items page, allowed items are shown with an alert level. Items can be removed from the Allowed Items list by clicking them and selecting Remove.

NOTE While Defender is a nice addition, it shouldn't be your only line of defense against spyware. Spyware is nasty, and it comes in so many variations that it's a good idea to use more than one antispyware tool, like SpyBot (www.safernetworking.org) or Lavasoft's Ad-Aware (www.lavasoftusa.com).

Enterprise environments can use Vista-ready software distribution solutions to manage the deployment of Defender updates, allowing them to control how the updates are rolled out to a large number of managed desktops.

In order to keep your system safe and secure, it isn't enough that Microsoft has included these tools—it's up to you to use them and use them properly. Naturally, this isn't the only way security is delivered to your computers and your network. Network security is another important issue—one we'll cover in the next chapter.

CHAPTER 11

Network Security

The last security-related topic we'll cover in this book is network security. Obviously, network security is so vast a subject that a number of books have been written on various areas that fall under the "network security" category. For the purposes of our discussion, we're going to look specifically at how a Windows Vista client can be secured to mitigate the risk posed by some of the most common threats to network security.

This chapter also looks at virtual private networks, which allow you to connect to your network remotely and securely via the Internet (or other untrusted networks) by encrypting the traffic as it traverses those networks. From there, we'll take a look at how Group Policy is implemented in Windows Vista and how you can use it to manage your clients' privileges and rights. We'll round things out with a discussion of network access protection, a mechanism that aims to keep "unhealthy" and unauthorized computers and users from hurting your network.

VIRTUAL PRIVATE NETWORKS

Virtual private networks (VPNs) have been around for well over a decade. VPNs are, simply put, encrypted connections between two or more computers or two or more networks. The connection, or tunnel, can be established over a public network, such as the Internet, or over a private internetwork, such as a corporate intranet. To ensure secure communication, data transmitted between the two VPN end points is encrypted. The encrypted data is then routed over a dial-up, wide area network (WAN), or local area network (LAN) connection, just like normal unencrypted Transmission Control Protocol/Internet Protocol (TCP/IP) network traffic. VPNs are commonly used to establish secure communication channels between offices or users over the Internet. VPN tunnels between end points within the same LAN are less common, but certainly possible if required. This process is illustrated in Figure 11-1.

In Figure 11-1, the computer icons marked 1 and 2 represent the same computer and same connection. The physical connection is illustrated by number 1, and the logical connection that represents the encrypted VPN session traveling over the physical connection is number 2. Once a Vista client creates a VPN tunnel between itself and a remote network, traffic over that channel is isolated through encryption. Packets encrypted over a VPN tunnel can flow alongside public traffic with a high degree of logical isolation, providing a reasonably secure option for distributed networking over the public Internet. Before VPNs, companies had to establish dedicated links between offices to secure communications between remote locations and remote users. Dedicated links (typically point-to-point network circuits, switched virtual circuits, and even Integrated Services Digital Network [ISDN] or plain old telephone service [POTS] dial-up) of this type are still heavily used, but they are great deal more expensive than conventional public IP circuits provided by Internet service providers (ISPs). Therefore, many organizations find that VPNs over public networks are a more cost-effective solution.

New Features in Vista

Vista has added features for Remote Access connections. Like Windows Server 2003, "Longhorn" networks can enforce client suitability before connectivity is granted.

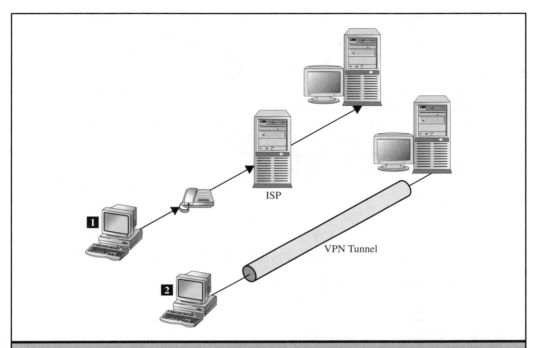

Figure 11-1. Virtual private networks provide secure data transfer over the Internet or public intranets.

Windows Server 2003 Service Pack 1 introduced Network Access Quarantine Control, which enforces, among other things, VPN connections. On the server side, and exclusive to networks running "Longhorn" (the code name for the next version of Windows Server), Network Access Protection (NAP) includes enforcement technologies that can be set to require services such as Internet Protocol Security (IPSec) and VPN tunnels.

Some of you may already be familiar with network access control in the form of Cisco's Network Admission Control (NAC). It's generally thought of as a direct competitor to Microsoft's NAP. This is because they both perform end-point network access control, and in all likelihood, you would not run both solutions in a single environment, as they are not particularly useful together.

NOTE There are a few things that you should know about NAC since it may already be at least somewhat available on your network. Cisco network access point control capabilities may already be in some of the Cisco networks on your network. If so, you could add and configure Cisco Secure Access Control Server and implement the Cisco Trust Agent on client computers to enable the service on your network. A simplified description of how it works is as follows: A client with the Cisco Trust Agent authenticates to the Access Control Server, is granted or denied permission (which is then passed to the Cisco hardware—usually a switch or access server). The Cisco device then blocks or allows a user on the network by enabling or disabling the user's specific network access port. It's a different approach from the one NAP takes, as you'll see in this chapter.

For Vista networks, NAP can enforce the type of VPN protocols allowed on the network and whether traffic can flow outside of a VPN tunnel. Vista includes an updated VPN client that integrates with NAP networks for smooth participation in secure networks. Since VPN enforcement through NAP is part of a consolidated and consistent platform, it can be easier to deploy, maintain, and troubleshoot than Network Access Quarantine Control (NAQC). Depending on your infrastructure, you can connect Vista to either NAP or NAQC.

Vista administrators may be interested to know that some of the authentication services that are handled by Internet Authentication Services (IAS) in Windows Server 2003 networks are now handled by a new service called Network Policy Server (NPS), first made available in "Longhorn." NPS uses policies to authorize clients with limited or unlimited access, working with NAP to ensure that clients operating on a network present less of a security risk.

Configuring a VPN

To successfully set up a remote-access VPN over the Internet, you'll need a few things:

▼ The IP address or the fully qualified domain name (FQDN) of the remote VPN end point to which you are connecting

■ An Internet connection

■ A VPN server at the remote end

▲ A VPN client (what we'll be setting up in this example)

Let's take a closer look at setting up the VPN client.

Set Up a Connection to the Internet

Before you use a VPN connection to a remote network, you should be connected to the Internet. The connection could be a dial-up, a broadband always-on connection, or another type of direct connection. Alternately, if the remote network has a direct-dial-access server, you can even configure your VPN client to use your modem to dial the remote access server.

If you have not already done so, see Chapter 5 and make sure that you have a working network configuration and a suitable connection to the Internet.

Create and Configure the Vista VPN Client

Once an Internet connection has been verified, the next step is to configure a VPN client. To configure a VPN client:

1. From the Start menu, click Connect To. The Connect To A Network window will open.

2. In the Connect To A Network window, shown in Figure 11-2, locate the links at the bottom of the window, and click Set Up A Connection Or Network to start the wizard.

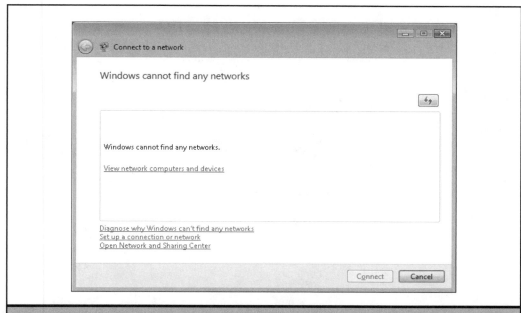

Figure 11-2.   The Connect To A Network window lets you pick the network to which you'll connect remotely.

3. In the Set Up A Connection Or Network page, scroll down and select Connect To A Workplace, and then click the Next button.

4. In the Connect To A Workplace page, shown in Figure 11-3, choose No, Create A New Connection, and then click the Next button.

5. On the How Do You Want To Connect page, shown in Figure 11-4, in most cases, you will want to click Use My Internet Connection (VPN). Click this option to move to the next page.

NOTE   The other option on this page is to use your modem to dial directly into the remote network's remote access server.

6. On the Before You Connect page, select an existing connection or elect to create a new one to use, and then click Next. The Internet connection can be a dial-up or broadband connection.

NOTE   See Chapter 5 for more information on how to configure a connection. In some cases, you will be setting up an Internet connection for a remote network that cannot be currently accessed, such as when configuring the computer for the user's home Internet connection. Click Skip to bypass the connection wizard, and click Set Up The Connection Anyway.

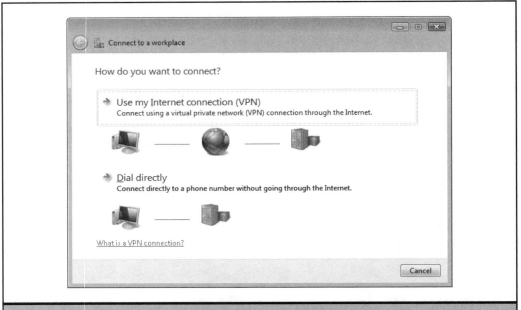

Figure 11-3. The Connect To A Workplace page helps build a VPN connection.

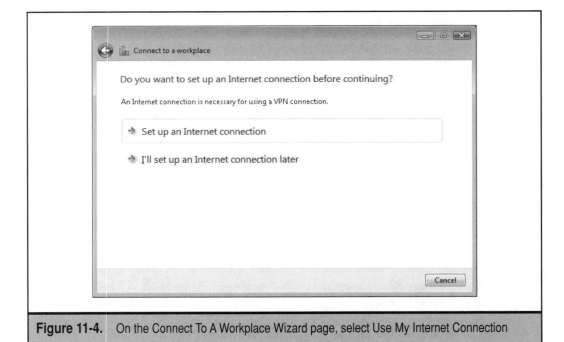

Figure 11-4. On the Connect To A Workplace Wizard page, select Use My Internet Connection

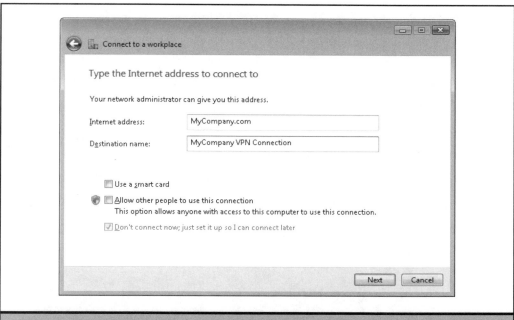

Figure 11-5.   Enter your network's IP address or FQDN to tell the VPN connection where to join.

7. In the next page, shown in Figure 11-5, you have to provide the address to your connection, as well as a few other details. Type the IP address or FQDN of the remote access server to which you are connecting, such as 68.110.4.23 or YourCompany.com. In most cases, this is the remote access server that has been configured for your office network.

8. Type a name for the connection in the Destination Name field so that you can distinguish it from other network connections.

9. If both the remote access server and your Vista client are configured to use a smart card for authentication, select the Use A Smart Card check box.

10. If you want the connection to be available to all users who log on to the Vista client, click the Allow Other People To Use This Connection check box. This is an appropriate choice when you plan to assign the connection through Group Policy.

11. Click Next. The next page gives you the option of providing a user name, password, and domain. This is shown in Figure 11-6. If you fill in these fields, Vista will happily use them each time the connection is launched. If you leave any of the fields blank, Vista will prompt the user for it when the connection is launched.

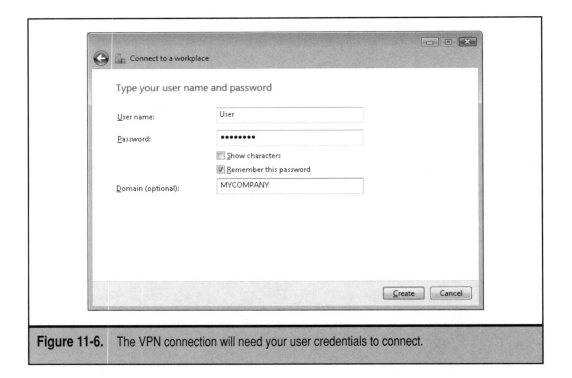

Figure 11-6. The VPN connection will need your user credentials to connect.

NOTE Selecting Remember This Password is not a best practice. Though convenient, should this Vista client be compromised, the VPN credentials can be compromised along with it. Also, if the connection is shared by more than one user, you cannot maintain security contexts per user.

12. Specify the logon domain in the Domain field, and then click Connect.

Additional Configuration

Once the VPN connection is created, you can further configure it by following these steps:

1. Locate the VPN connection by clicking Connect To from the Start menu. From the Connect To Network screen, locate the VPN connection and right-click it. Choose Properties from the context menu.

2. In the Connection Properties window, notice the five tabs at the top. The General tab, shown in Figure 11-7, allows you to update the remote access server name or IP address and select a connection to dial first. Configuring a VPN connection to use a dial-up connection first is usually done only when a broadband or local area connection is not available.

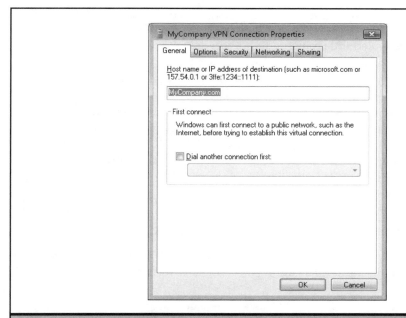

Figure 11-7. The General tab on your VPN connection allows you to manage the connection's IP address and which connection it will dial first.

3. The Options tab, shown in Figure 11-8, allows you to configure dialing options, redialing options, and Point-to-Point Protocol (PPP) settings. To configure PPP, click the PPP button. You then have the option to enable the following:

- **Enable LCP Extensions** Selected by default, Link Control Protocol (LCP) extensions are used to establish and configure link and framing settings, such as maximum frame size. LCP extensions include a callback option, time remaining, and identification packets, as defined in RFC 1570. The PPP standard framing format ensures that any vendor's remote access software can communicate and recognize data packets from any remote access software that adheres to the PPP standards. Contact your ISP to determine whether you should disable LCP extensions.

- **Enable Software Compression** Cleared by default, this option evokes PPP compression before packets are sent and evokes expansion upon receipt. Users should enjoy a performance boost with this option enabled, although some compatibility issues can occur.

- **Negotiate Multi-Link For Single-Link Connections** Cleared by default, this option enables the combination of multiple physical remote-access links into a single logical link to accelerate data transfers and reduce communications and connect-time costs. If your remote access server supports this feature, you may notice improved quality. This feature is incompatible with many remote access servers, however, so you should leave it disabled unless instructed otherwise.

4. The Security tab (shown in Figure 11-9) allows you to select between typical and advanced configurations. When selecting the typical option, you can elect to rely on a secure password or choose to use a smart card by clicking the down arrow; you also have the choice as to whether you wish to use the Windows user name and password automatically and whether you wish to require encryption. When choosing the advanced configuration option, shown in Figure 11-10, you have more choices than what you get with the typical settings. You can also select options for logon security and select allowed protocols. Your choices for data encryption include:

■ No Encryption Allowed (Server Will Disconnect If It Requires Encryption).

■ Optional Encryption (Connect Even If No Encryption).

■ Require Encryption (Disconnect If Server Declines). This is the default setting.

■ Maximum Strength Encryption (Disconnect If Server Declines).

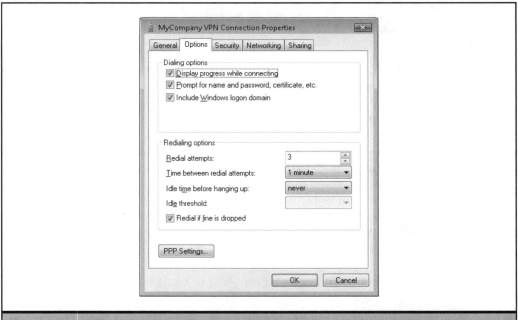

Figure 11-8. The Options tab of a VPN connection allows you to manage dialing options.

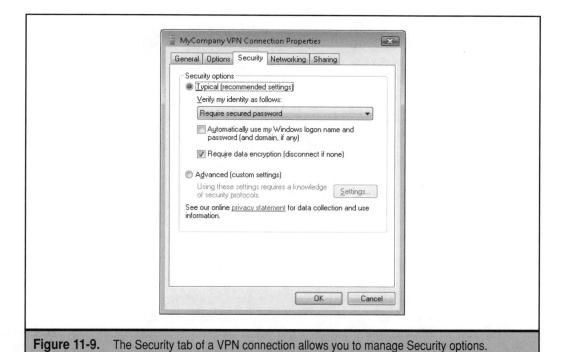

Figure 11-9. The Security tab of a VPN connection allows you to manage Security options.

5. When selecting logon security, you have these options:

- **Smart Card Or Other Certificate (Encryption Enabled)**   Smart cards combine the security of public-key cryptography with the portability of passwords. Before a smart card can be used for authentication, however, a logon certificate needs to be programmed into the card. You can do this by using the Smart Card Enrollment station, which is integrated with Microsoft Certificate Services in current Windows server operating systems.

- **Protected EAP (PEAP) (Encryption Enabled)**   With Protected Extensible Authentication Protocol (PEAP), you can use third-party authentication protocols as well as those supplied with Vista. EAP is the only authentication protocol supported by current Windows servers that enables you to use mechanisms other than passwords (such as digital certificates stored on smart cards) to verify a user's identity.

You have a few choices for authentication protocols as well, including:

- **Unencrypted Password (PAP)**   Password Authentication Protocol (PAP) is password-based and transmits passwords in clear text, which makes authentication traffic vulnerable to interception by packet captures. It is better than no authentication, although you should only use PAP as a fallback for clients that do not support any of the more secure protocols.

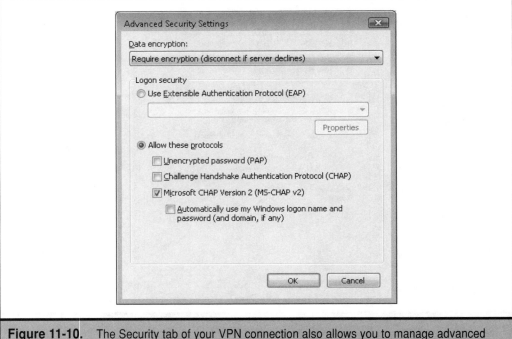

Figure 11-10.   The Security tab of your VPN connection also allows you to manage advanced security options.

- **Challenge Handshake Authentication Protocol (CHAP)**   CHAP uses one-way authentication and the same encryption key for both transmitted and received messages. It is not the optimal option, although it supports remote access clients running Windows 95 and Windows NT 3.51, which cannot use MS-CHAP v2.

- **Microsoft CHAP Version 2 (MS-CHAP v2)**   A password-based authentication protocol that enables the client and the server to mutually authenticate each other using encrypted passwords. This makes it all but impossible for potential intruders to compromise passwords by capturing packets. MS-CHAP v2 is the simplest and most secure option to use when your clients are running Microsoft Windows 98 or later.

6. Finally, you have the option to pass your Windows user name and password for authentication by default.

7. The Networking tab, shown in Figure 11-11, allows you to select between VPN protocols. Your choices include:

- **Automatic**   This option lets Vista detect the available VPN protocols and choose among the remaining options, preferring L2TP if it is available.

- **PPTP VPN** Point-to-Point Tunneling Protocol (PPTP) was developed by Microsoft for Windows NT 4.0. It builds upon standard PPP to encapsulate and encrypt IP traffic. It is common to use MS-CHAP v2 with PPTP to add authentication and provide a secure solution. PPTP is not easily integrated into non-Microsoft networks. If you need to support older Microsoft VPN clients (Window 98, etc.), or if a certificate distribution system is not available, PPTP is your best choice.

- **L2TP VPN** Layer 2 Tunneling Protocol (L2TP) was developed by Cisco and is known to be deployed in conjunction with IPSec. L2TP/IPSec encrypts and authenticates each password transmitted across the network. It is supported by multiple platforms, including UNIX-based and Macintosh systems. It requires a network certificate service, from which VPN end-point computers can receive encryption certificates. Windows 2000, Windows XP, and Vista all support L2TP/IPSec.

When using either automatic or L2TP VPN, you can also specify a few IPSec options. When selecting automatic and PPTP is ultimately used, IPSec will not be used, but you can provide the settings for those cases when L2TP VPN is automatically selected. Managing IPSec is shown in Figure 11-12.

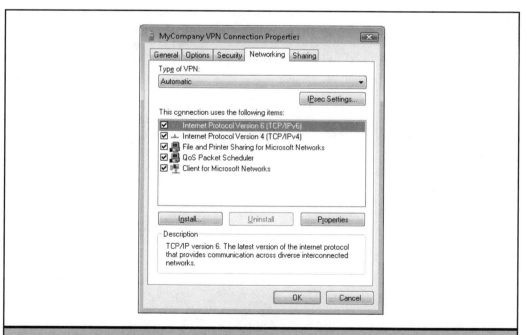

Figure 11-11.   The Networking tab allows you to manage the protocols your VPN connection will use.

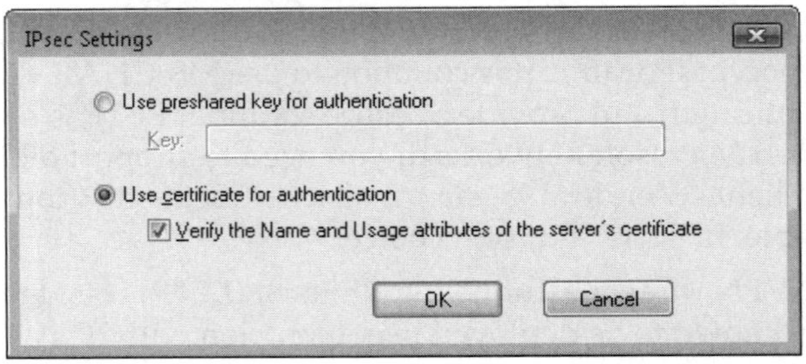

Figure 11-12. Within the VPN Properties menu, you can also manage IPSec settings.

8. The last tab is the Sharing tab, shown in Figure 11-13. Internet Connection Sharing (ICS) options on this tab include whether to share the VPN connection with other users on the same LAN, whether to dial up a connection when other users need the VPN connection first, and whether other users can turn ICS on and off.

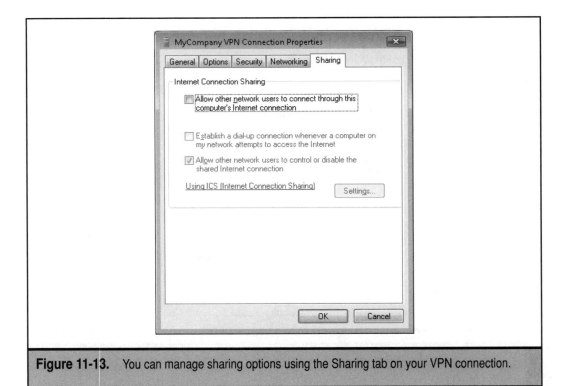

Figure 11-13. You can manage sharing options using the Sharing tab on your VPN connection.

Establishing a VPN Connection

As we pointed out previously, a VPN connection can be made over a dial-up connection or a broadband connection, such as a LAN or a Digital Subscriber Line (DSL) or cable service. Once you have successfully connected to the Internet, you can then connect to a VPN end point in a remote network.

To establish a VPN connection, from the Start menu, open the Network Connections window by typing **NCPA.CPL** into the Search field and pressing ENTER. Once the Network Connections window opens, shown in Figure 11-14, locate the connection you need, and double-click it. Alternately, you could follow these steps:

1. From the Start menu, click Connect To. In the Connect To window, choose Connect To A Network, and click the VPN connection you want to use. Click the Connect button to launch the VPN connection.

2. If the connection is configured to first dial another type of connection, Windows Vista tries to establish this connection before attempting the VPN connection. If prompted to establish this connection, click Yes. Then dial the connection as discussed in the Chapter 5.

3. Once the necessary connection is established, you'll see the Connect dialog box. After you confirm that the user name is correct and have entered the password for the account, click Connect.

Figure 11-14. When you connect to your VPN, Vista will prompt you for user name and password.

USING GROUP POLICY TO ACHIEVE NETWORK SECURITY

Vista improves upon Group Policy, an already invaluable administration tool. Administrators specify settings, or policies, that are applied to all computers or to a subset defined by you. Policies are stored on and synchronized among all domain controllers, which makes them resilient and easy to deploy across your environment. Chapter 14 discusses Group Policy management in detail, although the opportunity for reviewing the options for network security presents itself here. Network access and security settings policies affect network connections, dial-up connections, and Remote Assistance configurations. These policies affect a system's connectivity to the network, as well as remote access to the system.

Local Policies

Before we review the security policies, we should identify the containers where these policies are found. First, the Local Security Policy accompanies every Vista workstation. You can view these policies using the Local Security Policy Management Console, which you can launch from the Start menu by typing `secpol.msc` into the Search field and pressing ENTER. Looking at Figure 11-15, notice the parent node, Security Settings. Expand this, if it is not already, and expand the Local Policies node by double-clicking it. Finally, expand the Security Options node by double-clicking it. To edit a policy, or to learn more about what a particular policy does, simply double-click it.

Domain-Based Policies

The next area of policies is found in domain-based Group Policies. You can create policies and associate them with Active Directory sites, domains, and organizational units (OUs). The policies are then distributed to every domain controller where they apply. From the domain controllers, the policies are deployed to every workstation.

There are two main categories of domain-based policies: User Configuration policies and Computer Configuration policies. Both categories are found within every policy, although often one component is complete while the other is left blank. The computer policies are applied to every computer found within the Active Directory site, domain, or OU where the policy is associated. The user policies, likewise, are applied to users found in the Active Directory site, domain, or OU where the policy is homed.

Computer Policies

Computer Configuration policies cover most of the configuration options, ranging from printer settings to event viewer settings. As Figure 11-16 shows, there are thousands of settings, though here we settle on those that affect network access and security. From the computer level, you can control settings for these access technologies:

▼　ICS

■　Internet Connection Firewall

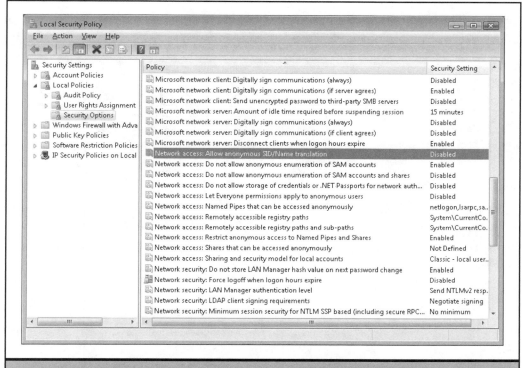

Figure 11-15. Use the Local Security Policies Management Console to edit local policies.

- Windows Firewall
▲ Network Bridge

There are hundreds of settings available, though from a security standpoint, some are more relevant than others. Table 11-1 includes some key policies that you may wish to review. You can find these network policies under User Configuration\Administrative Templates\Network\Network Connections.

You can increase the security of your network by deploying network policies. Network policies for workstations are intended to restrict user actions on the network. You can limit users' abilities to launch applications that may cause unwanted vulnerabilities. Stopping users from using ICS on your domain, for example, can help you maintain a safe network, though it does not prevent users with laptops from taking their computers home and using these features on their own networks. To deploy network policies:

1. From the Start menu, type **gpmc.msc** into the Search field and press ENTER. Keep in mind that you must be logged on to a domain for this tool to launch.

2. Right-click the top node, Group Policy Management, and choose Add Forest from the options. Provide the name of the Active Directory forest, and click OK.

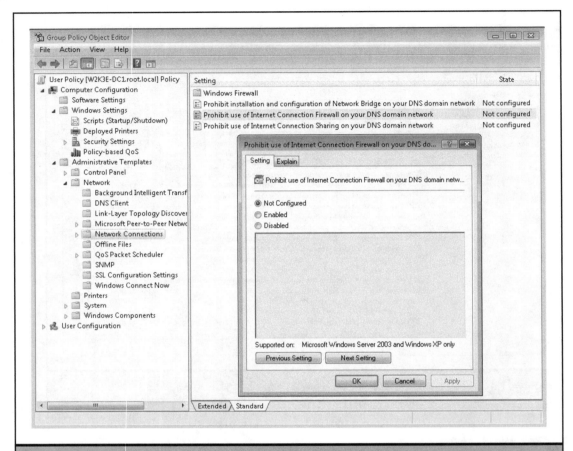

Figure 11-16. You can manage local computer policies using Group Policy.

3. Expand the forest-level node, and expand the Domains container by double-clicking it. Find and expand the domain of interest by double-clicking it.

4. Access the Network Connections node by expanding Computer Configuration\Administrative Templates\Network\Network Connections.

5. Double-click the policy that you want to configure. On the Settings tab, select either Enabled or Disabled. Click OK.

Policy Name	Description
Prohibit Installation And Configuration Of Network Bridge On Your DNS Domain Network	Determines whether users can install and configure network bridges. This policy only applies to the domain in which it is assigned.
Prohibit Use Of Internet Connection Firewall On Your DNS Domain Network	Determines whether users can enable the Internet Connection Firewall. This policy only applies to the domain in which it is assigned.
Prohibit Use Of Internet Connection Sharing On Your DNS Domain Network	Determines whether administrators can enable and configure connection sharing. This policy only applies to the domain in which it is assigned.
Windows Firewall Policies Container: Domain Profile	This container holds policies for configuring Windows Firewall. These policies will be applied while the computer running Vista is acting within a domain environment. This gives you the option to provide a Windows Firewall configuration for two separate working environments: connected and remote. The policies include: ■ Allow local program exceptions ■ Define inbound program exceptions ■ Protect all network connections ■ Do not allow exceptions ■ Allow inbound file and printer sharing exception ■ Allow Internet Control Message Protocol (ICMP) exceptions ■ Allow logging ■ Prohibit notifications ■ Allow local port exceptions ■ Define inbound port exceptions ■ Allow inbound remote administration exceptions ■ Allow inbound Remote Desktop exceptions

Table 11-1.   Computer Object Settings for Network Security

Policy Name	Description
	■ Allow inbound Remote Desktop exceptions ■ Prohibit unicast response to multicast or broadcast requests ■ Allow inbound Universal Plug and Play (UPnP) framework exceptions
Windows Firewall Policies Container: Standard Profile	In this container, you will find the same policies as those in the Domain profile. However, this duplicate set will apply while the computer running Vista is disconnected from the domain. This gives you the option to provide a Windows Firewall configuration for two separate working environments: connected and remote.

Table 11-1. Computer Object Settings for Network Security *(Continued)*

User Policies

User configuration options number in the thousands, as do the computer configurations. The User Configuration policies range from configuring driver search locations to enabling Internet Explorer settings. You make use of User Configuration policies, shown in Figure 11-17, to affect these network access areas:

▼ Network policies that control LAN connections

■ TCP/IP configuration

▲ Remote access

Table 11-2 lists the available settings that are especially relevant to network access and security. These policies are from the Network Policies container, found under Computer Configuration\Administrative Templates\Network\Network Connections And User Configuration\Administrative Templates\Network\Network Connections.

User Configuration policies for network connections usually prevent access to connection objects and the access configuration features. To configure and deploy these policies:

1. From the Start menu, type **gpmc.msc** into the Search field and press ENTER. Again, keep in mind that you must be logged on to a domain for this tool to launch.

2. Right-click the top node, Group Policy Management, and choose Add Forest from the options. Provide the name of the Active Directory forest, and click OK.

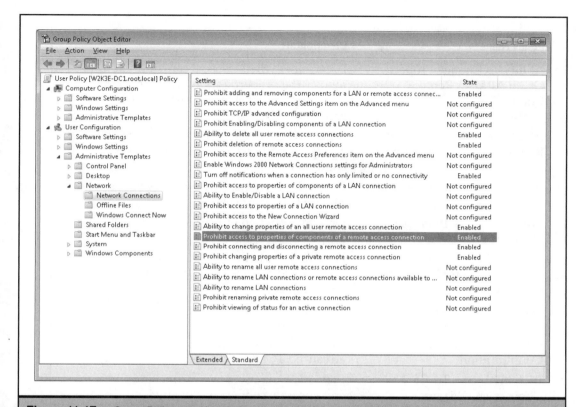

Figure 11-17.   Group Policy can also be used to manage individual user policies.

3. Expand the forest-level node, and expand the Domains container by double-clicking it. Find and expand the domain of interest by double-clicking it.

4. Access the Network Connections node by expanding User Configuration\Administrative Templates\Network\Network Connections.

5. Double-click the policy that you want to configure. On the Settings tab, select either Enabled or Disabled. Click OK.

SERVICE HARDENING

Your computer and network are further bolstered in Windows Vista through a mechanism that really runs under your radar. In fact, the threat itself was so under the surface that you wouldn't even consider it a risk—namely, individual services being given access to your system.

Policy Name	Description
Ability To Change Properties Of An All User Remote Access Connection	Determines whether users can view and modify the properties of remote access connections available to all users of the computer.
Ability To Delete All User Remote Access Connections	Determines whether users can delete remote access connections available to all users of the computer.
Ability To Enable/Disable A LAN Connection	Determines whether users can enable or disable LAN connections.
Prohibit Access To Properties Of A LAN Connection	Determines whether users can change the properties of LAN connections.
Prohibit Access To Properties Of Components Of A Remote Access Connection	Determines whether users can access and change properties of remote access connections.
Prohibit Deletion Of Remote Access Connections	Determines whether users can delete remote access connections.
Prohibit TCP/IP Advanced Configuration	Determines whether users can access advanced TCP/IP settings.
Prohibit Access To The New Connections Wizard	Prevents Vista users from launching and creating new connections of any kind.
Prohibit Adding And Removing Components For A LAN Or Remote Access Connection	Determines whether local administrators can add and remove network components for a LAN or remote access connection. This setting has no effect on nonadministrators.
Prohibit Enabling/Disabling Components Of A LAN Connection	Determines whether local administrators can enable and disable the components used by LAN connections.
Prohibit Connecting And Disconnecting A Remote Access Connection	Determines whether users can connect and disconnect remote access connections.

Table 11-2. User Object Settings for Network Security

Earlier versions of Windows granted access to system-level services, most of which ran under the LocalSystem account. A security breach could open up the computer and compromise system data, allowing malware to modify the system configuration, among other things.

Vista uses Windows Service Hardening to strengthen system security so that services cannot be used for nefarious purposes. It improves system security by doing the following:

▼ Limiting servers' privilege level by restricting the number of services that run in the LocalSystem account. Services that previously ran in the LocalSystem account now run in a less privileged account.

■ Critical Windows services are prevented from performing activities that influence the file system, registry, network, or other resources that could be used by malware to install itself or to attack other computers. Services can be prevented from modifying the registry or replacing system files. Some privileges, like performing debugging, have also been removed on a per-service basis.

▲ The default number of services that are running has been limited. To reduce the chance for attack, some services are configured to start as needed, rather than automatically.

Windows Service Hardening adds new features that are also used by Windows services.

Each service has a Security Identifier (SID)—like user accounts—which is used to manage the services' security permissions. Per-service SIDs allow per-service identities. Per-service identities allow access-control partitioning with the Windows access control model, including objects and resource managers that use access control lists. This allows services to apply access control lists to resources that are private to the service. This also prevents other services and users from accessing those resources.

NETWORK ACCESS PROTECTION

Windows Vista provides yet another way to prevent unauthorized computers and users from accessing the network via its Network Access Protection (NAP) mechanism. NAP is used to stop a Windows Vista–based client from connecting to a network if the client doesn't have current security updates and virus definitions.

How It Works

NAP is used to protect your network from both local clients and remote access clients whose computers are not as "healthy" as you want them to be. In this context, *health* refers to a computer's susceptibility to viruses, malware, or a configuration that you deem unsafe.

NAP utilizes three components:

▼ **Network Access Protection Agent**   This is a piece of software that allows clients running Windows Vista to participate in NAP. This agent is present on computers running Vista.

■ **NAP Client Configuration**   This is a tool used to define and enforce health policies on client devices. It also is used to designate trusted servers.

▲ **NAP Server Configuration**   This tool is used to manage NAP policies in your network. It is located on your "Longhorn" server.

The NAP Agent reports the health of a client to the server, which is called a Health Registration Authority. This report includes such information as:

▼ Overall health

■ Status of security updates

▲ Status of virus signatures

Protection

There are any number of scenarios in which you want your clients' health to be evaluated. There are times when foreign computers come to your network, and you want to ensure that they meet the health standards you've set for the rest of your network. There are also times when computers already on your network need to be checked to ensure that they are still healthy computers.

Roaming Laptops

While laptops provide a great deal of physical flexibility—users can take them home, take them to other networks, and so forth—it's that exact physical flexibility that can be a threat to the overall security health of the computer.

While they can come in contact with threats present on other networks, they can also suffer by not always being around when security updates are applied. They are also more likely to be exposed to viruses and other malware while connecting to the Internet. NAP allows network administrators to check the laptop's health, whether a user is connecting through a VPN or physically connecting to the network.

Desktops

With all the security mechanisms and prevention measures that you've laid down to prevent problems for your desktop clients, it's naive to assume that your clients are going to be totally safe. NAP provides another mechanism to ensure their health. These types of computers are still at risk from infection from malicious Web sites, e-mail, and files from shared folders, to name a few. NAP allows the network administrator to automatically initiate system checks to ensure that each desktop is in compliance with the network's health policies.

In addition to management applications, reports can be generated that the network administrator can check to look for unhealthy computers. In addition, computers that aren't healthy can be automatically updated. Finally, when administrators make a network-wide policy change on computer health, the changes can automatically be made to all computers.

Visiting Laptops

Naturally, it's not your network that's the source of a problem—it's the Internet and other peoples' networks that pose the threats. That's why roaming laptops need to be checked before they connect to your network, and that's why any visiting laptop needs to be treated like that monkey from the movie *Outbreak*.

Visitors to your network can be screened by NAP and a determination made as to whether the laptop is healthy enough to connect to your network. If the computer is not healthy enough, access can be limited, if allowed at all. As these devices are not your property or the responsibility of your organization, updates and configuration changes probably wouldn't be made.

Home Computers

There's another threat out there to your network: home computers. These are the devices that connect to your network through a VPN, but you have no control over how they are configured and managed. You don't have any say about whether antivirus and antispyware tools are installed and updated, or whether the user and anyone else in the home are practicing safe computing. Between what a user does on his or her own time and what little Jimmy downloads from some peer-to-peer (P2P) site, you probably want to check the health of these computers before you allow them to connect to your network.

NAP provides a way to do this. It allows network administrators to check for required programs, registry settings, and files each time a home computer makes a VPN connection to the network. If the computer is diagnosed as being unhealthy, it can be given limited access to the network until the computer's health has improved.

NAP Components

NAP utilizes four components to check a computer's health and limit its access, if necessary. Those components are:

- ▼ IPSec
- ■ IEEE 802.1X–authenticated network connections
- ■ VPNs
- ▲ Dynamic Host Configuration Protocol (DHCP)

These tools can be used individually or in cooperation to limit the access of unhealthy computers. Network Policy Server (NPS) is used as a health policy server for these technologies.

> **NOTE** In order to use NAP, your network's server must use Longhorn Server, and clients must use Vista or Longhorn Server.

Let's take a closer look at these technologies and what they do.

IPSec

IPSec enforcement includes two elements:

▼ Health Registration Authority (HRA)

▲ IPSec NAP Enforcement Client

The HRA issues X.509 certificates to clients when they are deemed to be healthy. The certificates are used to authenticate NAP clients when they try to communicate with other NAP clients via an IPSec-secured channel.

Since it uses IPSec, IPSec enforcement can define requirements for secure communications with other healthy clients based on IP address or TCP/ User Datagram Protocol (UDP) port number. Once they have successfully connected and obtained a valid IP address configuration, communication can be confined to those nodes.

802.1X

802.1X enforcement includes two elements:

▼ NPS Server

▲ EAPHost EAP Enforcement Client

An NPS server will instruct an 802.1X access point (be it an Ethernet switch or a wireless access point) to apply a restricted access profile on an unhealthy 802.1X client until it is deemed healthy enough.

Restricted access profiles can include IP packet filters or virtual LAN (VLAN) identifiers that will confine the client's traffic.

VPNs

VPN enforcement includes two elements:

▼ VPN NAP Enforcement Server

▲ VPN NAP Enforcement Client

VPN enforcement allows VPN servers to impose health policy requirements whenever a computer attempts a VPN connection to the network.

DHCP

DHCP enforcement includes two elements:

▼ DHCP NAP Enforcement Server

▲ DHCP NAP Enforcement Client

DHCP enforcement allows DHCP servers to enforce health policy requirements when a computer attempts to lease or renew an IP address configuration. This is the easiest way to deploy health policy enforcement, since all DHCP clients must lease IP addresses. Unfortunately, it is also the weakest form of enforcement.

Configuring NAP

Configuring NAP on clients is a fairly straightforward affair. At its heart, all you need to do is enable or disable certain forms of health examination. But that's not the only thing you can do when configuring NAP clients. The following sections examine some of the more common configuration tasks you might perform.

NAP Client Configuration

The NAP client is configured using the NAP Client Configuration tool, shown in Figure 11-18.

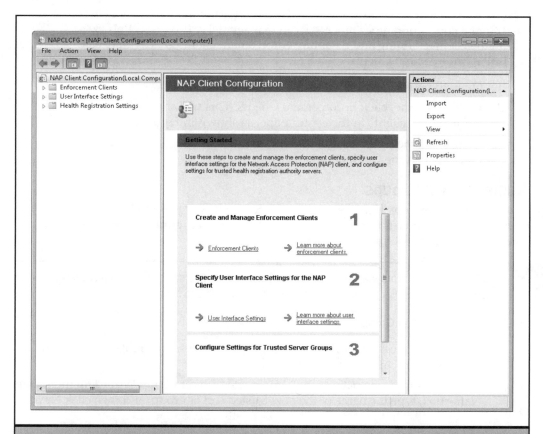

Figure 11-18. NAP is configured on a client by using the NAP Client Configuration tool.

To access the tool:

1. Click Start.

2. Click All Programs.

3. Click Accessories.

4. Click Run.

5. Type **napclcfg.msc**, and press ENTER, or launch Microsoft Management Console (MMC), and select the NAP Client Configuration snap-in.

Several steps must be followed to ensure that you've properly configured NAP on your Vista clients.

Configuring NAP Enforcement Clients

The NAP Client Configuration tool can be used to enable, disable, add, or delete NAP Enforcement Clients. These clients are responsible for requesting network access and communicating a client's health status to the NAP server. Earlier in this section, we talked about the different connection types that NAP can manage (DHCP, IPSec, VPNs, 802.1X).

On the client, enabling and disabling enforcement clients is extremely easy. To enable or disable Enforcement Clients:

1. Open the NAP Client Configuration tool.

2. In the left pane, click Enforcement Clients. This will show a list of available enforcement clients in the center pane, as shown in Figure 11-19.

3. Right-click the enforcement client you wish to manage, and select Enable or Disable from the Context menu.

Trusted Server Groups

In order to designate which server your Vista client will use to check its health, you manage trusted server groups using the NAP Client Configuration tool. With this tool, you indicate which HRA servers you wish to use.

NOTE   If there is more than one HRA server listed in a trusted server group, the client will attempt to connect to each HRA server in the order listed until it is able to connect.

Creating a Trusted Server Group   To create a trusted server group:

1. In the console tree, expand Health Registration Settings, right-click Trusted Server Groups, and then click New.

2. On the Group Name page of the New Trusted Server Group Wizard, in the Group Name box, type the name of the new trusted server group, and then click Next.

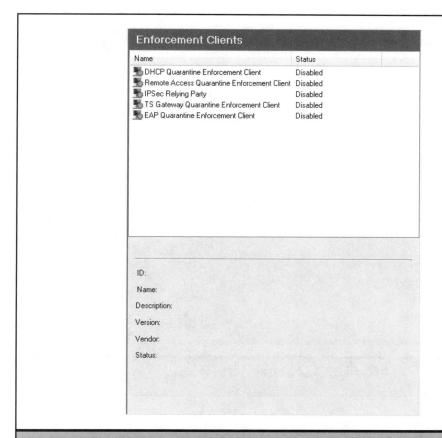

Figure 11-19.   The listed enforcement clients allow you to enable or disable NAP enforcement.

3. On the Add Servers page, shown in Figure 11-20, type the Uniform Resource Locator (URL) of an HRA server, and then click Add.

4. To add more HRA servers, repeat step 3.

5. If you want to change the order of the HRA servers in the trusted server group, do the following:

    a. In Trusted Servers, click the HRA server that you want to move up or down in the list.

    b. Click Move Up to move the HRA server up in the list; click Move Down to move the HRA server down in the list.

6. Click Next and then click Finish.

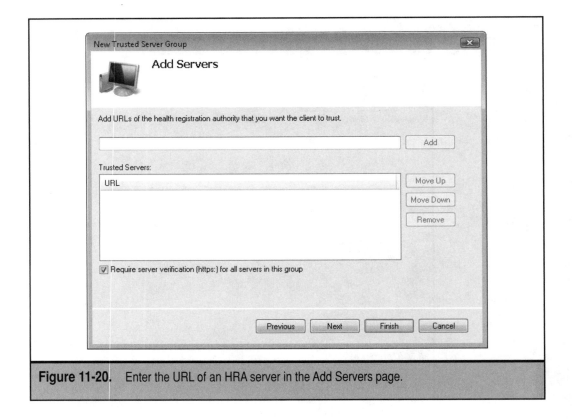

Figure 11-20. Enter the URL of an HRA server in the Add Servers page.

Adding an HRA to a Trusted Server Group To add HRA servers to a trusted server group:

1. In the console tree, expand Health Registration Settings, and click Trusted Server Groups.
2. Right-click the Trusted Server Group, and click Properties.
3. On the Trusted Server Group Properties dialog box, enter the URL of the HRA server that you want to add, and then click Add.

Changing the Order of the HRA Servers The order in which HRA servers within a trusted server group are checked can be changed by following these steps:

1. In the console tree, expand Health Registration Settings, and click Trusted Server Groups.
2. Right-click the Trusted Server Group, and click Properties.
3. On the Trusted Server Group Properties dialog box, click the URL of the HRA server that you want to move up or down the list, and then click Move Up or Move Down.

Changing an HRA Server's URL   Within a trusted server group, an HRA server's URL can be changed by following these steps:

1. In the console tree, expand Health Registration Settings, and click Trusted Server Groups.
2. Right-click the Trusted Server Group, and click Properties.
3. On the Trusted Server Group Properties dialog box, click the URL of the HRA server that you want to change, and then click Edit.
4. Type the new URL for the HRA server, and click OK.

Importing NAP Client Configuration Settings

Rather than configure each setting on multiple computers, it's much easier to first develop a standard configuration file and then import that file to each computer. You can import a configuration file either using the graphical user interface (GUI) or the command line.

GUI   To import a NAP client configuration file using the GUI:

1. In the console tree, right-click NAP Client Configuration, and then click Import.
2. In the Import NAP Configuration dialog box, in Look in, navigate to where the configuration file is stored.
3. In the File Name box, type the name for the configuration file.
4. Click Open.

Command Line   To import a NAP client configuration file from the command line:

1. Click Start.
2. Click Run.
3. Type **cmd**, and click OK.
4. Type netsh nap client import filename = <filename>.

NOTE   <filename> is the path and file name for the configuration file.

Exporting NAP Client Configuration Settings

Exporting settings is almost identical to importing settings. Again, it can be done using the GUI or command line.

GUI   To export a NAP client configuration file using the GUI:

1. In the console tree, right-click NAP Client Configuration, and then click Export.
2. In the Export NAP Configuration dialog box, in Look in, navigate to where the configuration file is stored.

3. In the File Name box, type the name for the configuration file.

4. Click Save.

Command Line To export a NAP client configuration file from the command line:

1. Click Start.

2. Click Run.

3. Type **cmd**, and click OK.

4. Type `netsh nap client export filename = <filename>`.

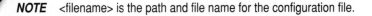

NOTE <filename> is the path and file name for the configuration file.

Network security is a huge topic that covers all sorts of computers and applications in your network. Windows Vista provides some of the old security favorites, along with some new stuff to keep your network protected.

PART IV

Working with Windows Vista

CHAPTER 12

Internet Applications

Included with Windows Vista are Microsoft's two latest Internet applications: Internet Explorer 7 and Internet Information Server (IIS) 7. Internet Explorer is the latest version of Microsoft's Web browser and the application most people use to navigate the World Wide Web. IIS is used to serve data on the Internet, an intranet, a local group, or home network.

In this chapter we'll take a closer look at these applications, examine what's new in their latest versions, and talk about how to use them and how to configure them. We'll start with an examination of Internet Explorer and explore how to use this updated tool. From there, we'll move on to IIS and talk about installing and configuring this Web server.

INTERNET EXPLORER 7

Internet Explorer 7 and Windows Vista were initially scheduled to be released together. However, when the Vista release was pushed back, Internet Explorer 7 came out several months before Vista and with a lot less fanfare than it probably would have had it been released alongside Vista.

To its credit, Microsoft listened to the user community and built a new browser based on what they wanted. They also released it when they had it ready, as opposed to delaying it so that it would be a part of the Vista marketing blitz. True, a lot of it was in territory already tilled by Firefox (like tabbed browsing, which we'll talk about in a moment), but it was a much-needed step forward for Internet Explorer.

Not only does Internet Explorer 7 contain a number of usability features, like Vista itself, it also offers new and improved security features. Security is included as part of the Dynamic Security Protection package. Its goal is to protect your computer and any information that you enter into Web pages.

This section examines Internet Explorer 7, its features, how you can use them, and then rounds out with a discussion of Internet Explorer 7's security enhancements.

Meet Internet Explorer 7

When you compare Internet Explorer 7 with Internet Explorer 6, it's easy to tell that there's more going on here than a new way to organize favorite Web sites. New user enhancements include tabbed browsing and integrated search, which makes Internet Explorer 7 much easier and powerful to work with than earlier versions.

When you look at the interface of Internet Explorer 7, shown in Figure 12-1, you can see some radical changes from Internet Explorer 6.

Improvements include:

▼ **A redesigned user interface** This gives more screen space to display Web pages, while the toolbar size is reduced.

■ **Tabbed browsing** Rather than open a new window for each Web site simultaneously visited, tabbed browsing allows all the windows to be managed within the same instance of Internet Explorer 7. This allows users to navigate quickly between sites by clicking a tab.

▲ **Web Search box** Another Firefox-like addition, Internet Explorer 7 doesn't require you to go to Google or Yahoo to perform a Web search—you can do it right from the Internet Explorer 7 Search box.

Figure 12-1. Internet Explorer 7 features a new, friendlier user interface.

Tabbed Browsing

While Firefox users have enjoyed this feature for a few years, Internet Explorer 7 is the first version of Internet Explorer to offer tabbed browsing. This feature allows you to view multiple Web pages in a single window. You can switch between pages by clicking the tabs at the top of the browser frame. You can still open new browser windows if you want, of course.

You can open a new tab by clicking the New Tab button. It is a nondescript, plain square that sits adjacent to the most recently opened tab. You can also press CTRL+T.

New tabs will appear to the right of the last tab created. Internet Explorer 7 gives you a couple of ways to manage your tabbed windows. When two or more tabs are opened, two additional buttons appear on the toolbar:

▼   **Quick Tabs preview button**   Shown in Figure 12-2, the Quick Tabs preview button shows the current contents of your tabs. For example, if you have five open browser screens, the contents of each screen are shown as thumbnail previews. You can access one of the pages by clicking its thumbnail. You can close the window by clicking the X in the upper-right corner of the screen.

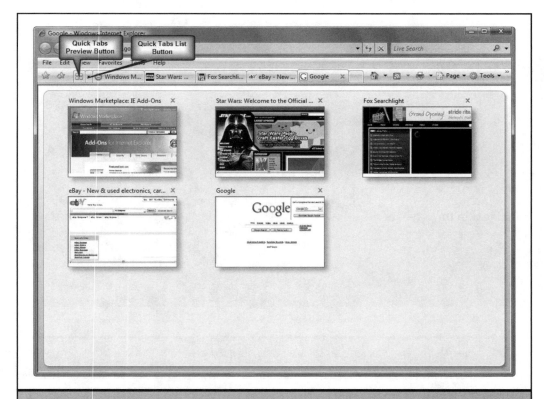

Figure 12-2.   The Quick Tabs preview button shows the contents of all your open browser windows.

▲ **Quick Tabs list button** Not nearly as sexy as the Quick Tabs preview button, the Quick Tabs list button displays a text list of the open Web pages. Just click the desired Web page's entry to go to it. While not containing the "cool" factor of the Quick Tabs preview button, it's a quicker way to navigate your open windows.

Once a tab is open, if you right-click it, you can elect to close just that tab or you can close all other tabs, if you are so inclined. You can also refresh the current tab or all open tabs.

Toolbars

While tabbed browsing is the most obvious change to Internet Explorer 7, it's not the only change. The toolbar has also undergone some considerable changes. There are, by default, four toolbars in Internet Explorer 7:

▼ Links bar

■ Standard toolbar

■ Address bar

▲ Status bar

This section examines what's new in these toolbars.

NOTE We don't really go into much depth on the Links bar. This bar hasn't changed from earlier versions of Internet Explorer. If you aren't familiar with the Links bar, it provides a nice, easy place to put URLs that you visit often. Rather than pulling the link from the Favorites menu, you can just click the desired link in the Links bar.

Standard Toolbar

The toolbar that you'll probably get the most action out of is the standard toolbar. Figure 12-3 shows this toolbar.

In Internet Explorer 7, iconography has really taken over. Rather than have a lot of initial text in the toolbars (like File, Tools, Edit, and so forth), these menu descriptors are replaced with icons. Chances are, if you spend some time with the icons, you'll figure out what they're for. However, if you don't like change, simply right-click the toolbar at the top of the screen, and select Menu Bar. This will call up the traditional menu. While it wasn't artsy, it was still useful.

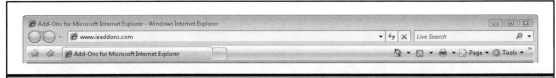

Figure 12-3. The standard toolbar in Internet Explorer 7 is an update of the classic menu bar from prior versions.

You can also press the ALT key to call up the menu bar for the Internet Explorer window you are using. Once you've selected the item you want from the menu bar, this toolbar disappears. You can also make the menu bar go away by pressing the ALT button again.

At the extreme left of the standard toolbar are a little star icon and a star with a little plus sign. The star icon is the Favorites Center button, and the other is the Add To Favorites button.

The Favorites Center is a new addition to Internet Explorer 7 that gives you a single location to view, access, and manage the following:

▼ **Favorites**   Your favorite Web sites

■ **Feeds**   Your favorite Really Simple Syndication (RSS) feeds

▲ **History**   Your recently accessed sites

Figure 12-4 shows the menu that appears when the Favorites Center button is clicked. Just click the icon of the area you wish to access, and then pick your favorite from the list.

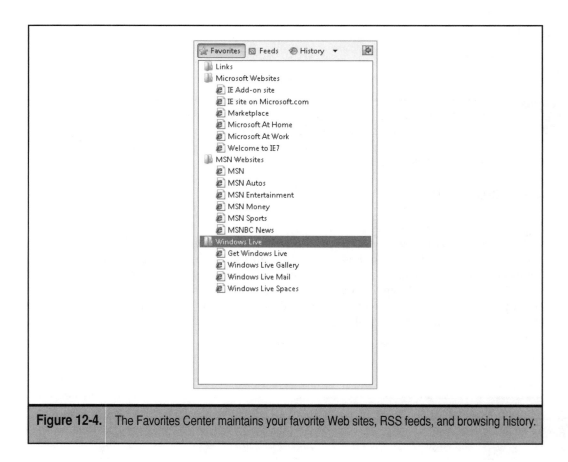

Figure 12-4.   The Favorites Center maintains your favorite Web sites, RSS feeds, and browsing history.

RSS Feeds   Yet another new addition to Internet Explorer 7 is the integration of RSS feeds. RSS feeds can contain any information: news headlines, podcasts—really anything the Web designer chooses to feed directly to your browser.

To display feeds in Internet Explorer 7:

1. Open Internet Explorer.
2. Click the Favorites Center button.
3. Click the Feeds tab.
4. Select the feed you want to view.

NOTE   If you're really into a certain feed, you can display it all the time by creating a gadget for your desktop. See Chapter 1 to learn how that's done.

Home Pages   Also new in Internet Explorer 7 is the ability to have more than one home page. The Home button on the right end of the standard toolbar allows you to go right to a default home page. However, the Home Options button (the icon is a downward-pointing arrow), located to the right of the Home button, allows you to select from a list of additional home pages and also gives you the ability to add, change, or remove them.

You can set a current page as a home page by clicking the Home Options button and then selecting Add Or Change Home Page. The Add Or Change Home Page dialog box appears, shown in Figure 12-5.

Choose the option you wish to set for this page, and then click Yes.

Printing   At the far right of the standard toolbar is a familiar printer icon. As with other versions of Internet Explorer—and, frankly, any application with a printer icon on it—clicking this button allows you to print the current view of the page you're visiting.

The Print Options button (again, a downward-pointing arrow), located to the right of the Print button, allows you to customize the print layout. Simply select Print Preview,

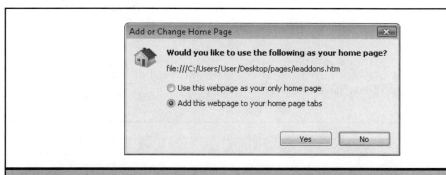

Figure 12-5.   Internet Explorer 7 allows you to have multiple home pages and to add new ones by clicking the Home Options button.

and you'll see a familiar preview screen of the page you want to print. While, so far, none of this is new, what Internet Explorer 7 brings to the printing party is the ability to scale Web pages to fit on the page. At the top of the screen is a drop-down menu that allows you to select a percentage size of the page. That is, you can print the page at 50 percent its original size, 200 percent its original size, and so forth.

Tools The Tools menu contains a lot of the behind-the-scenes functions of Internet Explorer 7. It's here where you can do things like delete your browsing history, diagnose connection problems, and a host of other options. The options you can perform include the following:

▼ **Delete browsing history** Erase all cached browsing information, including page history, cookies, saved passwords, and Web form information.

■ **Diagnose connection problems** Get help figuring out what's wrong with a failed connection.

■ **Full screen** Toggle Internet Explorer 7 to full-screen mode. This can also be done by pressing F11.

■ **Internet options** Display the Internet Options dialog box, where Internet Explorer 7 can be configured.

■ **Manage add-ons** Display a dialog box that shows currently installed add-ons. You can use this dialog box to enable, disable, or completely delete add-ons.

■ **Phishing filter** Specify options for your phishing filter. This is used to prevent malicious Web sites from stealing information you've already entered as form data.

■ **Pop-up blocker** Enable or disable pop-up blocking.

■ **Toolbars** Configure which toolbars are shown in the browser.

▲ **Work offline** Tell Internet Explorer 7 that you want to use the browser, but in offline mode. In this mode, Internet Explorer 7 will try to load content from its browsing cache. If the page is not cached, you'll see an error message and be asked if you want to go online.

Address Bar

Like so many other parts of Internet Explorer 7, the address bar has undergone some changes as well. The address bar is shown in Figure 12-6.

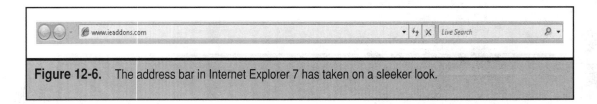

Figure 12-6. The address bar in Internet Explorer 7 has taken on a sleeker look.

You'll find the following components in the address bar:

▼   Forward and Back buttons

■   Address Path text box

■   Path History button

■   Refresh button

■   Stop button

▲   Search box

To open a new Web page, as with any other browser, enter the URL in the Address Path field, and then press ENTER or click the arrow button next to the box.

If you click the Path History button—the downward-pointing arrow—you'll be able to see paths you've already visited.

While this is fairly routine and standard fare for Web browsers, what's new in Internet Explorer 7 is the addition of the Search box. You can search the Web using a default search provider. Just enter the search text in the box, press ENTER or click the Search button, and your search will be conducted.

Next to the Search button is the Search Options button. Clicking this button allows you to do the following:

▼   Select an already configured search provider (like default provider MSN Search, Google, Yahoo, and so forth)

■   Find text on the current page rather than searching the Internet

■   Add new search providers from the Microsoft Web site

▲   Modify default search settings

Status Bar

The last toolbar is the status bar, located at the bottom of the screen and shown in Figure 12-7.

In earlier editions of Internet Explorer, the status bar was used to show browser status messages. In Internet Explorer 7, the status bar now shows the following information:

▼   **Phishing status indicator**   This shows the phishing status of the currently visited Web page. If it's a site that you haven't been to before (or as often), the phishing filter status indicator displays a warning icon. By clicking this icon, you can check the Web site's trustworthiness, report the Web site, or configure

Computer | Protected Mode: Off   100% ▾

Figure 12-7.   The status bar shows you information pertaining to the state of your browser's security status.

Check This Website
Turn On Automatic Website Checking...
Report This Website
Phishing Filter Settings

Figure 12-8.	Phishing filter options can be managed by clicking the open space to the left of the Internet Security indicator.

filter options. If you go to sites that aren't suspicious (like www.microsoft.com), the icon does not appear. You can still access all the phishing filter features by clicking in the empty space to the left of the Internet Security indicator. By doing so, you'll see a menu like the one in Figure 12-8.

- ■ **Internet Security indicator**   Indicates the current security zone and mode in use. Security zones are explained in more detail later in this section. Essentially, there are different zones for Internet, Local Intranet, Trusted Sites, and Restricted Sites.

- ▲ **View magnifier**   This allows you to zoom in or shrink a Web page. Anything greater than 100 percent will be zoomed in, while anything less than 100 percent will be reduced.

Internet Explorer Safety and Security

By now, you shouldn't be surprised when we tell you that a certain part of Windows Vista has improved security. Improvements are everywhere, and Internet Explorer 7 is no exception. In fact, one of the main areas of improvement in Internet Explorer 7 pertains to security with the inclusion of the Dynamic Security Protection package.

The Dynamic Security Protection package is comprised of four components:

- ▼ Parental controls
- ■ Protected Mode features
- ■ Privacy reporting
- ▲ Phishing filters

While parental controls are a nice feature, it's just not something that is likely to see the light of day in a corporate implementation. You'll get better use out of Group Policy, which we'll talk about later in this chapter. In this section, however, we'll talk about Protected Mode features, privacy reporting, and phishing filters.

Protected Mode

A lot of Vista seems to be integrated with other components by default, which is a nice usability feature. However, in the place where you would expect to see more of it—Internet

Explorer 7—deep and unfettered integration doesn't exist. Earlier versions of Internet Explorer have access to the operating system and active applications. However, Internet Explorer 7 makes a break from this behavior for the sake of system security. Rather than being able to access those applications, Internet Explorer 7 runs in Protected Mode.

In Protected Mode, Internet Explorer 7 is cut off from the operating system and running applications. It also prevents add-ons from saving information in any location beyond the temporary Internet folders without a user giving permission. This is a nice, secure step, because it prevents malware from damaging the computer.

By default, Internet Explorer 7 runs in Protected Mode, but you can disable it by clearing the Protected Mode check box on the Security tab in the Internet Options dialog box.

There are three more ways in which Protected Mode isolates Internet Explorer 7 from potential damage, as the following sections explain.

Add-on Restrictions   In order to prevent add-ons from harming your computers, Internet Explorer 7 includes a new Add-Ons Disabled Mode. In this mode, all browser extensions are disabled.

> **NOTE**   Actually, not all add-ons are disabled. Add-ons that are critical to the core browser components are still active.

To start Internet Explorer 7 in Add-Ons Disabled Mode:

1. Click Start.

2. Point to All Programs.

3. Click Accessories.

4. Click System Tools.

5. Click Internet Explorer (No Add-Ons).

Alternately, you can right-click the Internet Explorer desktop icon, and select Internet Explorer (No Add-Ons).

If you do elect to use add-ons, Internet Explorer 7 makes it easier to manage installed add-ons by using the Manage Add-Ons dialog box, shown in Figure 12-9.

Using this tool, you can see which add-ons have been installed. You can also disable or delete add-ons, if you choose.

To start the Manage Add-Ons tool:

1. In Internet Explorer, click Tools, click Manage Add-Ons, and then select Enable Or Disable Add-Ons.

2. In the Show drop-down list, select Downloaded ActiveX Controls.

3. Click the add-on you want to work with.

4. To disable the add-on, click the Disable option in the Settings area. The add-on is still installed, but nonfunctional.

5. To delete the downloaded add-on, click the Delete button in the Delete ActiveX section.

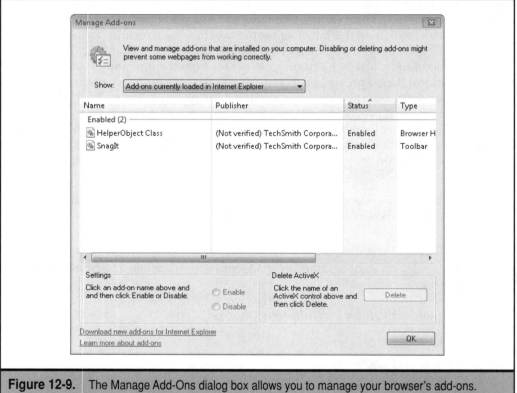

Figure 12-9. The Manage Add-Ons dialog box allows you to manage your browser's add-ons.

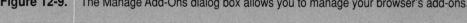

NOTE Add-ons aren't the devil! There are certainly add-ons you can use to the benefit of your productivity. Microsoft has a whole Web site dedicated to Internet Explorer 7 add-ons, located at www.ieaddons.com. The add-ons are divided into categories for home, security, timesavers, browsers, and entertainment. Some of the add-ons are free, but others will cost a few bucks.

Domain   Internet Explorer 7 allows domain names to be entered in English or as international letters and characters. However, realizing the potential for users to be tricked by authentic-looking domain names using these characters, Microsoft has implemented international domain name anti-spoofing. This is a way to protect your browser from sites that would normally seem authentic and above board. If you visit a site that uses characters that look like those of a trusted site, Internet Explorer 7 will display a warning message.

Security Levels and Zones Security levels and zones are not new to Internet Explorer, but they are key to Internet Explorer 7's security lineup. To see your security options in Internet Explorer 7:

1. Open Internet Explorer.
2. Click Tools.
3. Select Internet Options.
4. Click the Security tab in the Internet Options dialog box. The resulting dialog box looks like the one in Figure 12-10.

Security zones and levels might be somewhat confusing, but it's easy to think of them this way: Security levels define specific actions or behaviors from Internet Explorer 7, like not allowing ActiveX content to be downloaded. Security zones, on the other hand, tell Internet Explorer 7 which level of security to use for different sites.

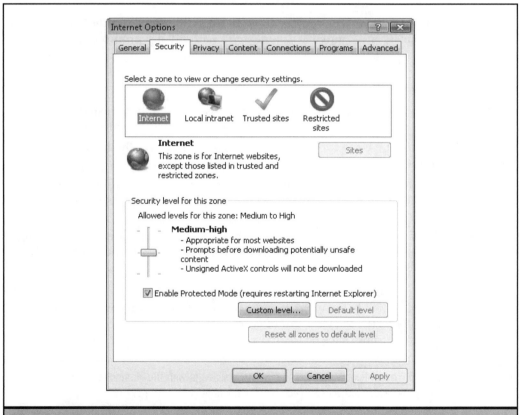

Figure 12-10. Security levels and zones are key to security in Internet Explorer 7.

There are five standard levels of security that you can use. As you look at them, you can think of them like the doneness of steak, except instead of "well" and "rare," use the terms "high" and "low," respectively. They are:

▼ **High**   Used for sites that you suspect contain harmful content. At this level, Internet Explorer 7 runs in its most protected state, and less-secure features are disabled.

■ **Medium-high**   New for Internet Explorer 7 and used for most sites. Internet Explorer 7 prompts you before downloading anything, and it disables the downloading of unsigned ActiveX controls.

■ **Medium**   Used for trusted sites. At this level, Internet Explorer 7 prompts you before downloading anything potentially unsafe and disables the downloading of unsigned ActiveX controls.

■ **Medium-low**   Used for sites on your internal network. Internet Explorer 7 runs most content without prompting for permission, but does disable the downloading of unsigned ActiveX controls.

▲ **Low**   Used for sites you unquestionably trust. Internet Explorer 7 uses almost no safeguards, and content is downloaded without any prompting.

To decide when the aforementioned security levels should be used, Internet Explorer 7 uses four different security zones:

▼ **Internet**   Used for Internet sites, except those listed in the Trusted and Restricted zones. By default, this zone is set at the medium-high level.

■ **Local Intranet**   Used for sites on your internal network. By default, this zone is set at the medium-low setting.

■ **Trusted Sites**   Used for sites that you have specifically identified as being trusted and needing the lowest level of protection against. These sites use a custom security level.

▲ **Restricted Sites**   Used for sites that you have specifically identified as being dangerous or that you've decided you need the most protection against. By default, these sites are protected at the high level.

The behavior for different sites can be managed per your liking. For instance, maybe you want to throw caution to the wind and just set everything to the low level of security. Once you've cleaned all the spyware out of your computers, you can beef up security by indicating that local intranet sites be treated with medium or medium-high security.

NOTE   The only exception to your customization abilities is with the Restricted Sites zone. Those sites will always be accessed with the high level of security.

Privacy

The sad thing about the Internet is that so much of what is bad about it started out as good ideas—like pop ups, and mechanisms to make Web life more pleasurable and productive have been usurped and turned into things we dread. Internet Explorer 7 includes some tools to deal with these good ideas gone bad.

Cookies Cookies are little pieces of information, stored on your computer, that allow Web sites to recognize and remember you from visit to visit. Cookies store all sorts of information, from user names to e-mail addresses to your real name and mailing address. To keep that information out of the wrong hands, Internet Explorer 7 uses privacy settings.

In the Internet zone, certain cookies are blocked. Internet Explorer can tell the difference between the site you are visiting and other sites that might use the same sorts of information. It does this by defining the Web site that you're visiting as a *first party*. Other Web sites that might display that content are considered *third parties*. For instance, if you are visiting www.google.com, some of the content might also come from maps.google.com. Here, www.google.com is the first party, while maps.google.com is the third party.

You can see a privacy report for the current page by clicking Page and then clicking Web Page Privacy Policy. A report, like the one in Figure 12-11, is generated.

The report will tell you if cookies were restricted based on your privacy settings and which Web sites have content on the page.

Clicking the Settings button displays the Internet Options dialog box with the Privacy tab selected. By default, cookies set by first-party sites are subject to different privacy levels than are third-party sites.

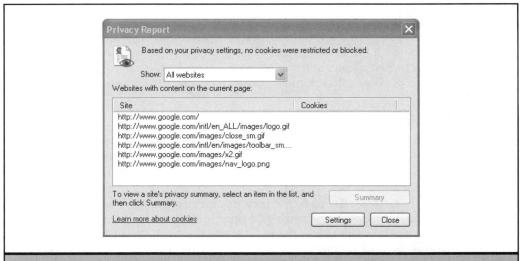

Figure 12-11. A Web page's privacy report can tell you information about its privacy attributes.

Privacy levels can be managed under the Privacy tab in the Internet Options dialog box. Privacy levels include:

▼ **Block All Cookies**   Used to block all cookies from every Web site

■ **High**   Used to block cookies from sites that do not have a compact privacy policy, blocks cookies that save information

■ **Medium High**   Used to block third-party cookies that do not have a compact privacy policy, blocks cookies that save information, blocks first-party cookies that save information

■ **Medium**   Used to block third-party cookies that do not have a compact privacy policy, blocks third-party cookies that save information, restricts first-party cookies that save information

■ **Low**   Used to block third-party cookies that do not have a compact privacy policy, restricts third-party cookies that save information

▲ **Accept All Cookies**   Used to accept cookies from any Web site

Phishing   Phishing is a means through which an attacker tries to learn sensitive—and ultimately valuable—information about you through deceptive tactics. This is commonly accomplished by sending genuine looking e-mails with links to imposter Web sites. Once a user is directed to an imposter Web site, he or she may be prompted to enter account information and other personal data, all the while assuming that they are doing so with a trusted Web site. As we discussed earlier, Internet Explorer 7 has a phishing filter that warns you if it suspects a malicious site. If the Web site is a known phishing site, it will block access to it, effectively preventing a user from giving out personal information.

The phishing filter, shown in Figure 12-12, is accessed by clicking Tools and then clicking Phishing Filter.

As you visit different Web sites, a warning icon is displayed in the status bar to remind you that you aren't at a known site. That icon doesn't mean that there is necessarily any trouble; it just means that the site is not well-known. If you go to a site like www.amazon.com or some other popular commercial site, the icon won't even appear.

Group Policy Settings

Group Policy is an enormously useful tool that you can use to manage most facets of your users' computing lives. While there isn't enough space in this book to talk about each and every setting in Group Policy, we can point out some of the areas where you are most likely to use it and the best way to do so—for example, with Internet Explorer.

As we noted in Chapter 11, Group Policy has been greatly enhanced in Windows Vista. Microsoft has added 800 new settings, bringing the total to about 2,400.

Internet Explorer is managed in three places in Group Policy. The first is reasonably straightforward, and will get you in and out of the Internet Explorer configuration door fairly quickly. It is located in Local Computer Policy/User Configuration/Windows Settings/Internet Explorer Maintenance. When you start it, the screen shown in Figure 12-13 appears.

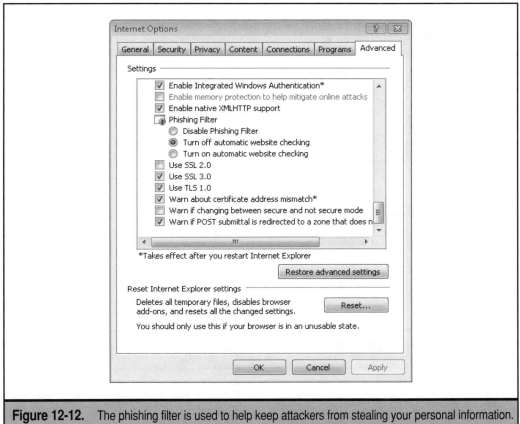

Figure 12-12.   The phishing filter is used to help keep attackers from stealing your personal information.

The two other areas are more complex and really drill down into Internet Explorer's functionality. They are located at:

▼   Local Computer Policy/Computer Configuration/Administrative Templates/ Windows Components/Internet Explorer

▲   Local Computer Policy/User Configuration/Administrative Templates/ Windows Components/Internet Explorer

Settings

So what exactly can you manage with Group Policy? A better question is: What can't you manage? Under the various settings in Group Policy, you can manage such items as:

▼   Which buttons appear on the toolbar

■   Bitmap textures behind menus

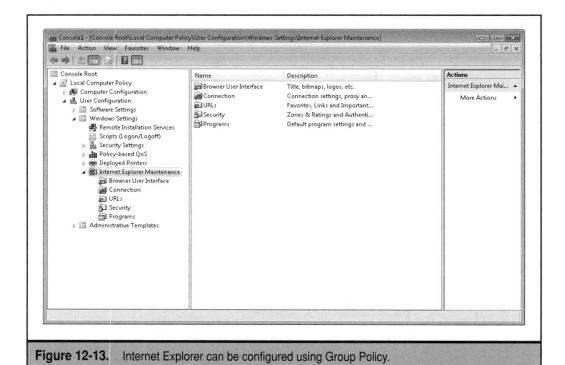

Figure 12-13. Internet Explorer can be configured using Group Policy.

- ■ Custom logos
- ■ Browser title
- ■ Pop-up blocking
- ■ Link underlining
- ■ User-friendly error messages
- ■ The ability to play music in Web pages
- ■ The ability to play video in Web pages
- ▲ Resetting Internet Explorer 7 to default settings

The list goes on and on. We don't have the space to examine each and every Group Policy setting for Internet Explorer 7, but take a look at the policy in Figure 12-14 for an idea of the sorts of things you can manage.

Figure 12-14 shows the Configure Toolbar Buttons Properties dialog box. We've selected this property to show how this particular one is managed. If you enable the policy, the dimmed center portion becomes active, and you can select which buttons will appear on your clients' Web browsers.

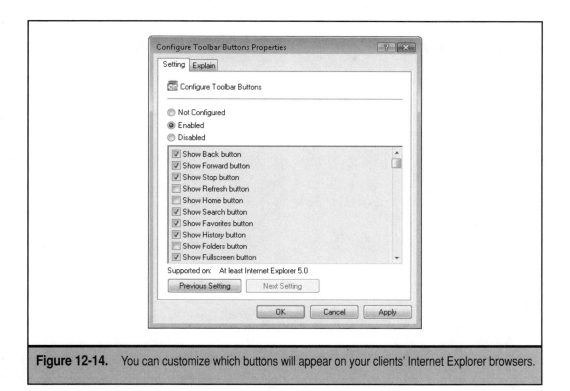

Figure 12-14. You can customize which buttons will appear on your clients' Internet Explorer browsers.

If, for some reason, you decided not to allow the Folders button to appear—as we have done—simply clear the check box next to it.

Again, there are far too many settings to get into, but it is worth your while to open Group Policy and poke around the Internet Explorer settings.

Changing a Policy

Let's take one more look at managing a Group Policy element. We'll do something that you might find yourself doing with your own organization—adding a company name to the browser's title.

First, open Group Policy and then navigate to User Configuration/Windows Settings/Internet Explorer Maintenance. Next, expand Browser User Interface in the left pane. The resulting Group Policy window will look like the one in Figure 12-15.

Next, double-click Browser Title. This will display a policy dialog box like the one shown in Figure 12-16. As you can see, we've entered the name of our company: Lyle's Chicken Farm, and we've also selected the Customize Title Bars check box.

Once you've entered the text you want, click OK and close out of Group Policy. The next time you open Internet Explorer, you'll see your title at the top of the browser window. Our example is shown in Figure 12-17.

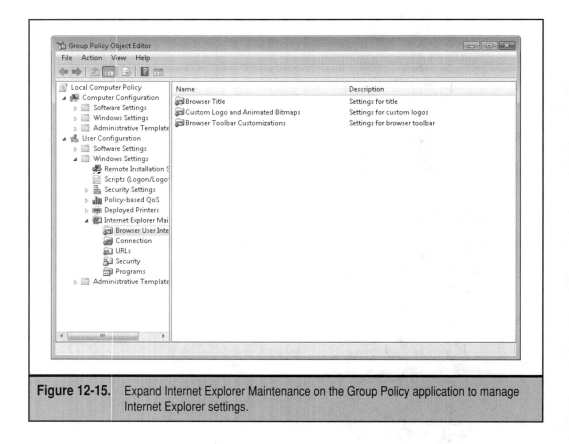

Figure 12-15. Expand Internet Explorer Maintenance on the Group Policy application to manage Internet Explorer settings.

Group Policy is a powerful application, and one that you should explore if you want to gain control over the browser's look, feel, and operability in your organization.

INTERNET INFORMATION SERVER 7.0

Internet Information Server (IIS) is a Web server service that comes with every Microsoft server operating system and some versions of the desktop operating system. IIS has been around since 1996 and has not had a new major release since Windows Server 2003. With IIS installed, you can host Web applications and leverage the wide array of Internet and intranet technologies that accompany IIS to solve a universe of business opportunities. It provides a platform for serving Web sites and File Transport Protocol (FTP), as well as support for FrontPage extensions and transactions, Active Server Pages (ASP), ASP.NET, Common Gateway Interface (CGI) applications, and database connections. The major releases of IIS are shown in Table 12-1.

Most major public Web sites are hosted on a fully robust server—or cluster of servers—using a server operating system such as Windows Server 2003 or Linux. A Web site

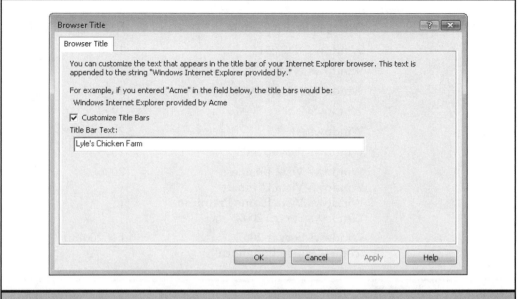

Figure 12-16. Enter the text you wish to appear on your Internet Explorer browser title bar.

that is hosted on a workstation-class computer or notebook with Vista will not normally be suitable for active public Web sites. IIS 7 on a computer running Vista can offer any number of solutions for a workgroup, however, or for a user who is currently logged on. Here are some of the common uses of IIS on a Vista platform:

▼ While developing Web site applications, use IIS 7 to host the draft Web site on the local Vista workstation to speed up development and simplify the network infrastructure.

■ Some applications may require IIS, such as certain scenarios using Microsoft Project Central and Microsoft SQL Server.

■ Use IIS to provide FTP services for your workgroup.

▲ Install IIS management tools locally, and configure them to manage remote servers, alleviating the need to use a network logon session.

Google - Windows Internet Explorer provided by Lyle's Chicken Farm

Figure 12-17. You can customize your browser's title, as well as many other environmental and behavioral settings.

Version of IIS	Operating System Platform	Release Year
1	Windows NT 3.51	1996
2	Windows NT 4.0	1996
4	Windows NT 4.0 Option Pack	1997
5	Windows 2000	1999
5.1	Windows XP	2001
6	Windows Server 2003	2003
7	Windows Vista Business Windows Vista Ultimate Windows Vista Home Premium Windows Server 2007	2006
7	Windows Server 2007 (code-named "Longhorn")	Est.2007

Table 12-1. Major Releases of IIS

IIS is available as an optional service for three versions of Vista: Business, Ultimate, and Home Premium.

NOTE With IIS installed on your workstations, you have management and security concerns to address. That is, you'll likely not allow it across enterprise desktops, unless there is a specific business requirement for it and all of the security implications of having local Web server functionality have been taken into account.

IIS 7 was released among great expectations for a new Web services platform. Some of the key benefits that it promises include:

▼ Granular control over the IIS footprint, reducing security risk and patching intensity

■ A new extensibility framework that enables you to delegate authority over finite components

▲ Improved Web infrastructure management, including building, deploying, migrating, and monitoring

Installing IIS

IIS is an optional service that you install by choice. For simple Web sites, you can install and configure it in a matter of minutes. For more complex Web applications, you can easily get lost in the myriad configuration options. To speed up the process and ensure consistency, you can automate the installation using the options discussed in the following sections.

Requirements for Installing IIS

There are no real requirements for IIS, other than authorization. To install IIS 7 onto a computer running Vista, you need to be a local administrator. If the computer is a member of a domain, you may leverage the Web Administrators Group. The install bits are contained on the Vista media, so keep the disk handy.

Installing IIS Manually

To manually install IIS 7 on a computer running Vista:

1. Click the Start button, and select the Control Panel link from the right pane.
2. In Control Panel, click the Programs link.
3. From the Programs window, click the Programs And Features link.

NOTE   Alternately, from the Start menu, you can type `appwiz.cpl` in the Search box and press **ENTER**.

4. In the left pane of the Programs And Features window, click Turn Windows Features On or Off. The Windows Features window will open and load. It can take a few moments for the window to fully load.
5. The list of Windows features is in alphabetical order. Locate Internet Information Services, and double-click it. Once opened, three folders become available, as shown in Figure 12-18:

   ■ FTP Publishing Service

   ■ Web Management Tools

   ■ World Wide Web Services

6. Depending on the role you wish IIS to perform, select the desired components for IIS, and click the OK button.

Automated Installs: Then and Now

You may wish to automate the installation of IIS for any number of reasons—for example, if you are installing IIS on 50 Vista workstations and you want to save time and ensure that the installations are configured the same. There a few ways in which you can automate the installation of IIS. In Vista, the same setup technology used to install it is also used to install optional features, such as IIS 7. Prior to Vista, the Windows setup infrastructure had multiple technologies to upgrade, service, and add optional features. The legacy installation technology tool chest includes:

▼ Setup.exe to install operating system

■ Sysocmgr.exe and answer files (unattend.txt) to install optional features

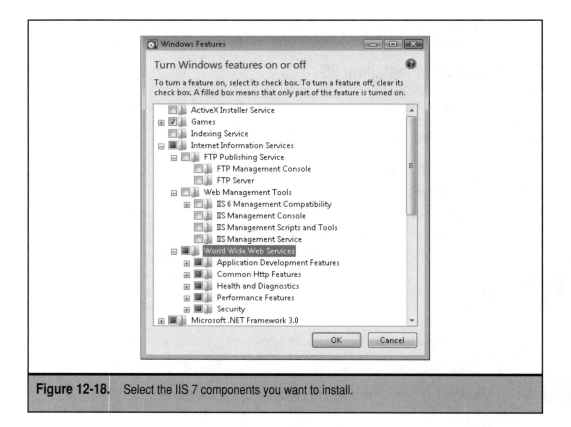

Figure 12-18. Select the IIS 7 components you want to install.

- Update.exe to install service packs
- Microsoft Installer (MSI) packages

In Vista, we now have a single setup infrastructure that unifies the installation and servicing of Vista and optional features. Sysocmgr.exe is no longer applicable for Vista components like IIS. The new feature installation engine is Pkgmgr.exe, and the unattended installation file is now eXtensible Markup Language (XML)–based.

Package Manager

The Windows Package Manager (pkgmgr.exe) is used to install and uninstall Windows optional features; it replaces sysocmgr.exe. You can use the tool to update your IIS 7 feature set using a command shell. Figure 12-19 shows this tool.

The following sample script will install IIS 7 with the limited default features and add the FTP service:

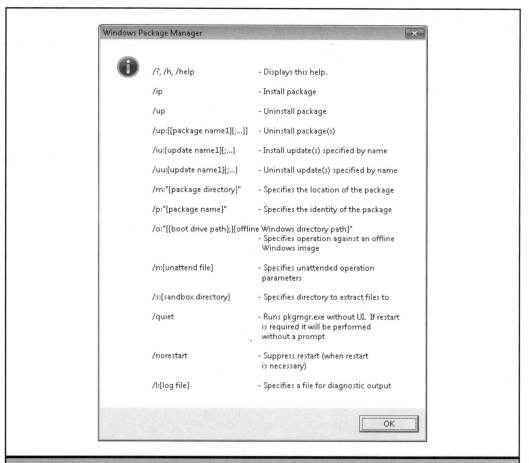

Figure 12-19. Windows Package Manager is the new way to install, service, and update optional components.

```
start /w pkgmgr /iu:IIS-WebServerRole;WAS-WindowsActivationService;WAS-
ProcessModel;
WAS-NetFxEnvironment;WAS-ConfigurationAPI;IIS-FTPPublishingService;IIS-
FTPServer;IIS-FTPManagement
```

For more information about pkgmgr.exe, see the Windows Automated Installation Kit (WAIK) User's Guide for Windows Vista, which can be download from the Microsoft Web site (go.microsoft.com/fwlink/?LinkId=63893).

Pkgmgr.exe also can accept input from an unattend.xml file. The unattend file lists the components to be installed or uninstalled. When using an unattend file, you use a different naming scheme for the components than the one you find in the Windows Features window. Instead of selecting components when adding features, you name the "update" as it's called. Each component in the Windows Features window has an update name. You can map all the features to update names by referencing the Microsoft IIS Web site at www.iis.net. To launch the Package Manager and leverage the instructions held in an unattend file, type the following into a command line:

```
start /w pkgmgr /n:unattend.xml
```

where the /n switch is filled with the path and name of the unattend file. The following text is a sample unattend.xml file used to provide instructions to pkgmgr.exe for installing IIS 7:

```
<?xml version="1.0" ?>
<unattend xmlns="urn:schemas-microsoft-com:unattend"
  xmlns:wcm="http://schemas.microsoft.com/WMIConfig/2002/State">
<servicing>
 <!-- Install a selectable update in a package that is in the Windows Foundation
namespace -->
 <package action="configure">
 <assemblyIdentity
 name="Microsoft-Windows-Foundation-Package"
 version="6.0.5308.6"
 language="neutral"
 processorArchitecture="x86"
 publicKeyToken="31bf3856ad364e35"
 versionScope="nonSxS"
 />
  <selection name="IIS-WebServerRole" state="true"/>
  <selection name="IIS-WebServer" state="true"/>
  <selection name="IIS-CommonHttpFeatures" state="true"/>
  <selection name="IIS-StaticContent" state="true"/>
  <selection name="IIS-DefaultDocument" state="true"/>
  <selection name="IIS-DirectoryBrowsing" state="false"/>
  <selection name="IIS-HttpErrors" state="true"/>
  <selection name="IIS-HttpRedirect" state="true"/>
  <selection name="IIS-ApplicationDevelopment" state="true"/>
  <selection name="IIS-ASPNET" state="true"/>
  <selection name="IIS-NetFxExtensibility" state="true"/>
  <selection name="IIS-HealthAndDiagnostics" state="true"/>
  <selection name="IIS-HttpLogging" state="true"/>
  <selection name="IIS-LoggingLibraries" state="false"/>
  <selection name="IIS-RequestMonitor" state="true"/>
  <selection name="IIS-Security" state="true"/>
  <selection name="IIS-WindowsAuthentication" state="true"/>
  <selection name="IIS-WebServerManagementTools" state="true"/>
  <selection name="IIS-ManagementConsole" state="true"/>
  <selection name="IIS-ManagementService" state="true"/>
```

```
    <selection name="WAS-WindowsActivationService" state="true"/>
    <selection name="WAS-ProcessModel" state="true"/>
    <selection name="WAS-NetFxEnvironment" state="true"/>
    <selection name="WAS-ConfigurationAPI" state="true"/>
  </package>
  </servicing>
  </unattend>
```

Migrating to IIS 7

The good news for IIS 6 users is that by applying an in-place upgrade from Windows XP to Vista, the IIS platform will also be upgraded. Moving IIS 6 Web sites to IIS 7 is not currently supported by Vista, but you can expect either Microsoft or a third-party software vendor to provide a toolset for this in the near future.

IIS 6 Compatibility

IIS 6 uses APIs and the Windows Management Instrumentation (WMI) interface to manage metabase settings. These APIs are not part of the IIS 7 default installation and must be explicitly selected for install. To ensure continued access to APIs, such as ABO and ADSI, as well as support for WMI, be sure to select these modules:

▼   IIS metabase and IIS 6 configuration compatibility

■   IIS 6 WMI compatibility

▲   IIS 6 scripting tools

IIS 7 Architecture

The new architecture for IIS 7 merits a few remarks. For starters, the platform is split into over 40 distinct *modules* that can be switched on or off, depending on the role your IIS 7 service will play. This can greatly reduce the attack surface of your IIS service and help it perform speedily without excess baggage in the way of unnecessary services to slow it down. Interestingly, you can replace the modules with custom versions to extend IIS in ways never thought of with previous versions.

The complete installation of IIS 7 includes 44 *components*, many of which are not installed by default. Again, this helps reduce the attack surface and enhance performance. IIS 7 also includes a new *configuration system* that is based on clear-text, XML files that hold the configuration settings for the entire IIS platform, including IIS, ASP.NET, and all components.

Configuration Files

All the settings for an IIS server—for application pools, Web sites, and applications—are stored in XML configuration files. The configuration files are collectively referred to as the *configuration store*. Different levels of the configuration hierarchy may be delegated by the computer administrator to other users, such as the site administrator or the application developer.

An IIS server has two levels of configuration: server and application. Server-level configurations are server-wide, and they affect every Web site and application running on the server. The application-level configurations pertain to settings affecting a single Web site or application only. The server-level configuration files include the following, applied in this order:

1. **Machine.config** Stores the global defaults for the .NET framework, including some of the ASP.NET settings (the rest are in the root web.config file, discussed next). This file is located in the .NET install folders in the %SystemRoot%\ microsoft.net\framework\[.NET Framework version number]\config\folder, where the default .NET Framework version number is v2.0.5072.

2. **Web.config (root)** Stores the global defaults for some of the ASP.NET settings (the rest of these are in the machine.config file in the same folder). This file is located in the .NET install folders in the %SystemRoot%\microsoft.net\ framework\[.NET Framework version number]\config\ folder, where the default .NET Framework version number is v2.0.5072.

3. **ApplicationHost.config** Stores the global defaults for Web server (IIS) settings, found in the %SystemRoot%\System32\Inetsrv folder.

4. **Web.config (application)** Application-specific configuration files may contain IIS, ASP.NET, or any other .NET Framework configuration settings that can be specified at the application level. By default, there are no web.config files. These files are stored in the content folders for each application.

The application-level files are optional. If you wish to have alternate or supplemental settings for a single Web site, they are stored in a web.config file. One key difference between IIS 7 and IIS 6 is that configuration is not maintained separately in memory for II 7; configuration is maintained exclusively in the configuration store files. In IIS 6, it was the in-memory configuration database that acted as the master set, which was flushed to disk periodically. A change to a configuration file in IIS 7 will be immediately picked up by the service. Also, the IIS 6 metabase is no longer part of IIS 7. However, Microsoft claims that IIS 7 will properly translate web.config files and application code, which makes IIS 7 compatible with IIS 6 applications (at least when it comes to storing configuration in a metabase).

IIS Installable Components

There are a total of 44 installable components available in the Windows Features setup of IIS. The components are grouped into three main categories:

▼ FTP Publishing

■ Web Management Tools

▲ World Wide Web Tools

Table 12-2 outlines the available components and subcomponents of IIS.

Installed by Default	Component Name (bold) and Subcomponents	Description
	FTP Publishing Service	Installs FTP service and FTP management console. Provides support for upload and download of files
	FTP Management Console	Installs FTP management console for administration of local and remote FTP servers
	FTP Server	Installs FTP service
Yes	**Web Management Tools**	Installs Web server management console and tools
	IIS 6 Management Compatibility	Allows you to use existing IIS 6.0 APIs and scripts to manage this IIS 7 Web server
	IIS Metabase and IIS 6 Configuration Compatibility	Installs IIS metabase and compatibility layer to allow metabase calls to interact with new IIS 7 configuration store
	IIS 6 WMI Compatibility	Installs IIS 6.0 WMI scripting interfaces
	IIS 6 Scripting Tools	Installs IIS 6.0 configuration scripts
	IIS 6 Management Console	Installs the IIS 6.0 Management Console Provides support for administration of remote IIS 6.0 servers from this computer
Yes	IIS Management Console	Installs the Web server management console, which supports management of local and remote Web servers
	IIS Management Scripts and Tools	Manages a local Web server with IIS configuration scripts
	IIS Management Service	Allow this Web server to be managed remotely from another computer via the Web server management console
Yes	**World Wide Web Services**	Installs the IIS 7 Web server. Provides support for Hypertext Markup Language (HTML) Web sites and optional support for ASP.NET, classic ASP, and Web server extensions

Table 12-2.   The 44 Components of IIS

Installed by Default	Component Name (bold) and Subcomponents	Description
	Application Development	Installs support for application development, such as ASP.NET, classic ASP, CGI, and ISAPI extensions
	ASP.NET	Enables your Web server to host ASP.NET applications
	.NET Extensibility	Enables your Web server to host .NET Framework–managed module extensions
	ASP	Enables your Web server to host classic ASP applications
	CGI	Enables support for CGI executables
	ISAPI Extensions	Allows Internet Server Application Programming Interface (ISAPI) extensions to handle client requests
	ISAPI Filters	Allows ISAPI filters to modify Web server behavior
	Server Side Includes	Provides support for .stm, .shtm, and .shtml include files
Yes	Common HTTP Features	Installs support for static Web server content, such as HTML and image files, custom errors, and redirection
Yes	Default Document	Allows you to specify a default file to be loaded when users do not specify a file in a request Uniform Resource Locator (URL)
Yes	Directory Browsing	Allows clients to see the contents of a directory on your Web server
Yes	HTTP Errors	Installs Hypertext Transfer Protocol (HTTP) error files. Allows you to customize the error messages returned to clients
	HTTP Redirection	Provides support to redirect client requests to a specific destination
Yes	Static Content	Serves .htm, .html, and image files from a Web site

Table 12-2.   The 44 Components of IIS *(Continued)*

Installed by Default	Component Name (bold) and Subcomponents	Description
	Health and Diagnostics	Enables you to monitor and manage server, site, and application health
	Custom Logging	Enables support for custom logging for Web servers, sites, and applications
Yes	HTTP Logging	Enables logging of Web site activity for this server
	Logging Tools	Installs IIS 7 logging tools and scripts
	ODBC Logging	Enables support for logging to an Open Database Connectivity (ODBC)-compliant database
Yes	Request Monitor	Monitors server, site, and application health
	Tracing	Enables tracing for ASP.NET applications and failed requests
	Performance Features	Allows improved ability from the application
Yes	Static Content Compression	Compresses static content before returning it to a client
	HTTP Compression Dynamic	Compresses dynamic content before returning it to a client
	Security	Enables additional security protocols to secure servers, sites, applications, vdirs, and files
	Basic Authentication	Requires a valid Windows user name and password for connection
	Windows Authentication	Authenticates clients using NT LAN Manager (NTLM) or Kerberos
	Digest Authentication	Authenticates clients by sending a password hash to a Windows domain controller

Table 12-2.   The 44 Components of IIS *(Continued)*

Installed by Default	Component Name (bold) and Subcomponents	Description
	Client Certificate Mapping Authentication	Authenticates client certificates with Active Directory accounts
	IIS Client Certificate Mapping Authentication	Maps client certificates one-to-one or many-to-one to a Windows security identity
	URL Authorization	Authorizes client access to the URLs that comprise a Web application
	Request Filtering	Configures rules to block selected client requests
	IP Security	Allows or denies content access based on Internet Protocol (IP) address or domain name

Table 12-2.   The 44 Components of IIS *(Continued)*

IIS Modules

Modules are IIS server components that handle requests from users according to how the modules are programmed and configured. When you enable a module for Web site or Web application, you ensure that IIS will leverage the module for user requests at that level. For example, you can enable and configure an authentication module for a server that will check user credentials for all installed Web sites and applications. There are two types of modules:

▼ **Global or native modules**   These modules are also called *native modules*, and to confuse us more, they are also known by Microsoft as *unmanaged modules*, because they are not created using the ASP.NET model. By default, most of the features included in the Web server are implemented as global modules.

▲ **Managed modules**   These modules are created using the ASP.NET framework of managed code, or assemblies, as they are known to programmers.

You will typically install a module onto a server (native modules only) and then enable the module for each Web application. By installing the module, it is registered globally with the server, making it available (but not active) for each Web application. Enabling the module in the application allows the application administrator to control the features enabled for the application (without bugging the server administrator). This allows installed modules to be enabled as needed, per application, and frees up the server administrator to manage other tasks. There are three methods for installing a native module:

▼   Manually edit the IIS 7 configuration store

■   Use the IIS Manager (this is shown in Figure 12-20)

▲   Use the IIS 7 command-line tool (AppCmd.exe)

All three of these options will result in an entry being added to the <globalModules> IIS 7 Configuration section, which applies only at the global server level and is not configurable per Web application. You can examine the contents of the <globalModules> tag by opening the root configuration file located in %SysemRoot%\system32\inetsrv\config\applicationhost.config and searching for the string "<globalModules>." After a full IIS 7 install, the <globalModules> section will contain an entry for each of the native modules shipped with IIS 7, specifying a name and the path to the module or assembly dynamic-link library (DLL).

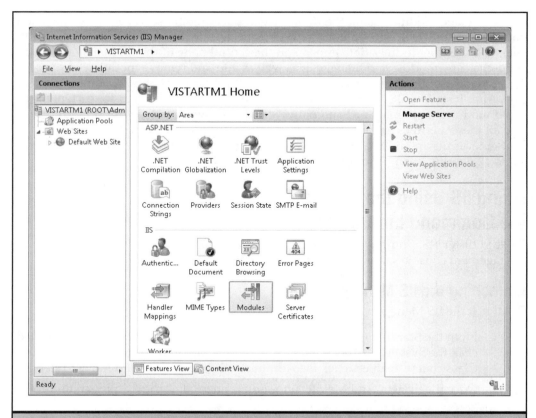

Figure 12-20.   Modules are located in the center pane of the IIS Manager.

Enabling a module allows it to provide its service for a particular application. To enable a native module, it must first be installed on the server (see the preceding paragraph). A managed module does not require installation, and can be enabled directly for each application. This allows applications to include their managed modules directly within the application by registering them in the application's web.config file, and providing the implementation in /BIN or /App_Code directories. To enable a module:

1. Manually edit the IIS 7 configuration store:

    a. Edit the store globally to enable the module for all applications on the server. To modify the global store configuration, open %SysemRoot%\system32\inetsrv\config\applicationhost.config in an XML editor and search for the <modules> tag.

    b. Edit the web.config file located within each application for which you would like to enable this module.

2. Use the IIS Manager (this is shown in Figure 12-21).

3. Use the IIS 7 command-line tool (AppCmd.exe).

To manage modules using the IIS Manager, select the IIS server in the Connections pane, and notice the IIS group in the middle pane. Locate the Modules icon, and double-click it. Once the Modules data appears in the central pane of the IIS Manager, you can right-click any module and manage it, as well as add and remove modules.

Using any of these options adds an entry to the <modules> IIS 7 Configuration section. After installing IIS 7, the <modules> section will contain an entry for each of the enabled modules (both managed and native) that you have installed with IIS 7, indicating that all these modules are enabled by default for all applications on the server.

Some of the modules are worth considering in more detail. By way of reference, Table 12-3 holds a sample of the more than 40 modules.

Managing IIS Using the IIS Manager, the Command Line, and WMI

To administer IIS, you have the options of using command-line tools or the main IIS management console snap-in, known as the IIS Manager.

Launching the IIS Manager

To launch the IIS Manager:

1. From the Start menu, click Control Panel. If you have the default view enabled, click the System And Maintenance link at the top of the page. If you have the Classic view enabled, click the Administrative Tools icon, and move to step 3.

2. Once the System And Maintenance link is open, click the Administrative Tools icon.

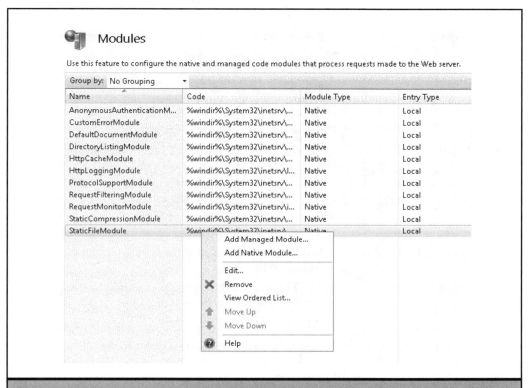

Figure 12-21.   Modules are managed in the IIS Manager.

3.   Locate and double-click the Internet Information Services (IIS) Manager icon. The resulting screen is shown in Figure 12-22.

NOTE   You can also launch the IIS Manager by typing `Inetmgr.msc` into the Search field in the Start menu.

The IIS Manager uses Microsoft Management Console (MMC) 3.0, which includes three panes. In the left pane, called the Connections pane, note the tree view that holds the IIS server and all its constituent objects: application pools and Web sites. View the elements of a server by double-clicking it to expand the list. By clicking various elements in the Connections pane, note how the available options for managing the element change in the middle pane. The right pane, the Actions pane, has a few common administration commands, such as a link to restart the IIS service.

Module Name	Description	Dependencies
AnonymousAuthentication Module	Implements anonymous authentication (that is, this module would generate the HttpUser object if a URL is configured to allow anonymous authentication)	None
CgiModule	Implements CGI on top of IIS 7	None
DefaultDocumentModule	Implements default document functionality (that is, requests that come in with a trailing / will be rerouted to a document in the default document list)	None
DirectoryListingModule	Implements directory browsing functionality	None
HttpCacheModule	The HttpCacheModule implements the IIS 7 output cache and also the logic for caching items in the http.sys cache. The cache size, output cache profiles, etc. can be set via configuration	None
HttpLoggingModule	Implements standard IIS logging by telling http.sys what to log	None
IpRestrictionModule	Implements an authorization scheme based on the IPv4 address of the client request	IPv4 stack has to be installed
TracingModule	Implements Event Tracing for Windows (ETW) tracing	None
UrlCacheModule	Implements a generic cache for a URL-specific server state, such as configuration. With this module, the server will only read configuration for the first request for a particular URL, and reuse it on subsequent requests until it changes	None

Table 12-3. Modules available in IIS 7

Module Name	Description	Dependencies
WindowsAuthentication Module	Implements Windows authentication (NTLM) or Negotiate (Kerberos).	Bottom of form

Table 12-3.   Modules available in IIS 7 *(Continued)*

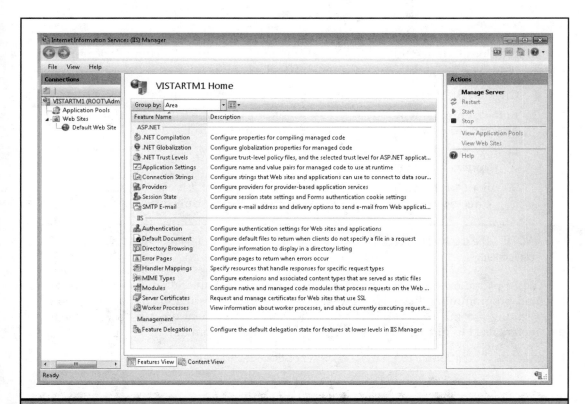

Figure 12-22.   The IIS Manager is used to configure and manage IIS on your computer running Vista.

The IIS 7 Command-Line Tool

In IIS 7, Microsoft introduces a special command-line tool for managing IIS and ASP.NET configurations, named AppCmd.exe. You can do a great many things with this tool, such as script changes and store your commands in a file. You can also:

▼ Create Web sites, application pools, and virtual directories

■ Start and stop Web sites, worker processes, and the IIS service themselves

▲ Report on processes for current IIS transactions

You can also use the command-line tool to run sophisticated queries, provide conditionals, and launch complex tasks—all in a sequence that you could not do otherwise in the IIS Manager. For example, you can query the state of all running processes and, based on the results, stop any Web site with requests over 60 seconds, and if all sites have delayed requests, restart the IIS service itself. This can substantially help when diagnosing IIS problems.

The tool resides in the %SystemRoot%\system32\inetsrv directory, which is available only to local administrators. To launch the tool, first launch a command prompt window and type the path of the executable. The steps are as follows:

1. Click the Start menu button, type **cmd** in the Search field, and then press ENTER.

2. In the command window, type **%SystemRoot%\system32\inetsrv\ AppCmd.exe**, and press ENTER. This is shown in Figure 12-23:

   ■ To view the available options for the appcmd tool, add the /? switch to your calling statement.

   ■ For 64-bit systems, the tool is located in the LocalDrive\system32\inetsrv directory, not the LocalDrive\syswow64\inetsrv directory.

NOTE The display has been changed from "Icons" to "Details" to display the description for each component.

The AppCmd.exe tool can be tricky at first, and those who are familiar with object-oriented programming, like VBScript, will find the principles familiar. The tool works by executing a command on one of the supported management objects, with optional parameters used to further customize the behavior of the command:

```
APPCMD.EXE <COMMAND> <OBJECT> <ID> [/parameter:value]
```

The syntax for the AppCmd.exe command is as follows:

▼ **<COMMAND>** One of the commands supported by <OBJECT>. Most objects support the following commands at a minimum:

   ■ **LIST** Display the objects on the computer. Optionally, provide a value for the <ID> parameter to specify a unique object to list.

   ■ **ADD** Create a new object with the specified object properties.

Figure 12-23.   IIS can be managed from the command line using the IIS 7 command-line tool.

- ■   **DELETE**   Delete the object specified by the <ID>.
- ■   **SET**   Set parameters on the object specified by <ID>.

NOTE An object will often support additional commands, such as START and STOP, for the Site object.

- ■   **<OBJECT>**   One of the management objects supported by AppCmd.exe. The objects available through AppCmd by default include:
    - ■   **SITE**   Administration of virtual sites
    - ■   **APP**   Administration of applications
    - ■   **VDIR**   Administration of virtual directories
    - ■   **APPPOOL**   Administration of application pools
    - ■   **CONFIG**   Administration of general configuration sections

- ■ **BACKUP** Management of server configuration backups
- ■ **WP** Administration of worker processes
- ■ **REQUEST** Display active HTTP requests
- ■ **MODULE** Administration of server modules
- ■ **TRACE** Management of server trace logs

- ■ **<ID>** The object-specific identifier for the object instance you want to specify for the command. The format of the identifier is specific to each object type. For example, the Site object uses the site name, the App object uses the application path, and the AppPool object uses the application pool name.

- ▲ **[/parameter:value]** Zero or more parameters for the command. Each command supports a different set of parameters, depending on the object.

For more information about the IIS 7 command-line tool, launch the tool using the /? switch or view the Help file from the IIS Manager and search for "AppCmd.exe."

A sample use of the AppCmd.exe tool includes the following code. This code allows you to list the sites installed on the server:

```
AppCmd list sites
```

This code lists sites that are stopped:

```
APPCMD list sites/state:Stopped
```

Using WMI Scripts

IIS 7 includes a Windows Management Instrumentation (WMI) class to support scripts for Web administration. Some of the tasks you can use WMI for include reading and modifying configuration files, such as applicationHost.config and Web.confg. You can add or remove modules and configure commonplace features, such as custom HTTP errors, Multipurpose Internet Mail Extensions (MIME) maps, Secure Sockets Layer (SSL) bindings, and ASP settings. You can also leverage the new Vista features exposed by the Runtime Status And Control API (RSCA) to monitor and diagnose the IIS service and the state of Web sites.

To use WMI scripts to manage IIS:

1. Make sure you are logged on as a local administrator, using either the local administrator account or an account that is a member of the local administrators group.

2. To add support for WMI:

   a. From the Start menu, type **AppWiz.cpl** into the Search field and press the ENTER key.

   b. From the Programs And Features window, click the Turn Windows Features On Or Off link on the left pane. This opens the window shown in Figure 12-24.

Figure 12-24.   Vista requires that you add support for WMI.

   c. In the Windows Optional Features window, locate the Internet Information Services node, and expand it by double-clicking it.

   d. Locate the Web Management Tools node, and expand it by double-clicking it.

   e. Select the check box next to the IIS Management Scripts And Tools node.

   f. Click OK to start the update.

  3. Install optional WMI tools, such as the WMI Administration Tools suite, from the Microsoft Download Center (www.microsoft.com/downloads/details .aspx?FamilyID=6430f853-1120-48db-8cc5-f2abdc3ed314&DisplayLang=en) and the WMI Code Creator (www.microsoft.com/downloads/details .aspx?FamilyID=2cc30a64-ea15-4661-8da4-55bbc145c30e&DisplayLang=en).

  4. It's a good practice to back up your configuration files before making any changes so that you can facilitate a rollback if needed. Make a copy of all the files mentioned in the previous section "Configuration Files."

The IIS 7 WMI namespace is WebAdministration, and it contains objects and methods that enable you to script administration of the IIS service, Web sites, and

Web applications. The following sample code, written in VBScript, illustrates how to create a new Web site:

```
Dim oIIS, oBinding, oSiteDefn
Dim strName, strPhysicalPath, arrBindings
Set oIIS = GetObject("winmgmts:root\WebAdministration")

' Get the IIS Site object and create a binding for the site
Set oSiteDefn = oIIS.Get("Site")
Set oBinding = oIIS.Get("BindingElement").SpawnInstance_
oBinding.BindingInformation = "*:80:www.MyNewSite.com"
oBinding.Protocol = "http"

' Provide parameters for the Create new site method
strName = "NewSite"
strPhysicalPath = "C:\inetpub\wwwroot"
arrBindings = array(oBinding)

' Create a new IIS web site
oSiteDefn.Create strName, arrBindings, strPhysicalPath

WScript.Echo "Site created successfully!"
```

For more information on how to use WMI scripts, visit the Microsoft scripting Web site (www.microsoft.com/technet/scriptcenter/). For more information on how to use WMI to administer IIS 7, visit the Microsoft IIS 7 Web site (www.iis.net).

IIS Management Task: Creating a Web Site

There is far more to managing the IIS service than what can be adequately covered in this book. You can find operational advice from the IIS 7 Help file, the Microsoft IIS 7 Web site (www.iis.net), and from the Microsoft IIS 7 Operations Guide (technet2 .microsoft.com/windowsserver/en/technologies/featured/iis/default.mspx).

An example of one of the common key tasks that all IIS administrators must be aware of includes creating Web sites. You can create Web sites using the IIS Manager, the AppCmd.exe command-line tool, or by using a WMI script. You can view the IIS 7 Web site (www.iisnet.com) and the AppCmd.exe /? output for more information on how to manage IIS using the command-line tool and WMI. To create a new Web site using the IIS Manager:

1. Open the IIS Manager from the Start menu by typing **Inetmgr** into the Search field and pressing the ENTER key.

2. In the Connections pane on the left, expand the server that you are managing by double-clicking it. Expand the Web Sites node under the server by double-clicking it.

3. You can launch the Add A Web Site Wizard by either:

   a. Clicking Add Web Site in the Actions pane to right of the IIS Manager.

   b. Right-clicking the Web Sites node in the Connections pane and choosing Add Web Site from the context menu.

4. In the Add Web Site window, shown in Figure 12-25, type a site name in the Name text box.

5. Select the application pool for the Web site from the Application Pool drop-down list, or click New to create a new application pool.

6. To complete the Content Directory section:

   a. In the Path text box, type the physical path to the folder where the content for the Web site will reside, or click the Browse button to navigate the file system to find the folder.

   b. Optionally, provide credentials for the Web site. Credentials are required if you are delegating administration of this site to a user who is not a member of the local Administrators group on the Web server.

Figure 12-25. New Web sites can be created using the IIS Manager.

7. To complete the Binding section:

   a. Select the binding type for the Web site from the Protocol drop-down list (your options, by default, are HTTP for normal sites and HTTPS for SSL-encrypted sites):

      i. If you choose HTTP, continue to the next step.

      ii. If you choose HTTPS, note that new fields appear that allow you to associate an SSL certificate to this site. The certificate must be already installed.

   b. In the IP Address box, leave the default setting if your computer running Vista has one physical IP address and you will make only one Web site available. If your computer has more than one address and you wish for IIS to respond only to one address for this particular Web site, specify a static IP address for the Web site.

   c. Type a port number in the Port text box if you wish to obscure your traffic from the normal port or if the port number is taken already by another Web site that uses the same IP address. The default port numbers are the RFC standard port 80 for HTTP Web traffic and 443 for HTTPS Web traffic.

   d. Optionally, type a host header name for the Web site in the Host Header text box.

8. Click OK to create the Web site.

While Internet Explorer and IIS are not new tools, their latest versions promise to offer new and improved functionality and services. By leveraging these tools, you can be more effective and efficient in your Web endeavors.

CHAPTER 13

Mobile Devices

T he first "laptop" computer couldn't actually be used on your lap. It was big, it was bulky, and it needed to be wrestled into place. One might not believe it now, but the portly, 22-pound Osborne 1 was once considered a "portable" computer. There were, of course, many that came after, each losing weight and gaining functionality. Twenty-five years later, portable computers are truly sleek, streamlined, light, and can do everything their deskbound brothers can do. Now, as if laptops weren't portable enough, there are now powerful Tablet PCs and palmtop computers that are on the leading edge of portability.

Because they are so prevalent and important, Microsoft has developed a number of tools for managing portable computing devices into Windows Vista. In this chapter we'll look at some of the functionality that Vista brings to the portability party. We'll talk about power management, synchronization, and the Vista utilities that are geared specifically to Tablet PC users.

POWER MANAGEMENT

The big selling point of laptops and Tablet PCs is their portability. You can use them—disconnected from a primary power source—on an airplane, in a coffee shop, on a park bench...wherever. Of course, that most important feature is only possible if you have a charged-up battery.

To help your laptop or Tablet PC use its power efficiently, Vista employs *power plans*. These are schemes that you can use to automatically tell Vista how to manage power on your computer. If you have managed power on your laptops and Tablet PCs before, this may sound like nothing new. Frankly, it isn't new. Earlier versions of Windows employed power schemes as well. What is new, however, is that in Vista, the power plans are a lot easier to work with, thanks to a new and improved interface.

Let's take a look at Vista's power plans.

Power Plans

Vista includes three default power plans, half of what was offered in Windows XP, and they are simpler to use. The power plans are presented as a tradeoff between power and performance. That is, the power plans can either offer you a higher-performing computer but with less battery life or a longer battery life but with the central processing unit (CPU) running at a reduced rate.

To view the power plans:

1. Click the Start button.
2. Click Control Panel.
3. Click System And Maintenance.
4. Click Power Options. The power options are shown in Figure 13-1.

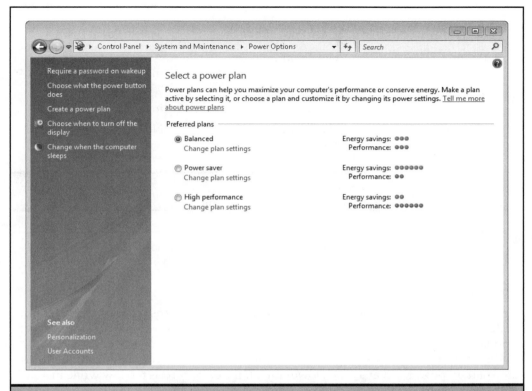

Figure 13-1.   Vista offers three power plans: Balanced, High performance, and Power saver.

The Plans

The power plans are:

- ▼ **Balanced**   The default plan strikes a balance (as the name suggests) between power consumption and computer performance. The processor accelerates when more resources are used and slows down as fewer are needed.
- ■ **Power saver**   This plan utilizes low power for maximum battery life. In order to reduce power consumption, processor usage is decreased.
- ▲ **High performance**   This plan allows high power usage so that graphics-intensive programs can easily be run. It also consumes the most power.

Laptops and Tablet PCs also contain a notification area on the taskbar with a Power icon. If you aim the mouse pointer at this icon, the battery state and the power plan you're using are displayed. You can right-click the Power icon to display a shortcut menu to go to the Power Options utility or the Windows Mobility Center.

Power Plan	Screen Power Down	System Power Down
Balanced	After 20 minutes of inactivity	After one hour of inactivity
Power saver	After 20 minutes of inactivity	After one hour of inactivity
High performance	After 20 minutes of inactivity	Never

Table 13-1.   Vista Power Plan Specifics

NOTE   We'll talk about the Windows Mobility Center later in this chapter.

Controls

The power plans are also used to govern when a computer turns off its display and powers down. Table 13-1 shows the default screen and system power-down settings for the various power plans.

When laptops and Tablet PCs are running on battery power, they continue to consume battery power, but at a much lower rate. If the battery runs too low while in a sleep state, the working environment will be saved to the hard disk, and the computer will be completely shut down.

NOTE   Remember that Standby and Hibernation modes are not power-saving options. As we noted in Chapter 1, powering down and shutting down mean new things in Vista. Most times, when you turn off the computer, Vista will enter a sleep state. The computer will only completely shut down when you turn the power off completely.

These are good, functional, easy-to-use plans. But what if you need to fine-tune them to meet your specific needs? Like so many other parts of Vista, you get the broad strokes of a task right up front, and if you want to get into some detail, you just have to click the right button or link.

Configuring a Plan

Let's say you conceptually like what the Balanced power plan has to offer, but you want to tweak it just a little bit. These plans aren't carved in stone, and you can manage them as you desire. To change the options of a power plan:

1. Open the Power Options utility.
2. Click Change Plan Settings for the plan you want to modify. This displays a screen like the one shown in Figure 13-2.

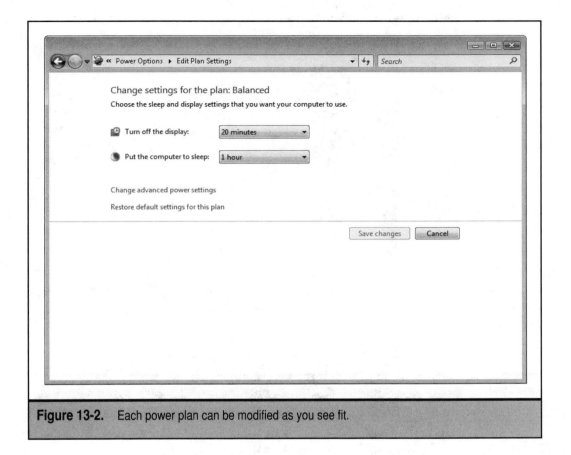

Figure 13-2.   Each power plan can be modified as you see fit.

3. Use the Turn Off Display list to indicate if and when the computer's display turns off.

4. Use the Put Computer To Sleep list to indicate if and when the computer enters Sleep mode.

Advanced Settings

But that isn't the last level of configuration. If you want to get even more granular, you can control the advanced settings for a power plan. From the dialog box shown in Figure 13-2, you can click the Change Advanced Power Settings link.

This link displays the Advanced Settings tab, shown in Figure 13-3, and you can use it to manage all sorts of power management settings, including:

▼   Requiring a password when the computer wakes up

■   Setting the maximum and minimum processor states

■   Defining power button and lid actions

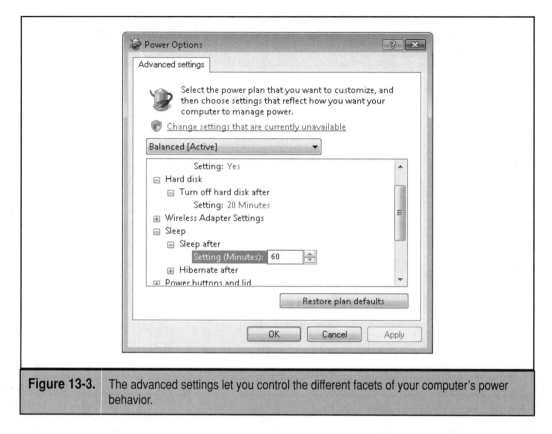

Figure 13-3. The advanced settings let you control the different facets of your computer's power behavior.

- Establishing power modes for wireless adapters and PCI Express links
- ▲ Configuring sleep and hibernation options

Wakeup Behavior

Even though Vista's power plans are seemingly point and click—and to a degree they are—you can still assign global options for the power button and password protection on wakeup across all of your power plans.

To manage these features:

1. Open the Power Options tool.

2. In the left pane, click Choose What The Power Button Does.

3. In the When I Press The Power Button list, indicate whether the computer should shut down, sleep, or hibernate when the power button is pressed. This is shown in Figure 13-4.

4. Select the relevant Password Protection On Wakeup option to indicate whether the computer requires a password on wakeup.

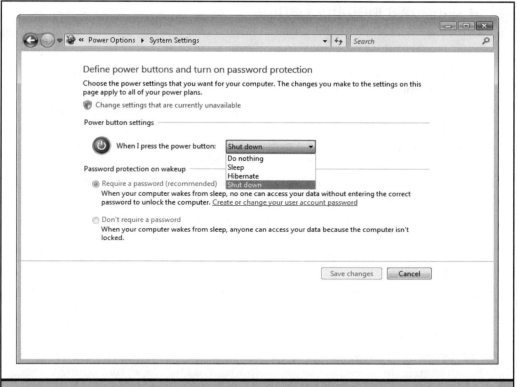

Figure 13-4. You can specify how the computer should behave when the power button is pressed.

WINDOWS MOBILITY CENTER

Like the Windows Security Center we talked about in Chapter 10, Vista provides a way to manage all your mobile settings in one centralized location, so you don't have to remember to point here and click there for these different attributes.

Getting Started

The Windows Mobility Center is a set of tiles that give quick access to the most commonly used mobile PC settings. You can access the Center by right-clicking the Power icon in the taskbar's notification area, and then selecting Mobility Center.

Each tile on the tool allows you to manage a different setting. These tiles will differ, based on whether you're using a Tablet PC or a laptop, as well as on the PC's manufacturer. Normally, laptops contain seven tiles, while Tablet PCs have eight.

Using the Windows Mobility Center

The tiles in the Windows Mobility Center allow you to quickly manage settings using sliders and toggle buttons. Control tiles include:

- ▼ **Brightness**   Indicates the current brightness settings and allows you to manage the setting with a slider

- ■ **Volume**   Indicates the current volume setting for audio and allows you to manage the setting with a slider

- ■ **Battery Status**   Indicates the status of the computer's battery. The selection list can be used to quickly change between power plans

- ■ **Wireless Network**   Indicates the status of your wireless network connection. You can quickly toggle the connection on or off

- ■ **External Display**   Indicates options for connecting a secondary display. You can quickly toggle the external display on or off

- ■ **Sync Center**   Indicates the status of file synching. You can start a new sync by clicking Start Sync

- ■ **Presentation Settings**   Indicates whether your computer is in Presentation mode. While in Presentation mode, the PC's display and hard drive do not go into Sleep mode because of inactivity. You can start Presentation mode by clicking Turn On

- ▲ **Primary Landscape**   Indicates the current display orientation for Tablet PCs. You can change the screen's orientation (portrait or landscape) by clicking Change Orientation

These are just a few of the tiles available with Windows Mobility Center. Different tiles are provided by different PC makers.

TABLET PCS

Laptop PCs have evolved to suit the needs of their users. But it isn't just more random access memory (RAM), bigger hard drives, and wireless capabilities that have improved the laptops—it's also their physical function. Tablet PCs are operable without a keyboard (actually, the keyboard tends to be tucked away behind the screen), and user input is accomplished through a touch screen.

Windows Vista builds on the Tablet PC functionality first introduced to the Windows world with Windows XP. It offers a number of ways—and a number of applications—that will help the Tablet PC user get the most out of his or her device.

The Pen

The chief way to enter data into a Tablet PC is via the pen. Vista is not only capable of performing handwriting recognition, but it will also interpret pen taps and pen motions as specific commands.

Taps

Pen taps are the Tablet PC equivalent of using your desktop PC's mouse. If you double-tap somewhere on the screen, that's like double-clicking your mouse. Holding down the pen is the same as right-clicking with a regular mouse.

To manage pen tap settings:

1. Click Start and then click Control Panel.

2. Click Hardware And Sound, and then click Pen And Input Devices.

3. As shown in Figure 13-5 , the Pen And Input Devices dialog box appears. Make sure the Pen Options tab is selected.

4. To configure double-tapping, double-click Double-Tap in the Pen Actions section. Next, adjust how quickly you must tap the screen and the distance the pointer is allowed to move between taps.

5. Click OK.

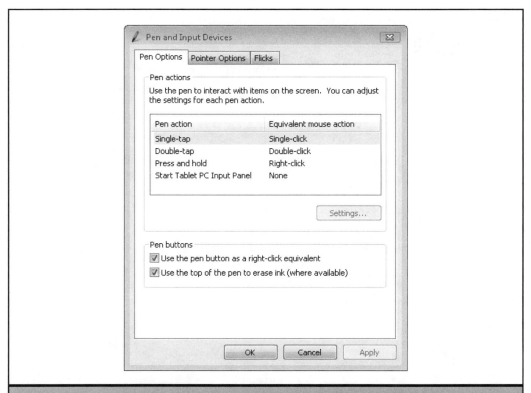

Figure 13-5.   You can manage your pen tap settings from the Pen And Input Devices dialog box.

6. To configure pressing and holding, double-click Press And Hold in the Pen Actions section. Adjust the amount of time you must press and hold down the pen to the screen to perform a right-click and the amount of time to perform the right-click action.

7. Click OK to save the settings.

You can also change visual feedback options by following these steps:

1. Click Start and then click Control Panel.

2. Click Hardware And Sound, and then click Pen And Input Devices.

3. In the Pen And Input Devices dialog box, click the Pointer Options tab. This is shown in Figure 13-6.

4. Each pen action elicits a different type of visual feedback. If you'd rather not see any visual feedback, clear the checkbox.

5. You can elect to use mouse cursors or pen cursors. Select or clear the Show Pen Cursors Instead Of Mouse Cursors When I Use My Pen check box, as needed.

6. Click OK to save the settings.

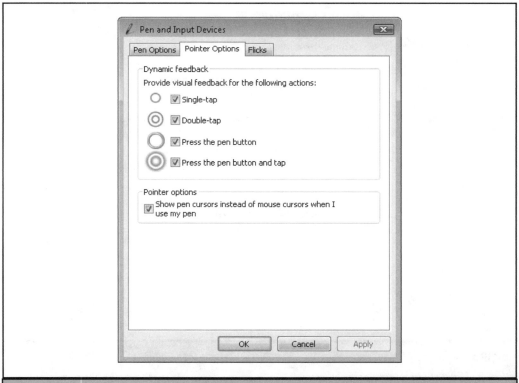

Figure 13-6. You can manage the visual feedback options in the Pen And Input Devices dialog box once you select the Pointer Options tab.

Flicks

Since the pen is the Tablet PC's mouse, you use a series of flicks to move the cursor around the screen. You can perform both navigation and editing functions using pen flicks. Those settings are configured separately, but, by default, navigational pen flicks are enabled.

Table 13-2 explains the behavior of the various pen flicks.

To manage pen-flick options:

1. Click Start and then click Control Panel.

2. Click Hardware And Sound, and then click Pen And Input Devices.

3. In the Pen And Input Devices dialog box, select the Flicks tab. This is shown in Figure 13-7.

4. Check the Use Flicks To Perform Common Actions Quickly and Easily check box to configure the types of flicks you wish to enable.

5. To configure pen flicks for both navigation and editing, select the Navigational Flicks And Editing Flicks option.

6. The Sensitivity slider is use to adjust how easily pen flicks are recognized. If you find that you're experiencing a lot of accidental pen flicks, set the sensitivity a bit lower.

7. Click OK to save the settings.

Pen Flick Direction	Action	Equivalent Action
Left	Go back	Same as clicking the Back button in Internet Explorer
Right	Go forward	Same as clicking the Forward button in Internet Explorer
Up	Scrolls up	Same as using a scroll bar in an extended window
Down	Scrolls down	Same as using a scroll bar in an extended window
Up and left	Copy	Same as copying an element or text using a menu
Up and right	Paste	Same as pasting an element or text using a menu
Down and left	Undo	Same as undoing an action using a menu
Down and right	Delete	Same as deleting an element or text using a menu

Table 13-2.   Explanations of Default Pen-Flick Behavior

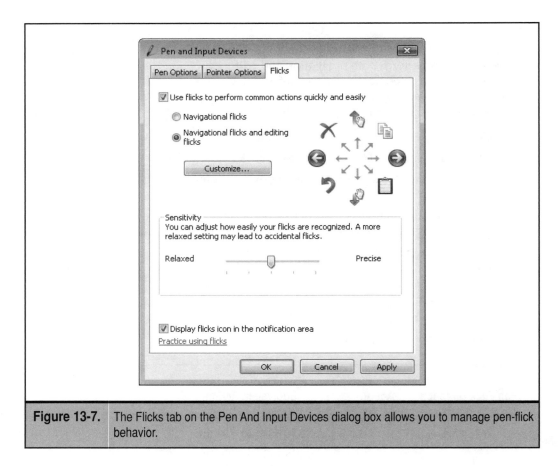

Figure 13-7. The Flicks tab on the Pen And Input Devices dialog box allows you to manage pen-flick behavior.

Tablet PC Applications

Windows Vista includes several applications that are meant to improve your Tablet PC experience. Among those applications are:

▼ Input panel

■ Snipping tool

■ Sticky notes

▲ Windows Journal

This section examines those applications and explains how you can use them.

Input Panel

The Input Panel is used to enter text into your Tablet PC rather than using the keyboard. It converts your handwriting into typed text. In Vista, Input Panel includes such features as AutoComplete, Back-Of-Pen Erase feature, and scratch-out actions.

Using Input Panel   Some applications that accept handwriting input from a pen (like Word or Windows Mail) display the Input Panel icon next to text-entry areas. Tap the icon, and Input Panel is displayed, allowing you to enter your handwritten text, which will then be converted to typed text when you tap the Insert button.

NOTE   The Insert button is located below and to the right of your converted text.

To display the Input Panel:

1. Click Start and point to All Programs.
2. Click Accessories.
3. Click Tablet PC.
4. Select Tablet PC Input Panel.

When Input Panel runs, it is shown as a tab on the left side of the screen. To open it, move the cursor over the tab and tap. Input Panel then slides out from the edge of the screen. The Input Panel is shown in Figure 13-8.

The Input Panel can be moved by dragging it to your preferred location or by docking it at the top or bottom of the screen. If you hide Input Panel, it will reappear at that location the next time you open it.

The Input Panel offers three input modes:

▼ **Writing pad**   Gives you a space for entering handwritten text, as if you were writing on a sheet of lined paper. As you write a word, it is converted into text and displayed. Clicking the word allows you to correct the letter case, change punctuation surrounding the word, or modify letters. The writing pad is the default mode and is shown in Figure 13-8.

■ **Character pad**   Gives you a space for entering single letters or characters. When you write a character, it's converted into text. By clicking below a character, an Options menu is displayed, with a list of related characters that look similar to the one you just entered. You can select one of the other characters from the menu. The character pad is shown in Figure 13-9.

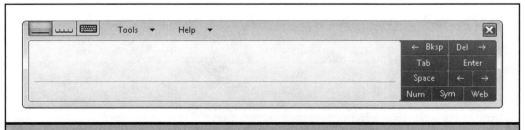

Figure 13-8.   The Input Panel is used to enter handwritten text, which Vista then converts to typed text.

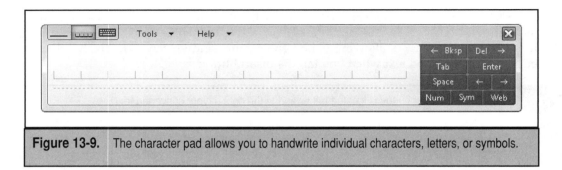

Figure 13-9. The character pad allows you to handwrite individual characters, letters, or symbols.

▲ **On-screen keyboard** Gives you a keyboard on the screen that you can use to tap characters for data entry. The on-screen keyboard is shown in Figure 13-10.

The character pad also contains three buttons you can tap to provide more features:

▼ Clicking Num displays the number pad, containing digits 0 through 9 and arithmetic symbols.

■ Clicking Sym displays the symbols pad. This contains options for commonly used characters.

▲ Clicking Web displays the Web pad. This contains character shortcuts for entering URL information.

AutoComplete A new feature for Tablet PC users in Windows Vista is the AutoComplete feature. In a Tablet PC, AutoComplete works much like it does in other applications. As you enter text, a list of possible matches is generated, so you don't have to write out the whole entry. If an item in the list matches text you want to enter, just tap the word, and it'll be used.

NOTE If the constant popping up of AutoComplete suggestions annoys you, or if you just don't want to use it, it can be disabled in the Options dialog box. In the Input Panel, click Tools and then click Options. On the Settings tab, clear the Suggest Matches In Input Panel When Possible check box.

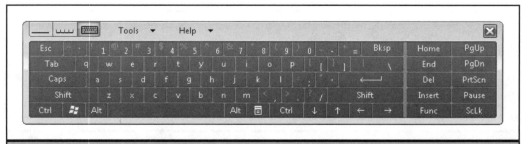

Figure 13-10. The on-screen keyboard allows you to use the pen to tap desired characters.

Back-of-Pen Erase Some Tablet PC pens have "erasers." The Back-Of-Pen Erase feature allows you to use this functionality. This can be used to delete entries from Input Panel. This feature is available depending on your hardware vendor.

Scratch-Out Gestures Scratch-out gestures are another way to delete entries. In essence, you write over your entries. Based on the symbol you draw, a different action is taken. Table 13-3 explains the different scratch-out gestures and how to perform them.

If these are just too many ways to delete something and you just want to stick with the standard Z-shaped scratch-out, you can disable the others by following these steps:

1. In the Input Panel, click Tools.
2. Click Options.
3. On the Gestures tab, select the Only The Z-Shaped Scratch-Out Gesture option.
4. Click OK.

Snipping Tool

The Snipping tool is used to capture and edit snippets of documents. It includes a pen selection, highlighter, and eraser functions. The Snipping tool isn't just used for text, however. You can use it to snip out any screen element, including text and images.

To display the Snipping tool:

1. Click Start and point to All Programs.
2. Click Accessories.
3. Click Snipping Tool.

The Snipping tool operates in two modes: New Snip mode and Edit mode.

Scratch-Out Gesture	How to Do It
Z-shape	Draw a Z over an entry or series of entries
Strike-through	Draw a horizontal line across an entry or series of entries (The line can be drawn left to right or right to left)
Angled	Draw an angled line across an entry or series of entries (The line can be drawn left to right or right to left)
Vertical	Draw an M or a W over an entry or series of entries. The M or W should be larger than the entries you want to delete
Circular	Draw a circle over an entry or series of entries. The circle should be drawn around or within the entries

Table 13-3. Scratch-Outs and How to Perform Them

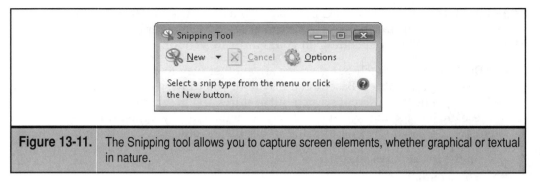

Figure 13-11.	The Snipping tool allows you to capture screen elements, whether graphical or textual in nature.

New Snip Mode   When the Snipping tool starts, it starts in New Snip mode. This mode is used for capturing—as the name implies—a new snip.

A capture is started by clicking the New Snip button on the toolbar. This will display the snipping window in the foreground, while rest of the screen is brightened to make it easier to determine which elements you are capturing.

Figure 13-11 shows the Snipping tool in New Snip mode. The buttons on the toolbar are, from left to right:

▼ **New**   Starts a new capture

■ **Options**   Sets capture options

▲ **Cancel**   Cancels the current capture

There are four snip modes that the Snipping tool utilizes. Table 13-4 explains these modes and how to perform the capture.

Snip Mode	Explanation	How It's Done
Freeform Snip	Captures an area you indicate by drawing around it	Tap and then drag around the area you want to capture
Window Snip	Captures an entire window	Move the pointer over the window you want to capture, and then tap the pen
Rectangular Snip	Captures an area you indicate by drawing a rectangle around it	Tap and then drag around the area you want to capture
Full-Screen Snip	Captures the full-screen display	The full screen is automatically captured when this mode is selected

Table 13-4.	Snipping Tool Snip Modes

By default, the snip mode is set to rectangular. You can change the snip mode by tapping the Capture Mode button and selecting the mode you prefer.

Edit Mode   Once a snip has been captured, the Snipping tool automatically changes to Edit mode. This is shown in Figure 13-12.

As with the New Snip mode, different buttons are displayed. From left to right, the buttons used in Edit mode are:

▼ **New Snip**   Switches to New Snip mode. Tapping this button will erase the current snip

■ **Save As**   Snips can be saved as an HTML, JPG, PNG, or GIF file

■ **Copy**   Copies the snip to the Clipboard

Figure 13-12.   Edit mode on the Snipping tool allows you to make changes to the snip.

- ■ **Send Snip** Sends the snip to someone as an e-mail attachment. Additional send options can be configured by clicking the Options button
- ■ **Pen** Used to change the pen color and ink thickness
- ■ **Highlighter** Used to highlight areas of the snip
- ▲ **Eraser** Used to erase pen ink and highlights

Sticky Notes

If you want to quickly jot a note, the Sticky Notes application gives you a pad of virtual sticky notes. You can use the Sticky Notes application for both written and voice memos.

> **NOTE** While Sticky Notes are meant for the Tablet PC users out there, there's nothing that says you can't use it on your desktop and laptop PCs as well. It's a handy way to jot down notes.

To open the Sticky Notes feature:

1. Click Start and point to All Programs.
2. Click Accessories.
3. Click Tablet PC.
4. Select Sticky Notes.

The application is shown in Figure 13-13.

Writing a sticky note is easy—just start writing or click the Record button to record a voice memo. A new note can be created by clicking the New Note button. New notes will be added to your stack of sticky notes.

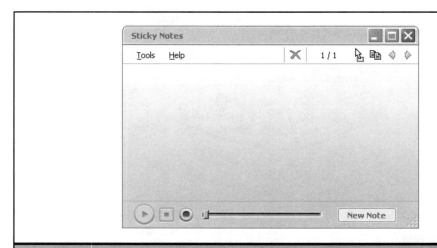

Figure 13-13. The Sticky Notes feature allows you to write handwritten notes or record voice memos.

You can navigate through your stack of sticky notes by using the Previous Note and Next Note buttons on the toolbar. To delete a sticky note, tap the red X on the toolbar, and then confirm its deletion.

Remember the scratch-out gestures from the earlier section? You can erase notes by writing a Z over them. As you lift the pen, the notes will be removed.

The idea of sticky notes is to have a quick tool that you can use to jot down notes. It's a bit cumbersome to have to navigate through the Start and All Programs menus to start it, however. If it is something you or your users intend to use regularly, it's a good idea to configure Sticky Notes for automatic startup. To do that, follow these steps:

1. Click Tools on the Sticky Note toolbar.
2. Click Options.
3. Select Open At Startup.

Windows Journal

Sticky Notes is a nice tool for jotting down a quick note. But if you need to write down more information, use the Windows Journal. Sticky Notes are like, well, a pad of sticky notes on your desk (we can't legally call them Post-it ® Notes, but you know that's what we're talking about), while Windows Journal is like a notebook.

To start Windows Journal:

1. Click Start and point to All Programs.
2. Click Accessories.
3. Click Tablet PC.
4. Select Windows Journal. This is shown in Figure 13-14.

When Windows Journal starts, it looks like a notepad with lined paper. Beneath the scrollbar are three buttons:

▼ **Previous**   Moves to the previous page.

■ **Next**   Moves to the next page.

▲ **New Page**   Creates a new page. This is normally used at the end of a journal to add a new page.

Selecting Stationery   The default setting for the stationery style in Windows Journal is lined notebook paper. This can be changed to narrow-ruled, wide-ruled, standard-ruled, or some other type of stationery. To change the stationery style:

1. In Windows Journal, on the Tools menu, click Options.
2. Click the Note Format tab.
3. In the Stationery section, click Default Page Setup.
4. Click the Style tab.

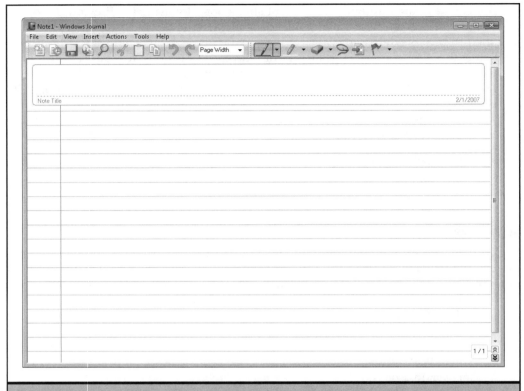

Figure 13-14. Windows Journal is the virtual equivalent of a notebook or stationery.

5. From the Line Style drop-down list, choose the style you want. Styles include:
   - Standard Ruled
   - Narrow Ruled
   - Wide Ruled
   - Large Grid
   - Small Grid
   - Blank

6. Click OK twice.

Handwriting Conversion   If you've entered text into your Windows Journal that you want to copy and use in other Windows applications, it can be done by following these steps:

1. Press and hold the pen to the screen.
2. Drag the pen around the handwriting you want to convert and copy.

3. When you release the pen, a shortcut menu is displayed. Select Copy As Text. The Copy As Text dialog box appears. Windows Journal automatically converts the handwriting to text.

4. If there are words or characters that didn't convert correctly, tap the word or character that you want to correct.

5. Choose a replacement from the Alternative list.

6. Click Copy, and the text will be saved to the Clipboard.

SYNC CENTER

Mobile users face troubles other than whether their laptops and Tablet PCs will run out of juice. A big headache comes when a file is maintained on the office network, but is modified by the user when he or she is out in the field. Okay, that's sort of a minor headache, but what if the user has dozens of files that have been modified, but others that haven't? That's where Vista's Sync Center helps out.

Microsoft's first jab at trying to resolve file synchronization issues was with Windows 95. Windows 95 introduced us to a tool called Briefcase. What you'd do is drag files to the Briefcase icon, and then drag the icon to a floppy disc (remember those?). When you brought the floppy disc back, you'd double-click the desktop's Briefcase icon, and the synchronization process would begin.

Synchronization has continued to develop through further editions of Windows, as well as with occasional standalone updates. The evolution continues with Vista, which introduces Sync Center.

To open the Sync Center:

1. Click Start.

2. Click All Programs.

3. Click Sync Center.

When Sync Center starts, you see an interface like the one in Figure 13-15.

Getting Started

Before you can start using Sync Center, there are a couple of prerequisites. First, both computers must be running Vista. You cannot mix and match Windows operating systems. So if you have a desktop running Windows XP in the office and a laptop running Vista, unfortunately, the two won't be able to use Sync Center. Next, both computers must be connected to the network, and you must be able to log on to both of them.

NOTE For the sake of clarity, Sync Center isn't just used between a desktop computer and a laptop. It can keep files up to date on mobile devices (music players, digital cameras, mobile phones), folders on your network's server, and programs that explicitly support Sync Center.

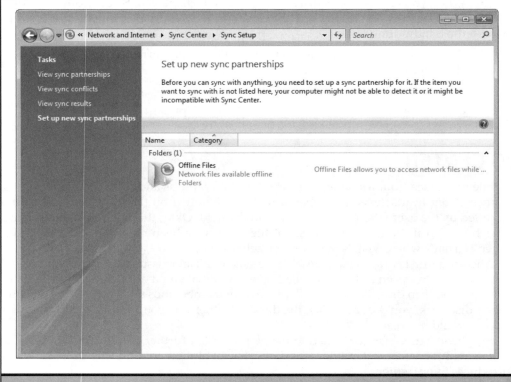

Figure 13-15. Sync Center helps you manage offline files for synchronization.

You probably don't need to sync every file on your computers, so take some time to look at the data you've got stored on the desktop, and decide which files need to go to the laptop and be synched and which ones should just remain on the desktop.

Sync Modes

Sync Center uses two types of synchronization:

▼ **One-way sync** In this scenario, files are copied from a primary location to a secondary location, but no files are ever copied back to the primary computer. For example, if you are transferring files to a music player, it's usually not necessary to transfer files back from the music player, so only new files would be copied to the player.

▲ **Two-way sync** In this scenario, files are compared on both computers, and changed copies are transferred both ways. You might use this on a network folder and your computer. In this case, Sync Center will transfer new copies of files between the network and your PC.

If you use two-way sync, that scenario poses another good reason to keep your synched files in as centralized a location as possible. There's going to be a lot going on back and forth, and with multiple folders, it's going to be a lot of work.

Synchronization

To synchronize your files, there are a couple of steps you must complete first. You must set up your files and folders as being "offline files." Next, you have to establish the partnerships between your computers, folders, and devices.

Offline Folders

In order to use Sync Center, you must indicate which files and folders you want to synchronize by marking them as *offline files*. This is accomplished by right-clicking the file or folder and selecting Always Available Offline from the Context menu.

Marking files as offline accomplishes a couple of things. First, it's necessary to use as part of Sync Center. Second, if you are working on a document and you cannot access the network, those offline files will be used instead. Then, once you are able to reconnect to the network, Sync Center can help you synchronize the files.

NOTE The Offline Files feature must be enabled. It is enabled by default, but if you are having problems, that's a good place to check. You can check to see whether you have the feature enabled or disabled by opening Control Panel and then clicking Network And Internet. Next, click Offline Files. On the General tab, make sure that Offline Files is enabled.

Establishing a Partnership

The next step is establishing what you will be synchronizing. This is called setting up a sync partnership. This is done between your computer and a mobile device, a folder on your network, or some other program that is compatible with Sync Center.

To establish a partnership:

1. Open Sync Center.
2. In the left pane of Sync Center, click Set Up New Sync Partnerships.
3. Click the name of the file or folder from the list of available sync partnerships.
4. On the toolbar, click Set Up.
5. Manage any settings and scheduling options you wish to make.
6. If you want to sync immediately, click View Sync Partnerships. Click your file or folder in the list of sync partnerships, and then click Sync.

You can also establish a sync schedule, which is helpful, because it allows Sync Center to automatically perform synchronization. This isn't necessarily helpful if you are synching a laptop or mobile device that isn't connected regularly. However, if you are synching files between a wired computer and the network, this is a handy feature.

Synching

If you want to manually sync files—for instance, between your laptop and desktop PCs—you can either sync one partnership or all partnerships.

To sync an individual partnership:

1. Open Sync Center.

2. Click the sync partnership you want to sync with, and on the toolbar click Sync.

To sync all your partnerships:

1. Open Sync Center.

2. On the toolbar, click Sync All.

Conflicts

What happens if a file has been changed on both the laptop and the PC? Which version of the file will Sync Center keep? If both files have been changed, then you will be presented with a *sync conflict*. In such a case, synchronization stops, and you'll see a window asking you which file is the master file. That file will be kept, and the other file will be updated.

If conflicts have arisen during scheduled syncs, you can review those issues at a later time by following these steps:

1. Open Sync Center.

2. In the left pane, click View Sync Conflicts to see any sync conflicts.

You can also see if you have sync conflicts via an icon on the taskbar. When a sync conflict is present, the Sync Center icon will have a little yellow warning sign on it. If you see this icon, you can right-click it to open Sync Center and proceed from there.

If a conflict arises, you will see a Resolve button that will take you through the process of fixing the conflict. When you click Resolve, a new Resolve Conflict dialog box appears that gives you options to fix the problem, like deleting both copies of the file or selecting which copy should be the master version.

Synching Devices

Sync Center can also synchronize files with your personal digital assistant (PDA), MP3 player, cellular phone, and any other James Bondesque gadget you may have. To use Sync Center with these and other gadgets:

1. Turn on the device, and plug it into your computer. You can also connect wirelessly, but ensure that a wireless connection is established between your device and computer.

2. Open Sync Center.

3. In the left pane of Sync Center, click Set Up New Sync Partnerships.

4.   Click the name of the device from the list of available sync partnerships.

5.   On the toolbar, click Set Up.

6.   Manage any settings and scheduling options you wish to make.

7.   If you want to sync immediately, click View Sync Partnerships. Click your device in the list of sync partnerships, and then click Sync.

MANAGING MOBILE USERS

Laptop and Tablet PCs are no different from other computers. If they need to be on your network, they need to be able to follow your rules. In this final section, we'll examine how you can manage your mobile users with as little fuss as possible.

Chances are, your mobile users will take their laptops and Tablet PCs on the road and then hook them up to another network, whether a network at a branch office or a client's network. In order for the computer to work properly on all these different networks, it's necessary to configure different options for computer management. But different environments require different addressing schemes. For example, if they are connecting to another corporate network, chances are they need to get their IP address from a DHCP server. However, if they are taking their PCs home or to a small branch office, maybe static IP addressing is necessary. We'll show you how to configure those properties on your mobile computers.

Finally, we'll revisit power management and show you how, using Group Policy, you can manage your road warriors' power plans.

DHCP

Dynamic Host Configuration Protocol (DHCP) can help you manage the IP addresses of thousands of computers. Rather than having a notebook with everybody's IP address jotted down, a DHCP server can just automatically dole out an IP address as needed. Once you enter some basic information, your mobile computer will grab its own IP address automatically.

To configure dynamic IP addressing with your mobile computer:

1.   Click Start.

2.   Click Control Panel.

3.   Under the Network And Internet heading, click View Network Status And Tasks.

4.   In the left pane in Network And Sharing Center, click Manage Network Connections.

5.   A list of all network connections configured for your computer is displayed. Right-click the connection you want to configure, and then select Properties from the Context menu.

6.   Double-click Internet Protocol Version 4 (TCP/IPv4). The Internet Protocol Version 4 (TCP/IPv4) Properties dialog box appears, as shown in Figure 13-16.

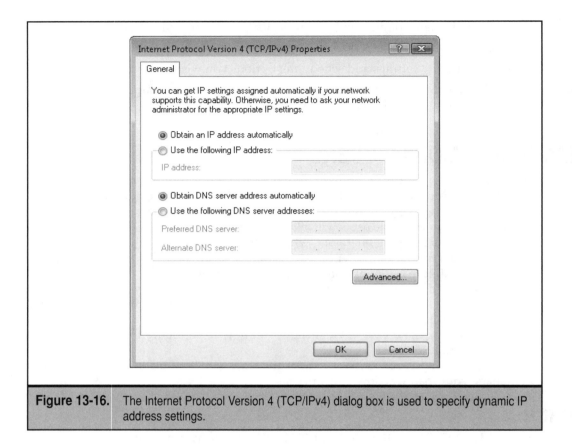

Figure 13-16. The Internet Protocol Version 4 (TCP/IPv4) dialog box is used to specify dynamic IP address settings.

7. Select Obtain An IP Address Automatically. If you need to use a static address for a DNS server, select Use The Following DNS Server Addresses, and then type the preferred and alternate DNS server addresses.

8. Click OK.

If your organization uses Internet Protocol version 6 (IPv6), follow these steps:

1. Double-click Internet Protocol Version 6 (TCP/IPv6) to open its Properties dialog box.

2. Select Obtain An IP Address Automatically. If you need to use a static address for a DNS server, select Use The Following DNS Server Addresses, and then type the preferred and alternate DNS server addresses.

3. If needed, configure alternate private IP addressing and Windows Internet Naming Service (WINS).

Alternate Private IP Addresses

If your mobile computer is trying to connect to a network but cannot find a DHCP server, it can still connect using an automatic private IP address (APIPA).

NOTE   APIPA is only used with IPv4, not IPv6.

APIPA addresses are in the range from 169.254.0.1 to 169.254.255.254, with a subnet mask of 255.255.0.0. Since the computer using APIPA isn't finding a default gateway, DNS, or WINS servers, the computer is on its own private network.

If you know that your mobile computer will be venturing into a network without a DHCP server—like a home network—you can configure a static IP address when no DHCP server is available.

NOTE   It's time to turn the tables on your users. Before you configure this setting, you need to know what their home networking settings are, including IP address, gateway, and Internet service provider (ISP) Domain Name System (DNS) server addresses.

To configure an alternate private IP address:

1. Click Start.
2. Click Control Panel.
3. Under the Network And Internet heading, click View Network Status And Tasks.
4. In the left pane of Network Center, click Manage Network Connections.
5. A list of all network connections configured for your computer is displayed. Right-click the connection you want to configure, and then select Properties from the Context menu.
6. Double-click Internet Protocol Version 4 (TCP/IPv4). The Internet Protocol Version 4 (TCP/IPv4) Properties dialog box appears.
7. Click the Alternate Configuration tab.
8. On the Alternate Configuration tab, select the User Configured option.
9. In the IP Address field, enter the IP address you want to use.

NOTE   A friendly reminder: The IP address you use should be a private IP address and not used anywhere else in the network.

10. Vista should insert a default value into the Subnet Mask field. If the network doesn't use subnets, the default value may work fine. On the other hand, if it does use subnets, you'll need to enter the correct subnet mask.

11. Enter the address for a network's default gateway. You might not need this entry if the computer does not need to access the Internet.

12. Enter a preferred and alternate DNS server address in the fields provided.

13. You may or may not need to enter a WINS address. This is used for backward compatibility with earlier versions of Windows. If WINS is needed, go ahead and enter a preferred and alternate WINS server.

14. Click OK twice.

15. Click Close.

Managing Power Plans with Group Policy

You don't need to leave it to your users to be custodians of their own power plans, and power plans don't just have to apply to mobile users. You can make power management a part of your regular Group Policy settings and establish them across your entire organization.

While it may sound a little iron-fisted to control your organization's power plans, there is some good, solid, fiscal responsibility behind power governance. If you want to save some money, power plans is one way to do that. Think about this: The average desktop PC with a flat-screen monitor consumes between $100 and $150 in electricity each year. If your organization has hundreds of PCs, you could save thousands of dollars each year by implementing a power plan that will turn off the display and put the computers into Sleep mode when they're not being used.

A word of warning, however: The stricter you are with your power plans, the greater the performance impact will be felt by your users. For instance, if you set the power plan to put the computers to sleep after 15 minutes of inactivity, users will wind up being less productive, because now they have to wait for their computers to wake up. There's a balance that needs to be struck.

Like so many other areas of Group Policy, there are scores of minute settings that you can tinker with for power management. You can do such things as define a power plan to be distributed across your network. You can name a power plan. You can reset power plans to default settings. You can customize power plans before you conduct a system-wide Vista installation. There's so much you can do with Vista's power plans with Group Policy, we'll let you poke around Group Policy for yourself and see what you can do that might be advantageous for your organization. But to get the ball rolling, let's look at how to perform a basic power plan rollout using Group Policy.

The power management policies in Group Policy are located in the Group Policy Object Editor. To find the policies, navigate to Computer Configuration | Administrative Templates | System | Power Management.

NOTE   There are no power management policies under User Configuration.

Establishing a Power Plan

The quickest and easiest way to establish power management settings is to use one of the three default power plans included with Vista. Once you establish this policy, users cannot change their power plans. To distribute a system-wide power plan:

1. In the Group Policy Object Editor, choose Properties for the Select An Active Power Plan policy. The Select An Active Power Plan Properties dialog box is shown in Figure 13-17.

2. Enable the Active Power Plan drop-down list by clicking Enabled.

3. Select one of the default power plans in Windows Vista:
    - ■ Automatic
    - ■ High Performance
    - ■ Power Saver

4. Click OK to save the policy setting value.

5. Use Group Policy Management to deploy the edited Group Policy object (GPO) to one or more systems.

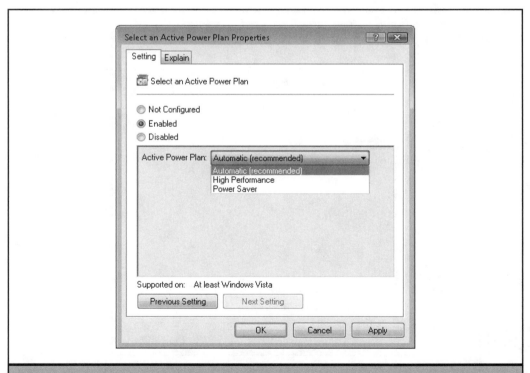

Figure 13-17.   You can establish a power plan for your entire organization through the Select An Active Power Plan policy.

This is a quick and easy way to distribute a power plan to computers in your organization. But it's not the only way. If you have customized settings you want to use, Group Policy can help with that, too.

Turning Off the Display

Once you've opened Group Policy and navigated to the power management section, let's talk about turning off the display after a period of inactivity. Follow these steps:

1. Choose Properties for the Turn Off The Display (Plugged In) policy. Windows Vista displays a dialog box like the one in Figure 13-18.

NOTE In this example, we're showing how to turn off a monitor that is plugged into alternating current (AC) power. While this chapter is specifically aimed at mobile devices, we wanted to show that power management and Group Policy can be used not only for laptops, but also for desktop PCs.

2. Click Enabled and enter a display idle timeout value in the Turn Off The Display (Seconds) box. This value is represented in seconds. If you enter 0, then the display will never turn off. In this example, 600 seconds means 10 minutes.

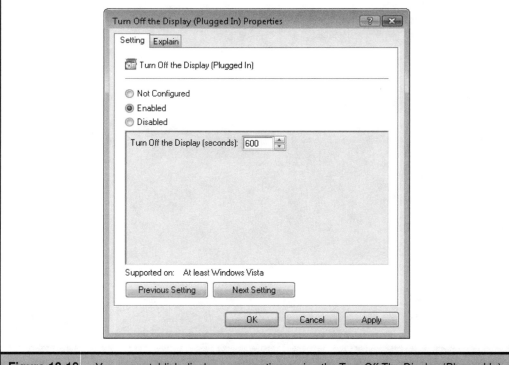

Figure 13-18. You can establish display power options using the Turn Off The Display (Plugged In) policy.

3. Click OK to save the policy setting value.

4. Use Group Policy Management to deploy the edited GPO to one or more systems.

You can check to ensure that this policy has been sent to client computers by viewing the setting in the Power Options Control Panel item. Figure 13-19 shows that the display will turn off after 10 minutes. The drop-down box is dimmed, so the user cannot change this setting.

Again, this might seem a little harsh that the user can't manage this setting, but Microsoft has included a message indicating that some settings are managed by the administrator and cannot be changed.

Setting the Sleep Mode

The next step is to determine at what point your organization's PCs will just go into Sleep mode after a period of inactivity. To establish that policy:

1. Choose Properties for the Specify The System Sleep Timeout (Plugged In) policy. The resulting dialog box is shown in Figure 13-20.

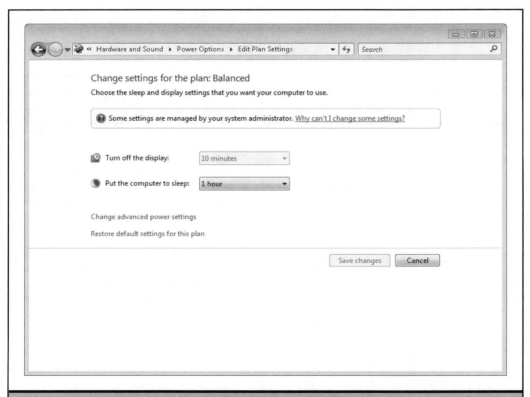

Figure 13-19. The display on this computer will turn off after 10 minutes of inactivity. It is a mandatory policy, so the user cannot change the setting.

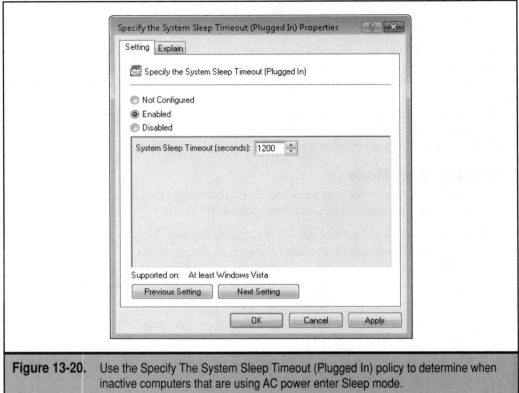

Figure 13-20.   Use the Specify The System Sleep Timeout (Plugged In) policy to determine when inactive computers that are using AC power enter Sleep mode.

2. Click Enabled and enter the sleep idle timeout value in the System Sleep Timeout (Seconds) box. This value is represented in seconds. If you enter 0, then the display will never turn off. In this example, 1200 seconds means 20 minutes.

3. Click OK to save the policy setting value.

4. Use Group Policy Management to deploy the edited GPO to one or more systems.

Mobile computers are the workhorses of road warriors, as well as of workers who need some mobility around the office. Vista has included a number of useful tools to meet this need, in addition to improving the way mobile devices were used in the past.

CHAPTER 14

Supporting Vista

Several tools are included with the operating system that help you keep your Vista clients running at peak performance. Most of the tools are familiar, but have been improved upon—things like the Microsoft Management Console (MMC) and Performance Monitor.

This chapter looks at the tools you can use to identify potential issues, prevent problems, and fine-tune your computers running Vista. We'll start with the "framework," MMC, which provides a platform for many of the applications you'll use. Next, we'll examine how Vista provides backup and restoration services. From there, we'll look at some common system configuration and support tools before we talk about Performance Monitor. We'll wrap the chapter up with a look at the new Group Policy options and how you can use them to support your Vista environment.

MMC 3.0

Microsoft has provided a nice tool for computer management in its Microsoft Management Console (MMC). Windows Vista uses version 3.0 of this powerful tool. In this section, we'll look at what's new with MMC, including some of the new snap-ins.

The MMC Interface

The MMC is launched as it was in earlier versions of Windows—just open a command prompt and type mmc. The MMC, shown in Figure 14-1, launches, sans snap-ins.

When the MMC is launched, at first blush, it looks a lot like it did in Windows XP, except for the Vista-style window. However, a new pane is present to the right side of the screen. The Actions pane displays different actions, or commands, that are associated with a selected snap-in, and it also provides you with easy access to the MMC.

Probably the biggest change to the MMC is that the Add Or Remove Snap-ins interface has been streamlined. Rather than having to click through two dialog boxes to get a snap-in installed, MMC 3.0 combines them into one dialog box. This is shown in Figure 14-2.

Adding and Removing Snap-ins

To add or remove a snap-in:

1. Click the File menu of the MMC 3.0 console.
2. Click Add/Remove Snap-in.
3. Select the snap-in you want to add in the Available Snap-ins list.
4. Click Add to add the snap-in to the Selected Snap-ins list.

NOTE   You can read a description of a given snap-in in either list by clicking it. Its description will appear in the Description box at the bottom of the screen. Be aware, however, that not every snap-in comes with a description.

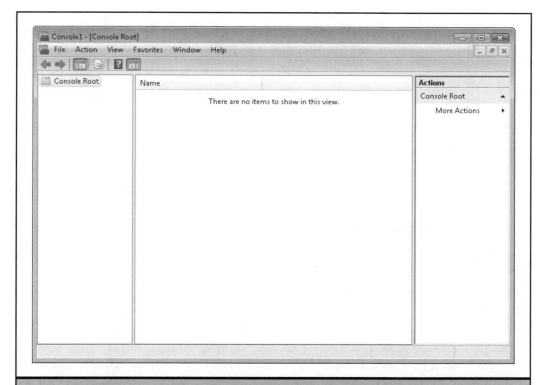

Figure 14-1. MMC 3.0 looks a lot like its predecessors, but it offers new functions and features.

5. If you want to change the order of the snap-ins in the console, just select the snap-in in the Selected snap-ins list, and then click Move Up or Move Down.

6. Remove a snap-in by selecting it in the Selected Snap-ins list and then clicking Remove.

7. Click OK when you're finished.

Setting the Parent Node

You can also set a parent node for a given snap-in. To do so, follow these steps:

1. With the Add or Remove Snap-ins dialog box open, click Advanced.

2. Select the Allow Changing The Parent Snap-in check box, and then click OK.

3. The Add Or Remove Snap-ins dialog box now shows the Parent Snap-in drop-down list. This contains the console root and all the snap-ins that are in the Selected Snap-ins list.

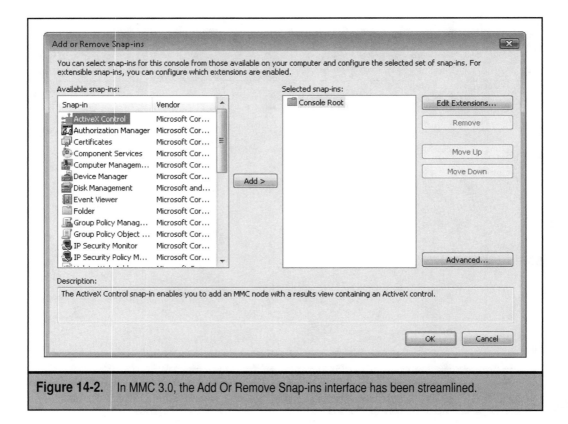

Figure 14-2.   In MMC 3.0, the Add Or Remove Snap-ins interface has been streamlined.

4. Select the desired parent node from the Parent Snap-in drop-down list.

5. Click the child snap-in in the Available Snap-ins list.

6. Click Add.

NOTE   If you want to move a snap-in that is already in the Selected Snap-ins list from one parent node to another, you must remove it and then add it to the new node.

BACKING UP AND RESTORING

Microsoft continues to improve the backup and restore features of Windows with its Backup And Restore Center. Not only do you get the protection of system backups, but Vista can also help you restore individual files with a couple clicks of the mouse.

In this section we'll talk about how you can back up and restore your system, as well as providing the means to protect single files.

System Restore

With Windows XP came the ability to restore a computer to a preexisting configuration. The System Restore tool automatically backs up registry and system files whenever you install new software or drivers. This is extremely useful when you install a piece of software or a driver and your system goes haywire (or, worse yet, doesn't work at all). Vista improves upon this feature.

NOTE   System Restore will not run on hard disks smaller than 1 gigabyte (GB).

Starting System Restore

You can start the System Restore tool in three different ways, depending on what kind of a pickle you've gotten yourself into.

Command Prompt   You can start the System Restore tool from the command prompt window if your computer does not start normally or in Safe Mode. To start the tool using this method, restart your computer and press F8 during startup.

From the boot options, select Safe Mode with a command prompt. This allows you to log on to your computer using administrative privileges.

Next, launch the System Restore tool. You do this by typing the following at a command prompt:

```
C:\Windows\System32\rstrui.exe
```

If you're in Vista and you want to run it from the command prompt, open the Run dialog box, then type **rstrui.exe**, and then press ENTER.

Vista Graphical User Interface (GUI)   System Restore is located by following these steps:

1. Click Start.
2. Click Control Panel.
3. Click System And Maintenance.
4. Click Backup And Restore Center.
5. In the left pane, click Repair Windows Using System Restore.

NOTE   You can also start System Restore by typing **restore** into the Start menu Search box. System Restore will appear at the top of the Start menu.

Next, you see a screen like the one in Figure 14-3, where you can choose to roll back the system to the last restore point.

You can select Recommended Restore and click Next, or you can choose a different restore point. If you elect to choose a different restore point, you'll see a dialog box like the one in Figure 14-4.

Click one of the restore points, and then you'll have to confirm and restart your computer to complete the procedure.

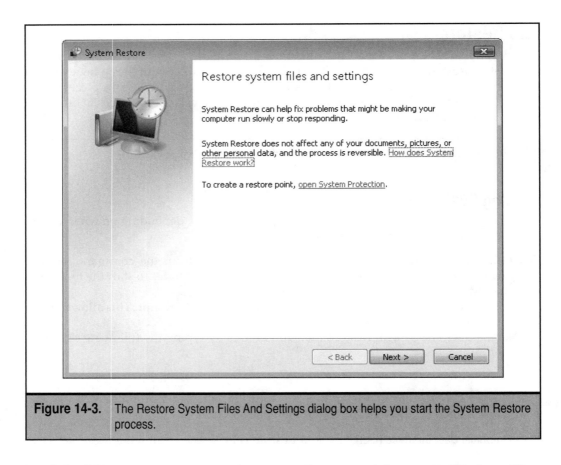

Figure 14-3.   The Restore System Files And Settings dialog box helps you start the System Restore process.

Install the DVD   You can also start the System Restore tool from your Windows Vista installation DVD. To do this, follow these steps:

1. Boot from the DVD. A dialog box will appear, and in the lower-left corner there is an option to perform a system restore.
2. Click Repair Your Computer, and then click Next on the next screen.
3. Choose System Restore from the System Recovery dialog box. It'll take a few moments to appear, but the screen looks like it does if you start the tool from within Windows.
4. Click Next and on the next screen indicate on which drive your copy of Vista is installed.
5. Click Finish, and Vista will roll back to the earlier restore point.

Undoing a Restore

What happens if you're not happy with the restore point you've selected? Can you un-restore? Absolutely.

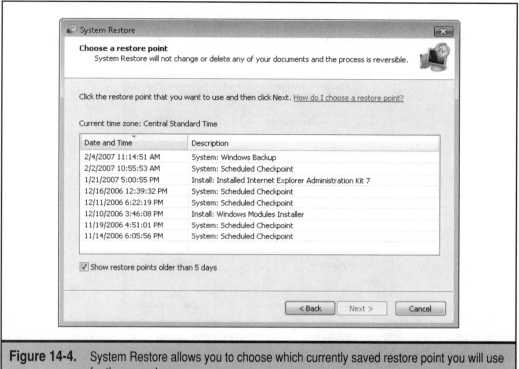

Figure 14-4. System Restore allows you to choose which currently saved restore point you will use for the procedure.

Whenever you use System Restore, another restore point is created, so you can undo a restore. You can either elect to go back to the original computer configuration, or you can pick another restore point.

To undo a system restore:

1. Open System Restore.
2. Click Undo System Restore, and then click Next.
3. Review your selection and then click Finish.

Restore Points

A restore point is automatically created every day and whenever a significant system event occurs, like the installation of a program or device driver. You can also manually create a restore point.

To create a restore point:

1. Click Start.
2. Right-click Computer.

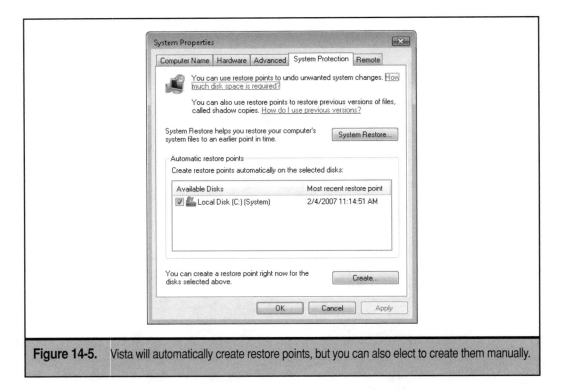

Figure 14-5.   Vista will automatically create restore points, but you can also elect to create them manually.

3. In the left pane, click System Protection. A dialog box like the one in Figure 14-5 appears.

4. Click the System Protection tab, and then click Create.

5. In the System Protection dialog box, type a description and then click Create. The restore point will be added to the list of restore points maintained on your computer.

Backup

Vista also provides an easy means to back up and restore the contents of your system. In the event of a catastrophe, you can rebuild your system using the backed up files. This section explains how to use the Backup And Restore Center to back up your complete system configuration, along with your saved files.

Backing Up Your System

To back up your system:

1. Click Start.

2. Click Control Panel.

3. Click Backup And Restore Center. This is shown in Figure 14-6.

4. Click the Back Up Computer button in the center of the dialog box.

5. Vista will scan your computer, looking for suitable drives on which to store backup files. Select the drive to which you want to save the backup.

6. In our case, we've selected to back up our computer to a DVD-ROM drive. As Figure 14-7 shows, Vista gives an estimate as to how many blank DVDs we'll need for the procedure.

Restoring Your System

If you want to restore your computer from backed up DVDs or other media, you follow a similar process. Open the Backup And Restore Center, and then click the Restore Computer button.

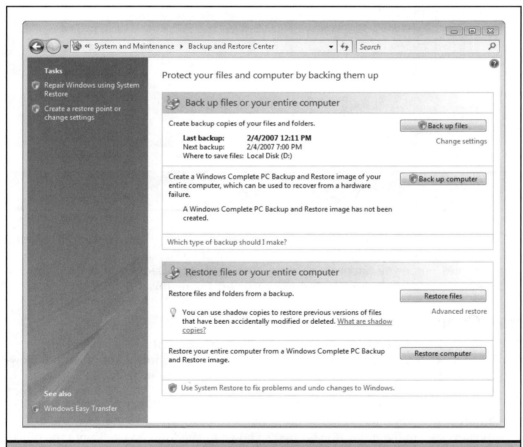

Figure 14-6.   The Backup and Restore Center is useful when you want to perform all sorts of protection-related tasks.

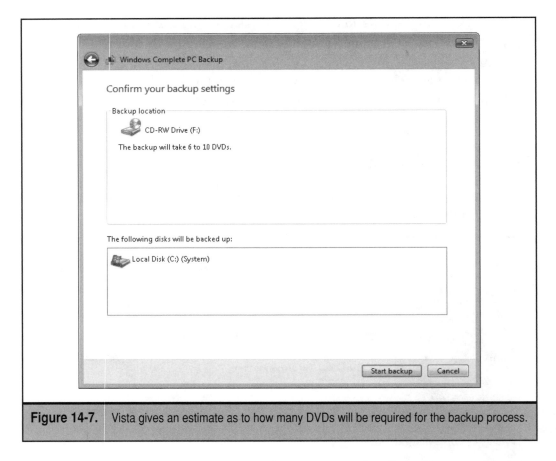

Figure 14-7.   Vista gives an estimate as to how many DVDs will be required for the backup process.

Before committing to a system restore, however, consider all your options. Restoring the entire computer from a backup is a drastic move. If you are able to access the Backup And Restore Center, you can probably access many other tools in Vista that can help you. Make sure you've exhausted all your options before taking this drastic step.

Shadow Copies

In the past, if a user without special recovery tools deleted a file, it was essentially gone. Poof. Vanished. Since then, Microsoft added dialog boxes confirming this action. However, that wasn't even enough for people, so Microsoft added the Recycle Bin. You could delete a file (and still be asked if you want to delete it), but it wasn't completely gone until you "emptied" the Recycle Bin.

Still this wasn't enough for some users.

The next step in file protection is what's known as shadow copies. It's not the title of the latest Tom Clancy book. Rather, it is a way to get back files if you accidentally erase them or save over a file you didn't mean to save over.

For example, let's say you've got an important presentation coming up and you've been artfully crafting your PowerPoint presentation. It's almost perfect. Regrettably, one wrong mouse click later, and you've copied over the file with some stupid PowerPoint presentation about mullets that your buddy across town e-mailed you. It's gone, right?

Not with shadow copies.

Turn It On

The ability to make shadow copies isn't turned on by default. Enabling it will take some time, but it'll be well worth your effort. To enable shadow copies:

1. Open the Backup And Restore Center.
2. Click the Back Up Files button from the Back Up Files Or Your Entire Computer section of the dialog box.
3. You'll be asked where you want to save the backup. Select from the pull-down list, or select a network location.

NOTE   If you want to know specifically which types of files are to be shadowed, point your mouse cursor at the selection, and you'll see a list of file types.

4. Click Next.
5. Vista will present you with another dialog box in which you are asked to select which file types you want to make shadow copies of. This is shown in Figure 14-8.
6. Click Next.
7. The next dialog box asks you how often you want to make backups of your files, as Figure 14-9 shows. Set your schedules and then click Save Settings And Start Backup.
8. Once the process starts, a dialog box like the one in Figure 14-10 appears.

NOTE   If, for some reason, you're still using the File Allocation Table (FAT) file system, you won't be able to use shadow copies.

The backup process will take some time, especially at first. When you want to enable the Shadow Copies process, expect it to have to run a little while.

Recover a File

If you've altered a file and want to recover a previous version, right-click the file in question, and then select Properties. Click the Previous Versions tab, and Vista will start looking for other versions of the file. The results of such a search are shown in Figure 14-11.

You can preview each file in a read-only version to find out which version you want to restore. To restore it, just drag the file to a folder, or select it and click Restore to restore it to its original location.

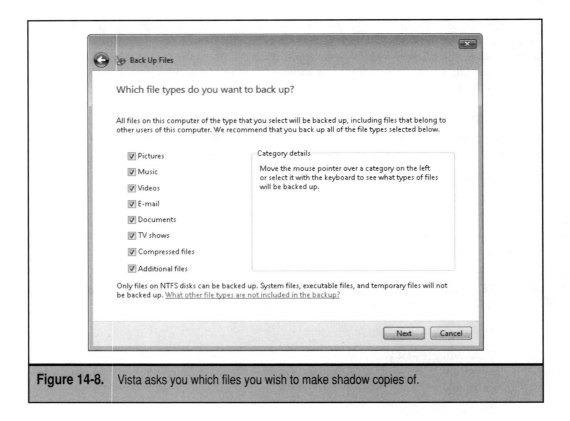

Figure 14-8. Vista asks you which files you wish to make shadow copies of.

This works on individual files as well as entire folders. When you restore a file, all previous versions of the file that are different from the live copy on the disk are shown. When you're examining previous versions of a folder, you can browse the folder's hierarchy as it used to exist.

CONFIGURATION TOOLS

There are a lot of tools within Vista that can help you manage all sorts of functions on your Vista clients. You can do everything from monitoring your hard drives to automatically sending yourself an e-mail if something goes awry on the system. In this section, we'll take a closer look at some of the tools that aim to make your Vista experience more rewarding.

Computer Management

The Computer Management application contains a number of administrative tools that you can use to manage a local or remote computer running Vista. It can be started from the command line by typing compmgmt.msc.

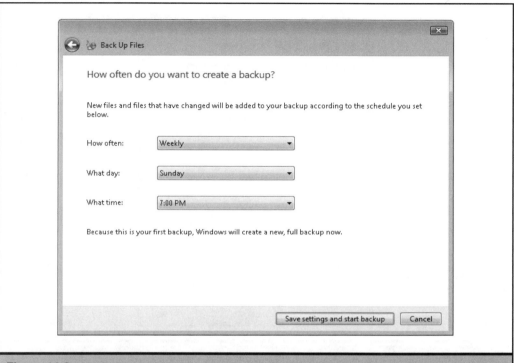

Figure 14-9.   Vista asks how often you want to back up your files.

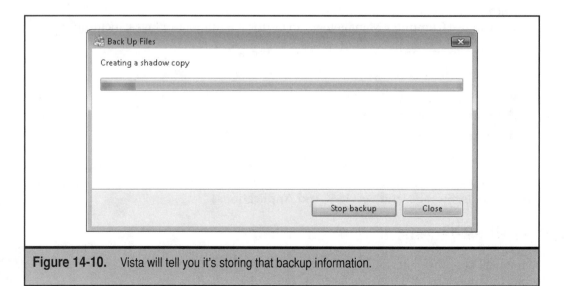

Figure 14-10.   Vista will tell you it's storing that backup information.

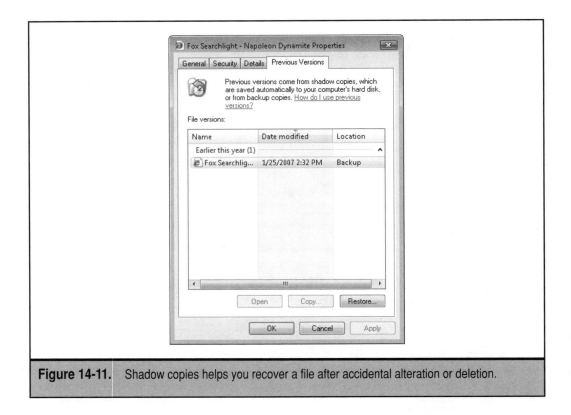

Figure 14-11. Shadow copies helps you recover a file after accidental alteration or deletion.

Once started, you'll see a window like the one in Figure 14-12.
You can use Computer Management to perform a number of tasks, including:

▼ Monitoring system events, like logon times

■ View a list of users connected to a computer

■ Start and stop system services

■ Manage properties for storage devices

■ Manage shared resources

▲ Manage applications and services

Computer Management is divided into three separate areas in the console tree: System Tools, Storage, and Services And Applications.

System Tools

The first item in the Computer Management console tree is System Tools. This is used to manage system events and performance. The section is further broken down into five tools, the functions of which are listed in Table 14-1.

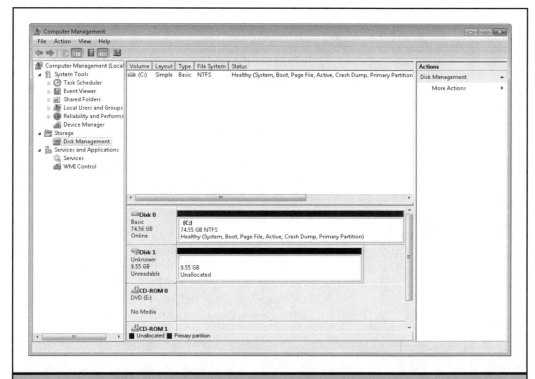

Figure 14-12.   Computer Management is a collection of administrative tools used for managing a local or remote computer.

Storage

The second item in the Computer Management console tree is Storage. This displays storage devices that are installed on the computer. This tool allows you to perform disk-related tasks, like creating and formatting partitions and volumes, and assigning drive letters.

Services And Applications

The final item in the Computer Management console tree is Services And Applications. It contains a number of default tools that help you manage services and applications. Table 14-2 lists the default tools.

Startup Applications

When you start Vista, you may decide it advantageous to have certain applications automatically start as well. For example, maybe Microsoft Word is a lynchpin of your organization, and it is helpful for the word-processing program to start every time you start Vista. Vista provides a way to do that.

Tool	Description
Task Scheduler	Create and manage tasks that the computer will automatically perform when a defined trigger is activated.
Event Viewer	Monitor events recorded in the Application, Security, and System logs.
Shared Folders	Manage shared resources on a network. You can control user access permissions, session activity, and shared resource properties.
Local Users And Groups	Manage user and group accounts on the local computer.
Performance Logs And Alerts	Collect performance data from local or remote computers. Logged data can be viewed using System Monitor or exported to spreadsheet or database programs.
Device Manager	Update drivers in hardware, modify hardware settings, or troubleshoot.

Table 14-1.   The System Tools

Configuring Startup Applications

To start a program every time Vista starts:

1. Click the Start button.
2. Click All Programs.
3. Right-click the Startup folder, and click Open.

Tool	Description
Services	Manage service applications, like Web servers, database servers, and so forth.
WMI Control	Manage Windows Management Instrumentation (WMI) settings on local or remote computers.

Table 14-2.   The Services And Applications Tool

4. Open the location of the item for which you want to create a shortcut.

5. Right-click the item and click Create Shortcut.

6. Drag the shortcut to the Startup folder.

Disabling Startup Applications

You might discover that too many startup applications are more trouble than they're worth, causing performance hits and a longer boot time. To disable programs from starting automatically:

1. Click the Start button.

2. Click All Programs.

3. Click Windows Defender.

4. Click Tools and then click Software Explorer.

5. In the Category box, click Startup Programs.

6. Select the program you want to stop running, and click Disable.

7. Click Yes to confirm your choice.

8. If you have more programs you want to disable, repeat steps 6 and 7.

Windows PowerShell

While the command prompt is—and has been—a utilitarian tool for computer management, it is still somewhat lacking. To allow more complex actions from the command prompt, Microsoft introduced the Windows PowerShell in January 2007.

PowerShell is a new command-line shell and scripting language providing greater productivity and control of system administration. It is built on the .NET common language runtime and .NET Framework. It accepts and returns .NET objects. This differs from other shells, and brings new tools and methods of management and configuration to Vista.

PowerShell is not a default part of Vista and must be downloaded and installed separately. You can download it from www.microsoft.com/technet/scriptcenter/topics/msh/download.mspx.

Cmdlets

Windows PowerShell uses cmdlets (pronounced "command-let"). These are simple, single-function command-line tools built into the shell. Each cmdlet can be used separately, but can also be used together to perform complex jobs.

Windows PowerShell includes more than 100 basic cmdlets, but you can write your own. Cmdlets are recognizable by their name format—a verb and a noun separated by a dash, like `get-help` or `start-service`.

Cmdlets are simple and designed to be used in conjunction with other cmdlets. They are grouped by the actions they perform, including:

▼ `get` Used only to retrieve data

■ `set` Used only to establish or change data

■ **format** Used only to format data

▲ **out** Used only to direct output to a specified destination

Objects

Without wandering too far down the path into the world of programming, let's talk about Windows PowerShell and its use of objects.

.NET objects are data entities that have properties (you can think of them as characteristics) and methods (which are actions that are performed on the objects).

For instance, when you get a service in Windows PowerShell, what you really get is an object that represents the service. Viewing information about that service is really viewing properties of the object. When you start the service, you change the status property to "started" by using a method of the object.

Error Handling

Cmdlets inherit options that allow the user to choose such details as the level of interaction and how to deal with errors. Cmdlets that can produce errors support the –WhatIf and –Confirm options. –WhatIf tells the user what would have happened but takes no action. –Confirm tells the user what is about to happen and allows the user to decide whether it should take place.

When an error does occur, one way that Windows PowerShell deals with it is by invoking a *suspend* feature. This allows the user to open a new command shell, research the problem, and resume the original command.

Starting Windows PowerShell

Once you've downloaded and installed Windows PowerShell, start it by following these steps:

1. Click Start.
2. Click All Programs.
3. Click Windows PowerShell 1.0.
4. Click Windows PowerShell.

You can also start it from the Run box or from the command prompt by typing `powershell`.

Getting Help

If you're stuck in Windows PowerShell and you need help, remember this command:

`get-help`

This cmdlet is useful for learning about Windows PowerShell and its various cmdlets. It will also give information about the Help system in PowerShell.

To learn about a given cmdlet, like **get-help** or **get-service**, enter the request like this:

```
get-help get-service
```

You can get detailed information about a cmdlet by adding the **–detailed** parameter. Our previous cmdlet looks like this now:

```
get-help get-command –detailed
```

You can get all of the available help information for a cmdlet by using the **–full** parameter. For instance:

```
get-help get-command –full
```

If that's information overload, or if you know specifically what part of the Help file you want to see, you can request just that information by entering that parameter. For instance, if we just want to see the –examples parameter, we would type:

```
get-help get-command –examples
```

Using Cmdlets

Cmdlets are simple, single-function tools built into the shell. You use cmdlets just as you would use commands and utilities in the command prompt.

The following snippet shows the **get-date** cmdlet:

```
C:\PS> get-date
Tuesday, February 5, 2007 8:49:20 PM
```

You can list all the cmdlets in your session by using the **get-command** cmdlet without any command parameters, as shown:

```
PS> get-command

CommandType Name Definition
----------- ---- ----------
Cmdlet Add-Content Add-Content [-Path] <String[...
Cmdlet Add-History Add-History [[-InputObject] ...
Cmdlet Add-Member Add-Member [-MemberType] <PS...
```

The default get-command shows the command type, its name, and its definition. The definition shows the syntax of the cmdlet.

As you can see Windows PowerShell is a robust tool—have fun with it and don't be afraid to explore. For more information on Windows PowerShell, visit Microsoft's Web site at: www.microsoft.com/windowsserver2003/technologies/management/powershell/default.mspx.

New Command-Line Tools

As any seasoned Windows IT professional knows, there's more to Windows functionality that what you can point and click. Often, it's easier—and more powerful—to run a command directly from the command line. Windows Vista includes a number of new command-line tools that perform new features. Table 14-3 lists some of the new commands and describes what they do.

Tool	Description
auditpol	Modify audit polices
bcdedit	Edit the Boot Configuration Data Store
bitsadmin	BITS administration utility
change	Change terminal server settings for logons, COM port mappings, and install mode
chglogon	Enable or disable session logons
chgport	List or change COM port mappings for DOS application compatibility
chgusr	Change install mode
choice	Allow users to select one item from a list of choices and return the index of the selected choice
clip	Redirect the output of command-line tools to the Windows Clipboard
cmdkey	Create, display, and delete stored user names and passwords
diskraid	Launch the diskraid application
dispdiag	Display diagnostics information
forfiles	Select a file (or files) and execute a command on that file
icacls	Display or modify access control lists (ACLs) of files; an updated version of cacls
iscsicli	The Microsoft iSCSI Initiator
muiunattend	The MUI Unattend Action
netcfg	The WinPE Network Installer
ocsetup	The Windows Optional Component Setup
pkgmgr	The Windows Package Manager

Table 14-3.   Vista's New Command-Line Tools

Tool	Description
pnpunattend	Used for unattended online driver installation
pnputil	The Microsoft Plug and Play (PnP) Utility
quser	Display information about users logged on to the system
robocopy	The Robust File Copy for Windows tool
rpcping	Ping a server using Remote Procedure Call (RPC)
setx	Create or modify environment variables in the user or system environment
sxstrace	The WinSxs tracing utility
takeown	Recover access to a file that was denied by reassigning file ownership
timeout	Accept a timeout parameter to wait for the specified time period or until any key is pressed
tracerpt	The TraceRpt tool
waitfor	Send or wait for a signal on a system
wbadmin	Start the backup tool
wceutil	The Windows Event Collector utility
wevtutil	The Windows Event command-line utility
where	Display the location of files that match the search pattern
whoami	Retrieve user name and group information, along with the respective security identifiers (SIDs), privileges, logon identifier (logon ID) for the current user (access token) on the local system
winrm	The Windows Remote Management tool
winrs	The Windows Remote Shell tool
winsat	The Windows System Assessment tool

Table 14-3.   Vista's New Command-Line Tools *(Continued)*

SUPPORT TOOLS

For better or for worse, some of the classic desktop support tools have been revamped for Vista. The underlying improvements have given Microsoft a chance to likewise improve upon the feature set for even the most fundamental tools. The improvements to these core tools will have mixed reviews from administrators. While the new features include some useful benefits, some of the features do not have an intuitive purpose. The somewhat drastic change in format will undoubtedly take some administrators by surprise, and require all administrators to slow down and learn before they leap. We recommend that you do just that: spend some time learning about the new version of these trusted tools before using them.

Event Viewer

The Event Viewer has been around since the early days of the Windows operating system. Today, the viewer is an MMC snap-in that enables you to browse and manage Vista event logs. It is an indispensable tool for learning how Vista and applications run, and for troubleshooting issues when they arise. The new Event Viewer for Vista is more than just a way to display entries in the log files, as it has been in previous versions. Leveraging the new MMC 3.0 platform, the viewer is a robust, complex application in its own right. The basic functionality of the Event Viewer includes:

▼ Viewing events from multiple event logs, both individual and compiled views from multiple logs

■ Saving event filters as custom views that can be reused

■ Scheduling tasks to run in response to an event

▲ Collect, store, and act on events from remote computers using event subscriptions

The data architecture for event logging has been completely revamped in Vista. Information about each event conforms to an eXtensible Markup Language (XML) schema, and you can access the XML representing any event. You can also build XML-based queries against event logs, making it possible to search log files without complicated scripts and third-party tools.

The logs themselves have a revamped scope. The standard log files are there, and Microsoft has broken the logs up into three different scopes:

▼ **Standard, system-wide logs**   Track events that affect every user, common applications, shared resources, and the operating system itself

■ **Application-specific**   Logs that track events on the Vista system and your installed applications that are virtualized and have no effect on the system itself

▲ **Application-specific – verbose**   These logs are subtypes of the application logs and hold details normally of no interest to operations but that may have great value when troubleshooting issues.

Opening the Event Viewer

There are three ways to open Event Viewer. You can open it from the Windows interface, from the shell Search field, and from the MMC snap-in interface. To open the Event Viewer from the Windows interface:

1. Click the Start button, and then click the Control Panel link on the right pane.

2. In the default Control Panel view, click System And Maintenance (skip this step if you are in the Classic view).

3. Click the Administrative Tools icon, and then double-click Event Viewer.

You can type EventVwr in the Search field from the Start menu or from any Windows Explorer window and press ENTER to launch the Event Viewer. For your third choice, you can add the Event Viewer to a custom console using the MMC tool, which you can start by typing **MMC** into the Search field from the Start menu (see the preceding section on how to add snap-ins to a custom MMC console).

Navigating Around the New Event Viewer

The Event Viewer in Vista is based on MMC 3.0 and includes the standard MMC panes (of which there are three). The Event Viewer is shown in Figure 14-13.

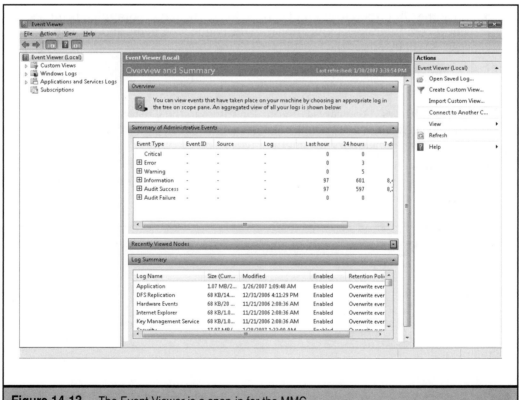

Figure 14-13.   The Event Viewer is a snap-in for the MMC.

The first pane on the left holds the computer object of which you wish to view and the event logs on that computer. You can add computers to the pane by connecting them as follows:

1. Right-click the Event Viewer parent node, located in the top of the left pane.

2. From the context menu that appears, click the Another Computer option, as shown in Figure 14-14.

3. In the Select Computer window, provide the resolvable name for the target computer (fully qualified domain name or NetBIOS name, depending on your network name resolution service) in the Another Computer field, or click the Browse button to navigate your network and select the target computer from the list of detected computers.

4. Optionally, provide alternate credentials if the account currently in use does not have access to the logs on the target computer. Select the Connect As Another User check box, and then click the Select User button to provide the user credentials.

5. Click the OK button to attempt connection to the target computer. If successful, a new computer object will appear in the connection pane, and the logs it carries will be accessible by double-clicking them.

Once you expand the computer node, you will see the major log containers. The containers include:

▼ **Custom Views**   You can save your log filters in the Custom Views container. The Vista Event Viewer enables you to stitch together output from multiple logs and save the query for ongoing use.

■ **Windows Logs**   The Windows Logs container holds the five system logs that track the system events for later viewing. The logs include the Application, Security, Setup, System, and Forwarded Events logs:

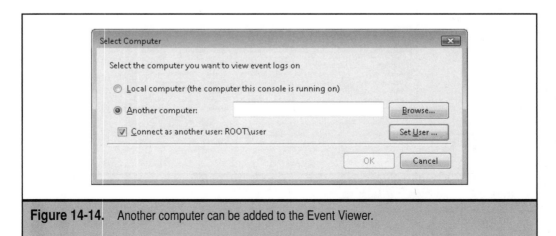

Figure 14-14.   Another computer can be added to the Event Viewer.

- ■ **Application log** The Application log contains events logged by installed applications or programs. The application developers decide which events to log.

- ■ **Security log** The Security log contains events such as valid and invalid logon attempts, as well as events related to resource use, such as creating, opening, or deleting files or other objects. You can affect what events are sent to the security log using Group Policy and Local Security Policy.

- ■ **Setup log** New for Vista, the Setup log contains events related to application setup, including installation activities and configuration updates. Be aware, however, that legacy applications may still send these events to the Application log.

- ■ **System log** The System log has events logged by Windows system components. For example, if a service fails to start, the event is sent to the System log.

- ■ **ForwardedEvents log** New for Vista, the ForwardedEvents log is used to store events collected from remote computers. To collect events from remote computers, you must create an event subscription.

- ▲ **Applications And Services Logs** New for Vista, logs in the Applications And Services Logs container hold events from a single application or component rather than events that may have system-wide impact. The logs are listed by activity type and vendor. The list of logs varies, depending on the services and applications that you have installed. A log file is shown in Figure 14-15. Common logs include:

  - ■ **DFS Replication log** The Distributed File System (DFS) Replication Service activities are tracked here

  - ■ **Hardware log** Device and peripheral activities are tracked here

  - ■ **Internet Explorer log** Activities tracked by the default Vista Web browser

  - ■ **Key Management Service log** Local events created by security associations between this computer and remote computers

  - ■ **Microsoft\Windows Log container** This container is different from the other log files listed. It is itself only a container and holds no events. Under the container, however, are hundreds of logs that are included with Vista and other Microsoft applications you may have installed on your computer

The log containers, like the Microsoft\Windows container, within the Applications And Services Logs container have four log subtypes. Events for these types of logs are stored within the following log folders: Admin, Operational, Analytic, and Debug (both Analytic and Debug logs are hidden and disabled by default):

- ▼ **Admin log** The events that are found in the Admin channels indicate a problem and a well-defined solution that an administrator can act on. An example of an admin event is an event that occurs when an application fails to connect to a printer. These events are either well documented or have a message associated with them that gives the reader direct instructions on what must be done to rectify the problem.

- **Operational log** Operational events are used for analyzing and diagnosing a problem or occurrence. They can be used to trigger tools or tasks based on the problem or occurrence. An example of an operational event is an event that occurs when a printer is added to or removed from a system.

- **Analytic or Diagnostic log** Analytic events are published in high volume. They describe program operation and indicate problems that cannot be handled by user intervention. Analytic and diagnostic logs are hidden and disabled by default. See the next section to learn how to enable them.

- ▲ **Debug or tracing log** Debug events are used by developers troubleshooting issues with their programs. Debug and diagnostic logs are hidden and disabled by default. See the next section to learn how to enable them.

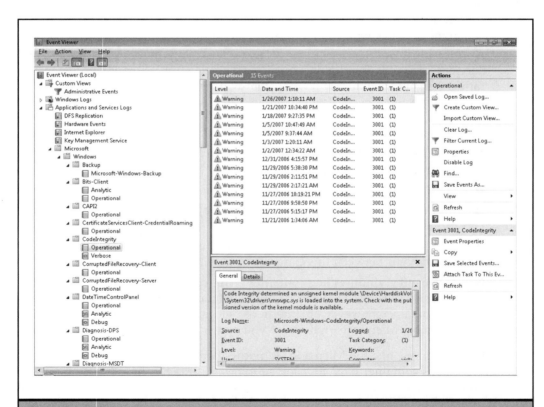

Figure 14-15. Vista includes hundreds of application containers, each with subtype log files.

Enable Analytic and Debug Logs Analytic and debug logs are disabled and hidden by default. When enabled, the logs will fill quickly with events. The logs are best left disabled for everyday operations and switched on to gather troubleshooting data, and then turned off again when you have your data. You can hide/unhide and enable/disable the logs using either the Windows interface or the command line. To enable analytic and debug logs using the Windows interface:

1. Launch the Event Viewer from the Start menu by typing **Eventvwr** in the Search field and pressing the ENTER key.

2. Select the Applications And Services log in the right pane, and then click the View menu option in the Actions pane. From the options that appear, choose the Show Analytic And Debug Logs option. This is shown in Figure 14-16.

3. In the left pane of the Event Viewer, select the analytic or debug log you want to enable.

4. On the Action menu in the right pane of the viewer, click the Properties menu option.

5. On the Properties dialog box, select Enable Logging.

6. Before the log is enabled, Vista will clear it. A warning message appears, informing you of this and giving you chance to consider the consequence. If you can afford to lose the log entries, click OK.

To enable analytic and debug logs using the command line:

1. From the Start menu, click Run, type cmd, and click OK.

2. Type the following text into the Open field: wevtutil sl <logname> /e: true.

Event Properties

Events have varying levels of information, depending on how thorough the developer who wrote the application was when working on the logging aspect. No matter how

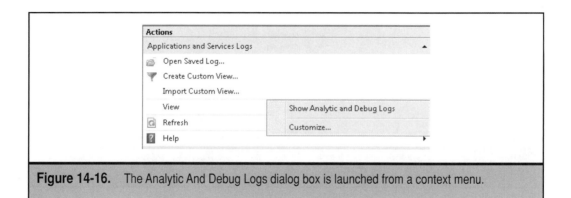

Figure 14-16. The Analytic And Debug Logs dialog box is launched from a context menu.

much data is provided by an application, at least the format in which Vista presents it to you is consistent. An example of an event's properties is shown in Figure 14-17.

Table 14-4 lists the common event properties. For more information about event properties and the underlying XML schema, see the Event Representation for Event Consumers topic in the Windows Event Log Software Development Kit (SDK), found at: msdn2 .microsoft.com/en-us/library/aa385780.aspx.

Note some other features of the Event Properties window. By clicking the Copy button, you copy the XML for the event to the Clipboard, and can paste it into any text editor. You can view the Details tab, which allows you to see the raw payload of the event in either a user-friendly view or in XML. You can also resize the Event Properties window itself to get a better view.

Create and Manage Custom Views

Custom views are stored filters that you create to suit a specific need. After creating and saving a custom view, you can reuse it anytime you wish. To reuse a custom view, navigate to the Custom Views node in the console tree, and select the name of the custom view. By selecting the custom view, you launch the filter automatically, and the results are displayed in the center pane of the Event Viewer.

Note that you can export a custom view by right-clicking it and choosing Export A Custom View. Likewise, you can import a custom view by selecting the Custom View node, right-clicking it, and choosing Import A Custom View. To create a custom view using the Vista interface:

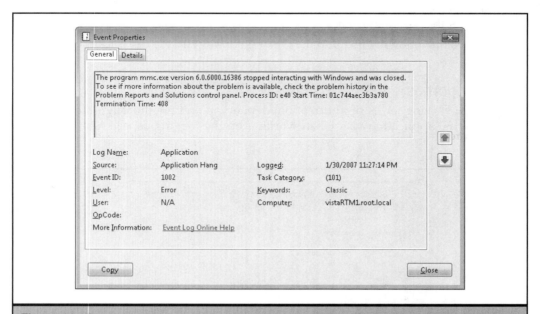

Figure 14-17.   Event details can be examined on the Event Properties dialog box.

Property Name	Description
Source	The application or subcomponent of an application that logged the event.
EventID	A number identifying the particular event type. The EventID can be used to identify an event online and look up more details about an event. A great resource for this is www.eventid.net.
Level	A classification of the event severity: error, information, or warning in the system and application logs; success audit or failure audit in the security log. In the Event Viewer normal list view, these are represented by a symbol.
User	The name of the user on whose behalf the event occurred. This name is the computer name if the event was actually caused by a computer process.
OpCode	A numeric value that identifies the point within an operation when the application performed the event, such as "initialization" or "closing." This can be a numeric version of the Task Category (see below).
Logged	The date and local time when the event occurred.
Task Category	Represents a subcomponent or activity of the application responsible for the event. This can be a text version of the OpCode (see above).
Keywords	Tags used by filters and custom views that qualify an event. You can search the logs based on these descriptive words, such as "Printer," or "Printing."
Computer	The name of the computer on which the event occurred.
More Information	A hyperlink that will search the online Microsoft database of events for more information. You must be online for this work correctly.

Table 14-4.   Common Event Properties

1. Launch the Event Viewer by clicking the Start button, typing **EventVwr** into the Search field, and pressing the ENTER key.

2. On the Action menu, click Create Custom View. The resulting dialog box is shown in Figure 14-18.

Create Custom View

Filter | XML

Logged: Last hour

Event level: ☑ Critical   ☐ Warning   ☐ Verbose

               ☑ Error   ☐ Information

◉ By log   Event logs: System

◯ By source   Event sources:

Includes/Excludes Event IDs: Enter ID numbers and/or ID ranges separated by commas. To exclude criteria, type a minus sign first. For example 1,3,5-99,-76

<All Event IDs>

Task category:

Keywords:

User: <All Users>

Computer(s):   <All Computers>

Clear

OK   Cancel

Figure 14-18.   You can create a custom view using the Vista interface.

NOTE   Be aware that there are two Action menus in the Event Viewer window. Do not use the one on the top bar.

3. Using the Logged drop-down list, filter events based upon the date and time when they occurred.

4. Click on the Custom Range if you wish to provide a specific range filter. In the Custom range dialog box, specify the earliest date and time from which you want events and the latest date and time from which you want events then click OK. This is shown in Figure 14-19.

5. In the Event Level area, click the check boxes next to the event levels that you wish to include.

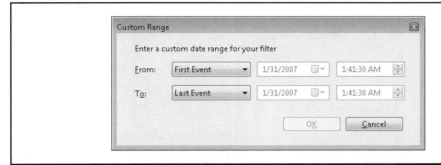

Figure 14-19.   Your filter will sort events by date and time.

6. Select between By Log and By Source. By Log allows you to use a combo list box to select the log you wish to target. By Source allows you to specify the application or technology provider, such as the .NET Framework.

7. In the Event IDs field, type the event IDs that you want your custom view to display:

   ■   Separate multiple event IDs by commas.

   ■   To provide a range of IDs, hyphenate the range, as in 1000-2000.

   ■   If you want your filter to display events with all IDs except certain ones, type the IDs of those exceptions, preceded by a minus sign.

8. In the Task Category field, select the check boxes next to the task categories in the drop-down list that you want included in the custom view. This drop-down list is only enabled if there are categories available for the log or source you chose in step 6.

9. In the Keywords field, click the check boxes next to the keywords in the drop-down list that you want included in the custom view.

10. In the User section, enter the name(s) of the user accounts on whose behalf the event is posted that you wish to qualify events against. Enter multiple users by separating them with a comma.

11. In the Computer(s) section, enter the name(s) of the computers that you want your custom view to include. Enter multiple computers by separating them with a comma.

12. Click the OK button to launch the Save Filter To Custom View dialog box. This is shown in Figure 14-20.

13. In the Save Filter To Custom View dialog box, type a name for the custom view.

14. In the Description field, type a description of the custom view (this is optional).

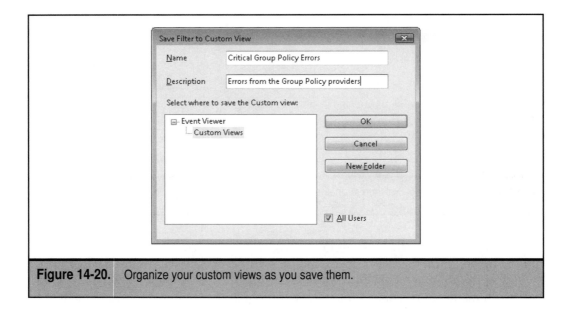

Figure 14-20.   Organize your custom views as you save them.

15. Select the folder in which you want to store the custom view. Custom views can be stored in the Custom Views folder or in any subfolder of the Custom Views folder. You create new subfolders in the Custom Views folder by clicking the New Folder button.

16. You can make the custom view accessible to either anyone using the computer or only to someone logged on to your current user account:

   ■ To save the custom view and make it accessible to anyone using the computer, ensure that the All Users check box is selected, and click OK.

   ■ To save the custom view and make it accessible only to someone logged on to your current account, ensure that the All Users check box is not selected, and click OK.

You can also modify a custom view by editing the XML query directly. Before you save the custom view, click the XML tab at the top of the Create Custom View dialog box, click the Edit Query Manually check box, and then click OK in response to the warning dialog box. This is shown in Figure 14-21.

Run a Task in Response to a Given Event

You can configure a task to run when a specific event occurs. You have to provide the event definition and assign the text using the Event Viewer interface. The task object is a new Task Scheduler job that gets posted to the Event Viewer folder in the Task Scheduler Library. The task is run on demand as the event you wish to track is posted to the Vista event logs. To run a task in response to an event:

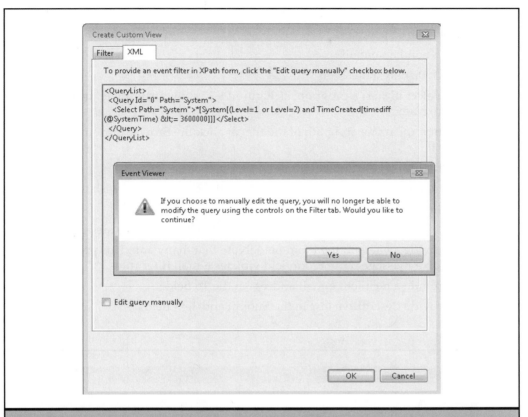

Figure 14-21. You can modify a custom view using the XML tab.

NOTE This can also be set up using Group Policy and distributed across all your organizations' computers.

1. Launch the Event Viewer by clicking the Start button, typing **EventVwr** into the Search field, and pressing the ENTER key.

2. In the console tree, navigate to the log that contains the event you want to associate with a task.

3. Right-click the event and select Attach Task To This Event.

4. Perform each step presented by the five-page Create Basic Task Wizard:

   a. In the first page of the wizard, provide a name and description for the event-task association, and click Next.

   b. In the When an Event Is Logged page, note the details of the event, and click Next.

   c. In the Action page, select between:

- Start a program
- Send an e-mail
- Display a message

5. If you elect to start a program, as Figure 14-22 shows, complete the details on the program:

   a. Enter the name and path of the file, or click the Browse button and navigate to it.

   b. Provide any arguments for the program.

   c. Optionally, provide the parent path of the program you wish to launch.

   d. Click the Next button.

6. If you elect to have an e-mail sent, complete the details on the message to be sent:

   a. Provide a value in the From field. Note that many antivirus programs will stop a message if the From field violates e-mail filter rules.

   b. Provide a recipient e-mail address in the To field.

   c. Provide descriptive text in the Subject and Text fields.

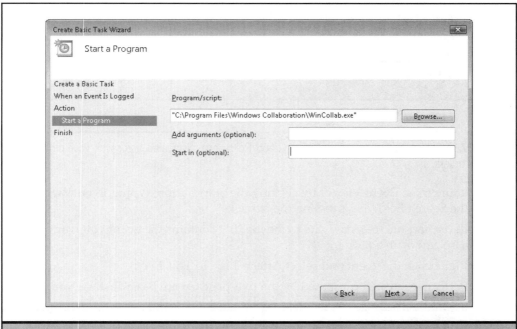

Figure 14-22.   Associating a program with an event is done using the Create Basic Task Wizard.

    d. Fill in the name and path to any attachments you wish to send.

    e. Be sure to provide the Internet Protocol (IP) address or name of the Simple Mail Transfer Protocol (SMTP) server that will accept a request from your computer to send an e-mail.

    f. Click the Next button.

    Figure 14-23 shows the dialog box seeking this information.

7. If you wish to modify the new task upon completing it, click the Open The Properties Dialog When I Click Finish check box, and then click the Finish button.

    Note these restrictions on associating tasks with events:

- You cannot assign a task to an event in a saved log.

- You cannot assign a task to an event in an analytic or debug log.

Upon completing the task, you view or edit it through the Vista Task Scheduler by following these steps:

1. Launch the Task Scheduler by clicking the Start button, typing **Task Scheduler** into the Search field, and pressing the ENTER key.

2. In the left pane, locate the Event Viewer folder, and open it by double-clicking it.

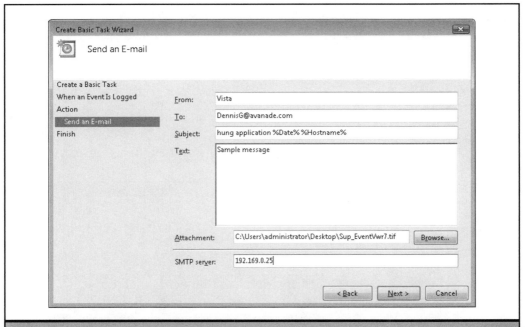

Figure 14-23. Using the Create Basic Task Wizard, you can have an e-mail sent when an event occurs.

3. In the middle pane of the Task Scheduler, locate the task you wish to audit or update, right-click it, and then choose Properties from the context menu.

4. The task will load, rendering a series of tabs that allow you to view and edit the task configuration. This is shown in Figure 14-24.

Note that you can do more with event-driven tasks:

▼ On the Actions tab of the task, you can add actions to the one that you created in the Event Viewer, making your event-driven task more robust.

▲ You do not have to wait until an event is logged to associate a task with it. You can create a task in the Task Scheduler and configure it to launch based on an event in an event log. Click the Triggers tab of a new task, add a trigger by clicking the New button, and select On An Event from the drop-down menu of the Begin Task On section.

Device Manager

The Device Manager is one great way to manage hardware. You can get the status of any device, resolve issues, update drivers, roll back drivers, and more. Incorrectly altering your device configurations can affect your system stability, so be sure to read any instructions provided by the manufacturer before making changes to your hardware configuration. To open the Device Manager:

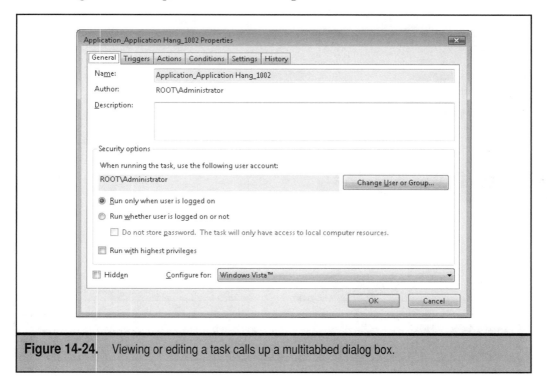

Figure 14-24.   Viewing or editing a task calls up a multitabbed dialog box.

1. From the Start menu, click the Control Panel link on the right side.

2. In the Control Panel window, click the System And Maintenance link.

3. Click Administrative Tools and then double-click Computer Management.

4. In the Computer Management console tree, expand the System Tools node by double-clicking it. Optionally, you can accomplish this by typing `CompMgmt.msc` into the Search field in the Start menu and pressing the ENTER key.

5. Select Device Manager from the Systems Tools node. By default, the list of devices is organized by device type. The Device Manager is shown in Figure 14-25.

Optionally, you can type `DevMgmt.msc` into the Search field in the Start menu and press the ENTER key.

In Device Manager, you can work with any installed device. Note that the list that appears in Device Manager upon launch is a set of categories. To view the devices within each category, double-click the category. If you right-click a device, a context menu appears. The options available depend on the device type and generally include the following:

▼   **Properties**   Displays the Properties dialog box for the device. The Properties dialog includes these tabs:

■   **General**   Displays information on the device, including the device type, manufacturer, location, and status

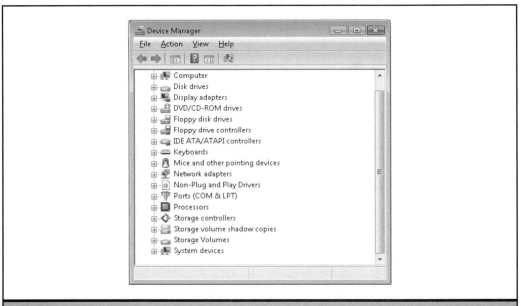

Figure 14-25.   The Vista Device Manager is used to manage your system's hardware.

- ■ **Driver** This tab gives you information and configuration tools. You will find the driver provider or vendor, the published date, version, and digital signer. The configuration options include updating the driver, rolling back the driver to a previous version, and disabling and uninstalling the driver (and hence the device). This tab is shown in Figure 14-26.

- ■ **Details** This tab has a drop-down menu from which you can select any number of properties to have the value displayed in the field below it. Note that Figure 14-27 shows the drop-down list, and behind it is the value box. Once you select a property, the menu collapses to one line, revealing the value.

- ■ **Resources** This tab gives you the current configuration of the memory resources allocated to that device. This is also where you need to resolve conflicts between competing devices vying for the same resources. This tab is shown in Figure 14-28.

- ■ **Uninstall** Uninstalls the device and its drivers

- ■ **Disable** Disables the device but doesn't uninstall it

- ■ **Enable** Enables a device if it's disabled

- ■ **Update Driver** Starts the Hardware Update Wizard, which you can use to update the device driver

- ▲ **Scan For Hardware Changes** Tells Vista to check the hardware configuration and determine whether there are any changes

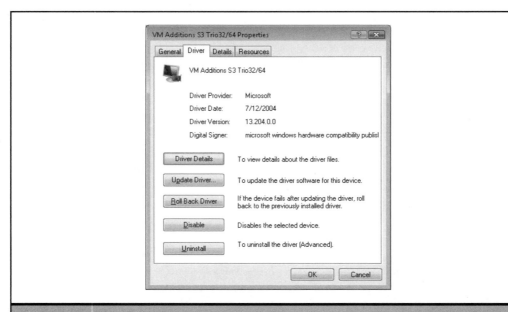

Figure 14-26. The Driver tab on the Properties dialog box within the Device Manager provides information and configuration tools.

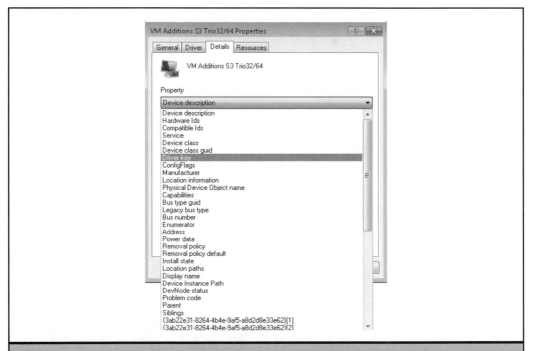

Figure 14-27.   The Details tab on the Properties dialog box within the Device Manager allows you to select properties to be displayed.

The device list shows warning symbols if there are problems with a device. A yellow warning symbol with an exclamation point indicates a problem with a device. A red X indicates a device that was improperly installed or disabled by the user or the administrator for some reason.

You can use the options on the View menu from the top menu bar to change the defaults for which types of devices are displayed and how the devices are listed. The options are as follows:

- ▼ **Devices By Type**   Shows devices listed by the type or category of device. This is the default view

- ■ **Devices By Connection**   Shows devices listed by connection type, such as audio and video codecs

- ■ **Resources By Type**   Shows the status of resources listed by type of device using the resource. A resource type is a Direct Memory Access (DMA) channel, an input/output (I/O) port, an interrupt request (IRQ), or a memory address

- ■ **Resources By Connection**   Shows the status of all allocated resources listed by connection type

- ▲ **Show Hidden Devices**   Shows non–Plug and Play devices and inactive devices (those that have been removed but the drivers remain)

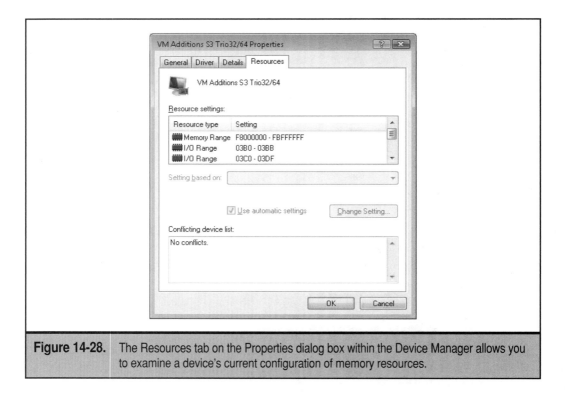

Figure 14-28. The Resources tab on the Properties dialog box within the Device Manager allows you to examine a device's current configuration of memory resources.

Enabling and Disabling Hardware

On occasion, you will want to uninstall or disable a device. Some reasons for doing so include a failed driver install, a corrupt driver, or a conflict between devices. Uninstalling a device unloads the driver, although the driver files and physical device remain. Uninstalling a device makes it appear that the device has been removed. The next time you restart Vista or execute the Scan For Hardware Changes feature, Vista will reinstall any Plug and Play device.

Another less drastic option is to disable the device. Disabling a device stops Vista from processing any threads using the driver and prevents Vista from using the device. Because a disabled device does not use system resources, you can be sure that it isn't causing a conflict on the system. To uninstall or disable a device:

1. Open Device Manager by typing `DevMgmt.msc` in the Search field in the Start menu and pressing the ENTER key.

2. Open a device category by double-clicking it, exposing the devices within the category.

3. Right-click the device you want to manage, and then select one of the following options:

   ■ Enable

   ■ Uninstall

   ■ Disable

4. If prompted to confirm the action, click Yes or OK as appropriate.

Task Manager

The Task Manager, shown in Figure 14-29, holds a wealth of information. You can get real-time data on your resources and processes, as well as information on logged on users and applications. Some of the uses of the Task Manager include the following:

▼ **Performance monitoring**   View real-time performance metrics from key components, including processor, memory, network throughput, hard disk drive I/O, and more

■ **Performance tuning**   You can align processes with processors using the Processor Affinity property of running processes, and terminate any process that may be using too much of any given resource.

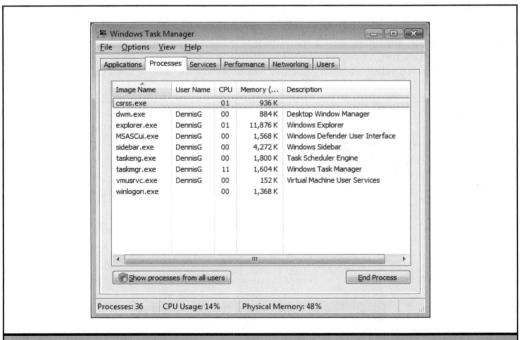

Figure 14-29.   The Task Manager is an extremely versatile tool.

- **Managing services** Associate services with running processes and start and stop services
- ▲ **Managing processes** View details on the running processes, including the resources allocated, descriptions, and associated files

To open the Task Manager, follow these steps:

1. Mouse over an open space on the task bar (the lowest menu on your screen).
2. Right-click the task bar and from the context menu that appears (see the figure below), click Task Manager. This is shown in Figure 14-30.

Alternatively, you can press CTRL+ALT+DELETE to display the screen shown in Figure 14-31. From the options presented, click Task Manager.

The last option for opening the Task Manager is a variation on the preceding method: press CTRL+SHIFT+ESC.

Managing Services from the Task Manager

The Services tab is a new addition to Task Manager in Vista. You can use the Services tab to start and stop services, and view several important aspects of the services, both running and available, on your computer. You can also use this as a shortcut to the Services MMC console. This is shown in Figure 14-32.

To view more of the information displayed on the Services tab, enlarge the Task Manager window, and adjust the column widths to suit your needs. To start or stop a service, right-click its name on the Services tab, and then click either Start Service or Stop Service. Using the Services tab, you can map a running service to its Process Identifier (PID), which can be useful when running scripts to automate the management of services.

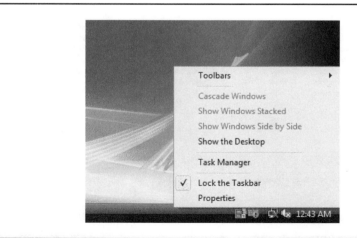

Figure 14-30. The Task Manager can be launched from the task bar.

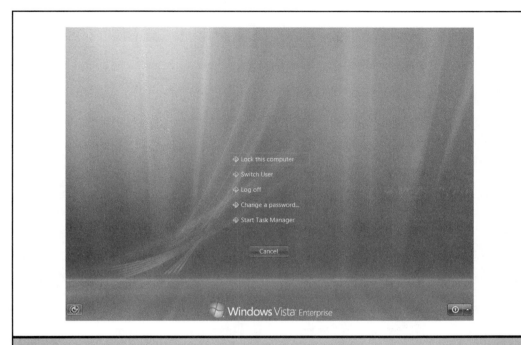

Figure 14-31. The Task Manger can be pressing CTRL+ALT+DELETE.

You can also map services to running processes. When right-clicking one of the services, you see two options: one to stop the service and one called Go To Process. By clicking Go To Process, the Processes tab is displayed, with the particular process highlighted that is associated with the service. Most service-related processes run under an account other than your own and, therefore, aren't available when you attempt to use the Go To Process option. To view these processes, select the Show Processes From All Users option on the Processes tab in Task Manager before clicking Go To Process.

PERFORMANCE MONITORING

Monitoring system performance has not changed much in Vista in comparison to previous platforms.

Performance Information and Tools

A great way to view Vista's collection of performance-related tools is to visit the Performance Information And Tools window. You may be impressed with the array of options that you can access from this area. To open the main window, shown in Figure 14-33:

1. Click the Start button, and then click Control Panel on the right side of the Start menu.

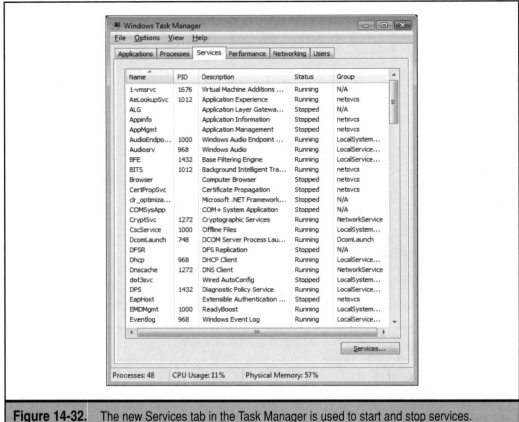

Figure 14-32.   The new Services tab in the Task Manager is used to start and stop services.

2. From Control Panel, click the System And Maintenance link.
3. Locate and click the Performance Information And Tools link.

The entry window for the Performance Information And Tools area shows you the Windows Experience index base score. This indicates the performance and overall capability of the local system. The index base score is calculated as the lowest of the subscores given to a set of hardware components that defines the overall performance of a computer. Those components include the processor, memory, graphics card, and hard disk drive. The overall base score is not nearly as useful as the individual subscores, because the base score simply takes the lowest subscore. If you have a fast process, for example, with a base score of 5.9, and a nominal gaming graphics capacity of 2.0, then the base score is 2.0. If software is processor-dependent and not a game, then the 2.0 score may mislead you into thinking that your system may not be optimal for the application. In fact, software vendors are planning to have recommendations for the minimum index to run their applications. Vista has been given the following recommendations by Microsoft:

▼ **Index Base Score 1-2**   Minimum level to run Vista at the basic level and operate general computing functions, including Microsoft Office

■ **Index Base Score 3**   Minimum level to run Vista with the Aero Glass interface and the multimedia functions

▲ **Index Base Score 4-5**   Minimum level to run all of Vista's features and high-end graphic applications

To access Vista's collection of performance tools, click the Advanced Tools link on the left pane of the Performance Information And Tools window. This is shown in Figure 14-34. The tools available from this window are described in Table 14-5.

Reliability And Performance Monitor

This tool is available in two modes. The mode available from the Performance Information And Tools window gives you a reporting interface that covers system health metrics. You can use the Reliability And Performance Monitor to identify how programs affect your computer performance, both in real time and through collecting log data for later analysis.

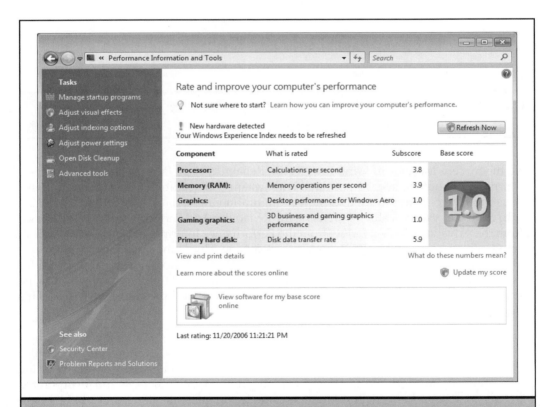

Figure 14-33.   The Performance Information And Tools window gives an overview of system performance.

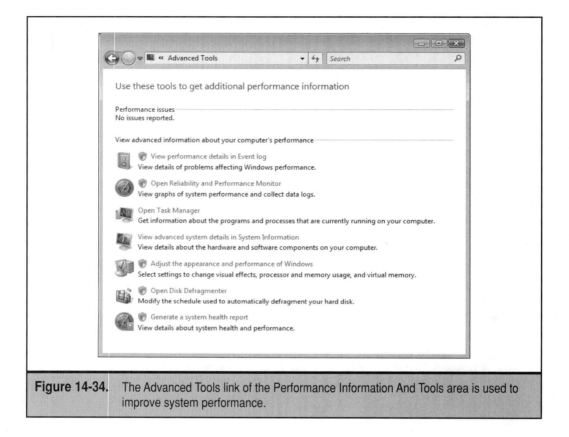

Figure 14-34. The Advanced Tools link of the Performance Information And Tools area is used to improve system performance.

Like the System Monitor in Windows XP, the Reliability And Performance Monitor uses performance counters, event trace data, and system configuration information. In Vista, you can roll the counters, trace data, and configuration into a data collector set.

To open the system health report using the Reliability And Performance Monitor, launch it from the Advanced Tools window from the Performance Information And Tools window. Click Generate A System Health Report in the left pane. This is shown in Figure 14-35.

There is another mode of the Reliability And Performance Monitor that provides access to the full console and configuration options. To launch this version, type Perfmon.exe in the Search field from the Start menu, and press the ENTER key. This is shown in Figure 14-36.

Data Collector Sets With Vista's Reliability And Performance Monitor comes a new configuration concept known as data collector sets. A data collector set allows you to organize multiple data-collection points into a single component that can be used to review or log performance. It can be created and then recorded, grouped with other sets and incorporated into logs, viewed in Performance Monitor, configure to generate alerts, and used by non-Microsoft applications. You can create a data collector set in one of three ways:

Link	Tool	Description
View Performance Details In Event Log	Event Log (EventVwr)	View events in the Windows System logs that describe performance
Open Reliability And Performance Monitor	Perfmon.exe	View graphs of the system performance, and collect data logs
Open Task Manager	Task Manager (Taskmgr.exe)	Get information on the programs, processes, services, and users that are currently running on the local computer
View Advanced System Details In System Information	SystemInfo	View details on the hardware and software installed on the local computer
Adjust The Appearance And Performance Of Windows	Performance Options dialog box from the SystemProperties Advanaced.exe tool	Select settings to change visual effects, processor and memory usage, and virtual memory
Open Disk Defragmenter	Disk Defragmenter	Modify the schedule used to automatically defragment your hard disk drive
Generate A System Health Report	Reliability and Performance Monitor (perfmon.exe)	View details about system health and performance

Table 14-5.   Advanced Tools Used to Improve System Performance

▼   **Create it from Performance Monitor**   Create a data collector set using the counters loaded in Performance Monitor by right-clicking anywhere in the Performance Monitor display pane, pointing to New, and clicking Data Collector Set to launch the wizard.

- **Create it from a template** This is the simplest way to create a new data collector set. There are several templates from which to choose. Templates are XML files and be exported and imported, too. To build a set from a template, open the Reliability And Performance Monitor. Locate the Data Collector Set node in the navigation pane, and double-click it. Right-click the User Defined node, choose New, and then click Data Collector Set to start the wizard. After providing a name for your new data collector set, choose Create From A Template, and click Next. Complete the wizard.

▲ **Create it manually** Open the Reliability And Performance Monitor, expand the Data Collector Sets node by double-clicking it, right-click the User Defined node, point to New, and click Data Collector Set to start the wizard. After providing a name for your new data collector set, choose Create Manually and click Next. Complete the wizard.

You can obtain system diagnostics and generate a report detailing the status of local hardware resources, system response times, and processes on the local system, along with system information and configuration data. This report includes suggestions for

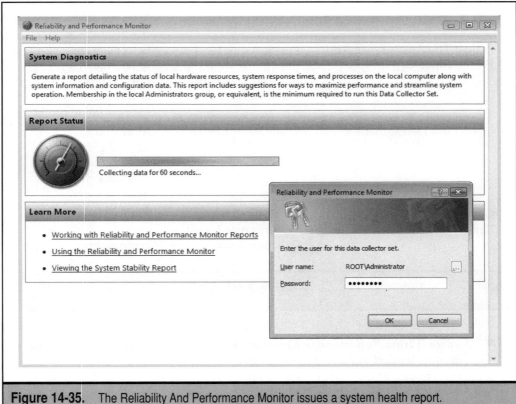

Figure 14-35. The Reliability And Performance Monitor issues a system health report.

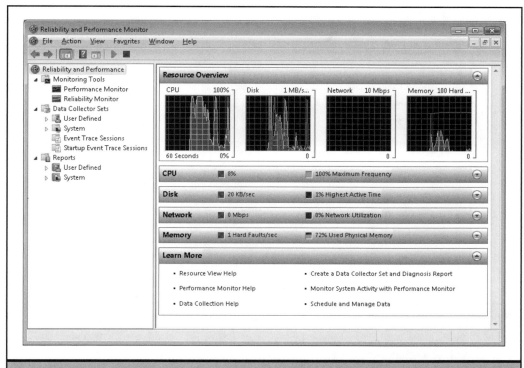

Figure 14-36.   The Reliability And Performance Monitor helps you monitor your system's performance.

ways to maximize performance and streamline system operation. Membership in the local Administrators group is required to run the default data collector set.

Performance Monitor   Performance Monitor is a visualization tool used for viewing performance data, both in real time and from data stored in log files. You can render the data in graphs, histograms, or a tabular report. To configure Performance Monitor, add counters by clicking the green plus sign (+) and using the Add Counters screen to select performance objects and counters to monitor. Be sure the Show Description check box is selected to view a helpful description of the counters as you browse through them. This is shown in Figure 14-37.

Reliability Monitor   The Reliability Monitor provides an overview of your system's stability and details events that affect system reliability. You are presented with a stability index, which is calculated over the lifetime of the system based on daily measures that are displayed in a graph on the main pane.

The index is an integer that ranges between 1 and 10, where 10 means that the system was most stable. The daily index is a weighted measure derived from the number of specified failures seen over a rolling historical period. Reliability events in the system stability report describe the specific failures. This is shown in Figure 14-38.

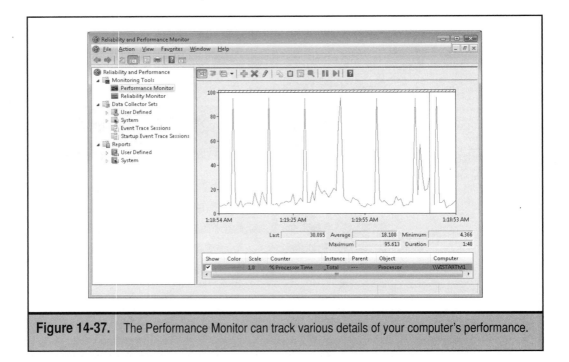

Figure 14-37.   The Performance Monitor can track various details of your computer's performance.

USING LOCAL AND GROUP POLICIES

Vista improves upon an already invaluable administration tool with a new implementation of Group Policies. Active Directory Group Policies are an administration tool for managing configuration settings for both users and computers. Administrators can specify settings, or policies, that can be applied to all computers and users or to a subset defined by you. Group Policy settings govern the behavior of services, applications, and operating system components. Group Policies are stored on domain controllers and distributed by them, which makes them resilient and easy to deploy across your environment. The benefits of using Group Policies to set configuration is a long list, so here we include an abridged version. Chief features of using policy-based configurations include the following:

▼   Set configurations covering the full range of desktop and network settings, including Internet Explorer, internetworking, printers, power management, and more

■   They are centrally managed from Active Directory.

■   Resilient distribution technology (multimaster synchronization using domain controllers)

■   Applied to users and computers based on criteria you establish

■   Use policies to enable or restrict user authorization for access to local and network resources

▲   Manage applications centrally, installing or disabling them

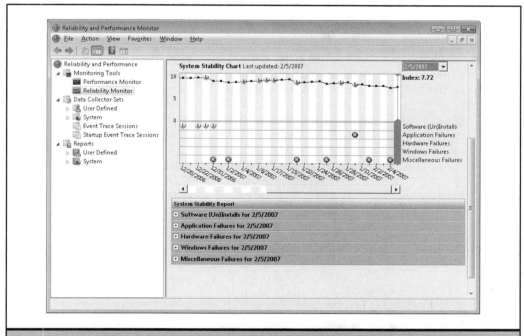

Figure 14-38. The Reliability Monitor tracks system reliability based on hardware and software performance.

Group Policies can be managed using a number of free and fee-based tools. Table 14-6 lists some of the available options.

Local Policies use the same technology to offer many of the same configuration management features found in Group Policies, though they apply to only the local computer and logged on users, and are not centrally managed using Active Directory. Local Group Policy Objectives (LGPOs) contain fewer policy settings than domain-based Group Policy Objects (GPOs), particularly security settings. LGPOs do not support folder redirection, Remote Installation Services, or Group Policy software installation when they are configured as standalone client computers, but you can use them to provide a secure operating environment on such computers.

Multiple Local Group Policy Objects

Multiple Local Group Policy objects (MLGPOs) is a new feature included in Vista that improves upon previous Local Group Policy technology. MLGPOs allow you to apply different configuration policies (LGPOs) to users. This can be especially handy for shared computing environments where domain-based management is not available, such as shared library computers and public Internet kiosks. It can be a great time saver, too, for notebook computers when you need one LGPO for a standard user and another for an administrator.

Name	Description	Location
Group Policy Management Console (GPMC) v2	GPMC is a scriptable MMC snap-in that provides a single administrative tool for managing Group Policy across the enterprise. The GPMC can back up and restore your policies, and is highly scriptable. It is integrated directly into Vista and is available as a download for Windows XP and Windows Server 2003.	Type **gpmc.msc** in the Search field from the Start menu, and press ENTER. Follow this link for more information on using GPMC: www.microsoft .com/downloads/details .aspx?familyid=D8291B79- 922A-439C-88E9-54041A295 3DD&displaylang=en
Group Policy Object Editor	An MMC snap-in used for configuring and modifying Group Policy settings within a single Group Policy object (GPO). It is the default tool for editing Local Group Policy objects (LGPOs). Like the GPMC, this tool is integrated into Vista and is available as a separate download for Windows XP and Windows Server 2003.	Type **gpedit.msc** to the Search field from the Start menu, and press ENTER.
Advanced Group Policy Management (AGPM) tool, formerly GPOVault	In 2007, GPOVault Enterprise from DesktopStandard will be transformed into AGPM, part of the Microsoft Desktop Optimization Pack. It integrates enhanced Group Policy management features into the GPMC, adding comprehensive change control, offline editing, role-based delegation, difference reporting, and GPO templates	Microsoft Desktop Optimization Pack

Table 14-6. Policy Management Tools for Configuring Users, Applications, and Computers

Name	Description	Location
Group Policy Inventory (GPInventory)	Group Policy Inventory (GPInventory.exe) allows administrators to collect Group Policy and other information from any number of computers in their network by running multiple Resultant Set of User Policy (RSOP) or WMI queries. The query results can be exported to either an XML or a text file, and can be analyzed in Excel.	www.microsoft.com/downloads/details.aspx?familyid=1D24563D-CAC9-4017-AF14-8DD686A96540&displaylang=en
ADMX Migrator	A snap-in for the MMC that simplifies the process of converting your existing Group Policy ADM templates to the new ADMX format and provides a graphical user interface for creating and editing administrative templates.	Download from the Microsoft Downloads page (www.microsoft.com/downloads) or directly (www.microsoft.com/downloads/details.aspx?familyid=0F1EEC3D-10C4-4B5F-9625-97C2F731090C&mg_id=10050&displaylang=en)
Group Policy Log View	A utility you use to export Group Policy event data from the system and operational log into a text, Hypertext Markup Language (HTML), or XML file.	Download from the Microsoft Downloads page (www.microsoft.com/downloads) or directly (www.microsoft.com/downloads/details.aspx?familyid=0F1EEC3D-10C4-4B5F-9625-97C2F731090C&mg_id=10050&displaylang=en)
Group Policy Manager from Quest	Group Policy Manager augments the GPMC with GPO version control, offline editing, change notification and approval, and more	www.quest.com/active_directory/

Table 14-6.   Policy Management Tools for Configuring Users, Applications, and Computers *(Continued)*

Name	Description	Location
	to give you control of Group Policy across your enterprise.	
Group Policy Extensions for Desktops from Quest	Group Policy Extensions for Desktops allows desktop administrators to remotely manage Outlook profiles and reconfigure desktop settings through Group Policy extensions. This product extends Group Policy substantially.	www.quest.com/active_ directory/
GPOADmin from NetPro	GPOADmin enhances Vista's GPMC, providing significant version control capabilities, as well as a robust GPO comparison feature, including complete comparisons between GPOs over time and GPO versions both within and across domains. It also features GPO lock capabilities to prevent unwanted changes, a GPO cloak feature designed to hide and protect pre-production GPOs, check-in/ check-out for secure editing, advanced searching and reporting, and GPO backup and link restoration.	www.netpro.com/ products/gpoadmin/
Group Policy Guardian from NetIQ	NetIQ's Group Policy Guardian helps reduce risks associated with GPO change management and provides the visibility you	www.netiq.com/products/ gpg/

Table 14-6. Policy Management Tools for Configuring Users, Applications, and Computers *(Continued)*

Name	Description	Location
	need to help protect your Windows infrastructure from security exposures and service disruptions.	
Group Policy Administrator from NetIQ	NetIQ's Group Policy Administrator assists in planning, managing, troubleshooting, and reporting on Group Policies.	www.netiq.com/products/gpa/

Table 14-6. Policy Management Tools for Configuring Users, Applications, and Computers *(Continued)*

New Administrative Templates

Vista introduces a new template format for managing policy-based configuration settings. The Group Policy Administrative Templates, known as ADM files, are now XML-based files that use the ADMX file extension and have a richer feature set.

These new files replace ADM files, which used their own markup language. The Group Policy tools—Group Policy Object Editor and Group Policy Management Console—remain largely unchanged. Group Policy tools will continue to recognize custom ADM files you have in your existing environment, but will ignore any ADM file that has been superseded by ADMX files, including:

▼ System.adm

■ Inetres.adm

■ Conf.adm

■ Wmplayer.adm

▲ Wuau.adm

If you have edited any of these files to modify existing settings or created new policy settings, the settings will not be read or displayed in the Vista-based Group Policy tools.

ADMX files are not stored in individual GPOs, unlike ADM files. Administrators can create a central store location of ADMX files. The store is accessible by anyone with permission to create or edit GPOs. The Group Policy Object Editor automatically reads and displays Administrative Template policy settings from ADMX files that are stored either locally or in the ADMX central store. Important facets of ADMX files include the following:

▼ The Group Policy Object Editor will automatically read and display Administrative Template policy settings from custom ADM files stored in the GPO.

■ You can still add or remove custom ADM files with the Add/Remove Template menu option.

■ New Vista settings can be managed only from Vista-based or Windows Server "Longhorn"–based administrative computers running Group Policy Object Editor or Group Policy Management Console. Such policy settings are defined only in ADMX files and are not exposed on previous operating systems.

■ The reporting function of GPMC on Windows Server 2003 and Windows XP will display new Vista Administrative Template policy settings as extra registry settings.

■ The Vista version of Group Policy Object Editor and Group Policy Management Console can be used to manage all operating systems that support Group Policy (Vista, Windows Server "Longhorn," Windows Server 2003, Windows XP, and Windows 2000).

■ Administrative Template policy settings that are part of ADM files from Windows Server 2003, Windows XP, and Windows 2000 can be configured from all operating systems that support Group Policy (Vista, Windows Server "Longhorn," Windows Server 2003, Windows XP, and Windows 2000).

■ The Vista version of Group Policy Object Editor and Group Policy Management Console support interoperability with versions of these tools on Windows Server 2003 and Windows XP. Custom ADM files stored in GPOs will be consumed by Group Policy Object Editor and GPMC on Vista, Windows Server "Longhorn," Windows Server 2003, and Windows XP.

▲ The Vista version of Group Policy Object Editor supports interoperability with versions of Group Policy Object Editor on Windows Server 2000. Custom ADM files stored in GPOs will be consumed by Group Policy Object Editor on Vista, Windows Server "Longhorn," and Windows 2000.

Ultimately, the devil, as they say, is in the details. There are an abundance of details in Microsoft Vista, and if you can master them—or at least understand what they do—you will have excellent control over the management of your system.

But what happens when things just don't go right? That's when you need to start troubleshooting. We'll finish our look at Microsoft Vista in the next chapter, dedicated to troubleshooting problems with Vista.

CHAPTER 15

Troubleshooting

I n the future, we'll drive flying cars. There will be no disease. Fast food will be the best way to lose weight and stay healthy. And while we're at it, man will live in harmony with his fellow man, and computer books won't need chapters on troubleshooting.

But wait…it seems that the future is not quite yet upon us. So until that utopian time, we still have to figure out how to fix our computers, and we still have to write chapters on troubleshooting.

Troubleshooting at its simplest involves the tried and true "reboot process." It seems that a great many errors result from a unique scenario and can be resolved by restarting an application or by restarting Vista. After a reboot, the error goes away. However, we have all encountered other, more persistent errors. These are the ones that come back after a reboot with the intention of staying for a while. So let's start with a few general steps that may help eliminate a persistent error:

1. Install the latest updates from Microsoft for Vista, using the Windows Update or Microsoft Update feature.

2. Install the latest service packs and patches from software vendors.

3. Install the latest device drivers from hardware vendors.

4. Install the latest firmware on hardware that has firmware (e.g., hard disk drives).

5. Update the motherboard Basic Input Output System (BIOS) to the latest version.

6. Make sure that you have enough memory or random access memory (RAM) installed for both Vista and the applications you wish to run.

7. Make sure that your hard disk drives are not full or nearly full. Vista needs around 25 percent free space on the system volume to run properly.

8. If the issue first occurred recently, consider restoring to a previous restore point to undue any system changes that may have caused the issue.

If these steps don't cure the problem, there are a number of tools available and other steps to take. In this chapter we'll talk about troubleshooting in general and trouble-shooting Vista in particular. From alerting you to a problem to fixing the problem all on its own, Vista has a broad set of features designed to help. This chapter covers a variety of common troubleshooting scenarios.

BUILT-IN DIAGNOSTICS

It's nice to have logs and such to check in on and see if there is a problem with your computer, but wouldn't it be nice if your operating system would just tell you when there's a problem? In Vista, this is a reality. Built-in diagnostics keep you informed when Vista encounters trouble with hardware, system performance, memory, and the network.

The system is remarkably automated and self-correcting. It will tell you if there's a problem and then help guide you through the process of fixing it.

Built-in diagnostics can identify and help fix such issues as:

▼ Hardware errors

■ Failing disks

■ Subpar performance

■ Memory problems

▲ Driver issues

Do these diagnostics work? They sure do. While preparing this book, one of our computers had a sketchy hard drive. Vista kept popping up messages, like the one in Figure 15-1, warning about the drive's impending failure. Sure enough, after a few days, the drive failed.

This section looks at Vista's built-in diagnostics and explains how you can use them to prevent your own loss of data and maybe even a hard drive or two.

Hardware, Performance, and Memory Diagnostics

The core of Vista's self-correcting architecture is hardware, memory, and performance diagnostics:

▼ **Hardware diagnostics**   Will detect error conditions and either repair the problem automatically or notify the user, walking them through the corrective actions. If a drive is suspected of failing, the user is walked through the backup procedure. An example of the sorts of help Vista offers in this regard is shown in Figure 15-2.

■ **Performance diagnostics**   Will detect problems with a slow application startup, slow booting, and network delays. These diagnostics can automatically

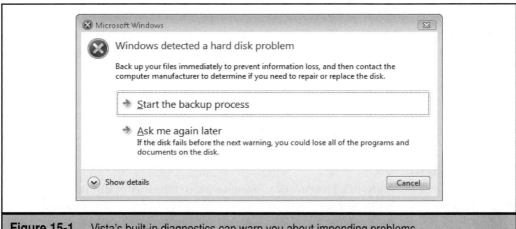

Figure 15-1.   Vista's built-in diagnostics can warn you about impending problems.

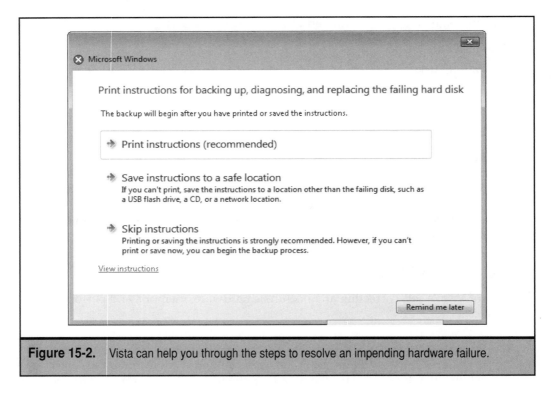

Figure 15-2.   Vista can help you through the steps to resolve an impending hardware failure.

tune your system's performance. In addition, Vista includes a new Performance console that offers more information and expanded performance counters than earlier versions of Windows.

▲ **Memory diagnostics**   Will detect problems with memory leaks and failing memory. These diagnostics work in tandem with the Microsoft Online Crash Analysis tool to prevent system crashes that would be caused by failing memory.

All built-in diagnostic scenarios are recorded in the event log. The log provides a record of built-in diagnoses that have been repaired and gives information as to how to resolve problems that can't automatically be resolved. Figure 15-3 shows a log entry from Event Viewer.

The log provides a record of problems that the built-in diagnostics have automatically repaired and also provides information for IT professionals to help them solve problems that can't be resolved automatically.

Network Diagnostics

We talked about the Network Diagnostics Framework in Chapter 5, but it bears repeating here. This framework allows Vista to examine and fix networking problems. It is managed with the Windows Network Diagnostics tool, which can be started by doing the following:

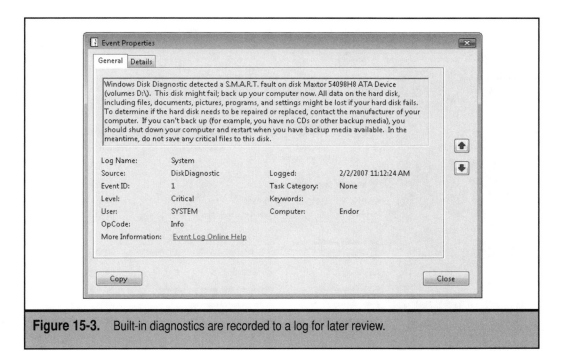

Figure 15-3.   Built-in diagnostics are recorded to a log for later review.

1. Click Start.

2. Click Control Panel.

3. In Control Panel, under the Network And Internet heading, click View Network Status And Tasks. This is shown in Figure 15-4.

4. Click Diagnose And Repair in the left pane to begin diagnosing the problem.

The result, shown in Figure 15-5, will tell you about the problems that are occurring and offer some suggestions for its repair.

HARDWARE PROBLEMS AND DIAGNOSTICS

Identifying and resolving hardware problems can be much easier in Vista than in previous Microsoft operating systems. If you think about it, there are two types of hardware problems: configuration issues and physical failures. To resolve physical failures, you will often replace the failing component. Configuration issues are a different matter. Greatly improved stability and self-healing features promise to reduce the occurrence of hardware configuration issues, but when they do happen, you have some terrific tools to use.

Event Viewer

Upon discovering an issue or evidence of one, the first step you should take is to view the event logs for an explanation. If a user reports a clicking sound, for example, you can check

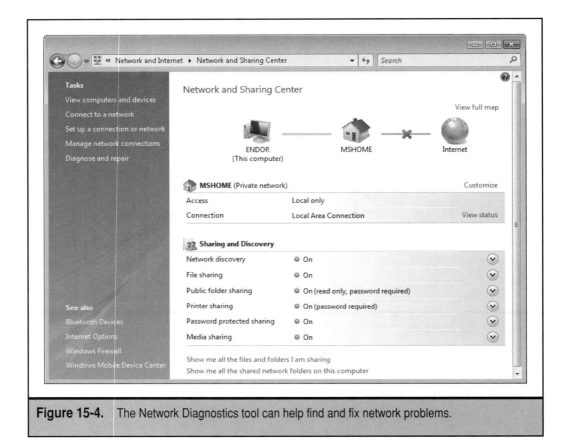

Figure 15-4. The Network Diagnostics tool can help find and fix network problems.

the event logs for failed input/output (I/O) write errors. If I/O write errors were posted, then other helpful data will also be posted, such as which hard disk drive is suffering.

The Vista Event Viewer is enhanced to present a wide array of activities, while also offering the same kinds of events and formats as you may be used to from Windows XP and other Microsoft operating systems. In addition to performance, diagnostics, warning, and information activities, the Event Viewer in Vista offers diagnostic, analytic, and debug activities. These new types of posts hold great promise, but there is a caveat. No activity will be posted unless the vendor who wrote the hardware driver has embedded such tracking in the device driver. If the Hardware Events log is empty, it is not necessarily because there are no hardware events. It could be because the events were sent to the standard logs. The Event Viewer is shown in Figure 15-6.

At least until drivers are updated for Vista, you may have a better chance of finding hardware-related events in the system log, one of the standard logs in the Windows Logs folder. To launch the Event Viewer, launch the Computer Management console, or type **EventVwr.exe** in the Search field from the Start menu and press the ENTER key. For more information about the Event Viewer, see Chapter 14.

545

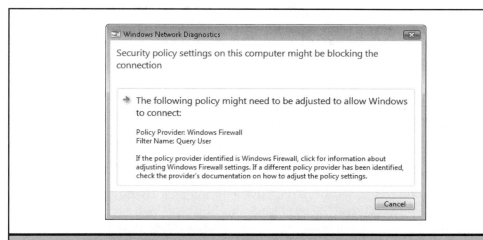

Figure 15-5. The Network Diagnostics tool can offer suggestions to fix a problem.

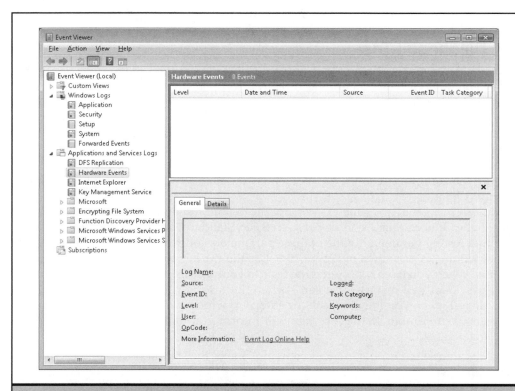

Figure 15-6. The Event Viewer has a special log for hardware events.

Device Manager

Hardware devices are loaded in the Device Manager and can be managed from there. The status of a device is indicated in the Device Manager and can be:

▼   Operating normally

■   Not functioning properly

▲   Disabled

Some details on the Properties dialog box for a device can help you troubleshoot issues you might find. Right-click the device and choose Properties. On the General tab, you will find the device status, and if there is a problem, you will find a result code in some cases. You can use the result code to look up advice using the Internet. There will also be a Find A Solution button, which will send the result code to a Microsoft Web site, where the device and result code will be used to look up advice that Microsoft may have in its database.

Drivers can also be updated, restored to a previous version, reinstalled, or uninstalled to alleviate an operational issue by right-clicking the device and choosing the appropriate option from the context menu. To launch the Device Manager, launch the Computer Management console or type `devmgmt.msc` in the Search field from the Start menu and press the ENTER key. For more information about the Device Manager, see Chapter 14.

Memory Diagnostic Tool

Vista includes a diagnostic tool that tests your installed system memory to verify that each memory module is functioning properly. To open the tool, click the Start menu, and type **memory** or **mdsched.exe** into the Search field, and then press ENTER. Click the Memory Diagnostic Tool as it appears in the pane above the Search field. In the Windows Memory Diagnostic Tool dialog box, shown in Figure 15-7, click Restart Now And Check For Problems if you wish to execute the check immediately, or click Check For Problems The Next Time I Start My Computer if you are not ready to restart the computer.

Once the computer reboots, the tool loads automatically. The running tool is shown in Figure 15-8.

You can press F1 at any time to interrupt the default test and enter the Options menu. While in the Options menu, choose between Basic, Standard, and Extended tests, and provide other testing parameters. One of these parameters controls the number of test passes the tool will make, as shown in Figure 15-9. Use the TAB key to move between testing parameters. When you have configured the tests to your satisfaction, press F10 to continue.

Your system will restart—if it can—when the testing is complete. The results will be displayed when you log on. Look for a pop-up window in the lower-right corner of the screen. With any luck, the message will inform you that "There were no memory problems detected."

Registry Helpers

There are many applications that provide logging options in the registry. To open the Registry Editor, type `regedit` in the Search field from the Start menu, and press ENTER. Be extremely careful when editing the registry, and be sure you have a backup of it before

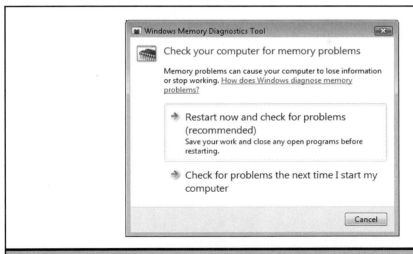

Figure 15-7.   Vista includes the Memory Diagnostic tool to help locate problems with your system's memory.

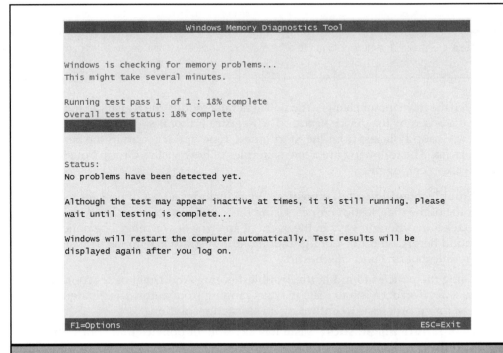

Figure 15-8.   The Memory Diagnostic tool checks your system memory for any issues that might compromise your computer.

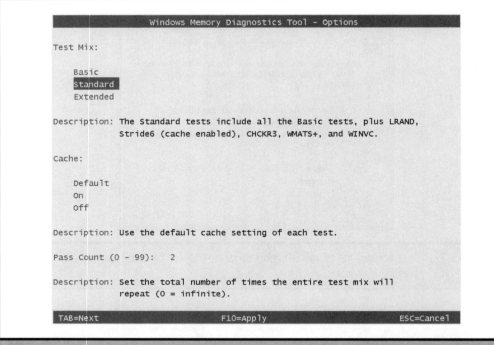

```
              Windows Memory Diagnostics Tool - Options

Test Mix:

    Basic
    Standard
    Extended

Description: The Standard tests include all the Basic tests, plus LRAND,
             Stride6 (cache enabled), CHCKR3, WMATS+, and WINVC.

Cache:

    Default
    On
    Off

Description: Use the default cache setting of each test.

Pass Count (0 - 99):   2

Description: Set the total number of times the entire test mix will
             repeat (0 = infinite).

 TAB=Next                       F10=Apply                    ESC=Cancel
```

Figure 15-9.   The Options menu for the Windows Memory Diagnostic tool allows you to choose which test to run.

making even the most minor change. You will generally modify the registry to improve logging only if advised by the device vendor. The Registry Editor is shown in Figure 15-10.

To view Group Policies, from the Start menu, type gpedit.msc in the Search field, and press ENTER. The following are a few examples of how Vista's Group Policies can affect hardware event logging:

▼   **Troubleshooting and diagnostics**   Vista includes a host of policies that control some of the diagnostic engines. Using these policies, you can instruct Vista to react in different ways in the event of an error or warning. The policies are found here: Computer Configuration\Administrative Templates\System\ Troubleshooting and Diagnostics.

Using the policies found in the Troubleshooting And Diagnostics container, you can instruct Vista to react in ways ranging from automatically detecting and fixing problems to indicating an assisted resolution.

■   **Disk failure diagnostics**   Vista has a couple of policies that control the information displayed by the disk failure diagnostics engine. The two policies allow you to specify custom text for errors and decide whether to advise your users on how to back up their data in the event a disk error is detected.

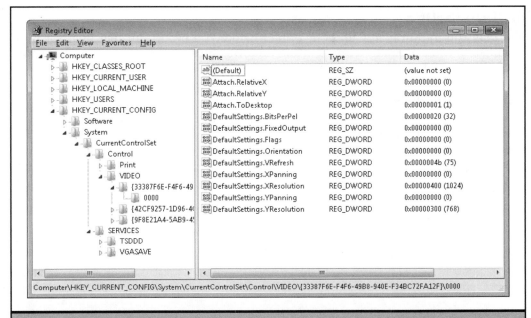

Figure 15-10. You can adjust logging for some applications using the Registry Editor.

The policies are found here: Computer Configuration\Administrative Templates\System\Troubleshooting and Diagnostics\Disk Diagnostics.

▲ **Windows error reporting** Disables Windows Feedback for Windows or for all components. By default, Windows Feedback is turned on for all Windows components. The policy is available in both the User and Computer nodes, found here:

■ Computer Configuration\Administrative Templates\Windows Components\Windows Error Reporting

■ User Configuration\Windows Components\Administrative Templates\ Windows Error Reporting

PRINTING PROBLEMS AND DIAGNOSTICS

As electronic as our lives have become, we still need things printed on paper. Whether it's the quarterly report or a simple correspondence, we need our printers. In this section, we talk about printer problems—from installing them to using them—and then discuss some options for fixing them.

Installation Issues

You may run into trouble with your printer before you even print that first test page. Installation, while normally a breeze with Windows, can sometimes turn into a hurricane. Let's examine different problems you might encounter with printer installation.

Manual Installation

When you try to add a network printer, ideally, Vista will automatically detect it. However, if it does not recognize the printer and give you the option to install it, you can manually install it by following these steps:

1. Click Start.
2. Click Control Panel.
3. Click Hardware And Sound.
4. Click Printers. This is shown in Figure 15-11.
5. Click Add A Printer.

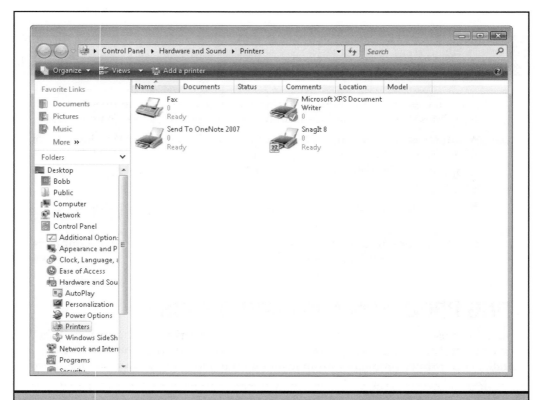

Figure 15-11.   The Printers folder is used for much of your printer troubleshooting.

6. In the Add Printer Wizard, select Add A Network, Wireless, or Bluetooth Printer.

7. On the Choose A Network Printer page, click The Printer That I Want Isn't Listed. The dialog box shown in Figure 15-12 appears.

8. On the Find A Printer By Name Or TCP/IP Address page, indicate how to find the printer, and then click Next.

9. The wizard will present some additional pages. When you're finished, click Finish.

If you are still unable to find your printer, the following sections provide more steps you can try.

Printer Not Listed in the Network Folder

If the printer you want to add is not listed in the Network folder, check to make sure that your network is working properly. If, however, there's nothing wrong with the network, check these issues:

▼   If you are connected to a domain, ensure that you are logged on with the correct permissions to access that domain's resources. The permissions you're logged on with might not allow you to access the printer to which you want to connect.

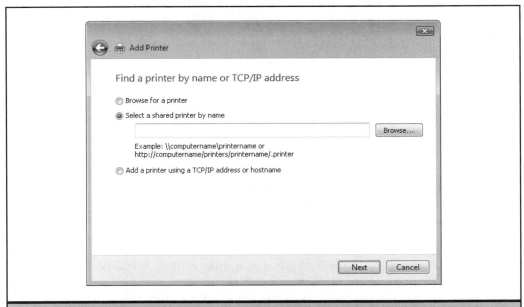

Figure 15-12.   You can specify a printer's name or Transmission Control Protocol/Internet Protocol (TCP/IP) address if Vista doesn't automatically detect it.

▲ If the printer is plugged into another computer on the network, make sure that computer is powered up. Check also to see if that computer user has changed the name of the printer.

Wireless Issues

If you're having trouble locating a Bluetooth-connected printer, make sure that the Bluetooth adapter to the computer is plugged in and turned on. Also, check to make sure that the Bluetooth printer is turned on. Try removing your connection to the Bluetooth printer and then using the Add Printer Wizard again.

Printing Problems

Once you get your printer installed and working properly, there may come a time when it simply ceases to work correctly. Perhaps the printer just suddenly stopped working for no apparent reason, or it failed to print right after a seemingly unrelated change in configuration.

New Problems

If the printer is installed properly and you've used it in the past with no problems, check these issues:

▼ Make sure that the network is working properly and that your computer is connected to the network.

■ Check the status of the printer in the print queue.

■ Ensure that the printer is turned on. Does it have any maintenance issues, like low toner or paper?

■ If the printer is plugged into another computer on the network, make sure that computer is turned on.

▲ If your printer was added to the network using a TCP/IP address instead of a name, ensure that the computer is connected to the Internet or the network where the printer is installed. If you've recently had a power outage, the printer's TCP/IP address might have changed. In that event, try to add the printer again.

New Configuration

If you just upgraded to Windows Vista from Windows XP or changed the printer driver, then you have a good idea what the culprit probably is. The best fix for this is to make sure that your printer driver is compatible with Vista.

Microsoft tries to put as many drivers for as many peripherals as they can in Vista. The driver you need may already be on your computer, waiting to be installed. However, sometimes, a driver you need isn't included. These drivers might be available through Windows Update, or they might be available through the printer manufacturer, either on a CD or DVD that came with the device or through the manufacturer's Web site.

Update via the Printers Folder   The first place to look for the right driver is right on your computer. It may already be located there, just not installed. To check your computer for the driver:

1. Open the Printers folder.
2. Right-click the printer for which you want to install a new driver. Select Run As Administrator, and then click Properties.
3. Select the Advanced tab.
4. Click New Driver and then follow the steps in the Add Printer Driver Wizard.

From the Manufacturer   Because Vista is a new operating system and, depending on what brand of printer you have, you might need to get the driver directly from the manufacturer.

Go to the manufacturer's Web site, and search for a printer driver that is compatible with Windows Vista. Once you've downloaded it, see if the manufacturer has any special installation instructions. Some manufacturers have special installers that bypass the Windows printer wizard.

Performance Problems

If the printer is installed, recognized by Vista, and printing, now we wander into the realm of performance problems. Many little things can go wrong with a printer that is really out of the purview of this chapter. For example, if the printer is out of paper, then you probably don't need us to tell you to add more paper. But who hasn't been stymied by that at least once? Go ahead and check the paper tray anyway.

That said, one way to improve a slow printer is to check the print spooler. The print spooler is a little application that temporarily stores print jobs on the computer's hard drive or in memory until the printer is ready to print them. If you've been waiting a long time and see an error message that mentions the print spooler, you might need to restart the Print Spooler service on your computer. To do that, follow these steps:

1. Click Start.
2. Click Control Panel.
3. Click System And Maintenance.
4. Click Administrative Tools.
5. Double-click Services.
6. Right-click the Print Spooler service, and select Properties. This is shown in Figure 15-13.

NOTE   For more information about managing services in Vista, see Chapter 14.

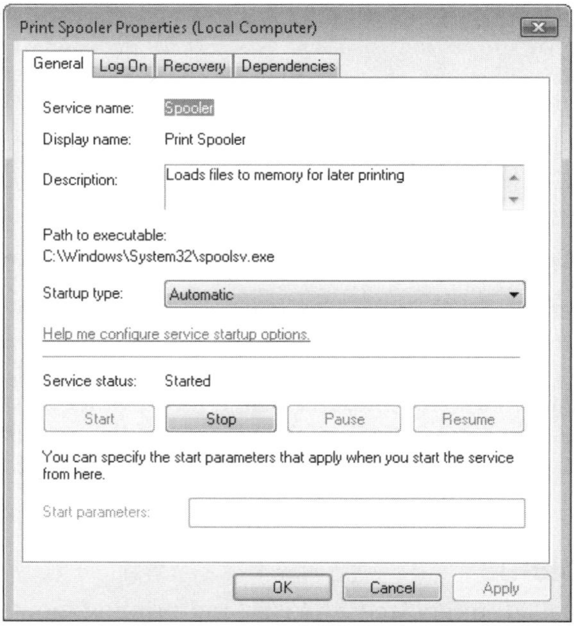

Figure 15-13. The Properties tab of the Print Spooler service is used to manage the service.

7. On the General tab, in the Startup Type drop-down list, select Automatic.

8. If the service is not running, under Service Status, click the Start button, and then click OK.

Printer Permissions

One of the best security practices that an administrator can follow is to not routinely log on to Vista using an administrator account. That is, you should only use your administrator privileges for managing certain parts of Vista that require administrator privileges. The rest of the time you should log on with a more limited user account. However, you should take the administrator privileges out of its sheath long enough to assign printer permissions.

Printer permissions are used to establish which printer properties yourself or your users can manage. Permissions can be managed (locally) by the person who installed the printer or by the network administrator.

Vista includes four types of printer permissions:

▼ **Print** Users have the default permission level that allows them to print and cancel, pause, or restart files that they send to a printer.

- ■ **Manage documents**   This permission allows users to manage all jobs for a printer that are waiting in the print queue, including documents or files that are being printed by other users.
- ■ **Manage printers**   This permission allows users to manage printer preferences, including the ability to rename, delete, and share the printer. This permission is granted by default to members of the administrator group for a computer.
- ▲ **Special permissions**   This permission is normally only used by the system administrator, and is used to change the printer owner.

Permissions are germane to troubleshooting, because a user might be trying to do something he or she is not authorized to do. For example, if the user is trying to move a document to the head of the print queue and cannot do it, there may not be a problem beyond the fact that the user doesn't have the permission to do so.

Print Management

To round out the discussion on printer troubleshooting, let's talk about how you can manage your printers. Solving a problem may be as easy as deleting the file from the print queue and asking the user to resend it.

Starting Print Management

The Print Management tool is part of the Microsoft Management Console (MMC). To start it, you can either type `printmanagement.msc` at the command prompt or you can follow these steps:

1. Click Start.
2. Click Control Panel.
3. Click Administrative Tools.
4. Click Print Management. The tool is shown in Figure 15-14.

Viewing Printers

There are three places where printer information is stored on the Print Management console tree:

- ▼ **Custom Printer Filters**   This file contains the All Printers, Printers Not Ready, and Printers With Jobs objects. If you create your own filter for your printers, it will be contained in this folder as well.
- ■ **Print Servers**   This file contains your network's print servers, all of which are given four objects that serve as filters for the servers' printer information. Those objects are: Drivers, Forms, Ports, and Printers.
- ▲ **Deployed Printers**   This file maintains a list of all the printers located in Print Management that are managed by Group Policy objects.

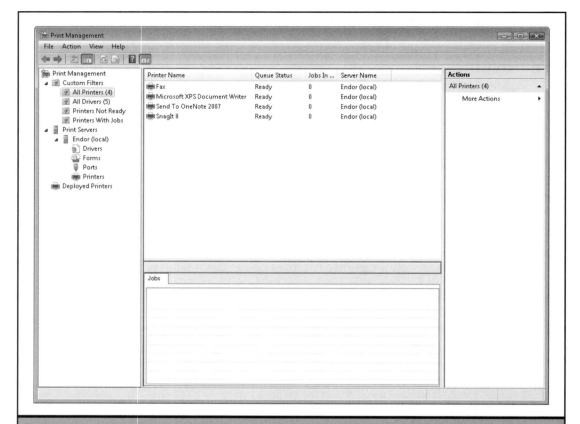

Figure 15-14.   The Print Management tool is used to manage your local and network printers.

Offline Print Servers

You can easily tell if a print server goes offline, because the server's icon will change and "(Offline)" is added to the end of the server name. Also, all the printers on that server will be hidden from view until the server comes back online.

Details

When you click a printer, its details are listed in the Jobs pane of the console, like the one shown in Figure 15-15.

NOTE   In Figure 15-15, extended view has been selected to show more details.

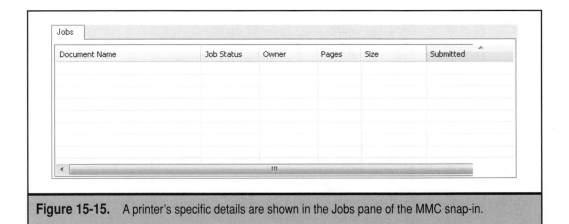

Figure 15-15.   A printer's specific details are shown in the Jobs pane of the MMC snap-in.

Displayed are such details as:

▼   Printer name

■   Queue status

■   Jobs in queue

▲   Server name

The snap-in allows you to add and remove columns to show the characteristics you want to see. You can also filter among the print servers in your organization to show only printers with the characteristics you're looking for.

When you double-click a printer, more details are displayed, as shown in Figure 15-16, that allow more granular management of your printer.

RECOVERING FROZEN APPLICATIONS

Mac guys out there love to snicker and laugh whenever a Windows application freezes up. You know what, though? It happens to everyone. But to Microsoft's credit, they've developed different ways to minimize the deleterious effects of an application freeze.

This section talks about frozen applications and what you can do, in part, to reduce lost time thanks to a noncooperative application.

Release and Recovery

In earlier versions of Windows, when you would run out of virtual memory, you'd be told of the impending problem, but Windows wouldn't do anything more to avoid trouble. Windows Vista, on the other hand, tries to avoid the problem of unresponsive applications by using the Restart Manager.

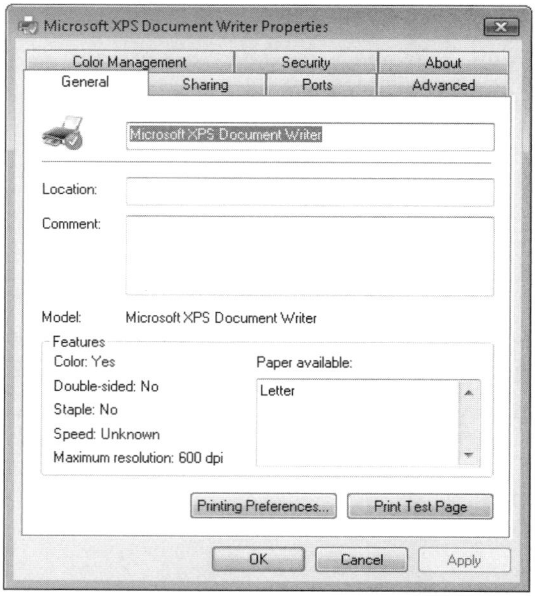

Figure 15-16. Double-clicking a printer displays a detailed listing of your printer and its properties.

The Restart Manager is able to shut down and restart unresponsive applications. While the application has still failed, you're spared the time drain of having to get involved, log out, or even restart the computer.

To help avoid running out of virtual memory, Vista employs the Resource Exhaustion Detection And Recovery system. This monitors your system's virtual memory and warns you when you're running low. While this is what earlier versions of Windows did, Vista goes an extra step and tells you what processes are using the most memory. At this point, you can close applications using the Close Programs To Prevent Information Loss dialog box.

The exhaustion of system resources is also logged to the system event log, that can be reviewed later.

Terminating Frozen Applications

If the worst does happen and the application does freeze, you can use the Task Manager to terminate a nonresponsive application.

Conventionally, you can start the Task Manager by pressing CTRL+ALT+DELETE and then clicking Task Manager. Alternatively, you can right-click the taskbar, and select Task Manager. You can also open a command prompt window and type taskmgr.

When the Task Manager, shown in Figure 15-17, starts, locate and select the application that is not responding, and click End Task.

Ideally, that will end the frozen program and free up its resources for your system.

Figure 15-17. The Task Manager can help you stop an unresponsive application.

Stopping Services or Processes

In a perfect world, Vista will keep all your programs running smoothly. Plan B is to use the Task Manager to stop an unresponsive application. But if even that doesn't stop an errant program, there's another step you can take.

While still in the Task Manager, click the Processes tab. This is shown in Figure 15-18. Examine the processes and look for the one that is causing trouble. For example, if you are having problems with an open Word document, look for "winword.exe." Highlight it and then click End Process.

A Task Manager Warning dialog box, saying "Terminating a process can cause undesired results, including loss of data and system instability. The process will not be given the chance to save its state or data before it is terminated. Are you sure you want to terminate the process?" will appear. Confirm the process by clicking OK or End Now.

Advanced Boot Options

Every so often, the installation of a device causes Windows Vista to crash (thus, Microsoft's Device Driver Approval Program). If you've fallen victim to this, you can use Windows Vista's Advanced Boot Options to restart Vista, ferret out the problem, and eliminate it.

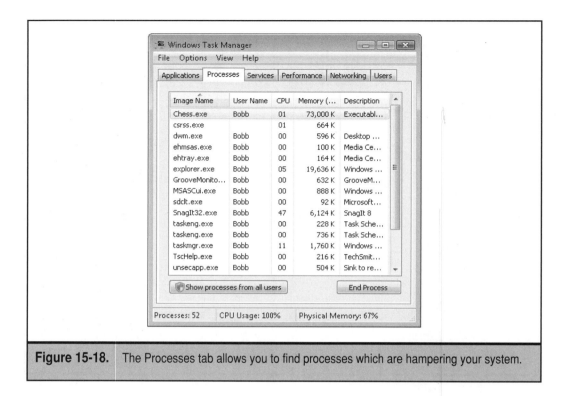

Figure 15-18. The Processes tab allows you to find processes which are hampering your system.

Advanced Boot Options give you a number of different ways to restart Vista. Some options, like Safe Mode, start Windows in a limited state, where you only have the bare essentials to run the computer. If the problem does not reappear, you can rule out default settings and device drivers as the source of the problem. Other options start Windows with advanced features that you can use to solve your problem. Safe Mode, for instance, is shown in Figure 15-19.

In prior versions, the Advanced Boot Options were known as "Safe Mode," but Vista has a more robust suite of tools that you can use. Advanced Boot Options can be entered by pressing F8 during bootup. Vista's Advanced Boot Options are as follows:

▼ **Safe Mode** Starts Vista with minimal drivers (mouse, monitor, keyboard, mass storage, and default system services) and in Video Graphics Array (VGA) mode.

■ **Safe Mode With Networking** Starts Vista in Safe Mode, but allows network connectivity.

■ **Safe Mode With Command Prompt** Starts Vista in Safe Mode, but instead of a traditional desktop, a command prompt is displayed.

■ **Enable Boot Logging** Starts Vista and logs all drivers and services that were or were not loaded. The list is saved in a file called ntblog.txt, located in the C:\Windows directory.

Figure 15-19. Starting Vista in Safe Mode uses a minimal amount of drivers so that you can locate the source of problems.

- **Enable Low Resolution Video (640 × 480)**   Starts Vista with a basic VGA driver. This option allows users to repair their system if they install a video driver improperly.

- **Last Known Good Configuration (Advanced)**   Starts Vista using the registry information from the last time that the system loaded properly. This mode does not repair anything, and changes made since it was last loaded will be lost.

- **Directory Services Restore Mode**   Starts Windows domain controller running Active Directory so that directory services can be restored.

- **Debugging Mode**   Starts Vista while sending debugging information via a serial cable to another computer.

- **Disable Automatic Restart On System Failure**   Stops Vista from automatically restarting if an error causes a crash.

- **Disable Driver Signature Enforcement**   Allows drivers that have not been approved by Microsoft to be installed.

- ▲ **Start Windows Normally**   This starts Windows normally.

Troubleshooting Services

Vista uses many different services, and quite often, you may want to enable or disable them for the purposes of troubleshooting. Some services are installed by default, while others must be added later through Control Panel.

Services can be managed using the Services snap-in located under Administrative Tools on the Start menu. This console allows you to start, stop, pause, resume, disable, and review service status. You can also have the computer restart if a particular service fails to start.

To install additional services:

1. Click Start.
2. Click Control Panel.
3. Click Programs and then click Programs and Features.
4. From the list of tasks, click Turn Windows Features On or Off.
5. Select the check box beside the service you want to install, and click OK.

To disable a given service, use the Services applet. To disable a service:

1. Click Start.
2. Click All Programs.
3. Click Administrative Tools.
4. Click Services.
5. In the list of services, shown in Figure 15-20, double-click the one you want to disable.
6. In the General tab, click the arrow by the Startup Type option, and select Disabled.
7. Click OK.

NOTE   Remember, disabling a service does not uninstall it.

If the service fails, you can tell Vista how it should respond. Clicking the Recovery tab, as shown in Figure 15-21, presents you with different options as to how the service should behave.

Task Scheduler

Windows Vista allows you to perform services in response to events or system state changes, or simply on a schedule that you establish. This functionality was present in earlier versions of Windows, but Vista brings a new level of utility and usefulness.

Task Scheduler is useful, because when events occur, you can automatically set up Vista to respond, thus minimizing problems. You can configure your computers to react

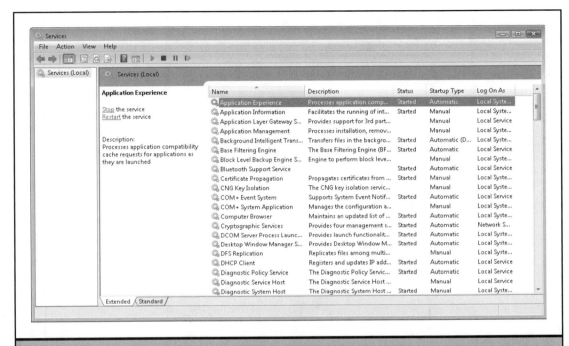

Figure 15-20.   Locate the service you want to disable in the Services applet.

to problems that may be hard to reproduce, and you can also set up complex tasks to run in response to multiple triggers. You can also configure Vista to send you an e-mail when an event is triggered.

Task Scheduler, which was a standalone application in earlier versions of Windows, is now a snap-in for the MMC. While it provides the core functionality of being able to schedule an event, it is also able to react to more complex issues. It is able to respond this way because of a host of improvements.

Triggers

Tasks can be triggered by any event captured in the event log. This allows you to send an e-mail or launch an application automatically when an event occurs. Tasks can be set up to launch when an event occurs using the Create Basic Task Wizard, shown in Figure 15-22.

Other triggers include:

▼   The computer being idle

■   At startup

■   User logon

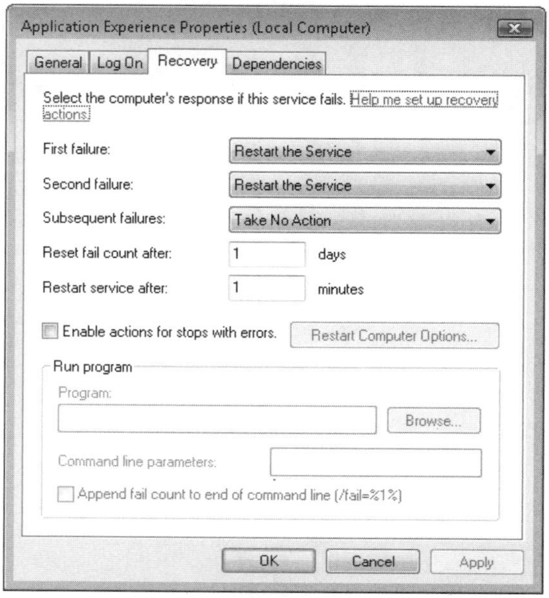

Figure 15-21. The Recovery tab gives additional options for managing a given service.

- ■ Terminal Service connect or disconnect
- ▲ Workstation lock and unlock

A delay can also be added to a trigger, or it can be set so the trigger must occur a certain number of times. The controls available for creating and managing triggers are shown in Figure 15-23.

Conditions and Settings

Conditions are used to restrict a task to run if the computer is in a given state. In Vista, new conditions are based on the idle state of the computer, network connectivity, and the computer power source. Figure 15-24 shows the dialog box for setting conditions.

If a task fails to run correctly, settings can be used to tell Task Scheduler what to do. Settings include:

- ▼ The number of times to retry a task
- ■ If the computer is not powered on when the task was scheduled, it can be set to retry when the power is on
- ▲ The maximum execution time for the task

Figure 15-25 shows the Settings tab and the execution options.

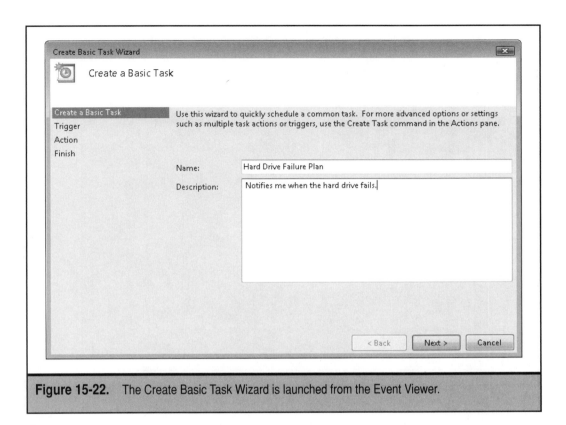

Figure 15-22. The Create Basic Task Wizard is launched from the Event Viewer.

Multiple Triggers and Actions

Vista allows multiple triggers to be attached to a task. For instance, an error condition might be present only if two separate events occur. The administrator can define the task that will launch when these events occur.

Task Scheduler can also launch multiple events when a single trigger occurs. Operations can be performed in synchronization or by chaining the events. For example, you could set up Task Scheduler to check a disk for errors, clean the disk, compress the files, and back up the disk. These events can all be performed using a single task.

Figure 15-26 shows how multiple actions can be defined for a single task.

PROBLEM REPORTING AND ASSISTANCE

In Windows XP, if you had a problem, like a crashed application, Windows would offer to generate a report to be sent back to Redmond for analysis. Don't trick yourself into believing Microsoft had a room full of people analyzing each and every crash message that came back to them, but they would take a look at the issues, add them to a database, and presumably use the information to patch and improve the operating system.

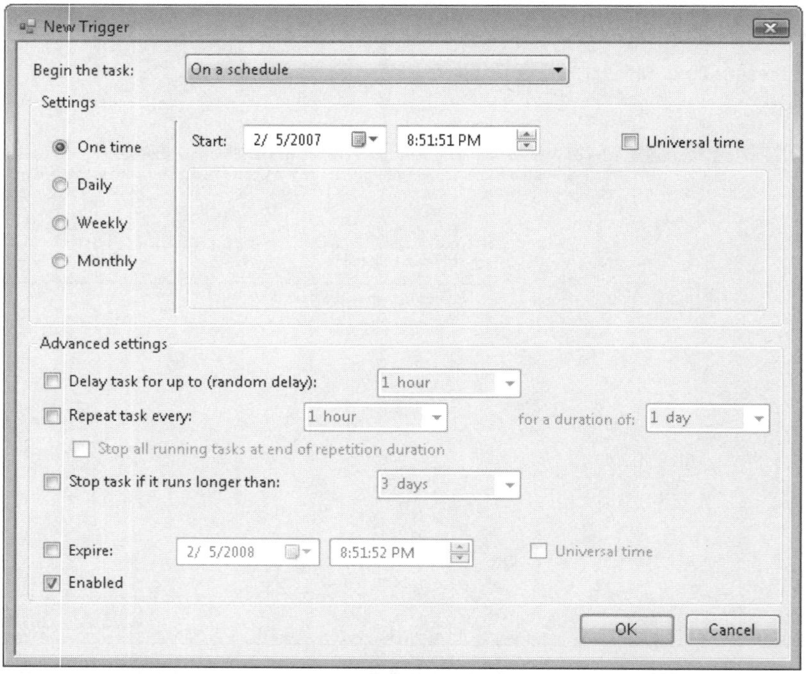

Figure 15-23. Administrators can use advanced options to tweak their triggers.

In this section, we'll examine the tools that you can use to report your problem to Microsoft. Will you get immediate help with the problem? Maybe, maybe not. It depends on the problem. But the best way to see if Microsoft can help you is to send in your report and hope for the best.

Problem Reports and Solutions

A new tool in Vista is the Problem Reports And Solutions tool. It is the Vista replacement of the venerable Windows Dr. Watson tool. Problem Reports And Solutions helps you check your computer for hardware and software problems, and then helps you find solutions for those problems.

Vista can be set to report problems and check for solutions automatically, or you can choose to check for solutions when a problem arises. Problems and their solutions are saved, so you can go back and check them any time.

The Problem Reports And Solutions tool is shown in Figure 15-27.

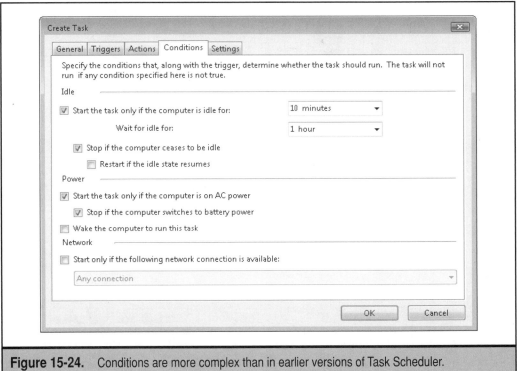

Figure 15-24.   Conditions are more complex than in earlier versions of Task Scheduler.

Privacy

You don't have to send any information to Microsoft when a problem occurs. It's advantageous, but if you worry that Microsoft is culling information about your organization or your users, then simply elect not to send information back to them.

When a problem does occur and a problem report is generated, the following information is included:

▼   Program name

■   Date and time of the problem

▲   The version of the program that encountered the problem

Once a report is sent to Microsoft, you'll be told if a solution is available. If there is not a solution available, Microsoft might ask you for more information about the problem to help develop a solution. For example, you might be asked about files or parts of files that can help identify the problem or explain what it did to your computer.

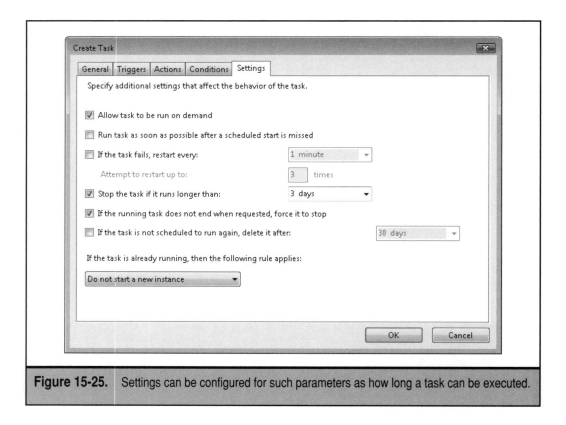

Figure 15-25. Settings can be configured for such parameters as how long a task can be executed.

Problem Reports

If a problem report is generated, it will contain information about your system and what was going on before the problem occurred. You can view the contents of a problem report before it is sent, if you like. If you've had a problem and Vista generates a problem report, click the View Problem Details button to examine the contents of the report.

Vista also maintains a historical record of your computer's problems. To go back later and check out the contents of problem reports:

1. Click the Start button.
2. Click Control Panel.
3. Click System And Maintenance
4. Click Problem Reports And Solutions.
5. In the left pane, click View Problem History.
6. Double-click the problem you want to examine. An example problem report is shown in Figure 15-28.

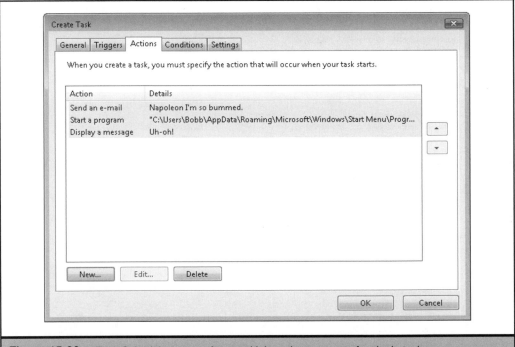

Figure 15-26.   Task Scheduler can perform multiple actions as part of a single task.

Solutions

Vista checks for solutions to problems in a couple of ways. Let's take a closer look at how you can get help when a problem is detected.

Automatically Checking

The easiest way to check for solutions is to have Vista automatically check for solutions. If a program stops working, Vista can automatically send a report of the problem and check for a solution. To configure Vista to do that:

1. Click the Start button.
2. Click Control Panel.
3. Click System And Maintenance
4. Click Problem Reports And Solutions.
5. In the left pane, click Change Settings.
6. Select Check For Solutions Automatically (Recommended).
7. Click OK.

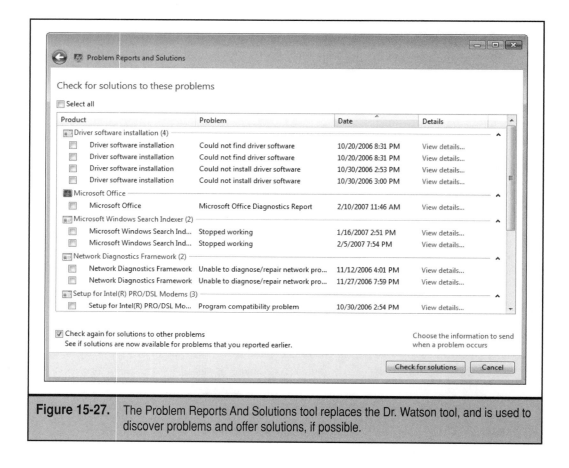

Figure 15-27. The Problem Reports And Solutions tool replaces the Dr. Watson tool, and is used to discover problems and offer solutions, if possible.

If a problem does arise, this will automatically prepare a problem report. If a solution is available, you'll be notified.

Manually Checking

If you elect not to automatically check for solutions, or if you've missed the notification and want to view it later, Vista maintains a library of your computer's problems and available solutions. To view them:

1. Click the Start button.
2. Click Control Panel.
3. Click System And Maintenance
4. Click Problem Reports And Solutions.
5. To view a solution, click the solution's title.

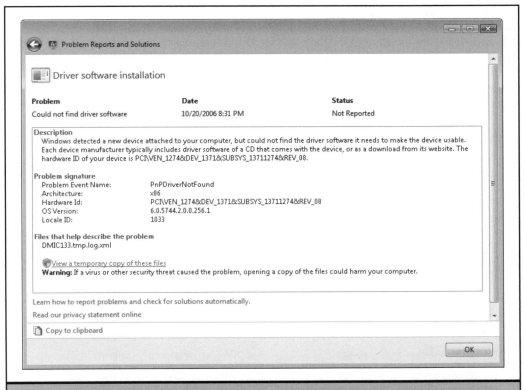

Figure 15-28.   Problem reports can be sent to Microsoft, and if a solution exists, Microsoft will share it with you.

NOTE   You can right-click a solution to see more options for working with it.

STOP ERRORS AND THE BSOD

Vista is empowered with a special mechanism for protecting itself when it detects a threat to the system kernel. A *stop error* is a failure in the mechanics of Vista itself, one that causes enough trouble to halt the operating system. In contrast, a *runtime error* is one where an application fails. Vista handles stop errors differently from runtime errors. In many cases, runtime errors will be posted to an event log and the application will continue to run, and so will Vista. In some cases, the application will freeze or terminate unexpectedly, but Vista will continue to operate and other applications are not affected. Stop errors, however, will halt Vista and make the computer completely unusable.

When Vista encounters a stop error, it displays a blue screen and shows text messages with a white font. In deference to the severity of a stop error and the poignant blue screen, the errors are known colloquially as "blue screen errors," and the screen itself is known as the dreaded Blue Screen of Death (BSOD). This is shown in Figure 15-29.

To help you manage stop errors, we will first talk about the components of stop errors, and then show you how to tell Vista to handle stop errors. Finally, we'll review some of the common errors and how to solve them.

Composition of a Stop Error

The format of a stop error is consistent, though the content varies, depending on the error. To understand stop errors, take a look at the following sample:

```
STOP 0x000000ED (0xC000000A,0xC0000032,0xC0000501,0xC0000000)
UNMOUNTABLE_BOOT_VOLUME
```

Note that all stop errors begin with the word *stop*. Following the stop notice is the error number and up to four parameters that include more information about the specific error. The details on the stop message are as follows:

```
*** STOP: 0x0000001E (0x80000003,0x80106fc0,0x8025ea21,0xfd6829e8)
Unhandled Kernel exception c0000047 from fa8418b4 (8025ea21,fd6829e8)

Dll Base Date Stamp - Name          Dll Base Date Stamp - Name
80100000 2be154c9 - ntoskrnl.exe    80400000 2bc153b0 - hal.dll
80258000 2bd49628 - ncrc710.sys     8025c000 2bd49688 - SCSIPORT.SYS
80267000 2bd49683 - scsidisk.sys    802a6000 2bd496b9 - Fastfat.sys
fa800000 2bd49666 - Floppy.SYS      fa810000 2bd496db - Hpfs_Rec.SYS
fa820000 2bd49676 - Null.SYS        fa830000 2bd4965a - Beep.SYS
fa840000 2bdaab00 - i8042prt.SYS    fa850000 2bd5a020 - SERMOUSE.SYS
fa860000 2bd4966f - kbdclass.SYS    fa870000 2bd49671 - MOUCLASS.SYS
fa880000 2bd9c0be - Videoprt.SYS    fa890000 2bd49638 - NCC1701E.SYS
fa8a0000 2bd4a4ce - Vga.SYS         fa8b0000 2bd496d0 - Msfs.SYS
fa8c0000 2bd496c3 - Npfs.SYS        fa8e0000 2bd496c9 - Ntfs.SYS
fa940000 2bd496df - NDIS.SYS        fa930000 2bd49707 - wdlan.sys
fa970000 2bd49712 - TDI.SYS         fa950000 2bd5a7fb - nbf.sys
fa980000 2bd72406 - streams.sys     fa9b0000 2bd4975f - ubnb.sys
fa9c0000 2bd5bfd7 - usbser.sys      fa9d0000 2bd4971d - netbios.sys
fa9e0000 2bd49678 - Parallel.sys    fa9f0000 2bd4969f - serial.SYS
faa00000 2bd49739 - mup.sys         faa40000 2bd4971f - SMBTRSUP.SYS
faa10000 2bd6f2a2 - srv.sys         faa50000 2bd4971a - afd.sys
faa60000 2bd6fd80 - rdr.sys         faaa0000 2bd49735 - bowser.sys


Address dword dump Dll Base                                - Name
801afc20 80106fc0 80106fc0 00000000 00000000 80149905 : fa840000 - i8042prt.SYS
801afc24 80149905 80149905 ff8e6b8c 80129c2c ff8e6b94 : 8025c000 - SCSIPORT.SYS
801afc2c 80129c2c 80129c2c ff8e6b94 00000000 ff8e6b94 : 80100000 - ntoskrnl.exe
801afc34 801240f2 801240f2 ff8e6df4 ff8e6f60 ff8e6c58 : 80100000 - ntoskrnl.exe
801afc54 80124f16 80124f16 ff8e6f60 ff8e6c3c 8015ac7e : 80100000 - ntoskrnl.exe
801afc64 8015ac7e 8015ac7e ff8e6df4 ff8e6f60 ff8e6c58 : 80100000 - ntoskrnl.exe
```

Figure 15-29.   Stop errors are fatal events that can be resolved with research.

▼   **Error number**   The text following the stop note includes the error number in an eight-digit hexadecimal number. The error number is commonly written in a shorthand notation, where a STOP 0x0000000A error may also be written as Stop 0xA. The error number is determined by Microsoft. In the preceding example, 0x000000ED is the hexadecimal error number.

■   **Error parameters**   Every stop error is followed by up to four parameters, which are enclosed by parentheses. The parameters, like the error number itself, are in eight-digit hexadecimal form. The parameters' values are unique to the stop situation and the computer.

■   **Symbolic error name**   This is the message that the component of Vista that failed returned. It is also displayed at the bottom of the screen. In our example, the symbolic error name is UNMOUNTABLE_BOOT_VOLUME.

▲   **Troubleshooting recommendations**   Vista gives you a spot of generic advice based on the type of error. You may be told to check the available free disk space, to uninstall hardware, or to update a recently installed driver.

Responding to a stop error should start by allowing Vista to reboot normally. Be sure that all your data and configuration is safely backed up, and then try to reproduce the stop error. Should the stop error occur again, perform the following steps:

▼   **Follow the advice in the stop error**   Though generic, the advice given with the stop error can quickly point you in the right direction.

■   **Research the error**   Search www.microsoft.com, www.google.com, forum .aumha.org/, or your favorite Vista Web site for more information, using both the full and short formats of the error number and the symbolic error name.

■   **Research events**   Comb the event logs for any events related to the crash. Rarely does a stop error occur without some matching events posted to the logs. The additional data can help you identify other hardware or software that might be involved. Also, look for recent changes to system or hardware configurations—recent changes are a common cause for stop errors.

■   **Adjust device drivers**   The error message may include a file name, and you can trace that file to a driver for a specific hardware device. Then you may be able to solve the problem by disabling, removing, or rolling back that driver to an earlier version. The devices that are commonly involved in stop errors include video cards, network interface cards, and disk controllers.

■   **Check the memory**   Vista includes a Memory Diagnostic tool that you can use to check system memory. See the previous section on hardware issues for more information on the Memory Diagnostic tool.

▲   **Identify changes**   Changing a processor, updating a driver, or installing a utility can have unintended effects on Vista, especially if the change involves hardware or software that is not listed on a Vista compatibility list and is, therefore, a higher risk for failure.

Configuration Options

Before we talk about how you can configure Vista to respond to stop errors, let's review what happens when a stop error occurs. When Windows encounters a fatal error that causes it to fail, it takes these actions:

▼ **Stop message**   The system displays a stop message.

■ **Crash dump**   Vista can write debugging information to the page file (pagefile .sys) if configured to do so. If Vista does write debugging information to the page file, when the computer restarts, the information is saved to a crash dump file. This file can be used by Microsoft support experts to debug the error.

▲ **Restart**   Based on the current preferences, Vista either pauses with the stop message on the screen or restarts normally after the crash dump information has been saved.

You can control this process in the following ways:

■ Define the size of the crash dump files

■ Specify whether you want Vista to restart automatically after a stop message appears

By default, Vista will restart after a stop message. If you are experiencing chronic stop errors, however, you may need to control when Vista starts, in which case you follow these steps to change the restart policy:

1. Open the System Properties dialog box from the Start menu, type **SystemPropertiesAdvanced** in the Search field, and press ENTER.

2. In the Startup And Recover section of the Advanced tab of the System Properties dialog box, click the Settings button.

3. In the System Failure section, note the configuration options, which can be modified by selecting the respective check boxes, shown in Figure 15-30:

■ Write An Event To The System Log

■ Automatically Restart

■ Overwrite Any Existing File

From the dialog box, you can also define the settings for crash dump files. Vista saves a kernel memory dump by default. A kernel memory dump includes data held in memory that is allocated to kernel-mode drivers and programs. It does not include un-allocated memory or memory allocated to user-mode applications. The file size will be about a third of your installed RAM, but usually no less than 256 megabytes (MB). The crash file path is %SystemRoot%\ Memory.dmp. Make sure to specify a page file size on the system volume that is at least one and one-half times larger than the size of your installed memory so that you can store all the crash data.

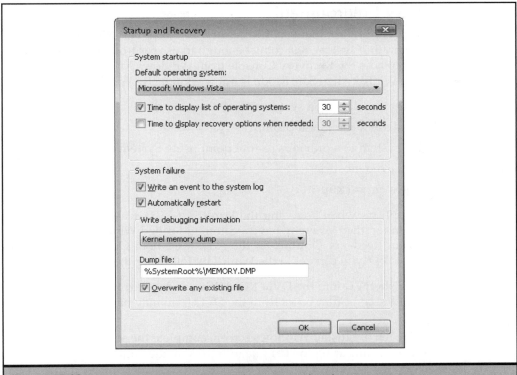

Figure 15-30.   You can adjust the startup and recovery options in response to stop errors.

RECOVERING THE SYSTEM

In the event that your Vista system will not boot normally, you can make use of Vista's recovery tools.

Advanced Boot Options

If you press F8 while your system is starting up, Vista displays a menu of diagnostic startup options. The first and most important of these is Safe Mode, which lets Vista start with only its most essential drivers and services. After you have started in Safe Mode, you can start and stop services, uninstall programs or drivers that might be causing problems, and run System Restore to return your system to an earlier, more stable state.

If Vista was preinstalled on the computer by the vendor, you may have a command called Windows Recovery Environment or System Recovery Options on the Advanced Boot Options menu.

Windows Recovery Environment

The Windows Recovery Environment (WinRE) is new in Vista. It is a stripped-down version of the Vista operating system, just robust enough to use for troubleshooting and repairs. The WinRE replaces the Recovery Console from Windows XP and Windows 2000.

You can use the WinRE when Safe Mode is not working. Use WinRE to:

▼   Repair or replace damaged system files

■   Perform tasks at a command prompt

■   Return the system to a previous restore point using System Restore

■   Run memory diagnostics

▲   Restore a system backup

You have two options when accessing the WinRE. If Vista was preinstalled on the computer by the vendor, then you may have a command called Windows Recovery Environment or System Recovery Options on the Advanced Boot Options menu. If you have a Vista media DVD, you can get to the WinRE by following these steps:

1. Insert the Vista DVD into the DVD-ROM drive and restart the computer. Ensure that the computer boots from the DVD (you may have to adjust BIOS settings).

2. Once you reach the Install Windows screen, complete the selections that work for you when configuring the Language To Install, the Time And Currency Format, and the Keyboard Or Input Method screens. Click the Next link to get to the install menu. This is shown in Figure 15-31.

3. Click Repair Your Computer, found at the bottom of the screen. The System Recovery Options dialog box appears.

4. In the System Recovery Options dialog box, ensure that the correct operating system is selected, and then click Next to launch the System Recovery Options menu, shown in Figure 15-32.

From the System Recovery Options menu, you can choose among the Vista recovery tools that can best help you. The different options in this menu are covered in the following sections.

Startup Repair

The Startup Repair option is designed to get you back up and running when Vista fails because of a missing or damaged system file. Startup Repair is a great place to begin when you are not sure why Vista will not load. This option might run automatically when Vista fails to boot.

System Restore

You can use the System Restore tool to return the core Vista system to a previous state when the operating system is unstable and you cannot undo the cause otherwise.

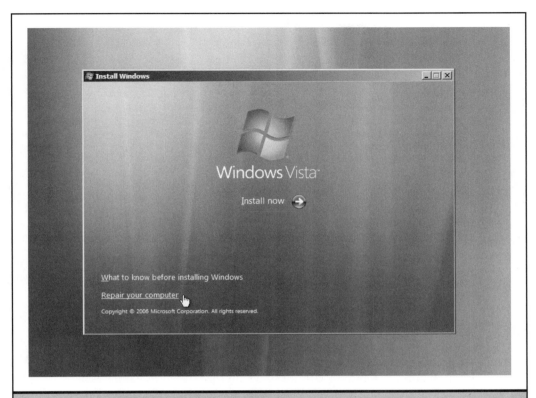

Figure 15-31.   The install menu gives you the option to choose Vista repair tools.

Using a previous snapshot of the system, System Restore rolls back the image to a known good state. For information about using System Restore, see Chapter 14.

You can run System Restore either while Vista is fully loaded or within WinRE. The difference between the two is that while running System Restore in WinRE, a new restore point is not created. If you run System Restore from the WinRE, you will not be able to undo the restore.

Complete PC Restore

Use the Complete PC Restore command in the WinRE to restore an image of the computer. Beware—all data on the computer is at risk of being lost when restoring this way. Restoring a backup image of a computer replaces the current contents of the disk with images made previously. When you restore the computer this way, the hard disk drive is formatted and wiped clean. Afterward, the Vista operating system, your installed applications, your configurations, and your data are all returned to the state they were in at the time you made the backup.

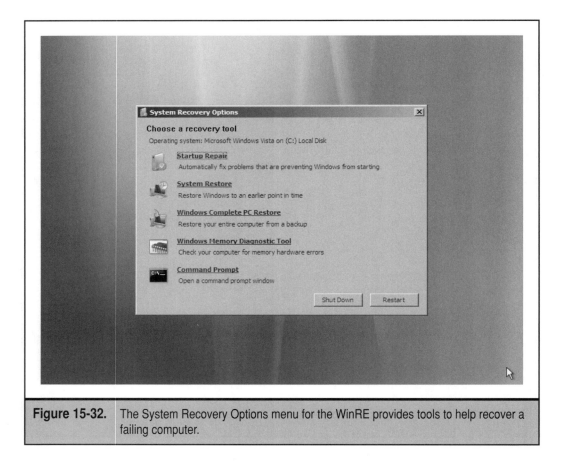

Figure 15-32.	The System Recovery Options menu for the WinRE provides tools to help recover a failing computer.

This is a great option when you do not have time to troubleshoot a stubborn issue, and you have a recent backup. You have to exercise caution, however, when restoring a computer using the Complete PC Restore option. Before you use this option, take note of all the changes to the computer that were made before the backup was taken. All those changes will be lost, including any application that was installed, configuration changes made, and updates to the user's documents. Hopefully, the user has not made any significant changes, but if he or she has then you will serve them well by helping them plan to restore the differential changes.

You can use Windows Complete PC Restore to restore image backups that are stored on the local hard disk drives or from backup media like a CD or DVD. Be sure the media is inserted into the DVD-ROM drive before you launch the restore tool. Vista is quirky in that if you have more than one media in your backup set, you need to insert the last disk in the set to start with, or else the restore tool will not recognize your backup.

Another quirk includes the volume structure of the disk you wish to restore. If it has changed since the time at which the backup was made, you need to select the Format And

Repartition Disks check box, or Vista will try to apply the backup and fail. Also, if you are restoring an image to a new hard disk drive, then be sure to select this check box.

The last tip we offer has to do with restoring to multiple new hard disk drives. If you wish to use the Complete PC Restore option to apply images to two or more hard disks that are at manufacture defaults, without disk signatures and partitions, you must first partition the drives. Using the Format And Repartition Disks option will only work if there is one raw disk, not if there are more. To prepare your hard disk drives, go to the WinRE command prompt, and use the Diskpart.exe command-line tool to create and format volumes on the new disks. The Diskpart tool is shown in Figure 15-33.

For more information about how to use the Diskpart tool, see Chapter 10.

Windows Memory Diagnostic Tool

We talked about the Windows Memory Diagnostic tool in the section "Hardware Problems and Diagnostics." The tool performs low-level tests on your computer memory

Figure 15-33.   Use the DiskPart.exe command-line tool to prepare raw hard disk drives.

to ensure that the system's RAM is fully functional. Memory failures can be subtle and manifest in ways that mask the true nature of the failure, such as applications freezing or closing inexplicably.

The main benefit of using the Windows Memory Diagnostic tool from the WinRE is that you do not have to reboot the computer to perform the test, whereas if you launch the tool from inside Vista, you will have to wait until the next reboot to get your results.

Command Prompt

The last option on the System Restore menu is to use the command prompt. Click this option to access a command-line shell from which you may launch any number of troubleshooting tools. The current directory for the command prompt will be the Sources folder, hosted on a RAM disk with the drive letter X. Unlike the Recovery Console in previous operating systems, the Vista command-line environment is largely unrestricted and grants you unfettered access to Vista's improved fleet of command-line tools.

From the Sources folder, you can access nearly a hundred command-line tools, including the disk management utilities (such as Chkdsk, Format, and Diskpart), as well as file management commands (such as Copy, Rename, and Delete). You can also affect system configurations. For example, you can make use of the "net" commands to manage users, groups, shares, and services.

Note, however, that network functionality is not available by default at the WinRE command prompt. To enable it, type wpeinit.

Security

A major point about the WinRE concerns security. You need to understand that the System Recovery Options tools run under the local system account, giving anyone who has a Vista DVD and a bit of knowledge free access to every file on a computer running Vista. Like every computer with a Microsoft operating system, physical access and data encryption are two of your major concerns for keeping data safe.

To minimize your security risk, restrict users from storing sensitive data on their local workstations. Keep confidential information encrypted, using any number of third-party products or Vista's native Encrypted File System (EFS) option. You should also deploy Vista's drive encryption option, BitLocker, when you can. For more information about BitLocker, see Chapter 10.

We're not there with the flying cars. Nor do we have 100 percent trouble-free computers yet, but Vista makes some nice strides in that direction. By following the basic troubleshooting steps we laid out at the beginning of this chapter and by using Vista's new troubleshooting tools, you should be able to spend less time fixing and more time using Vista.

INDEX

B

D

G

H

I

▼ J

O

P

S

▼ T

V

U

Z

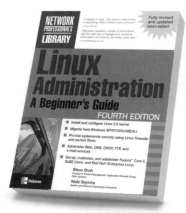
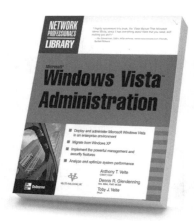

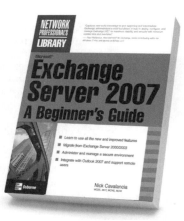
GEORGE BROWN COLLEGE
CASA LOMA LIBRARY LEARNING COMMON